"Well before the transdenominational convergence of what we now call the evangelical church, B. B. Warfield spent forty years as the Presbyterian Horatius, holding the bridge that leads into the citadel of the Westminster Standards against those he saw as spoilers from the wastelands of liberalism. A heavyweight academic and a complete player in the fields of systematic, exegetical, historical, and polemical theology, he scattered his wisdom in hundreds of articles, which this book surveys and integrates with great skill. Warfield can now be seen in his full stature as the godly giant that he was, thanks to Fred Zaspel's labor of love. Best thanks, and hallelujah!"

J. I. Packer, Board of Governors' Professor of Theology, Regent College

"B. B. Warfield's distinguished achievements as a systematic theologian have been obscured by the episodic, ad hoc publication of his major theological statements. But even if Warfield did not think it necessary that he write a single, connected systematic theology, it is nonetheless most welcome that Fred Zaspel has done the job for him! The result is a very useful compendium that gives both admirers and detractors of Warfield a full and coherent account of his theology. All who are in the least interested in Warfield or who care at all about vigorous Calvinist theology will find this a most valuable book."

Mark Noll, Francis A. McAnaney Professor of History, University of Notre Dame; author, *America's God: From Jonathan Edwards to Abraham Lincoln*

"Serious Christians who have dipped into Warfield find his writings to be a wholly admirable mix of rigorous exegesis, mature theological synthesis, and frank devotion to Christ. Much of his work is known only to specialists, not least because when Warfield first published it, it was scattered over many journals and books. Indeed, a fair bit of it was never published. Zaspel's *Theology of B. B. Warfield* remedies the problem admirably. One hopes and prays that it will entice a new generation of readers to delve deeply into Warfield's contributions."

D. A. Carson, Research Professor of New Testament, Trinity Evangelical Divinity School

"The 'Lion of Old Princeton' roars and purrs in this helpful survey. The author finely displays the passion and wit as well as intellectual credibility of Warfield's remarkable work."

Michael Horton, J. Gresham Machen Professor of Systematic Theology and Apologetics, Westminster Seminary California

"B. B. Warfield was the last towering figure in a long line of Old School Presbyterian intellectuals known for their unshakable faith in the truth of Scripture and their practical, experiential Calvinism. Both profound and prolific, Warfield produced an invaluable body of theological and polemical writings that remain deservedly influential today. Fred Zaspel's work is the first detailed, readable digest of Warfield's theology, and it is an immensely helpful volume. Dr. Zaspel puts Warfield's published writings in clear perspective against the theological issues that dominated that era. He also shows how those same issues—and Warfield's clear and persuasive teaching—remain relevant to us today. Dr. Zaspel writes with such clarity and simplicity that this volume will be a valuable help and encouragement to lay people and serious theologians as well—a highly recommended addition to anyone's library."

John MacArthur, Pastor, Grace Community Church, Sun Valley, California; President, The Master's College and Seminary

"B. B. Warfield was without doubt the greatest of the theological minds of Old Princeton, and he remains a towering influence within both his own confessional Presbyterian tradition and wider conservative evangelicalism. Nevertheless, while his writings are still in print, clearly written, and very accessible, their occasional nature means that there is no convenient way of gaining from them a good grasp of the overall shape of his theology. Until now, that is. In this volume, pastor-theologian and passionate Warfield aficionado Fred Zaspel has produced a work of historical and theological synthesis that sets Warfield's thought in context and offers a comprehensive account of his thought on the major loci of theology and the controverted points of his day. In this, Fred has left us all—the veteran Warfield fan and the neophyte—deeply in his debt."

Carl Trueman, Academic Dean and Vice President,
Westminster Theological Seminary

"B. B. Warfield does not need an introduction for evangelical Christians. He is well known as a major conservative theologian at the close of the nineteenth and the beginning of the twentieth centuries. His scholarship in biblical, historical, and doctrinal fields was often without a match. As a Professor in Didactic and Polemic Theology in Princeton Theological Seminary, he was content to use the three volumes of Charles Hodge's *Systematic Theology* as the textbook and to pour out the fruits of his labor in a flow of searching articles in a number of theological reviews. Many of these have been republished in book form, but they have not been systematically arranged in one text. That is what Dr. Zaspel has done in culling from the great mass of Warfield's writings his actual statements in the order they could have followed had Warfield written a one-volume Reformed theology. In this form Warfield may enjoy a renewed effectiveness for our age. With great enthusiasm I highly recommend this volume and hope it will receive a wide reception."

Roger Nicole, Professor of Theology Emeritus,
Reformed Theological Seminary, Orlando, Florida

"The great B. B. Warfield was essentially an occasional writer. His works are largely made up of learned articles, encyclopedia entries, and popular journalism. Fred Zaspel had the great idea of rendering this vast body of material into a compendium, a Warfield systematic theology. He clearly has what it takes to do the job superbly well: a love for his subject, care and attention to detail, and, above all, a thorough knowledge of Warfield's writing. The result is a book that does not replace the Warfield volumes, but provides an accurate, thematic entry into them. It will be of inestimable benefit to all students of this outstanding Reformed theologian. Well done!"

Paul Helm, Teaching Fellow, Regent College; author, *Faith with Reason*

"This work is long overdue. That a theologian of the stature of B. B. Warfield should not have had a comprehensive overview of his entire corpus, such as this one by Dr. Zaspel, says far more about the thinking of evangelicals and the ranks of the Reformed in the twentieth century than it does about Warfield. This truly excellent and eminently readable work will serve both as a primer to Warfield's thought and as an outline of the systematic theology he never wrote. Highly recommended."

Michael G. Haykin, Professor of Church History and Biblical Spirituality,
The Southern Baptist Theological Seminary; Director,
The Andrew Fuller Center for Baptist Studies

THE THEOLOGY OF
B. B. WARFIELD

THE THEOLOGY OF
B. B. WARFIELD

A Systematic Summary

FRED G. ZASPEL

Foreword by Sinclair B. Ferguson

CROSSWAY

WHEATON, ILLINOIS

The Theology of B. B. Warfield: A Systematic Summary
Copyright © 2010 by Fred G. Zaspel
Published by Crossway
        1300 Crescent Street
        Wheaton, Illinois 60187

Cover design: Amy Bristow
Cover image: *Benjamin Breckinridge Warfield*, by Ernest Ludvig Ipsen (1925)
        Special Collections, Princeton Theological Seminary Libraries
Typesetting: Lakeside Design Plus
First printing 2010
Printed in the United States of America

Except for scattered phrases translated by Warfield, Scripture quotations not otherwise identified are from the ESV® Bible (The Holy Bible, English Standard Version®), copyright © 2001 by Crossway. Used by permission. All rights reserved.

Scripture quotations marked KJV are from the King James Version of the Bible.

Scripture quotations marked NASB are from The New American Standard Bible.® Copyright © The Lockman Foundation 1960, 1962, 1963, 1968, 1971, 1972, 1973, 1975, 1977, 1995. Used by permission.

All emphases in Scripture quotations have been added by the author.

Hardcover ISBN: 978-1-4335-1395-4
PDF ISBN: 978-1-4335-1396-1
Mobipocket ISBN: 978-1-4335-1397-8
ePub ISBN: 978-1-4335-2435-6

Library of Congress Cataloging-in-Publication Data

Zaspel, Fred G.
  The theology of B. B. Warfield : a systematic summary / Fred G. Zaspel.
      p. cm.
    Includes bibliographical references (p.   ) and indexes.
    ISBN 978-1-4335-1395-4 (hc)

    1. Warfield, Benjamin Breckinridge, 1851–1921. 2. Theology, Doctrinal. I. Title.

BX9225.W236Z37 2010
230'.51092—dc22

                                  2010009037

Crossway is a publishing ministry of Good News Publishers.

SH	22	21	20	19	18	17	16	15	14	13	12	11	10
14	13	12	11	10	9	8	7	6	5	4	3	2	1

To James and Connie Zaspel,

loving and beloved parents
who faithfully pointed me to Christ,
and through whom God first instilled in me
a love for himself and his Word.

CONTENTS

FOREWORD

Sinclair B. Ferguson

It is a high privilege to write a few words of introduction and commendation to this important survey of the theology of B. B. Warfield. Many (I included) have expressed disappointment that, for a variety of reasons, Warfield never wrote a systematic theology of his own. One of these reasons was undoubtedly his deep sense of *pietas* toward Charles Hodge (of whom he said that he never made a major decision without asking himself, What would Dr. Hodge say about this?). But few who have read the work of both Hodge and Warfield doubt that the disciple would have produced a greater work than his teacher.

The result has been that, by and large, Warfield has been regarded as a theologian focused on expounding and defending one doctrine alone, that of the inspiration and authority of Scripture.

Dr. Fred G. Zaspel's work will put that misunderstanding to rest. Warfield's interests and acumen ranged much wider and deeper. He was prodigiously learned in a variety of areas of theology. Whereas lesser men become typecast by publication in a narrow field of interest, Warfield wrote at the highest scholarly level in the areas of biblical studies, Patristic theology, Reformation theologians, confessional history, and biblical and systematic theology proper.

Dr. Zaspel has quarried the ten volumes of Warfield's collected works, as well as the published *Selected Shorter Writings*, but has also mined his lecture notes (and notes of his students), as well as Warfield's other published works. Wisely, this has included his sermons, which, as one of his colleagues noted, were preached in his rich, educated Kentucky accent that made words come from his lips "as if they walked on velvet." These are often minor theological treatises on their own and well express Warfield's spiritual drive and pastoral sensitivity. In addition, we find here reference to materials published in places sufficiently obscure as to guarantee that Warfield's articles would share their fate of oblivion.

In contrast to the caricature of Warfield as a one-doctrine theologian, any student of his who has attempted to read widely in his work soon realizes that to some degree his thinking and writing covered the bases of the whole theological system. Of course there are some *loci* to which he paid special attention. The mountain peaks are found not only in the doctrine of Scripture but also in his studies in the person and work of Christ, and soteriology. In addition are impressive mountains of learning in his studies in Calvin and the Westminster Assembly. And Dr. Zaspel has paid careful attention to Warfield's enduring concern, expressed in his critical reviews (born, perhaps from his early studies in Europe), to inform his fellow Americans of the latest theological thinking emerging from the continent—and in the process, along with characteristically generous comments where merited, to provide his own devastating critique.

Here then is spread before us the entire mountain range of *Warfieldiana* as we are given the privileged position of surveying the encyclopedia of Warfield's thought. *The Theology of B. B. Warfield* is, therefore, as its title suggests, a systematic summary of his thought; but it is also an ordnance survey map with copious notes directing the traveler in *Warfieldiana* to some of the best places to linger, find nourishment, or rest—or simply pause to admire.

These pages represent a labor of love of Herculean proportions. The Warfield corpus is substantial and wide ranging. Few writers today are capable of the breadth of interest that made Warfield a scholar of Renaissance-man proportions. Not only so, but Warfield's tendency was to write according to older principles—paragraphs extending to three pages are not uncommon in his writings—and so his work makes demands on the reader's powers of both concentration and perseverance.

Having known of Fred Zaspel's intentions from the commencement of this work, I am filled with admiration that he has successfully completed it—not least since Warfield has been a companion to me throughout most of my Christian life. I had just turned seventeen and recently arrived at university in Scotland when I first heard the name of B. B. Warfield spoken in reverential terms by an older student. It was clear that one could not afford to remain ignorant of the man or his writings. And so I obtained (from what was then the Craig Press) the abbreviated set of his works, the ten-volume Oxford edition (though now widely available) having been long out of print.

The patient scholarship of his essays in *The Inspiration and Authority of the Bible* was, of course, immediately impressive. The scholarship represented in his studies in *Calvin and Augustine* were enormously informative to a relative novice only beginning to read in Calvin. The *Studies in Perfectionism* were sufficient to immunize me for life against all forms of "higher life" teaching! But the deepest impression was made by his *Biblical and Theological Studies* and *The Person and Work of Christ*—though perhaps the deepest impression of all, on me and many others, was made by Warfield's striking essay "The Emotional Life of Our Lord" (curiously absent from the Oxford ten-volume edition). Here, for a younger Christian, was at last serious and stretching theology that enhanced understanding of Christ and enriched faith in him and love for him.

I felt then, as I feel now, that here was a theologian who understood what theology was *for*. Benjamin Breckinridge Warfield (who could ever think of him as "Ben" or "Benny"?) has been a mentor and friend ever since. Now that *The Theology of B. B. Warfield* is being published, hopefully many more in our generation and beyond will come to discover the same riches. Dr. Zaspel deserves our congratulations and our profound gratitude for producing this invaluable volume.

PREFACE

On more than one occasion historian Mark Noll, among others, has lamented that no one has yet produced a comprehensive account of the theology of Benjamin Breckinridge Warfield.[1] This work is intended to fill that void and reintroduce Warfield to today's theological discussion. This Princetonian's writings are widely diverse, filling many thousands of pages spread over many hundreds of articles, books, pamphlets, and book reviews, and covering virtually the entire spectrum of Christian theology. Since his own day many have wished that he had produced a systematic theology of his own. Yet no one has attempted to bring his work together in such an order.

There may be several reasons for this, such as the sheer magnitude of the task. Warfield's literary output is staggering, and bringing it all together in condensed form is a monumental task indeed. Perhaps the task has been left undone simply because it is difficult to represent Warfield well without representing him completely. His theological arguments are extensive, precise, and detailed but not verbose or redundant. And so the task of condensing Warfield becomes frustrating: how can we reduce in size what is already so densely packed?

But as Noll's remark indicates, the need is real. If for no other reason, this work is necessary because few will ever have the luxury of reading all that Warfield had to say on a given subject, much less read all of Warfield! And so this book is born.

It is ironic that B. B. Warfield is both appreciated and neglected. He is appreciated in that he still speaks with commanding authority, and scholars today continue to reference him accordingly. But he is neglected in that he is seldom read fully. Of course there have been a few who have sought to provide holistic analysis of his doctrine of inspiration, and there has been some interest in his apologetic understanding and method. And here and there an article or essay has appeared touching this or that aspect of his theology. But to view Warfield's theology from a global perspective, students heretofore could only set themselves to the daunting task of reading many thousands of Warfield pages. It is to assist in that task that this book has been written. That is not to suggest—shudder to

---

[1] E.g., his introduction to Gary L. W. Johnson, *B. B. Warfield: Essays on His Life and Thought* (Phillipsburg, NJ: P&R, 2007), 4.

think!—that the larger task is no longer of value, but it is to reduce that task for those who need assistance and perhaps to introduce Warfield in such a way that will inspire others to go to the source themselves.

My own interest in Warfield began when I was an undergraduate student working my way through school in a Christian bookstore. That is when I first laid eyes—and hands!—on *The Lord of Glory, Faith and Life, The Plan of Salvation*, and the two volumes of his *Selected Shorter Writings*. What a feast it was. Immediately I was struck both with the breadth and depth of Warfield's learning and with the passion of his heart for Christ. Eventually I was given the ten volumes of his *Works* (Thank you, Neil and Ruth!), and for many years now I have sought to read every word Warfield published. As a result my initial impressions of him have become increasingly confirmed, and it has been a joy to study him "whole." As few others I had read, Warfield seemed to understand the Christian faith at its heart, with all its various teachings in proper relation. Along the way I came to see the value of reintroducing him to today's theological discussion, condensing his whole thinking on the various theological themes in ways that faithfully reflect his approach and method.

A few remarks by way of clarification are in order. You will notice at some points a certain inequality of treatment of given doctrines, but this reflects Warfield's own writing. Warfield was an "occasional" writer, addressing specific issues as the need and interest arose. Also, in digesting Warfield's various arguments, I needed at virtually every turn to bring together statements from various writings. Often a single sentence in this work reflects thoughts and statements that Warfield expressed in multiple places. This, in turn, made footnote referencing impossibly cumbersome. And so an editorial decision was made to group references together, usually at the end of the paragraph. I trust that those who wish to follow the references will find themselves only somewhat inconvenienced by this.

Of course it is to be expected that there will be areas of disagreement with Warfield—in questions of baptism and eschatology, for example, common areas of much dispute. But the goal here has been to present Warfield's arguments accurately on their own terms. There has been no attempt either to confirm or refute his views, his arguments, or even his understanding of other writers—an endeavor that would increase the length of this study exponentially. Nor have I entered discussion with others who have attempted to criticize Warfield's views. The purpose is not to critique or evaluate but to clarify the views Warfield actually held and the arguments he advanced in their support. And with this object kept in mind I have had to leave aside the arguments of others, whether in support of or opposition to Warfield. My interaction with others, rather, is restricted to those who in my judgment have misstated Warfield's position on a given issue.

In such cases I seek to clarify Warfield against such misunderstandings or misrepresentations of him.

There have been men in the past whose voices were needed, and, it would seem, God sent them for just the occasion and context in which they lived. Warfield was such a man. But he deserves a new hearing. I trust you will find it so.

I owe many thanks to Bram van de Beek and Michael Haykin for their helpful input throughout this project. Without them the book would be of much less value indeed. Many thanks to Ryan Kelly, as well, for encouraging me to undertake this work in the first place. Many thanks are due to Ken Henke for his invaluable assistance with the Warfield Archives in the Princeton Theological Seminary Library. Many thanks also to Reformed Baptist Church of Franconia, Pennsylvania, for their patient and even enthusiastic listening to so much of Warfield. And many thanks to my wonderful family, who have at least pretended so much interest as I have rattled on and on of Warfield on countless occasions upon returning to them from my study. Surely no writer has ever had a more supportive wife than mine. All throughout these years of research—beset though they were with so much suffering in our home—she has been a mainstay of constant loving encouragement to see the work to its completion. Thank you, Kim.

ABBREVIATIONS

BBW	*B. B. Warfield: Essays on His Life and Thought*, ed. Johnson
BSac	*Bibliothecra Sacra*
BT	*The Banner of Truth*
BTS	*Biblical and Theological Studies*, Warfield
BTSp	*Biblical and Theological Studies*, the faculty of Princeton Theological Seminary, ed. Warfield
CA	*Calvin and Augustine*, Warfield
CC	*The Centennial Celebration of the Theological Seminary of the Presbyterian Church in the United States of America*, ed. Warfield, Armstrong, and Robinson
CM	*Counterfeit Miracles*, Warfield
CP	*The Cumberland Presbyterian*
CT	*Christian Thought*
EQ	*Evangelical Quarterly*
ESS	*Evolution, Science, and Scripture*, Warfield
FL	*Faith and Life*, Warfield
HS	*The Holy Spirit*, Warfield
ITCNT	*An Introduction to the Textual Criticism of the New Testament*, Warfield
JETS	*Journal of the Evangelical Theological Society*
JGM	*J. Gresham Machen: A Biographical Memoir*, Stonehouse
JPH	*The Journal of Presbyterian History*
LG	*The Lord of Glory*, Warfield
NSHERK	*The New Schaff-Herzog Encyclopedia of Religious Knowledge*
P	*The Presbyterian*
PB	*The Presbyterian Banner*
PCUSA	The Presbyterian Church in the United States of America
PGS	*The Power of God unto Salvation*, Warfield
PJ	*The Presbyterian Journal*
PQ	*Presbyterian Quarterly*
PR	*The Presbyterian Review*
PRR	*The Presbyterian and Reformed Review*
PrS	*Princeton Sermons*, Warfield

PS	*The Plan of Salvation*, Warfield
PSB	*The Princeton Seminary Bulletin*
PTR	*The Princeton Theological Review*
PWC	*The Person and Work of Christ*, Warfield
SBET	*Scottish Bulletin of Evangelical Theology*
SPR	*Southern Presbyterian Review*
SSW	*Selected Shorter Writings of Benjamin B. Warfield*, 2 vols.
SW	*The Savior of the World*, Warfield
TBS	*The Bible Student*
TBST	*The Bible Student and Teacher*
W	*The Works of Benjamin Breckinridge Warfield*, 10 vols.
	W, 1 *Revelation and Inspiration*
	W, 2 *Biblical Doctrines*
	W, 3 *Christology and Criticism*
	W, 4 *Studies in Tertullian and Augustine*
	W, 5 *Calvin and Calvinism*
	W, 6 *The Westminster Assembly and Its Work*
	W, 7 *Perfectionism, Part One*
	W, 8 *Perfectionism, Part Two*
	W, 9 *Studies in Theology*
	W, 10 *Critical Reviews*
WTJ	*Westminster Theological Journal*
WCF	Westminster Confession of Faith

Whence, then, arises the plaint which we hear about us,
that the right of Criticism is impugned and the rights of Criticism
denied? From the ineradicable tendency of man to confound the right
of Criticism with the rightness of his own criticism. We may safely
recognize this to be a common human tendency; for, as all of us
doubtless know by this time, humanum est errare. *But as soon as*
our attention is directed to it, the way seems to be opened
to remind ourselves of a few distinctions, which it will be well for
the Presbyterian Church to attend to in the crisis which is at present
impending over her—a crisis the gravity of which cannot be
over-estimated for a church of Christ, to which has been committed
the function of being the pillar and ground of the truth.

SSW, 2:596; the Latin reads, "To err is human."

Benjamin Breckinridge Warfield (Nov. 5, 1851–Feb. 16, 1921)

Princeton Theological Seminary

Princeton, The Presbyterians, and Beyond

"Christian Supernaturalism": Warfield in Summary

1

HISTORICAL CONTEXT

Benjamin Breckinridge Warfield (Nov. 5, 1851–Feb. 16, 1921)

The life of Benjamin Breckinridge Warfield[1] is a story of theology, a story told in his own extensive writings. He wrote no autobiography and almost nothing about himself. Most of what we know of his life circumstances and experiences—which is relatively little for such a noted figure—comes from his correspondence and a few reports from others who knew him. To date, no Warfield biography has been written, although at least one is in the making. We do know that he did comparatively little other than teach, preach, and write in Princeton. But his literary output in this regard was enormous, and by anyone's measure, Warfield's writings are themselves his legacy. It is in these more than forty books and booklets, nearly seven hundred periodical articles, more than a thousand book reviews, hundreds of brief book notices, other lesser works, and unpublished manuscripts and lecture notes—all covering the entire spectrum of theological discussion—that we find who he was and how he spent his life.

B. B. Warfield is widely recognized as the leading Reformed theologian of the late nineteenth and early twentieth centuries. When he was born in 1851,

---

[1] The personal and biographical information about Warfield highlighted here comes from the following sources: the Warfield correspondence preserved in the Princeton Theological Seminary archives; newspaper archives from the time; Ethelbert D. Warfield, "Biographical Sketch of Benjamin Breckinridge Warfield," in *W*, 1:v–ix; "Benjamin Breckinridge Warfield" (death notice), *PTR* 19, no. 2 (1921): 329–30; Francis L. Patton, "Benjamin Breckinridge Warfield: A Memorial Address," *PTR* 19, no. 3 (1921): 369–91; Samuel G. Craig, "Benjamin B. Warfield," in *BTS*, xi–xlviii; J. Ross Stevenson, "Benjamin Breckinridge Warfield," *The Expository Times* 33, no. 4 (1922): 152–53; personal letter from Charles Brokenshire to John Meeter dated June 25, 1942; Hugh T. Kerr, "Warfield: The Person behind the Theology," *PSB*, new series, 25, no. 1 (1994): 80–93; David B. Calhoun, *Princeton Seminary*, vol. 1, *Faith and Learning 1812–1868*; and *Princeton Seminary*, vol. 2, *The Majestic Testimony 1869–1929* (Carlisle, PA: Banner of Truth, 1994, 1996); John Meeter, "Foreword," in *SSW*, 2:vii–x; Bradley J. Gundlach, "'B' Is for Breckinridge: Benjamin B. Warfield, His Maternal Kin, and Princeton Seminary" and "'Wicked Caste': Warfield, Biblical Authority, and Jim Crow," in *BBW*, 13–53, 136–68; also private correspondence with Bradley Gundlach, whose biographical studies of Warfield are the most thorough to date, and whose forthcoming biography will be an invaluable contribution to Warfield studies.

just outside Lexington, Kentucky, the Warfield and Breckinridge family names (the latter, his mother's) were already rich with heritage. Behind him were military officers, educators, influential ecclesiastical leaders, and governmental and political figures, even a United States vice president. Warfield's father, William Warfield, was descended from English Puritan forebears who had fled to America to avoid persecution.[2] The atmosphere of the Warfield home was one of "vital piety." The Warfields were members of Lexington's Second Presbyterian Church, the only local Presbyterian church to affiliate with the Northern Presbyterians in the division between the North and South around the time of the Civil War, and it was here at age sixteen that Benjamin made public profession of faith. William was a successful cattle breeder, and Benjamin was reared in some degree of privilege. He received a private education and developed particular interest in mathematics and especially science, devouring with intense interest the newly published works of Charles Darwin. With a touch of humor, his brother Ethelbert (1861–1936) reports that Benjamin

> was so certain that he was to follow a scientific career that he strenuously objected to studying Greek. But youthful objections had little effect in a household where the shorter catechism was ordinarily completed in the sixth year, followed at once by the proofs from the Scriptures, and then by the larger catechism, with an appropriate amount of Scripture memorized in regular course each Sabbath afternoon.[3]

Not quite aged seventeen, Warfield entered the sophomore class at the College of New Jersey (now Princeton University) in the fall of 1868. At Princeton his friends called him "Wo-field," imitating his southern drawl. School records indicate his involvement in a Sunday afternoon fistfight, of which it seems Warfield was the instigator! His maternal grandfather Robert Jefferson Breckinridge (1800–1871) had been suspended from the school for a similar incident many years before. This incident earned Warfield the nickname, "pugilist"—which some have found somewhat prophetic. But Warfield evidently applied himself well as a student, over all, attaining "foremost rank in every department of instruction" and, as Ethelbert reports, "perfect marks" in mathematics and science, graduating with highest honors, first in his class in 1871 at age nineteen.[4] He also won awards for essays and debate in the American Whig Society and was an editor for the *Nassau Literary Magazine*, for which he wrote several poems and other pieces. Following Benjamin's graduation his father persuaded him to study in Europe, and in the

---

[2]It was for a distant cousin of Warfield's, Wallis Warfield Simpson, that King Edward VIII of England would abdicate in 1936.

[3]*W*, 1:vi.

[4]Stevenson, "Benjamin Breckinridge Warfield," 152; *W*, 1:vi.

spring of 1872 he began study in Edinburgh and then Heidelberg. Midsummer the family was surprised to receive word that he would enter Christian ministry, and in 1873, after a brief stint as editor of the *Farmer's Home Journal* in Lexington, he entered Princeton Seminary, where he received instruction from men whom he deeply admired—especially the famous and by then elderly Charles Hodge (1797–1878) and his son Caspar Wistar Hodge (1830–1891). The younger Hodge was professor of New Testament, and he became something of a personal mentor of Warfield, a relationship that developed into an intimate and lasting friendship. It would be C. W. Hodge who on behalf of the seminary would write to Warfield in late 1886, inviting him to consider joining their faculty. For his entire life Warfield maintained deep affection for both the college and the seminary in Princeton, appreciating both the illustrious history of each institution and what he had learned from them.

In May of 1875, Warfield was licensed to preach by the Presbytery of Ebenezer, meeting at Lexington, Kentucky, and he served that summer as stated supply at Concord Church in Nicholas County, Kentucky. After graduating in 1876, Warfield was the stated supply of the First Presbyterian Church of Dayton, Ohio, from which he received a unanimous call to the pastorate. He declined the call, determining instead to pursue further studies again in Europe. Warfield was married on August 3 of that year to the brilliant, witty, and beautiful Annie Kinkead, and then very soon took up studies in Leipzig. He endured extended health problems that kept him from some studies while in Germany, but over the winter of 1876–1877 he took in lectures from such notables as New Testament scholar Ernst Luthardt (1823–1902), historical theologian Adolf von Harnack (1851–1930),[5] and the famous Hebraist and Old Testament commentator Franz Delitzsch (1813–1890).

Warfield's new wife, Annie, was the daughter of a prominent Lexington attorney who in 1855 defended Abraham Lincoln. In the brief biographical sketches of Warfield that are commonly available, Annie is often reported to have been an invalid their entire married life, but it does not seem that this degree of debilitation came until perhaps 1893. A notice in the *New York Times* dated May 1, 1892, notes that Mrs. Warfield, Mrs. Woodrow Wilson, and other prominent ladies of Princeton served as "Patronesses" at a lecture event sponsored by the American Whig Society in Princeton on April 30. Then in July of 1893, Warfield sent a paper to be read at an event in Staten Island, New York, which he was unable to attend

---

[5]Harnack was a German scholar at (in turn) Leipzig, Giessen, Marburg, and Berlin. His views cost him official ecclesiastical recognition. Harnack's primary area of study was Patristic thought, and his views, which he confessed were shaped by Ritschlian liberalism, later brought him into conflict with his former pupil Karl Barth (1886–1968). Harnack, whose brilliant scholarship Warfield firmly opposed yet held in high esteem, is widely regarded as the most influential German church historian and theologian prior to World War I.

"owing to illness in his family."[6] It would seem that Annie's illness became severe during this period. There are reports of her ill health from others at Princeton at the time, and by all accounts Warfield was a devoted husband in a very happy marriage. The Warfields had no children, and for many years he left his home only for the classroom. He was otherwise nearly always in the company of his wife. In the providence of God, without doubt, this contributed to his time in writing so extensively on so many subjects.

While Warfield was studying in Europe, Western (now Pittsburgh) Theological Seminary in Allegheny, Pennsylvania, contacted him and offered him an appointment to teach Old Testament. Old Testament had been his earlier interest, but ironically, and perhaps due to the influence of C. W. Hodge, his interests had now turned to (previously eschewed!) Greek and New Testament studies. The young couple returned home in the late summer of 1877, and Warfield served again as stated supply, this time at the historic and prestigious First Presbyterian Church in Baltimore, Maryland. While in Baltimore he was contacted by Western Seminary once again, but this time with an appointment to teach New Testament, a work he took up with great interest in September 1878. Warfield was ordained as an evangelist by the Ebenezer Presbytery at their meeting in Frankfort, Kentucky, on April 26, 1879. And by the early 1880s he already had begun to gain international recognition as a force of conservative Reformed theological scholarship. His inaugural lecture, "Inspiration and Criticism" (1880), his "Syllabus on the Canon of the New Testament in the Second Century" (1881), his landmark "Inspiration" (1881) coauthored with Archibald Alexander Hodge (1823–1886), and his "Canonicity of Second Peter" (1882) were especially noted, portending the brilliant career that quite obviously lay ahead for this young scholar.

In 1886 he became the first American to publish a textbook in New Testament textual criticism, a title that received accolades from all quarters and established him as a leading authority in the field. The Theological Seminary of the Northwest in Chicago offered Warfield their chair of theology in 1881, but he declined. It was otherwise highly unusual that a historic and prestigious chair such as that of didactic and polemic theology at Princeton should be offered to such a young man, Warfield being just thirty-five at the time. But in a letter dated November 30, 1886, C. W. Hodge wrote Warfield that he was the only man the board had in sight for the position. They were uncertain he would even consider, but they were hopeful, requesting only that he affirm that he would not dismiss the possibility out of hand. Warfield replied with tones of deepest affection and honor, affirming that he would be willing to consider the matter prayerfully. A. A. Hodge had

---

[6]Introductory note to Warfield, "The Bible Doctrine of Inspiration," *Christian Thought* 11 (1893–1894): 163.

died unexpectedly, and the historic chair that had belonged to his father Charles, and to Archibald Alexander before him, now fell to Warfield, a position he would occupy with famous distinction for the next thirty-four years.

Decades before, Charles Hodge had also moved from New Testament to theology, and for both men the previous work would prove foundational to their new endeavors. But Warfield's move was not met with universal approval, for what the department of theology had gained, the world of New Testament studies had lost. Then and since, many have speculated that Warfield would have been one of the great New Testament commentators of the age. John Broadus, professor of New Testament and soon to be president at Southern Baptist Theological Seminary in Louisville, Kentucky, was one who had made such predictions in the classroom. In a letter dated January 31, 1897, Broadus wrote Warfield with a touch of humor, bemoaning that his move to systematic theology would now give Broadus's students proof that he was no true prophet! In a letter dated February 5, 1897, the British New Testament scholar William Robertson Nicoll (1851–1923) wrote to congratulate Warfield. The communication was very cordial but marked clearly by disappointment, even hinting of disapproval. Evidently Warfield had agreed to provide a commentary for the multivolume *Expositor's Bible*, which Nicoll edited.

> Permit me first of all to congratulate you on your new position. I do not know whether I can do so with unmixed feelings. You will no doubt do a great work in Princeton for us all but I grudge very much that you should be taken away from the study of the New Testament. . . . I do not release you from the Expositors Bible though you be a professor of Dogmatic Theology now. You owe this debt to the . . . position[7] you have forsaken.

But despite such reservations, expressions of support were unanimous, and congratulations were characterized by expectations of helpful contributions to theological studies.

Warfield was not the first in his family either to attend or to teach at Princeton. His grandfather Robert Breckinridge and Robert's brother (Warfield's great-uncle) John Breckinridge (1797–1841) had attended the seminary also, and John was professor of pastoral theology from 1836 to 1838 and the son-in-law of Samuel Miller, Princeton's renowned second professor.[8] Robert Breckinridge was an influential leader of the Old School Presbyterians and in 1853 became founding

---

[7]Nicoll's handwriting here is difficult to decipher, but it seems "position" is the word used here, though immediately before it is an illegible word.

[8]Joseph H. Dulles, *Princeton Theological Seminary: Biographical Catalogue* (Trenton, NJ: MacCrellish & Quigley, 1909), 8, 17, 43, 102.

president of the new Presbyterian seminary in Danville, Kentucky. He had been well acquainted with the early Princetonians, but his relationship with Princeton had been strained since his fighting days at the college, and later with Charles Hodge in particular, due to significant disagreements and (at least perceived) betrayal. Indeed, that it was Breckinridge who became the president of the new seminary in Kentucky seemed to carry more implications than simply that a new seminary was needed in the West. Warfield's appointment to Princeton, there-fore, was from the standpoint of the family somewhat ironic to say the least, as well as a prestigious honor of which they were proud. So in 1887 he assumed his appointment to the theological department at Princeton, and he did so with a deep and expressed sense of sobriety and responsibility.[9] Quite appropriately he moved into the house next door to Alexander Hall that had been the home of his revered and beloved predecessor, Charles Hodge.

We know relatively little of Warfield personally other than what his writings reveal of his personality. J Gresham Machen (1881–1937) makes passing reference to Warfield's "glaring faults," but this is not what stood out in his mind in regard to his former teacher and senior colleague: "With all his glaring faults he was the greatest man I have known."[10] This is the only remark we have in reference to War-field's personal faults, and Machen does not elaborate. Overwhelmingly Warfield is described by those who knew him as a "model Christian gentleman," a man of grace, great personal charm, generosity, kindness, good humor, and wit. One of Warfield's acquaintances summarizes his impressions of Warfield memorably:

> After a lapse of more than twenty years, Dr B. B. Warfield stands out as the most ideal Christian Character that I have ever known. . . . Dr Warfield possessed the most perfect combination of faculties of mind and heart that I have ever known in any person. His mind was keen and analytical in understanding facts and thoughts; and it was comprehensive in seeing all sides of a subject. He was so devoted to the truth as a man and teacher that his pupils could always trust his statements implicitly; and their confidence in him was never betrayed in any sense. He not only had the power of thought to comprehend a truth; but he also had a perfect command of language to give expression to his thoughts. His diction was precise and complete.
>
> But if Dr Warfield was great in intellectuality, he was just as great in goodness. Over a long period of years this man stands out in my mind as the most Christ-like man that I have ever known. In spite of his brilliance of mind, there was no spirit of superciliousness, no purpose to offend the dullest pupil, no haughtiness of heart. With him there was never any sign of pretence [sic], or false front; for there was no

---

[9]"Inaugural Address: The Idea of Systematic Theology" in *Inauguration of the Rev. Benjamin B. Warfield, D.D., as Professor of Didactic and Polemic Theology* (New York: Anson D. F. Randolph, 1888), 40.
[10]*JGM*, 310.

spirit of hypocrisy in his inner heart. Rather there was always the spirit of humility and meekness and the spirit of kindness and gentleness toward others.[11]

Warfield was tall and erect, pleasant but dignified, rather heavy, something of an imposing figure, ruddy cheeks, hair parted in the middle, sparkling eyes, and a full graying beard. Former student Charles Brokenshire (1885–1954) recalled, "He walked with head erect and well thrown back, and his face beamed with intelligence and amiability." He was "somewhat deaf," which made classroom recitation to him frustratingly difficult, but he was known for this method of teaching nonetheless. Brokenshire continues:

> His most interesting method of instruction appeared when he heard and answered some question in the classroom. Sometime he would use the Socratic method on a reciter and lead some student disposed to argue into a series of statements which drove the young liberal into the orthodox corner where "Benny" wanted him.[12]

"Benny" was the name used by his family—and by his students, but only behind his back, of course. He was always of good humor but also serious, somewhat reserved, and, as one former student reports, with a commanding air of authority. Thoroughly informed as he was, on the one hand he could appear aloof and indifferent to the theological opinions of others, but on the other hand he displayed an obvious love for others and especially children. And he was always demonstrative in his support of gospel endeavors both at home and abroad.

Warfield conducted wide correspondence with Christian leaders of the day from all quarters—Nicoll, Broadus, Charles A. Briggs (1841–1913), William G. T. Shedd (1820–1894), Charles Spurgeon (1834–1892), J. Henry Thayer (1828–1901), Samuel H. Kellogg (1839–1899), George Frederick Wright (1838–1921), Herman Bavinck (1854–1921), Abraham Kuyper (1837–1920), to name only a few. He was held in highest admiration by his peers and was a recognized giant. Throughout his time at Princeton he also conducted continuous correspondence with his former students "with an interest and affection that never waned." His "marvelously retentive memory" enabled him to quote poetry at length and provide librarian-like references for any theme of biblical or theological inquiry. After it was known that Warfield had been offered the position at Princeton, a former seminary classmate wrote to congratulate him in a letter dated February 7, 1887, and remarked, no doubt reflecting Warfield's own sense of humor, "Ben you know you were a wayward kind of a boy in college [Warfield notes, "Seminary"]

---

[11]Letter from F. T. McGill to John Meeter, in *BT* 89 (Fall 1971): 18.
[12]Charles Brokenshire letter to John Meeter, June 25, 1942, p. 2.

& would not take my advice then, but I know you will now, when I tell you by all means accept the chair offered you in Princeton Seminary." Warfield enjoyed good humor and would on occasion employ it in his most involved theological writings, sometimes as biting wit and even sarcasm. He was well spoken, with his pleasant southern accent. He preached in a conversational tone that was calm, deliberate, and unaffected but marked by deep spirituality and impassioned with the truth he expounded, yet without demonstrative oratory. Not his scholarship only but his Christlikeness also deeply impressed his students, and he was a man who was himself profoundly affected by the gospel he preached. It was written of him that he was a "devout and sweet-spirited Christian" and a "Christ-like man." He was recognized as a Christian and a scholar in the best senses of both.[13]

Long-time friend and colleague Francis Landey Patton (1843–1932), in his Warfield memorial address in Princeton, remarked that Warfield "was pre-eminently a scholar and lived among his books." He did not spend a great deal of time with social pleasantries such as after-dinner conversation. He was something of a recluse with his books and his pen, always diligent in his theological studies, well read in all other fields of literature also, especially science. The theological journal was to him much more than an available resource in the dissemination of the faith. It was a most highly valued resource, which he utilized to maximum potential. Throughout his career the bulk of his publishing was in the journal— primarily the *Presbyterian Review*, which he edited for a brief time, the *Presbyterian and Reformed Review*, which he planned and edited for twelve years, and then the *Princeton Theological Review*. His articles regularly appeared in these and other theological journals throughout his career, along with the many hundreds of book reviews that he understood as an important means of addressing contemporary theological issues. Some of these reviews, which he provided continuously of works published in English, German, Dutch, and French, were substantive monographs in their own right. His range of scholarly learning extended over every theological domain, and judging from his citations and footnotes, it seems he read more of his opponents than of his comrades. He was manifestly an independent thinker and a theologian of broadest scholarship, and his reputation attracted many students to Princeton from around the world.

Warfield received the honorary degrees Doctor of Divinity in 1880 and Doctor of Laws in 1892 from the College of New Jersey, his alma mater. He also received the Doctor of Laws from Davidson College in 1892, the Doctor of Letters from Lafayette College in 1911, and the *Sacrae Theologiae Doctor* from the University of Utrecht in 1913. A brief note in the December 5, 1913, *New York Times* mentions that this last

---

[13]*BSac* 78, no. 310 (1921): 124; *Watchman*, Boston, March 3, 1904, cited in *SSW*, 2:718.

degree was a special honor, given as it was, without precedent, *in absentia*. Warfield had decided instead to remain with his wife in her illness and afterward responded to the Dutch institution with deep expressions of honor and gratitude.

One of Warfield's closest friends was Geerhardus Vos (1862–1949), whom Warfield had helped bring to Princeton for the new chair of biblical theology. It was their regular practice for many years to walk together for refreshment and fellowship. On December 24, 1920, Warfield was walking along the sidewalk to the Vos home, just a few hundred yards across campus from his own home, when suddenly he grasped his chest and collapsed.[14] Warfield spent the next few weeks recovering until Wednesday, February 16, 1921, when he was finally ready to resume teaching. At the close of the class he returned home where that evening a heart attack took him, this time fatally. A former student remarked that Warfield had passed to his bright and happy reward where he can "continue his studies to all eternity." J. Ross Stevenson, president of the seminary, wrote of Warfield's death almost a year later, "The Reformed Theology and the cause of evangelical religion have lost one of the ablest interpreters and defenders which America has ever produced." Patton remarked in his memorial address that it was a loss that was unquestionably felt throughout the greater part of the Christian world. "Nothing but ignorance of his exact scholarship, wide learning, varied writings, and the masterly way in which he did his work," he surmised, could prevent anyone "from uniting with us today in the statement that a prince and a great man has fallen in Israel." Warfield's younger colleague J. Gresham Machen lamented in a letter to his mother after Warfield's funeral that as they carried him out, Old Princeton went with him and that he was certain there was not a man in the entire church who could fill one quarter of his place.[15]

Princeton Theological Seminary[16]

In the early years of the nineteenth century, Presbyterians in America began to sense the need for a theological seminary of their own to train and supply

---

[14]This personal report came from the elderly Johannes Vos, son of Geerhardus Vos, in private conversation with R. C. Sproul, as Sproul reports in *Tabletalk*, April 2005, 4. Sproul has some details wrong, however, when he reports this event as occurring in 1921 and as the event that took Warfield in death. The heart attack Vos describes would have been December 24, 1920.

[15]*JGM*, 309.

[16]See Calhoun, *Princeton Seminary*, vols. 1 and 2; Lefferts A. Loetscher, *Facing the Enlightenment and Pietism: Archibald Alexander and the Founding of Princeton Theological Seminary* (Westport, CT: Greenwood, 1983); William K. Selden, *Princeton Theological Seminary: A Narrative History* (Princeton: Princeton University Press, 1992); Samuel Miller, *A Brief Account of the Rise, Progress and Present State of the Theological Seminary of the Presbyterian Church in the United States of America at Princeton* (Philadelphia: A. Finley, 1822); Mark A. Noll, "The Founding of Princeton Seminary," *WTJ* 42, no. 1 (1979): 72–110.

ministers for their churches. There was a shortage of ministers, and the choices for their adequate training were few and, from their perspective, inadequate. Harvard had drifted, appointing a Unitarian professor in 1805, and Congregationalists had responded with the founding of Andover Seminary, providing a model—and incentive—for the Presbyterians. There was no school of their own to prepare their ministers with a focus on their concerns of orthodox Reformed theology and fervent, practical piety. The College of New Jersey (now Princeton University), founded primarily for the purpose of training men for the Presbyterian ministry, had broadened its curriculum, giving less attention to ministerial concerns, and there were suspicions of the orthodoxy of its leadership also. The cry, "Give us ministers!" was growing, and the church increasingly felt the need for a seminary.

Several men in the church took up the cause, most prominently Ashbel Green (1762–1848), Samuel Miller (1769–1850), and Archibald Alexander (1772–1851)—men of learning, deep theological conviction, and pastoral concern. After much prayer, deliberation, and planning, "The Theological Seminary of the Presbyterian Church in the United States at Princeton" opened its doors in August of 1812 with three students and one professor (Alexander) to embark on a mission whose influence would prove greater and farther reaching than any could have imagined at the time. The seminary classes first met in the college's famous Nassau Hall, but this soon became inadequate. By spring of 1813 the seminary had nine students and had hired a second professor (Miller), and in 1814 the General Assembly (PCUSA) passed a resolution authorizing the purchase of new property for the seminary's own facilities nearby on Mercer Street, its present location. Of the two hundred and fifty-six men in the first ten graduating classes from Princeton, there came six moderators of the General Assembly of the Presbyterian Church (USA), two bishops of the Protestant Episcopal Church, fifteen college presidents of such noted institutions as Princeton and Yale, and missionaries and pastors in every part of the country, even to the Pacific Ocean; in but a few years Princeton would have graduates ministering around the world.[17] Most notably, very soon into its life the seminary at Princeton became recognized at home and abroad as the bastion of the Reformed faith.

The seminary was founded to promote more than theological orthodoxy. Its official "Plan" described the school's purpose to supply the church with ministers who both understood and loved the gospel, men of high learning and deep piety, men who could expound and apply the Word of God pastorally as well as defend it against all heresies and infidelity. The "Plan" states that the seminary's aim was

---

[17]William L. McEwan in *CC*, 408–9; *PSB* 13, no. 3 (1919): 6–8; cf. *PTR* 17, no. 1 (1919): 98–117.

to form men for the Gospel Ministry, who shall truly believe, and cordially love, and therefore endeavor to propagate and defend, in its genuineness, simplicity, and fulness, that system of religious belief and practice which is set forth in the Confession of Faith, Catechisms, and Plan of Government and Discipline of the Presbyterian Church; and thus to perpetuate and extend the influence of true evangelical piety, and gospel order. . . . It is to unite in those who shall sustain the ministerial office, religion and literature; that piety of the heart which is the fruit only of the renewing and sanctifying grace of God, with solid learning: believing that religion without learning, or learning without religion, in the ministers of the Gospel, must ultimately prove injurious to the Church. . . . It is to provide for the Church, men who shall be able to defend her faith against infidels, and her doctrines against heretics. It is to furnish our congregations with enlightened, humble, zealous, laborious pastors, who shall truly watch for the good of souls, and consider it as their highest honor and happiness to win them to the Saviour, and to build up their several charges in holiness and peace.[18]

The intent was that neither the academic nor the affective aspects of the faith would be neglected, but that both would be vigorously advanced and, insofar as humanly possible, instilled in the students. Samuel Miller described their goal as that of a "union of piety and learning." It was in many respects a combining of both the Old Side and the revivalistic New Side Presbyterian ideals. Archibald Alexander, the seminary's founding professor, had witnessed revivals firsthand, and from the founding of the seminary onward the Princetonians labored to see God's self-revelation shape both the theology and the lives of its faculty and graduates alike. Its conscious ideal was a union of the most rigorous academic studies with a cultivation of the deepest evangelical piety. Since its beginning, this goal had been achieved in recognizable degree. Warfield had witnessed it in his own student days, and he would come to embody this ideal himself.

Throughout its first century Princeton boasted a faculty of exemplary piety and unsurpassed erudition. Archibald Alexander, Samuel Miller, and Charles Hodge were the first three professors, and after them came Joseph Addison Alexander (1809–1860), John Breckinridge, James Waddell Alexander (1804–1859), William Henry Green (1825–1900), Alexander Taggart McGill (1807–1889), Caspar Wistar Hodge, James Clement Moffat (1832–1861), Charles Augustus Aiken (1827–1892), Archibald Alexander Hodge, Francis Landey Patton, and William Miller Paxton (1824–1904). They all served as professors of eminent distinction before or with Warfield, equipping hundreds of men for gospel ministry and earning for the institution an international reputation of Christian learning, faithfulness, and grace.

[18]Miller, *A Brief Account*, 16–18.

Alongside and after Warfield came professors of similar renown, such as John D. Davis (1854–1926), George T. Purves (1852–1901), John DeWitt (1842–1923), William Brenton Greene (1854–1928), Geerhardus Vos, William Park Armstrong (1874–1944), Robert Dick Wilson (1856–1930), and Caspar Wistar Hodge Jr. (1870–1937), the last of whom worked alongside Warfield for twenty years in the department of theology, finally inheriting his chair. From these men came thousands of graduates heavily influenced by their tutelage and an endless literary output in books and theological journals to further the faith entrusted to them. For Princeton, sometimes dubbed "the Oxford of America,"[19] it was a century of biblical and theological giants of international renown.

Paul Helseth observes correctly that "it has become something of an article of faith in the historiography of American Christianity that the theologians at Old Princeton Seminary were scholastic rationalists whose doctrine of Scripture was shaped by the Scottish Common Sense Realism of the 'Didactic Enlightenment' in America."[20] But Helseth,[21] David Smith,[22] and Andrew Hoffecker[23] have questioned the extent to which the Princetonians were influenced by the Scottish philosophy and have demonstrated at length that all the major Princetonians were marked equally by the academic rigor and the fervent piety idealized in the seminary's Plan. Men such as Archibald Alexander, Samuel Miller, Charles Hodge, and J. W. Alexander in particular were known for their pastoral instincts. The sermons preached by Warfield and others at the Sabbath afternoon conferences in Miller Chapel demonstrate that while the Princetonians excelled in learning, they were men deeply affected by the gospel, with a keen sense of dependence upon God and consciously aware of the need of the supernatural influences of his Spirit in them. The seminary's centennial celebration (May 5–7, 1912) was an important milestone for the Princetonians and for the Presbyterian Church. Churchmen and scholars from around the world were invited to represent their respective

---

[19]Roland Bruce Lutz, "Keeping Out of the Rut," *PSB* 14, no. 5 (1921): 13.

[20]Paul Kjoss Helseth, "'*Re*-Imagining' the Princeton Mind: Postconservative Evangelicalism, Old Princeton, and the Rise of Neo-Fundamentalism," *JETS* 45, no. 3 (2002): 427.

[21]Paul K. Helseth, "Right Reason and the Princeton Mind: The Moral Context," *JPH* 77, no. 1 (1999): 13–28; Helseth, "'*Re*-Imagining' the Princeton Mind," 427–50; Helseth, "B. B. Warfield's Apologetical Appeal to Right Reason: Evidence of a Rather Bald Rationalism?" *SBET* 16 (Autumn 1998): 156–77; republished as "A 'Rather Bald' Rationalist? The Appeal to 'Right Reason,'" in *BBW*, 54–75.

[22]David P. Smith, "B. B. Warfield's Scientifically Constructive Theological Scholarship" (PhD diss., Trinity International University, 2009).

[23]Andrew Hoffecker, "The Relation between the Objective and Subjective Aspects in Christian Religious Experience: A Study in the Systematic and Devotional Writings of Archibald Alexander, Charles Hodge, and Benjamin B. Warfield" (PhD diss., Brown University, 1970); later published under the title, *Piety and the Princeton Theologians* (Phillipsburg, NJ: Presbyterian and Reformed, 1981). See also Hoffecker, "The Devotional Life of Archibald Alexander, Charles Hodge and Benjamin B. Warfield," *WTJ* 42, no. 1 (1979): 110–29; and Hoffecker, "Benjamin B. Warfield," in David F. Wells, ed., *The Princeton Theology* (Grand Rapids: Baker, 1989), 65–91; republished also in Wells, ed., *Reformed Theology in America: A History of Its Modern Development* (1985; repr., Grand Rapids: Baker, 1997), 65–91.

institutions at the event, and in their letters sent ahead and their speeches during the celebration, seemingly endless expressions of "indebtedness" and praise were given to the seminary for the incalculable service it had rendered the cause of Christ via the "piety, scholarship, teaching power, and writings [that] have carried the name and fame of Princeton throughout the world." Much was made of its zeal for the truth and its stalwart defense and propagation of the sacred faith.[24] Those who knew the school well testified that the hearts of the Princetonians ran deeper than immense scholarship alone. For Warfield himself, as we will see in the next chapter, all theological learning had as its very practical goal the experiential knowledge of God.

Even so, the theological acumen for which the "Old Princetonians" were known served notably to advance their treasured Reformed orthodoxy, and more important to the Princetonians than their fame was their fidelity and influence for divine truth as they understood it. At the seminary's centennial celebration much praise and thanksgiving were offered to God on this score. Speakers and correspondents perceived it as no small measure of grace that throughout a century that was marked by rationalism and that in virtually every way conspired against such ideas as divine sovereignty and human depravity, the Reformed theology of "Old Princeton" remained powerfully influential.

Charles Hodge had remarked on several occasions that a new idea had never originated at Princeton,[25] and opponents have used his words against him to cast the Old Princeton as out of touch with the times. But of course the quote is capable of a much more sympathetic understanding. Certainly Hodge intended to affirm their conservative stance and the faithful continuation of Reformed theology. He—and they collectively—regarded their Reformed heritage as entrusted to them, and it was a matter of conscience and faithfulness for them not only to preserve it but to perpetuate it. At the 1912 centennial celebration, seminary president Francis Landey Patton made the point that they were bound to this by the school's founding charter and constitution.[26] But it should not be inferred that they merely rehashed theological sentiments centuries old. As with every new generation, theirs brought its own challenges, and in the process of meeting these challenges the Princetonians labored to bring the old faith to bear on the thinking of the new day and its changing culture. Patton affirmed on the one hand that the seminary's theological position was "exactly the same" in 1912 as it had been at the school's inception a century before. But he also clarified that this was to be understood only in terms of "the distinctive dogmatic content of

---

[24]E.g., see CC, 92, 232; cf. 123, 221, 233, 266, 286, passim.
[25]A. A. Hodge, The Life of Charles Hodge, D.D., LL.D. (London: T. Nelson and Sons, 1881), 256, 430, 521, 594.
[26]CC, 347; cf. Wells, Reformed Theology in America, 66.

the Reformed Theology." The Princetonians were "not content with a repetition of the old formulas" but were receptive to new learning on all fronts and eager to bring that learning to use in the defense and propagation of the old faith. Their teaching was "not novel in its essential features, but built up in full view of opposing systems, and with constant reference to the science and philosophy and criticism of the time."[27]

In the end they constructed a traditional Reformed theology that was yet distinctively Princetonian. "Old Princeton" was a term used already before the end of the nineteenth century to describe their distinctive theology. The phrase "the Princeton theology" reflects the same, which historian Mark Noll defines as "a distinctly American and a distinctly nineteenth-century expression of classical Reformed faith."[28] In terms of their theology historically considered, the Princetonians taught nothing new. They labored conscientiously to perpetuate the historic faith, and they would not alter it, no matter the demands of the new age. Their theological anchor held firmly in place. But in terms of their methodology, organization of thought, and points of contemporary application, they labored just as vigorously to bring the old faith to bear on the modern world and the American culture. And this they did with distinguished success. From its inception in 1812 to its reorganization in 1929, Old Princeton was the recognized force in the contemporary defense and propagation of the historic Reformed faith.

Russell Cecil, pastor of Second Presbyterian Church in Richmond, Virginia, and moderator of the General Assembly, reported at the centennial that

in all these hundred years Princeton Seminary has been true to the ideals and standards of its first great organizers, and it has been loyal to the Word of God. No student has, by reason of any teaching from any professor, had his reverence for or belief in the Word of God, as the only infallible rule of faith and practice, weakened or destroyed. No student has here learned to question the essential deity of the Lord Jesus Christ, or has lost any of the passionate loyalty of his heart for Him as Saviour and Lord. No student passes through these halls without having it impressed upon his heart and mind and conscience that the only salvation for a lost world of sinful men is that gospel which is the power of God unto salvation to all them that believe. Men who have the spirit of this Seminary go forth to their solemn calling as preachers of the gospel, caring for the vital and essential truths of revelation, and putting these things above the temporal and the accidental.

From this Seminary have been graduated about six thousand men, the greater part of whom (a little over half) remain until this present day. From more than

---

[27]CC, 349–50.
[28]Noll in Wells, *Reformed Theology in America*, 15.

two thousand pulpits every Sabbath day they preach the Gospel of Jesus Christ to multitudes of men and women. Year after year they stand in their places, the broken ranks being re-filled, proclaiming the everlasting righteousness and the infinite love of God. Who can estimate their influence upon the thought and life of this nation?[29]

Of the stars that made up the Princeton constellation, Charles Hodge had shone most brightly. It was reported that a student from Princeton who had taken up study in Germany, upon asking his professor if he would receive credit for courses taken at Princeton under Hodge, was told he perhaps "should receive double!" Such was his international reputation. But for all his deserved acclaim, first place in learning among the Princetonians would later be given to Warfield. No less than Caspar Wistar Hodge Jr., the grandson of Charles Hodge and Warfield's assistant for twenty years and then successor at the seminary, remarked at his inauguration that in erudition Warfield excelled all the illustrious professors that held the chair of theology before him, and that he was "without an equal in the English speaking world."[30] Samuel Craig reports that

> John DeWitt, long the professor of Church History in Princeton Seminary and himself a man of no mean scholarship, once told the writer that he had known intimately the three great Reformed theologians of America of the preceding generation—Charles Hodge, W. G. T. Shedd, and Henry B. Smith—and that he was not only certain that Warfield knew a great deal more than any one of them but that he was disposed to think that he knew more than all three of them put together.[31]

Both friends and foes acknowledge Warfield as "possibly the most intellectually gifted professor ever to teach on that [Princeton] faculty."[32] The breadth and depth of his voluminous works have impressed Christian students and scholars of all theological persuasions. Warfield was by all accounts one of the most outstanding and influential orthodox theologians of the era. The congratulatory correspondence that poured into the school from church leaders and religious institutions from around the world for the centennial celebration, as well as speakers at the event, brought remarks of praise not only of past Princeton professors, which is to be expected, but also of Warfield, then in his prime, a leading "ornament" of

---

[29]*CC*, 416–17.
[30]Calhoun, *Princeton Seminary*, 1:353; *PTR* 20, no. 1 (1922): 1.
[31]Samuel G. Craig, "Benjamin B. Warfield," in *BTS*, xvii.
[32]Ernest R. Sandeen, *The Roots of Fundamentalism: British and American Millenarianism, 1800–1930* (1970; repr., Grand Rapids: Baker, 1978), 115.

the seminary and a scholar who had already become "a household name" both in America and abroad. Such was the esteem in which he was held in his own day.[33] Among Reformed orthodox theologians few have stood taller. This was the reputation he earned in his own lifetime, and the breadth and depth of his scholarship and exhaustive acquaintance with the theological, scientific, and philosophical literature and thought of his day constituted the high-water mark of Old Princeton.

Princeton, The Presbyterians, and Beyond

The late eighteenth century through the nineteenth century was a time marked by change. Political and philosophical upheavals and scientific and technological advances were dramatically transforming life and culture. Learning itself and new understandings grew at a record pace. In the academy new ways of thinking were advanced in virtually every discipline. It was a new and "enlightened" world, and this inevitably brought new pressures to the church. Theologians and church leaders of the day felt this pressure very keenly, and as responses varied, the Christian world and church denominations of the early twentieth century were shaped and reshaped accordingly.

At the heart of the Enlightenment ideal, eighteenth-century rationalism, was the optimistic contention that human reasoning—rationality—is the final arbiter of truth. This starting point, and its close sibling naturalism, resulted in a higher criticism of Scripture and an attack on virtually everything Christian. Then came Darwin's *On the Origin of Species* (1859), which demanded a new consideration of the early chapters of Genesis, raising questions regarding God and his involvement in the universe. These and other expressions of naturalism came against the historic Christian faith in force, and the rapid change of the world at large was reflected in no small measure in the world of Christian theology. Professing Christians were becoming ever less satisfied with traditional Christianity, its institutions, and its creeds. Change was demanded, and the church became increasingly divided between conservative and liberal patterns of thought. Change in one respect or another was unavoidable. Sizing it up well, Friedrich A. G. Tholuck (1799–1877) is reported to have remarked to Henry Boynton Smith (1815–1877) that "the controlling and central feature of the theological thought of the day" is "*Ent-wick-el-ung*" (emphasizing each syllable

---

[33]*CC*, 123, 471, 525.

of *Entwicklung* emphatically)—"development."[34] Historic doctrines could no longer be assumed stable.

By the close of the nineteenth century, students of Scripture had come to recognize that century as one of unprecedented advance in biblical scholarship and learning. Warfield agreed with this assessment, but he was careful to nuance the observation with a larger contextual note, namely, that biblical students of the nineteenth century were standing on the shoulders of those of previous centuries. It was not the nineteenth century that invented or discovered the Bible. Its discovery was the great gift of the Reformation, and "the light that was then turned upon the Word of God has been shining steadily upon it ever since." Men such as Johann Reuchlin (1455–1522) and Erasmus (c. 1466–1536) gave us the Scriptures in their original languages, and these treasures also have been kept under close scrutiny. "The Reformation age grasped at the heart of Scripture; the age of systematization investigated its substance; the age of rationalism occupied itself with its shell. But each point of view and each age had its own contribution to make to the common store of ascertained fact, and still knowledge grew." It was this continuously advancing and "accumulated mass of learning," Warfield says, that "was laid at last in the lap of the nineteenth century" and enabled it to achieve its own progress.[35]

Biblical scholars of the nineteenth century, in turn, furthered the work of their predecessors in the study of the biblical text, the biblical languages, biblical history and archaeology, and of course biblical criticism. C. W. Hodge Jr. remarked in 1894 that "the state of philosophy all over the world to-day is one of criticism rather than construction," and this was no less the case in biblical and theological studies. This is not surprising, Warfield remarked, for an age of investigation and development in knowledge is by the nature of the case an age of criticism. By this growth of knowledge the total body of old knowledge is tested and tried. It is to be expected that the progress of knowledge should bring with it new challenges to the faith. Warfield was neither afraid of nor opposed to scientific criticism, even in reference to the Bible. Indeed, he championed the right of criticism and was confident that by it the historic faith of the church had been all the more vindicated. "An inspired statement which cannot stand the test of criticism is not foundation enough to build faith on," he remarked. But immediately he added, "A criticism which cannot be trusted to accord independently with inspired statements, cannot be trusted where we have no such divine authority to check its vagaries." That is, he insisted that criticism must be honest and objective and

---

[34]Cited in George W. Richards, "The Mercersburg Theology: Its Purpose and Principles," *Church History* 20, no. 3 (1951): 45; cf. *W*, 9:25–31.
[35]*SSW*, 2:3–4.

not driven merely by the unbelieving, negative, naturalistic spirit of the age. To disallow flawed criticism is not to deny criticism per se. The supposed findings of a criticism marred in its methodology or by its ill-founded presuppositions cannot be naively accepted simply because it is called criticism. And just as the "old facts" must be checked by the "new facts" criticism discovers, so also the old facts must check the new. Warfield's complaint was that the antisupernaturalistic criticism of the day had run too long unchecked. Its assaults on Scripture were grounded in a naturalistic presupposition and were driven by the goal of ridding Christianity of the supernatural. Its "findings" were not objectively obtained and were in the largest measure unjustified.[36]

But an era of change it was, and "progressive orthodoxy" increasingly became the slogan of the day. Warfield was eager to affirm that the church ought to be progressive in its understanding of God's revelation in Scripture until in glory our understanding is made perfect. But the "strange connections" in which the phrase was most often used left the expression self-contradictory. Modern theology had taken its stand not first in Scripture but in other sources of ideas. For Warfield this is necessarily the makings of heresy, and he lamented that although so many in his day were in supposed "pursuit of truth," very few seemed to have found much of it.[37]

Modern liberal theology is generally said to have its origin in the German preacher-theologian Friedrich Schleiermacher (1768–1834), who, reacting against philosophical skepticism, grounded theology in experience and feeling, specifically the feeling of God-consciousness and its corollary, a sense of absolute dependence. Schleiermacher led the way for the rejection of external authority, in favor of an anthropological point of reference, the religious consciousness. This grounding of theology in the experience and feelings of the inner life became a permanent fixture in Christian theology and opened a path for rationalism and mysticism alike. Indeed, resting on such an uncertain and shifting basis as the human psyche, "Christian doctrine" could have no certain meaning and no room for authoritative dogma. Christianity itself now could be considered but one of the world religions, and it could be weighed accordingly. Though Christianity could be viewed as superior, for whatever reasons, "comparative religions" rather than divine revelation became the point of reference, and "theology" rather than the study of God as he has revealed himself became the study of religious experience. Schleiermacher marks this turn in

---

[36]*PRR* 7, no. 26 (1896): 211; *SSW*, 2:4–8, 124–31, 595–603; *W*, 9:25–31; "Dr. Briggs' Critical Method," *Interior* 14 (Feb. 4, 1882): 2.

[37]*W*, 9:78; *SSW*, 2:672–79; "The Hibbert Journal," *TBS*, new series, 7, no. 1 (January 1903): 55.

Christian theology from a recognition of divine revelation to a confidence in the human psyche.[38]

The ramifications of this new thinking played out in succeeding generations of theological endeavor. Despite the enormous stature of Schleiermacher, Albrecht Ritschl (1822–1889) is recognized, by reason of influence more than originality, as the father of the later classic Protestant liberalism that prevailed in Warfield's day. The son of a Lutheran (Prussian) minister, Ritschl made his name as Germany's leading theologian at Göttingen, where he taught from 1864 until his death in 1889. The hallmark of Ritschlianism is its attempt "to clear theology of all 'metaphysical' elements. Otherwise expressed, this means that nothing will be admitted to belong to Christianity except facts of experience." Any elaboration of these "facts" into "dogmas" necessarily entails metaphysical elements and questions of ontology and is therefore ruled out of court. Heavily influenced by Schleiermacher's theology of religious experience and by Immanuel Kant (1724–1804), who emphasized the moral character of Christianity and taught that the human mind is incapable of investigating matters beyond the immediate experience of the human senses and the dictates of reason, Ritschl left theoretical speculations about such matters as the nature and being of God to "science." "Religious" investigation had to do only with religious experience, "value judgments," morals, and ethics. God may be known as love, for this is how we experience him. But beyond that is beyond experience and the realm of religion. Christ is Lord in that this is how we experience him as we bow to his example and teaching. There is nothing knowable about him apart from this. Ritschl never explicitly denied the future state, but for him religion had to do with life on earth. Life's highest goal is the pursuit of the kingdom of God, which for Ritschl is the Christian community that has collectively made this value judgment. Ritschl had no room for metaphysical or (its related) mystical theology, and doctrine itself came to be held in utmost disdain as obstructive of true religion and "essential Christianity." Warfield therefore often characterized Ritschlianism as a reduced Christianity and a mere system of ethics. As Paul Tillich later described it, "Ritschlianism was a withdrawal from the ontological to the moral." Indeed, in one of Ritschl's leading American disciples, Walter Rauschenbusch (1861–1918), Ritschlianism gave birth to the "social gospel," an understanding of the gospel in humanitar-

---

[38]*W*, 9:657–60; R. A. Finlayson, *The Story of Theology* (London: Tyndale, 1969), 56; James C. Livingston, *Modern Christian Thought: The Enlightenment and the Nineteenth Century* (Minneapolis: Fortress, 2006), 93–105; Louis Berkhof, *Recent Trends in Theology* (Grand Rapids: Eerdmans, 1944), 11–12, 16–17; Colin Brown, *Philosophy and the Christian Faith: A Historical Sketch from the Middle Ages to the Present Day* (London: Inter-Varsity, 1969), 110–16.

ian terms only. Ritschl was the most influential theologian of the time, and Ritschlianism dominated the late nineteenth and early twentieth centuries. His enormous influence continued after his death until about 1925, when the eschatological nature of the kingdom of God became more widely recognized and the "new orthodoxy" of Karl Barth (1886–1968) began to erode the older liberal theology.[39]

Warfield observes that this liberalism did not arise directly from unbelief but indirectly, in an attempt to rescue what was considered "essential Christianity" from the onslaught of philosophical and scientific materialism. Increasingly traditional Christian doctrines were deemed indefensible to modern criticism, and they were abandoned as needless accretions to the true faith of the historical Jesus. Early in the history of the church the religion *of* Jesus was corrupted into a religion *about* Jesus. All such "doctrines" now were to be abandoned. Virtually all metaphysical elements and the supernatural were yielded over in an attempt to preserve "essential Christianity." But what was surrendered in the process, Warfield contended, was precisely that which was distinctive to Christianity— supernaturalism, and its attending notions of divine revelation and external authority.

Accommodation to unbelief had resulted in a Bible that was something other than the divine word and a Jesus who was something less than the divine Christ. In the hands of the liberals all the miraculous elements of Scripture came quickly under assault. The supernatural aspects of Christ's person and work were espe- cially the object of criticism—his virgin birth, deity, transfiguration, vicarious atonement, resurrection, and miracles were all given naturalistic explanations, ranging from theories of fraud and prescientific naivety to lessons of moralistic instruction. Kenotic theories of Christ's incarnation multiplied with attempts to explain him as other than divine, and various fictitious lives of Jesus were published, all to explain Jesus in human terms. Stripped of metaphysical ele- ments, the church's historic doctrines of sin, grace, and regeneration were also eliminated, as well as any meaningful doctrine of prayer and vital communion with the exalted Christ. "And," Warfield wryly quips with Acts 19:2 in mind, "like the disciples that Paul met at Ephesus, [Ritschlianism] 'did not so much as hear whether there is a Holy Ghost.'" Christianity was reduced to an ethic and a phi- losophy to which no naturalistic philosopher or unbelieving scientist could

---

[39]*SSW*, 2:244–46, 448–51; *W*, 9:591–92, 657–60; Finlayson, *The Story*, 57–58; Brown, *Philosophy*, 154–55; Gary Dorrien, *The Word as True Myth: Interpreting Modern Theology* (Louisville: Westminster John Knox, 1997), 52; Livingston, *Modern Christian Thought*, 270–90; Paul Tillich, *A History of Christian Thought* (New York: Simon and Schuster, 1967), 514. Note that already in 1898 Warfield observed that the influence of Ritschlianism "seems distinctly on the wane in the land of its birth." *SSW*, 2:450.

find objection. All that is distinctively Christian was lost, the term "Christian" itself was rendered meaningless, and "essential Christianity" was but another naturalistic religion. Warfield approvingly cites James Orr's characterization of Ritschlianism as simply "an attempt to show how much of positive Christianity can be retained compatibly with the acceptance of the modern non-miraculous theory of the world."[40]

Harvard dean Willard Sperry (1882–1954) described liberalism as the "Yes, But" religion in a volume by that title (1931).

> Yes, I believe in the deity of Christ, but the language of Chalcedon has become mean-ingless. We must redefine the doctrine so as to make it intelligible to us who live in the twentieth century. Yes, I believe in the Virgin Birth of Christ, but the important thing is not any biological fact but the value of Jesus for us.[41]

William Robertson Smith (1846–1894), a flashpoint of the new theology in the Free Church of Scotland, provides a clear example. When accused of denying the deity of Christ, he responded: "How can they accuse me of that? I've never denied the divinity of any man, let alone Jesus."[42] Traditional terminology was used, but sharply different meanings were attached. Such was the theological world of Protestantism at the close of the nineteenth century. The Christian faith had come to mean many different things, and its resemblances to traditional orthodoxy were becoming increasingly distant. H. Richard Niebuhr (1894–1962) famously described early twentieth-century theology this way: "A God without wrath brought men without sin into a kingdom without judgment through the ministrations of Christ without a cross."[43]

In his 1894 "Evading the Supernatural," Warfield severely exposes the dialectic of liberal theologians. They affirm that their destructive critical views nevertheless leave the doctrine of inspiration intact and serve only to enhance Scripture's prof-itability to God's people. Stripping Christianity of all its dogmas, they yet assure us that Christianity itself stands all the more firm. And having reduced Jesus to mere humanity, they assure us still that he is worthy of our adoration. Warfield understands all this as deceptive doublespeak and warns that no rightly guarded Christian will be taken by it. "A tendency to the minimizing of the importance of the high supernaturalism of the creeds of the Church has taken possession of the world." In such an atmosphere Christianity itself hangs in the balance, for "Chris-

---

[40]*W*, 9:31, 588–91; *W*, 10:321–23; *SSW*, 2:242, 295–96, 448–51; Brown, *Philosophy*, 151–56; cf. *W*, 3:349–50; *W*, 10:1–25.
[41]Cited by Kenneth Kantzer, "Liberalism's Rise and Fall," *Christianity Today*, February 18, 1983, 10.
[42]Cited in Millard Erickson, *Christian Theology* (Grand Rapids: Baker, 1984), 740.
[43]*The Kingdom of God in America* (1937; repr., Middletown, CT: Wesleyan University Press, 1988), 193.

tianity, in its very essence, is supernaturalism."[44] These issues are nonnegotiable. "No one will doubt that Christians of to-day must state their Christian belief in terms of modern thought," Warfield acknowledges. "Every age has a language of its own and can speak no other." But he quickly cautions, "Mischief comes only when, instead of stating Christian belief in terms of modern thought, an effort is made, rather, to state modern thought in terms of Christian belief."[45] Warfield repeatedly insists that in this struggle Christianity itself is at stake. The Christianized language of unbelief masks an entirely different religion.[46] We might as well commit to fetishism, he argues: take away Christian doctrine, and no difference between Christianity and fetishism remains.

> It is the gravest kind of self-deception to imagine—to bring the matter to its sharpest point—that we can discard the religious conceptions of Paul, or of Jesus, and remain of the same religion as Paul or Jesus, because forsooth we feel that we too, like them, are religious beings and function religiously. Christianity is not a distinctive interpretation of a religious experience common to all men, much less is it an indeterminate and constantly changing interpretation of a religious experience common to men; it is a distinctive religious experience begotten in men by a distinctive body of facts known only to or rightly apprehended only by Christians.[47]

As an example, in 1906 the *American Journal of Theology* asked Warfield, among others, to respond to the question of whether the supernatural birth of Jesus is essential to Christianity. Much of what was called "Christianity" in his day, endeavoring to preserve the name, did not hold that Jesus' supernatural birth is at all essential, and this was the answer given by others in the article. For his part, before answering, Warfield sought to clarify just "what 'Christianity' it is we are talking about." Without the doctrines taught in Scripture and held by the church historically, Warfield insists, the very term "Christianity" has been evacuated of all meaning. "If everything that is called Christianity in these days is Christianity, then there is no such thing as Christianity. A name applied indiscriminately to everything, designates nothing."[48]

One difficulty liberalism faced in all this is that while it formally dismisses all metaphysical aspects of theology, it could not define itself apart from meta-

---

[44]*SSW*, 2:680–84.

[45]*W*, 10:322.

[46]E.g., *W*, 10:268, 404–5. Doubtless this emphasis in Warfield is at least in part where Warfield's famous student J. Gresham Machen received his inspiration for his celebrated exposé of liberalism, *Christianity and Liberalism*.

[47]*W*, 10:325–26.

[48]"The Supernatural Birth of Jesus," *The American Journal of Theology* 10, no. 1 (January 1906): 1–30; *W*, 3:447–58; *W*, 2:396; cf. *W*, 10:321–34.

physical references. To speak even of God requires the metaphysical elements that Ritschlianism disallowed. "It is a matter of metaphysical opinion whether we worship a fragment of bone or the God of heaven and earth; what separates the fetish-worshipper from the Christian here is a little matter of metaphysical opinion."[49] But this was an inconsistency Ritschlianism was willing to live with. Ritschlianism also faced a problem with history. It gave itself to destroying the whole system of historical Christian dogma yet clung to the name Christian. The problem is that "Christianity" is not an empty word able to fit any given system of belief. It has a historical content and meaning, and history knows of no undogmatic or nontheological Christianity at all. Warfield scarcely overstated the matter when he wrote, "The history of Christianity is the history of doctrine." Thus Ritschlianism was left "to explain the origin and development of doctrinal Christianity in such a manner as to evince essential Christianity to be undogmatic." In other words, it must "explain doctrinal Christianity as corrupted Christianity" and the rise and development of theology as accretions from without, obscuring the original faith. This task fell chiefly to Ritschl's brilliant and most outstanding student, Adolf von Harnack, and to Harnack's foremost American student and America's foremost Ritschlian representative, Arthur C. McGiffert (1861–1933)[50] of Union Theological Seminary in New York. Both labored vigorously to demonstrate the influence of pagan Greek philosophy in the forming of Christian doctrine in the early centuries of the church and, in turn, to tear away this "husk" so as to restore the pure and original kernel of the gospel—"essential Christianity"—that lay hidden beneath it. The "kernel," of course, is subjective faith in God our Father taught us by a human and non-miraculous but ethical Jesus who did not spread dogma but set the example of perfect love and taught us to love both God and man, thus proclaiming the kingdom of God.[51]

Beneath all this was, simply, rationalism—a rationalism that can admit no external authority. Liberalism by definition is "the idea that Christian theology can be genuinely Christian without being based upon external authority."[52] Warfield describes this attitude toward the authority of Jesus and the apostles as "the fundamental evil" of Ritschlianism. He repeats this charge often, as in his "Recent

---

[49] SSW, 1:365–66.

[50] McGiffert was a Presbyterian and Congregational church historian and educator at Lane Theological Seminary and Union Theological Seminary. His History of Christianity in the Apostolic Age (1897) led to heresy charges in the Presbyterian Church and resulted in his move to the Congregationalists in 1900.

[51] W, 9:591–94, 609–14; W, 10:115–18; SW, 201–2; SSW, 2:292; Tillich, A History of Christian Thought, 515–19; Livingston, Modern Christian Thought, 286–90; Earle E. Cairns, Christianity in America (Chicago: Moody, 1964), 151–52.

[52] Gary Dorrien, The Making of American Liberal Theology: Imagining Progressive Revelation 1805–1900 (Louisville: Westminster John Knox, 2001), xiii.

Reconstructions of Theology" (1898), where he characterizes the theological and religious scene of his day as, above all else, "a crisis of authority." It is not a new interpretation of Scripture so much as a new attitude toward Scripture itself. The "recent reconstructions of theology" have as their leading feature a refusal of all external authority, and the primitive church is represented as holding no "rule of faith" or "canon." "The only authority that was recognized was the Holy Spirit; and He was supposed to speak to every believer as truly as He spoke to an apostle." This is the significance of the new covenant as the age of the Spirit, according to Ritschlianism; primitive Christianity was individualistic and had no notion of apostolic authority. Scripture was denied any revelatory significance; instead, authority was found within the human spirit.

Warfield observes that not all liberals acknowledge this refusal of external authority with equal frankness. They may speak of a Christian consciousness or the witness of the Spirit, and they may cling to the fragments of Scripture that criticism has left and profess adherence to them. "But it is undeniable that 'recent theological reconstruction' holds at best but a crumbling Bible in its hands." The Ritschlian will not be made subject to biblical doctrines simply because those doctrines are biblical, for the Bible is denied that authority. Warfield cites McGiffert as an example, who not only "lays aside whole tracts of the New Testament as not in his judgment apostolic in origin, or trustworthy in narrative, or authoritative in teaching"; but "even to those parts the apostolic origin of which he can bring himself to allow," he will deny any peculiar authority above that which "belongs to the utterances of any Christian man who is led (as are all Christians) by the Holy Spirit."[53] This relocation of religious authority and rejection of biblical authority was the turning point of nineteenth-century theology.

In the absence of external doctrinal authority and with human reason the supreme arbiter of truth, other traditional Christian doctrines came under suspicion. "The nineteenth-century liberals refused to accept religious teachings that offended their moral, intellectual, and spiritual sensibilities. They began with the Calvinist doctrines of human nature, atonement, and divine predestination, which for them failed the moral test."[54] Douglas Macintosh wrote in the *Harvard Review* that the traditional theory of redemption as represented by Warfield "is not only not essential to Christianity, because contrary to reason, but moreover essentially unchristian, because opposed to the principles of sound morality."[55]

---

[53]*SSW*, 2:291–93, 448–51; *W*, 9:595–96, 619–28; *W*, 10:321–34; *W*, 3:323–24.
[54]Dorrien, *The Making of American Liberal Theology*, 399.
[55]Douglas Clyde Macintosh, "What Is the Christian Religion?" *The Harvard Theological Review* 7, no. 1 (1914): 18.

Religious authority resided now in the human psyche, and teaching grounded in Scripture could be rejected if offensive to the modern mind. But in our rejection of external authority, Warfield observes, we have but naively assumed infallibility for ourselves.[56]

But the rejection of the authority of Scripture carries further ramifications, even more fundamental, and Warfield presses the issue often: "Of course men cannot thus reject the Bible, to which Christ appealed as authoritative, without rejecting also the authority of Christ, which is thus committed to the Bible's authority." Questions of the nature and character of Scripture necessarily entail questions of christology, and for Warfield this is the deciding factor. We cannot have the Jesus of the Bible without also having the Bible of Jesus. But liberalism rejects all external authority, and by various arguments that limit the knowledge and/or teaching of Jesus, and by various kenotic theories, even Christ is divested of binding authority. Creative evasions do not change the reality of the case, however, and Warfield insists that it is all or nothing: "We may be theists without authority," he concedes, "but not Christians."[57]

An era of change it was. Christianity was being offered a new set of beliefs. Prominent among these was a new understanding of man and his origin, as well as a higher estimate of human potential and worth. Not only had humanity itself advanced from lower forms, but with it civilization itself had advanced. Religion had advanced also, and it was needful for Christianity to shed its ancient relics in order to keep up with the times. Such an atmosphere, which breathes naturalism, inevitably affects the church. Just how much is God involved in this world? Did he really create it? And if so, just how are we to understand that? Does he govern the universe? Is he transcendent or immanent? And in what way does this make a difference? Did he speak to the apostles in such a way that their writings constitute his word? Of course in all this, questions quickly arise regarding providence, predestination, inspiration, incarnation, redemption, and so on. The very nature of the church is thrown into question. Just what is the church? Is it the pillar and ground of the truth? Or is it more a religious society, or a business? And by what rule are such questions decided? What is the source of authority? Change was the leading characteristic of the day, and virtually all that was distinctively Christian hung in the balance.

Now the age in which we live is anything but supernaturalistic: it is distinctly hostile to supernaturalism. Its most striking characteristic is precisely its deeply rooted

[56]*W*, 10:322.

[57]*W*, 9:590; Warfield, "'Sixty Years with the Bible': A Record of Drifting," *TBST* 12 (February 1910): 128; *W*, 10:125–26, 431; *SSW*, 2:127–28.

and wide-reaching rationalism of thought and sentiment. . . . It has invaded with its solvent every form of thought and every activity of life. It has given us a naturalistic philosophy (in which all "being" is evaporated into "becoming"), a naturalistic science (the single-minded zeal of which is to eliminate design from the universe); a naturalistic politics (whose first fruits was the French Revolution, and whose last may well be an atheistic socialism); a naturalistic history (which can scarcely find place for even human personality among the causes of events); and a naturalistic religion, which says, "Hands off" to God—if indeed it troubles itself to consider whether there be a God, if there be a God, whether He be a person, or if He be a person, whether He can or will concern Himself with men.[58]

The Reformed branch of Protestantism, largely speaking, had proven a haven of historic Christian orthodoxy. Its Reformed faith was not ashamed to admit mystery, yet neither were its adherents ashamed to demonstrate the reasonableness of that faith and its internal cohesiveness. But change would come, and it was in the late nineteenth century that Warfield's Presbyterian Church in the United States of America experienced it.[59]

In his 1880 inaugural lecture at Western Theological Seminary, Warfield referred to "a certain looseness of belief" that had "invaded" several quarters of the church.[60] With many controversies behind it, the American body had a history of maneuvers that resulted in preserving an external unity of dissonant theological voices. The 1801 Plan of Union, acknowledging Congregational and Presbyterian ministers alike in the denomination, was finally overturned in the Old School–New School schism of 1837. But new issues and the climate of healing following the Civil War served to minimize and promote tolerance of previous differences. The reunion of 1869 marked a healing of sorts, at least externally, as differences were laid aside. The early 1890s witnessed various heresy trials over the higher criticism, that of Charles Briggs and the loss of Union Seminary being the most famous. Although the Old School conservatives could claim victory in these trials, significant opposition remained, owing often to the safe refuge afforded by several New School–dominated presbyteries. In 1889 many in the Presbyterian Church began calling for confessional revision. "It is an inexpressible grief," Warfield wrote, to see the church "spending its energies in a vain attempt to lower its testimony to suit the ever changing sentiment of the world around it."[61] The movement did not gain all that it sought, but it did

---

[58]*CA*, 504.
[59]Perhaps the most helpful study of this period in the Presbyterian Church is Lefferts A. Loetscher, *The Broadening Church* (Philadelphia: University of Pennsylvania Press, 1954), 1–89.
[60]*W*, 1:393.
[61]"Revision or Reaffirmation?" *Daily True American* (June 29, 1900); *PJ* 25, no. 27 (July 5, 1900), 7f.; *Southwestern Presbyterian* (July 19, 1900); and elsewhere.

finally result in the amendments of 1903 and a softening in tone of the strict Calvinism that had historically marked Presbyterianism. This, in turn, opened the way to the 1906 reunion with the Arminian Cumberland Presbyterians in the South. Warfield vigorously opposed all calls for confessional revision on grounds that the proffered changes would not improve at all but rather blur the precision already attained by the Westminster Confession of Faith.[62] He opposed reunion with the Cumberland Presbyterians on the ground that given their Calvinist-Arminian differences, gospel issues were at stake.[63] And he led the cause for the advancement of the historic faith against the higher criticism newly arrived from Germany. In article after article Warfield defended the faith on all fronts, answering the encroaching Arminianism and critics on all sides and launching a counterattack of his own.

Although Warfield remained ever confident of the ultimate triumph of the historic Christian faith, he seems gradually to have seen the cause as lost in his

---

[62]"What Is the Confession of Faith?" (address given before the Presbytery of New Brunswick, June 25, 1889), *PB* 76 (September 4, 1889); reprinted in *Shall We Revise the Confession of Faith?* (Trenton, NJ: n.p., 1889); also *On the Revision of the Confession of Faith* (New York: Randolph, 1890); "The Presbyterians and the Revision of the Westminster Confession," *The Independent* 41 (July 18, 1889): 914–15; "Revision of the Confession of Faith I–III," *Herald and Presbyter* 49, nos. 51–52, and 50, no. 1 (1889): 2 (in all three issues); "The Presbyterian Churches and the Westminster Confession," *PR* 10, no. 40 (1889): 646–57; "Confessional Subscription and Revision," *PQ* 76 (November 1889); "God's Infinite Love to Men and the Westminster Confession," *P* 59, no. 44 (1889): 6; "The Meaning of Revision of the Confession," *PJ* 14, no. 46 (1889); "The Present Status of the Revision Controversy," *The Central West* 4 (March 20, 1890); "As Others See Us," *The New York Observer* 68 (August 25, 1890): 266; "True Church Unity: What It Is" (December 1890), *SSW*, 1:299–307; "The Final Report of the Committee on Revision of the Confession," *PRR* 3 (April 1892): 322–30; "The Revision of the Westminster Confession before the Presbyteries," *The Independent* 44 (September 22, 1892): 1316–17; "The Significance of the Westminster Standards as a Creed" (November 13, 1897), *SSW*, 2:660–62; "The Significance of Our Confessional Doctrine of the Decree" (May 17 and 24, 1900), *SSW*, 1:93–102; "Revision or Reaffirmation?"; "Is There No Danger in the Revision Movement?" *PJ* 25, no. 29 (1900): 8; "The Revision Movement in the Presbyterian Church," *The Independent* 52 (August 1900): 1906–9; "Is It Restatement That We Need?" *PJ* 25, no. 27 (1900): 7–8; also *P* 70, no. 33 (1900): 8–10; "Revision and the Third Chapter," *PB* 87 (August 23, 30, September 6, 1900): 12–13 (in all three issues); "Predestination in the Reformed Confessions" (January 1901), *W*, 9:117–231; "A Declaratory Statement," in *Papers Submitted to the General Committee on Confessional Revision for Information* (n.p., 1901): 5–8; "The Making of the Westminster Confession, and Especially of Its Chapter on the Decree of God" (1901), *W*, 6:75–161; "The Confessional Situation," *The New York Observer* 79 (May 16, 1901): 63; "The Proposed New Statement of Presbyterian Doctrine," *P* 71, nos. 27–31 (1901): 10–11, 8–9, 8–9, 8–9; "On the Diction of the Revision Overtures," *P* 73, no. 12 (1903): 8–9; *PB* 89 (March 26, 1903): 1323; also *PJ* 28, no. 13 (1903): 7–8; also *Herald and Presbyter* 74, no. 12 (1903): 10–11; "Dr. Warfield's Reply," *P* 53, no. 14 (1903): 8–9; "The Proposed Union with the Cumberland Presbyterians," *PTR* 2, no. 2 (1904): 295–316; see also *P* 74, nos. 15–19 (1904): 7–8 (in each issue); "An Humble Defense," *CP* 67, no. 17 (1904): 519–20; "Christian Unity and Church Union: Some Primary Principles," *PB* 91 (July 7, 1904): 103–4; "In Behalf of Evangelical Religion," *P* 90, no. 39 (1920): 20; reprinted in *SSW*, 1:385–88. After the amendments to the confession were ratified, Warfield lent his general support, affirming that the changes that were finally adopted did not alter the confession's system of theology ("The Confession of Faith as Revised in 1903," *SSW*, 2:370–419). Perhaps, but the Cumberland Presbyterians en masse understood them as sufficiently overcoming their differences and thus allowing the reunion.

[63]Letter to *CP* (quoted in part in an editorial) 68, no. 16 (1904): 484, and printed in full at Warfield's request 68, no. 21 (1904): 655; "On the Misapplication of Historical Names," *P* 74, no. 52 (1904): 8–9. This article had been refused by *CP*; "The Basis of the Proposed Union—Theoretical and Practical," *P* 75, no. 9 (1905): 8–9; "Vote of the Cumberland Presbyteries on Union," *P* 75, no. 19 (1905): 8.

Presbyterian Church. As early as 1882 he wrote that the gravity of the crisis could not be overestimated, being so severe that he suggested getting rid of the critics.[64] In 1889 even Charles Briggs, Warfield's archrival at Union Seminary in New York, could write of their church:

> The Westminster system has been virtually displaced by the teachings of the dogmatic divines. It is no longer practically the standard of the faith of the Presbyterian Church. The Catechisms are not taught in our churches, the Confession is not expounded in our theological seminaries. The Presbyterian Church is not orthodox, judged by its own standards. . . . It is drifting toward an unknown and a mysterious future.[65]

In May of 1893 Charles Briggs was suspended from Presbyterian ministry for his critical views of Scripture, but he responded with increasing confidence. In his July 1893 "The Future of the Presbyterianism in the United States," he questioned whether liberals would be able to stay in their respective denominations or if they would eventually need to leave and form a union of their own. Either way, he stated confidently, the "ultra conservatives," as he called them, would certainly be "crushed" and in due time left behind.[66] Later in his controversial 1909 *Church Unity* he wrote more confidently, "It is evident to intelligent observers that Christianity is passing through a process of change which is gradually transforming it." He wrote this as one laboring to advance that transformation and establish the "coming Catholicism" that he envisioned would be marked by a "deeper and richer religious experience, higher and broader comprehension of divine truths and facts," and free of "fruitless controversies." He recognized the pivotal significance of his era, and with confidence that was at times triumphalistic, he spoke of "The Passing and the Coming Christianity" as though this new and truly "Catholic" church had already emerged, leaving the historic faith behind it.

> The antitheses of the sixteenth century are to a great extent antitheses of one-sidedness, which the modern world has outgrown. The world has moved since then. The world has learned many things. We have new views of God's universe. We have new scientific methods. We have an entirely different psychology and philosophy. Our education is much more scientific, much more thorough, much more accurate, much more searching, much more comprehensive. All along the line of life, institution, dogma, morals, new situations are emerging, new questions pressing for solution;

---

[64]*SSW*, 2:596, 603.
[65]Charles A. Briggs, *Whither?* (New York: Charles Scribner's Sons, 1889), 223–24.
[66]*North American Review* 440 (July, 1893): 9–10.

the perspective is changed, the lights and shadows are differently distributed. We are in a state of enormous transition, changes are taking place whose results it is impossible to foretell—reconstruction is in progress on the grandest scale. Out of it will spring, in God's own time, a rejuvenated, a reorganized, a truly universal Christianity, combining in a higher unity all that is true and real and worthy in the various Churches which now divide the world.[67]

Briggs had lost his own case with the church body, but so fast-paced were the theological changes and so overwhelming was this wave of new thinking that he felt nonetheless assured he was on the winning side.

It was this onslaught exactly that Warfield labored to halt and even destroy. As Raymond Cannata remarks, "At the height of what Sydney Ahlstrom calls the 'Golden Age of Liberal Theology,' B. B. Warfield was a spoiler."[68] Intellectually and academically well equipped and with a literary output comparable to Augustine or Calvin, he was a towering figure in the counterattack against liberalism. Devastating in his critical analysis of liberalism, Warfield is often referred to as, simply, "the Princeton apologist." Theology and not apologetics was his department of instruction and focus of attention, but it was in large measure a theology polemically maintained and advanced, driven by the circumstances of his day. What marked the Protestant landscape was to him all that smacked of unbelief dressed in new clothing, and he was supremely confident that the facts were on his side and that no critical scholarship or antisupernaturalistic bias would ever overthrow the faith once for all delivered to the saints. James McClanahan observes insightfully that Warfield "may be studying Tertullian, but he has an eye on Harnack. He may be describing the Westminster Assembly, but he's watching Briggs and McGiffert, too."[69] "There was no one in the English-speaking world who could surpass the massive learning, lucid pen and sheer intellectual powers of the seminary's own B. B. Warfield."[70] Always ready to step up and raise a banner for the historic faith of the church and always ready to address unbelief both inside and outside his denomination, he throughout his career was marked by fervency of spirit, keen insight, and massive learning.

For nearly a century before Warfield arrived on its faculty, Princeton Seminary had stood out as the scholarly bastion of the historic Reformed faith. And due in large measure to the towering influence of Old Princeton, much of the new

---

[67]Charles A. Briggs, *Church Unity* (New York: Charles Scribner's Sons, 1909), viii, 416, 426–27, 435.

[68]Raymond Cannata, "History of Apologetics at Princeton Seminary," in William A. Dembski and Jay Wesley Richards, eds., *Unapologetic Apologetics* (Downers Grove, IL: InterVarsity, 2001), 71.

[69]James Samuel McClanahan, "Benjamin B. Warfield: Historian of Doctrine in Defense of Orthodoxy, 1881–1921" (PhD diss., Union Theological Seminary, 1988), 630.

[70]Cannata, *Unapologetic Apologetics*, 113.

liberalizing tendencies in the church had been held back in significant degree. By means of his 2,700 students and his endless literary output, Warfield played an enormous role in this. But the undercurrent was always present, and within a decade after his death, liberal currents of thought would gain prominence in his Presbyterian church and at his beloved Princeton also. Warfield once met the wife of the seminary president J. Ross Stevenson while walking down a Princeton street, and she implored him: "Dr. Warfield, I hear there is going to be trouble at the General Assembly. Do let us pray for peace." To this he replied, "I am praying that if they do not do what is right, there may be a mighty battle."[71] Warfield's younger colleague J. Gresham Machen reports a conversation with Warfield some weeks before Warfield's death.

> I expressed my hope that to end the present intolerable condition there might be a great split in the Church, in order to separate the Christians from the anti-Christian propagandists. "No," he said, "You can't split rotten wood." His expectation seemed to be that the organized Church, dominated by naturalism, would become so cold and dead, that people would come to see that spiritual life could be found only outside of it, and that thus there might be a new beginning.[72]

This was Machen's last conversation with Warfield, and it reveals Warfield's thinking regarding the state of his church: it had fallen irreparably into naturalism. Hence Machen's further comment, after the funeral, that he felt as they carried Warfield out, that Old Princeton went out with him.

"Christian Supernaturalism": Warfield in Summary

In his 1896 opening address, "Christian Supernaturalism," delivered before the faculty and students of Princeton Seminary, Warfield criticizes the antisupernaturalistic bias of the age and highlights the necessary supernaturalism of Christianity. In doing so he provides for us a concise outline of the frame of reference that shaped his polemic throughout his career. He charges that the antisupernaturalistic bias of modern rationalism is rooted in a pantheistic—or at least pantheizing—philosophy that blurs the distinction between the natural and the supernatural. This is a dominant feature of the rationalist's "God," whose immanence is championed at the expense of his transcendence. Warfield cites

---

[71] W. J. Grier, "Benjamin Breckenridge Warfield, D.D. LL.D. Litt.D.," *BT* 89 (Fall 1971): 8.
[72] *JGM*, 310.

theistic evolution as an example of giving a nod to "God" but explaining all things in terms of naturalistic development. Warfield suggests that perhaps as in no other era, this antisupernaturalistic bias has dominated and thus driven the thinking of his own age.[73]

Warfield acknowledges that it would be impossible for such thinking not to affect the church in some ways. And he observes that although "the supernatural is the very breath of Christianity's nostrils" and that there is nothing more deadly to it than such an antisupernaturalistic atmosphere, still the chief characteristic of contemporary "Christian" thought is its naturalistic bias. "The real question with them seems to be, not what kind and measure of supernaturalism does the Christianity of Christ and His apostles recognize and require; but, how little of the supernatural may be admitted and yet men continue to call themselves Christians." To which he adds, "The effort is not to Christianize the world-conception of the age, but specifically to de-supernaturalize Christianity so as to bring it into accord with the prevailing world-view." Hence, the "speculative theism" known commonly as "non-miraculous Christianity" and "that odd positivistic religion" of the Ritschlians,

> who, under color of a phenomenalism which knows nothing of "the thing in itself," profess to hold it not to be a matter of serious importance to Christianity whether God be a person, or Christ be God, or the soul have any persistence, and to find it enough to bask in the sweet impression which is made on the heart by the personality of the man Jesus, dimly seen through the mists of critical history.

This "bias" is the presupposition of the era's attempted reduction of Christianity, a "starting point in unbelief" that determines ahead of time the "findings" of its critical investigations and leaves us with a merely naturalistic Christianity.[74]

In the remainder of his lecture Warfield outlines "the frankness of Christianity's commitment to the absolute supernatural," beginning with "the supernatural fact": God. When the Christian says "God," he by definition refers to a God who is more than merely immanent, "entangled in nature" so as to render him indistinguishable from it. For the Christian, God is neither confined to nor limited by the comparatively small forces of the universe. God is indeed a God in nature, but he is a God above nature also, who "transcends all the works of His hands," a supernatural transcendent God, the Maker and Supporter of the universe. From this it follows that the Christian believes also in "the supernatural act": creation. What we call "nature" did not simply come into existence.

---

[73]W, 9:25–29.
[74]W, 9:29–31.

It was made. It is neither self-made nor self-existent. It is not the result of evolution or modification. It was created, supernaturally, called into being by the transcendent God. The universe is therefore dependent on God, and he is not only its Creator but its Governor and Lord also. His activities in the world are not confined to its activities, but rather it owes both its existence and its persistence to his mighty will. Second causes he may well use, but they are his nonetheless.[75]

This leads the Christian, next, to affirm and cherish "a supernatural redemption." As surely and as soon as the Christian recognizes the fact of sin that alienated him from God, he must look for a corrective and recovery not to natural causes or simply to providential agencies operating through natural causes. By the nature of the case he must look to the supernatural, the miraculous. The Christian must affirm, further, "the supernatural man"— the man "from heaven," as Paul calls him (I Cor. 15:47)—who came to redeem sinners, Christ, the eternal Son sent from the Father, who was born of a virgin, lived a supernatural life, died bearing the sinner's curse, conquered death, and returned to heaven, whence he came, "in an obviously supernatural ascension."[76]

Next, Warfield argues, the Christian must maintain a hearty faith in a "supernatural revelation," for "how shall we be advantaged by a supernatural redemption of which we know nothing?" Who is competent to reveal and explain the meaning of God's redemptive acts, but God himself? The Christian, by definition, must affirm divine revelation and not in deed only but in word also. It is one thing to speak of a baby born in Bethlehem, but it requires a divine word "to tell us who and what this child was, why He lived and what He wrought by His death, what it meant that He could not be holden of the grave, and what those cloven tongues of flame signified—before they can avail as redemptive facts to us." Only God can reveal these things, and he has done so by his Word, given to us supernaturally by the apostles and prophets. "That we may believe in a supernatural redemption, we must believe in a supernatural revelation, by which alone we can be assured that this and not something else was what occurred, and that this and not something other was what it meant."[77]

Finally, as Christians we must heartily affirm also a "supernatural salvation." It is not enough to know that God has accomplished a supernatural redemption in this world and that he has made it known to us. A supernatural redemption beyond our reach is of no profit to us at all. There must also be a supernatural application of that redemption to us, raising us from our sinful slumber to union

---

[75] W, 9:31–33.
[76] W, 9:38–41.
[77] W, 9:41–43.

and fellowship with Christ in faith. And this is accomplished by the creative operations of the Holy Spirit upon the human heart. The Christian is neither the product of natural forces, however divinely led, nor an "evolution" out of natural man: he is a new creation. He is not self-made but divinely created, made a new man in Christ Jesus by the mighty power of the Holy Spirit. The Christian is himself a living, walking miracle, the result of the supernatural workings of God.[78] As Warfield says again elsewhere:

> The religion of the Bible is a frankly supernatural religion. By this is not meant merely that, according to it, all men, as creatures, live, move and have their being in God. It is meant that, according to it, God has intervened extraordinarily, in the course of the sinful world's development, for the salvation of men otherwise lost.[79]

Here is the Christian worldview, a frank confession of the "absolute supernatural" that pervades the Christian faith that is "incumbent on every Christian"—a supernatural God, a supernatural redemption, accomplished by a supernatural Savior, interpreted by a supernatural revelation, and applied by the supernatural operations of his Spirit. "This confession constitutes the core of the Christian profession. Only he who holds this faith whole and entire has a full right to the Christian name: only he can hope to conserve the fullness of Christian truth . . . and witness a good confession in the midst of its most insidious attacks." Supernaturalism is, in short, "the very heart of the Christian religion."[80]

This was Warfield's frame of reference from which, throughout his career, he sustained continued and vigorous assault on the naturalistic criticism of his day. From this standpoint he championed the Calvinistic concept of divine sovereignty and opposed all lesser notions, whether Pelagian, Socinian, deistic, Arminian, or Ritschlian. From this vantage point he opposed philosophical evolutionism, the contemporary kenotic theories of Christ's incarnation and person, all nonsubstitutionary interpretations of Christ's death, notions of self-salvation and self-sanctification, and naturalistic accountings of Scripture. Everything rises or falls with the question of supernaturalism. If supernaturalism, then Christianity—Christianity in its biblical and historic expression and Christianity in its deepest evangelical and Reformed piety and its most profound sense of dependence upon God. Here in brief summary is the career of B. B. Warfield.[81]

---

[78] W, 9:43–45.
[79] W, I:3.
[80] W, 9:45–46; SW, 73.
[81] Samuel Craig provides a nice summary of Warfield's concern for supernaturalism in BTS, xxiii–xxix.

Christianity has from the beginning ever come to men as the rational religion, making its appeal primarily to the intellect. It has thus ever evinced itself not merely, as Dr. Macgregor puts it, preeminently as the apologetical religion, but also as the doctrinal religion. Above all other religions, it consists in doctrines: it has truth to offer to men's acceptance, and by their acceptance of this truth it seeks to rule their lives and save their souls. . . . The commission is, Go, preach. . . . Is the foolishness of preaching after all a useless evil, inflicted on men? Was Paul mistaken when he declared that Christ had sent him forth above all to preach the gospel? We may think as we will; but it is very evident that the founders of Christianity earnestly believed, not that the so-called Word of God is the product of faith and its only use is to witness to the faith that lies behind it and gives it birth, but that the veritable Word of God is the seed of faith, that faith cometh by hearing and hearing by the Word of God, or, in other words, that behind the Christian life stands the doctrine of Christ, intelligently believed. When for example the apostle asks the Galatians, "This only would I learn of you, Received ye the Spirit by the works of the law or by the hearing of faith?" he intimates with entire distinctness that it is in connection with the truth of God offered to faith that the Holy Spirit is given; and therefore elsewhere, although the gospel is naught save as it is attended with the demonstration of the Spirit and with power—and Paul may plant and Apollos may water in vain if God do [sic] not himself give the increase—yet this very gospel itself and its preaching is called the "power of God unto salvation."

SSW, 2:277–79 (emphasis original).

The Apologetic Task

The Theological Enterprise

2

APOLOGETICS AND THE THEOLOGICAL ENTERPRISE

Warfield is without doubt best known as the theologian of the doctrine of inspiration. This was the issue of his day, and he above all others rose to meet the challenges that called for its defense, clarification, and restatement. Indeed, in this and every other area of Christian theology he was eager to propagate and give clear voice to historic Christian teaching and to silence and discredit the encroaching advance of unbelief. Often echoing the words of the apostle Peter, Warfield sought at length to give reason for the faith.[1]

Warfield was professor of didactic and polemic theology. Today we refer to the discipline more simply as systematic theology, as they did in Warfield's day also. But it was part of his responsibility in this, quite clearly taken to heart, to keep a watchful eye on the theological expressions of the day and to inform and equip his students—and his many readers—accordingly. Willing to contend earnestly for the faith, he was indeed a polemic theologian whose pen was his sword, ever ready to be put to the defense and the advance of the faith once for all delivered to the saints.

One of the distinctive features of Warfield's wide-ranging works is his frequent emphasis that Christianity, unlike all other religions, is a revealed religion. Its doctrines are not the product of human thought but are specifically communications from God. Accordingly, Christianity is marked by its message, and it

---

[1]Warfield treats this subject primarily in the following: "Calvin's Doctrine of the Knowledge of God," in *W*, 5:29–130; "Apologetics," in *W*, 9:3–21; "The Idea of Systematic Theology," in *W*, 9:49–87; "The Task and Method of Systematic Theology," in *W*, 9:91–105; "On Faith and Its Psychological Aspects," in *W*, 9:313–42; "The Right of Systematic Theology," in *SSW*, 2:219–79; "Introduction" to Francis R. Beattie's *Apologetics*, in *SSW*, 2:93–105; "Review of Herman Bavinck's *De Zekerheid des Geloofs*," in *SSW*, 2:106–23; "Christian Evidences: How Affected by Recent Criticisms," in *SSW*, 2:124–31; "Theology a Science," in *SSW*, 2:207–12; "Christianity the Truth," in *SSW*, 2:213–18; and "The Indispensableness of Systematic Theology to the Preacher," in *SSW*, 2:280–88.

stakes everything on the truth of that message. In turn, it is the responsibility of Christians to propagate this message and bear witness to its truth. And it is in this context that Warfield speaks so famously of Christianity as the distinctively apologetic religion, a religion whose goal is to *reason* its way to dominion.

These expressions by Warfield have given rise to much discussion in recent years, and not always with the clearest understanding of his intended meaning and connotations. The distinction he makes between theology and apologetics and his assessment of the potential and the limitations of apologetics are frequently overlooked. What follows here is intended as neither a critique nor a defense of Warfield but rather an attempt at clarification, a descriptive exposition and summary of his understanding of the apologetic task.

The Apologetic Task[2]

APOLOGETICS AS PRIMARY

Warfield lamented the confusion surrounding the question of the role of apologetics in his day. Since Immanuel Kant, Friedrich Schleiermacher, Albrecht Ritschl, and the relocation of authority to the human psyche, the prevailing influence of subjectivism in faith had led many to hold the discipline of apologetics in more or less disdain. Not the establishing of faith but the individual subjective experience of faith was deemed important. Under such a conception, faith does not have to do with reason, does not consist in metaphysical doctrines, and does not rest on facts objectively demonstrable; it is purely an affair of the heart. On

---

[2]It should be noted that much has been made of the influence of the Scottish Common Sense philosophy on Warfield's theology generally and his apologetic methodology. This allegation comes most recently from an otherwise friendly quarter in Robert L. Reymond's *Faith's Reasons for Believing* (Fearn, Ross-shire: Mentor, 2008), 246. See also John Vander Stelt, *Philosophy and Scripture: A Study of Old Princeton and Westminster Theology* (Marlton, NJ: Mack., 1978); Sydney Ahlstrom, "The Scottish Philosophy and American Theology," *Church History* 24, no. 3 (1955): 257–72; and George M. Marsden, *Fundamentalism and American Culture* (New York: Oxford University Press, 1980), 110–16. This question does not fit within the scope of this section, the purpose of which is merely to provide clarification and summary exposition of Warfield's view of the apologetic task. But a significant dependence by Warfield on the Scottish philosophy is by no means certain. Curiously, in 1912 seminary president Francis L. Patton, unaware of these criticisms, which would come so much later, addressed the question specifically, even if only in briefest passing, stating that although the common sense philosophy was taught at the college, it was never a significant factor in the theological endeavors of the seminary (*CC*, 348). For a fuller analysis, see especially David P. Smith, "B. B. Warfield's Scientifically Constructive Theological Scholarship" (PhD diss., Trinity International University, 2009). See also Paul K. Helseth, "Right Reason and the Princeton Mind: The Moral Context," *JPH* 77, no. 1 (1999): 13–28; Helseth, "'Re-Imagining' the Princeton Mind: Postconservative Evangelicalism, Old Princeton, and the Rise of Neo-Fundamentalism," *JETS* 45, no. 3 (2002): 427–50; Helseth, "B. B. Warfield's Apologetical Appeal to Right Reason: Evidence of a Rather Bald Rationalism?" *SBET* 16 (Autumn 1998): 156–77; republished as "A 'Rather Bald' Rationalist? The Appeal to 'Right Reason,'" in *BBW*, 54–75; Donald Fuller and Richard Gardiner, "Reformed Theology at Princeton and Amsterdam in the Late Nineteenth Century: A Reappraisal," *Presbyterion* 21, no. 2 (1995): 89–117.

another level, Warfield felt that the seeping influence of mysticism on Christianity had showed itself in an increasing disregard of apologetics in favor of the "witness of the Spirit." For many, the discipline of apologetics simply had no right to exist. And among those who did allow the discipline, little agreement had been reached as to its specific role. Complaining of all this, Warfield lamented that "there is scarcely a corner in the theological encyclopedia into which it has not been thrust"—whether a subset of exegetical, historical, systematic, or practical theology—and that apologetics was "treated very much like a stepchild in the theological household. The encyclopaedists have seemed scarcely to know what to do with it."[3] Nor was he satisfied with the subordinate role given apologetics by his highly esteemed friend Abraham Kuyper in his survey of Christian theology, *Encyclopedia of Sacred Theology* (1898), even though Warfield wrote a generous introduction to that work.

In Warfield's view all of this missed the point entirely. For Warfield, apologetics bears a primary role. Apologetics does not merely teach men how to defend Christianity; if it were only this, then it would belong to the discipline of practical theology. Nor does apologetics set out merely to vindicate Christianity, in its various branches of thought, against opposing thought; if it were this, it would presuppose the faith it defends and, thus, properly take its place as "the culminating department of systematic theology." But for Warfield, apologetics stands *first* in theological method and discussion. It undertakes not merely the defense or even the vindication but the establishment of Christianity. More specifically, it seeks to establish "that knowledge of God which Christianity professes to embody." It is the business of theology to explicate this knowledge of God in its various details, but it is the business of apologetics to establish it as a fact. Apologetics may, because of the particular circumstances of a given context, enter into the defense and/or vindication of this or that aspect of the Christian faith, but its "essential character" is "positive and constructive" and would be as necessary were there no opposition or contradiction to overcome. Its need is grounded in the basic needs of the human spirit: we believe only if we have reason to believe. The function of apologetics is "to investigate, explicate, and establish the grounds on which a theology—a science, or systematized knowledge of God—is possible." As the basis on which theology rests, it necessarily takes its place "at the head of the departments of theological science," finding its task in "the establishment of the validity" of their respective areas of subsequent inquiry. That is to say, all other branches of theology—exegetical, historical, systematic, and practical—presuppose apologetics. "Apologetical Theology prepares the way

---

[3]*W*, 9:5; *SSW*, 2:93–94.

for all theology by establishing its necessary presuppositions without which no theology is possible."[4]

Warfield explains. Theology is not the science of faith or of religion, in which case its subject matter would be the subjective experiences of the human heart, and the role of apologetics would be that of establishing the validity of those experiences. Nor is theology the science of the *Christian* religion, in which case the role of apologetics would be more historical, establishing the validity of the various articles of Christian belief. Theology is the science of God, in which case it deals with a body of objective facts, truth God has revealed about himself. These facts are assumed by theology and explicated in their various branches of thought. But it would be absurd to assume and develop these facts before they are established, indeed, as facts. Theology is the science of God, and the science of God has no right to exist until it is first established that God does exist, that he may be known, and that we have a trustworthy means of learning about him. This is the role of apologetics, and it therefore stands first.[5]

Put another way, apologetics establishes the exclusive truth of Christianity "directly only as a whole, and in its details only indirectly." It does not seek to establish Christianity in all its details, and neither does it seek to establish the essence of Christianity. It seeks to establish Christianity itself "in its unexplicated and uncompressed entirety," the "foundations on which the temple of theology is built." It establishes the regulative principles of theology from which, in turn, the details of Christian theology are derived. Apologetics is basic. It establishes those foundational and determinative truths that give Christianity its shape and could therefore as easily be referred to as "fundamental theology" or "principal theology."[6]

What, then, are these principal facts upon which Christianity is built and that give it its shape and constitute the specific focus of apologetics? The presuppositions of any science, Warfield observes, are three: "the reality of its subject-matter, the capacity of the human mind to receive into itself and rationally to reflect this subject-matter, the existence of media of communication between the subject-matter and the percipient and understanding mind." These presuppositions underlie all the sciences. Psychology, for example, as a science, rests on the objective reality of "a mind to be investigated, a mind to investigate it, and a self-consciousness by means of which the mind as an object can be brought under the inspection of the mind as subject." Similarly, he argues, "There could be no astronomy were there no heavenly bodies to be investigated, no mind capable

---

[4] *W*, 9:3–5, 55, 63–65, 73–74, 97–99; cf. *SSW*, 2:304–5.
[5] *W*, 9:7; *SSW*, 2:99, 219.
[6] *W*, 9:9.

of comprehending the laws of their existence and movements, or no means of observing their structure and motion." So also, "There can be no theology, conceived according to its very name as the science of God, unless there is a God to form its subject-matter, a capacity in the human mind to apprehend and so far to comprehend God, and some media by which God is made known to man." It is the role of apologetics, therefore, to establish these three: "the existence of God, the capacity of the human mind to know Him, and the accessibility of knowledge concerning Him." In short, its specific subject matter is God, religion, and revelation, and with these three facts established, theology then becomes possible.[7]

These three principal facts, however, do not lead to a specifically Christian theism, unless the third—revelation—entails the establishing of Holy Scripture as divine revelation. And if the Scriptures are thus established, Christianity itself becomes included in the domain of apologetics. So to the three principal facts—God, religion, and revelation—Warfield adds two more with which apologetics must concern itself—Christianity and the Bible. These five domains constitute the specific focus of apologetics:

1. The existence of God as a personal being, or philosophical apologetics
2. Religion, or psychological apologetics, which entails the study of man's religious sense, philosophy, comparative religions, and the history of religions
3. Revelation, which entails the establishing of supernaturalism, God's government of the world, and how he makes himself known
4. Christianity, or historical apologetics, which entails establishing "the divine origin of Christianity as the religion of revelation in the special sense of that word"
5. Scripture, or bibliological apologetics, which seeks to establish the trustworthiness of the Christian Scriptures as the revelation from God for the redemption of sinners[8]

In a summary paragraph in his introduction to Beattie's *Apologetics*, Warfield traces the necessary conditions for deriving the knowledge of God from the Scriptures. This is the work of exegetical theology, which in turn leads to historical and then systematic and then practical theology.

---

[7] *W*, 9:11, 53–56; *SSW*, 2:219.

[8] *W*, 9:12–13. Elsewhere Warfield noted that in his day it was scarcely necessary to defend the notion of general revelation. This in some form was acknowledged on virtually all sides. With special revelation the case was much different. Notions abounded that sought to mediate between deistic or pantheistic conceptions and those of a truly Christian theism, "and," Warfield said, "in meeting the subtlety and variety of these Christian apologetics finds today its chief task." *SSW*, 1:25–26.

But certainly, before we draw it [theology] from the Scriptures, we must assure ourselves that there is a knowledge of God in the Scriptures. And, before we do that, we
must assure ourselves that there is a knowledge of God in the world. And before we
do that, we must assure ourselves that a knowledge of God is possible for man. And,
before we do that, we must assure ourselves that there is a God to know. Thus we
inevitably work back to first principles. And, in working thus back to first principles,
we exhibit the indispensability of an "Apologetical Theology," which of necessity
holds the place of the first among the five essential disciplines.[9]

All this Warfield views as the specific task of apologetics. He describes Kuyper as
"one of the really great theologians of our time" but complains that his discussion
of apologetics is "hidden away as a subdivision of a subdivision" of systematic
theology, a relatively minor discipline whose function is confined only to the
narrow task of defending developed Christianity against its various philosophical assaults. This is a "standing matter of surprise" to Warfield, for it contentedly
leaves Christianity unfounded, "the great assumption," and leaves the work of
the theologian suspended on air. Certainly, Warfield insists, the theologian cannot take his standpoint in the Scriptures until he *has* the Scriptures, and this
more fundamental work is the task of the apologist. His work does not consist in
the elaboration of assumptions but like all the sciences must first establish "its
right to rank as such." Apart from this role of apologetics the theologian's work
"would hang in the air" unsupported as "an elaboration of pure assumptions."
Apologetics is primary, and it therefore has an offensive or constructive and not
merely a defensive role.[10]

EVIDENCE AND FAITH

All this raises the larger question of Warfield's understanding of the relation of
apologetics and evidence to faith. Both Kant and Ritschl disallowed any connection between faith and reason. Religious knowledge and theoretical knowledge
are distinct realms of thought. Similarly for Schleiermacher it is the subjective
experience of faith that matters. Mysticism also made its mark in Christendom,
leaving a disregard of objective truth and an overdependence upon inner lights
and the "witness of the Spirit."[11] Faith is considered the immediate creation of
the Holy Spirit apart from external means.

---

[9]*SSW*, 2:97–98, 304–5.

[10]*W*, 9:16; *SSW*, 2:96–100, 117.

[11]It would seem that this interest in apologetics on Warfield's part accounts for his repeated critiques of
mysticism in his latter years. See his "Mysticism and Christianity," in *W*, 9:649ff., and his 1913, 1914, 1916
reviews in *W*, 10:334ff., 357, 366ff.

Closer to home, although Warfield held Abraham Kuyper and Herman Bavinck in the very highest regard, he took sharp exception to the "subordinate" role they gave to apologetics and what he understood as a mystical tendency in it: because of the noetic effects of sin, apologetics was essentially useless in regard to the unbeliever. Hence, apologetics is relegated to the defense of that which is given in systematics, not the establishing of fundamental truths. For Warfield, the task of apologetics is to "vindicate" the *sensus divinitatis* in man (natural or general revelation) and proceed from there to vindicate special revelation in order then to allow theology its work. Moreover, Warfield argues that for his esteemed Dutch colleagues, evidence played no significant role in faith. In their view, he alleges, no attempt need or should be made to demonstrate the divinity and infallibility of Scripture, for example, for faith is the immediate creation of the Holy Spirit in the human heart. Warfield heartily agrees that regeneration is necessary to faith, and he acknowledges the ineffectiveness of evidential proof of miracles to those previously committed to the impossibility of the supernatural. That is, he recognizes the controlling presuppositional bias of the unbeliever. But the failure to present evidence, he insists, renders faith blind and ungrounded, and it smacks of a retreat to mysticism.[12]

Warfield insists that "if it is incumbent on the believer to be able to give a reason for the faith that is in him, it is impossible for him to be a believer without a reason for the faith that is in him; and it is the task of apologetics to bring this reason clearly out in his consciousness, and make its validity plain." Indeed, "We can conceive of no act of faith of any kind which is not grounded in evidence: faith is a specific form of persuasion or conviction, and all persuasion or conviction is grounded in evidence." Faith is "a moral act and the gift of God," but as with all kinds of conviction and confidence, it rests—and must, by the nature of it, rest—on evidence as its ground. That is to say, with Augustine (354–430), faith is an act of rational creatures. We may believe what we do not fully comprehend, and in that sense faith precedes understanding. But even in this case we believe because we have judged the testimony sufficiently credible and authoritative. Faith is not a blind but a rational act. In words that echo both Augustine and Aquinas (1225–1274), Warfield says, "We never believe anything until we have found it worthy of our belief."[13] That is to say, faith by its very nature is grounded in evidence.

---

[12]*SSW*, 2:94–97, 100; *SSW*, 2:167–204. The Latin term *sensus divinitatis*, which Warfield uses, following Calvin, indicates man's inherent "sense of divinity" or awareness of God. See also below, *sensus deitatis*, or "sense of deity."

[13]*W*, 9:4, 314–15, 326; *SSW*, 2:112–13; *W*, 4:171–72.

Warfield investigates this at length in his "On Faith in its Psychological Aspects" (1911). Faith, he argues, necessarily connotes reason, the grounds on which we believe.

> When we say "faith," "belief," our minds are preoccupied with the grounds of the conviction expressed: we are speaking of a mental act or state to which we feel constrained by considerations objective to ourselves, or at least to the act or state in question. The conception embodied in the terms "belief," "faith," in other words, is not that of an arbitrary act of the subject's; it is that of a mental state or act which is determined by sufficient reasons.

Faith is a "mental act or state to which we feel constrained by considerations objective to ourselves." Faith is not arbitrary but "determined by sufficient reasons." It is not a product of the will but a "forced consent" to evidence that is perceived as relevant, true, and real. We never believe anything unless we consider the evidence objectively adequate. This is the nature of faith. It does not follow from this that all faith necessarily corresponds with reality. Strictly speaking, faith does not follow evidence immediately but our judgment of the evidence. And our convictions and our perceptions are fallible. But faith is the product of evidence nonetheless. Moreover, following Augustine, Warfield explains that the difference between knowledge and faith is not that one rests on evidence while the other does not. The difference lies only in the kinds of evidence: knowledge rests on "sight" and faith on "testimony." Faith is produced by sufficient or persuasive testimony according to the perceived authority of that testimony.[14]

Evidence, therefore, plays a part in conversion, and apologetics has a part—a "primary" and "conquering part"—to play in the Christian witness to the world.

> It is the distinction of Christianity that it has come into the world clothed with the mission to *reason* its way to its dominion. Other religions may appeal to the sword, or seek some other way to propagate themselves. Christianity makes its appeal to right reason, and stands out among all religions, therefore, as distinctively "the Apologetic religion." It is solely by reasoning that it has come thus far on its way to its kingship. And it is solely by reasoning that it will put all its enemies under its feet. . . . It stands calmly over against the world with its credentials in its hands, and fears no contention of men.[15]

Warfield argues that from the beginning, Christianity has "made its appeal . . . to men's reason." From the beginning Christianity has presented itself as a ratio-

---

[14]*W*, 9:214–15, 313–15, 318–19, 326.
[15]*SSW*, 2:99–100 (emphasis original); cf. 119–20, 213, 216–17.

nal religion whose truth claims must be understood and embraced, and it is the corresponding duty of the Christian evangelist to declare and press these truth claims to the world. As Romans 7:23 implies, Christianity "makes its appeal to the 'mind' and secures the affection of the 'inward man' first, and thence advances to victory over the 'flesh' and 'members.'" Similarly in Romans 12:2 it is by the "renewal of your mind" that sinners are to be transformed so as no longer to be fashioned like the world. Similarly in Ephesians 4:18–24. When the apostle Paul inquires of the Galatians, "Did you receive the Spirit by works of the law or by hearing with faith?" (Gal. 3:2), he expressly implies that it is by means of truth offered to the mind to be believingly embraced that the Holy Spirit is given. Warfield demands that "the noetic root of salvation is continually insisted on in the Scriptures." Precisely because Christianity is a revealed religion, it has at its center a message to proclaim, and it is therefore the Christian objective to "*reason the world into acceptance of the 'truth.'*" Christianity does not make its advance from soul to soul the way a prairie fire spreads in tall grass or a virus passes from body to body. Christianity makes its advance only by the propagation of its truth claims.[16] And the establishing of these truth claims, very simply, is the role Warfield assigns apologetics.

This is not to imply human neutrality in reference to God or that faith is anything other than a divine gift. Throughout his sustained attack on modern criticism Warfield charges that modern unbelief is driven by a presuppositional bias steeped in naturalism, a bias that precludes genuine objectivity in the interpretation of evidence. Possessed by such a bias, men are left with an aversion to truth; indeed, they have "no faculty for truth." Due to their "lamentable and constitutional inaccuracy" their thinking is "deficient" and "will always consider an appeal to truth an evil." Warfield never assumes that either the Christian message or the evidence for it could ever itself suffice to make men Christian. Such a notion he repeatedly describes as "absurd." "Is it not plain to you that it is not evidence alone that produces faith?" Only the "Spirit of Life" can accomplish such a feat. This is a favorite theme in Warfield. He argues rather that "apologetics supplies to Christian men the systematically organized basis on which the faith of Christian men must rest." In every act of saving faith is the conscious conviction "that there is a God, knowable to man, who has made Himself known in a revelation of Himself for redemption in Jesus Christ, as is set down in the Scriptures." Such faith may or may not be aware of the full grounds of such convictions, but it rests

---

[16]*SSW*, 2:213 (emphasis original), 277–79, 469.

nonetheless on these perceived grounds. And it is these grounds that apologetics seeks to explicate.[17]

> Though faith is the gift of God, it does not in the least follow that the faith which God gives is an irrational faith, that is, a faith without cognizable ground in right reason. We believe in Christ because it is rational to believe in Him, not even though it be irrational. Of course mere reasoning cannot make a Christian; but that is not because faith is not the result of evidence, but because a dead soul cannot respond to evidence. The action of the Holy Spirit in giving faith is not apart from evidence, but along with evidence; and in the first instance consists in preparing the soul for the reception of the evidence.[18]

Or again:

> It certainly is not in the power of all the demonstrations in the world to make a Christian. Paul may plant and Apollos water; it is God alone who gives the increase. But it does not seem to follow that Paul would as well, therefore, not plant, and Apollos as well not water. Faith is the gift of God; but it does not in the least follow that the faith that God gives is an irrational faith, that is, a faith without grounds in right reason. It is beyond all question only the prepared heart that can fitly respond to the "reasons"; but how can even a prepared heart respond, when there are no "reasons" to draw out its action? . . . The Holy Spirit does not work a blind, an ungrounded faith in the heart. What is supplied by his creative energy in working faith is not a ready-made faith, rooted in nothing and clinging without reason to its object; nor yet new grounds of belief in the object presented; but just a new ability of the heart to respond to the grounds of faith, sufficient in themselves, already present to the understanding. We believe in Christ because it is rational to believe in him, not though it be irrational. Accordingly, our Reformed fathers always posited in the production of faith the presence of the "*argumentum propter quod credo*," as well as the "*principium seu causa efficiens a quo ad credendum adducor.*" That is to say, for the birth of faith in the soul, it is just as essential that grounds of faith should be present to the mind as that the Giver of faith should act creatively upon the heart.[19]

Again, in his review of Bavinck he writes similarly:

> No one is in danger of believing that "the evidences" can produce "faith": but neither can the presentation of Christ in the gospel produce "faith." "Faith" is the gift

[17]*FL*, 98; *SSW*, 2:99, 120; cf. *SSW*, 2:274; *W*, 5:89. See also the section of chapter ten on "Human Inability and Divine Initiative"; *W*, 9:16.

[18]*W*, 9:15; cf. *SSW*, 2:98.

[19]*SSW*, 2:98–99. The Latin here translates, first, "arguments on account of which I believe," and next, "the principle or efficient cause by which I am brought to believing."

of God. But it does not follow that the "faith" that God gives is not grounded in "the evidences." Of course it is only the prepared heart that can fitly respond to the force of the "evidences," or "receive" the proclamation.... But this faith that the prepared heart yields—is it yielded blindly and without reason, or is it yielded rationally and on the ground of sufficient reason? Does God the Holy Spirit work a blind and ungrounded faith in the heart? What is supplied by the Holy Spirit in working faith in the heart surely is not a ready-made faith, rooted in nothing and clinging without reason to its object; nor yet new grounds of belief in the object presented; but just a new power to the heart to respond to the grounds of faith, sufficient in themselves, already present to the mind.[20]

In his 1909 article "The Deity of Christ," written for *The Fundamentals*, Warfield provides a helpful insight into his thinking in this regard. In this essay he voices the favorite themes that this doctrine is too obvious to need demonstration and that it is the presupposition of every word of the New Testament. Nonetheless, true to form, he highlights the major arguments and stresses in particular the clarity of the biblical teaching in this regard. Finally, as he concludes, he refers to the transforming power of Christ that is experienced by everyone who believes. And then he remarks that this inner experience is "the supreme proof to every Christian ... the most convincing proof ... which he cannot escape.... Whatever else he may or may not be assured of, he knows that his Redeemer lives." He says that this is the supreme proof *to the Christian*, but this is just the point of significance here: what makes a man a believer, in the last analysis, is not something objective only but objective truth now subjectively understood—or, perhaps better, objective truth now rightly understood because of a subjective change. Saving faith has its reasons, to be sure, but it grows only in a God-awakened heart, a heart that has been persuaded by God of the truth of those reasons.[21]

In short, Warfield denies that apologetics has in itself the potential to conquer the world for Christ. Rather, "We are arguing that faith is, in all its exercises alike, a form of conviction, and is, therefore, necessarily grounded in evidence."[22]

In his "On Faith in Its Psychological Aspects," Warfield argues at length that faith is "forced consent" grounded on evidence. Faith is not a mere act of the will. Rather, it is a response to evidence. When adequate evidence is perceived, the person is driven by the persuasive force of that evidence to give consent. Of course this does not mean that all faith necessarily is justified, for the human mind may very easily mistake bad evidence for good or lend undue credence to the authority

---

[20]*SSW*, 2:114–15.
[21]*SSW*, 1:156–57.
[22]*SSW*, 2:99.

by which it is presented. Nor does it mean that when presented with adequate evidence on proper authority, faith will necessarily follow. Compelling evidence though it may be, considered in itself, it may be misunderstood due to a man's subjective state of mind. More to the point, the evidence for the truthfulness of Scripture and the adequacy of Christ, impeccable as it is, will not always be rightly perceived, in which case faith will not be forthcoming. Indeed, Scripture plainly teaches that the natural man's heart is "inhabile" to the evidence on which his faith must rest. He is at enmity with God and *cannot* perceive the truth of Christ rightly. For this he is utterly dependent upon the sovereign workings of God in the heart, restoring the man and enabling him to believe. The human mind is not passive in the acquisition of knowledge; rather, the acquisition of knowledge is conditioned by the nature or ethical state of the soul. Still, Warfield insists, in order to give rise to faith, there must be both—evidence on which faith is grounded and a subjective condition of the heart that is receptive to that evidence. Evidence is essential, but only as the mind is open to receiving it is it compelling.[23]

By way of illustration, a mathematical demonstration may prove absolutely the proposition demonstrated, but that demonstration will not produce conviction in a mind incapable of following it. If a man is tone deaf or otherwise unable to appreciate music, he will not be impressed with even the best of musical presentations. So also the evidence for faith, although it is altogether adequate, will be effective in producing faith only when the heart has been prepared for it by the Spirit of God. The relation of evidence to faith is not a mechanical one. Faith cannot exist without evidence, but even the best of evidence does not guarantee faith. The subjective condition of the mind will determine the efficacy of the evidence. Faith on the part of unregenerate man is, therefore, impossible. "The sinful heart—which is enmity towards God—is incapable of that supreme act of trust in God." It is for this reason that Scripture describes faith as a gift of God, an exercise of trust that can only result from the *testimonium Spiritus Sancti*.[24]

In his sermon on Acts 26:18, Warfield summarizes his understanding of the role of truth and the role of the Holy Spirit in the apologetic task. In fulfillment of his divine commission, the apostle Paul was to "open [the] eyes" of the Gentiles. This, Warfield exhorts, is the function assigned not just to Paul but to all Christ's witnessing servants. But Warfield also reminds us carefully that this is of course a work only God the Holy Spirit can do. However, while it is the Holy Spirit alone who does this work, he does it by means of truth. And so in a "lower sense" it was required of Paul, and it is required of every Christian witness also,

---

[23]W, 9:313–42, 336–40; W, 4:149.
[24]W, 9:335–37; SSW, 2:114–16.

to "open the eyes" of unbelievers by the presentation of truth. This is their need, and this is our duty. One plants, and another waters. But it is God who gives the increase. This, in brief, is Warfield's understanding of the role and function of the apologist.[25]

Warfield develops this point at length in his interpretation of Calvin's under-standing of the *testimonium Spiritus Sancti* and the *indicia*. Calvin stresses repeat-edly that the evidences of the Scripture's divinity, though sufficient and compel-ling, are not in themselves able to produce faith in the fallen heart. But neither is the faith produced by the Spirit an ungrounded or blind faith. Nor is the testimony of the Spirit a supplemental revelation, adding new ground of faith. Rather, the testimony of the Spirit is given "to confirm" the already evident divinity and trustworthiness of Scripture. Warfield finds repeated confirmation of this in Calvin's *Institutes*.

> Thus we find him [Calvin] repeatedly affirming that these *indicia* will produce no fruit *until* they be confirmed by the internal testimony of the Spirit (I. vii. 4, 5; viii. 1, 13): "Our reverence may be conciliated by its internal majesty [the Scripture's], but it never seriously affects us, *till* it is confirmed by the Spirit in our hearts" (I. vii. 5). "*Without this certainty*, . . . in vain will the authority of Scripture be either defended by arguments or established by the consent of the Church, or of any other supports: since, unless the foundation be laid, it remains in perpetual suspense" (I. viii. 1). The *indicia* "are *alone* not sufficient to produce firm faith in it [the Scriptures], *till* the heavenly Father, discovering His own power therein, places its authority above all controversy" (I. viii. 13).

Once again, faith is grounded conviction. It is brought about by the Spirit's illu-mination of the mind, to be sure, but it is grounded conviction nonetheless. It is conviction grounded in evidence that is sufficiently appreciated only by the Spirit's enablement. For Calvin, Warfield insists with hearty agreement, it is the Spirit *and* the Word. "We are as helpless, then, without the Word as we are without the Spirit, for the whole function of the Spirit with respect to the truth is, not to reveal to us the truth anew, much less to reveal to us new truth, but efficaciously to confirm the Word." The work of the Spirit is that of illumination and persuasion, bringing the human soul, by means of evidence, to faith. With the Spirit and the Word the subjective and objective are brought together. Neither by itself is effica-cious. Each must have the other. As he summarizes in a footnote, "The question between the testimony of the Spirit and the *indicia* is not a question of which gives the strongest evidence; it is a question of what each is fitted to do." The *indicia*

---

alone provide objective evidence. But the objective evidence is ineffective, given the fallen condition of the human mind, and it is this, the repair of the mind, that the Spirit accomplishes so that the truth is now rightly apprehended.[26]

Citing 1 Corinthians 2:14, Warfield remarks:

> None but the Christian man can understand Christian truth. . . . There is no creative power in doctrines, however true; and they will pass over dead souls leaving them as inert as they found them: it is the *Creator Spiritus* alone who is competent to quicken dead souls into life; and without him there has never been and never will be one spark of life produced by all the doctrines in the world.[27]

More eloquently, he writes in his "Christian Supernaturalism":

> It is upon a field of the dead that the Sun of righteousness has risen, and the shouts that announce His advent fall on deaf ears: yea, even though the morning stars should again sing for joy and the air be palpitant with the echo of the great proclamation, their voice could not penetrate the ears of the dead. As we sweep our eyes over the world lying in its wickedness, it is the valley of the prophet's vision which we see before us: a valley that is filled with bones, and lo! they are very dry. What benefit is there in proclaiming to dry bones even the greatest of redemptions? How shall we stand and cry, "O ye dry bones, hear ye the word of the Lord!" In vain the redemption, in vain its proclamation, unless there come a breath from heaven to breathe upon these slain that they may live. The redemption of Christ is therefore no more central to the Christian hope than the creative operations of the Holy Spirit upon the heart: and the supernatural redemption itself would remain a mere name outside of us and beyond our reach, were it not realized in the subjective life by an equally supernatural application.[28]

Ernest Sandeen is clearly mistaken, then, when he alleges that "the witness of the Spirit, though not overlooked, cannot be said to play any important role in the Princeton thought. It is with the external not the internal, the objective not the subjective, that they deal."[29] It would seem that for Warfield to satisfy Sandeen on this score, he must place but little, if any, emphasis on evidences and simply wait for God to work as in a vacuum. In fact Warfield places great stress on the

---

[26]*W*, 5:81, 86, 89 (Warfield's emphasis). The Latin *testimonium Spiritus Sancti* indicates inward witness or "testimony of the Holy Spirit" to the divinity and authority of Scripture. *Indicia* is Latin for the "evidence," "marks," or "indications" of the same. See also the discussion of "The Self-Attesting Character of Scripture and the *Testimonium Spiritus Sancti*" in chapter 4.
[27]*SSW*, 2:274.
[28]*W*, 9:43–44.
[29]Ernest R. Sandeen, *The Roots of Fundamentalism: British and American Millenarianism, 1800–1930* (1970; repr., Grand Rapids: Baker, 1978), 118.

Acts 16:14
The Lord opened Lydia's
heart to receive Paul's msg.

role of the Holy Spirit, repeatedly and consistently throughout his writings. This aspect of "Christian supernaturalism" is a frequent and favorite theme of his.[30] But he understands the evangelist's or apologist's role as one thing and the Holy Spirit's role as another. And so he will not be forced to choose *either* evidence *or* the work of the Spirit. He insists he must have both. The evangelist-apologist must faithfully fulfill his own role and present the truth, but always in conscious awareness that God alone opens the heart.

Jack Rogers and Donald McKim are clearly wide of the mark when they assert that Warfield (and the Old Princetonians generally) "held an almost Pelagian confidence that the mind was essentially undisturbed by sin's influence."[31] Similarly, both McKim and Cornelius Van Til misunderstand Warfield in a similar way when they allege that Warfield attributes the power of "right reason" to the unregenerate.[32] This very clearly was not Warfield's position. When Warfield speaks of "right reason," he is not assuming ability on the part of the unregenerate. Warfield does argue in this context that there is a significant level of understanding that the unbeliever does possess. His *sensus deitatis* is unshakable, and Warfield seeks to build on this ground accordingly, pressing the unbeliever with truths of which he is already aware. This is in one sense the ground of Warfield's apologetic method: the unbeliever's ignorance is inexcusable. Unregenerate man *knows* that God is, and from this he is able to see the compelling force of "right reason" as the Christian presses him with it. In this connection Warfield understands the value of the theistic proofs as reminders of what the unregenerate man is already inescapably aware. But he does not attribute "right reason" to the unbeliever. He also argues in this same context, "The depraved man neither thinks, nor feels, nor wills as he ought; and the products of his action as a scientific thinker cannot possibly escape the influence of this everywhere operative destructive power." Warfield makes much of the fact that Christianity is objectively true and can provide evidences that are accessible even to the sinful mind, and he argues that the knowledge of God impressed on the soul is itself clearly understandable to every "normal man." But he equally emphasizes the necessity of regeneration and a "prepared heart" for the right understanding of truth. And by way of clarification,

---

[30]*W*, 9:29, 43–45.

[31]Jack B. Rogers and Donald K. McKim, *The Authority and Interpretation of the Bible: An Historical Approach* (Eugene, OR: Wipf and Stock, 1999), 290.

[32]"Van Til and Warfield on Scripture in the Westminster Confession," Jack B. Rogers, in *Jerusalem and Athens: Critical Discussions on the Philosophy and Apologetics of Cornelius Van Til*, ed. E. R. Geehan (Nutley, NJ: Presbyterian and Reformed, 1971), 154; Cornelius Van Til, *The Defense of the Faith* (Philadelphia: Presbyterian and Reformed, 1955), 362. See also Van Til, *A Christian Theory of Knowledge* (Nutley, NJ: Presbyterian and Reformed, 1969), 244–45. In a letter to John Vander Stelt in 1969, Van Til went so far as to characterize Warfield's apologetic as "Arminian" (*The Works of Cornelius Van Til, 1895–1987*, CD-ROM, Logos Library System).

he explicitly characterizes the persuaded reasoning of the unregenerate mind as ineffectual, borrowing from the proverb—"the man convinced against his will is of the same opinion still." It is the regenerate man who has the "stronger and purer thought" as a gift of God. And so, while the evidence is available even to the unregenerate mind, and while these facts are clearly understandable to the "normal man," the reality is that fallen man is not in his "normal state," and so these accessible truths will never be grasped aright apart from the regenerative work of God. Warfield asks rhetorically, "Though 'pure reason' be sufficient for the religion of pure nature, what warrants the assumption that its sufficiency is unimpaired when nature is no longer pure?" Moreover, faith "is a moral act and not merely an intellectual assent. It is the response of the whole being to its appropriate object." This necessarily implies a renewal. The fall and sin have left man with an "intellectual imbecility" that only God can overcome, thus restoring a "right reason."[33]

Warfield further states that "the condition of right thinking . . . is, therefore, that the Christian man should look upon the seething thought of the world from the safe standpoint of the sure Word of God." He even goes so far as to criticize that "concessive" attitude of some Christian men that leads them "to accept the tenets which have originated elsewhere than in the Scriptures." His point is clearly that Scripture alone can shape "right thinking." More to the point, only the regenerate man can think rightly about God, and thus he has infinite advantage over the man of the world in pressing his argument. The thinking of the world is hostile to truth; it is the Christian mind, informed by Scripture, that possesses the advantage of right thinking.[34]

Warfield presses the clarity of God's natural revelation and insists that it renders the unbeliever responsible and without excuse. But nothing could be clearer than that for Warfield "right reason" does *not* belong to the unregenerate mind. "Right reason" for Warfield belongs to the truth claims of the Christian faith and to the regenerate mind made right by the inner workings of the Spirit of God and informed by the infallible Word of God—in the context of the apologetic task, the weapon to be used against all forms of unbelief. The unregenerate mind, under the sway of sin, is closed to right thinking about God. The same evidence presented to both the unregenerate man and the regenerate will be rejected by the one and welcomed by the other. But it is not faulty evidence that leaves the one in unbelief, and neither is it without evidence that the other is brought to faith.[35] Hence, it is

---

[33]*W*, 3:15, 151, 339; *W*, 5:32, 43, 150–51; *W*, 2:496; *W*, 4:156; *W*, 9:159; *SSW*, 2:98–100, 111–15; *SW*, 219.
[34]*SSW*, 2:103, 674–75.
[35]*W*, 9:70; *SSW*, 2:99–115; *W*, 3:339; *W*, 4:156; *W*, 5:41–42. See Helseth, "Right Reason and the Christian Mind," 13–28. Also Helseth, "B. B. Warfield's Apologetical Appeal to 'Right Reason,'" 156–77.

the apologist's role to press the truth claims of Christianity against the unwilling conscience of the unbeliever, thus laying the groundwork for, but consciously waiting for and relying on, the sovereign Spirit to persuade.

APOLOGETICS AND FAITH

Warfield argues that Bavinck confuses certainty of the truth of the Christian religion with assurance of faith, and that these do not always go together. The unregenerate mind may very well be convinced of the truth of the Christian religion without ever coming to saving faith in Christ, the Founder of that religion. Bavinck himself acknowledges this, Warfield observes, when he describes apologetics as useful to "silence gainsayers." Such a use is of course impossible unless the unregenerate and unbelieving mind is, in fact, able to assess Christianity's truth claims. So Warfield affirms that evidence cannot produce saving faith; and for that matter neither can the preaching of the gospel, by itself, produce faith. But evidence—and, therefore, apologetics—can serve to establish the grounds of that faith to which, in turn, only the "prepared heart" can rightly respond and yield. God the Spirit gives the faith, but it is not a blind and ungrounded faith that he gives.[36]

In his distinction between historical faith and saving faith—or faith in a fiducial sense, "humble trust"—Warfield argues that while saving faith is the gift of God and can only be had as a sovereign gift, historical faith is something toward which the Christian *ought* to press the unregenerate. No human being can escape the consciousness of dependence upon God. He is as dependent upon God as the believer and therefore cannot help believing in God in a historical sense. However, in his unregenerate state his dependence upon God is not one of glad and loving trust. "On the contrary, faith in this sense has been transformed into its opposite—faith has passed into unfaith, trust to distrust." In a word, the sinfulness of his condition renders faith impossible. But because of this innate sense of dependence upon God, the presentation of the evidences on which faith rests cannot be a hopeless endeavor. Indeed, the Christian must "use and press this advantage that God has given him" and carry this "assault" to the world. It is ours to present the evidence on which faith is grounded. It is God's to give the faith.[37]

Evidence, therefore, plays a part in conversion, and apologetics has a part—a "primary" and "conquering part"—to play in the Christian witness to the world.

---

[36]*SSW*, 2:112–15, 120. Henk van den Belt makes a compelling case that Warfield's "friendly and instructive" (Bavinck's words) critique shows its influence in Bavinck's later Stone Lectures on "The Philosophy of Revelation." See Hendrik van den Belt, "An Apology for the Lack of Apologetics: The Influence of the Discussion with B. B. Warfield on H. Bavinck's Stone Lectures." A paper delivered at the annual conference of the Abraham Kuyper Center for Public Theology in celebration of Herman Bavinck's Stone Lectures, "The Philosophy of Revelation," April 17, 2009.

[37]*SSW*, 2:116–20.

SUMMARY OF THE APOLOGETIC TASK

It may be helpful to note once again that for Warfield the apologetic task is necessary irrespective of unbelieving opposition. Its object is not, first, evangelistic. Its concern is the objective establishing of the basic facts of Christianity. Paul Helseth may well be right to say that it is this consideration that explains Warfield's dismay with Kuyper's approach to apologetics. Contrary to popular assessments, Warfield and Kuyper shared a presuppositional epistemology in this respect. Warfield understood very clearly—he insisted!—that the unregenerate mind was incapable of rightly receiving divine truth. But this does not render the basic facts of Christianity or their objective establishment irrelevant. The Christian worldview is not subjective merely. Kuyper's relegation of apologetics to secondary status was to Warfield "a standing matter of surprise" simply because the apologetic task of objectively establishing primary truths on which Christian theology is built, the grounds of faith, is necessary in any case. It is basic. Thus Helseth suggests that Warfield was bewildered that

> Kuyper was reluctant to do what Warfield believed that the Christian must of necessity do even when there is "no opposition in the world to be encountered and no contradictions to be overcome," namely, establish the integrity of the grounds of faith by urging "his stronger and purer thought" continuously, and in all its details, upon the attention of men.

Indeed, a failure to do so would result in fideism.[38]

Very simply, Warfield's point is, first, that apologetics deals with basic or first principles. It is positive and constructive and thus stands first in the theological enterprise. And, second, faith by its very nature, although subjectively conditioned, rests in evidence, and the presentation of this evidence is the task of apologetics.

The Theological Enterprise

THE NATURE OF THEOLOGY AND THE THEOLOGICAL TASK

If it is the task of the apologist to establish Christianity as such—that God is and that he has revealed himself climactically in the Scriptures—then it is the task of the theologian, in turn, to explicate that revelation in all its details. Here Warfield adopts the common fourfold distribution of the theological disciplines. In order

---

[38]Paul Kjoss Helseth, "Warfield on the Life of the Mind and the Apologetic Nature of Christian Scholarship," in *BBW*, 129; *SSW*, 2:96, 103–5, 117.

they are exegetical theology, historical theology, systematic theology, and practical theology. Warfield tweaks this only by prefixing to them the department of apologetical theology.[39] As we have discussed above, he views apologetics as positive and constructive, preparing the way for all theology by establishing its necessary presuppositions. In brief, it "places the Scriptures in our hands for investigation and study." Next, exegetical theology investigates the meaning of Scripture and presents us with a body of detailed and substantiated results, "culminating in a series of organized systems of Biblical History, Biblical Ethics, Biblical Theology, and the like." In turn, historical theology investigates the unfolding understanding of Christianity in the thought, worship, and experience of men throughout the centuries, issuing in a full account of the history of Christianity and in a body of facts thus accumulated. Systematic theology draws from historical theology in great detail but only as it is sifted by the sister discipline of exegetical theology, its primary source guide. It is in exegetical theology, itself culminating in biblical theology, that systematic theology finds the material out of which its system is built. Within this relationship of the disciplines, systematic theology is the crown and head. It is named "systematic" theology simply because it presents its material, gleaned from the other disciplines, in the form of a comprehensive system. Warfield illustrates with a military analogy:

> The immediate work of exegesis may be compared to the work of a recruiting officer: it draws out from the mass of mankind the men who are to constitute the army. Biblical Theology organizes these men into companies and regiments and corps, arranged in marching order and accoutered for service. Systematic Theology combines these companies and regiments and corps into an army—a single and unitary whole, determined by its own all-pervasive principle. It, too, is composed of men—the same men which were recruited by Exegetics; but it is composed of these men, not as individuals merely, but in their due relations to the other men of their companies and regiments and corps.[40]

---

[39] As many have noticed (e.g., Henk van den Belt, *The Authority of Scripture in Reformed Theology: Truth and Trust*, Studies in Reformed Theology 17 [Leiden: Brill, 2008], 220n152), Warfield incorporated this understanding of the proper arrangement of the theological disciplines in his ordering of the book reviews in *PRR*. Beginning with the October issue of 1893 the reviews are arranged in the following sequence: apologetic theology, exegetical theology, historical theology, systematic theology, practical theology, and general literature.

[40] *W*, 9:49, 63–68, 91–93, 97–99; *SSW*, 2:209. Lints points out, curiously, that although Warfield emphasized the importance of biblical theology as necessarily prior to systematic theology, this priority does not seem evident in Warfield's own theological method. Richard Lints, "Two Theologies or One? Warfield and Vos on the Nature of Theology," *WTJ* 54, no. 2 (1992): 235–54. This observation is valid to some extent, with these two caveats: (1) the discipline of biblical theology was young in Warfield's day, and (2) in several of his theological essays Warfield conscientiously addresses the subject from the standpoint of the developing canon.

Systematic theology, then, collects all the facts of Christianity and presents them in the form of a comprehensive system. It is not a historical discipline. It does not seek to discover or to elucidate what Christians have held or do hold to be true. It seeks to discover and elucidate what is true. "It deals with absolute truth and aims at organizing into a concatenated system all the truth in its sphere." This is a necessary step, Warfield argues, for the human mind is not content with bare facts in isolation. The mind is constituted such that it demands to understand those facts in their mutual relations and in a rational body of correlated thought. That is to say, theology is a "science" properly so called. A science, by the nature of it, "reduces a section of our knowledge to order and harmony," and it is the task of systematic theology to do exactly this with our knowledge of God as he has made himself known.[41]

Warfield cautions that it must be held firmly in mind that systematic theology is not the study of religious experience or of faith. It is not subjective but objective. Nor is it a historical discipline, comparing, say, Christian theology with Buddhist theology or Lutheran with Baptist. Systematic theology is a science, and as a science it seeks to discover and explain what is. It seeks to explain what is true about God, and as such it is exclusive and allows no other theology at all. Warfield illustrates by comparing theology to other sciences: "Geology is a science, and on that very account there cannot be two geologies; its matter is all the well-authenticated facts in its sphere, and its aim is to digest all these facts into one all-comprehending system." He continues, "There may be rival psychologies, which fill the world with vain jangling; but they do not strive together in order that they may obtain the right to exist side by side in equal validity, but in strenuous effort to supplant and supersede one another: there can be but one true science of mind." It is of the nature of a science to gather all the facts within its sphere and present them in a single comprehensive system of thought. "In like manner, just because theology is a science there can be but one theology. This all-embracing system will brook no rival in its sphere, and there can be two theologies only at the cost of one or both of them being imperfect, incomplete, false." This is not to say that there are no competing theologies. There is Pelagian theology, and there is Augustinian theology. But these "are not two coordinate sciences of theology; they are rival theologies. If one is true, just so far the other is false, and there is but one theology." Just so, theology is not the science of religion or of religious experience or of faith. It is the science of God, and it belongs

---

[41]W, 9:50, cf. 51–54, 91–96.

to systematic theology to reduce God's self-revelation to a self-consistent and comprehensive system.[42]

As we have just alluded, then, the theologian's task is possible only insofar as God has made himself known. "If God be a person, it follows by stringent necessity, that He can be known only so far as He reveals or expresses Himself." The subject of God's self-revelation will be taken up in some detail in the following two chapters, but suffice it to say at this point that although the theologian may well mine his data from the created order, general revelation, it is to his distinct advantage that God has revealed himself more clearly and specifically in the words of human language, culminating in Scripture, God's very word. Indeed, theology has this advantage over all the other sciences. The theologian is not left to discover hidden data in the natural world, gathered slowly and uncertainly and incompletely, and then to determine of himself the significance of it all. Yet just as the astronomer must look to the stars as the instruments by which his science is developed, so the theologian is privileged to examine God's written revelation, which affords a certain lucidity and completeness that is unavailable to the other sciences.[43]

This is not to say that theology is not a progressive science. To be sure, it does not progress in the sense that new revelations of truth are expected to complete the theologian's task, although there is a sense in which this is true also, when in the eschaton God reveals himself still more fully, and the saints will see him as he is. Then, "in the mind of perfected humanity," the perfected theology will be realized. But we do not in this age look for an increase of theological material. Rather, theology progresses as we progress in "gathering, defining, mentally assimilating, and organizing these facts into a correlated system." Indeed, theology has a history, and "the body of Christian truth has come down to us in the form of an organic growth." There has been an Augustine and an Anselm and a Luther and a Calvin. And we do not expect the history of theology to close in our own day, however complete our body of truth may seem to us. Systematic theology is the study of God's self-revelation, and as any other science, it entails our progressive understanding of it.[44]

THE RIGHT OF SYSTEMATIC THEOLOGY

That God has revealed himself in the written Word is a gift to be cherished, and with this blessing comes a corresponding privilege and obligation to learn and

---

[42] W, 9:51–52, 54, 56–58, 96–97.
[43] W, 9:58–63, 74–76, 97–105.
[44] W, 9:74–79, 104–5; SSW, 2:102; cf. W, 5:21.

understand that Word. Yet Warfield complains, "Nothing can be a clearer indication of a decadent theology or of a decaying faith, than a tendency to neglect the Word in favor of some one or of all of the lesser sources of theological truth." Valuable as general revelation is, even in all its combined manifestations—in the human psyche, in conscience, in God's providence and our experience with him in grace—it is inadequate, particularly for the sinner. Warfield's leading criticism of mysticism stems from this very consideration. Seeking to know God by inner lights and natural revelation, it ignores the clarity and completeness of the external and authoritative revelation of God in Scripture.[45]

Indifferentism

Mysticism is not the only enemy of the methodical study of theology. Warfield also gives sharp criticism of the doctrinal "indifferentism" that prevailed in his day. It had been customary to regard theology as the queen of the sciences and systematic theology as the queen among the theological disciplines. But, Warfield complains, few in his day would affirm such lofty claims. Of course, by the nature of the case, indifferentism is difficult to combat—it does not care! But with many the sentiment is much stronger, and indeed the very right of systematic theology to exist is widely challenged. In the July 1896 issue of *The Presbyterian and Reformed Review*, Warfield published the lengthy article, "The Right of Systematic Theology." (This was also published the following year in Edinburgh as a separate book under the same title, with an introduction by James Orr, along with commendations by several religious leaders in Edinburgh.) The essay is given to the justification of systematic theology in light of the contemporary indifferentism and its related assaults. "There are few phenomena in the theological world which are more striking indeed than the impatience which is exhibited on every hand with the effort to define truth and to state with precision doctrinal presuppositions and contents of Christianity." The theological enterprise is scornfully designated "intellectualism" or "dogmatism" and characterized as mere ingenious hairsplitting over things that do not matter. Warfield charges that at the root the problem is not a mere indifference to but a dislike of theology—and this coupled with antipathy to external authority in matters of religion. Doctrine is not only useless but noxious, a genuine threat to true religion and religious experience. This, Warfield complains, is the relentless appeal that meets us at every turn. What religious "truth" is needed is sufficiently ascertained by the human feeling and experience.[46]

---

[45]W, 9:58–61, 649–66; cf. SSW, 2:293–94.
[46]SSW, 2:220–24, 242, 294.

For proof that doctrine is not essential we are offered "highly colored portraitures of 'good Christians' of every name and no name, of every faith and no faith, under each of which stands the legend written that since good Christians arise under every form of faith or no faith alike, it cannot be of much importance what men believe." But Warfield warns that this line of reasoning would inevitably "banish Christianity from the earth. For if doctrine be of no value, because some, who theoretically deny or neglect it, nevertheless exhibit the traits of a good life, what truth will remain to which we can attach importance?" Surely, these portraits would "prove" to us that a man can deny *any* doctrine and yet remain a "good Christian." Inevitably we would be driven to conclude that "not only those doctrines which divide Christian sects but those also which constitute the very elements of Christianity are of no real moment."[47]

This "indifferentism" is built entirely on the supposition that religious sentiment and life are what constitute Christianity. But such is the possession of every man alike, whether Christian or pagan. This is simply "natural religion." To reduce Christianity to religious sentiment and experience is to cut it up by its roots and leave nothing that is distinctively Christian. With this presupposition—that doctrine does not matter—we have disposed of all that is peculiar to Christianity. What distinguishes Christianity "is not the religious sentiment and its working, but its message of salvation—in a word, its doctrine." Warfield warns that the conclusion is inescapable: "To be indifferent to doctrine is thus but another way of saying we are indifferent to Christianity."[48]

Nor is this to push the argument to an illegitimate extreme, for it is of the very essence of this indifferentism to affirm that doctrine is useless. To disallow this objection is to renounce indifferentism altogether.

> If there can be any doctrines, however few, which justly deserve the name of essential doctrines and stand at the root of the Christian life as its conditions, foundations, or presuppositions, it surely becomes the duty as well as the right of the Christian man to study them, to seek to understand them in themselves and in their relations, to attempt to state them with accuracy and to adjust their statement to the whole body of known truth—in a word, the right and function of Systematic Theology is vindicated.

Simply put, for the "indifferent" man to claim that any doctrine at all is essential to Christianity is to evacuate his own position. If he recognizes the objective valid-

---

[47]*SSW*, 2:223–24.
[48]*SSW*, 2:227.

ity of a body of religious truth as a condition of religious life, he has become, in spite of himself, a systematic theologian.[49]

Doctrinal indifferentism, then, for the Christian, cannot logically be sustained, and where it is maintained at all, it eviscerates Christianity of all that makes it Christian.

Facts versus Doctrines

To deny the right of systematic theology to exist, then, some positive argument must be found to demonstrate that doctrine lacks all significance. And in fact the prevailing antipathy for doctrine has become more polemic. Christ, we are told, did not come to teach a doctrine, and the church must be stripped of all such human artificialities. For many this cry is "only the expression of an innate antipathy to clear thinking and of a not very rare incapacity for truth—a sort of color-blindness to truth." Truth itself has become distasteful, and on such minds, exact statement of theology is like an irritant and appears an enemy of true religion. "Men who have no faculty for truth will always consider an appeal to truth an evil."[50]

Warfield has little time for this, for it is of the very essence of Christianity that it claims to be "the truth," and it is as "the truth" that the gospel offers itself to men and seeks to propagate itself in the world. Christianity does not advance by sword or any means other than that by which "truth" makes its way. This is what Warfield has in mind so often when he speaks of Christianity's mission to "reason" its way to dominion and "to reason the world into acceptance of the truth." At its very heart Christianity is a revelation from God, and it has this message—this message of truth—to proclaim. Apart from this there is no Christianity at all.[51]

This is not to say that the assault on doctrinal Christianity comes only from those who are unwilling to think but who would still keep their religion. "Theology is killing religion" is also "the reasoned assertion of masters of theological science whose professed object is to preserve Christianity in its purity and save it from the dangers which encompass it in this weak and erring world."[52]

One of these schools of thought is noted by its watchword, "Christianity consists of facts, not dogmas." Our faith for salvation rests not on theories and intellectual constructions, it is said, but on a series of mighty divine acts in human history. We are not saved by some theory of the person of Christ but by his incarnation, not by

---

[49]*SSW*, 2:227–28; *W*, 9:587–89.
[50]*SSW*, 2:228–30.
[51]*SSW*, 2:213, 228–30, 294, 469.
[52]*SSW*, 2:230.

any theory of atonement but by the great fact of his death for us, and not by any theory of his high priesthood but by the great fact that he reigns in heaven over all things for his church. Christianity consists in these *facts*, not in its dogmas.[53]

Of course there is an element of truth to this, Warfield acknowledges. Our faith does rest in historical facts. Indeed, the facts of the incarnation, atonement, and heavenly high priesthood of Christ are of the very center of Christianity. But the antithesis here between facts and doctrines is a false one. What are facts without their interpretation? A fact without its accompanying interpretation—doctrine— is simply a fact not understood. "An event whose significance remains foreign to us cannot have the least direct importance for our salvation."

> No one would contend that Christianity consists in doctrines as distinguished from facts, far less that it consists in doctrines wholly unrelated to facts. But neither ought anyone contend that it consists in facts as distinguished from doctrines, and far less that it consists in facts as separated from doctrines. What Christianity consists in is facts that are doctrines, and doctrines that are facts. The Incarnation is a doctrine: no eye saw the Son of God descend from heaven and enter the virgin's womb: but if it be not a true fact as well, our faith is vain, we are yet in our sins. The Resurrection of Christ is a fact: an occurrence in time level to the apprehension of men and witnessed by their adequate testimony: but it is at the same time the cardinal doctrine of Christianity.

If we contend that Christianity consists in facts wholly separated from their interpretation, their doctrines, then the bare facts lose all significance, and we destroy Christianity altogether. These historical facts are indeed essential, but they are meaningless until they are understood and their significance is ascertained. It is surely of utmost importance, Warfield concludes, that the Christian man investigate and determine the meaning of Christianity's facts—and this, very simply, is the task of systematic theology.[54]

Warfield further notes carefully that "there lies at the basis of Christianity not only a series of great redemptive facts, but also an authoritative interpretation of those facts." And he queries, Who has such knowledge and the right to interpret these facts for us authoritatively? Of course, there is no answer but the obvious: that authority belongs only to Christ. It is therefore in the teaching of Christ and in his commissioned apostles that we find authoritative Christian dogma. It follows, then, that this dogma—doctrine—is of the very essence of Christianity.[55]

---

[53]*SSW*, 2:230–31.
[54]*SSW*, 2:230–38, 242.
[55]*SSW*, 2:238–39.

One Fact Only

Albrecht Ritschl represents an extreme form of the contention that Christianity consists not in doctrines but in facts. Ritschl taught that Christianity's doctrines were corruptions of Christianity, and that if Christianity is to be rescued from the destruction that awaits it by modern criticism, it must rid itself of its metaphysical accretions, which have brought it into conflict with modern knowledge. What this means, of course, is that it must be stripped of its supernatural. The whole sweep of its metaphysical dimensions must be abandoned, and only that which is "purely religious" may be retained. If Christianity is to be safe and remain in this modern world, religion must be separated from metaphysics. But the attack is not on the side of metaphysics only; it is also on the side of history. Once we yield up the church's doctrines, might we defend its history? If doctrines do not matter, then what of Christianity's facts? The Ritschlian response is the same—they do not matter either. Just this one fact is essential: Jesus Christ. This is the Ritschlian position in its most characteristic form.[56]

But Warfield is not impressed, and he finds it difficult to take seriously a teaching that is less concerned with truth and history than "playing to the galleries" of an unbelieving age already steering clear of metaphysics. He asks what might be left after so much has been surrendered. If we eliminate all metaphysical conceptions, can we then even speak of the human soul? Indeed, how can we speak of God? "Every religious truth, however primary, contains a metaphysical element." Can we follow Ritschl and believe in God? That he is infinite? That he is a person? That he exists? None of this is allowed us on Ritschlian grounds. For Ritschl, God is a "necessary assumption" for the Christian, but scientifically God remains an open question. What of the Holy Spirit? And what of Ritschl's one allowed fact, Jesus Christ? Which Jesus is it? The "historical Jesus" is, according to the Ritschlians, a nonsupernatural Jesus. Not Jesus the miracle worker or Jesus resurrected or Jesus ascended—these metaphysical accretions have nothing to do with the historical Jesus. But, Warfield wonders, how could they know this? All the historical records are of a supernatural Jesus only. Where in the historical records is this other, nonmiraculous Jesus? The Jesus they want is nowhere to be found but in Ritschl's own preconceived theories.[57]

The Ritschlian procedure, then, first strips Christianity of its metaphysical doctrines and demands a historical Jesus only. It then delivers this "historical Jesus" to the unbelieving critics to do with him as they please. And thus the whole essence of Christianity has evaporated. Surely, they have surrendered too much.

---

[56]*SSW*, 2:244–46, 294–95.
[57]*SSW*, 2:246–52.

Such an "eviscerated Christianity" is not worth the world's notice and hardly worth its preservation. Ritschlian Christianity is an absurdity. If we would have the Jesus that the apostles give us, the only Jesus known to history, it is a Jesus whose person and acts demand understanding. And this is the business of systematic theology. "Call it metaphysical, call it Greek, if you will. But remember that it is of the essence of Christianity."[58]

Doctrine versus Life

A final and more popular attack on systematic theology contends that Christianity is not a doctrine but a life. Its ethic and its experience are essential, but these may be independent of both facts and doctrines. The purpose of the Bible is to quicken life, not to satisfy our curiosity, and as we focus on doctrine, we steer away from its proper and intended use. By the Bible, God implants life and leads us to depend solely on God—and not facts or doctrines—for that life.[59]

Again Warfield notes that there is an element of truth in this line of thinking that makes it attractive. Christianity is indeed a life, a blessed life in communion with the Son of God, and the whole body of Christian doctrine is in order to this blessed life. And no, it is not doctrine that creates this life but the Spirit of God enabling us to hear the truth and respond to it. This is all fundamental to Christianity. But to make such sharp separation of life from doctrine is entirely foreign to Christianity and in fact turns it on its head. In this inverted view, feeling comes first and then ideas, experience and then doctrine. God produces life within us, and from this we learn divine things. Life is before doctrine "not merely in importance but in time: and doctrine is only a product of the Christian life." Christian doctrine is but "the manifestation of precedent Christian life." God reveals himself, but in Christian life, not in objective revelation. And so it follows that doctrine may change and evolve. The fluctuations of the spiritual life produce varying ideas and ideals, and while we may speak the same words as our fathers, it is with different meanings. But no matter—Christianity is about life, not doctrine. Under some conceptions of this, Jesus represents the climactic moment of this progress in the perfect realization in his life of God's love, and it is for this that we look to him and follow him. But what is important is life, and this is what Christianity is all about.[60]

Once again Warfield charges that this amounts to a formal renunciation of Christianity and denies Christianity's claim to absolute truth. And again the logic

---

[58]*SSW*, 2:252–56.
[59]*SSW*, 2:256–57.
[60]*SSW*, 2:257–61.

offered is self-defeating. If, as some contend, our religious experience (and so its thinking) evolves, on what ground should we think that Jesus, two millennia ago, should remain the example? Would not the logic demand that by now, surely, he has been surpassed? The demands of the theory leave no room for Christ whatever. This is mere indifferentism dressed in other clothes. Or, whatever may be said of Jesus, if religion is just a feeling, a feeling that is ever fluctuating, then Christianity is reduced to a natural religion with nothing distinctively Christian about it, and it is left only to be surpassed by a still higher religious feeling. But most to the point, Warfield asks simply, "What produces the specific form of the religious feeling which is distinctive of Christianity?" Holding that which is common to all natural religions, Christianity would have nothing that can explain its distinctive religious experience. A feeling apart from knowledge is meaningless, "and would be suggestive of disease rather than of the divine." Clearly, it is Christianity's thinking, its doctrines, that gives shape to its distinctive experience. But if this is so, then life does not precede doctrine after all; rather, "doctrine precedes life and is the cause of the specific form which the religious life takes in Christianity." Once again Warfield concludes, "To be indifferent to this doctrine as if it were only an index of the life flowing on steadily beneath it and independently of it, is therefore to be indifferent to distinctive Christianity itself."[61]

Biblical Reflections

Warfield acknowledges that there is a very important sense in which it is true that life precedes doctrine, and that is bound up in the Bible's teachings of the noetic effects of sin and of the sovereignty of grace (see, e.g., 1 Cor. 2:14). "I believe in order that I may understand" and "faith precedes understanding" are long-accepted watchwords of Christianity. This is a favorite emphasis in Warfield, and it will be explored in the following chapters. But of course this is not the sense intended by those who oppose doctrine or hold that life precedes it.[62]

More to the point, Warfield references the distribution of material in the letters of the apostle Paul, in which doctrine is regularly made to precede life, and indeed life is built upon doctrine. The transition that is marked in Romans 12:1 stands as an example. "I appeal to you *therefore*, brothers." The "therefore" is significant, indicating "because this is so." "In these 'tremendous therefores' is revealed Paul's conception of the relation between truth and life." The same was true of Christ before him when he made so much of his Father's word given to his disciples, that they might know the truth and have the eternal life and joy

---

[61]*SSW*, 2:261–75; *W*, 9:283–86, 587–88.
[62]*SSW*, 2:273–74.

that it affords. His prayer for them was that they would be sanctified by the truth of God's word.[63]

Warfield remarks further that there is a moral basis in faith, and that Jesus did teach, "If anyone's will is to do God's will, he will know whether the teaching is from God or whether I am speaking on my own authority" (John 7:17)—"that is, it is only in the good ground of a good heart that even the good seed of the gospel can produce fruit." Warfield clarifies:

> But nowhere did he or any of his apostles ever teach that the good seed is unnecessary for the harvest—that the unsowed soil, however good, is competent of itself to produce the golden return. Knowledge of God's will with them was ever the condition of doing God's will, and lay at the root of all good conduct and true religion.

This has from that day onward been the conviction of the church, that it has truth to proclaim to the world. Christianity is preeminently a doctrinal religion, and it seeks by the propagation of these truths to save the lost and rule their lives. "Go and preach" is its commission, and we do so with the conviction that this word gives birth to faith and life. God gives increase, but he does so by means of the word planted by Paul and watered by Apollos (1 Cor. 3:6). By this word the Spirit is given (Gal. 3:2). Hence, Paul describes the gospel as "the power of God for salvation" (Rom. 1:16). And it is for this reason that he urges Christians at all costs to preserve that gospel in its purity.[64]

THE GOAL OF THEOLOGY

Life, then, is founded on truth, and this constitutes the goal of the theological task. The study of theology is not an end in itself, valuable as that study is. Nor is theology purely theoretical. It has an end in view beyond itself—the salvation and sanctification of the soul. It is designed and intended to make one wise unto salvation (2 Tim. 3:15). We might say that "to make one wise" describes the task of systematic theology, and "unto salvation" describes the task of practical theology. But such fine distinctions must not leave the impression of a sharp division between the two disciplines. The science of systematic theology does not exist independently or for its own sake. It is part of the larger theological task, laboring toward and culminating in this practical issue. It does not seek to elucidate a theory left to hang in the air. It is intended to issue in life. Put in other terms,

---

[63]SSW, 2:276.
[64]SSW, 2:276–79, 280.

the goal of the theological sciences, in all its branches, is "the knowledge of God," and such knowledge is not merely abstract but experiential.[65]

Here then is established not only the right of systematic theology but its absolute necessity. If doctrine shapes life, then not only must we give attention to doctrine, generally, but we must give our most diligent attention to it. The character of our theology will shape the character of our religion, and any defective view of God's character will be reflected in the soul and the peace of conscience. "No convictions, no Christianity. Scanty convictions, hunger-bitten Christianity. Profound convictions, solid and substantial religion."[66] "We must think right thoughts of God if we would worship him as he desires to be worshipped, if we would live the life he wishes us to live, and enjoy the peace which he has provided for us." More fully:

> We do not possess the separate truths of religion in the abstract: we possess them only in their relations, and we do not properly know any one of them—nor can it have its full effect on our life—except as we know it in its relations to other truths, that is, as systematized. What we do not know, in this sense, systematically, we rob of half its power on our conduct; unless, indeed, we are prepared to argue that a truth has effect on us in proportion as it is unknown, rather than in proportion as it is known.[67]

> That the knowledge of the truth is an essential prerequisite to the production of those graces and the building up of those elements of a sanctified character for the production of which each truth is especially adapted, probably few will deny: but surely it is equally true that the clearer, fuller, and more discriminating this knowledge is, the more certainly and richly will it produce its appropriate effect; and in this is found a most complete vindication of the duty of systematizing the separate elements of truth into a single soundly concatenated whole, by which the essential nature of each is made as clear as it can be made to human apprehension. It is not a matter of indifference, then, how we apprehend and systematize this truth. On the contrary, if we misconceive it in its parts or in its relations, not only do our views of truth become confused and erroneous, but also our religious life becomes dwarfed or contorted. The character of our religion is, in a word, determined by the character of our theology: and thus the task of the systematic theologian is to see that the relations in which the separate truths actually stand are rightly conceived, in order that they may exert their rightful influence on the development of the religious life.[68]

---

[65]*SSW*, 1:415; *SSW*, 2:209–11; *W*, 9:79, 85, 92.
[66]*SSW*, 1:368.
[67]*W*, 9:83–87, 285–86.
[68]*W*, 9:80.

If this is the value and end of doctrine, then the study of theology is the solemn obligation of every preacher. Indeed, the systematic theologian himself "is preeminently a preacher of the gospel." The aim of both theology and preaching is not merely to arrange truths in logical order but by the power of these truths to move men to love God, to trust in Christ and hold him precious, and to experience the Spirit-ministered blessings intended for him. Inasmuch as this is the function and use of theology, it is an indispensable treasure.[69]

Here two important themes of Warfield's works come together. First, Warfield consistently views Christianity in redemptive terms. Christianity is distinctively at its very heart a redemptive religion. Revelation itself is a redemptive act, and its purpose is to restore the sinner to fellowship with God. Second, it is important for Warfield that this saving truth be preached, for it is the means by which this rescue is realized. God saves, but he does not save in a vacuum—he saves by means of the truth understood. Specific differences in roles allowed, the communication of this truth is the responsibility of the apologist, the theologian, and the preacher alike. Christianity has a message to proclaim, and it is a message that saves and transforms life.

---

[69]SSW, 2:276–79, 280–88; W, 9:79, 86.

Now when man fell, the relation in which he stood to God was fundamentally altered. Not as if he ceased to be dependent on God, in every sphere of his being and activity. Nor even as if he ceased to be conscious of this his comprehensive dependence on God.

Even as sinner man cannot but believe in God; the very devils believe and tremble. He cannot escape the knowledge that he is utterly dependent on God for all that he is and does. But his consciousness of dependence on God no longer takes the form of glad and loving trust. Precisely what sin has done to him is to render this trust impossible. Sin has destroyed the natural relation between God and His creature in which the creature trusts God,

and has instituted a new relation, which conditions all his immanent as well as transient activities Godward. The sinner is at enmity with God and can look to God only for punishment. He knows himself absolutely dependent on God, but in knowing this, he knows himself absolutely in the power of his enemy. A fearful looking forward to judgment conditions all his thought of God. Faith has accordingly been transformed into unfaith; trust into distrust.

He expects evil and only evil from God. Knowing himself to be dependent on God he seeks to be as independent of Him as he can. As he thinks of God, misery and fear and hatred take the place of joy and trust and love. Instinctively and by his very nature the sinner, not being able to escape from his belief in God, yet cannot possibly have faith in God, that is trust Him, entrust himself to Him.

W, 9:339.

The Existence of God

Divine Revelation

DEFINITION, DESCRIPTION, AND CLASSIFICATIONS
REVELATION AND AUTHORITY
REVELATION AND THE KNOWLEDGE OF GOD

3

PROLEGOMENA

The Existence of God

In Warfield's apologetic method, establishing the existence of God[1] is primary, laying the necessary groundwork for theological explication. He grounds his argument—following Calvin, he notes—"in the very constitution of man" and seeks to "vindicate" the *sensus divinitatis* that he insists is intuitive, ineradicable, and unavoidably part of the consciousness of every person. He finds it significant that even among the remotest of peoples, awareness of God—understood not just metaphysically but religiously—is universal and "strikingly pure and complete." He readily affirms that lapse into practical atheism is evident even among professing Christians, but he argues that "positive" or dogmatic atheism is impossible. For Warfield, dogmatic atheism is but antitheism and merely seeks to conceal the universally "instinctive and indestructible sense of the divine" that cannot finally be erased. Not just in the Scriptures but in the human consciousness also the existence of God is a given.[2]

Warfield acknowledges that positive atheism has found formal expression in a number of systems of thought, in his day primarily by the doctrine of evolution that was given scientific standing by Darwin's *On the Origin of Species*. But with a note of cynicism he complains that while evolution is allowed to give account for everything, evolution itself strangely needs no accounting for! This is more than a complaint: Warfield is arguing that groundless, bald assertions are the best arguments the atheist can muster. God's existence remains an "intuitive truth" that is altogether unavoidable.[3]

---

[1]Warfield's primary treatments of this subject may be found in the following: "Agnosticism," *SSW*, 1:34–36; "Atheism," *SSW*, 1:37–40; "God and Human Religion and Morals," *SSW*, 1:41–45; "God," *SSW*, 1:69–74; "Calvin's Doctrine of the Knowledge of God," *W*, 5:29–130; and "Calvin's Doctrine of God," *W*, 5:133–85.
[2]*W*, 5:145; *W*, 10:54–55; *SSW*, 1:37–39; *SSW*, 2:97, 116–17; *PGS*, 232–33.
[3]*SSW*, 1:40, 70.

Warfield acknowledges the validity of the standard "proofs" of the existence of God, and he affirms that their usefulness is recognized in the Scriptures themselves. Nevertheless he describes them as functioning first to remind us of or confirm the already settled, innate conviction that God is. Intuitively we are "under necessity" to believe in "the real existence of the infinitely perfect Being," who is the uncaused cause of this contingent universe, the intelligent designer of this universe of order, and the lawgiver and judge for "dependent and moral beings," who possess "an ineradicable feeling of responsibility." That is to say, the standard arguments for God's existence are useful precisely because—and only because—they elucidate that of which by nature all men are intuitively aware.[4]

In his "God and Human Religion and Morals," Warfield cites the words of Jesus in Matthew 12:12—"Of how much more value is a man than a sheep!"—and inquires *why*. What is it that makes a man better than a sheep? Warfield acknowledges that there are numerous superficial answers that could be given the question, such as self-consciousness and freedom. But most fundamentally, he argues, what makes human beings of more value than the lower creation is their "irresistible sense of dependence and an ineradicable sense of obligation." It is not that other creatures are any less dependent or less obligated than man. All God's creation is equally dependent and obligated; this is the nature of the Creator-creature relationship. It is rather the "constant and profound" awareness of these in the consciousness of mankind that places man above other creatures. "It is because man is conscious of his dependence that he is a religious being. And it is because he is conscious of his obligation that he is a moral being." Because man is so aware of his dependence upon God, he is "necessarily" a religious being. And his corresponding sense of obligation unavoidably shows itself in "the whole range of his activities that we speak of as moral." Echoing Calvin, Warfield summarizes: "In other words, our native endowment is not merely a *sensus deitatis*, but also a *semen religionis*. . . . For what we call religion is just the reaction of the human soul to what it perceives God to be." Or, again echoing Calvin, Warfield argues that if we know ourselves, we must know ourselves as we truly are, "and that means we must know [ourselves] as dependent, derived, imperfect, and responsible beings." That is to say, both man's knowledge of God, skewed as it may be, and his consequent perception of himself as a religious being, are intuitive.[5]

---

[4]*SSW*, 1:70–71; *SSW*, 2:137–41. An article entitled "God," written by A. A. Hodge and later revised by Warfield, states, "All the 'arguments' for the being of God are intended either to quicken and confirm this innate idea, or to expand and render it definite by showing *what* God is, as well as proving *that* he is." *Johnson's Universal Encyclopedia*, new edition, ed. Charles Kendall Adams, vol. 3 (New York: D. Appleton and Company, 1899), 821.

[5]*SSW*, 1:41–42; *W*, 5:31, 35, 37; cf. *PGS*, 230–36. *Semen religionis* indicates the religious nature or "seed of religion" common to every man.

Further, if because of man's sense of dependence and obligation atheism is impossible, agnosticism is likewise impoverishing, degrading human life by secularizing it and denying its highest significance. Arguing on the ground that knowledge of God is unattainable, agnosticism "bids men think and feel and act as if there were no God and no spiritual life and no future existence. It thus degenerates into a practical atheism. Refusing to declare there is no God, it yet misses all there may be of value and profit in the recognition of God."[6] Again, for Warfield, man's awareness of God and corresponding sense of dependence and obligation is so constant and so strong that it necessarily gives human life its dignity, value, and meaning. To reject this knowledge of God or even to question it is to strike at the heart of what renders man king of creation.

Without question this sense of dependence and obligation has been radically weakened by the entrance of sin. The image of God in man, while not erased, became defaced. Sinful man was "thrown into terror by his sense of responsibility" to God. His innate sense of religion and morality gave way to religions and moralities in countless varieties. In the words of Romans 1, man now seeks to suppress his knowledge of God and sense of obligation to him. Because man is now guilty, he fears God with great terror, and because man is now corrupt, he hates God. The result is a profound sense of inward moral conflict between right and wrong. But God's image in man has not been eradicated altogether. In all this, man's sense of dependence and obligation remains and remains evident—from this awareness of God he cannot escape. "Escape from the apprehension of a being on whom we are dependent and to whom we are responsible is no more possible than escape from the world in which we live. God is part of our environment." "As God is as much a part of the environment of man as the earth on which he stands, no man can escape from religion any more than he can escape from gravitation."[7] Warfield insists that God is the universally recognized given.

Divine Revelation[8]

Warfield often emphasizes that there are two classes of religion in the world. The one is man-made, the product of human thought and arising from the human consciousness. The other is altogether of divine origin. The one, therefore, is natu-

---

[6]*SSW*, 1:35–36.

[7]*SSW*, 1:39, 42–44; *W*, 9:649.

[8]The primary articles in which Warfield treats this subject include the following: "The Biblical Idea of Revelation," in *W*, 1:3–34; "The Idea and Theories of Revelation," in *W*, 1:37–48; "Christianity and Revelation," in *SSW*, 1:23–30; "Under Orders," in *SSW*, 2:729–34; "Calvin's Doctrine of the Knowledge of God," in *W*, 5:29–130; "Mysticism and Christianity," in *W*, 9:649–66; and "The Christian Doctrine of Revelation," *The New York Observer* 73 (July 4, 1895): 4–5.

ral and the other supernatural. Similarly, we cannot read Warfield even cursorily without noticing his deep commitment to supernaturalism and, specifically, to the supernatural character of Christianity. Repeatedly throughout his works, Warfield insists that this is what distinguishes Christianity from all other religions: Christianity is distinctly and uniquely a revealed religion. It originates not in man seeking after God but in God making himself known to men. Its doctrines are not the product of human thought but communications from God. It is the supernatural, because divinely revealed, religion.[9]

DEFINITION, DESCRIPTION, AND CLASSIFICATIONS

Warfield defines divine revelation in light of its varying shades of usage. In its active sense it is "the act of God by which he communicates to man the truth concerning himself—his nature, works, will, or purposes." That is, divine revelation is God's making himself known to men. In its passive sense revelation is the knowledge of God that humanity possesses as a result of God's self-disclosure. All this is the necessary implication of theism. Divine revelation is also understood in a wider sense—general revelation—and a narrower sense—special revelation.

> In its wider sense it includes all modes in which God makes himself known to men; or, passively, all knowledge concerning God however attained, inasmuch as it is conceived that all such knowledge is, in one way or another, wrought by him. In its narrower sense it is confined to the communication of knowledge in a supernatural as distinguished from a natural mode; or, passively, to the knowledge of God which has been supernaturally made known to men.[10]

General revelation is so called both because of the nonspecific and rather inarticulate nature of the information it provides, and because its reception is by means of the normal exercises of the human psyche. Warfield therefore refers to it also as "natural" and "cosmical" revelation. He stresses that all knowledge of God is necessarily revealed knowledge. To be sure, there can be no religion at all except on the ground of revelation, and wherever it or any knowledge of God exists, there revelation must be inferred, "for it is only as God makes himself known that he can be known, in any measure whatever." Our intuitive awareness of God, our sense of dependence and obligation, is due to his self-disclosure to humanity created in his image. General revelation is "communicated through the

---

[9]*SSW*, 1:23; *W*, 9:649. On Warfield's supernaturalism, see for example his "Christian Supernaturalism," in *W*, 9:25–46, 649–66.
[10]*W*, 1:37; cf. 58–59; *SSW*, 1:24.

media of natural phenomena, occurring in the course of Nature or of history." It is "addressed generally to all intelligent creatures, and is therefore accessible to all men." There has never been a time in history in which God has been silent; since the creation of the world he has been making himself known. Warfield points to Acts 14:17; 17:27; Romans 1:20ff.; and Psalm 19 to accent the truth that God has continuously made himself known in the created order—"nature." The seasons, the rains, the harvests, the provision of food and gladness are all tokens of his divine care for his creatures. All of it harks back to the One who gives it, and all of it is designed to draw attention to him and thus "woo" his creatures to himself (Acts 17:27). The created order further displays with clarity the Creator's eternality, power, deity, and glory, even if in sinful rebellion humanity has suppressed such revelation (Rom. 1:20ff.; Ps. 19:1–4). God, who does nothing unconsciously or without intention or purpose, has in all his works of creation and providence displayed his glory to his intelligent creatures for the purpose of "awaking and nourishing religion" in them and bringing them into relation with himself. More importantly, it is not in the created order only, generally speaking, that God has left his impress, but (as noted in the previous chapter) in the very consciousness of every human being, made in his image, there is the inescapable awareness of God and a corresponding sense of dependence on him and obligation to him. Man knows himself as a dependent creature, and there is in him not merely a *sensus deitatis* but therefore a *semen religionis*. In all these ways, God is purposefully and very effectively making himself known to his intelligent creatures with the result that our awareness of him, both intuitive and augmented from without, is unavoidable and ineradicable.[11]

Essential, valuable, and trustworthy though general or natural revelation is, it has severe limitations. It is nonspecific and rather inarticulate. There is a sense in which all revelation, general or special, is supernatural, for it all comes to us from God. But for the acquisition of general revelation nothing is required beyond the usual operations of the human psyche. The mode of communication is in no way "special" or extraordinary but emerges merely in the human consciousness. Warfield emphasizes that general revelation is characterized, further, by insufficiency. That is, the knowledge of God it provides lacks in detail and specificity. Special revelation, by contrast, is marked by its objectivity and the extraordinary operations of the Spirit of God. Special revelation culminates not merely in divine acts within history but consummately in the divinely spoken Word. God has given man the high gift of language, not just for man to communicate with man, but for God to communicate with him also.

---

[11] *W*, 1:4–6, 42, 45–46; *SSW*, 1:24, 26.

The characteristic element in the Bible idea of revelation in its highest sense is that the organs of revelation are not creatively concerned in the revelations made through them, but occupy a receptive attitude. The contents of their messages are not something thought out, inferred, hoped, or feared by them, but something conveyed to them, often forced upon them by the irresistible might of the revealing Spirit.[12]

This is the biblical idea of special revelation: it originates with God and is communicated immediately to man apart from second causes. It does not arise from within the human psyche. It is, simply, God's speaking to man as Spirit to spirit so as to be heard and understood.

Most significantly, Warfield emphasizes, general revelation is insufficient for our necessities as sinners, "and by its very insufficiency [it] awakens a longing for a fuller knowledge of God and his purposes." It is adapted to man as man, a creature, but not man as a sinner. It provides an awareness of God, but it leaves us, as sinners, unable to know him as Savior. There is in general revelation a disclosure of the God of nature but not of the God of redemptive grace. For this knowledge of God something further is required. And for this reason Warfield characterizes special revelation not only as supernatural but also as redemptive or soteriological. It is the disclosure of God in his redemptive activity, and it is itself a redemptive act and part of his redemptive purpose. Special revelation presupposes man's fallenness, and its purpose is not merely "to inform men's understanding (which would be intellectualism); or merely to correct their conduct (which would be ethicism); or merely to quicken within them religious emotions (which would be mysticism)." Rather, it is always perceived as within the great organic process by which God is glorifying himself in the rescue of mankind from sin. Special revelation may take the form of "external manifestation," such as theophany or miracle, or "internal suggestion," such as visions or dreams and the giving of the "prophetic" word. But it is all designed with a redemptive end in view. This soteriological revelation culminates, of course, in the incarnation of Christ, the divine Word. But again, God's self-disclosure in the rescue of sinners is not by act only, and it will never do justice to the biblical representation of divine revelation to speak of it in terms of saving acts only. Providence, miracle, theophany, and dream by themselves will not suffice: they require explication. Divine acts apart from words are but "naked messages." The incarnation is God's supreme self-revelation, but even this could not be understood aright or fully apart from words. It is supremely in the spoken word that God has made himself known. He has *spoken* to make manifest his works, his will, and his purpose. In this respect

---

[12] W, 1:9, 44–45.

special *verbal* revelation not only gives explanation to God's redemptive activity but is itself a redemptive act. God's special, redemptive revelation climaxes in the objective communication of words to sinners concerning his gracious and powerful saving work.[13]

Warfield treats this further in his discussions of the doctrine of inspiration, but here also he emphasizes that God's revelation in word is yet a "concursive operation" in which the Holy Spirit works in, with, and through human will and activity in such a manner that God's Word is communicated by means of human spokesmen, whether in their speaking or in their writing. Of Moses it is said that he knew God face to face (Deut. 34:10) and that God spoke to him mouth to mouth (Num. 12:8), and Scripture distinguishes him as the model prophet (*nabhi'*) or spokesman for God. But the entire series of Israel's prophets were "like Moses" in this same way—they spoke for God. In Deuteronomy 18:15–18, God promises that he will raise up a prophet like Moses: "And I will put my words in his mouth, and he shall speak to them all I command him" (v. 18). Here Warfield finds a precise description of the process of divine verbal revelation—God puts *his* word in *their* mouths. And so the prophets themselves ever asserted: "Then the LORD put out his hand and touched my mouth. And the LORD said to me, 'Behold, I have put my words in your mouth'" (Jer. 1:9; cf. 5:14; Isa. 51:16; 59:21; Num. 22:35; 23:5, 12, 16). "Accordingly, the words 'with which' they spoke were not their own but the Lord's" (Ezek. 3:4; 2 Sam. 14:3, 19). By contrast, what constitutes the false prophets is that they speak "from their own heart," and "speak visions of their own minds, and not from the mouth of the LORD" (Ezek. 13:2–17; Jer. 23:16, 26; cf. 14:14). Warfield refers to Exodus 4:10–17 and 7:1–7 as "the fundamental passage" that describes the prophetic function exactly. Here God specifically declares that he who made the mouth can be with it to teach it what to speak, and here he describes the prophet as a mouth of God, one who speaks not his own words but the words of God. That is, the prophet is a spokesman. Hence the common prophetic assertion "The word of the LORD came to me," or the brief "says the LORD." That is to say, divine revelation is climactically verbal. God spoke directly to the prophets, and by them directly to his people at large.[14]

Warfield further clarifies the nature of this special revelation in word by means of a series of affirmations. First, it was given progressively in historical development and not all at once (Heb. 1:1–2). Second, its progressive unfolding was in keeping with the progressive unfolding of God's redemptive work. Its focus advanced continually throughout the centuries of its unfolding development toward its culmination in

---

[13]*W*, 1:6, 11–13, 37–46, 512–19; *W*, 5:68; *SSW*, 1:24, 29–30; *SSW*, 2:152–66.
[14]*W*, 1:15, 18–19, 22.

It is in this sense that special communication is itself considered a redemp-
. Third, in this progressive unfolding the divine revelation was verified by
miracles. Here Warfield states briefly a theme more fully developed in his *Counterfeit Miracles*, namely, that the primary purpose of miracles was to serve as credentials of God's spokesmen. Fourth, predictive prophecy is both itself revelation and a credential of that fuller revelation of word of which it is organically a part. And fifth, all this serves to underline the nature of Scripture, through inspiration, as God's climactic revelation, intended for the permanent and universal possession of humanity and, thus, "a substantial part of his redemptive work" itself.[15]

All this is to say that divine revelation climaxes in the Bible, which is "just the Word of God written" and therefore is designated by such expressions as "the word of the Lord," "word of God," "law," or simply "the word" or, in a very high sense, "Scripture." All this reflects an understanding on the part of the biblical authors themselves that their writings constitute a divine revelation. And in this, Christianity is shown to stand apart from all other religions as *the* revealed religion. "The religion of the Bible thus announces itself, not as the product of men's search after God, if haply they may feel after Him and find Him, but as the creation in men of the gracious God forming a people for Himself, that they may show forth His praise." Warfield takes sharp issue with the claim of Charles Augustin Sainte-Beuve (1804–1869) that "Christianity is only the perfection of the total body of universal beliefs." If this were so, then Christianity would also be but a natural religion, having risen merely from the cumulative consciousness of men. Warfield admits that there is a "high and true sense" in which Christianity is the fulfillment of all the natural religions, for these religions also possess the idea of God, a consciousness of guilt, and the longing for redemption. "Israel's Promise, Christianity's Possession, is also the Desire of all nations." God makes himself known, in measure, in both spheres, and only this can account for the very idea of religion. Other religions are based in varying degree on general revelation. "The real difference between Christianity and other religions turns thus precisely on their diverse initiation: in the ethnic religions men are seeking after God if haply they may feel after him and find him; in Christianity God is seeking men and finding them." Or again, Christianity comes to man from outside him, from God alone, while other religions flow merely "from no higher source than the human spirit itself." Christianity alone is grounded in special revelation. And so Warfield summarizes, "Were there no 'general revelation' there would be no religion in the world of any kind: were there no 'special revelation' there would be no Christianity."[16]

---

[15]*W*, 1:11, 13, 28, 46–48; "The Christian Doctrine of Revelation," 4–5.
[16]*W*, 1:4, 1–33; *SSW*, 1:23–25; *W*, 9:649–50. Warfield notes on a couple of occasions that the reality of general revelation is acknowledged by virtually all brands of theists as a necessary implication of theism itself

It follows from all this that the relation of general and special revelation is not one of absolute contrast or opposition but of supplement and completion. Nor are the two entirely separate; rather, each is incomplete without the other. Together they form a complete "organic whole." Special revelation, then, may indeed correct misapprehensions of general revelation, but it does not in any way correct the general revelation itself. God has not been misleading in any of his self-disclosures. He does all things well. Nor can general revelation merely be set aside in favor of special revelation. Rather, the purpose of the one is to supplement and complete the other. "Without special revelation, general revelation would be for sinful men incomplete and ineffective" and would only issue in leaving them without excuse (Rom. 1:20). But without general revelation, special revelation would lack the foundation of man's fundamental knowledge of God as almighty, wise, righteous, good, the Maker and Ruler of all things. Apart from general revelation God's redemptive interventions in the world would be unnoticed or unintelligible. Special revelation builds on general revelation. But more specifically, special revelation is occasioned by the need that arose because of human sin, and its purpose is to meet these new circumstances. To redeem fallen man, a new method and a new content of revelation was required. General revelation is in no way imperfect or even incomplete in itself considered; it is not designed to address the needs of fallen man. It is special revelation that is designed to meet the sinner's need and to disclose God in grace. It is to be expected, for example, that apart from Israel's special revelation from God the heathen nations around her remained heathen: they had no revelation. Once again, special revelation is part of the redemptive process and a substantial part of the redemptive act itself.[17]

REVELATION AND AUTHORITY

It also follows from this that special revelation provides the singular authority in religion, an external source that can arbitrate truth from error. "The principle of authority is inherent in the very idea of a revelation." It is thus designated "law" or "instruction," and reference to it—"it is written"—settles all matters of dispute.[18]

---

and foundational to the very idea of religion, but that this agreement is not shared in regard to special revelation. Here Warfield affirms again that it is the task of apologetics to validate not special revelation only but specifically the special revelation on which Christianity—as over against pantheism, deism, mysticism, rationalism, and any other anti- or otherwise inadequate theistic notion—rests. See *SSW*, 1:25; *W*, 1:37, 48. This establishing of Scripture as divine special revelation is an area of study to which Warfield himself gives so much attention, and in so many attending details, that its development must be taken up in a separate chapter (chap. 4). It should be kept in mind, however, that for Warfield the doctrine of Scripture very decidedly falls properly under the domain of theology proper and of divine revelation specifically.

[17]*SSW*, 1:27; *W*, 1:6–7, 10, 47–48.
[18]*W*, 1:31–33; cf. *W*, 9:650.

least three times in his writings Warfield quotes Rudyard Kipling (1865–1936), who in one of his works has a certain character declare,

> The 'eathen in 'is blindness bows down to wood an' stone;
> 'E don't obey no orders unless they is 'is own.[19]

It is the nature of "unrevealed religion" that it lacks authority. Being man-made, any particular religious idea in question is shaped by the individual himself, in whose consciousness the religious idea has been discovered.

This is the point at issue between Christianity and all forms of mysticism and rationalism. The dignity of the Christian is that, unlike the heathen, he is not a law unto himself. He is "under orders." He lives unto the King and submits to his authority. It is the mark of Christianity that it is a revealed religion and that Christians, therefore, march to orders from without. By contrast, the mystic or rationalist, seeking the knowledge of God from within his own psyche, has confused himself with God and has therefore left himself with no authoritative touchstone of truth—in which case truth itself becomes a merely relative, individual matter. God, then, becomes many different things, and "the history of mysticism only too clearly shows that he who begins by seeking God within himself may end by confusing himself with God." Mystics of all varieties "rest on religious sentiment as the source of knowledge of divine things." Naturalistic mysticism conceives religious feelings in terms of man's natural religious consciousness as shaped by the individual. Supernaturalistic mysticism explains those feelings as the workings of God in the human heart. Theosophical mysticism "goes a step further and regards the religious feelings as the footprints of Deity moving in the soul, and as, therefore, immediate sources of knowledge of God, which is to be obtained by simple quiescence and rapt contemplation of these His movements." Pantheistic mysticism identifies the soul with God, who is known by the simple axiom, "Know thyself." Even "Christian" mysticism becomes ultimately indistinguishable from that of all other religions in its seeking the Holy Spirit, the Christ within, as its source of knowledge of divine things. Against all this, Warfield insists that external revelation must be given its right and that a refusal of external, normative authority of the written Word is to revert to natural religion, heathenism, and to discard Christianity altogether. True knowledge of God is not found in "inner lights" within ourselves but in his objective Word. Apart from the external authority of special revelation there is no authority and no message of redemptive grace. No one can do without the natural, religious sentiment. It is a gift of God

---

[19] *W*, 9:650; *SSW*, 2:729, 731; *FL*, 160.

bound up with our creation in his image. But it is not an adequate religion for sinners. There is no gospel in it, and therefore no Christianity. This, ultimately, is what sets Christianity apart: it is the revealed religion.[20]

REVELATION AND THE KNOWLEDGE OF GOD

Man's knowledge of God, then, is innate. In his own soul, man possesses an unmistakable awareness of God (*sensus deitatis*) as he sees himself as a responsible and dependent creature (*sensus religionis*). God has made himself known in the very psyche of his image bearers. This basic knowledge of God is augmented in the created order, in which God's power and glory are clearly and continually displayed. All this is God's gracious self-disclosure in general revelation. But it is in special revelation that God makes himself known redemptively and with detailed specificity and clarity.

Standing above all other modes of revelation in a class by itself is the revelation of God in Christ incarnate. "He does not so much make a revelation of God as Himself is the revelation of God." In comparison to his manifestation of God in the flesh, even the previous theophanies are but faint shadows of God. The prophets could foretell of him by the Spirit of Christ testifying in them. But in Christ, God himself speaks and makes himself known. And yet although all revelation culminates in him and is summed up in him, that revelation would remain sealed up in him "had it not been thus taken by the Spirit of truth and declared unto men." And that is to say, therefore, that the New Testament in its entirety is but the explanatory word about Christ. Here divine revelation reaches its climax—in Christ, yes, but in the revelation of him by word in the New Testament Scriptures. "And when this fact was in all its meaning made the possession of men, revelation was completed and in that sense ceased. Jesus Christ is no less the end of revelation than He is the end of the law."[21]

Still, there is more that is required if man is to know God. Warfield notes in this context that because of human sin and its noetic effects, the reception of this revelation fails, "special" and clear though it is. Sin has so "disordered" the human mind that even written revelation cannot bring someone to know God. If man were in "his normal state," unfallen, he "by the very necessity of his nature would have known God, the sphere of his being, the author of his existence, the standard of his excellences," and "he could not under this double revelation, internal and external, fail to know God as God would wish to be known." There is no shortcoming in the revelation itself; the problem is only in the corruptions

---

[20]*W*, 9:649–66; *SSW*, 2:729–34.
[21]*W*, 1:28.

of the human nature. Man in his "normal" condition may know God and rightly perceive the things of God, but "man as we know him is not normal man." Sin has darkened his mind and clouded his vision so that his knowledge of God is obscured. For man to know God aright a "repairing operation" is required. He not only needs more light—"he needs the power of sight." And this can be achieved only in the *testimonium Spiritus Sancti.* "In other words, what is needed, is a special supernatural revelation on the one hand, and a special supernatural illumination on the other." To meet this need God not only has provided external revelation but also works inwardly,

> creating within them new hearts by his regenerating grace and illuminating their minds for the apprehension of divine things. Thus he creates over against the new objective manifestations of himself in his redemptive acts, a new subject to apprehend and profit by them. To this new subject, the revelations of God in nature and providence and grace appeal with new power; and in him they beget a new knowledge of God, indefinitely higher and truer and more adequate than is possible to the natural man.

And so no one can know God but by the powerful work of God's Spirit. Yet, echoing Calvin, Warfield says, "Men do not wring the knowledge of God from a Deity reluctant to be known: God imparts the knowledge of Himself to men reluctant to know Him: and therefore none know Him save those to whom He efficaciously imparts, by His Word and Spirit, the knowledge of Himself." This, as we shall see, is a theme Warfield returns to often. Christianity is at its heart a redemptive religion, and God reveals himself in grace that we may know him.[22]

---

[22]W, 4:156; W, 5:36, 43, 47, 79, 83, 150–51; "The Christian Doctrine of Revelation," 4–5. For more on this theme in Warfield see chapters 2, 4, 9, and 10.

Christianity is often called a book-religion. It would be more exact to say that it is a religion which has a book. Its foundations are laid in apostles and prophets, . . . but Christ Jesus alone is its chief corner-stone. He is its only basis; he, its only head; and he alone has authority in his Church. But he has chosen to found his Church not directly by his own hands, speaking the word of God, say for instance, in thunder-tones from heaven; but through the instrumentality of a body of apostles, chosen and trained by himself, endowed with gifts and graces from the Holy Ghost, and sent forth into the world as his authoritative agents for proclaiming a gospel which he placed within their lips and which is none the less his authoritative word, that it is through them that he speaks it. It is because the apostles were Christ's representatives, that what they did and said and wrote as such, comes to us with divine authority. The authority of the Scriptures thus rests on the simple fact that God's authoritative agents in founding the Church gave them as authoritative to the Church which they founded. All the authority of the apostles stands behind the Scriptures, and all the authority of Christ behind the apostles. The Scriptures are simply the law-code which the law-givers of the Church gave it.

SSW, 2:537.

4

BIBLIOLOGY

Context

HISTORICAL AND ECCLESIASTICAL MILIEU

It is not overstating the case at all to say that the doctrine and character of Scripture[1] were *the* issue of Warfield's day. This was Warfield's own assessment, and it was the assessment of his archrival, Charles Briggs.[2] Warfield complained pointedly and repeatedly of the confusion that abounded in the ecclesiastical world in this regard. Arguments from "the Babel of voices" of "unbelieving and half-believing speculation" proceeded in every conceivable direction, and, he surmised, from every five "advanced thinkers" on the subject at least six theories of inspiration would emerge. The only point of agreement among them was that "inspiration is less pervasive and less determinative than has heretofore been thought, or than is still thought in less enlightened circles," and that in the Bible there is less truth and more error than previously believed by the church. "A radical change in our

---

[1] The most significant works in which Warfield treats bibliology include the following: "The Biblical Idea of Revelation," in *W*, 1:3–34; "The Idea of Revelation and Theories of Revelation," in *W*, 1:37–48; "The Inspiration of the Bible," in *W*, 1:51–74; "The Biblical Idea of Inspiration," in *W*, 1:77–112; "'Scripture,' 'The Scriptures,' in the New Testament," in *W*, 1:115–65; "The Real Problem of Inspiration," in *W*, 1:169–226; "'God-Inspired Scripture,'" in *W*, 1:229–80; "'It Says:' 'Scripture Says:' 'God Says:'" in *W*, 1:283–332; "'The Oracles of God,'" in *W*, 1:335–91; "Inspiration and Criticism," in *W*, 1:395–425; "The Divine Origin of the Bible," in *W*, 1:429–47; "Augustine's Doctrine of Knowledge and Authority," in *W*, 4:135–225; "Calvin's Doctrine of the Knowledge of God," in *W*, 5:29–130; "The Westminster Doctrine of Holy Scripture," in *W*, 6:155–257; "The Doctrine of Inspiration of the Westminster Divines," in *W*, 6:261–333; review of *Bible Problems and the New Material for Their Solution*, by T. K. Cheyne, in *W*, 10:112–18; review of *The Bible, Its Origin and Nature*, by Marcus Dods, in *W*, 10:118–27; review of *Revelation and Inspiration*, by Reinhold Seeberg, in *W*, 10:231–42; "The Bible the Book of Mankind," in *SSW*, 1:3–22; "Christianity and Revelation," in *SSW*, 1:23–30; "Inspiration," in *SSW*, 1:31–33; "God's Providence Over All," in *SSW*, 1:110–15; "Calvin and the Bible," in *SSW*, 1:397–400; "The Authority and Inspiration of the Scriptures," in *SSW*, 2:537–41; "The Divine and Human in the Bible," in *SSW*, 2:542–48; "The New Testament Use of the Septuagint, and Inspiration," in *SSW*, 2:549–59; "The Westminster Doctrine of Holy Scripture," in *SSW*, 2:560–71; "The Westminster Doctrine of Inspiration," in *SSW*, 2:572–79; "The Inerrancy of the Original Autographs," in *SSW*, 2:580–94; "The Westminster Confession and the Original Autographs," in *SSW*, 2:588–94; "The Rights of Criticism and of the Church," in *SSW*, 2:595–603; "Review of Three Books on Inspiration," in *SSW*, 2:604–13; "Inspiration," in *SSW*, 2:614–36; "Under Orders," in *SSW*, 2:729–34.

[2] A. A. Hodge and B. B. Warfield, *Inspiration*, ed. Roger Nicole (Grand Rapids: Baker, 1979), 38–39; Charles Briggs, "Critical Theories of the Sacred Scriptures in Relation to Their Inspiration," *PR* 2, no. 7 (1881): 550.

conception of the Scriptures as the inspired Word of God is thus pressed upon us as now necessary by a considerable number of writers, representing quite a variety of schools of Christian thought."[3]

The "present crisis in regard to the inspiration and authority of the Scriptures," Warfield says, "is largely an imported one." He refers, of course, to the German rationalism, the "evil leaven" of which was so influential in shaping the nineteenth-century American modernism.[4] Throughout the latter half of the nineteenth century and into the twentieth, a steady stream of American students (Warfield among them!) studied in German universities, where theological innovations of men such as Friedrich Schleiermacher, Ferdinand Christian Baur (1792–1860), Albrecht Ritschl, Wilhelm Hermann (1846–1922), and Adolf von Harnack, as well as the historical-critical theories of men such as Julius Wellhausen (1844–1918), were virtually unrivaled. Added to these were the pressures brought against Christianity from the realm of science and, since Charles Darwin's *On the Origin of Species*, the question of the reliability of Genesis. This European "liberalism" was brought back to America, where, by the beginning of the twentieth century, it had become a major theological force.[5] The higher-critical theories, rationalism and its corresponding rejection of external authority, the determined attempt in favor of "modern scientific knowledge" to expunge the supernatural from Christianity in virtually all of its forms, and the various theological innovations of the day had convinced many that the traditional Christian understanding of the nature and character of Scripture had been hopelessly destroyed. If the evangelical faith would be saved, it would be only by concession to the "findings" of the new criticism. Errors and discrepancies in the biblical text were alleged to have been demonstrated, and the time had come for the doctrine of plenary verbal inspiration to "get out of the way."[6]

The debate over biblical inspiration loomed large in Warfield's own Presbyterian Church as the two sides on this issue clashed and vied for dominance. In 1880 the opposing forces, best represented by Union Theological Seminary and Princeton Theological Seminary, joined in the creation of the *Presbyterian Review*, edited jointly by Charles Briggs and A. A. Hodge. Although the relationship was cordial, discussions of matters related to inspiration and the new criticism were unavoidable. With growing interest in biblical criticism, spurred by the heresy trials of William Robertson Smith of the Free Church of Scotland, Briggs and Hodge

[3]*W*, 1:51–52, 170.
[4]*PRR* 4, no. 15 (1893): 488.
[5]See Gary Dorrien, *The Making of American Liberal Theology*, 403–5. Also Mark Noll, *Between Faith and Criticism: Evangelicals, Scholarship, and the Bible in America* (Grand Rapids: Baker, 1986), 12–15.
[6]*W*, 1:169–72; *PRR* 4, no. 15 (1893): 491.

published a series of eight articles, four from each viewpoint.[7] The first of these was the landmark "Inspiration" by Warfield and A. A. Hodge.[8] Whatever else was accomplished by these articles, they at least defined the issues in the conflict. In 1890, Union Seminary moved Charles Briggs to the newly created chair of biblical theology, and his inaugural address on January 20, 1891, marks a watershed moment in the history of the American Presbyterian church. The lengthy address (one and three-quarter hours) constituted an attack on the traditional view of inspiration, and its contemptuous and offensive tone proved embarrassing even to Briggs's supporters.[9] The outcome was predictable: from one side some rose to his defense, but from the other came calls for his removal. Warfield complained that the defense mounted by Henry Preserved Smith (1847–1927)[10] and Llewellyn J. Evans (1833–?), both professors at Lane Theological Seminary, took more the form of an attack on the doctrine of inspiration. They were much less concerned to argue that the Bible was the only infallible rule for faith and practice than they were to argue that it was not an infallible rule in anything else.[11] The furor was brought to a formal end in late 1892, when, after the case was heard, Briggs was suspended from ministry. A similar and related case was also successfully brought against Henry Preserved Smith. Official pronouncement was given, but the issue itself was by no means settled and was not about to go away.

It was in this context that Warfield sought energetically to expound and preserve the church's historic high view of inspiration. In the face of the relentless encroachment of critical thought, Warfield remained unmoved, indeed, unthreatened, undaunted, and unembarrassed. He understood the vital significance of the debate, and he was eager to meet the challenge on all fronts. Warfield read and digested virtually all of the literature liberalism had produced, and throughout the years of his career he reviewed and critiqued a seemingly endless list of such scholars who had "explained away" the doctrine of verbal inspiration or denied it altogether. Besides Briggs and Smith, Thomas Kelly Cheyne (1841–1915),[12] Washington Gladden (1836–1918),[13] William Sanday (1843–1920),[14] Marcus Dods (1834–1909),[15] and

---

[7]See Noll, *Between Faith and Criticism*, 15–16. Also Lefferts A. Loetscher, *The Broadening Church* (Philadelphia: University of Pennsylvania Press, 1954), 29–39.
[8]*PR* 2, no. 6 (1881): 225–60. This article was later republished along with related Warfield correspondence and various studies by Roger Nicole in Hodge and Warfield, *Inspiration*.
[9]See Loetscher, *The Broadening Church*, 48–62.
[10]Smith was an American Old Testament scholar at Lane Theological Seminary and later Andover Theological Seminary.
[11]"Professor Henry Preserved Smith on Inspiration," *PRR* 5, no. 20 (1894): 600, 650.
[12]Cheyne was an early and influential Old Testament critic at Oxford.
[13]Gladden was an influential Congregationalist pastor in Columbus, Ohio.
[14]Sanday was a British theologian and New Testament scholar; one of the first to introduce the Continental critical scholarship to the English and the Anglican world.
[15]Dods was a professor of New Testament, New College, Edinburgh.

Reinhold Seeberg (1859–1935)[16] are a few whose views of inspiration drew Warfield's sharp criticism. With complete confidence he brushed off the "vast majority" of alleged contradictions in Scripture as unfounded and "irrelevant" objections, and scoffed at those who characterize the doctrine of verbal inspiration as in distress, suffering beneath the findings of critical investigation and forced now to adapt itself to the lesser status to which it has been relegated. To the contrary, he demanded that attacks against and denials of the trustworthiness of Scripture do not, *ipso facto*, render Scripture any less reliable. "It is clear enough, then, that a problem has been raised with reference to inspiration by this type of criticism. But this is not equivalent to saying that the established doctrine of inspiration has been put in jeopardy."[17]

This was Warfield's posture throughout his career, and his intense interest in this issue marked his life. In 1880 he chose for his inaugural lecture at Western Seminary the topic "Inspiration and Criticism," in which he labors to demonstrate that the attacks against Scripture have yet to prove anything against it. His second article on this subject was his famous "Inspiration," coauthored with A. A. Hodge in 1881, when Warfield was still at the threshold of his celebrated career. These were but the first two of nearly one hundred articles and book reviews on the subjects of inspiration and canon that Warfield eventually produced. These articles range from the more brief and popular to the detailed and polemic, and from the intensely exegetical and even lexical to the more broadly systematic and/ or historical. In all, he published perhaps 1,500 pages on this subject.[18] Clearly, for Warfield, this was a subject of pivotal significance.

COMPETING THEORIES OF INSPIRATION

In his 1909 article for *Universal Cyclopaedia*, Warfield provides a summary of the views of inspiration competing for prominence. The variations are many, but he classifies them under three broad categories. First, there are the theories that refer inspiration to religion generally but not to Scripture specifically. In this view the biblical religion is of divine origin, but the Bible is not, except secondarily. This position may be expressed in terms of that divine influence that is generally common to all men; in this natural or intuitional or even providential theory, the Bible is the product of human genius. Or, scarcely better, this position may be expressed in terms of that divine influence that is generally common to all Christians: Scripture is the product of Christian men of peculiar spiritual attainments. Or a still

---

[16]Seeberg was a German Lutheran theologian, University of Berlin.
[17]*W*, 1:169, 171.
[18]See Roger R. Nicole, "Warfield on Scripture: A Chronological Bibliography," appendix 3 in Hodge and Warfield, *Inspiration*, 83–90. See also xi n9.

higher form of this position maintains a recognition of the prophetic office and function but makes a distinction between what was revealed and the record of what was revealed. Divine revelation was given to the biblical writers, according to this understanding, but it was then left to them to provide a written record of it, a record not itself produced by special divine influence or oversight.[19]

Next, there are theories that understand God as involved directly in the production of Scripture but deny that he is author of the entire book. In this general view, inspiration is restricted to certain portions or elements of Scripture only. Not all of Scripture is of direct revelation. This theory is often presented as "partial inspiration." Some on this understanding hold that the Bible is inspired throughout but only in certain of its elements—its mysteries, matters of faith and practice, its ideas or thoughts or concepts. Others hold to "graded" inspiration, understanding—as the name implies—that some portions of Scripture are more inspired than others. This last position confuses inspiration with other processes by which a divine element has entered the Bible—all divine influences are alike, whether generally providential or specifically supernatural, revelation generally or inspiration specifically. As a result it sees some elements as "more" inspired, but in broad terms this position differs very little from the traditional understanding (see next), which sees all the Bible as equally inspired.[20]

Finally, there are theories that maintain that God so superintended the process of the production of Scripture and so influenced the biblical writers that his Word was infallibly given through them. All parts of the Bible are "the Word of God written and as such are infallibly true and divinely authoritative in all their declarations." This view is called "plenary" inspiration to distinguish it from the view above that holds that only parts or elements of Scripture are inspired, and it is known as "verbal" inspiration to distinguish it from the view above that holds that only the thoughts or ideas or concepts of Scripture are inspired, but not its words. The very words of Scripture—all of them—are of divine origin.

This view is the traditional understanding of the church and has been held in two variations. First, the theory of dictation holds that God the Spirit employed the biblical writers as mere pens, more or less passive instruments in his hands. Their contribution to Scripture, in this understanding, is not recognized, and Scripture is seen as simply the work of God alone. The more common and historic understanding is captured in the word *concursus* ("running together") and understands that Scripture is the product of both human and divine activities.

---

[19] *SSW*, 2:622–25.
[20] *SSW*, 2:625–27; cf. *W*, 1:58–59.

cifically, it holds that God so superintended the biblical writers that through their words he gave his own Word. This is both the church doctrine, traditionally, and the teaching of the Bible itself.[21]

Warfield's Doctrine of Scripture in Summary

PRESUPPOSITION

For Warfield, the controlling factor in shaping the doctrine of Scripture is that it is God's self-revelation. This is its first and most fundamental characteristic. The Bible's inspiration rests on its underlying claim that it is God's self-disclosure. Bibliology, therefore, falls properly under the domain of theology proper, or more specifically, divine revelation.[22] Scripture is not merely a record of divine revelation, nor is it a mere vehicle for conveying that revelation; it is a mode of divine revelation and is itself the very climax of that revelation. This notion pervades and controls Warfield's entire discussion of the doctrine: Scripture is before all else the spoken word of God.

For Warfield this spells the fundamental difference between Christianity and all other religions: Christianity is a religion that is grounded not in human thought or speculation but in divine revelation. If Scripture is God's word, then it is the arbiter of truth, infallibly and supremely authoritative in all matters of faith and its related practice.

SPECIFIC FORMULATION

Definitions

The underlying implication of the word *inspire* is that of "an influence from without, producing in its object movements and effects beyond its native, or at least its ordinary powers." In theological nomenclature the word has taken on specific reference to the biblical writers and their books as products of the Holy Spirit's activity. The biblical writers are said to be inspired in the sense that God the Holy Spirit breathed into them, as it were, and so exerted influence over them that "the product of their activities transcends human powers and becomes Divinely authoritative." And so Warfield frequently defines inspiration as "a supernatural

---

[21]*SSW*, 2:15, 627–29.

[22]Warfield clearly treats bibliology as a subset of divine revelation, but he also argues that the traditional ordering of bibliology and then theology proper is justified, given that Scripture is our source of knowledge of God (*SSW*, 2:302–7).

influence exerted on the sacred writers by the Spirit of God, by virtue of which their writings are given Divine trustworthiness."[23]

In his definition of inspiration Warfield carefully emphasizes that the influence on the writers of Scripture is a distinctly supernatural one and not the "inspiration" experienced by a poet or man of genius. Moreover, it is more than the "ordinary" actions of the Spirit in the sanctification and guidance of believers. The doctrine of inspiration entails "the entire divine agency operative in producing the Scriptures," from the preparation of the men themselves, to the actual point of their writing. In other words, he insists that Scripture is in its every detail both human and divine. Every word is thoroughly human and yet thoroughly divine. In inspiration God so prepared and guided the biblical writers that his word was given through theirs. As he summarizes briefly, "We rest in the joyful and unshaken certainty that we possess a Bible written by the hands of men indeed, but also graven with the finger of God."[24]

Authority, Inerrancy

To say that Scripture is God's word—"God's word written," as Warfield often describes it—is by the nature of the case to acknowledge its divine authority. Not by the acknowledgment of church councils but by virtue of its very nature, Scripture is supremely authoritative. Moreover, this understanding of inspiration necessarily entails, therefore, the notion of inerrancy also. The inerrancy of Scripture is bound up with its authority. Inerrancy cannot be viewed as an additional consideration but is a necessary corollary and belongs to "the core" of the doctrine of inspiration. If Scripture in its every detail is the word of God, who cannot err, then by the nature of the case it is and must be entirely trustworthy and reliable in every respect. Warfield complains that the controversy in the Presbyterian Church is misrepresented by those who allege that "the sole bone of contention" is the bare question of inerrancy. Such a characterization misses the root issue. The issue goes much deeper to the trustworthiness of Scripture and therefore its authority and inspiration, and the reliability of the claims it makes concerning itself. "A proved error in Scripture contradicts not only our doctrine, but the Scripture claims, and therefore its inspiration in making those claims." The entire notion of inspiration rests on the factual truthfulness of all of the claims of Scripture. The two issues—inspiration and inerrancy—are so inextricably bound together that the one cannot be true without the other. These

[23]W, 1:77–78, 396–97; cf. SSW, 2:615.
[24]W, 1:77–78, 100–105, 396–98; W, 10:123; SSW, 1:111–13; SSW, 2:543–44, 606, 608, 615, 627, 629, 631; Hodge and Warfield, Inspiration, 71.

are not separate notions. Inerrancy is a vital issue precisely because it is a necessary entailment of inspiration as biblically defined, and for this reason Warfield
insists that "there is no standing ground between the two theories of full verbal
inspiration and no inspiration at all."[25]

Autographs Only

It should be noted that Warfield's doctrine of inspiration necessarily concerns the
autographs specifically, and the copied texts only by implication and only insofar
as they are accurately copied. As did the Westminster Confession of Faith, Warfield argues that while translations of Scripture may faithfully convey the Word
of God, and while the text of Scripture has in God's providence been substantially
preserved in its purity, it is the original text alone that was immediately inspired
of God. The human biblical authors and their writings are the focus of concern
in this discussion.[26]

Sufficiency

Finally, although Warfield seldom addresses the question formally and nowhere
argues it at length, he does at times register his hearty confidence in the Scripture's sufficiency, its "absolute objective completeness" for its given purpose.
In agreement with the Westminster Confession, he denies the need for either
new revelation or tradition. What is taught in Scripture, and nothing else, is
binding on the church—that is, only what was "imposed" by the apostles. "The
Bible, and the Bible only, is the religion of Protestants." This "formal principle of
Protestantism"—*sola scriptura*—was not the specific point of debate in Warfield's
context, but it was clearly his shared conviction and point of reference. "This is
the corner-stone of universal Protestantism; and on it Protestantism stands, or
else it falls." Warfield does not deny but in fact often affirms that there has been
a progressive development of doctrine in the history of the church. It should not
be expected that the first generation of Christians had already sounded all the
depths of divine revelation; nor do we make our appeal for authority to the early
church. Rather, the church has always recognized its obligation continuously to
explore and discover truth revealed in the written Word. But all the while it recognizes also the difference between the Spirit's illumination of our minds to what
is written and new revelations by which some suppose to add to the substance
of what has been once for all delivered to the saints. "'The word of God written'
stands through all ages as a changeless witness against human additions to, and

---

[25]*W*, 1:173, 396–97, 423; *SSW*, 2:581; Hodge and Warfield, *Inspiration*, 41.
[26]*SSW*, 2:580–81.

corruptions of, God's truth." Or, as he says in a more personal vein: "We cannot do without the Scriptures; having them we need no other guide. We need this light to light our pathway; having it we may well dispense with any other."[27]

Inspiration a Church Doctrine

It is important to Warfield that this view of inspiration is the understanding the church has maintained from the beginning, and he condemns other views as serious departures, not from the understanding of a given individual here or there or even of past believers, but from the settled faith of the entire church universal, past and present. Since its inception the church has regarded the Bible as an oracular book, as a book divinely given, indeed, "as the Word of God in such a sense that whatever it says God says." This view of Scripture did not grow and develop over the years in the church: the church was born with this settled instinct. Christians since the beginning have held the Bible to be not a book in which we can find the word of God here and there but a book that is itself the very word of God. Accordingly, Christians have universally approached the Scriptures with singular reverence, unquestioningly receiving all its statements of fact, humbly submitting to all its demands, trembling before its threats, and resting in its promises with entire trust in its every word.[28]

SURVEY OF THE HISTORIC WITNESS

Warfield is eager to demonstrate that the whole body of Christian literature gives testimony that, since its beginning and through all the ages of the church, this high view of the divinity of Scripture has indeed been its universal and continuous conviction. Clemens Romanus (c. 90–100) refers to Scripture as "the true utterances of the Holy Ghost." Clement of Alexandria (c. 150–211) affirms that the Christian faith is "received from God through the scriptures." Origen (c. 185–254) holds that the coauthorship of the Holy Spirit precludes any mistake on the part of the biblical writers. Irenaeus (d. c. 200) describes Scripture in terms of its "perfection" as God's spoken words. Polycarp (69–155), the disciple of the apostle John, describes Scripture as the voice of the Most High and condemns as the firstborn of Satan all who would pervert its words. All the church fathers continue unanimously in the same vein. Tertullian (c. 160–225) refers to the Scriptures as "the writings and the words of God." Augustine teaches that since Scripture is God's word, the human

---

[27]*SSW*, 2:567–68, 570–71; *W*, 9:600–606.
[28]*W*, 1:52–53; *SSW*, 2:617–18.

authors could not and did not err at any point. The earliest Christians and the early and later church fathers knew no other doctrine. Similarly the Reformers insist that Scripture, because divine, cannot err and that all that Scripture teaches must be humbly received by the church with the same reverence given to God. Samuel Rutherford (1600–1661) characterizes the Bible as surer than a direct oracle from heaven. Richard Baxter (1615–1691) affirms the complete truthfulness, without error, of all the words of Scripture. All of the great worthies of the church—Martin Luther (1483–1546), John Calvin (1509–1564), John Knox (1510–1572), George White-field (1714–1770), John Wesley (1703–1791), Thomas Chalmers (1780–1847)—and all of the church's formal creeds, Catholic and Protestant alike, Lutheran and Reformed, unite in a common assumption of the Bible's divine authority and complete trustworthiness and, therefore, carefully ground their teachings on it. Down to his own century in the writings of New School Presbyterian theologian Henry B. Smith and Warfield's revered mentor, Charles Hodge, Warfield traces this unbroken understanding of the church regarding Scripture. Creeds of every branch of the church, theologians, commentators, preachers, and representatives of every kind share this doctrine in common. "In every way possible, the church has borne her testimony from the beginning, and still in our day, to her faith in the divine trustworthiness of her Scriptures, in all their affirmations of whatever kind." In his famous Bampton Lectures on inspiration—"in which, unfortunately, he does not teach the church-doctrine"—William Sanday acknowledges that a high doctrine of verbal inspiration was held by the church "almost from the very first." Warfield comments, "He might have spared the adverb 'almost.' The earliest writers know no other doctrine." Warfield also cites Herman Schultz (1836–1903), and other critical scholars who, themselves having departed from this tradition, yet acknowledge that the earliest Christians knew no other doctrine. Indeed, in the very words of the critics seeking a "modern" and "more enlightened" view, Warfield finds tacit confession of the novelty of any competing theory.[29]

Warfield acknowledges just two exceptional cases to this in the history of the church. The first was rationalism, whose characteristic feature was to distinguish between the inspired and uninspired elements of Scripture. This position, in varying forms, was adopted by the humanists, the Socinians, the syncretists in Germany, the Remonstrants, the Jesuits in Roman Catholicism, some defend-ers of Christian supernaturalism in the Enlightenment era, and finally, in the nineteenth century, some who affirmed either that only the mysteries of the faith (things undiscoverable by unaided reason) are inspired, or that only mat-ters of faith and practice are inspired, or that only the thoughts or concepts of

---

[29]W, 1:51–68, 175–76, 406–7; W, 4:178–81; Hodge and Warfield, *Inspiration*, 41; SSW, 2:617–19, 634.

the Bible are inspired. Warfield finds it significant that while these views often made their way into print and have affected the faith of many, they nonetheless have never made their way to creedal recognition or to the hearts of the people of the church at large.[30]

The second movement of thought that tended to a lower conception of the inspiration and authority of Scripture was that of mysticism, the essentially naturalistic understanding that subjects all external revelation to the judgment of inner light and subjective reason and defines inspiration accordingly. This view also, in its varying forms, reaching its high point in the genius of Schleiermacher,[31] influential as it has been in many ways, has likewise failed to make its way into the creeds of the church or the hearts of its people. The "instinctive" position of the church has remained.[32]

More to date, for Warfield the ministerial ordination vows required in his own Presbyterian Church did not allow anything less than a full acknowledgment of plenary verbal inspiration and inerrancy. Llewellyn J. Evans had argued that the clause the ordinands must affirm, that they believe the Scriptures "to be the Word of God, the only infallible rule of faith and practice," means only that the Bible is infallible in the two realms of faith and its related practice, and that it allows for factual errors in matters such as history and science. This Warfield would not allow. The double-phrase formula—"word of God, the only infallible rule"—declares the Scriptures "*to be* the Word of God, not merely to contain somewhere in them the Word of God"; the confession is that the Bible *is* the word of God. Moreover, what is affirmed is not that Scripture is only the rule for matters of faith and practice; what is affirmed is that, being the word of God, Scripture is *the only* infallible rule of faith and practice. The second phrase grows out of the first: because Scripture is itself the word of God, it is therefore the only infallible guide.[33]

SUMMARY OF THE CHURCH'S TESTIMONY

Hendrik van den Belt observes, probably rightly, that Warfield emphasized the church's testimony to the Scriptures in order to rescue the question from the prevailing mystical subjectivism fostered by Schleiermacher. Calvin, on the other hand, emphasized the *testimonium* in order to rescue believers from dependence on the uncertain and unstable authority of the church. But in the end, both shared

---

[30]*W*, 1:58–59.
[31]Friedrich D. E. Schleiermacher was a German philosopher and theologian who sought to ground religious experience in human emotion, especially the feeling of dependence, rather than on reason.
[32]*W*, 1:59–60, 67.
[33]"Professor Henry Preserved Smith on Inspiration," *PRR* 5, no. 20 (1894): 602 (emphasis original).

the same goal, and neither would deny what the other affirmed.[34] In any case, Warfield does not rest the doctrine of inspiration on the authoritative pronouncements of the church. He specifically denies the church any such authority. But it is important to him that this doctrine is, in fact, common to all the church. Most to the point, he is eager to stress that this doctrine belonged to the church from its inception. It was given to her from Christ and his apostles. It is in this light that Warfield speaks of inspiration as a "church doctrine" and of the testimony of the church as a "proof" of that doctrine: it is a doctrine the church was given at her birth and so a doctrine she has never been without.[35]

HISTORICAL ACCURACY OR RECONSTRUCTION?

Charles Briggs was Warfield's most bitter and outspoken opponent concerning verbal inspiration. In successive works, especially his 1889 *Whither?* he vehemently insisted that Warfield's (and Princeton's) "idolatrous" view of inspiration was not the church's official or historic position but a mistaken novelty and unprecedented innovation.[36] Warfield, however, finds Briggs's contention impossible, and in "The Doctrine of Inspiration of the Westminster Divines" and "The Westminster Doctrine of Inspiration," he exposes it in detail. Warfield demonstrates at great length, citing passages that "might be multiplied without other limit than that imposed by the amount written by the Westminster men on the subject," that these divines consistently and self-consciously contended for the doctrine of verbal inspiration. He insists that "it would be difficult to believe that there was a single member of the Westminster Assembly who did not attach the sense of verbal inerrant inspiration" to their doctrine of Scripture. And he expresses surprise at Briggs's attempt to "explain away" the "obvious" teaching of verbal or plenary inerrancy in the Westminster Confession. He further contends that in his many quotations from the Westminster divines, Briggs falls into the "fallacy of quotations"—"alleging passages from well-known authors as proving some disputed point, when they do not prove it at all, but something resembling it as far as words go, though quite different from it in reality." Warfield contends still further that Briggs's use of these quotations is colored by his own bias, which leaves him twisting the intended meaning of the Westminster divines exactly backwards. Most significantly, Warfield proves Briggs duplicitous in his misrepresentation of John Lightfoot, demonstrating that he (Briggs) gives evidence in other of his

---

[34]Henk van den Belt, *The Authority of Scripture in Reformed Theology: Truth and Trust*, Studies in Reformed Theology 17 (Leiden: Brill, 2008), 218–19.

[35]*W*, 1:52–68; *W*, 5:72–74; *W*, 9:641; *W*, 10:233; *SSW*, 2:538, 612–13.

[36]Charles A. Briggs, *Whither?* (New York: Charles Scribner's Sons, 1889), 64–73; Briggs, "Critical Theories of the Sacred Scriptures," 554.

published works that he himself knew that Lightfoot held to the inspiration of even the Hebrew vowel points and accents. Warfield then writes with a touch of sarcasm as he examines extensively the published views of Lightfoot concerning inspiration in order to find "which of Dr. Briggs's Lightfoots is the true one." Warfield concludes that it is a "desperate cause" that seeks to wrench any other view than verbal inspiration from the Westminster divines.[37]

Besides briefer historical surveys of the traditional view found here and there in his treatment of figures such as the Fathers, the scholastics, Richard Baxter, Martin Luther, and Samuel Rutherford, as outlined above, Warfield wrote lengthy essays demonstrating the same not only from the Westminster Confession and divines[38] but also from Augustine[39] and Calvin.[40] On Briggs's charge that his view was a novelty, Warfield would not yield.

In more recent years a few scholars have attempted to pick up Briggs's cause, most notably Ernest Sandeen, followed by Jack Rogers and Donald McKim. In *The Roots of Fundamentalism* Sandeen, like Briggs, argues vigorously that the Old Princeton doctrine of verbal inspiration—especially Warfield's—was historically naive and far beyond the view taught in the Westminster Confession.[41] Similarly, in *The Authority and Interpretation of the Bible: An Historical Approach*,[42] Rogers and McKim, relying somewhat on Sandeen, and on Rogers's earlier doctoral thesis, "Scripture in the Westminster Confession: A Problem of Historical Interpretation for American Presbyterianism";[43] and, reflective of Rogers's essay "Van Til and Warfield on Scripture in the Westminster Confession,"[44] they launch a similar assault on Warfield and the Princetonian doctrine of Scripture. Although somewhat more tempered in tone than Sandeen's polemic, the charge remains that Warfield misrepresented history in defense of his innovative and unprecedented doctrine. According to Sandeen, Rogers, and McKim, the doctrine of inerrancy is the result of rationalistic scholasticism, Warfield's historical arguments were skewed by his apologetic motive, and his case was built on unsubstantiated assumptions, historical inaccuracies, and dogmatic precommitments. However, in his *Biblical Authority: A Critique of the Rogers/McKim Proposal*, John Woodbridge takes Rogers

---

[37]*W*, 6:279, 333; *SSW*, 2:572–79.

[38]*W*, 6:155–257, 261–333; *SSW*, 2:560–71, 572–79, 588–94.

[39]*W*, 6:178–225.

[40]*W*, 5:29–130.

[41]Ernest R. Sandeen, *The Roots of Fundamentalism: British and American Millenarianism, 1800–1930* (1970; repr., Grand Rapids: Baker, 1978), 119–21.

[42]Jack B. Rogers and Donald K. McKim, *The Authority and Interpretation of the Bible: An Historical Approach* (Eugene, OR: Wipf and Stock, 1999), chapter 6.

[43]ThD diss., Free University of Amsterdam, 1966.

[44]In *Jerusalem and Athens: Critical Discussions on the Philosophy and Apologetics of Cornelius Van Til*, ed. E. R. Geehan (Nutley, NJ: Presbyterian and Reformed, 1971), 154–65. See also Rogers, "The Church Doctrine of Biblical Authority," in *Biblical Authority*, ed. Jack Rogers (Waco, TX: Word; 1977), 17–46.

and McKim to task for their own historical reconstructions and selective use of the sources. Woodbridge surveys the whole of church history and so thoroughly vindicates Warfield's representation of history that it is difficult to imagine this question ever being raised again.[45]

Inspiration a Biblical Doctrine

Warfield argues that there is only one way to account for this immediately adopted, continuously held, and universally common conviction regarding Scripture on the part of the church: "This church-doctrine of inspiration was the Bible doctrine before it was the church-doctrine," and it is "the church-doctrine only because it is the Bible doctrine." Although in many of Warfield's published works he labors to show the biblical grounding of the doctrine of inspiration, in "The Inspiration of the Bible" he argues instead that it is scarcely necessary to offer such detailed biblical evidence. This is for three very obvious reasons. First, we who have read the Bible understand instinctively that it teaches its own inspiration and divine origin. It would be nearly insulting to us to have to demonstrate it, for any reading of the New Testament leaves this firm impression with every reader. That is to say, to read the New Testament is to know already of its divine claims. Second, the critics themselves acknowledge that the biblical writers claim inspiration. This is the common ground between believing and unbelieving students of Scripture: we all know, by any level of acquaintance with the Bible, that it claims to be an inspired book. It is simply unnecessary to prove what is so frankly confessed by all sides. And third, it is evident to all readers of the Bible, even the critics, that this high view of inspiration was the understanding and teaching of the Lord Jesus Christ himself. Moreover, every attempt to modify this biblical teaching must for its justification make appeal to the Scripture for its authority, explaining away what it has seemed clearly to teach—in which case is implicitly conceded the very doctrine being explicitly denied. Indeed, even to disallow, as circular reasoning, the appeal to the Bible for testimony of its inspiration is to acknowledge that the Bible does, in fact, teach inspiration. On any reading it is unmistakably

---

[45]John D. Woodbridge, *Biblical Authority: A Critique of the Rogers/McKim Proposal* (Grand Rapids: Zondervan, 1982). See also Woodbridge and Randall H. Balmer, "The Princetonians and Biblical Authority: An Assessment of the Ernest Sandeen Proposal," in *Scripture and Truth*, ed. D. A. Carson and John D. Woodbridge (1983; repr., Grand Rapids: Baker, 1998), 251–79. See also John Gerstner, "Warfield's Case for Biblical Inerrancy," in *God's Inerrant Word*, ed. John Warwick Montgomery (Minneapolis, MN: Bethany House, 1974), 115–42. Also Randall H. Balmer, "The Old Princeton Doctrine of Inspiration in the Context of Nineteenth-Century Theology: A Reappraisal" (MA thesis, Trinity Evangelical Divinity School, 1981). Also Raymond Cannata, "Old Princeton Doctrine of Scripture," in William A. Dembski and Jay Wesley Richards, eds., *Unapologetic Apologetics* (Downers Grove, IL: InterVarsity, 2001), 120–27.

obvious that the Bible teaches its own inspiration. As Warfield concludes, "The issue is not, What does the Bible teach? but, Is what the Bible teaches true? And it is amazing that any or all of such expedients can blind the eyes of any one to the stringency of this issue."[46]

For Warfield, therefore, the Bible's own claim of divine inspiration is a given, immediately recognized by all who read it. But of course Warfield will not leave the matter here. Still he labors in extensive detail to demonstrate the obvious— that the biblical writers everywhere claim inspiration and the divine origin of their message.

A BRIEF OVERVIEW OF THE BIBLICAL TESTIMONY

In this vein a favorite approach for Warfield is simply to point out the language the biblical writers use in regard to their own writings. It would be a complete misconception to think that the doctrine of the plenary inspiration of the Scriptures is taught only in a passage here or there. Some passages are indeed exceptionally clear on the matter, such as Jesus' declaration that the Scriptures cannot be broken (John 10:35), Paul's affirmation that every Scripture is inspired of God (2 Tim. 3:16), and Peter's assertion that the biblical writers were moved along by the Holy Spirit (2 Pet. 1:21). These passages, while of such clarity to be sufficient of themselves to establish the doctrine of inspiration in its entirety, are by no means unique but merely give culminating expression to a pervasive biblical testimony to the divine origin and character of the Bible. In particular, Warfield customarily highlights the lofty titles given to God's Word—"scripture," "the scriptures," "the oracles of God"—and the significant formulae employed in quoting Scripture—"It is written," "It is spoken," "It says," "God says," and other such phrases that demonstrate the biblical writers' understanding that "scripture says" is equivalent to "God says." The biblical authors use this terminology in a way that makes evident their awareness that even the narrative portions of Scripture are divine utterances. Add to this the many passages that attribute divine qualities and acts to Scripture, as in the expression, "the scriptures foresaw." Further, Warfield would have us consider the often-repeated reference to the Holy Spirit as the author of Scripture in all its various parts, and this while the human authors are viewed merely as his media of expression. To this Warfield reminds us of the position of unrivaled authority that Scripture retains among the biblical writers and throughout the believing community, and the corresponding attitude of reverence and trust

---

[46]W, 1:60–64; cf. SSW, 2:618–19.

given it. "It would seem to require a dogmatic prejudice of the very first order to blind one to a fact so obvious as that with Paul 'Scripture,' as such, is conceived everywhere as the authoritative declaration of the truth and will of God." This line of evidence is seemingly without end, so that, Warfield concludes, to explain away inspiration will require much more than explaining away select passages such as 2 Timothy 3:16 or the like: it would require explaining away the whole New Testament. This doctrine pervades the whole of Scripture and is its constant testimony to itself.[47]

ANALYSIS OF THE PRIMARY PASSAGES

The Old Testament Prophets

In Deuteronomy 18:15–20, God promises that Moses will not be his last spokesman, but after him God will send another in whose mouth God will put his own word (v. 18). In this promise God secures for Israel a succession of prophets who will come to them and speak on his behalf. This, in turn, is precisely what the prophets themselves unanimously and consistently asserted, that the message they proclaimed was from God himself. "The LORD said to me, 'Behold, I have put my words in your mouth'" (Jer. 1:9; cf. 5:14; Isa. 51:16; 59:21; Num. 22:35; 23:5, 12, 16). The prophets' commission from the Lord, as perhaps best illustrated in Moses, was to speak his words to his people (Ex. 4:10–17; 7:1–7; Ezek. 3:4). Because the role of the prophets was to speak for God, they continuously and unanimously prefaced their message with words such as "Thus says the LORD" and "The word of the LORD came to me saying" (see Isa. 1:10; 2:1, 3; 50:4–5; Mic. 1:1; 4:2; Hab. 1:1; Jer. 38:21; Ezek. 1:3–4; 13:3). For this reason the prophets are said to be empowered by the Spirit of God (1 Sam. 10:6, 10; Neh. 9:30; Zech. 7:12; Joel 2:28–29; Hos. 9:7; Isa. 42:1; Mic. 3:8). That is, as they spoke, they did so under such guidance and control of God, that their words were in fact his words proclaimed through them. The prophets therefore insisted that they were not the authors of their own message: their message was given to them. While always employing their own vocabulary, experience, and learning, they yet understood themselves to be instruments of the divine word. Warfield sees this line of evidence as so pervasive and clear that only a brief survey of it establishes the point firmly that the prophets were God's mouthpiece and that their words were his word. Accordingly, the Old Testament Scriptures written by these men are referred to as torah, divine instruction. And that the Old Testament was recognized as such by the Lord Jesus is obvious to all.[48]

---

[47]W, 1:64–66, 299 (see 283–332); SSW, 2:634–35.
[48]W, 1:18–33.

The Claims of the New Testament Writers

It is of greatest importance to Warfield to emphasize that the New Testament writers themselves, like the Old Testament prophets before them, claimed inspiration for their own writings. The Lord Jesus promised that his Spirit would be granted the apostles to give them supernatural guidance in teaching (John 14:28; 16:12–15; cf. Matt. 10:19–20), and the apostles, in turn, enjoined their teaching upon the church as divinely given and supremely authoritative (1 Cor. 2:13; 7:40; 14:37; 2 Cor. 10:7–8; Gal. 1:7–8; 1 Thess. 4:2, 11; 2 Thess. 2:15; 3:6–14; 1 Pet. 1:12; 1 John 5:10; Rev. 22:18–19). They specifically placed each other's writings "in the same lofty category in which they place the writings of the Old Testament," which they manifestly recognized as inspired of God (1 Tim. 5:18; cf. Luke 10:7; 2 Pet. 3:16). This claim of the New Testament writers is a point Warfield returns to often, as we will see in due course. Foundational to the doctrine and to Warfield's exposition of the doctrine is that the men who wrote the Scriptures claimed that they did so with divine guidance and authority.[49]

2 Timothy 3:16

With the designation "sacred writings" (v. 15) the apostle Paul reflects his conviction of the Bible's divine origin (see below) and its unique value for all holy purposes. As the Word of God it is a book singularly suited to making one wise to salvation in Christ. But the full import of the apostle's teaching regarding the nature of Scripture is expressed in the term θεόπνευστος ("God-breathed"), a term Warfield argues is beset by misunderstandings. Θεόπνευστος appears only here in the New Testament and is found nowhere earlier in all extant Greek literature. Still, its meaning is rather easy to ascertain. In his lengthy "God-Inspired Scripture," Warfield searches the uses of the term from all other sources, particularly in Jewish and Christian contexts, and concludes that it consistently connotes the notion of "given by God," "God-given," "provided by God," and so on. More to the point, in no instance does it convey an active sense—"God breathing" or "breathing the divine spirit" or the like—but everywhere it carries a passive significance "rooted in the idea of the creative breath of God" and expressing "production by God,"[50] that is to say, "God-breathed." Θεόπνευστος very certainly does not mean

---

[49] W, 1:401–5.

[50] W, 1:256, 259. This was Warfield's view in his 1881 "Inspiration" coauthored with A. A. Hodge. Interestingly, in his 1889 article "Paul's Doctrine of the Old Testament," PQ 5, no. 3 (1889): 389–406, leaning on the strength of Hermann Cremer's 1880 article in the second edition of Herzog's Realencyklopædie and then the third edition of Cremer's lexicon, Warfield reversed his position and defined the term in an active sense. Then in his 1900 "God-Inspired Scripture," in W, 1:229–80, Warfield retracted his reversal, confessing that he had followed Cremer too hastily. In this later article Warfield traces out all the lexical evidence himself and thoroughly discounts Cremer's view, returning again to the passive idea of θεόπνευστος.

"inspired of God," nor even as the Authorized Version renders it, "given by inspiration of God." These misleading paraphrases imply an in-breathing of God into the biblical writings that gives them a divine quality. But this is much less than what the word connotes. Θεόπνευστος assures us that Scripture is *breathed out* by God (which is the ESV wording), and no word other than θεόπνευστος could have been chosen to make this point more emphatically. "What Paul declares is that 'every scripture,' or 'all scripture' is the product of the Divine breath, 'is God-breathed.'" That is to say, Scripture is the very spoken word of God. Timothy had faithful instructors (vv. 14–15), but most importantly he had a Bible in which God himself speaks (v. 16).[51]

Warfield leaves undecided the other translation questions in the verse—whether it should be "every scripture" or "all scripture," and whether it should be "every [or all] scripture is God-breathed and [therefore] profitable," or "every [or all] scripture, being God-breathed, is as well profitable." He sees these questions as unimportant. Whether Paul speaks in distributive terms ("every") or of Scripture as a whole ("all"), or whether he affirms specifically that "all scripture is God-breathed" or that "all scripture, being God-breathed, is also profitable," little has changed. Without explanation he expresses preference for the translation, "Every scripture, seeing that it is God-breathed, is as well profitable." Paul's affirmation, as Warfield sees it, is that the sacred Scriptures "in their every several passage" are "the product of the creative breath of God," and, because of this divine origin, Scripture "is of supreme value for all holy purposes."[52]

2 Peter 1:21

Here the apostle Peter takes us further into the doctrine of inspiration than Paul's statement in 2 Timothy 3:16. Peter assures his readers that Scripture is even more reliable than eyewitness testimony. The phrase "every prophecy of scripture" is probably a reference to the whole of Scripture in all its parts viewed as prophetic, a word from God. It is, then, the equivalent of Paul's "every scripture." Peter begins with an emphatic denial that this Scripture arose from human thinking or inquiry or will. The Bible does not owe its origin to human initiative in any sense. Then he emphatically affirms that its source lies in God: it is a divine gift. Men spoke "from God" as they were borne along by the Holy Spirit. That is, the biblical writers spoke not from themselves but from God.[53]

Throughout his changing definition of the term and interpretation of 2 Tim. 3:16, however, his definition and understanding of inspiration remained constant.
[51] *W*, 1:78–80, 99, 267–70.
[52] *W*, 1:80.
[53] *W*, 1:82.

But this passage takes us still further. It tells us not only of the divine origin but also of the means and method by which God has given his Word. Scripture was given "through the instrumentality of men," yes, but it was through men who "spoke from him." If in 2 Timothy 3:16 the apostle Paul affirms that Scripture came by means of the influence of the Holy Spirit exerted upon them as they spoke and wrote, the apostle Peter here describes that operation of the Holy Spirit as "bearing" them. The biblical writers spoke "from God" in that they were "taken up by the Holy Spirit and brought by His power to the goal of His choosing. The things which they spoke under this operation of the Spirit were therefore His things, not theirs." Spoken through men though the prophetic word is, it is God's Word, for these men were carried along by him as they spoke. The stress of Peter's comment is not laid on the spiritual value of Scripture, however much that is involved. The stress is laid on the complete trustworthiness of Scripture precisely because it is divinely given. As such, Scripture "affords a more sure basis of confidence than even the testimony of human eyewitnesses" (v. 19). Scripture is altogether trustworthy simply because it comes from God. And this he affirms is true of "every prophecy of scripture," the equivalent of Paul's "all scripture."[54] Scripture in its entirety and in all its parts is divinely given, God's word given through men.

John 10:34–35

Here our Lord tells us just how far this supreme trustworthiness of Scripture extends. In verse 33 the Jews are offended because Jesus claims deity, making himself God. Jesus responds by pointing out that in Psalm 82:6 human judges are referred to as "gods," and his point is that it cannot always be wrong to use the word *god* in reference to men. Jesus' response is certainly not complete: he made himself "God" in a much higher sense than that of Psalm 82:6. But his response is sufficient for the occasion. If it is not blasphemous to refer to judges as "gods" who represent God, then surely it is not blasphemous to so designate God's Son, whom he sent into the world as his emissary. With that there is a note of satire marking Jesus' defense: the Jews could allow "that corrupt judges might properly be called 'gods,'" but they could not tolerate "that He whom the Father had consecrated and sent into the world should call Himself Son of God."[55]

The point of note here, however, is the way Jesus appeals to Scripture and the attitude toward Scripture he displays. He refers to this passage from Psalms as "law," thus recognizing its rightful place in Holy Scripture and its consequent legal or binding authority. But, more basically, Jesus rests his case on Scripture, which

---

[54] *W*, 1:82–83.
[55] *W*, 1:86.

both he and his enemies recognized as having final authority. For this purpose, however, it would seem to have been sufficient for him to say, "Is it not written in your Law?" But to drive home his appeal to Scripture he adds with emphasis, "and Scripture cannot be broken." This is why Jesus cites what is written in the law: because it cannot be broken. It cannot be annulled, its authority cannot be denied, and its declarations cannot be contravened. Jesus' argument rests on the irrefragable authority of every part of Scripture. Warfield characterizes this as "the strongest possible assertion of the indefectible authority of Scripture; precisely what is true of Scripture is that it 'cannot be broken.'" In even its most casual clauses, "more than that, the very form of its expression in one of its most casual clauses," it bears divine, incontrovertible authority. "It belongs to Scripture through and through, down to its most minute particulars, that it is of indefectible authority."[56]

JESUS' VIEW OF INSPIRATION

John 10:34–35 leads Warfield to the larger discussion of Jesus' view of Scripture evident throughout the Gospels. It is "scripture," after all. In Matthew 19:4–5, Jesus treats the words of Moses as the words of God, and in Matthew 22:43 he states that in his psalms David spoke "in the Spirit." Jesus speaks similarly, in advance, of the writings of the apostles: his teaching would be given to them in all truth and in infallible remembrance by the Spirit (John 14:28; 16:12–15; cf. Matt. 10:19–20). And as in John 10:35, our Lord everywhere cites Scripture as to "the indefectible authority whose determination is final." These appeals are made "indifferently to every part of Scripture, to every element in Scripture, to its most incidental clauses as well as to its most fundamental principles, and to the very form of its expression." Is Jesus merely conceding his opponents' view of Scripture as something he does not share? No, this is common ground: both he and they hold this high regard for Scripture and appeal to it accordingly. This attitude is intimated by his use of the term "Scripture" and the authoritative "It is written" (Matt. 4:4, 7, 10; Luke 4:4, 8), giving these writings his own imprimatur. Further, the Lord Jesus regularly explains that events occur "that the Scripture might be fulfilled" (John 17:12; similarly Mark 14:49; John 13:18; cf. 12:14; Mark 9:12–13). Similarly he speaks with utter confidence, again on the basis of declarations of Scripture, that certain future events must occur: "*for* it is written . . ." (Matt. 26:31; Mark 14:27; cf. Luke 20:17). Indeed, in its every last detail what Scripture says will come to pass (Matt. 5:18). His own approaching sufferings "must be," for so the Scriptures have

---

[56] *W*, 1:84–86.

declared (Matt. 26:54). Still again, he expresses wonder that some are surprised at certain events, for had they read the Scriptures, these things (the rejection of Messiah) would have been expected (Ps. 118:22; Mark 12:10; Matt. 21:42; cf. Matt. 22:29). Again, in Mark 12:24 he directly implies that those who rightly know the Scriptures do not err.[57] For Jesus, failure to read and understand Scripture warrants rebuke (Luke 24:44). Commenting on Luke 24:44–46 Warfield remarks:

> Among the last words which He spoke to His disciples before He was received up was a rebuke to them for not understanding that all things "which are written in the law of Moses, and the prophets, and psalms" concerning Him—that is (ver. 45) in the entire "Scriptures"—"must needs be" (very emphatic) "fulfilled" (Luke 24:44). "Thus it is written," says He (ver. 46), as rendering all doubt absurd. For, as He had explained earlier upon the same day (Luke 24:25ff.), it argues only that one is "foolish and slow at heart" if he does not "believe in" (if his faith does not rest securely on, as on a firm foundation) "all" (without limit of subject-matter here) "that the prophets" (explained in ver. 27 as equivalent to "all the scriptures") "have spoken."[58]

This was our Lord's view of Scripture—that it is supremely authoritative and indefectibly trustworthy in its every detail. "Jesus' occasional adduction of scripture as an authoritative document rests on an ascription of it to God as its author. His testimony is that whatever stands written in Scripture is a word of God." And this was his conviction both in his state of humiliation and in his resurrection.[59] There can be no doubt that the high view of Scripture traditionally held by the church was taught by and learned from the Lord Jesus Christ.

RELATED CONCEPTIONS AND BIBLICAL TERMINOLOGY

Warfield is quick to point out that the New Testament writers held the very same high view of Scripture as did Jesus; in fact, this view was already established by their Lord and was merely left for them to accept in following him. To demonstrate that they did, in fact, continue with this same understanding and doctrine, Warfield makes much of their use of that same "pregnant name"—"Scripture" (γραφή/ γραφαί), a term that Warfield notes was used in the New Testament exclusively in its high and technical sense, most always of the Old Testament Scriptures, conveying always the sense of divine authority (e.g., 1 Chron. 15:15; 2 Chron. 30:5, 18; Matt. 22:29; John 10:35; Rom. 1:2; 2 Tim. 3:16; 1 Pet. 2:6). The same is true, of course, of the more complete phrase ἱερὰ γράμματα ("holy Scripture," 2 Tim.

---

[57] W, 1:87, 183–84, 185–86, 86–90; "The Angel of Jehovah and Critical Views," *TBS* 8, no. 1 (July 1903): 60.
[58] W, 1:87.
[59] W, 1:89–90.

3:15). Accordingly, the New Testament writers made appeal to the Scriptures' same solemn "It is written," betraying, as did Jesus, their understanding that whatever is written in Scripture bears divine authority (cf. Matt. 4:4; Mark 1:2; Acts 8:35; 17:3; 26:22; Rom. 1:17; 3:4, 10; 4:17; 11:26; 14:11; 1 Cor. 1:19; 3:19; 1 Cor. 15:3–4, 45; Gal. 3:10, 13; 4:22, 27). Similarly, they regularly cited the Scriptures as "what was spoken through the prophets" and "by the Lord" (Matt. 1:22; 2:15, 23; 13:35; 21:4; 22:31; Acts 1:16; 4:25; 28:25). So also they were confident that the gospel they proclaimed rested on Scripture and therefore was true (Acts 17:2; 18:24, 28), and they encouraged others to test that gospel by the Scriptures (Acts 17:11). Continuously they grounded their counsel, arguments, and commands in the text of Scripture with utter confidence that with this they cannot err (cf. Acts 1:16; 18:5; Rom. 2:26; 8:36; 9:33; 11:8; 12:19; 15:9, 21; 2 Cor. 4:13; James 2:8; 1 Pet. 1:16; 2:6). The fulfillment of Scripture was viewed as altogether necessary, inevitable (Acts 1:16), and this was so because in the writers' view, as in Christ's, what the Scripture says, God says (Rom. 9:17; Gal. 3:8). It is with this conviction that the apostle James insists that Scripture cannot speak in vain (James 4:5). The terms "God" and "scripture" were used often interchangeably, a practice grounded in the conviction that God is the author of Scripture, and that what it declares, he declares. It was not "Scripture" that spoke to Pharaoh or to Abraham but God. Yet the New Testament writers could as easily say "Scripture" spoke to them (e.g., Rom. 9:17; Gal. 3:8). What God says, Scripture says, and yet the more common practice was the reverse: what Scripture says, God says (Heb. 3:7–11, quoting Ps. 95:7–11; Acts 4:25, quoting Ps. 2:1; Acts 13:34, quoting Isa. 55:3 and Ps. 16:10). The conclusion is inescapable: "When we take the two classes of passages together, in the one of which the Scriptures are spoken of as God, while in the other God is spoken of as if He were the Scriptures, we may perceive how close the identification of the two was in the minds of the writers of the New Testament."[60]

Warfield lists as an example the many Old Testament passages cited successively in Hebrews 1: Psalm 2:7; 2 Samuel 7:14; Deuteronomy 32:43; Psalms 97:7; 104:4; 45:6–7; 102:25–27; 110:1. He comments, "Here we have passages in which God is the speaker and passages in which God is not the speaker, but is addressed or spoken of, indiscriminately assigned to God, because they all have it in common that they are words of Scripture, and as words of Scripture are words of God." He then provides a similar list of Old Testament quotations from Romans 15:9ff.: Psalm 18:49; Deuteronomy 32:43; and a third from Psalm 117:1; Isaiah 11:10. All

---

[60]*SSW*, 2:617; *W*, 1:90–92, 130, 145, 148 (see 115–65), 283–84, 335–91; cf. 404. Warfield draws this argument out at great length in "'It Says:' 'Scripture Says:' 'God Says:'" in *W*, 1:283–332.

this demonstrates that the New Testament writers understood the Old Testament as "a compact mass of words of God."[61]

Reflecting this understanding the New Testament writers refer to the Old Testament as "the oracles of God" or "the living oracles" (τὰ λόγια, Rom. 3:2; cf. Acts 7:38; Heb. 5:12; I Pet. 4:11). Warfield analyzes this expression in detail in "The Oracles of God." In the Septuagint, Philo, and elsewhere, the term, used both of words spoken and words written, consistently parallels ἡ γραφή ("the Scripture") and connotes not words merely but words of God and, therefore, oracular utterances or sacred writings, "divinely authoritative communications, before which men stand in awe and to which they bow in humility: and this high meaning is not merely implicit, but is explicit in the term." In Romans 3:2, for example, the distinct privilege of Israel is said to be that they were the recipients of "the oracles of God," by which the apostle means, simply, "the Holy Scriptures in their entirety, conceived as a direct Divine revelation." Warfield explains that from the point of view of this designation, "Scripture is thought of as the living voice of God speaking in all its parts directly to the reader." Similarly, the use of the eminent term "Scripture" and its citation by the formula "It is written" reflect primarily the "indefectible authority" the writers understood Scripture to possess, an authority that clearly rests on its divine origin. When Scripture speaks, God speaks.[62]

Accordingly, the New Testament writers cite Scripture with such formula as "it is said" as an alternative to "it is written" (Luke 4:12, replacing the "it is written" in Matt. 4:7; Heb. 3:15; cf. Rom. 4:18). Similarly, the New Testament writers cite Scripture not merely as what God *said* but as what he "says" (present tense), thus "emphasizing the living voice of God speaking in the Scriptures to the individual soul" (Heb. 3:7; Acts 13:35; Heb. 1:7, 8, 10; Rom. 15:10). Once more, the New Testament writers often cite Scripture with the simple "says" without an expressed subject, "the subject being too well understood, when Scripture is adduced, to require stating; for who could be the speaker of the words of Scripture but God only" (Rom. 15:10; I Cor. 6:16; 2 Cor. 6:2; Gal. 3:16; Eph. 4:8; 5:14). Just as, for the Old Testament writers, the name of God was often too obvious to need explicit mention as the subject (Job 20:23; 21:17; Ps. 114:2; Lam. 4:22), so also the New Testament writers, when quoting the Old Testament, often see no need to state explicitly whose word they are citing: it could be none other than God's word, and they are manifestly conscious in these citations that the words they cite are, in fact, the words of God (Gal. 3:16; cf. John 10:34; Matt. 22:32, 43). In Galatians 3, Paul's argument rests not only on the word that God spoke to Abraham but on

---

[61] *W*, 1:93.
[62] *W*, 1:31–33, 94, 96, 145, 387; cf. 335–91.

the particular form of that word ("seed" vs. "seeds"). Again, Warfield's point here is that the New Testament writers make no distinction between the words of Scripture and the words of God.[63]

All this is to say that in the view of the New Testament writers, the Old Testament Scriptures are the very word of God.

This, in turn, has definitive bearing on the nature of Scripture's authority. Such terms as "law" and "scripture," understood in the highest sense ("oracles of God"), reflect the biblical writers' understanding of Scripture as divinely authoritative. Reference to Scripture—"It is written"—is final, settling all matters of dispute, for what Scripture says, God says; and as his word it bears his very own authority. "It is a mark of the Christian man that the Word is his source and norm of truth, and wherever it has spoken he asks no further evidence, nor can he admit any modification whatever to its deliverances, no matter from what quarter they may be drawn." Warfield faults H. Wheeler Robinson on this score exactly: his "Christian doctrine of man" is ever changing because he has disallowed the biblical doctrine of man. The "Christian" doctrine of man is, properly, not that understanding which Christians today tend commonly to hold. Properly speaking, Christian doctrine cannot be in a state of flux. Christian doctrine is given authoritatively for Christians of all time to embrace faithfully. Warfield will not allow uncertainty; nor will he allow subjectivity to rule. It will not do to accept only those teachings of Scripture that we ourselves sense as "intrinsically true," nor can we profess a high regard for Jesus while rejecting what he taught. To the contrary, precisely because Scripture is divine revelation to man, it supplies a universally authoritative standard of truth to the whole church. This is among Scripture's most "fundamental assertions." Scripture is not and does not profess to be a record of the ideas current among the Jewish people of ancient times. It professes to be a revelation from God to those people. That we can learn in Scripture many of the ideas held by ancients is, from the standpoint of Scripture itself, merely incidental. Biblical authority rests on its character as the spoken and written word of God, and as such it is objective and final.[64]

SUMMARY OF THE BIBLICAL WITNESS

Some of the critics sought to get around the traditional doctrine of inspiration by explaining away such primary passages as 2 Timothy 3:16. Warfield regarded

---

[63]W, 1:94–95, 285, 300.
[64]W, 1:31–33; SSW, 2:674; W, 10:321–34, 373–76. Henry Wheeler Robinson (1877–1945) was an English Baptist minister and Old Testament theologian, principal of his alma mater Regent's Park Baptist College, 1920–1942.

this as an ironic turn of events—appealing to Scripture as authoritative in order to disprove its inspiration! But more to the point, he insisted that it reflected a complete failure to grasp the pervasiveness of Scripture's claim to inspiration. It would be a gross misunderstanding of the case, he argued, to think that Scripture bears witness to its own inspiration by means of the great primary passages alone. "These are but the culminating passages of a pervasive testimony to the divine character of scripture, which fills the New Testament." The inspiration of the Scriptures is established not only by such direct assertions but also by "an endless variety of expressions of confidence in, and phenomena of use of" Scripture. The lofty titles given it by the New Testament writers reflect the highest regard in which they held it: "Scripture," "the Scriptures," and (notes Warfield) "even that almost awful title, 'the Oracles of God.'" Beyond this there are the introductory formulas by which it is quoted: "It is written," "It is spoken," "It says," "God says." Still further, the writers' absolute equating of "what Scripture says" with "what God says," their attributing divine qualities and acts to Scripture in such phrases as "the Scriptures foresaw," the ascription of the Scripture in whole or in part to the Holy Spirit as its author, the reverence they show to Scripture, the unrivaled authority they ascribe to it, and their "general attitude of entire subjection to every declaration of scripture of whatever kind" reveal plainly their conviction that Scripture is from God. The New Testament writers' witness to the divine inspiration of Scripture is so pervasive that any attempt to explain away the doctrine by emptying this primary passage of its import is rendered futile.[65]

> Our Lord and his apostles looked upon the entire truthfulness and utter trustworthiness of that body of writings which they called "Scripture," as so fully guaranteed by the inspiration of God, that they could appeal to them confidently in all their statements of whatever kind as absolutely true; adduce their deliverances on whatever subject with a simple "it is written," as the end of all strife; and treat them generally in a manner which clearly exhibits that in their view "Scripture says" was equivalent to "God says."[66]

It is so pervasively evident that even the critics must acknowledge that Christ and his apostles understood Scripture as verbally inspired, and taught it accordingly. For Warfield this is the deciding factor in the discussion: our Lord himself and his apostles clearly believed and plainly taught this.

---

[65] W, 1:64–66.
[66] SSW, 2:580.

A DIVINE-HUMAN BOOK

While arguing at length that the Bible is a thoroughly divine book, Warfield is careful to stress that this does not in any way minimize the fact that the Bible is also a thoroughly human book. Scripture was given from God but through human agency. Warfield clarifies that it would be inexact to speak of a "human element" in Scripture. The New Testament writers do not conceive of Scripture as partly human and partly divine, or in some of its parts human and in other parts divine. Rather, Scripture in all its "least minutiae, in form of expression as well as in substance of teaching, is from God." Yet that very same Scripture, in all its parts, was given from God through human instrumentality. In their citing of Old Testament Scriptures the New Testament writers may as easily say "Moses says" (Rom. 10:19; cf. Matt. 22:24; Mark 7:10; 12:19; Luke 20:28; Acts 3:22; Rom. 10:5) or "Isaiah says" (Rom. 10:20; cf. Matt. 15:7; Mark 7:6; John 1:23; 12:39; Rom. 9:27, 29) or "David says" (Luke 20:42; Acts 2:25; cf. Mark 12:36; Rom. 11:9) as they could say "God says" (Acts 2:17; cf. Matt. 19:4–5) or "the Holy Spirit says" (Heb. 3:7), or even simply "he [God] says" (Rom. 9:15; 15:10; 2 Cor. 6:2; Gal. 3:16; Eph. 5:14; Heb. 1:6). Or they may speak at once of the Holy Spirit's speaking through the mouth of David (Acts 1:16; 4:25; cf. Matt. 13:35) or of David's speaking by the Spirit (Mark 12:36). All of these designations are equally appropriate, but none of them is appropriate in a sense that would exclude the others. The biblical writers view Scripture as thoroughly human and thoroughly divine at the same time. There are human and divine *aspects* to Scripture, and the writers give full recognition to both.[67]

Second Peter 1:21 provides a crisp example: Scripture came not by the will of man, but holy men of God, as they were "carried along by the Holy Spirit," "spoke from God." The whole initiative is God's, and throughout the process he maintained complete control over the human writers so that the end product was his Word given through them. Jesus speaks similarly in Mark 12:36, quoting Psalm 110:1: "David himself, in the Holy Spirit, declared." Our Lord's argument here rests on the fact that it was David himself who spoke his own very words; yet he spoke only as he was borne along by the Spirit (cf. Acts 1:16; 3:18, 21; 4:25; cf. 2 Sam. 23:2). Again Warfield presses the significance of the fact that although the New Testament writers freely cite Scripture as the words of the human agents—"Moses says," "Moses said," "Moses writes," "Moses wrote," "Isaiah says/said/cries," "David says," and so on—yet, as surveyed above, they also introduce Old Testament quotations with the formula, "God says." They freely speak in both ways. That is to say, in

---

[67]*W*, 1:96–98, 183, 284; cf. *SSW*, 2:15, 542–48.

the understanding of the New Testament writers, Scripture is both thoroughly human and thoroughly divine.[68]

BIBLICAL FORMULATION

The biblical writers do not state with precision exactly how God gave his Word through these human agents. They are content merely to affirm that God gave his Word through them—through their speaking and through their writing. God "bore them along" in such a way that their word was in fact God's Word "breathed out" through them. There is only a sense in which the word *dictation* can be used to describe this process. God gave his words to the prophets, and it was his words they spoke (e.g., Deut. 18:15–18). This is the very nature of the prophetic function. But the biblical descriptions of this process reflect a much more intimate relationship between God and the biblical writers than the idea of dictation can adequately express. We cannot account for the Scriptures by a disregarding of the human element any more than by a disregarding of the divine. The process was not merely mechanical or artificial, and the apostles and prophets were not merely the pens but the penmen of the Holy Spirit. Their words were their own words, reflecting their own experiences, backgrounds, culture, education, thinking, and investigation. Yet God had so prepared them that their words were in fact his words given through them. "The sacred writers were under the influence of the Spirit of God in the whole process of their writing, in such a sense that, while their humanity was not superseded, the Holy Spirit so cooperated with them in their work that their words were made to be at the same time the words of God." Returning to his definition of θεόπνευστος, Warfield again insists that this is the biblical representation of "inspiration": God did not "breathe in" to Scripture, thus giving it a divine quality; Scripture is his own word "breathed out" by him through the biblical writers.

> Just as the first act of loving faith by which the regenerated soul flows out of itself to its Saviour, is at once the consciously-chosen act of that soul and the direct work of the Holy Ghost; so, every word indited under the analogous influence of inspiration was at one and the same time the consciously self-chosen word of the writer and the divinely-inspired word of the Spirit.[69]

Warfield refers to this divine-human relationship in Scripture as *concursus* and insists that only this conception of both the divine and the human working together

---

[68] *W*, 1:97–99.
[69] *W*, 1:19, 22, 25, 99; cf. 397–99, 419; "The Bible Doctrine of Inspiration," *CT* 11 (1893–1894): 166–67; *SSW*, 2:543–45.

in the production of Scripture does justice to the biblical teaching of inspiration. The theological basis for this is the Christian understanding of God as both transcendent and immanent in all his providence and activity with men—such as in his grace "wherein we work out our own salvation with fear and trembling, knowing that it is God who is working in us both the willing and the doing according to his own good pleasure." The biblical basis of this understanding is seen in the many repeated representations of the coauthorship of Scripture, its constant recognition as both divine and human in character, and its explicit claims that its human authors were carried along by the Holy Spirit. Once again, the fundamental principle of this understanding is that the divine activity does not supersede the human authors but works harmoniously with them and through them so that Scripture is in its every part both thoroughly human and thoroughly divine. The Spirit of God did not exert influence on the biblical writers from the outside, as it were, but worked "in, with and by them, energizing them so that, as His instruments they rise above themselves and under His inspiration do His work and reach His aim."[70]

In his treatment of the subject of divine revelation Warfield writes that the Scriptures "affirm, indeed, with the greatest possible emphasis that the Divine word delivered through men is the pure word of God, diluted with no human admixture whatever." Warfield has been criticized for overstating his case here and going beyond what he himself teaches everywhere else regarding *concursus*. The criticism may be valid, but it seems more likely that Warfield was simply speaking in terms of ultimate origins and intending to emphasize the divine source of Scripture. This is the context of the remark in his article on divine revelation. A few pages later he says with more clarity, "In the prophets' own view they were just instruments through whom God gave revelations which came from them, *not as their own product*, but as the pure word of Jehovah." He is speaking in terms of origins. Similarly, in the context of his discussion of inspiration Warfield speaks freely in terms of the "co-authorship" of Scripture, emphasizing that it is God's speaking through men (*concursus*). However, when speaking specifically of revelation (as distinct from inspiration) he is careful to emphasize that the prophets themselves, with their repeated "the word of the Lord came to me" (and related expressions), are intent on stressing that "they are in no sense co-authors with God of their messages." That is, Warfield is content to speak of them as coauthors in terms of the delivering of their message but not in terms of the origination of that message.[71]

The intimacy of relationship with men by which God gave us his Word, moreover, assumes a "complex of processes" by which God actively assured the result. The

---

[70] *SSW*, 2:15, 546–48, 627, 629, 631; *W*, 1:15, 22, 26–27, 173, 398–99.
[71] *W*, 1:18, 23–24 (emphasis added), 173.

various books of the Bible were not produced suddenly by miraculous act or fiat or handed down complete out of heaven. They are the result of many long processes in final convergence. Before the writing of history there was the preparation of the history to be recorded. And before the writing there was the preparation of the material and the preparation of the writer himself—his religious experiences; revelations of divine truth; his education; his physical, intellectual, emotional, and spiritual development; his gifts and biases and vocabulary; and so on. God did not decide finally to give his Word and choose men at random, any of whom would do for the conveyance of that Word. No, before giving a series of letters to the churches he first prepared a Paul—called from his mother's womb—to write them; and in preparing Paul, God made him all that would be necessary for the writing of these letters. To provide us with the psalms, God first prepared a David. In his providence God first provided a fervidly impetuous Peter, a tender and saintly John, a practically wise James, each of whose personalities dominate their writings. All these considerations contribute to the many "marks of human authorship" so evident in Scripture. And so the idea of inspiration entails not only the final product but the entire process by which God gave us his Word through human agents. "God's providence is over all," and we should bear in mind this fact in our understanding of the doctrine of inspiration. "The production of the Scriptures is, in point of fact, a long process." "Inspiration" is the final act of God in a sustained work of providence, producing a book that is thoroughly human and yet superhuman: "a trustworthiness, an authority, a searchingness, a profundity, a profitableness which is altogether Divine" and speaks the divine Word still to each individual heart that reads it.[72]

Inspiration, then, while it cannot be equated with revelation absolutely, is nevertheless a mode of revelation. It is "that operation of the Spirit of God by which He 'bears' men in the process of composing Scripture, so that they write, not of themselves, but 'from God.'" God so prepared the writers of Scripture that in speaking and writing their own words, they spoke his.[73]

OLD AND NEW TESTAMENTS INSPIRED

Without question, when the apostle Paul speaks of "the scriptures" that young Timothy had to make him wise to salvation, it is the Old Testament Scriptures of which he spoke. This is the point of reference all throughout the New Testament discussion of inspiration. But it would be a mistake to think that the New Testament writers' discussion of inspiration is limited to the Old Testament Scriptures, for what the New Testament writers consider "Scripture" extends to their own writings

---

[72] W, 1:22–27, 100–105, 398; W, 10:123; SSW, 1:111–13; SSW, 2:543–44, 606, 608, 615.
[73] W, 1:107; SSW, 2:611.

also. Never do the apostles imagine themselves as less in possession of the Spirit of God than their Old Testament counterparts. They present their teaching in full confidence that they speak "by the Holy Spirit" (1 Pet. 1:12; 1 Cor. 2:13). Having been made sufficient by the Holy Spirit they minister a covenant that is of surpassing glory compared to the former (2 Cor. 3:4–11). They therefore speak with supreme assurance of the truth of their message (Gal. 1:7–8), and they issue commands with the most complete authority (1 Thess. 4:2; 2 Thess. 2:15; 3:6, 12; 1 Cor. 14:37). Both their spoken and written words are considered of divine authority (Gal. 1:7–8; 1 Cor. 14:37; 2 Thess. 3:14). And so it is not surprising to observe them referring to the writings of other New Testament writers as "Scripture." The same apostle who insists that "all Scripture" is God-breathed (2 Tim. 3:16) already in 1 Timothy 5:18 referred to Luke 10:7 as "Scripture"; his conception of what constitutes "Scripture" clearly is not limited to the Old Testament. Similarly, the same apostle who writes that the Scripture came as men were "carried along" by the Holy Spirit and "spoke from God" (2 Pet. 1:21) also ranks the writings of the apostle Paul with whatever other books deserve the title "Scriptures" (2 Pet. 3:16). It is clear that the New Testament writers understand their writings as on par and in unity with the Old Testament Scriptures. It was a mere matter of detail, then, to determine precisely what new writings were to be so understood and received.[74]

In the view of the New Testament writers, the Old Testament Scriptures are the very word of God. And they do not hesitate to place alongside these books their own writings, which were likewise given by the Holy Spirit. They do not in any way consider their own writings in a lesser category but see themselves as completing what was earlier begun. In their view the Scriptures, both Old and New Testaments, are authoritative, completely trustworthy, without error, speaking only and always truth from God himself. That the Scriptures are inspired is not only the church doctrine, then, but it is the doctrine held by Christ and his apostles and commended to us by them.[75]

Canon

HOW THE CANON CAME TO BE

The books of our Old Testament became recognized as "canon"[76] in the same way that the Old Testament itself was formed—gradually, as holy men of old spoke

---

[74]*W*, 1:109–10, 213, 401–5, 451–52; *SSW*, 2:539, 618–19.

[75]*W*, 1:73.

[76]Works in which Warfield treated canonicity include the following: "The Apologetical Value of the Testament of the Twelve Patriarchs," *PR* 1, no. 1 (1880): 57–84; Warfield, "Syllabus on the Canon of the New

and wrote, being moved of the Holy Spirit. In various ways and at various times throughout the old covenant times, God spoke to his people through the prophets, and as they delivered God's word to the people, it was received as of divine origin. Gradually these canonical books were gathered together and became known among the Jews as the Law, the Prophets, and the Scriptures; or, briefer, the Law and the Prophets; or in briefest shorthand, the Law. Grecian Jews may have borrowed somewhat the phraseology of γράφω, γραφή, and γράμμα—words freighted with implications of divine authority. But this idea was already prevalent among the Jews themselves, as is evident in their use of terms such as the "sacred books" (ἱεραὶ βίβλοι or ἱερὰ βιβλία) or "sacred scriptures" (ἱερὰ γράμματα) or more fully the "books of the sacred scriptures" (αἱ ἱερῶν γραφῶν βίβλοι). Ancient Israel possessed a body of writings, regarded as "sacred scriptures," and these were recognized as the authoritative word from God, that is, canonical. Accordingly, it was further understood that Israel's teachings required for their verification demonstrable grounding in these writings, and so from within this context arose the expressions, "for it is said," or "as it is written," and the like (cf. 1 Chron. 15:15; 2 Chron. 30:5, 18; 2 Esdras 6:18; 7:22; Matt. 4:4; Mark 1:2; Acts 1:20; 13:33; Rom. 1:17; etc.). These Scriptures, recognized by our Lord as such (Luke 24:44), constituted the word of God to Israel and as such formed the authoritative basis for her teaching. Given Christ's recognition and endorsement of them, the church receives its Old Testament "canon" on his authority.[77]

The idea of canon, then, was inherited by the church from ancient Israel and given by the Lord Jesus Christ himself. Again the use of "Scripture" or "Scriptures" is important for Warfield here. As already noted, the term is used in the New Testament exclusively in the technical sense of divinely inspired writings. Warfield comments further that the anarthrous use of γραφή (its use without an article) in such passages as 1 Peter 2:6 and 2 Peter 1:20 (cf. 2 Tim. 3:16) "is explicable only on the presupposition that ἡ γραφή had become so much the proper designation of Scripture that the term had acquired the value of a proper name, and was therefore treated as definite without, as with, the article." Moreover, the terms are used in such a way as to make evident that in the understanding of the biblical writers "Scripture" or "Scriptures" form an "irreducible unity"—a single document, "as constituting in their entirety a single divinely authoritative 'writing.'" This "Scripture" was the church's recognized canon. To the earliest Christians the

Testament in the Second Century" (Pittsburgh, 1881); "Dr. Edwin Al Abbott on the Genuineness of II Peter," SPR 34 (1883): 390–455; "The Christian Canon," The Philadelphian 1 (June 1887): 300–304; Warfield, The Canon of the New Testament (Philadelphia: American Sunday School Union, 1902); review of The Rise of the New Testament (1900), by David S. Muzzey, in PRR 11, no. 44 (1900): 712–13; "The Formation of the Canon of the New Testament," in W, 1:451–56; "The Canonicity of 2 Peter," in SSW, 2:48–79.
[77] W, 1:115–17; W, 9:639.

"old covenant" Scriptures (2 Cor. 3:14), "the holy Scriptures" (Rom. 1:2), comprised Israel's canon, which they too referred to as "the Law . . . and the Prophets and the Psalms" (Luke 24:44), or more briefly as "the Law and the Prophets" (Matt. 7:12; Luke 16:16; cf. Acts 28:23; Luke 16:29–31), or simply as "the Law" (John 10:34; 1 Cor. 14:21) or even "the prophets" (Rom. 16:26 KJV). These were the "holy Scriptures" of the early church (Rom. 1:2; cf. 2 Tim. 3:16; Acts 13:15), and like ancient Israel before them, so the early church adduced the authority of these "Scriptures" with the same authoritative "It is written." There was "nothing left for Christianity to invent" in the way of the recognized authority (canonicity) or usage of the Old Testament Scriptures, and in this sense it added nothing new but merely adopted an understanding and practice already well recognized and exemplified even in our Lord himself.[78]

It would be a mistake, however, to assume that the Bible of the early church consisted only of these Old Testament books. As mentioned above, the apostles of Christ saw themselves as possessing the Spirit of inspiration as fully as did the prophets of the old covenant. They spoke with the authority of Christ and issued commands in his name. They claimed to speak by means of the Holy Spirit and imposed their teaching and directives on the church as from God. The apostles themselves, as well as the churches to whom they wrote, recognized their word as on par with that older revelation (1 Tim. 5:18; 2 Pet. 3:16; cf. 1 Thess. 2:13), and as this new revelation came to them, it was revered as from Christ. Beginning immediately in the apostolic age these new spokesmen for our Lord began to impose upon the church additional writings that were to be regarded—and were regarded by the apostles themselves—as divinely given and divinely authoritative. One by one, writings came from the apostles' pens and along with the Old Testament Scriptures were imposed on the church and received by the church as canon (e.g., Gal. 1:7–8; 1 Cor. 2:13; 7:40; 14:37; 1 Thess. 2:13; 4:1–2; 2 Thess. 2:15; 3:6, 14; 1 Tim. 6:3; Rev. 1:10–11; 2:1, etc.). That the apostles produced writings that the church was responsible to receive as divinely binding is plain to every reader of the New Testament. The church possessed a canon from the very beginning, and in that first century that canon grew as the apostles so provided.[79]

This apostolic authority was not self-made. Christ had commissioned his apostles to this task, in advance, and this was to be the role they would serve in the history of the church. He appointed these men as his personal legates, directing them to be his spokesmen. He had brought the revelation of God to them, and

---

[78]W, 1:115, 118–19, 130, 140, 144–45, 147 (see 115–65), 451; W, 9:639; "The Christian Canon," 300–304.
[79]W, 1:119–21, 402–3, 406–7, 451–52; SSW, 2:14–15, 539; W, 9:639–41; cf. W, 4:178–79.

they, in turn, were to take this revelation to the world. They were to continue his teaching. In order to equip them to fulfill this role successfully Christ sent them "another Helper" (John 14:16–18), his replacement, the Holy Spirit of God who would teach them "all things" and "bring to [their] remembrance" all that Jesus himself had taught them (vv. 24–26). The promised Spirit of Christ was to speak for Christ and guide the apostles into "all the truth," revealing to them "things that are to come" (John 16:12–13). They would be the final repositories of God's full and final revelation in Christ. Their written witness to Christ was, in fact, Christ's continued revelation to his church, and bound up with their authority is our Lord's endorsement of the same.[80]

HISTORICAL AND CRITICAL CONSIDERATIONS

Warfield is very aware of "the critical school of scepticism," especially that of the Tübingen School. He describes its aim as being "to undermine the received account of the first and second centuries" with regard to the New Testament canon and to "reconstruct their whole history in accord with its own theories." Denying a personal God and, consequently, the concept of revelation, it was left to explain both Christianity and its canon in terms of natural growth in time. In their view the New Testament "becomes a *human growth* instead of a *divine gift*." Through the ordinary interplay of human follies, divisions, and strife, the canon is simply the product of time and finally took the shape of those who prevailed in such struggles. Advocates of these theories are forced by their presuppositions to demand a second-century date for the composition of the New Testament books. In order to secure this result "they have gone systematically to work to discredit all the records which have come down to us from that century, and overturn all we know of the period. . . . The result is a complete reconstruction of the history of the second century."[81]

On several occasions, therefore, Warfield takes up the question of whether critical scholarship can show that the apostles' claim of inspiration was disallowed by their contemporaries, whether they viewed the writings of the apostles in any lower regard than those of the Old Testament prophets. He insists that just as the New Testament itself abounds with implications of the church's submissive reception of the writings of the apostles, so also does the record of the earliest centuries. Following the lead of his predecessor Archibald Alexander, Warfield demonstrates at length that the various books of the New Testament were from the beginning held in the highest regard by the church. "No church writer of the

---

[80]*W*, 1:187–88, 401.
[81]"Syllabus on the Canon of the New Testament," 3–4 (emphasis original).

time can be pointed out who made a distinction derogatory to the New Testament, between it and the Old Testament," the divine authority of the latter having already been fully acknowledged. Polycarp (AD 69–155) refers to the new apostolic books as *sacrae literae*. Dionysius of Corinth (AD 148–176) refers to them with the standard γραφαί ("Scripture"). Similarly, Justin in *Trypho* cites Matthew's Gospel with "the sacred formula" γέγραπται ("it is written") and refers to the Gospels as "The Memoirs of the Apostles" (*Ta Apomnemoneumata ton Apostolon*), holding them in equal regard with "*Ta Suggrammata of the Prophets*." Irenaeus refers to the New Testament Scriptures as *ta Logia* and *ta Kyriaka Logia* ("the oracles of the Lord"), and Clement of Alexandria as "oracles (Logia) of truth" and "the inspired Oracles." Similarly, the author of *The Testaments of the Twelve Patriarchs* (AD 100–120) betrays dependence on Matthew, Luke, John, Acts, Romans, 1 Corinthians (probably), 2 Corinthians, Ephesians, Philippians, Colossians, 1 Thessalonians, 1 Timothy, Hebrews, James, 1 Peter, 2 Peter (probably), 1 John, and Revelation. And still more impressively, he makes specific mention of Acts and Paul's epistles, describing them as βίβλοι ἁγίαι ("holy Scriptures"), and this as part of a collection of books of which the Old Testament was also a part. Warfield argues that if the author of *The Testaments* indisputably possessed so many other of the New Testament books, and if he referred to Paul's as part of a collection of βίβλοι ἁγίαι, it is not a long step at all to expect on a priori grounds that "the New Testament canon had been already practically formed at the outset of the second century." This line of evidence Warfield traces out at considerable length in order to demonstrate that the early Christian writers unanimously treated the writings of the apostolic company with the very highest respect and held their teachings in the highest honor. Even the early "Christian" heretics recognized the unique status of these books as they labored by "ridiculous exegesis" to ground their teachings on their mutually acknowledged authority. After thorough investigation of all the earliest Christian writers, Warfield finds that they all "without exception" treat the New Testament books as on par with those of the Old Testament and as distinct from all other writings.[82]

In summary, "If the historical authenticity of our Canon is to be denied, it must be done at the expense of all our historical sources; at the expense of the falsification of history herself; at the expense of the destruction of the grounds of all historic inquiry."

---

[82] *W*, 1:405–7; *W*, 9:639–45; "The Descriptive Names Applied to the New Testament Books by the Earliest Christian Writers," *BSac* 42, no. 166 (1885): 551–52, 561; "Syllabus on the Canon of the New Testament," 38–39, 50–51, 56–57, 60–61; "The Apologetical Value of the Testament of the Twelve Patriarchs," 77–80. Cf. Archibald Alexander, *The Canon of the Old and New Testaments Ascertained* (Philadelphia: Presbyterian Board of Publication, 1851), part 2.

It appears that there was, from the beginning of the second century, a collection (Ignatius, 2 Clement, Marcion) of "New Books" (Ignatius), called the "Gospel and Apostles"
(Ignatius, Marcion), esteemed as the "Oracles" of God (Polycarp, Papias, 2 Clement)
and "Scripture" (1 Timothy, 2 Peter, Barnabas, Polycarp, 2 Clement, Basilides), which
was attached to the "Old Books" as part of one "Holy" Canon (Testt. XII Patriarchs)
with them.

As the decades progress, the evidence grows only stronger. "Every particle of
evidence" from the earliest days exhibits the early church as not disallowing but
giving full recognition to "the absolute authority of the New Testament writings."
From the first Christian authors there is no distinction made between Old and
New Testament writers, but only between the biblical writers and extrabiblical
authors, such as themselves. This church, which already had accepted the full
authority of the Old Testament Scriptures, also accepted the New Testament writings as likewise inspired of God.[83]

By way of clarification, Warfield finds no evidence of a gradual elevation in the
early church's esteem for the New Testament books, from their original reception until their finally being regarded as the authoritative rule of faith. Rather,
from the very beginning these writings were recognized as divinely authoritative
Scripture and were immediately attached to the older canon as their number
grew and they were read in the assemblies accordingly (cf. 1 Thess. 2:13; 5:27; Col.
4:16; Rev. 1:3). The collection of New Testament writings finally increased to the
point of becoming viewed as another *section* of the Scriptures. Yet they were not
considered something separate or different, but following the lead of the apostles
themselves (1 Tim. 5:18; 2 Pet. 3:16, "*other* Scriptures"), the church held the new
books in the same regard as the older "Scriptures." Moreover, these newer books
were seen as divinely given not only individually and separately but collectively,
and as they accumulated, they became collectively designated as the Gospels
and the Apostles; or more briefly, the Gospel. Together with the older books they
were designated the Law and the Prophets with the Gospels and the Apostles; or
more briefly, the Law and the Gospel. Ignatius (d. c. 110) relates a custom already
in use that refers to the Old (books) and the corresponding Gospel, and in which
Ignatius himself speaks of the New Testament as lying hidden in the Old and the
Old being made clear in the New—again reflecting the common understanding
that the Old and New Testaments were viewed as a single body of Scripture. And
Warfield samples various other writings to establish that this is the consistent
understanding and witness of the early church. From the very beginning of the

---

[83]"Syllabus on the Canon of the New Testament," 45–46, 89–90; "The Descriptive Names Applied to the
New Testament Books," 561; *W*, 1:407, 454; *W*, 9:636–37, 643.

second century—that is, from the time immediately following the apostles—the "New Books" were regarded as one and equally authoritative with the Old.[84]

The New Testament canon grew, then, in a way similar to that of the Old Testament—as the revelation was given. Just as Israel's earlier canon grew over the centuries, so the church's canon grew over the course of the second half of the first century AD. It was a canon in progress. As the new books were received, they, like the books of the Old Testament, were to be read in the assemblies and recognized as divinely given.

The New Testament canon was completed when John wrote the Apocalypse, around AD 98. But whether the church of Ephesus, to whom he wrote, possessed a complete canon at that point is a separate question and would depend on whether all other apostolic writings had yet reached them. Of course, in the day before moveable type and mass reproduction and distribution, handwritten copies were slow in coming, and individual churches were slow in receiving the New Testament canon in full. Recognition by the churches depended on circulation to the churches, and so the "canon" that was recognized varied from locality to locality. As copies were made by a given locality, some incomplete "canons" were perpetuated unwittingly. However, statements from the early church (e.g., Polycarp, 69–155; Justin, 100–165; 2 Clement, c. 150; *The Testaments of the Twelve Patriarchs*, c. 100–120; Irenaeus, c. 175) demonstrate sufficiently that the New Testament canon in use then was the same as we presently acknowledge, "with the possible exceptions of Jude, 2 and 3 John and Philemon. And it is more natural to suppose that failure of very early evidence for these brief booklets is due to their insignificant size rather than to their non-acceptance." But as circulation increased, so also did recognition, and "from the time of Irenaeus down, the church at large had the whole Canon as we now possess it."[85]

The criterion for recognition of this growing canon was, simply, *apostolicity*—apostolic endorsement. "Any book or body of books which were given to the Church by the apostles as law must always remain of divine authority in the Church." Apostolic *authorship* was the norm, of course, but not exclusively so. Indeed, the apostle Paul himself endorsed as "Scripture" the writing of Luke, a nonapostle (1 Tim. 5:8). But apostolic *endorsement* was the test. The apostles were the "legislators to the Church," "agents of Christ," the Lord's spokesmen and founders of the church by divine appointment, and it was theirs to impose the new rule upon the church. This distinction (apostolicity vs. apostolic authorship) was forgotten at times, and because it was forgotten, doubts as to the proper canonicity of

---

[84]*W*, 1:452–54; *W*, 9:636–37, 641–42; "Apologetic Value of the Testaments of the Twelve Patriarchs," 81–83; "Syllabus on the Canon of the New Testament," 89.

[85]*W*, 9:643–44; *W*, 1:453–54.

Hebrews, James, and Jude were raised. But from the beginning the critical factor was imposition by the apostles, not apostolic authorship per se. Hence, Justin remarks that "The Gospel and the Apostles" were "written by the apostles and their companions."[86]

> It is because the apostles were Christ's representatives, that what they did and said and wrote as such, comes to us with divine authority. The authority of the Scriptures thus rests on the simple fact that God's authoritative agents in founding the Church gave them as authoritative to the Church which they founded. All the authority of the apostles stands behind the Scriptures, and all the authority of Christ stands behind the apostles. The Scriptures are simply the law-code which the law-givers of the Church gave it.[87]

Warfield therefore utterly rejects as a reconstruction of history the Ritschlian theory of a lately recognized canon. The notion of apostolic authority and therefore biblical canon was not the invention of the second century but the settled understanding of the primitive church. The church did not gradually form the canon by coming eventually to decide which books to include in it and then rendering official judgments accordingly. Apostolic authority was recognized from the beginning. The New Testament canon was "imposed on the Church by its founders, not evolved by the Church in the course of its controversies." Warfield insists that "the entire labored theory of the development of the Canon, of Old and New alike, which has been worked out by the 'critical' school is an invention which flies flat in the face of all the facts." Never was any such authority given to the church. The authority of the Scriptures does not rest on the authority of the church. It is "not the church, but the inspired apostles who gave the sacred books one by one to the Church, thus at once creating and filling up the total contents of the class of sacred books." There was never a "selection" of canon made on the grounds of judged fitness. The church "never had anything to do with [the canon] but to receive it." The church may bear witness to what it has received from the apostles as its divine authority, but it does not belong to the church to establish that authority "which rightfully belongs to [Scripture] whether she recognizes it or not." The point is not whether the church existed prior to the Scriptures, but whether the Scriptures are a product of the church, or the church the product of the Scriptures. And on this question Warfield carefully observes that "the Church certainly did not exist before the authority which Christ gave the apostles to found it, in virtue of which they have imposed the Scriptures on it as law." Each of the

---

[86]W, 1:455–56; W, 10:120–21, 233; SSW, 2:14–15, 538–39; W, 9:644–45.
[87]SSW, 2:537.

books, then, became canon as they came to the church from the apostolic company. It was the role of the apostles, under the personal endorsement of Christ, to provide the church with her canon.[88]

What is important to recognize in all this is that both the Old and New Testaments, coming to us before and after Christ respectively, are alike given by Christ through the apostles. He places his divine imprimatur on both—one after the fact and one before. It is therefore on his authority that the church recognizes its present biblical canon.[89]

2 PETER: A TEST CASE

If apostolicity is key to canonicity, then the denials of the critics must be answered. Warfield is bold in his rejection of the many critical assaults on the genuineness of some of the New Testament books and repeatedly insists that for all their attempts, they have never disproved the genuineness of any New Testament book.

Warfield offers the canonicity of 2 Peter as a test case for the critics' assault.[90] Second Peter is perhaps the most disputed book of the New Testament canon, and the evidence in its favor is admitted on all sides to be less compelling—even if not less in amount than that for, say, 2 John and Philemon—than the evidence for any other book. And so if the case for 2 Peter can be shown to be convincing, then the evidence in favor of the other books would seem to be overwhelming. Second Peter, then, the most disputed book, is Warfield's test case.

What must be demonstrated in order to establish canonicity is that the book in question was given to the church by the authority of the apostles. What is left for us at this date, then, is to answer two queries: (1) Is there evidence that the book dates from apostolic times? (2) Has the church from the beginning held it as its authoritative rule of faith? Warfield takes up these questions with vigor.

Peter's second epistle is well known to Christians at the opening of the third century, as witnessed by Origen and Clement of Alexandria. The critics would argue that this is as far back as we can find 2 Peter, but Warfield counters that they have not allowed sufficient weight to the fact that Clement's witness comes in the form of a commentary (as we learn from Eusebius) on the canonical Scriptures, including 2 Peter. It is impossible to assume that he would include in his commentary on canonical writings a book that was produced as recently as his own lifetime. Moreover, he wrote on books already recognized by others as Scripture.

---

[88]*W*, 10:120–21, 233; *SSW*, 2:14–15, 537–38, 612–13; *W*, 9:596–645.

[89]*SSW*, 2:538–40; *W*, 1:111, 401.

[90]"The Canonicity of Second Peter," in *SSW*, 2:48–79; cf. *W*, 1:411–13; cf. "Dr. Edwin A. Abbott on the Genuineness of Second Peter," *SPR* 34 (April 1883): 390–445; and "The Genuineness of 2 Peter," *TBS*, new series, 6, no. 3 (September 1902): 179; Warfield, "Syllabus on the Special Introduction to the Catholic Epistles" (Pittsburgh: W. W. Waters, 1883): 100–131.

These facts argue strongly that 2 Peter had been considered canonical all along, and Clement himself says as much when he claims that "he had traveled far and sat under many teachers of many names, and he holds only those books which he had found everywhere clung to as those which had come down from the apostles." Warfield concludes, "If we had no further evidence than Clement's, therefore, a probability of apostolical origin of 2 Peter would already exist, such as would require some weighty evidence to overturn. The burden of proof would certainly rest on those who denied its canonicity."[91]

But Warfield offers more than presumptive evidence of the recognition of 2 Peter prior to Clement. Most importantly, he finds in Irenaeus (d. c. 200) fragmentary yet unmistakable references to 2 Peter 1:15; 2:4–7; and 3:18, quotations that follow Peter's context as well as wording. And so Warfield concludes confidently that Irenaeus also possessed 2 Peter. Still further, Warfield finds similar references to 2 Peter 1:19 in Theophilus of Antioch (d. c. 185); 2 Peter 3:5–7, 10–12 in Melito Sardis (d. c. 180); 2 Peter 2:13, 15, 20 in Hermas (second century); 2 Peter 2:1 and 3:8 in Justin (100–165); 2 Peter 3:8 in Irenaeus; and other such parallels in Pseudo-Clement (c. 150), *The Testaments of the Twelve Patriarchs*, and even Polycarp (69–155), Barnabas, and Clement of Rome (d. c. 99). After surveying these, Warfield concludes that "to a moral certainty" Peter's second epistle was known of and used by Irenaeus (c. 175), Justin Martyr (c. 147), and Barnabas (c. 106). He insists that even one such probable quotation would provide sufficient presumptive evidence, but his fifteen or sixteen render the matter beyond reasonable doubt: 2 Peter comes to us from the first century. All this testimony is the more significant in that the single factor that decided canonicity for these writers was that the book had come to them from the apostles.[92]

Warfield further offers external evidence of the early acceptance of 2 Peter as canonical. He stresses first the weightiness of the fact that 2 Peter was finally accepted as genuine by the whole church, something very difficult to account for if the epistle were not genuine. Before the fourth century, only one branch of the church, the Syriac church, disputed 2 Peter. Its place is settled in codices B and X, and it is attested by all the great writers of the day and on down to our own time. With such abundant witnesses as this establishing the rightful place of 2 Peter in the canon, Warfield insists that the burden of proof lies with any who would exclude it. Furthermore, Warfield reminds us that it is only one corner of the church that omitted 2 Peter and that the testimony of this one sector of the church cannot possibly overthrow that of all the rest. Still further, it is far from

---

[91]*SSW*, 2:51.
[92]*SSW*, 2:52–58.

certain that the earlier Syriac church rejected this epistle. Prior to Chrysostom it seems to have been included, and its later exclusion seems clearly to be the result of critical Antiochene revision of the fourth century. These critical revisions were individual judgments by no means shared by the church at large. And finally, the Syriac church itself was not agreed as to the number of the General Epistles that should be included. Warfield sees nothing in all this that would possibly militate against the overwhelming positive evidence in favor of 2 Peter. "The testimony of the Church, as the Church, rings clear and strong above all doubt in favor of the letter."[93]

Finally, Warfield offers internal evidence in favor of the genuineness of 2 Peter. First, the letter bears Peter's name (1:1, cf. 14, 16). It is therefore either genuine or a malicious forgery. The tone of the letter is not that of a deceiver but of a holy apostle. There is "not a false note struck" in the entire book. Instead the author appears clearly to love truth above all things (1:3, 12), is in genuine earnest about Christian virtue (1:5), is fearful of the coming judgment (2:1) and believes in God's justice (2:9), and despises deceit and lying (1:16). He claims, further, to be an eyewitness of our Lord's transfiguration (1:16–18) and reflects a personal acquaintance with the Lord Jesus Christ. This hardly seems the work of a forger. Moreover, the style of the epistle is the same as that of the speeches of Peter recorded in the book of Acts. Once again, the author of 2 Peter is plainly the same as the author of 1 Peter. Whatever questions of differing style remain, "the same character underlies both writings; both are the outflow of an ardent, impulsive, yet chastened heart. The writers of both bear the same relation to Paul and are anxious equally to express approval and recommendations of his teaching"; and so on. Yet further, all antiquity testifies that Mark's Gospel is dependent on Peter. And so Warfield points out the striking parallels between 2 Peter 2:1 and Mark 13:22; 2 Peter 3:17 and Mark 13:23; 2 Peter 3:10 and Mark 13:36; and 2 Peter 3:4 and Mark 13:19. Still again, 1 Peter 5:13 reflects Peter's close relationship with Mark, and in 2 Peter 1:15, Peter seems to promise a Gospel. In short, "1 Peter testifies to Mark's intimacy with Peter; 2 Peter promises a Petrine Gospel; antiquity tells us that Mark was but Peter's mouthpiece." Then Warfield asks, "Who could have invented that middle term and so delicately inserted it into 2 Peter?"[94]

Warfield confidently concludes in the face of all critical scholarship that there is "a mountain mass of presumption in favor of the genuineness and canonicity of 2 Peter."[95] And this is a sampling of the posture held by Warfield throughout

---

[93]*SSW*, 2:65.

[94]*SSW*, 2:65–78.

[95]*SSW*, 2:78. Warfield wrote this defense of 2 Peter in 1882, just at the beginning of his career, at age thirty-one. Dr. John R. Mackay later commented of this "able article" that it was "among the first of Dr. Warfield's

his career. He holds no embarrassment whatever before the critical theories of the origin of the books of the Bible but asserts confidently that criticism "has not disproved the authenticity of a single book of our New Testament." He is assured that the critical theories "rest on no better basis than an over-acute criticism overreaching itself and building on fancies."

> Rationalism has expended its strength in an attempt to prove that this New Testament could not have come from the hands of its reputed authors, but the result of a half century's strife has been the total ignominious defeat of the attack. And today it has come about that we do not possess a tithe of the evidence for Caesar's authorship of his lucid commentaries, or Euripides' production of his sublime tragedies, that we do for the undoubted and indubitable fact that the books that make up our precious Testament came directly from the hands of Peter, and James, and John, and Paul.[96]

Inspiration an Evident Truth

GENERAL OBSERVATIONS

In "The Divine Origin of the Bible"[97] Warfield makes inquiry into the question of how to give account for the Bible. What ultimate factor gives adequate explanation for it? Specifically, is there reason to believe that the Bible is of divine origin? Is there evidence that would lead to this conclusion? In this inquiry Warfield provides a series of eighteen propositions under five general headings: (1) "The History of the Bible," (2) "The Structure of the Bible," (3) "The Teaching of the Bible," (4) "Special Characteristics of the Bible," (5) "Impossibility of Accounting for the Bible." He begins by pointing out that the Bible is unique among all books in the place it maintains among civilized people. Its influence on legislation, social habits, culture, and governmental forms is unparalleled. It has left its mark in the shaping and even transformation of every quarter of every society to which it has gone. Religious rituals of sacrifice forever embedded in the consciousness of men and societies suddenly fall into neglect when brought into contact with the Bible. Religion and morals, in their practice and in their very theory, have been revolutionized by this unique book. Moreover, its influence has always been beneficent. This is not to deny the abuses of professing Christians, but it is an unchallenged fact that where the Bible has gone, society has improved, and love has replaced hate and horror. Following its first arrival the Bible has deluged

---

contributions to New Testament studies which brought its author to the notice of British New Testament scholars." *Expositors*, July, 1922, 31; cited in *SSW*, 2:48n.

[96]*W*, 1:408, 418; Hodge and Warfield, *Inspiration*, 39–40; *The Daily Dayton Democrat*, July 25, 1876, 4.

[97]*W*, 1:429–47.

rld, crossing all boundaries and barriers. So pervasive has been its influ-
wherever it has gone, that it would be difficult to overstate the case. All
this has been accomplished without the commendation of royalty, against the
most determined and violent opposition, and by the efforts of a dozen unlearned
men bringing a message considered foolish by all who heard it. Yet all who are
encountered by it are left with the deep-rooted conviction that this book is from
God. If this is fanaticism, it is a remarkable fanaticism that has continued and
grown without precedent. Warfield inquires what might account for all this if
not what the Bible itself claims—that it is of divine origin.[98]

Warfield adds that God "authenticated" and "endorsed" the biblical writers by
the numerous miraculous signs he gave them to perform.[99] Not only do such miracles fit well with the overall supernatural character of Scripture, but they served
in their first instance as divine validation of the human authors and the message
that they gave. This is the position Warfield takes in his *Counterfeit Miracles* also.
Although he nowhere offers to demonstrate at length the historicity of these
apostolic miracles, he does argue that the historical evidence is irrefragable and
that all the related historical testimony unites in corroborating the claim. The
miracles were manifestly open and astounding to all, and they were witnessed
by the apostle's contemporaries, friend and foe alike. The Scriptures were born
with supernatural testimony that they are from God.

For Warfield, it does not appear that a Bible of merely human origin could
have been produced with the conscious intent of influencing the world as it has.
The Bible is in fact not one but sixty-six books of virtually every genre, written
by at least thirty different authors from all walks of life, education, and temperament, and scattered over a period of 1,500 years. Yet the Bible is not, as might be
expected, a conglomerate of unrelated literary debris finally thrust together by
some whirlpool of time. Rather, the Bible displays a remarkable unity in theme, in
moral and religious ideal, in subject matter, and in its leading figure, Jesus Christ.
Predictions and prophecy in the first half of the book are fulfilled so numerously
and so exactly in the second half that the two are manifestly designed for each
other. The former half clearly anticipates and is completed by the latter, and the
latter rests entirely upon the former. Each part contributes to the whole, and each
book adds something of an orderly and constantly progressive explanation, definition, or completion to the others. All of its parts very naturally dovetail together
into a single well-connected and consistent whole. Each part seems clearly to
be meant for the others, intentionally framed for its peculiar place. Although its

[98]*W*, 1:429–35.
[99]*W*, 1:435; Hodge and Warfield, *Inspiration*, 29.

production far outlasted the life span of any single man, the Bible seems by all accounts to be a book designed from the beginning to be what it is in its final form. All its varied parts fit together so well and so naturally that it appears to have been produced by a single mind.[100]

Moreover, not only does the Bible display a remarkable unity in its teaching, but the teaching itself is marked by a unique and otherwise unexplainable grandeur. The writers betray an advanced knowledge beyond their historical setting, an understanding of the universe that is in perfect accord with all that later, advanced learning has discovered. Their elevated conception of God, unprecedented in any other religious teaching before and unmatched since, and their correspondingly elevated conception of the nobility of man created in God's image likewise cry for explanation. Still further, the great truths they present are not suited for their own time and culture only but are universal truths that are instinctively recognized by all to be true, divinely insightful, personally and universally relevant, and of eternal bearing. Warfield inquires, what can account for this? Was Moses capable of this? Was an anonymous forger of his name capable of it? What accounts for all this but a single divine author?[101]

Warfield adds to all this the observation that nonsupernaturalistic attempts to account for the Bible have all failed. Some have sought to explain the miracles of the Bible in terms of exaggeration: people were healed, but by medicinal means; the "dead" were raised, but only from seeming death. But this attempted explanation has inevitably failed, requiring as it did, instead, "as great a series of miracles of wonderful coincidences as it explained away." Others have attempted to account for the miraculous in terms of growing myth: there was just a kernel of truth to the stories, but over time the legends grew to unrecognizable proportions. But this theory is discredited by the lack of time for such legends to grow within the generation of those who witnessed the events. Finally, others have attempted to explain the Bible in terms of party strife and forgeries and reforgeries to serve peculiar designs, all resulting finally in the New Testament of the party who won. This theory likewise fails for too little time for such an elaborate process before the proven existence of these books. The world still awaits a naturalistic theory able to account for the Bible. Warfield insists that the evidence does not allow an accounting for the Bible apart from God. And if this book cannot be accounted for apart from him, "we seem shut up to account for it as from him."[102]

---

[100] W, 1:435–41.
[101] W, 1:441–44.
[102] W, 1:446–47.

THE SELF-ATTESTING CHARACTER OF SCRIPTURE
AND THE *TESTIMONIUM SPIRITUS SANCTI*

The self-attesting character of Scripture (that it is *autopistia*, "trustworthy in and of itself") and the *testimonium Spiritus Sancti* have long enjoyed formal and consistent recognition in Reformed theology. Warfield's immediate context was one of polemics calling for demonstrable evidence and historic faith, and so by the nature of the case his emphasis was not on self-attestation. But this in no way reflects a lesser appreciation of this aspect of his Reformed theological heritage.

For example, in his famous 1881 article with A. A. Hodge on "Inspiration," Warfield offers the following as one of the basic "proofs" of the doctrine of inspiration:

> The moral and spiritual character of the revelation which the Scriptures convey of God, of the Person of Christ, of the Plan of Redemption, and of the law of absolute righteousness, and the power which the very words of the Record, as well as the truths they express, have exercised over the noblest men, and over nations and races for centuries; this is the characteristic self-demonstration of the Word of God, and has sufficed to maintain the unabated catholicity of the strict doctrine of Inspiration through all changes of time and in spite of all opposition.[103]

That is to say, the loftiness of the Bible's teachings reflects a heavenly origin, and in this way Scripture is self-authenticating and carries with it its own authority and convincing power. In the very character of its message and teaching it demonstrates itself to be of God.

Warfield's treatment of the *testimonium* comes almost exclusively in conjunction with his lengthy analysis of Calvin's teaching on the subject. The *testimonium Spiritus Sancti* lies specifically in the noetic effects of regeneration and the creation of genuine saving faith in the hearts of God's elect, thus persuading them of and opening their eyes to recognize the divine origin of Scripture. In other words, persuasion of the divinity and authority of Scripture is bound up with saving faith itself. It is for this reason that Warfield so often refers to the inspiration of Scripture as belonging to the Christian's very "instinct." Persuasion of the Bible's divine origin does not depend upon scholarly investigation but depends on the witness of the Spirit, and this is given to the heart of every believer.[104]

---

[103]Hodge and Warfield, *Inspiration*, 31–32.
[104]*W*, 5:29–130; see also *W*, 10:234. Warfield here never states in so many words that in expounding Calvin's doctrine he is expressing his own, but the tenor throughout seems clearly to demand this association; cf. *W*, 1:67–68.

Warfield further emphasizes that apart from this supernatural work of the Spirit no other evidential demonstration of the divinity of Scripture will prove effective.[105] Only the Holy Spirit can remove spiritual blindness and give faith. These themes of human inability and divine initiative are favorites of Warfield, frequently highlighted and reflective of his deep sense of rescue by the supernatural workings of divine grace. If we recognize Scripture to be God's word, then we are blessed, for this is his work in us.

However, it is important for Warfield to clarify the precise mode of this testimony. He offers three options: an "immediate revelation" to each individual, a "blind conviction" produced in each mind, or a "grounded conviction" produced in the mind by God's Spirit. Is the testimony revelation, ungrounded faith, or grounded faith? Taking up again his apologetic method, Warfield insists that it is a *grounded faith* that the Spirit gives. His witness within is not apart from the *indicia* (information, evidences) of Scripture's divinity. The faith he produces does not arise from nowhere but arises with and by means of the *indicia*. The Spirit of God attests to a divinity that is actually present in the Scriptures. His work "presupposes the objective revelation" and does not create a "new sense" in the person; rather, it "prepares the heart" by "restoring" to it a right spiritual sense "by which God is recognized in his Word." Although the Spirit's work is "equivalent to demonstration" in producing moral certitude, it is not so much of the nature of demonstration as it is *confirmation*. It is a restoring of that sense in man that enables him to "taste" the divinity of Scripture that is already present in them. There is nothing new given to Scripture; rather, there is a new recognition of it, "and of course recognition implies perception of *indicia*." The Spirit's work is one of persuasion and consists simply in enabling a recognition of this divinity that is objectively present but hidden because of the noetic effects of the fall. The Spirit does not add new evidence, and he does not attribute a divinity to Scripture that is not, in fact, present. Rather, the Holy Spirit works alongside the *indicia*, external and internal, to effect a grounded faith. Neither the Word nor the Spirit does this by itself. Writing of the role of miracles in Warfield's thought, Gerstner captures his thinking well: "Warfield of course recognized and emphasized the truth that the Holy Spirit must make the evidence appealing. . . . But it was 'evidence' that the Holy Spirit made appealing. . . . The internal testimony seals to the heart what external miracles [and *indicia* in whatever form] provide for the mind."[106]

---

[105] W, 5:70–83.

[106] W, 5:32–33, 84–90, 129–30; W, 10:74, 80; Gerstner, "Warfield's Case for Biblical Inerrancy," 124, 129. Warfield goes to pains to demonstrate that Calvin did not teach, as many have thought, that this testimony of the Spirit is apart from evidences. There is disagreement here as to the accuracy of Warfield's understanding of Calvin, but it falls outside our purpose here to explore the question at any length. Warfield himself,

Van den Belt helpfully observes that although the Greek word *autopistos* appears in Warfield only once, this should not be construed to mean that the notion was far from his mind. Warfield enthusiastically acknowledges the self-attesting nature of Scripture. But for him "the self-authenticating character of Scripture is related to the *testimonium*, because the *testimonium* renders the Scriptures self-authenticating for believers via the *indicia* of the divine origin of Scripture."[107] This summarizes Warfield's thinking well. In short, the *testimonium* provides no new information. And faith in the divinity of Scripture is not blind or without ground. Rather, the Spirit illumines the soul and enables it to perceive rightly the true character of Scripture, an objectively demonstrable supernatural character to which the natural man is otherwise blind.

Warfield characterizes Calvin's understanding of the *testimonium* similarly, that it is not in any sense a "third authority" in operation either apart from or in opposition to reason and the Scriptures. Rather, it is "a power of God clarifying reason in its use of the Scriptures and acting only confluently with them." As he summarizes, Calvin taught

> that the Spirit witnesses also to the divine origin and authority of Scripture in all its extent, through the noetic effects of His regenerating grace, by which the renewed spirit is enabled and led to perceive and estimate in their full validity the *indicia* of divinity in the Scriptures, and so to recognize the hand of God in the book of God.

Or again, "If he [Calvin] holds that the revelation of God is ineffective without the testimony of the Spirit, he holds equally that the testimony of the Spirit is inconceivable without the revelation of God in the Word."[108]

To the present day this position of Warfield on the relation of the *indicia* to the witness of the Spirit continues to attract debate and criticism. It seems to some that the important place Warfield allows the *indicia* is essentially Arminian. But this criticism overlooks two considerations. First, everywhere in his works Warfield emphasizes human inability and the utter necessity of divine initiative. This is in fact a favorite theme for Warfield, which he emphasizes with a deep sense of worshipful dependence in seemingly every connection—whether apologetic methodology, the nature and source of saving faith, the *testimonium*, or simply his expositions of related biblical passages. It would be an odd thing

---

however, is entirely convinced and argues the point in detail (*W*, 5:79–193); van den Belt, *Authority of Scripture*, 207–19.

[107] Van den Belt, *Authority of Scripture*, 216.

[108] *W*, 10:248, 234; *W*, 5:80–81; cf. *W*; 6:211–12.

indeed for a scholar of Warfield's stature to be so blind as to hold so vigorously a doctrine that fundamentally opposes another doctrine that he holds with at least equal vigor. In fact Warfield speaks to the question somewhat, first in his explication of the varying levels of faith. There is in every man an intuitive and unshakable "belief" in God. This *sensus deitatis* plays a foundational role in Warfield's apologetic, and he stresses repeatedly its significance in the religious understanding of every man. And in his apologetic task he seeks to build on this human faith in many ways. But never does he confuse it with but repeatedly and emphatically distinguishes it from saving faith that is only and always Spirit wrought. So also here in his understanding of the role of the *indicia*, while emphatically denying its ability to produce that certain conviction of the divinity of Scripture, he stresses that it is nonetheless conclusive and the means by which the Spirit gives faith.

More specifically, this criticism of Warfield overlooks his understanding of the nature of the *indicia* itself. At some points Warfield seems to understand the term in reference to all the external evidences of the divine origin of Scripture, whether historical or philosophical. But at other times, as his above reference to Calvin makes abundantly clear, Warfield understands by *indicia* simply Scripture itself and its own internal evidencing of divinity. That is, the *indicia* include the Scripture's own self-authentication already highlighted. As another example, Warfield writes that "the greater value of the witness of the Scriptures themselves, in form and contents, to their supernatural origin is affirmed and richly illustrated: *by the miracle of Scripture itself, it abundantly evidences itself to be the Word of God.*" This understanding of the Spirit's working by means of the *indicia* is nothing new to Reformed theology but is a familiar theme evident in Calvin himself.[109] There is nothing in Warfield's understanding of the role of the *indicia* that is self-contradictory or inconsistent with his cherished Reformed commitments.

God must persuade, and he does so in regeneration; but he does so by the use of means. The external evidences of the divine origin of Scripture are entirely conclusive. The internal testimony of the Scriptures themselves is conclusive also. But neither can remove the natural blindness over the heart of the lost. Warfield himself attempts endlessly to demonstrate the evidences for Scripture's divine origin. But he does so recognizing all the while that in the end that persuasion is something only God can effect.

---

[109] *W*, 6:211 (emphasis added). Man Chee Kwok provides a helpful discussion of this in his "Benjamin B. Warfield's Doctrine of Illumination in Light of Conservative Calvinistic Tradition" (PhD diss., Trinity International University, 1995), 212–42 (emphasis added).

Inspiration a Foundational Doctrine

Warfield does not argue that an inspired Bible is necessary to Christianity but frankly acknowledges, theoretically, that there could well be a Christian faith without it. Consistent with his own apologetic method, he argues that belief in the inspiration of Scripture comes logically not first but after other truths are established. Issues such as the existence of God, revelation, God's moral government, human accountability, the historical credibility of Scripture, and the divine origin of Christianity are all presupposed in the discussion of the nature and character of Scripture. In his joint article with Warfield, A. A. Hodge remarks similarly: "While the Inspiration of the Scriptures is true, and, being true, is a principle fundamental to the adequate interpretation of Scripture, it nevertheless is not in the first instance a principle fundamental to the truth of the Christian religion."[110] It is not quite accurate to say that the Christian faith rests on the doctrine of inspiration. It is an inspired and therefore trustworthy Bible that teaches our faith to us in a fully reliable way. But the Christian faith rests not on an inspired Bible but on the "previous fact" of divine revelation. Warfield continues:

> And it is important to keep ourselves reminded that the supernatural origin and contents of Christianity, not only may be vindicated apart from any question of the inspiration of the record, but, in point of fact, always are vindicated prior to any question of the inspiration of the record. We cannot raise the question whether God has given us an absolutely trustworthy record of the supernatural facts and teachings of Christianity, before we are assured that there are supernatural facts and teachings to be recorded. The fact that Christianity is a supernatural religion and the nature of Christianity as a supernatural religion, are matters of history; and are independent of any, and of every, theory of inspiration.[111]

Warfield admits, however, that this line of thinking is significant only to the Christian apologist. Whether inspiration is necessary to the Christian religion is not normally a question for the Christian. For the believer this doctrine is indeed foundational in virtually his entire faith. Every Christian's very "instinct" is that the validity of the church's doctrines all must rest on a reliable and authoritative revelation from God. This doctrine of the inspiration of Scripture has been held, therefore, with unique consistency and tenacity: the church has always instinctively felt that the trustworthiness of Scripture is fundamental, foundational to the entire system of Christian teachings. Apart from inspiration there is no sure

---

[110]W, I:209–11; SSW, 2:305, 540; Hodge and Warfield, Inspiration, 8–9.
[111]W, I:67.

reference point and therefore no well-grounded reason for the Christian hope or life. Without an inspired Bible the ground for any of Christianity's teachings is lost. Christians instinctively recognize the need for an external authority by which to measure their beliefs. And in that most important question of our standing before God, we recognize that we need more than inner light or impressions: we need a sure Word from God. We need from him a statement of his purpose of grace. To be assured of our safety beyond death, we need his own explicit assurance. For all this it is the church's instinct to look to Scripture, and indeed, this is what Scripture claims to provide for us. Here we learn of Christ, of God's grace, of faith, and of salvation. And so Warfield muses: Where would we be without an inspired Bible? Where would the church be? How would we have learned rightly of Christ? What a confused faith Christianity would be without an inspired guide. Though it is theoretically possible to have a genuine Christianity without an inspired book, the fact is, this is how Christianity has been given to us, and without that inspired Bible we would have no Christ, no salvation, and no hope. The church's instinctive appeal to Scripture for its faith is sound.[112]

> Wherever Christ is known through whatever means, there is Christianity, and men may hear and believe and be saved. But God has caused his grace to abound to us in that he not only published redemption through Christ in the world, but gave this preachment authoritative expression through the apostles, and fixed it with infallible trustworthiness in his inspired word. Thus in every age God speaks directly to every Christian heart, and gives us abounding safety to our feet and divine security to our souls. And thus, instead of a mere record of a revelation given in the past, we have the ever-living word of God; instead of a mere tradition however guarded, we have what we have all learned to call in a unique sense "the Scriptures."[113]

In this sense, at least, the inspiration of Scripture is a foundational doctrine. And in this sense Warfield can assert, "Apart from the revelation of God deposited for us in the Scriptures, there is no Christianity. Obliterate this revelation—theology may remain, but it is no longer a Christian theology; religion may remain, but it is no longer the Christian religion." As the revelation of God in Scripture is ignored, a purely natural religion is left to make its advance.[114]

By the same token, rejecting the verbal inspiration of Scripture would imply that any given teaching of the Bible may be safely neglected or repudiated. If Scripture is the word of men merely and not the word of God, then whatever value it may have, it cannot be trusted absolutely in any matter, even—or perhaps especially—

---

[112]W, 1:66–73.
[113]SSW, 2:541.
[114]SSW, 2:294–95.

of faith. "The authority which cannot assure of a hard fact is soon not trusted for a hard doctrine," and sooner or later the authority of Scripture will be retired in favor of that of human reason, or of "feelings," or of "Christian consciousness" and such. Without the doctrine of verbal inspiration not only will we have a very different Bible but—because we will then have to seek another basis for doctrine— we will have a very different theology altogether. The entire body of Christian teaching is bound up with the trustworthiness of Scripture.[115]

It should be mentioned at this juncture, at least in passing, that this redemptive purpose is what shapes Warfield's concern for biblical inspiration. It is true that this was not always the dominant note, for his own immediate context and purpose called him to argue on another level. But that this was Warfield's underlying concern is abundantly evident. Scripture, as all revelation, general and special, has a gracious and redemptive intent. The very need of special revelation lies in the first instance in our lostness: general revelation, valuable and necessary as it is, is not able to make one wise to salvation in Christ. For this, a word from God is required. Revelation—and inspiration, a specific mode of revelation—is itself a redemptive act, and if this revelation is marred, its saving value is diminished accordingly. As Warfield said in conclusion of his 1880 inaugural lecture, "Inspiration and Criticism," this saving revelation "is but half revelation unless it be infallibly communicated; it is but half communicated unless it be infallibly recorded." To which he solemnly added, "The heathen in their blindness are our witnesses of what becomes of an unrecorded revelation." Warfield believed that his day called for a clear defense of the integrity of Scripture, and so this is where he focused his treatment of the theme. But it is hardly accurate to charge that "the main problem with Warfield's procedure was that it tended to shift the focus of Scripture from Christ to the doctrine of inerrancy." This would be to overlook not only Warfield's context but also his own statements regarding the importance of the issue and the larger body of his writings in which the Christ-redemption theme remains paramount. For Warfield, inspiration touches the heart of what Christianity is—a redemptive religion. Inspiration is essential not as an abstract piece of theological data but because Scripture is given to tell us infallibly about Christ. "Let us bless God, then, for His inspired word! And may He grant that we may always cherish, love and venerate it, and conform all our life and thinking to it! So may we find safety for our feet, and peaceful security for our souls."[116]

---

[115]W, 1:51–52, 67, 181–82, 225–26.
[116]W, 1:424–25, 435; Robert James Hoefel, "The Doctrine of Inspiration in the Writings of James Orr and B. B. Warfield: A Study in Contrasting Approaches to Scripture" (PhD diss., Fuller Theological Seminary, 1983), 292.

Once more, given that the inspiration of Scripture is the clear and emphatic teaching of Christ and the apostles, this doctrine is bound up with their credibility. If, in fact, the Bible is not inspired, then Christ and his apostles are proved untrustworthy as teachers of religion altogether, and Scripture's claim to be the infallible guide in matters of faith is unfounded and misleading. And in this case, nothing the Bible teaches can be accepted with certainty. That is to say, if inspiration is disproved, we are left questioning not only the various doctrines of Scripture, but whether Scripture itself is an objective ground of faith. For Warfield it is all or nothing. Either Scripture is verbally inspired and therefore entirely truthful in all its parts, or we are left without a sure guide for faith and without a reliable Christ or apostolate. "We cannot modify the doctrine of plenary inspiration in any of its essential elements without undermining our confidence in the authority of the apostles as teachers of doctrine." This for Warfield is where the question rests and is ultimately settled. If the Bible is not verbally inspired, then Christ and his apostles were themselves deceived and have, in turn, misled us. This is "the real issue" and "the real problem of inspiration," and it renders the question to be of "infinite importance." If our Lord and the biblical writers "held and taught this doctrine, then this doctrine is true, and is to be accepted and acted upon as true by us all." At bottom, Warfield emphasizes, "We believe this doctrine of the plenary inspiration of the Scriptures primarily because it is the doctrine which Christ and his apostles believed, and which they have taught us."

> If we are to occupy the attitude towards Scripture which Christ occupied, the simple "It is written!" must have the same authority to us in matters of doctrinal truth, of practical duty, of historical fact and of verbal form that it had to Him: and to us as truly as to Him, the Scriptures must be incapable of being broken.[117]

To reject verbal inspiration is to repudiate our Lord and his apostles.

Warfield sees no way to escape this dilemma. We cannot pit Christ against the apostles, imagining as some have that although the apostles taught a high doctrine of inspiration, our Lord did not. As highlighted above, our Lord shared the view of his contemporaries and taught accordingly. And this Jesus who taught verbal inspiration is the Jesus we receive from the apostles. More to the point, it is Jesus himself who commissioned and endorsed these apostles (John 16:12–15), and therefore their authority is bound up with his: to reject them is to reject him. The critics cannot have it both ways: they cannot take the Christ given them by the apostles and then turn him against the apostles, and

---

[117]W, 1:73–74, 180–81, 186, 209; Hodge and Warfield, *Inspiration*, 34–35; cf. W, 10:124–27; SSW, 2:128, 635–36; W, 9:590; PRR 4, no. 15 (1893): 499.

they cannot take him and reject his endorsement of them. To accept either is to accept both. Nor is it possible to assume merely that Jesus and the apostles only accommodated the common understanding of the Jews of their day, for such an accommodation, in this case, would amount to deceptive and insincere adoption of what is, in fact (on this view), false teaching. Nor is it possible, as some have attempted, to draw a distinction between the belief and the teaching of the apostles on this matter and argue that although the New Testament writers did believe in verbal inspiration, they did not teach it—and that since they did not teach it, it is not a doctrine to be believed. Not only is it in this case impossible to empty formal statements on inspiration such as 2 Timothy 3:16 of their obvious didactic element; it is equally impossible to discern the beliefs of the apostles apart from their teaching. By means of what other source than their teaching could we possibly learn their beliefs on such matters? On what conceivable ground could such a distinction be made and held? Is it only what is dogmatically taught that is binding? And if so, how are such distinctions fairly to be made? It is impossible to take this course without undermining the apostles' credibility as reliable teachers of the faith. Finally, it is likewise impossible to establish "errors" in the Bible and then use them to correct its teaching of inspiration. If such errors can be established, we must choose between them and the Bible's teaching concerning its inspiration. We cannot have both. Again, for Warfield, it is all or nothing.[118]

Warfield confidently rests the question of inspiration on the reliability of Christ and the apostles as teachers of the faith. If the Scriptures are acknowledged to be even generally reliable, if the apostles are acknowledged to be even generally reliable, and if Christ is acknowledged to be even generally reliable, then we must take the next step and acknowledge with them their high doctrine of verbal inspiration. Only those who are willing to reject the authority of Christ and his apostles can refuse this doctrine. Thus, we believe this doctrine "because it is taught us as truth by Christ and his apostles." This, Warfield insists, is the real problem of inspiration: are Christ and his apostles reliable teachers or not.[119]

For these reasons Warfield considered the doctrine of verbal inspiration a foundational doctrine. Christianity is distinct as "a religion which has a book," a book by which it is formed and given its shape. And so he warned that the gravity of the controversy over this doctrine in his day "cannot be over-stated."[120] With this doctrine virtually everything else is at stake.

---

[118]*W*, 1:182–207.
[119]*W*, 1:207–14, 218, 225; *SSW*, 2:128.
[120]*SSW*, 2:537, 596.

Polemics: Inspiration and Criticism

THE RIGHT AND ROLE OF CRITICISM

Warfield remarks sarcastically that it is customary to spell *criticism* "with a big C, doubtless because it is 'Higher,'" and to champion "the right" of "Criticism," "with a certain air of conscious heroism," as though it "were being dreadfully opposed by somebody." His point is that no one would deny the right of criticism and that criticism is important in testing claims of truth. Indeed, when the book in question claims to be from God, critical inquiry is all the more important, for we would never want to cast our souls on untested or unproven assertions. "By all means let the doctrine of the Bible be tested by the facts and let the test be made all the more, not the less, stringent and penetrating because of the great issues that hang upon it."[121] So far from denying the right of criticism, Warfield sees it as a Christian responsibility.

Then why the fuss? Do both sides suddenly agree? The role of criticism consists, simply, in the "careful scrutiny of the facts," and this is a function Warfield championed. But criticism "is good or bad in proportion to the accuracy and completeness with which the facts are apprehended and collected, and the skill and soundness with which they are marshaled and their meaning read." That is to say, not all that is called criticism is worthy of the name—it must be thorough in its grasp of the facts, honest in following the evidence, and accurate in its analysis. The problem is not with criticism, per se. The problem arises when we confuse the right of criticism with the rightness of one's own criticism. "There is criticism and criticism," Warfield cautions. Critical scholars are not above bias, and the bias of the critics can easily skew their critical work such that its "findings" are simply not in keeping with the facts. So, for example, Karl Heinrich Graf (1815–1869) himself admitted the danger of circular argumentation in his theories. Warfield points out that to observe and expose such circular argumentation in those attempts to dislocate the Old Testament books from their apparent age and authors, is not to deny the right of criticism but simply to allow the facts, and not bias, to shape the conclusions. Similarly for New Testament studies, to begin with the assumption of the impossibility of the supernatural or miraculous and then to judge the New Testament accordingly is gratuitous. Of one such attempt Warfield writes pejoratively, "From the standpoint of reason, all this is very satisfying, provided it is useless; but unless one begins by denying that there is anything supernatural to explain, it does not explain anything." In such cases the critic

---

[121]*SSW*, 2:595–96; *W*, 1:172, 216.

inevitably presents a life of Jesus that is "clearly inconsistent in its every detail with the one document on which it is professedly founded." To expose such flaws in a critical method is not to deny criticism itself.[122]

While Warfield welcomes honest critical investigation, he also reminds the critic of the implications of his findings, specifically, implications of the testimony of Christ and the biblical writers in this regard. He emphatically will not allow the "mediating" view of many critics—that Scripture is inspired and trustworthy but only in specific matters of religion. This is impossible, Warfield insists, because the Scripture's religious claim is fully pervasive: Scripture in its every detail is inspired and therefore reliable. Such a claim has necessary implications and leaves us either to conclude that Scripture is, in fact, a reliable guide in teaching religion, or it is not. If its claim to infallibility is in fact false, then Scripture is discredited as a reliable guide even in religious matters. Similarly, if the trustworthiness of Christ as a teacher is curtailed in any degree, then we are not left with a teacher who is yet reliable in religious matters: he is discredited as the revelation of God he claims to be. We must be willing to acknowledge what is at stake. And so arguing within a "Christian" context, he feels free to turn the tables and argue that the onus lies on the critics and that "immense presumption" must meanwhile be given to inerrancy. Given that Jesus and his apostles so clearly taught biblical inspiration and infallibility, we in following them assume their reliability and therefore also assume the infallibility of Scripture. Warfield presses this with vigor and cautions that virtually everything is at stake in the question. If errors can be proved, then our Lord and his apostles are discredited as unreliable teachers of religion. The presumption is in favor of inerrancy. Even so, Warfield invites even the most stringent criticism, acknowledging that the question is too important to ignore uncritically. He concedes that there will be difficulties that must be faced. But he also insists that it is all or nothing—either our Lord was right as to biblical inspiration, or he himself is proven unreliable, in which case Christianity itself crumbles. And so, honest criticism must be welcomed. But we cannot fool ourselves—we must understand what is at stake.[123]

Moreover, once the critics hand Scripture back to us—this Scripture which they say is able still to teach us in matters of religion—"Which Jesus is it" they will give us? And what will he be allowed to teach? These questions inevitably reflect on the Lord Jesus himself, and the two issues—Jesus and the character of Scripture—are necessarily tied together.

---

[122]*SSW*, 2:596; *W*, 1:171; "Some Recent Apocryphal Gospels," *SPR* 35 (1884): 718–19, 724; *SSW*, 2:596–98.
[123]*W*, 1:214–26; *SSW*, 2:599–603.

The hardest thing to believe about the Bible, to our thinking, is that it can be a different kind of a book from what Jesus and His Apostles declare it to be. And the most difficult task we can conceive any one setting himself is that of holding to the Jesus of the Bible and at the same time not holding to the Bible of Jesus. It is a task we may feel sure has never been accomplished. He who no longer holds to the Bible of Jesus—the word of which cannot be broken—will be found on examination no longer to hold to the Jesus of the Bible. The new Bible he [the critic] has constructed for himself gives him a new Jesus, and his whole system of truth, brought into harmony with what he considers the spirit of this new Jesus, is eccentric to the system of truth which is taught us by the real Bible which is placed in our hands by the real Jesus, to whom it bears consentient witness.[124]

The critic seems to want to have his cake and eat it too, but Warfield will not allow it. Once again it is all or nothing.

THE CRITICS' BURDEN

In order to disprove the full verbal inspiration of Scripture, the critics have only a few options, Warfield argues. First, they might disprove the genuineness of the individual books of the Bible. This Warfield addresses in his discussions on canon, demonstrating that the various New Testament books were from the earliest times accepted as apostolic and thus divinely given. This need not detain us again here except to note in summary his contention:

The New Testament writings themselves bristle with the evidences that they expected and received a docile hearing; parties may have opposed them, but only parties. And again, all the evidence that exists coming down to us from the sub-apostolic church— be it more or less voluminous, yet such as it is admitted to be by the various schools of criticism—points to a very complete reception of the New Testament claims. No church writer of the time can be pointed out who made a distinction derogatory to the New Testament, between it and the Old Testament, the Divine authority of which latter, it is admitted, was fully recognized in the church. On the contrary, all of them treat the New Testament with the greatest respect, hold its teachings in the highest honor, and run the statement of their theology into its forms of words as if they held even the forms of its statements authoritative. They all know the difference between the authority exercised by the New Testament writers and that which they can lawfully claim. They even call the New Testament books, and that, as is now pretty well admitted, with the fullest meaning, "Scripture."[125]

---

[124] "'Sixty Years with the Bible': A Record of Drifting," *TBST* 12 (February 1910): 128. Cf. *W*, 10:125–26.
[125] *W*, 1:405–6.

Failing this option, the critic must prove that each alleged discrepant statement certainly occurred in the original autograph of the sacred book in which it is said to be found.

Second, it must be proved that the interpretation that occasions the apparent discrepancy is the one the passage intended to bear. It is not sufficient to show a difficulty that actually springs out of our defective knowledge of the circumstances. The true meaning must be definitely and certainly ascertained and then shown to be irreconcilable with other known truth. Or finally, it must be proved that, the true sense of some part of the original autograph is directly and necessarily inconsistent with some certainly known facts of history or truth of science, or some other statement of Scripture certainly ascertained and interpreted. Moreover, the alleged error must be one of substance—an untruth—and not merely a difference in style of thought or wording. Writers vary widely in their individual traits and modes of thought, expression, and argumentation. Stylistic differences do not constitute contradiction of truth or fact. Similarly, figures of speech, idioms, and accepted modes of expression that themselves may lack exactness do not preclude the truthfulness or accuracy of the ideas conveyed. Nor will it do to disprove authorship. Real error is what must be proved. This, Warfield vigorously contends, has never been done, and in defense of this conviction he is willing to take on all comers.[126]

SAMPLE POINTS OF ASSAULT

Historical and Geographical Accuracy

Although opponents of inspiration have argued that Scripture contains inaccuracies in historical and geographical details, Warfield eagerly points out that such allegations have become increasingly few with the advance of learning in these areas. As our confirmed knowledge of the biblical world increases, so also Scripture's accuracy is vindicated. He cites as an example Luke's supposed mistake in naming the fifteenth year of Tiberias as the beginning of John the Baptist's ministry (Luke 3:1). It is now widely understood that this date refers not to Tiberias's sole reign as Caesar but to his coregency with Augustus. Similarly, the allegation that Josephus disproves Luke regarding the time of the revolt of Theudas (Acts 5:36) depends on the assumption that the same Theudas is in view and, if so, that Josephus is a more reliable historian than Luke. Neither assumption, Warfield insists, can be sustained. There is no proven inaccuracy in Scripture here.[127]

---

[126]Hodge and Warfield, *Inspiration*, 36–38.
[127]Ibid., 45–46.

More criticism surrounds Luke's mention of the historical setting of Jesus' birth, for historians know nothing of a governorship of Cyrenius in Syria at that time or of a census under Augustus. Warfield responds that arguments from silence do not carry much weight and that in fact there is evidence that Cyrenius served twice in Syria, once within six months of the death of Herod. Further, Warfield argues that Luke does not say that Christ was born while Cyrenius was governor of Syria but that he was born during the census that was the first for Cyrenius to carry out: the census was begun under the previous governor and finished under Cyrenius.[128]

Concluding this discussion, Warfield surveys the many historical and geographical references in the New Testament, especially the book of Acts, and remarks that despite all the complexity of that historical setting, all testable references have been demonstrated to be accurate.[129]

Internal Inconsistencies

Another line of objection to inspiration alleges conflicting or otherwise inconsistent statements within the canon. Warfield mentions as an example the famous "sixth hour" of Jesus' crucifixion as per John's Gospel (John 19:14) as over against Mark's "third hour" (Mark 15:25). He notes that even more conservative writers such as Alford have conceded a contradiction here, but then he demonstrates that John and Mark simply employ differing modes of reckoning time. John follows the method common in Asia Minor, reckoning from midnight, and Mark the more typical Jewish method of reckoning from daybreak, or 6:00 AM. Hence, the supposed inconsistency vanishes.[130]

Warfield also takes up the question of internal consistency and the allegation that certain narrative events are inconsistent with related accounts elsewhere in the canon. The first concerns the narrative of events surrounding Jesus' birth in Matthew and Luke. Warfield insists that the respective accounts are not contradictory but "mutually supplementary," and in a lengthy footnote he lists in order the full series of events from the two accounts, demonstrating that Matthew and Luke are indeed consistent with one another. The other alleged inconsistency that Warfield takes up concerns Paul's visits to Jerusalem and his interactions with the apostles as recorded in Acts and Galatians. Here Warfield begins his defense by citing one critic who himself acknowledges that the allegation of contradiction between Luke and Paul is grounded in biased eisegesis. Consideration must be

---

[128]Ibid., 46–50.
[129]Ibid., 50–54.
[130]Ibid., 54–57; cf. "*Andover Review*'s Logic and Hermeneutics," *Herald and Presbyter* 45, no. 2 (1884): 2.

given to the fact that in Galatians, Paul does not profess to provide an exhaustive narrative of all his visits to Jerusalem, but he tells only of his opportunities there to learn from the apostles. Further, in varying contexts Paul uses the term "apostle" in its narrower (Gal. 1:19) and wider senses (Acts 9:27; cf. Acts 14:4, 14). Factors such as these, if conveniently overlooked, present an illusion of inconsistency where in fact no disharmony exists.[131]

The New Testament Use of the Old Testament and Septuagint

The argument has been made against inspiration that New Testament citations of the Old Testament are often incorrect, often from the Septuagint rather than the Hebrew, and sometimes from neither. These quotations are often not quotations at all, strictly speaking, but loose paraphrases. Some critics have made much of this, alleging that these misquotations of Scripture constitute errors on the part of the New Testament authors.

This argument was answered long before Warfield's time, and so he describes it as rising "from the waste basket of the past" and expresses surprise that it should be brought up again after having been so thoroughly discredited. Specifically, this argument is grounded in a misunderstanding of the doctrine of inspiration. Nowhere is the doctrine understood to require exact citations of other passages from inspired Scripture, much less to disallow faithful translation. Verbal inspiration ensures real inerrancy but not verbal exactness in quotation. In fact it is easy to show that in each New Testament citation from the Old the sense of the passage in question is conveyed, whether or not the citation is given verbatim. The New Testament writers in their paraphrasing of the Old Testament never falsify passages or use them for unwarranted purposes. Thus Warfield dismisses this argument against verbal inspiration as of no consequence. No one anywhere holds to the doctrine of inspiration addressed by this argument, and it seems to have been born less from the merits of the case than from the desperation of those who would discredit inspiration at any cost.[132]

The Bible a Human Book

Warfield complains of the increasingly frequent mischaracterization of Scripture in his day that so stressed the human origin of the Bible, its divine origin was relegated to insignificance if not altogether forgotten. Human beings were said to be incapable of conveying a pure word from God. For critics the mere evidence

---

[131]Hodge and Warfield, *Inspiration*, 57–61.
[132]Ibid., 62–70; *SSW*, 2:549–59.

of individual personal traits among the authors of Scripture demonstrates a humanity that is manifestly given to error.[133]

Warfield replies, first, that this constitutes a complete misrepresentation of the biblical doctrine of inspiration, "the core" of which is "the assertion of the coactivity of both the human and divine authors in the production of Scripture." He therefore warns that we must not exaggerate either side: Scripture is both thoroughly human and thoroughly divine. "It is all human—every word, and all divine." Some in the history of the church have overstressed the divinity of Scripture in the theory of mechanical dictation. But the human authors of Scripture were not merely the pens but the penmen of the Holy Spirit. Although few still hold this view, many are advancing the opposite error, overstressing Scripture's human authorship and thereby deprecating its trustworthiness. Warfield stresses in response that it is indisputable that men as men wrote the Bible: their individual personalities and traits are evident throughout. But if human authorship were to presuppose error, it would preclude the Bible's divine authorship, which is also evident throughout. The Bible's own claim is that it is *both* a human and a divine book, and neither aspect can be pressed to the exclusion of the other. The divine and human aspects of Scripture are not incompatible or opposing elements in conflict. Nor can we sort through Scripture and divide the human element from the divine. Rather, both are evident throughout the entire fabric of Scripture. Holy men of God spoke and wrote out of their own experiences and abilities, yet they did so only as they were carried along by the Spirit of God. The two aspects work together continuously, never excluding the other. In the biblical conception neither is denied, but full justice is given to both, and this to every word of Scripture.

> God did not give us these books, as he gave Moses the Ten Words, written without human intermediation, by his own finger, on the tables of stone. He gave them not only by, but through men. They are the Oracles of God, and every word of them is a word of God. But they are also the writings of men, and every word of them is a word of man. By a perfect confluence of the divine and human, the one word is at once all divine and all human.

Echoing B. F. Westcott, Warfield summarizes that as Scripture is the word of God, it is authoritative, and as it is the word of man, it is intelligible. "Because it is the

---

[133]See especially his "Review of Three Books on Inspiration," in *SSW*, 2:604–13; cf. *W*, 1:102; *SSW*, 2:543–48.

word of man in every part and element, it comes home to our hearts. Because it is the word of God in every part and element, it is our constant law and guide."[134]

Furthermore, Warfield argues that the all-pervasive divinity *and* humanity of Scripture rests on the all-pervasiveness of God's providence. The production of the Scriptures involved divine activity not only at the point of their writing but in all events prior. God prepared men for the task he would assign them, carefully bringing to them every experience necessary for the production of the word he would give them. Just as a stained-glass window may be designed by its architect for the express purpose of flooding the cathedral with the precise tone and quality of light that it is to receive, so God prepared the writers of Scripture, throughout the whole of their lives, so that when his word was given to them, they were capable of conveying it faithfully and accurately. Humanness does not necessitate error: God whose providence is over all was at work in all things beforehand and during the whole process of Scripture's production so that in the end it was his word given through men.[135]

Finally, in their joint article on inspiration, Hodge and Warfield specifically affirm the possibility of formal inaccuracies due to idiomatic conventions and even limited understanding. But they insist that such matters do not impinge on the claims of inspiration.

> [The Scriptures] are written in human languages, whose words, inflections, construc-
> tions and idioms bear everywhere indelible traces of error. The record itself furnishes
> evidence that the writers were in large measure dependent for their knowledge upon
> sources and methods in themselves fallible, and that their personal knowledge and
> judgments were in many matters hesitating and defective, or even wrong.[136]

This specific passage was written by Hodge and was afterward condemned by James Brookes in *Truth* as surrendering the doctrine of inerrancy. Warfield writes in response that Brookes has completely misunderstood the matter. Inspiration (or inerrancy) makes no claim of omniscience or personal infallibility on the part of the biblical writers. Nor does it preclude grammatical error or inexactness of speech. It simply ensures truth in what is affirmed. If Paul's "all the world" (Rom. 1:8) is proved to mean, merely, "the Roman world," the apostle is not thereby proved to be in error. Similar explanations should be given in respect to idiomatic expressions reflecting a formally incorrect cosmology (Eph. 4:26).[137] But these

---

[134]*SSW*, 2:15, 543–48, 604–12; *W*, 1:398–99.
[135]*SSW*, 1:111–13; *SSW*, 2:615; *W*, 1:101–2, 108.
[136]Hodge and Warfield, *Inspiration*, 28.
[137]*Truth* 8 (1882): 490–95; *Truth* 9 (1882): 124–29; reprinted in Hodge and Warfield, *Inspiration*, 43, 77–82. Also *W*, 1:196–97.

matters do not touch the claims of inspiration. Allowing all personal traits as well as personal ignorance and fallibility, inspiration precludes falsehood and error and ensures the truth of all that is affirmed. Scripture is fully human, but it is also fully divine.

Autographs Only

Warfield acknowledges the jeers of the critics against the claim that inspiration applies only to the autographs "which no living man has ever seen," but he is unmoved by this complaint. First, he argues that on no other ground could a doctrine of inspiration be maintained. The Bible as we have it is, simply, the original plus the errors that have crept into the text since. However striking has been the degree of providence in the preservation of the text, no one would advocate the immediate inspiration of the copies. And if we cannot advocate the inspiration either of the autographs because they do not exist or of the copies because they are so obviously not inspired, then we are left without any doctrine of inspiration whatever, and the biblical teaching is evacuated of all meaning. By the nature of the case, the discussion of inspiration concerns the autographs.[138]

Moreover, Warfield had great confidence in God's providential preservation of the biblical text. Having produced early in his career (1886) the first American textbook on New Testament textual criticism, *An Introduction to the Textual Criticism of the New Testament*, he established himself as an authority in textual issues and maintained that the relatively few variants that have crept in are virtually all without determinative theological significance, and most all are easily discernable by means of critical examination; that is, for all practical purposes the original is recoverable.

> The inerrant autographs were a fact once; they may possibly be a fact again, when textual criticism has said its last word on the Bible text. In proportion as they are approached in the processes of textual criticism, do we have an ever better and better Bible than the one we have now. . . . We already have practically the autographic text in the New Testament in nine hundred and ninety-nine words out of every thousand.[139]

Or again,

> If our controversial brethren could only disabuse their minds of the phantom of an autographic *codex*, which their excitement has raised (and which, apart

---

[138]*SSW*, 2:582–84; cf. 588–94.
[139]*SSW*, 2:557–58. See also *ITCNT*, 12–15; also Warfield's review of *The Greek Testament of Westcott and Hort*, *PR* 3, no. 10 (1882): 356; and *SSW*, 2:589.

from their excited vision "no living man has ever seen"), they might possibly see with the Church that genuine text of Scripture which is "by the singular care and providence of God" still preserved to us, and might agree with the Church that it is to it alone that authority and trustworthiness and utter truthfulness are to be ascribed.[140]

The critics' jeers overstate the case: we do have access to the original in most every disputed case. The nonexistence of the autographs does not in any way do harm to the doctrine of verbal inspiration.

Finally, in response to those who allege that this doctrine of inspired autographs only is new, Warfield marshals support from Richard Baxter, John Calvin, Martin Luther, John Lightfoot, Samuel Rutherford, and the Westminster Assembly.[141]

Circular Reasoning?

Warfield acknowledges that the doctrine of inspiration must rest primarily on the claims of the sacred writers. By the very nature of the case, the biblical writers themselves "are the prime witnesses of the fact and nature of their inspiration." This claim, in turn, was affirmed by their contemporaries. But to the critics who charge that it is circular reasoning to ground the doctrine of inspiration in the Bible's own claim, Warfield responds that they have misrepresented the case. In keeping with his apologetic method he argues that the question of inspiration rests first not on Scripture's own claims but on the previously established fact of its general trustworthiness as a theological guide. This previous fact is established in discussion of the general evidences for Christianity, and only then can the Scriptures address the question of its inspiration. Scripture comes to us only after theism has been established, and then the reality of divine revelation, and the authenticity and historical credibility of Scripture, and then the divine origin and character of the religion they present, and then the general reliability of their presentation of it. Only after all this can its claim to inspiration be taken as ground of the doctrine. But once Scripture is established as a reliable guide in Christian doctrine, then its claim to inspiration must be accepted just as its teachings on any other doctrine. Carl Henry summarizes it well: "For Warfield, the doctrine of plenary inspiration rests logically on the authority of Scripture, and not vice versa." It is indisputable that the Bible does, in fact, claim for itself divine inspiration. And once even a general reliability is attributed to it as a doctrinal guide, we are forced to accept this claim it makes for itself. When these claims

---

[140]*SSW*, 2:584.
[141]*SSW*, 2:569, 585–87, 588–94.

are tested, and contradictory evidence remains absent, the claim is verified still further. This reasoning is not circular.[142]

This is Warfield's formal answer to the question of circular reasoning. But elsewhere he argues along two additional lines. First, as discussed above, in the miracles marking the apostles' credentials, God has given us objective demonstration of his endorsement of their teaching, whether oral or written. It is on this ground that many of their contemporaries, in fact, acknowledged their divine authority (Heb. 2:3–4). With this supernatural endorsement necessarily comes God's own stamp of approval on what they have written. Warfield does not pursue this line of argument at great length in this context, but he does insist on it.[143]

More to the point, Warfield argues that the ultimate ground of our doctrine of inspiration is the authority of Christ. On any accounting it is undeniable that our Lord believed and taught this doctrine, and it comes to us from him.

> This, then, is the real question involved, and it is far from a small one: . . . Is the Bible authoritative as a teacher of doctrine? It cuts even deeper than that, and takes the form, Is Christ authoritative? For, seek to soften the statement of the matter as we will; say, with Schultz, that Christ held this doctrine of Scripture only as "a pious intuition," and not in the form of "a scholastic theory"; the fact remains that it was Jesus' conception of the nature of Scripture. What are we to do with Jesus?

Similarly, "We believe this doctrine of the plenary inspiration of the Scriptures primarily because it is the doctrine which Christ and his apostles believed, and which they have taught us." And again:

> If we accept the full authority of Christ and his apostles in all things, we must accept the infallible Bible at their hands. . . . If we are to occupy the attitude towards Scripture which Christ occupied, the simple "It is written!" must have the same authority to us in matters of doctrinal truth, of practical duty, of historical fact and of verbal form that it had to Him: and to us as truly as to Him, the Scriptures must be incapable of being broken.

It would be impossible for a Christian to hold to the Jesus of the Bible without also holding to the Bible of Jesus. To reject this doctrine is to reject Christ. But those who regard the authority of Christ as supreme will accept this doctrine also. For Warfield, this doctrine is settled for us by lordship. The word and reliability of

[142]W, 1:399–401; SSW, 2:632–64; Carl F. H. Henry, God, Revelation and Authority, vol. 4, God Who Speaks and Shows (Waco, TX: Word Books, 1979), 69.
[143]W, 1:47, 435; Hodge and Warfield, Inspiration, 29; CM, 21, 24–25; "Miracle," in Davis Bible Dictionary (Philadelphia: Westminster Press, 1917), 505; "The Christian Doctrine of Revelation," The New York Observer 73 (July 4, 1895): 4–5.

Christ are at stake in the question, for it is on his authoritative teaching on the subject that the doctrine rests.[144]

All these considerations combine to form the ground of our doctrine of inspiration, and by them the charge of circular reasoning is discarded.

SUMMARY OBSERVATIONS

Throughout his career Warfield gave himself to defending Scripture's claim to verbal inspiration. He acknowledged that difficulties present themselves from time to time to the doctrine, but he advised that we should expect this. There are difficulties in the way of believing anything—that God is, that Christ is God's Son, even that we ourselves truly exist. Many in giving attention to such questions have been perplexed at times. And it would be a strange thing if there were no difficulties in the way of our doctrine of inspiration. We expect difficulty in any area of faith. We surely cannot wait to believe a doctrine until all its difficulties are cleared away. How then could a Christian believe that God is three in one or that Christ is both human and divine? How then could a Christian believe in the predestination of the acts of free human agents? The question is not whether the doctrine of plenary inspiration faces certain difficulties. The question is whether the church and the apostles and Christ himself were all deceived in their understanding of Scripture as from God. This is the point at issue. At bottom, Warfield emphasizes, "We believe this doctrine of the plenary inspiration of the Scriptures primarily because it is the doctrine which Christ and his apostles believed, and which they have taught us." To reject verbal inspiration is to reject our Lord and his apostles, and the difficulty of rejecting them is much greater than any "difficulty" that presents itself to the truthfulness of Scripture. "It may sometimes seem difficult to take our stand frankly by the side of Christ and his apostles," Warfield acknowledges. But he adds, "It will always be found safe."[145]

Mere difficulties are not the final obstacle, and what is important to Warfield is that there has never been a *proven* error in Scripture. After examining the various attempts of the critics to discredit the full verbal inspiration of Scripture, Warfield confidently concludes that "modern biblical criticism has nothing valid to urge against the church doctrine of verbal inspiration, but that on the contrary it puts that doctrine on a new and firmer basis and secures to the church Scriptures which are truly divine."[146] So far from fearing criticism, Warfield invites

---

[144]*CT* 11 (1893–1894): 219; *W*, 1:73–74, 186–89; *PRR* 4, no. 15 (1893): 499; *SSW*, 2:635; *TBS* 12 (February 1910): 128.
[145]*W*, 1:73–74, 215–16, 421–23; cf. 180.
[146]*W*, 1:424.

it, assured that precisely because Scripture is God's word, it will always stand vindicated as such.

> The legitimate proofs of the doctrine, resting primarily on the claims of the sacred writers, having not been rebutted by valid objections, that doctrine stands doubly proved. Gnosis gives place to epignosis, faith to rational conviction, and we rest in the joyful and unshaken certainty that we possess a Bible written by the hands of men indeed, but also graven with the finger of God.[147]

---

[147]Hodge and Warfield, *Inspiration*, 70–71.

[God] tells us that he is a spirit, infinite, eternal and unchangeable in his being and attributes; and we hear the words with wonder, and our hearts go forth in praise; but we cannot comprehend them. He tells us that, though one and simple in nature, he exists in three persons, the same in substance, equal in power and glory— distinct and yet the same; not three Gods, but one God, and yet three persons, with one will, one thought, one purpose, and yet so separate that one can love and send another forth from himself, and each can say "I" and "Thou" and "He." Such are the mysteries of his being.

From Warfield's earliest-known sermon,
delivered Sunday, July 23, 1876,
First Presbyterian Church of Dayton, Ohio,
The Daily Dayton Democrat, July 25, 1876, 4.

Brief Survey of the Biblical Revelation of God

The Trinity

Predestination, Providence, and the Divine Decree

5

THEOLOGY PROPER

Brief Survey of the Biblical Revelation of God

Warfield nowhere provides extended exposition of the nature, character, and attributes of God. But on several occasions he provides a brief summary, in broadest strokes, of his understanding of what God has progressively revealed concerning himself, and a survey of this may serve well as our starting point.[1] God has made himself known first of all in general revelation, the created order and the consciousness of man made in his image. Here he displays his existence and such attributes as his self-existence, eternality, independence, unity, uniqueness, wisdom, power, and justice—"God the infinite Spirit" and "perfect Being" who stands as the cause of all that is and the One to whom all his moral creatures are responsible and on whom they are dependent. Of all this, men are "intuitively" and "unavoidably" aware. God's self-revelation in the created order and in the consciousness of man pales, however, in comparison to that supreme revelation of himself in his Word, Scripture, which Warfield is happy to refer to as "special" revelation. Warfield prefers to survey this biblical presentation of God along redemptive-historical lines and in fact insists at several points that this was God's own intention in his self-revelation. That is to say, it was only in the outworking of his redemptive purpose that God progressively revealed himself in his fulness.[2]

In the Old Testament such matters as God's existence and nature are not open to question. Nor is there question as to the accessibility of knowledge of him. God has made himself known to his people, and their business is not fumblingly to seek for him but to believe him and obey him as he has revealed himself to them. That is to say, "the fundamental note" of the Old Testament is *revelation*. It is not Israel's notions of God that the Old Testament displays but God's own self-revelation to Israel. Central to God's self-revelation is his *unity* (Deut. 6:4): he is

---

[1] See "God," "Godhead," and "The God of Israel." This section highlights these summaries, serving as a transition to Warfield's more extended treatment of God as Trinity.
[2] See especially *SSW*, 1:69–74, 82–87; *W*, 2:133–72.

one, and he is the only one. Within this emphasis of God's unity his *personality* or personhood lies at the heart.

> Over against themselves he stood, another Self, capable of communion with them as Person with persons; talking with them, concerning himself for them, showing himself their friend. They met with him walking in the garden in the cool of the day; they talked with him in the door of the tent; they reasoned with him and were sure he was open to their appeal. They looked to him to act, as persons do, under the influence of motives, and to be governed, as persons are, by rational consideration.[3]

Moreover, God is a *uniquely majestic* person, and Israel was taught to think of him with "intense reverence" (1 Sam. 6:20; Ex. 15:11). "The sense of the uniqueness of God was as strong in Israel as the sense of his unity. As he alone was God, there was none like him." To impress this upon the minds of his people, God forbade Israel from making any representation of him: he is a person, but not a person among other persons; he is the only one of his kind, infinitely exalted above all other persons and "immeasurably removed from all the weaknesses which belong to humanity."[4]

Further, in this divine self-disclosure God's *almighty power* formed a chief element of his incomparable glory. Indeed, Warfield stresses that God's personality and might are "the two most persistently emphasized elements" of the Old Testament conception of him. He is a person and thus acts always with purpose; and he is all-powerful, and thus his purpose cannot be frustrated. He is the Creator and Sustainer of all that is, the One who can do all his will and "the free determiner of all that comes to pass." This conception of God is prominent throughout the Old Testament narrative and in the names given him from the beginning—*El, Eloah, Elohim, El Shaddai*. But God's greatness is not displayed in his omnipotence alone. His is not bare power. He is *holy* and *righteous* also, exalted above all, and always and only acting as consistent with his person, doing only what is right. Evil he will "unfailingly rebuke." Yet his righteousness is not harsh—God is also *loving* and *good* (Ex. 34:6). "The God of Israel was not only a God who commanded and saw to it that he was obeyed. He was a God who loved and attracted love."[5]

That is to say, God revealed himself to Israel as a God of *grace*, "and it is here that we at last reach the real heart of the revelation of God to Israel." He, the great God over all, is Israel's Redeemer. He will himself visit his people with salvation

[3]*SSW*, 1:83–84; *W*, 2:7–8.
[4]*SSW*, 1:83–84.
[5]*SSW*, 1:85–86; *W*, 1:7–8.

from sin. In grace God calls even to the nations, "Look to me and be saved, for I am God, and there is no other" (Isa. 45:22).[6]

That this coming of God in redemption was to be identified with the coming of the anointed King and the Suffering Servant was not (in the Old Testament) revealed with great clarity. This further revelation awaited the saving event itself, when God revealed himself in supreme grace, rescuing sinners by bearing in his own person the penalty of their sin, in their place. Only in the New Testament, in the outworking of his saving purpose, does God plainly reveal himself as Father, Son, and Spirit—three in one.[7]

The Trinity

Trinitarian concerns loom large in Warfield.[8] Arguably, he is first and foremost a "christologian," but as an heir of the best of Reformed orthodoxy he manifests throughout his works an enthusiastic and robust Trinitarianism. He acknowledges his indebtedness to Tertullian, Augustine, Nicea, Calvin, and the Puritans, but Warfield's work on the Trinity is no mere rehash of what was offered before him. Both in method of exposition and in substance Warfield offers substantive contribution to the discussion.

BIBLICAL APPROACH: THE REVELATION OF THE TRINITY

Progressive Revelation

The common approach to the doctrine of the Trinity involves a successive examination of the following propositions: (1) There is but one God (Deut. 6:4; Isa. 44:6; 1 Cor. 8:4; James 2:19); (2) the Father is God (Matt. 11:25; John 6:27; 8:41; Rom. 15:6; 1 Cor. 8:6), the Son is God (John 1:1, 18; 20:28; Acts 20:28; Rom. 9:5; Heb. 1:8; Col. 2:9; Phil. 2:6; 2 Pet. 1:1), and the Spirit is God (Acts 5:3–4; 1 Cor. 2:10–11; Eph. 2:22); (3) the Father, Son, and Holy Spirit are distinct persons (John 15:26; 16:13–14; 17:1, 8, 18, 23). This traditional approach, found with slight variations in the standard theological texts, is useful for Warfield, and he summarizes it at various points.[9] Otherwise

---

[6]*SSW*, 1:86–87.

[7]*SSW*, 1:70–73, 86–87; *W*, 2:144.

[8]Warfield's primary writings treating Trinitarian themes include the following: "The Biblical Doctrine of the Trinity," in *W*, 2:133–72; "Tertullian and the Beginnings of the Doctrine of the Trinity," in *W*, 2:3–109; "Calvin's Doctrine of the Trinity," in *W*, 5:189–284; "God," in *SSW*, 1:69–74; "Antitrinitarianism," in *W*, 5:88–92; "God Our Father and the Lord Jesus Christ," in *W*, 2:213–31; "The Divine Messiah in the Old Testament," in *W*, 3:3–49; and *The Lord of Glory*; also numerous other articles and sermons on the person of Christ and of the Holy Spirit.

[9]*SSW*, 1:73; cf. *W*, 2:146–47.

he gives comparatively little attention to these propositions. For Warfield, the Trinity is a mysterious truth about God progressively revealed in connection with his unfolding saving purpose. The full benefit of the doctrine is found not in a systematic presentation of its static, constituent elements but in observing its unfolding revelation throughout gospel history. Accordingly, Warfield's primary method of treating this doctrine is exegetical and redemptive-historical.

Warfield takes this approach in his article titled "God," written for *A Dictionary of the Bible* (1898), which was edited by his Princeton colleague John D. Davis, professor of Oriental and Old Testament literature; but there Warfield states his case only concisely and in broad strokes. It is spelled out more fully in his article "Trinity," written originally for *The International Standard Bible Encyclopedia* (1915), edited by James Orr.

Warfield emphasizes that the doctrine of the Trinity is purely revealed truth. It is a truth about God that is neither discovered nor discoverable by natural reason. Nor is it provable by human reason. Nor are there any analogies to it in nature or even man himself, who is created in God's image. "In His trinitarian mode of being, God is unique; and, as there is nothing in the universe like Him in this respect, so there is nothing which can help us to comprehend Him."[10] This truth we know solely on the grounds of divine self-disclosure.

Warfield rehearses the attempts of theological worthies of the past, including Jonathan Edwards (1703–1758), to establish God's tri-unity on rational grounds. But Warfield concludes that they all have failed to achieve their goal. Their contributions at best lend rational "support" to the doctrine and are of value only "once that doctrine has been given us." These attempts are an aid to our understanding once the truth itself is conceived. Indeed, they enrich our understanding of God and prove very satisfying to the believing human mind.

> Difficult, therefore, as the idea of the Trinity in itself is, it does not come to us as an added burden upon our intelligence; it brings us rather the solution of the deepest and most persistent difficulties in our conception of God as infinite moral Being, and illuminates, enriches and elevates all our thought of God. It has accordingly become a commonplace to say that Christian theism is the only stable theism. That is as much as to say that theism requires the enriching conception of the Trinity to give it a permanent hold upon the human mind—the mind finds it difficult to rest in the idea of an abstract unity for its God; and that the human heart cries out for the living God in whose Being there is that fulness of life for which the conception of the Trinity alone provides.

---

[10] W, 2:135.

But for the establishing of this doctrine and for its demonstrable proof, only divine revelation will do.[11]

Further, God's tri-unity is not evident merely on the plane of general revelation. This "ineffable truth" requires special revelation. General revelation teaches us that God is, and it teaches us many of his necessary attributes, such as his power and glory. But to know this high truth requires more specific and more detailed information than is available in the created order generally.

Moreover, if God is triune, we would expect to see at least hints of this even in his Old Testament self-disclosure. "It is a plain matter of fact that none who have depended on the revelation embodied in the Old Testament alone have ever attained to the doctrine of the Trinity." But for one "already acquainted with the doctrine," it is entirely reasonable to expect to find indications of it in that older revelation. Warfield briefly summarizes the Old Testament Trinitarian evidences found commonly in the standard theological works: the plural form of the divine name, the use of plural pronouns and plural verbs in reference to God, those passages which seem to distinguish between God and God, the threefold liturgical formulas, the personification of the Wisdom and Word and Spirit of God, and the "remarkable phenomena" connected with the appearances of the angel of Jehovah.[12] In light of all these factors, Warfield argues that

> the Trinitarian interpretation remains the most natural one. This is not an illegitimate reading of the New Testament ideas back into the text of the Old Testament; it is only reading the text of the Old Testament under the illumination of the New Testament revelation. The Old Testament may be likened to a chamber richly furnished but dimly lighted; the introduction of light brings into it nothing which was not in it before; but it brings out into clearer view much of what is in it but was only dimly or even not at all perceived before. The mystery of the Trinity is not revealed in the Old Testament; but the mystery of the Trinity underlies the Old Testament revelation, and here and there almost comes into view.[13]

In his major article on the Trinity in *The International Standard Bible Encyclopedia*, Warfield gives only this passing attention to the Old Testament evidence for the doctrine. He acknowledges that all this remains inconclusive and cannot by itself establish firmly the doctrine of the Trinity. God's tri-unity is a "purely Christian doctrine." The Old Testament reflects the doctrine more clearly revealed by the New Testament writers, but it does not establish it on its own. However, in separate articles Warfield discusses the Old Testament teaching regarding the

---

[11] *W*, 2:135–39.
[12] *W*, 2:140–41.
[13] *W*, 2:141–42.

deity of the Messiah and the deity and distinct personality of the Holy Spirit, essays in which he lays out impressively the basic evidence for Trinitarianism provided in the Old Testament Scriptures. But he cautions that an understanding of the deity of the Messiah did not immediately necessitate an understanding of a multiplicity in the unity of the Godhead: it quite evidently did not. In fact, "In the history of doctrine the conviction of the Deity of Christ was the condition, not the result, of the formulation of the doctrine of the Trinity." Nevertheless, the Old Testament's presentation of the Messiah as a divine person clearly lays the groundwork for the doctrine of the Trinity. Similarly, the portrayal of the Holy Spirit as the transcendent God and yet immanent and sent from God "prepares the way for His hypostatizing and so for the Christian doctrine of the Trinity." Again, if the Old Testament does not by itself provide unmistakably a clear Trinitarianism, it does "tend" and "hint" toward it continuously in such a way that once the New Testament light is shed on it, Trinitarian conclusions very naturally emerge.[14]

Still Warfield observes that when we approach the New Testament, we cannot but notice that its inspired writers speak more freely and unguardedly of the one God as Father, Son, and Spirit. What was latent and scarcely discernable in the Old Testament becomes patent in the New Testament. The New Testament writers betray no sense of caution, no hint that they are presenting any new truth, much less a new god or two new gods. Their monotheism is intense (John 5:44; 17:3; 1 Tim. 1:17; 2:5; 6:15). They worship and proclaim the God of Israel, and their insistence on the unity of this God is at least as strong as that of the older prophets. And yet when they proclaim this same Jehovah as Father, Son, and Spirit, there is clearly no lurking suspicion on their part that they are making some new innovation. They freely apply Old Testament passages equally to Father, Son, and Spirit and feel no distance between themselves and their Jewish forebears. "The God of the Old Testament was their God, and their God was a Trinity; and their sense of the identity of the two was so complete that no question as to it was raised in their minds."[15]

This simple confidence on the part of the New Testament writers is significant. If they feel no sense of novelty in speaking of this one God in three persons, it is at least in part because this was, in fact, *not* a new doctrine to them or to those who heard them. We witness in the New Testament writings, in other words, not the "birth of a new conception of God" but a "firmly established conception of God underlying and giving its tone to the whole fabric." This explains why in the New Testament we do not find the doctrine of the Trinity established merely

---

[14] W, 3:3–49; W, 2:101–29; SSW, 1:88; SSW, 2:711–17.
[15] W, 2:143; cf. 102–3.

by select verses here or there; rather, we find a document and a community that are Trinitarian to the core. God's tri-unity is presupposed throughout. Allusions meet us without controversy at every turn, allusions that reveal a commonality and a familiarity with this doctrine on all Christian sides. From the earliest New Testament writings to the last, religious adoration and worship is freely given to one God and yet to three persons. "The doctrine of the Trinity does not appear in the New Testament in the making, but as already made."[16] Just as this truth was not revealed but only alluded to in the Old Testament, so it is established by allusion in the New Testament, even if these allusions are clearer and more frequent. But it is not a doctrine taught, so much as it is a doctrine presupposed and already universally accepted in the Christian community.

It is important for Warfield, for polemic reasons, to establish that Trinitarianism was part and parcel of the theological consciousness of the primitive church. In his day Ritschlianism—most prominently via Harnack in Europe and McGiffert in America—argued influentially that primitive Christianity was an undogmatic Christianity, without such notions as authority and doctrine. But Christianity soon began to undergo change until the fifth century, by which time it became a dogmatic and philosophical religion. Trinitarian and incarnational theology were the result of pagan Greek philosophical thought in contrast to the simple ethical religion of Jesus and the early church. The original church, so it was argued, knew nothing of such metaphysical dogmas. Warfield saw all this as striking at Christianity's heart and as threatening its very character as a redemptive religion, and it was important to him to demonstrate that the notion of plurality in unity—Trinitarianism—was already the settled, common faith of the aboriginal church, even if that common faith had not yet achieved formal statement.[17]

Warfield develops this notion in detail in his "God Our Father and the Lord Jesus Christ," in which he examines that phrase and its slight variations as they appear in Paul's epistles (1 Thess. 1:1; 2 Thess. 1:1–2; Gal. 1:1, 3; 1 Cor. 1:3; 2 Cor. 1:2; Rom. 1:7; Eph. 1:2; 6:23; Col. 1:2; Philem. 1:3; Phil. 1:2; 1 Tim. 1:2; Titus 1:4; 2 Tim. 1:2; also James 1:1; 2 Pet. 1:2; 2 John 3). Warfield notes first that this phrase, so commonly employed in the New Testament, appears already to have been long in use among Christians generally. "All the articles have been rubbed off, and with them all other accessories; and it stands out in its baldest elements as just 'God Father and Lord Jesus Christ.'" This mode of speaking of God evidently can as easily be reversed, as in Galatians 1:1, where Paul describes the divine origin of his apostleship as "not from men nor through man, but through Jesus Christ and God the Father."

---

[16]W, 2:143.
[17]W, 9:591–94, 609–14; W, 10:115–18; SW, 201–2; SSW, 2:292.

What is striking here is that God is referred to as "Jesus Christ and God the Father," and for Warfield the Trinitarian overtones are unmistakable. Similarly, in each occurrence of this phrase, the apostle is invoking divine blessing. He is praying that "grace, mercy, and peace" will be given "from God our Father and Lord Jesus Christ." Again, the divine source of blessing is spoken of in terms of both Christ and the Father. His prayer is not merely that the grace of God will come channeled through Jesus Christ. Rather, his prayer is that this grace will come from God our Father and the Lord Jesus Christ together, "as the conjoint object addressed in his petition." The God of blessing is freely spoken of in terms of a plurality. Two persons are brought together in closest possible relation, yet they are not absolutely identified. The Father is referred to as "God," and Christ is referred to as "Lord," both terms obviously reflecting deity. They are the one God, yet distinct persons. "The two, God our Father and the Lord Jesus Christ, are steadily recognized as two, and are statedly spoken of by the distinguishing designations of 'God' and 'Lord.' But they are equally steadily envisaged as one, and are stately combined as the common source of every spiritual blessing." Accordingly, they are united under the single governing preposition, "from"—"Grace to you and peace from God our Father and the Lord Jesus Christ." Further, this God spoken of in plural terms is yet spoken of in singular terms also. Warfield cites four passages (1 Thess. 3:11; 5:23; 2 Thess. 2:16; 3:16) in which the pronoun "himself" ($\alpha\dot{\upsilon}\tau\acute{o}\varsigma$) is employed, and he determines that "the $\alpha\dot{\upsilon}\tau\acute{o}\varsigma$ is to be construed with the whole subject"—"God" and "Lord." Both the plurality and the unity are maintained as God is referred to as "our Lord Jesus Christ and God our Father Himself." All this is to say, simply, that God the Father and the Lord Jesus Christ are essentially one yet personally distinct and, thus, that Trinitarianism is embedded in the very language of the earliest of Christian slogans. It is not formally taught in the pages of the New Testament as much as it is presupposed everywhere. It was the very natural and universal mode of reference to him, and the language reflects a doctrine that was common property to Christians everywhere, a firmly established understanding of the being of God.[18]

Warfield finds all this summarized nicely in 1 Corinthians 8:4–6 where Paul's argument rests on his firm assertion of monotheism: "There is no God but one" (v. 4). This truth governs Paul's point: false gods and lords are many (v. 5), but there is only one God. Paul reaffirms this statement of monotheism in language that reflects a settled Trinitarian understanding of God: "yet for us there is one God, the Father . . . , and one Lord, Jesus Christ" (v. 6). Two are mentioned, but his point is to refute pagan polytheism: "there is but one God—the Father and the

---

[18] W, 2:213–31, 235–52.

Lord Jesus Christ. This is the only God who exists." Paul could hardly be understood as saying that these two Gods demonstrate that there is only one God. His point, clearly, is that these two who are God, are one God, the only God who is.[19] Again, the language reflects a firmly established Trinitarian understanding that was shared by Christians universally.

The explanation for this "presupposed Trinitarianism" is evident. God's tri-unity was revealed not merely in word but in fact and in deed. The apostolic company and that first generation of Christians did not learn of the Trinity in a book or an apostolic letter. No, they had been personally acquainted with the incarnate Son; they were deeply convinced of his absolute deity, and on this pivot "the whole Christian conception of God turned." Their "eyes had seen and their hands had handled the word of life" (see 1 John 1:1), and they had heard him speak of "Father, Son, and Spirit." Moreover, they had themselves witnessed and experienced the outpouring of the Spirit of God. At Christ's baptism, they heard the Father speak and saw the Spirit descend as a dove. They heard the Father on the Mount of Transfiguration. They had seen firsthand that God had sent his Son to redeem and his Spirit to replace him. God's tri-unity was revealed "in the missions of the Son and Spirit." It was made known first in person, in fact, and in deed. The New Testament bears witness to this not only in its record of the events but also in its very natural, frequent, unguarded, and unchallenged allusions to God the Trinity.[20]

Gospel Revelation

All this brings Warfield to the point that for him is most significant: God's tri-unity is a matter of gospel revelation. This explains why the Trinity is not disclosed in the general revelation of the created order—"nature has nothing to say about redemption." This explains further why the Trinity was not clearly revealed in the Old Testament—God's redemptive program was not yet ready to be fulfilled. It had been revealed clearly that God was a saving God who would himself come to the rescue of his people, but it had not been so clearly revealed that this God is one with the anointed King who was to come or that this anointed King is one with the atoning Servant. "It required the fulfilment to weave together all the threads of the great revelation into one marvelous portraiture."[21] The revelation of the Trinity awaited the revelation of the gospel.

---

[19] W, 2:227–30.
[20] W, 2:144, 146, 167, 169; SSW, 1:73, 88.
[21] SSW, 1:87.

More specifically, it was the gospel of grace, the outworking of God's saving plan, that God was first concerned to reveal; and only in the revelation of this saving purpose is God's tri-unity made known also. In this sense, the doctrine of the Trinity, important as it is in itself, is "incidental" to the gospel. Its revelation became necessary only in the outworking of redemption. The promise and long hope of Israel was that God himself would come, bring deliverance to his people, and dwell with them, and it is in the fulfilling of that promise that he reveals himself and we learn of God the Father, Son, and Holy Spirit. This, God's highest self-disclosure, is a gospel revelation, the outworking of his saving purpose. God the Father sends his Son. The Son comes to redeem. And the Spirit comes to apply the merits of his work to the elect. Salvation is a work of the triune God, and in the fulfilling of this divine purpose of grace, God's tri-unity is made known. Indeed, apart from this there is no need for such revelation. "The doctrine of the Trinity, in other words, is simply the modification wrought in the conception of the one only God by his complete revelation of Himself in the redemptive process."[22]

Accordingly, the bulk of the apostolic Trinitarian statements and allusions are soteriological both in form and in substance. For example, in his hymn of praise, Paul traces the Christian's soteric blessings back to the Father, who chose and predestined us; to Christ, who redeemed us by his blood; and to the Holy Spirit, who seals us for our final inheritance (Eph. 1:3–14). The hymn is Trinitarian, to be sure, for the God who is thanked is Father, Christ, and Holy Spirit. But the structure is soteriological. God's tri-unity is a redemptive truth, a gospel revelation.

Similarly, in the apostolic benediction (2 Cor. 13:14), "the three highest redemptive blessings are brought together, and attached distributively to the three Persons of the Triune God." Again, Paul "habitually thinks of this Divine source of redemptive blessings after a trinal fashion." So also when the apostle traces the source of the "spiritual gifts" given to each believer, he sees standing behind them "the same Spirit," "the same Lord," and "the same God" (1 Cor. 12:4–6). The benefits of grace stem from the workings of the triune God. The apostle Peter follows a similar pattern. In greeting his fellow pilgrims, he designates them "elect . . . according to the foreknowledge of God the Father, in sanctification of the Spirit, for obedience to Jesus Christ and for sprinkling with his blood" (1 Pet. 1:1–2). Warfield treats a few of these passages as samples and references many others. His purpose is primarily to demonstrate that the New Testament writers spoke of God as triune with an "unstudied naturalness and simplicity" and that this presupposition underlay all of their thinking.[23]

---

[22] W, 2:144.
[23] W, 2:159–61.

"Accordingly, the doctrine of the Trinity and the doctrine of redemption, historically, stand or fall together." It is no surprise to Warfield that Unitarianism would teach a Pelagian anthropology and a Socinian soteriology. Drawing again from his acquaintance with the history of theological progress, Warfield observes that in the absence of a doctrine of the Trinity, there is an absence of a doctrine of redemption also.

> It is in this intimacy of relation between the doctrines of the Trinity and redemption that the ultimate reason lies why the Christian church could not rest until it had attained a definite and well-compacted doctrine of the Trinity. Nothing else could be accepted as an adequate foundation for the experience of the Christian salvation.[24]

Sabellianism and Arianism, for example, could not satisfy the biblical data regarding God's nature and relations. But their problem goes further—they could not satisfy the data of the Christian's consciousness of salvation. Thus, Warfield finds it only natural that as the discussions of the early Christian theologians and apologists shifted "from the cosmological to the soteriological aspect of Christian truth," the early *Logos* speculations were supplanted by a clearer doctrine of the Trinity. Playing off Augustine's famous quote, Warfield states, "Here too the heart of man was restless until it found its rest in the Triune God, the author, procurer and applier of salvation."[25]

For the Christian, a Trinitarian concept of God is a necessary one if this concept of God is to correspond to our own experience of salvation. This, at bottom, is what gives the doctrine its significance. For Calvin and all the Reformers, as for every Christian since the very beginning of Christianity, "the nerve of the doctrine was its implication in the experience of salvation, in the Christian's certainty that the Redeeming Christ and Sanctifying Spirit are each Divine Persons."[26] Warfield summarizes:

> The Trinity of the Persons of the Godhead, shown in the incarnation and the redemptive work of God the Son, and the descent and saving work of God the Spirit, is thus everywhere assumed in the New Testament, and comes to repeated fragmentary but none the less emphatic and illuminating expression in its pages. As the roots of its revelation are set in the threefold Divine causality of the saving process, it naturally finds an echo also in the consciousness of everyone who has experienced this salvation. Every redeemed soul, knowing himself reconciled with God through

---

[24] *W*, 2:168.
[25] *W*, 2:88, 169.
[26] *W*, 5:195.

His Son, and quickened into newness of life by His Spirit, turns alike to Father, Son and Spirit with the exclamation of reverent gratitude upon his lips, "My Lord and my God!" If he could not construct the doctrine of the Trinity out of his consciousness of salvation, yet the elements of his consciousness of salvation are interpreted to him and reduced to order only by the doctrine of the Trinity which he finds underlying and giving their significance and consistency to the teaching of the Scriptures as to the processes of salvation. By means of this doctrine he is able to think clearly and consequently of his threefold relation to the saving God, experienced by Him as Fatherly love sending a Redeemer, as redeeming love executing redemption, as saving love applying redemption: all manifestations in distinct methods and by distinct agencies of the one seeking and saving love of God. Without the doctrine of the Trinity, his conscious Christian life would be thrown into confusion and left in disorganization if not, indeed, given an air of unreality; with the doctrine of the Trinity, order, significance and reality are brought to every element of it.[27]

The Teaching of Christ

As we might expect, a strong sense of Trinitarianism pervades and underlies the teaching of Jesus, and it is from him, no doubt, that the first Christians learned most precisely how to speak of God as triune. But as with his apostles, Jesus' teaching *reflects* more than *teaches* Trinitarianism. Nonetheless, the Trinitarianism reflected in Jesus' teaching is fully developed. Warfield cites evidence primarily from the Gospel of John, chiefly the Upper Room Discourse (John 13–17), and from the Great Commission of Matthew 28:19–20.

In Jesus' teaching in the Gospel of John, Warfield finds all the essentials of Christian Trinitarian theology. "I and the Father are one," Jesus declares (10:30). There is a plurality of persons ("are") and singleness of being ("one," neuter singular). Christ is "one" with the Father (10:30; 17:11, 21, 22, 25) and shares a "unity of interpenetration" (10:38), an essential oneness (8:58), and coeternality in glory (17:5) with the Father. "His eternal home is in the depths of the Divine Being," and yet he and the Father are personally distinct (8:42). All this is true in relation to the Spirit also. "It would be impossible to speak more distinctly of three who were yet one." The Son makes request of the Father. The Spirit is "*another* comforter"—another like Jesus, granted, but "another" nonetheless. These three are kept distinct. "And yet the oneness of these three is so kept in sight that the coming of this 'another Advocate' is spoken of without embarrassment as the coming of the Son Himself (14:18, 19, 20, 21), and indeed as the coming of the Father and the Son (14:23)." Warfield summarizes, "There is a distinction between

---

[27] W, 2:167–68.

the Persons brought into view; and with it an identity among them; for both of which allowance must be made."[28]

In the Great Commission Warfield finds "the nearest approach to a formal announcement of the doctrine of the Trinity which is recorded from our Lord's lips, or, perhaps we may say, which is to be found in the whole compass of the New Testament." Specifically, of course, Warfield refers to the baptismal formula, "in the name of the Father and of the Son and of the Holy Spirit" (Matt. 28:19). Just as the "determining impulse" in the formulation of the doctrine of the Trinity in the early church was "the church's profound conviction of the absolute Deity of Christ," so also the baptismal formula was its "guiding principle." Here the Lord Jesus does not speak of "the names" (plural), as though the three were entirely separate beings. Nor does he speak of "the name of the Father, Son, and Holy Spirit," as though these were three designations of the same person. "With stately impressiveness it asserts the unity of the three by combining them all within the bounds of the single Name; and then throws up into emphasis the distinctness of each by introducing them in turn with the repeated article: 'In the name of the Father, and of the Son, and of the Holy Ghost.'"[29] There is distinction, but distinction within unity. Further significance is to be observed in the expression "the name." "The name," in Jewish contexts, was understood clearly as reference to God—so also in the baptismal formula.

> When, therefore, Our Lord commanded His disciples to baptize those whom they brought to His obedience "into the name of . . . ," He was using language charged to them with high meaning. He could not have been understood otherwise than as substituting for the Name of Jehovah this other Name "of the Father, and of the Son, and of the Holy Ghost"; and this could not possibly have meant to His disciples anything else than that Jehovah was now to be known to them by the new Name, of the Father, and the Son, and the Holy Ghost. The only alternative would have been that, for the community which He was founding, Jesus was supplanting Jehovah by a new God; and this alternative is no less than monstrous. There is no alternative, therefore, to understanding Jesus here to be giving for His community a new Name to Jehovah and that new Name to be the threefold Name of "the Father, and the Son, and the Holy Ghost. . . . This is a direct ascription to Jehovah the God of Israel, of a threefold personality, and is therewith the direct enunciation of the doctrine of the Trinity."[30]

---

[28]W, 2:149–52, 198.
[29]W, 2:153, 169; cf. W, 4:3–109.
[30]W, 2:153–54.

In another context Warfield summarizes crisply that the baptismal formula alone, in continued use, would guide Christians everywhere to Trinitarianism. It keeps before them the notions of the unity of God and the deity and distinctness of both Christ and the Spirit.[31] The three are the one God.

THEOLOGICAL FORMULATIONS: THE CHRISTIAN DOCTRINE OF THE TRINITY

Historical Development

It was because of the complexity of the questions involved and the uniqueness of the doctrine itself, Warfield assumes, that Trinitarian theology achieved its full, formal statement only slowly. He notes the struggle of the early Christian theologians to give full weight to both the distinction of persons in and the unity of the Godhead. In his lengthy, three-part article, "Tertullian and the Beginnings of the Doctrine of the Trinity," Warfield sets out to delineate the "inestimable service" that Tertullian rendered to the church in this regard.[32] He observes:

> No one earlier than Tertullian and few besides Tertullian, prior to the outbreak of the Arian controversy, seem to have succeeded in giving anything like a tenable expression to this potential Trinitarianism. If Tertullian may not be accredited with the invention of the doctrine of the Trinity, it may yet be that it was through him that the elements of this doctrine first obtained something like a scientific adjust-ment, and that he may not unfairly, therefore, be accounted its originator, in a sense somewhat similar to that in which Augustine may be accounted the originator of the doctrines of original sin and sovereign grace, Anselm of the doctrine of satisfaction, and Luther that of justification by faith.[33]

Warfield acknowledges that Tertullian was never quite free of the *Logos* specula-tions, which so dominated the Christian world of his day, but he labors to show how Tertullian pushed the contents of these speculations to their limits and beyond. "The Logos Christology, in other words, was stretched by him beyond its tether and was already passing upward in his construction to something better."[34]

Tertullian was forced to "establish the true and complete deity of Jesus, and at the same time the reality of His distinctness as the Logos from the fontal-deity, without creating two Gods." Warfield comments that "this is, on the face of it,

---

[31] *W*, 4:17–18.
[32] *W*, 4:4.
[33] *W*, 4:18–19.
[34] *W*, 4:25.

precisely the problem of the Trinity. And so far as Tertullian succeeded in it, he must be recognized as the father of the Church doctrine of the Trinity." But he also acknowledges that Tertullian was not entirely successful in this task. Warfield notes five areas of thought that Tertullian held in common with *Logos* speculations, all of which mar his doctrine of the Trinity to some extent. First, he held with them the "fundamental conception out of which the Logos doctrine grows—the conception of the transcendence of God above all possibility of direct relation with a world of time and space." That is, "the invisible God," as he is in himself, cannot be manifested in this world. His "invisibility," or what we might call transcendent majesty, precludes such revelation. Second, Tertullian held "with equal heartiness" that the *Logos* is "the world-form," a "prolation" or mediating form of the invisible God. This mode of thinking had been inherited from earlier Gnostic influences and tendencies. Third, Tertullian also held "the consequent view that the Logos is not God in His entirety, but only a 'portion' of God—a 'portion,' that is, as in the ray there is not the whole but only a 'portion' of the sun." The difference between the Father and the Son is one of both mode and measure. The Father is "the entire substance," but the Son is a derived portion of the whole. Fourth, Tertullian held in common with *Logos* christology that the prolation of the *Logos* was a voluntary act of God and not a necessary one. "The prolate Logos is dependent on the divine will." Finally, Tertullian shared the subordinationist tendencies inherent in *Logos* theology.[35]

These defects notwithstanding, Tertullian marks a significant advance in Trinitarian theology. Tertullian preserved *Logos* speculations, but in facing the Monarchian controversy he was compelled to "enlarge and modify" them and bring them into closer conformity to the biblical data. He insisted, against the Monarchians, that unity of the Godhead does not necessitate unity of person. Indeed, Tertullian was the first to speak of three in one and one in three—one in substance and yet three in number or persons—and this he emphasized with vigor. Warfield demonstrates that despite the defects of his *Logos* influence, Tertullian taught a real distinction of persons in the Godhead, that *in some way* these distinct persons were essential to the divine existence, that within these distinctions is an essential unity of God, that full and equal deity belongs to Christ, and that to the Holy Spirit also belongs eternal distinctness of personality and absolute deity. Indeed, in the course of his defense of the doctrine, "Tertullian's organizing principle had become no longer subordinationism but equalization," even if some subordinationist notion remained. And so Warfield asks, "What, then, lacks he yet of Nicene orthodoxy?" In answer to the question Warfield demonstrates in

---

[35]W, 4:24, 30–32.

some detail that Tertullian is, indeed, "the father of Nicene theology," even if his statement of the doctrine is only germinal and not fully developed.[36]

Warfield observes that the doctrine of the Trinity received its "completed statement" in Augustine, but he notes also that this articulation "came too late to affect the Greek construction of this doctrine, and accordingly gave form on this great topic only to the thought of the West." Accordingly, while the Trinitarianism of the Eastern church was marked by a subtle subordinationist tendency, as allowed by the famous θεὸς ἐκ θεοῦ ("God of God") of the Nicene formulary, Western Trinitarianism following Augustine, by contrast, was dominated by the principle of equalization. This principle of equalization, in turn, "found its sharpest assertion in the ascription of αὐτοθεότης to Christ by Calvin, whose construction marks the only new (subordinate) epoch in the development of the doctrine of the Trinity after Augustine."[37]

Warfield examines at length Calvin's contribution to the Christian doctrine of the Trinity. He admires the way Calvin "prepares" his readers to "expect depths in the Divine Being beyond our sounding" as he turns to speak of the Trinity. We should not expect God to be more or less like us; we should, rather, expect in learning of his essence to be struck with new facets of his greatness. This greatness of God's being is nowhere more evident, Warfield agrees, than in God's "tripersonality." The leading characteristics of Calvin's Trinitarian teaching are its simplicity, its consequent lucidity, and its final elimination of any remnants of subordinationism—"simplification, clarification, equalization." It is to the last of these that Warfield devotes his attention. To stress the absolute deity of Christ (as well as the Spirit), Calvin insisted on his self-existence and self-deity (aseity, αὐτοουσία, and αὐτοθεότης). To say anything less of Christ, he argued, would be sacrilege. This, Calvin demanded, is evident simply in the many occasions in Scripture in which the Holy Spirit names Christ Jehovah, the self-existent God.[38]

Calvin clarified (albeit inconsistently, in Warfield's judgment) that all this is in reference to Christ's being or essence, not his person. The person (not the essence) of the Father begets the person (not the essence) of the Son, and it is from the persons (not the essence) of the Father and Son that the person (not the essence) of the Spirit proceeds. It is the distinguishing property of the Son that is begotten, and it is the distinguishing property of the Spirit that is the product of the procession. The essence is common to all three persons. Calvin, then, did allow a doctrine of generation and procession and a proper order of Father, Son,

---

[36]W, 4:34, 36, 99, 100–109.
[37]W, 4:116; the Greek term αὐτοθεότης, "self-deity," indicates that Christ (as is each other person of the Trinity) is "of himself God."
[38]W, 5:230, 234.

and Spirit. But he had no use for the doctrine of eternal generation "as it was expounded by the Nicene Fathers." The Nicene theologians speculated both that the Son's generation "occurred once for all at some point of time in the past" and that it was "always occurring, a perpetual movement of the divine essence from the first Person to the second, always complete, never completed." This concept Calvin found meaningless. The Nicene Creed he accepted; these speculations of the Nicene theologians he did not. Θεὸς ἐκ θεοῦ is acceptable but confusing, given that a "non-natural personal sense" must be understood, and it is open to the abusive implication of a created God.[39]

The cornerstone of Calvin's Trinitarianism was that of equalization—a principle already well established in the Nicene Creed and especially dominant in the Athanasian Creed, even if certain subordinationist tendencies had survived. Warfield determines that Calvin "adjusted everything to the absolute divinity of each Person, their community in the one only true Deity; and to this we cannot doubt that he was ready not only to subordinate, but even to sacrifice, if need be, the entire body of Nicene speculations." He therefore incurred the unyielding opposition of all varieties of subordinationism, but any whose Trinitarianism was described along the lines of the traditional Nicene orthodoxy have, since Calvin, been thrown into more or less confusion, now feeling "compelled to resort to nice distinctions in order to reconcile the two apparently contradictory confessions of αὐτοθεότης and θεὸς ἐκ θεοῦ of our Lord." Warfield traces at length Calvin's influence and the opposition of his critics and concludes that Calvin's Trinitarianism created not only a theological stir but a theological party—a party that, despite its continued differences on various points, has shaped Reformed Trinitarianism ever since. Calvin raised the bar of theological discussion, and in his assertion that Christ is αὐτόθεος, "the ὁμοουσιότης of the Nicene Fathers at last came to its full right."[40]

Thus Warfield credits Tertullian, Augustine, and finally John Calvin as the chief contributors "to the exact and vital statement" of this Christian doctrine. Warfield nowhere delineates Augustine's completed Trinitarianism; on the historical development of the doctrine, he writes only of its early formulation in Tertullian and its most fully developed statement in Calvin.[41] Warfield himself follows self-consciously, even enthusiastically, in this tradition but never slavishly and always with a close eye on the biblical text. His exposition of these respective presentations of the doctrine is exhaustive, and throughout he tests them on exegetical grounds.

---

[39] W, 5:247, 249.

[40] W, 5:257, 251–52, 284; cf. 272–73; ὁμοουσιότης indicates "of the same substance."

[41] W, 2:171; W, 4:3–109; W, 5:189–284.

Warfield's Formulation

The question of the Trinity turns on the twin issues of God's unity and diversity. Warfield affirms with all of orthodox Christianity that in terms of "essence," the Son is "exactly like" the Father. That is, the "Divine Being" is shared with absolute equality by all three persons. They share "identical essence." They are "numerically one in essence, and can be represented as distinct only in person."[42]

Warfield is not inclined to affirm that the very essence of the Trinity is enshrined in the language of "Father, Son, and Spirit." To be sure, "Father" and "Son" are the terms regularly employed by our Lord and the apostle John, but the regular language of Paul is, rather, "God" and "Lord." The difference no doubt, in part at least, is one of perspective. For Christ, "Lord" would not be the most natural way to speak of his position in relation to the other two persons of the Trinity. "Son," however, "expresses his consciousness of close relation, and indeed of exact similarity, to God." But from the perspective of Paul, speaking as a worshiper, Christ is "Lord," and so this becomes for him the divine name for the second person. "God" and "Lord" he consistently places side by side in reference to what may otherwise be designated "Father" and "Son." Thus Warfield comments, "It remains remarkable, nevertheless, if the very essence of the Trinity were thought of by him as resident in the terms 'Father,' 'Son,' that in his numerous allusions to the Trinity in the Godhead, he never betrays any sense of this."[43]

Further, and somewhat startling, Warfield observes that the order, Father, Son, Spirit, is not necessarily essential to the relationships described by the terms, given that this order is not preserved but variable in Paul and the other New Testament writers. Indeed, the reverse order occurs in 1 Corinthians 12:4–6 and Ephesians 4:4–6; and in 2 Corinthians 13:14, the apostolic benediction, it appears, Lord, God, and Spirit. Warfield therefore suggests, on exegetical grounds, that the order of designations does not express the essence of the doctrine of the Trinity.[44]

Ultimately, Warfield does not deny that the terms "Father," "Son," and "Spirit" reveal to us the mutual relations of the Trinity. In fact he acknowledges that these designations specify the "distinguishing properties" of each personality and that it is by these designations that the persons of the Godhead are differentiated from each other.[45] But he does caution that we must take into consideration two attending factors: first, that these terms and their order—Father, Son, Spirit—are not strictly followed in the New Testament; and second, that the *implications* of these designations may be other than commonly assumed. Although the des-

---

[42] W, 5:214–15.
[43] W, 2:161, 162.
[44] W, 2:162.
[45] W, 5:214.

ignations "Son" and "Spirit" may to us naturally intimate subordination and derivation, Warfield questions whether this is even remotely suggested by the biblical usage of the terms. Sonship rather denotes likeness and equality with the Father, not subordination. Similarly, the term "only begotten" conveys the idea of uniqueness, not derivation. So also, "Spirit of God," as used so frequently in the Old Testament, does not convey the idea of derivation or of subordination; it is simply the executive name of God, "the designation of God from the point of view of His activity." It "imports accordingly identity with God." In fact, Warfield finds in the New Testament what resembles a formal definition of these terms. In John 5:18 Jesus' claim to sonship is taken as a claim to equality with God, and for this assumed blasphemy, he is opposed. And in 1 Corinthians 2:10–11, "the Spirit of God" is more or less defined as "just God Himself in the innermost essence of His Being." Warfield concludes that these terms do not imply any notion of subordination or derivation and that if these terms do not convey such notions, then there is no evidence in the New Testament for such notions at all.[46]

To speak of subordination or derivation, we must note the distinction between the economic Trinity and the ontological or immanent Trinity; or, in Warfield's preferred terminology, the "modes of operation" and the "mode of being" or "modes of subsistence."[47] That is, we must not assume that the order by which the triune God works toward the salvation of his people reflects the "necessary" relation of the three persons to one another. The order of "Father, Son, and Spirit" always has in view the operations of God in redemption.

> It may be natural to assume that a subordination in modes of operation rests on a subordination in modes of subsistence; that the reason why it is the Father that sends the Son and the Son that sends the Spirit is that the Son is subordinate to the Father, and the Spirit to the Son. But we are bound to bear in mind that these relations of subordination in modes of operation may just as well be due to a convention, an agreement, between the Persons of the Trinity—a "Covenant" as it is technically called—by virtue of which a distinct function in the work of redemption is voluntarily assumed by each.

Then Warfield advises, "It is eminently desirable, therefore, at the least, that some definite evidence of subordination in modes of subsistence should be discoverable before it is assumed."[48] This evidence Warfield cannot himself discover. For him,

---

[46] *W*, 2:163–65.
[47] Tertullian speaks of "that dispensation *which we call* the οἰκονομία" (emphasis added). Warfield interprets this as signifying "which is commonly so called." This, coupled with Tertullian's own assertion that his teaching is the traditional teaching of the church, leads Warfield to conclude that although this term is found first in Tertullian, it quite clearly predates him (*W*, 4:15).
[48] *W*, 2:166.

all "subordinationist passages" have in view the attending doctrines of the covenant of redemption, the incarnation, humiliation, and two natures of Christ.

> Certainly in such circumstances it were thoroughly illegitimate to press such passages to suggest any subordination for the Son or the Spirit which would in any manner impair that complete identity with the Father in Being and that complete equality with the Father in powers which are constantly presupposed, and frequently emphatically, though only incidentally, asserted for them throughout the whole fabric of the New Testament.[49]

In Warfield's commitment to the principle of equalization, then, it would seem that he has given Calvin's notion of Christ's αὐτοθεότης a fuller expression than did Calvin himself. This is perhaps his most outstanding contribution to Trinitarianism. If in Calvin's assertion of Christ's αὐτοθεότης "the ὁμοουσιότης of the Nicene Fathers at last came to its full right,"[50] then it seems Warfield has sought, in turn, to bring Calvin's αὐτοθεότης to its full right also.

Predestination, Providence, and the Divine Decree[51]

If the prevailing rationalism of the day created an atmosphere of naturalism, the Hegelian philosophy of evolutionary historical progress gave an optimistic tone to the entire nineteenth century. Not until the First World War did its slogan begin to lose credibility: "Every day in every way we are getting better and better." It was a day of advance in every conceivable field of learning, resulting in a realized betterment of the individual and of society in many ways. With all this came a pantheizing tendency in modern theology that minimized ideas of God's transcendence and his active government over the world. The Presbyterian Church in the 1890s witnessed sustained calls for revision of its Westminster Confession, and at issue, among other matters, was its doctrine of the divine decree. Historic articles of theology such as this just did not fit well with the optimism of the day. Lefferts Loetscher captures the atmosphere well: "Men could not forever bow as

---

[49] W, 2:167.

[50] W, 5:284; cf. 272–73.

[51] Warfield's primary treatments of this theme may be found in the following: "The Significance of the Confessional Doctrine of the Decree," in SSW, 1:93–102; "Some Thoughts on Predestination," in SSW, 1:103–10; "God's Providence over All," in SSW, 1:111–15; "What Is Calvinism?" in SSW, 1:389–92; "Election," in SSW, 1:285–98; "What Fatalism Is," in SSW, 1:383–86; "The Confession of Faith as Revised in 1903," in SSW, 2:370–410; "Calvinism," in SSW, 2:411–47; "A Review of Systematic Theology [by John Miley]," in SSW, 2:308–20; "Predestination," in W, 2:3–67; "The Making of the Westminster Confession and Especially of Its Chapter on the Decree of God," in W, 6:75–151; "Predestination in the Reformed Confessions," in W, 9:117–231; and "The Theology of the Reformation," in W, 9:461–79.

wretched sinners on Sunday and swell with self-confidence the other six days of the week."[52] The historic doctrine of God's sovereignty had come on bad times, and out of deep commitment to it Warfield addressed the issue at considerable length.

EXPLICATION OF THE DOCTRINE OF THE DIVINE DECREE

Warfield often makes reference to the varying conceptions of God—deistic, pantheistic, and theistic—a matter of formative significance in the discussion of the decree. Deism acknowledges God as Creator but denies his continued immanence in the creation. Though he endowed all the elements with their respective powers, he is but the first and remote cause of events. God is transcendent and not involved in his creation, and events are to be explained only in terms of second causes. "Deism involves a mechanical conception of the universe. God has made a machine, and just because it is a good machine, he can leave it to work out, not its, but his ends." Because deism represents God in such remote terms, disallowing his personal involvement in the affairs of the world, Warfield sometimes describes it as "natural" religion. Pantheism is the polar opposite: it identifies God with the universe as the form in which he exists, "or at least so confines him to it as to deny his transcendence beyond the universe as an extra-mundane Spirit and conscious Person whose actions are rationally determined volitions." For the pantheist, "God" is merely "an impersonal diffused force." Christian theism stands between these two extremes and insists on both the transcendence of God beyond and above the world and the immanence of God within the world. God is a conscious, personal Spirit who acts sovereignly and according to purpose. He ordinarily works by means of second causes, but he remains free always to intrude, whether miraculously or via second causes, to do the extraordinary. Transcendent, he rules over the universe, yet is always immanent within it, penetrating even "the inmost being of every element of every creature with the infinite energies of his free intelligent will" and working through them always to his own purpose and glory.[53]

It is virtually a given for Warfield that God's decree is singular and all-inclusive and that his providence is over all. This conviction is bound up with the very notion of his Godhood. If God is a personal being, then he acts in all things according to his purpose. And if he is almighty, God over all, then all that is has come about by his will and plan. He rules the universe teleologically, with a goal or end in view. Warfield often repeats that all this is simply the first postulate of true theism.[54] Over

---

[52]Earle E. Cairns, *Christianity in America*, 147; Loetscher, *The Broadening Church*, 9.

[53]*SSW*, 2:416–19; *PS*, 12–14; *PGS*, 236–37; *W*, 5:189.

[54]*W*, 2:8, 17, 58, 60, 62; *SSW*, 1:93–97, 103–4, 389. "He who has affirmed, with section 1 [of the Confession], that 'God from all eternity did by the most wise and holy counsel of his own will freely and unchangeably

against naturalism, which looks to "the laws of nature" as deciding the course of events in the world; over against deism, which denies the continued immanence of the Creator in the creation and the consequent immediate dependence of the creature on the Creator; and over against pantheism, which at least practically denies his transcendence and identifies the universe as God's form of existence, theism affirms and emphasizes that God is both infinitely transcendent beyond the creation and immanent within it. The necessary corollary of this is that God is the Almighty over all and stands behind all that is, ordering it all according to his own eternal, wise, and good purpose. The world's history, with all its complexity of events, is (in words borrowed from Charles Hodge) "not the result of accident or chance, nor yet of necessity or fate, nor of human caprice or Satanic malice—but the orderly working out of the purpose of our Father in heaven, the infinitely wise and holy One." This is of the essence of theism, the very basis of prayer, and the whole foundation of order in the universe. In all things, God acts with his own purpose in view. Once again, this is simply the fundamental presupposition of consistent theism. Warfield insists that Scripture is full of predestination precisely "because it is full of God, and when we say God . . . we have said Predestination."[55]

The "fundamental conception of God" throughout all the Old Testament and "the two most persistently emphasized elements" in that conception of God are his almighty power and his personality. "Before everything else," Warfield insists, "the God of Israel is the Omnipotent Person." This exalted majesty of the all-powerful person of God lies at the very core of the Old Testament idea of God, as we have seen. The biblical writers further employ varied terminology that makes explicit God's causative relation to all that is: words and phrases such as "elect," "chose," "ordained," "predestined," "appointed before," "determined before," and "fore-ordained" are common to every translation and reflect a wide variety of Hebrew and Greek vocabulary. They render the concept of God's all-inclusive decree and providence familiar to every reader of Scripture. But most fundamentally, through-out the biblical narrative the underlying conscious assumption of the narrators is that in all of his dealings with men, God the Creator rules over everything that he has made, directing it in every detail to his own ends. The varied terminology of predestination is impressive and telling, but by itself it cannot convey adequately the vivid awareness biblical writers maintained of God's all-inclusive providence, which is displayed in their narrative of God's dealings with men. For Warfield,

---

ordain whatsoever comes to pass,' has affirmed nothing but one of the most immediate implicates of a consistent theism." *SSW*, 1:97. Warfield similarly argues that theism demands Calvinism (*SSW*, 1:94; see also *PS*).

[55] *SSW*, 2:416–18; *SSW*, 1:93–95, 103, 106, 108–9, 393.

just a cursory glance over this narrative makes plain the Bible's fundamental assumption of God's all-pervasive sovereign direction. What the biblical writers convey is a pure and consistent theism.[56]

Moreover, if God made the universe for himself, then "he must be supposed to have made it precisely to suit himself." He surely did not make a universe he did not wish to have. He made the universe as he was pleased to make it. He is not left to put up with the best he could do. "A being who cannot make a universe to his own liking is not God." And similarly, "A being who can agree to make a universe which is not to his liking, most certainly is not God." Warfield scoffingly calls such a being a "godling" who, no longer God, must tolerate the universe as it is rather than as he would have it to be. All of this is nonsense. It is necessary from the very notion of Godhood that God controls in entirety all that he has made.[57]

Warfield argues further. If God were not in absolute control of all things, not only would he then cease to be God; he would be immoral. It would be an irresponsibly immoral act were God to make anything that he could not or would not control. To perpetuate chaos is an immoral act, and to conceive of God as creating a universe or a single being that he could not or would not control would be to dethrone him and demoralize him. As God, and as the kind of God he is, he necessarily controls all things.[58]

Once more, if God controls all that he has made, then he intended to control it and controls it according to his purpose. We could not imagine a "God" who acts willy-nilly, spur of the moment, without intention. God created and rules over all things as he pleases and according to his own design. This—God's acting according to intention—very simply, is the biblical doctrine of God's all-inclusive predestinating decree.[59]

Warfield argues exegetically as well as theologically. Surveying the Old Testament, he observes that God is continuously conceived of and portrayed as the "almighty maker" and "irresistible ruler" of all that he has made. The inspired writers maintain such a "vivid sense of dependence" upon God that they rarely speak abstractly of the rain or of famines and such: it is rather God who sends the rain, God who sends the famine, God who sends the wind and has his way in it, God who hurls the lightning to strike its intended mark, God who opens the womb, God who gives prosperity or calamity, God who directs the feet of men and even creates the thoughts and intents of the soul, and it is God who opens and hardens hearts. Even the seemingly chance happening—the occasional "it

---

[56]W, 2:3–10.
[57]SSW, 1:104–5.
[58]SSW, 1:103–4.
[59]SSW, 1:105–6; SSW, 2:310–13.

appened that" (cf. Ruth 2:3)—is not conceived as apart from God's direction and provision. Indeed, even the lot was understood to be at his disposal (Josh. 7:16; Prov. 16:33). All of heaven and earth are seen as the instruments of his hands working out his irresistible purpose. "All things without exception, indeed, are disposed by Him"—nations, nature, individual experiences, all alike are the disposition of his will. He is the "free determiner of all that comes to pass in the world."[60]

So pervasive and so specific is this kind of language about God that "an appearance is sometimes created as if everything that comes to pass were so ascribed to His immediate production as to exclude the real activity of second causes." It would be a mistake, however, to forget that God does indeed employ second causes, Warfield insists. Men are everywhere recognized as authors of their own actions and are therefore held accountable for those actions. Similarly the created order acts according to consistent "laws of nature." But, again, these are not conceived as independent of God; they are, rather, the instruments of his will. God has prescribed the laws by which nature functions, and he is the governor over even the hearts of men. Nor is his providence a blind force as in pantheistic thought; that would be to forget his personhood. God is at work in and by means of all that is, directing all things to accomplish his "all-inclusive and perfect plan." It is evident on the very face of the pages of the Old Testament that this is the world in which the biblical writers live and think.[61]

It is from this conscious awareness of God's working in and through all things that the biblical writers so repeatedly and consistently reflect such a vivid sense of absolute dependence upon God. And it is due to this consciousness that faith—trust—becomes the keynote of piety. "Standing over against God, not merely as creatures, but as sinners, the Old Testament saints found no ground of hope save in the free initiative of the Divine love." Accordingly, self-sufficiency is the characteristic mark of the wicked. The very heart of godliness is trust in God and his sovereign distribution of mercy.

> In the entire self-commitment to God, humble dependence on Him for all blessings, which is the very core of the Old Testament religion, no element is more central than the profound conviction embodied in it of the free sovereignty of God . . . in the distribution of His mercies. The whole training of Israel was directed to impressing upon it the great lesson enunciated to Zerubabel, "Not by might nor by power, but by my Spirit, saith the Lord of hosts."[62]

---

[60]W, 2:8–9; SSW, 1:103–4.
[61]W, 2:9–10; cf. SSW, 1:98–99; SSW, 2:420–21. The exception to God's use of second causes is what we call "miracle," and this, for Warfield, is of the essence of the definition of miracle—it is an act of God in which he does not employ the usual second causes (SSW, 2:169).
[62]W, 2:11.

Accordingly, the establishment of the kingdom of God is consistently represented in the Old Testament "not as the product of man's efforts in seeking after God, but as the gracious creation of God Himself." Its inception, as well as its development and accomplishment, is due to God's working in free grace through all things to fulfill his loving purpose of restoring fallen man to fellowship with himself. Throughout it all God is at work. He makes the covenant promise, he preserves the race from destruction in the flood, and he chooses a man and family through whom he will bring about his gracious purpose. "At every step it is God, and God alone, to whom is ascribed the initiative," and throughout the recipients of his favor are reminded that it is not their work or will that has given rise to his free and gracious provision. Israel is "emphatically not a people of their own making, but a people that God had formed that they might set forth His praise" (Isa. 43:21). In the complex details of the lives of the patriarchs it is not their own experiences that stand out as most significant; the "real plot of the story" is the advance of God's purpose through them. And so in every historical event.[63]

The New Testament presentation of the doctrine of predestination follows in the same vein. With the additional emphasis on God's fatherhood, God is "the great King" (Matt. 5:35) and "Lord of heaven and earth" (Matt. 11:25), who does all his pleasure, whose throne is in the heavens with the earth his footstool, and whose power knows no limitation, "whether on the score of difficulty in the task, or insignificance in the object." He rules and directs the rain, the flowers of the field, the birds of the air, the falling sparrow, and even the very hairs of our head. In the minutest details of the course of the world's history God is directing all things toward his appointed goal in the world to come. It is impossible not to think that if God presides over even the falling of the sparrow, then his providence is over everything in the most extensive detail. So also in the larger picture, the advance of the nascent church in the book of Acts is traced to its heavenly origin in the promise and bestowal of the Holy Spirit, in whose power the gospel made its promised and therefore inevitable progress. In the book of Revelation also the curtain is pulled back for us to see, from heaven's perspective, that history is but the unfolding of the divine purpose and will.[64]

Warfield considers it important in this connection to distinguish the relation between the divine purpose and foreknowledge. The understanding of the biblical writers is emphatically not that God works to accomplish his plan through all that he foresees will happen. The ground of God's knowledge is not his foresight; the ground of his knowledge is himself. His decree is not based on his perfect

---

[63] W, 2:12–13.
[64] W, 2:33; SSW, 2:26–28, 87.

understanding of all the causes in operation, as though he were enabled by this foresight to calculate and forecast the outcomes of events. Such a notion would be entirely contradictory to the biblical writers' conception of the almighty, all-sovereign ruler of the universe. This would be to render God contingent and "dethrone" him as the governor of the universe and "no longer God," making him ruled by rather than ruler of the course of events. God's purpose and works are not contingent on his foreknowledge; rather, this foreknowledge is dependent on the divine purpose. In the biblical conception, "God foreknows only because He has pre-determined." His foreknowledge is grounded in his purpose and "is at bottom a knowledge of His own will, and His works of providence are merely the execution of His all-embracing plan." It is his will that is "the real ultimate ground of the futurition of events." Warfield commends the Westminster Confession in this regard with its affirmation not only that God knows the future exhaustively but also that he knows the whole range of possibilities growing out of all supposable conditions. Accordingly, Warfield represents the Hebrew sages (in the Wisdom Literature of the Old Testament) as conceiving of God as "eternally contemplating all possibilities" and, again, in keeping with the purity of their theism, as "predetermining every event that comes to pass" in accord with his wise and all-embracing purpose.[65]

PROBLEMS AND OBJECTIONS

This understanding of God's foreknowledge and purpose reflects no discomfort with the notion of human freedom. Warfield treats this matter in two steps. First, God's foreknowledge of the actions of free human agents indeed implies the certainty of those actions, but it does not in any way impinge on human freedom any more than his foreknowledge of his own actions or choices impinges on his freedom. Warfield marvels that the Arminian John Miley[66] can see this but somehow not see that God's foreknowledge of his own free choices surely implies his foreintention of those same choices (which is just the doctrine of predestination). Warfield concludes that if this much is granted, there remains no objection to God's foreintention of human free choices. God orders even the free choices of men. Second, Warfield simply notes that "throughout the whole Old Testament there is never the least doubt expressed of the freedom or moral responsibility of man." There was no question at all in the minds of the biblical writers that men were free agents, and it was on this ground they were held

---

[65]*SSW*, 1:99–100; *W*, 2:16–29.
[66]John Miley (1813–1895) was a leading American Methodist theologian of the nineteenth century, serving as the chair of systematic theology at Drew University in Madison, New Jersey.

responsible. But at the same time the biblical writers supremely believed *God* to be free. And because God is free, he is never hampered or limited in the attainment of his goals. Just how he thus governs over the free acts of men in pursuit of his purpose is a subject the biblical writers scarcely address. But that he thus governs men "in even their most intimate thoughts and feelings and impulses" is their "unvarying assumption."[67]

Nor does the moral quality of the actions in question present any difficulty or exception to God's all-inclusive rule. It is never the case that God is the author of sin, and he is in no way implicated by the sinfulness of men's "misuse of creaturely freedom." He is always the Holy One, who is entirely separate from sin, and the blame for sin always remains with the sinner himself. Yet God's relation to the sinful acts is not purely passive: his involvement is not that of mere allowance. The biblical writers are nowhere embarrassed to maintain God's rule over all things, even sinful things. God presides over all the courses of history, sin included, and because of this there is a sense in which we may say, *O beata culpa*, for even sin is used by God to accomplish his purpose and display his glory (Ps. 76:10). It is in the doctrine of concurrence that Warfield unravels the tension: all that happens, good or evil, stems from God's positive ordering of it; but the moral quality of the deed itself is rooted in the moral character of the person who does it. Even evil actions trace back to God's all-embracing decree. He hardens hearts (Ex. 4:21, etc.), he sends evil spirits to trouble sinners (1 Sam. 16:14), and from him sinful impulses take their shape (2 Sam. 24:1). Yet he is not the immediate cause of all that comes to pass; that would be pantheism. Evil men and evil spirits do what is evil because they themselves are evil, and they therefore receive the blame and carry the guilt. But in it all, God remains God over all, acting and ordering according to his own purpose, so that no evil comes to pass apart from his wise providence, which orders all things for the highest good and directs all that is to return to his own praise (Ps. 76:10).[68]

Against the objection that it would be inconsistent with divine goodness to create souls whose ultimate destruction is foreknown, Warfield argues that to attribute ignorance to God on this score would not avert the problem: creation of souls with the known *possibility* of loss leaves God open to the same charge. For that matter, God's continuance of the human race after numerous such losses had occurred would likewise leave the same dilemma. Unless foreknowledge is denied altogether, we are left to see that God created souls knowing that some

---

[67] *SSW*, 2:310–13; *W*, 2:19.
[68] *W*, 2:20–22; *SSW*, 1:44–45, 98–99; *SSW*, 2:310–13; *FL*, 25–27. *Beata culpa* is a term Augustine used in reference to Adam's fall. His was a "happy fault" or "blessed crime" in that it brought about the wondrous display of God's saving grace.

would be lost. But to say this much is to say also that God *intended* to create souls that would be lost. The problem is not a Calvinist's problem only; this is a problem all Christians must face. And so Warfield sees only two options: deny foreknowledge altogether, in which case God is no longer God, or admit the Calvinistic and biblical doctrine of predestination.[69]

Evil has come into the world, then, in keeping with God's all-inclusive decree. God knows all that is and all that will be, but this foreknowledge—with its necessary corollary, foreintention—impinges neither on human freedom nor on human responsibility. Nor does this reflect poorly on God so long as it is understood that in his decree God had in view "an end great and glorious enough" to justify the evil involved in his plan.[70]

ELECTION

Warfield consistently treats the doctrine of special or soteriological predestination (election) against the larger backdrop of God's all-inclusive decree and views it as a specific application of that decree. He argues that the biblical writers themselves view election in this larger context—for example, in Ephesians 1:1–12, where God's elective choice is stated in the context of the One "who works *all things* according to the counsel of his will" (v. 11). Similarly, the "golden chain" of Romans 8:29–30 is rooted in the apostle's statement that God works *all things* together for good. Or more generally, Warfield states of the apostle Paul that "the roots of his doctrine of predestination were set in his general doctrine of God, and it was fundamentally because St. Paul was a theist of a clear and consistent type . . . that he was a predestinarian." Warfield sees predestination not as a purely soteriological truth but as a soteriological aspect of a larger truth concerning God's all-inclusive decree. Election to salvation is but an "entailment" and specific "application" of God's all-embracing, purposeful decree. The doctrine of the divine decree "lies at the basis of this doctrine of election," and out of it the doctrine of election "is made to grow."[71] Warfield is repeatedly explicit in clarifying that the doctrine of election is a subset of theology proper and of the doctrine of the all-inclusive divine decree.

However, he is just as careful to emphasize that Scripture maintains a redemptive focus throughout and that this redemptive focus is evident in the Bible's treatment of the doctrine of the decree: within the all-inclusive decretive purpose of God the redemptive purpose is central, and in the biblical treatment of the

---

[69] *SSW*, 2:311–12.
[70] *SSW*, 2:312.
[71] *W*, 2:45–48, 55; *SSW*, 1:96; *W*, 2:22.

doctrine of the divine decree the soteric focus dominates. Indeed, "we easily get the impression" in reading the biblical record that soteriological predestination (election) is "the core of God's general decree . . . and that His whole plan for the government of the universe is subordinated to His purpose to recover sinful man to Himself." Election, he emphasizes, is "the prime matter of importance."[72] In his extensive analysis "Predestination in the Reformed Confessions" (1901), Warfield notes that the confessions themselves maintain a "prevailing soteriological interest" and that treatment of the broader notion of predestination and the divine decree "is much less usual and full than that of Special Predestination or Election and Reprobation," the broader subject being more "commonly presupposed or incidentally alluded to rather than the doctrine fully expounded."[73]

All this is to be expected, he remarks, for the Bible is primarily a soteriological book. In Warfield's own presentation of the doctrine, it is the soteriological element that likewise dominates. In his major article on predestination he traces out the doctrine of the decree in large strokes throughout the history of biblical revelation and then presents a brief systematization of it. Throughout his lengthy essay the doctrine of God's gracious election to salvation is given special prominence within the context of the larger doctrine of the decree. Warfield stresses that predestination to eternal life bears all the characteristics of the doctrine of the decree itself—it is free, sovereign, just, and so on. In his article on election, however, the doctrine is presented within the framework of grace, and the emphasis is on God's sovereign mercy in rescuing sinners from their deserved condemnation.

It is difficult to discern whether Warfield, had he written a systematic theology, would have treated predestination under the domain of theology proper or under soteriology. He explicitly affirms that election belongs to the larger subject of the all-inclusive divine decree, stressing at times that viewing soteric election from this standpoint preserves its character as a sovereign act of grace. And so predestination properly falls under the domain of theology proper. But in his actual treatment of the subject, the soteriological focus intentionally dominates. It is not at all certain, therefore, that Warfield would even acknowledge this dichotomy. He conceives of God in holistic terms, as the sovereign Savior. His presentation of the doctrine follows closely the biblical presentation of it, and so, while both emphases are constant, it is the soteric element that inevitably dominates.[74]

---

[72] W, 2:22–23.

[73] W, 9:220; see more fully 218–28. Warfield himself does provide a rather thorough explication of predestination in its broader sense in his 1909 "Predestination," written for James Hastings, *A Dictionary of the Bible* (W, 2:3–67).

[74] In this, Warfield also falls in line with the Westminster Confession of Faith, to which he so heartily subscribes. There the doctrine is treated in chapter 3, under the heading of "God's Eternal Decree," but in

For our purposes here and in some way reflecting this understanding, Warfield's doctrine of predestination is reviewed under both headings, theology proper and soteriology.

SUMMARY OF THE DOCTRINE OF THE DECREE

Warfield summarizes his doctrine of the decree:

> In one word, the sovereignty of the Divine will as the principle of all that comes to pass, is a primary postulate of the whole religious life, as well as of the entire worldview of the Old Testament. It is implicated in its very idea of God, its whole conception of the relation of God to the world and to the changes which take place, whether in nature or history, among the nations or in the life-fortunes of the individual; and also in its entire scheme of religion, whether national or personal. It lies at the basis of all the religious emotions, and lays the foundation of the specific type of religious character built up in Israel. . . . Throughout the Old Testament, behind the processes of nature, the march of history and the fortunes of each individual life alike, there is steadily kept in view the governing hand of God working out His preconceived plan—a plan broad enough to embrace the whole universe of things, minute enough to concern itself with the smallest details, and actualizing itself with inevitable certainty in every event that comes to pass.[75]

In short, the *subject* of the decree is God, the *object* of the decree is the whole universe and all that is and occurs within it, and the *end* or goal of the decree is his own praise.

> The whole Bible doctrine of the decree revolves, in a word, around the simple idea of purpose. Since God is a Person, the very mark of His being is purpose. Since He is an infinite Person, His purpose is eternal and independent, all inclusive and effective. Since He is a moral Person, His purpose is the perfect exposition of all His infinite moral perfections. Since He is the personal creator of all that exists, His purpose can find its final cause only in Himself.[76]

USES AND IMPORTANCE OF THE DOCTRINE

Warfield is eager to clarify the difference between this doctrine of God's all-inclusive decree and fatalism, and to accomplish this he retells at length a story of a young Dutch boy.

---

that treatment also the doctrine points explicitly forward in the direction of soteriology. This is Warfield's approach exactly.

[75] W, 2:12–13.
[76] W, 2:60–62.

This little boy's home was on a dyke in Holland, near a great wind-mill, whose long arms swept so close to the ground as to endanger those who carelessly strayed under them. But he was very fond of playing precisely under this mill. His anxious parents had forbidden him to go near it; and, when his stubborn will did not give way, had sought to frighten him away from it by arousing his imagination to the terror of being struck by the arms and carried up into the air to have life beaten out of him by their ceaseless strokes. One day, heedless of their warning, he strayed again under the dangerous arms, and was soon absorbed in his play there—forgetful of everything but his present pleasures. Perhaps, he was half conscious of a breeze springing up; and somewhere in the depth of his soul, he may have been obscurely aware of the danger with which he had been threatened. At any rate, suddenly, as he played, he was violently smitten from behind, and found himself swung all at once, with his head downward, up into the air; and then the blows came, swift and hard! O what a sinking of the heart! O what a horror of great darkness! It had come then! And he was gone! In his terrified writhing, he twisted himself about and looking up, saw not the immeasurable expanse of the brazen heavens above him, but his father's face. At once, he realized, with a great revulsion, that he was not caught in the mill, but was only receiving the threatened punishment of his disobedience. He melted into tears, not of pain, but of relief and joy. In that moment, he understood the difference between falling into the grinding power of a machine and into the loving hands of a father.

"That," Warfield adds, "is the difference between Fate and Predestination. And all the language of men cannot tell the immensity of the difference."[77]

It is here that Warfield finds the value of the doctrine of the divine decree and our understanding of it. The difficulties that arise from the doctrine of predestination arise chiefly from our natural "unwillingness to acknowledge our selves to be wholly at the disposal of another." But Warfield is eager to point out that such unwillingness is misguided and not at all in our own best interests. Do we really not care "whether it be the everlasting arms or merely our own weak arms that we rest on in all our Christian life?" Do we really not care for the confident certainty of knowing that God works all things according to the counsel of his own will? What comfort can be derived from a God, infinitely caring though he may be, who stands impotent over the course of world and life events—watching from all eternity things that he does not wish to happen, seeing them coming, ever coming, until at last they come, and he is unable to stop them? Would we really prefer chaos to order? To deny God's all-sovereign control over all things is to do away with God altogether and leave us to the uncertain fate of our own making. So much better this doctrine of the divine decree in which we can rest and which inevitably evokes in us a deep sense of grateful dependence upon God. And so much better this assurance that despite appearances, "there is stretched beneath us the everlasting arm of the almighty Father" working all things together for the good of those whom he has called according to his purpose. In this doctrine we have provided for us the whole ground of our trust and hope. It establishes "all that gives us a right as individuals to trust in the saving grace of God alone for the inception, continuance, and completion of our salvation" and all that gives us a right to trust in God the governor of the universe. Commenting on Romans 8:28, Warfield counsels:

> The fundamental thought is the universal government of God. All that comes to you is under His controlling hand. The secondary thought is the favour of God to those that love Him. If He governs all, then nothing but good can befall those to whom He would do good. The consolation lies in the shelter which we may thus find beneath His almighty arms.

That is to say, here in the doctrine of the universal providence of God we learn that "all is well with the world," and in that realization we may rest confidently. Here we learn with grateful adoration that our eternal salvation depends absolutely on "the infinite love and undeserved favor of God." And here we come to worship God aright. Contemplation of this doctrine enhances our conception of God and strengthens our fundamental confession, *soli Deo gloria*. A deep realization of this truth drives us to a firm dependence upon divine mercy and to that highest and purest expression of religion—prayer. Here "the plummet is let down to the bottom of the Christian's confidence and hope. It is because we cannot be robbed of God's providence that we know, amid whatever encircling gloom, that all things shall work together for good to those that love him." Here, in short, is "the solution of all earthly troubles."[78]

---

[78]*SSW*, 1:95, 100–103, 107–11, 146; *SSW*, 2:411, 414–15; *FL*, 200–210.

The glory of the Incarnation is that it presents to our adoring gaze,
not a humanized God or a deified man, but a true God-man—
one who is all that God is and at the same time all that man is: on
whose mighty arm we can rest, and to whose human sympathy
we can appeal. We cannot afford to lose either the God in the man or
the man in the God; our hearts cry out for the complete
God-man whom the Scriptures offer us.

SSW, 1:166.

6

CHRISTOLOGY I: THE PERSON OF CHRIST

More than just a polemic theologian, Benjamin Warfield was first and foremost a christologian. The person of Christ[1] and his work clearly topped the list of Warfield's many interests as measured by his literary output and preaching, as well as his recurring mention of and express concern for the doctrine. His reasons were more than academic: he was deeply convinced that in this theme we are brought to the very heart of the Christian faith. For Warfield, to maintain vigorously and carefully the doctrine of Christ set forth in Scripture is to preserve Christianity itself. The contemporary denials of the historicity of Christ, his mighty works, his deity, his two natures, his vicarious death, and his triumphal resurrection all threaten the very essence of Christianity. If these issues are not understood scripturally, the entire Christian structure crumbles, and redemption from sin is only a dream. Warfield writes, therefore, as the polemic theologian he is—with

---

[1]Significant Warfield titles treating the theme of the person of Christ include, first, *The Lord of Glory*, Warfield's book-length treatment of the deity of Christ, and the following articles: "The Foresight of Jesus," in *W*, 2:71–97; "The Biblical Doctrine of the Trinity," in *W*, 2:133–72; "The Person of Christ," in *W*, 2:175–209; "God Our Father and the Lord Jesus Christ," in *W*, 2:213–31; "The Christ That Paul Preached," in *W*, 2:235–52; "Jesus' Mission, According to His Own Testimony," in *W*, 2:255–324; "The Divine Messiah in the Old Testament," in *W*, 3:3–49; "Misconception of Jesus and Blasphemy of the Son of Man," in *W*, 3:53–94; "Jesus' Alleged Confession of Sin," in *W*, 3:97–145; "Jesus Christ," in *W*, 3:149–77; "Concerning Schmiedel's 'Pillar Passages,'" in *W*, 3:181–255; "The 'Two Natures' and Recent Christological Speculation," in *W*, 3:259–310; "Christless Christianity," in *W*, 3:313–67; "The Twentieth-Century Christ," in *W*, 3:371–89; "The Supernatural Birth of Jesus," in *W*, 3:447–58; "Tertullian and the Beginnings of the Doctrine of the Trinity," in *W*, 3:3–109; "Calvin's Doctrine of the Trinity," in *W*, 3:189–284; "The Principle of the Incarnation," in *SSW*, 1:139–47; "John's First Word," in *SSW*, 1:148–50; "The Deity of Christ," in *SSW*, 1:151–57; "The Human Development of Jesus," in *SSW*, 1:158–66; "Incarnate Truth," in *SSW*, 2:455–67; "Why Four Gospels," in *SSW*, 2:639–42; "The Gospel of John," in *SSW*, 2:643–46; "Jesus the Measure of Men," in *SSW*, 2:688–92; "Introduction to Samuel G. Craig's *Jesus As He Was and Is*," in *SSW*, 2:693–97; "The Emotional Life of Our Lord," in *PWC*, 93–145; plus the many sermons published in *The Power of God unto Salvation*, *Faith and Life*, and *The Savior of the World*, as well as many significant reviews of books. This list is by no means exhaustive. As an example of Warfield's chief interest in this doctrine, in his review of *Dictionary of the Apostolic Church*, by James Hastings, he expresses dissatisfaction with the article by C. Anderson Scott on "Christ, Christology" by stating that this should have been "the central article of the volume" (*W*, 10:444). For his own part, Warfield gives more attention to the Gospels in his writings, particularly his christological writings, than to any other portion of Scripture.

penetrating analysis, careful exposition, and often devastating critique. Yet he consistently displays a sense of adoration of Christ and of utter dependence upon him for redemption from sin. Without question, in the person and work of Christ (the topics of this chapter and the next) we have reached the heart of Benjamin Warfield.

Warfield explicitly locates himself in the stream of orthodox christology, describing Chalcedon in fact as the necessary presupposition for understanding Scripture. That Christ in his incarnate state is both truly God and truly man, consubstantial with God and with us, is not only expressly taught by the biblical writers at times but also the underlying assumption throughout their presentation of him. But in the context of nineteenth-century liberalism, in which all such metaphysical concepts were disallowed, this doctrine was no longer the shared assumption of all professing Christians. In the Ritschlian theology that was attempting to dominate much of the Protestant world, Christ had become something much less—a great leader, a great example, a great teacher, a great man, even the best of men, but not the God-man. Warfield deplored "the widespread, the almost universal tendency to deprecate the uniqueness and the unapproachable majesty of the Son of God."[2] And while Warfield was prepared to answer heterodoxy on all fronts, a particular concern was this reduced christology. Here was teaching that spelled the undoing of the gospel, of Christianity itself, and Warfield labored vigorously to answer the assault in all its various inventive forms.

The Deity of Christ

Warfield treats the subject of the deity of Christ often, but the basic outline of his thinking is provided in *The Lord of Glory* (1907) while fuller expositions of specific New Testament passages abound in his works. Virtually his only treatment of the theme from the Old Testament is "The Divine Messiah in the Old Testament" (1916), which is more an exhibition of the failures of the critics who deny or attempt to conceal the deity of the Messiah in the Old Testament than a positive exposition of the theme. Warfield does focus on a few sample passages to demonstrate that the hope of ancient Israel centered on a divine deliverer. We will survey the later of the two works first in a more natural progression from the Old Testament to the New in Warfield's development of the doctrine.

---

[2]*W*, 2:196; *SSW*, 2:296; cf. *W*, 3:160.

THE MESSIAH IN THE OLD TESTAMENT

The Messianic Psalms

Warfield demonstrates at the outset of "Divine Messiah" that the New Testament writers and Christ himself all understand the Old Testament as recognizing and teaching that "the Messiah was to be of divine nature." This is evident in that all of them equally support their own assertions of Christ's deity with appeals to the Old Testament. Hebrews 1 provides as good an example as any. The writer makes use of the messianic psalms, specifically Psalms 2, 45, and 110. In Psalm 2 the very term meaning "Messiah," that is, Christ, is used and is applied to Jesus not only by the writer of Hebrews (1:5; 5:5) but also by the first apostles (Acts 4:24–26) and Paul (Acts 13:33), and "its language has supplied to the book of Revelation its standing phrases for describing the completeness of our Lord's conquest of the world (Rev. 2:27; 12:5; 19:15)."[3]

Psalm 110:1 provides the earliest biblical expression of the Messiah's session at the right hand of God,

> The LORD says to my Lord:
> "Sit at my right hand,
> until I make your enemies your footstool,"

and it is so cited in Hebrews 1:13; 5:6; 7:17–21; and 10:13. But the apostle Paul also employs its language when speaking of Christ's exaltation (1 Cor. 15:25), as does the apostle Peter in his initial proclamation of the gospel at Pentecost (Acts 2:32–36). Jesus himself references this psalm in order to silence his opponents, "who, harping on the title 'Son of David,' had forgotten that David himself recognized this, his greater Son as also his Lord" (cf. Mark 12:35–37; Matt. 22:45–46; Luke 20:41–44). Warfield shows that although the opinion of the day understood Messiah as a descendant of David, Jesus held that the Old Testament demanded something more, a higher estimate of him. Messiah is the Son of God, the heavenly Son of Man, who rides the clouds. Jesus saw in Psalm 110 "a reference to the transcendent Messiah in which He Himself very evidently believed. In Jesus' view, therefore, the transcendent Messiah is already an object of Old Testament revelation." It is this that shaped the conviction of the New Testament writers and their use of the messianic psalms; if Jesus so understood them, it is only natural that they would also.[4]

---

[3] W, 3:6.
[4] W, 3:6–7.

Warfield contends that "if a man reject the eternal Godhead of Christ, he must either lay the Psalms aside or sing them with bated breath." Indeed, "the latest phase of sceptical criticism" has itself thoroughly demonstrated that the doctrine of a divine Messiah "was native to pre-Christian Judaism." The entire house had been prepared and only awaited Jesus to enter it for faith to come to its full realization. "The whole secret of the Christology of the New Testament, explains Hermann Gunkel, lies in the fact that it was the Christology of pre-Christian Judaism before it was the Christology of Christianity." Warfield cites Psalm 96:11–13 as a clear example.

> Let the heavens rejoice, and let the earth be glad; let the sea roar, and the fulness thereof. Let the field be joyful, and all that is therein: then shall all the trees of the wood rejoice before the LORD: for he cometh, for he cometh to judge the earth: he shall judge the world with righteousness, and the peoples with his truth. (KJV)

Warfield asserts that no Christian can read this without thinking of the advent of Christ, and no Christian can doubt that the proper response to this must be that of the apostle John: "Amen. Even so, come Lord Jesus" (KJV).[5]

Warfield frankly admits that when liberal critics demonstrate this faith of pre-Christian Judaism, they have no interest or motive at all to justify the faith in a divine Jesus. They are noting the beliefs of ancient Israel only. As for themselves, they dismiss such a faith as a reflection of the mythical God-King, which they allege was common to Israel's neighbors. Nevertheless, the fact remains that the New Testament writers and Jesus himself maintain the faith of Israel and understand the Messiah as a divine being.

Warfield spends more time with Psalm 45:6—"Thy throne, O God, is forever and ever" (KJV)—and surveys the attempts of some to retranslate it as "Thy throne is God," or "Thy throne of God," "Thy throne is of God," and so on. He then observes others who "allow the Psalmist his own word," but attempt to reduce the meaning of it. "Violent avoidances" or "violent reductions," "evacuations," and other such "artificialities of interpretation" of the text are the only alternatives to seeing in it a testimony to the divine nature of the Messiah. Even critical scholars now acknowledge this, Warfield notes, even if they disallow such notions from their own "scientific interpretation." And for good reason, for what purely human Davidic king could be addressed as "God," and his sons be constituted as princes over the whole world (Ps. 45:7, 17)?[6]

---

[5]W, 3:10–11.
[6]W, 3:13–15, 17.

Warfield argues this interpretation against the broader backdrop of Israel's eschatology, which consisted in "the settled expectation of the universal establishment of the reign of Jehovah." The Old Testament repeatedly fans this hope—not only that Messiah would come, but that Jehovah himself would come to save his people. The recurring "he comes" (יָבוֹא) "stamps the religion of the Old Testament specifically a religion of hope"—a hope that the God of heaven and earth would come and bring the whole world eternally into his kingdom of peace and righteousness and worship of him. It is this twin hope—of a coming king and of a coming God—that coalesces into a hope for "the transcendent Messiah," even if the larger questions of the unity of God and the plurality of divine persons were not yet understood. This hope does not appear simply here and there; it is "involved in the entire drift of the eschatological expectations of the Old Testament," and it is against this background that we must read and understand specific expressions of that hope. "He who reads the Old Testament, however cursorily, will not escape a sense, however dim, that he is brought into contact in it with a Messiah who is more than human in the fundamental basis of His being, and in whose coming Jehovah visits His people in some more than representative sense." Only in an incarnate God can these two lines of promise be brought together, and only this gives justification for ascribing titles of deity—"God," "Lord," "the mighty God," "Jehovah our righteousness," and so on—and divine attributes and functions— eternality, holiness, forgiveness, and the like—to Messiah.[7]

Accordingly, the New Testament writers freely and unanimously refer all lines of messianic prediction to Jesus, "and they declare Him no less the Jehovah who was expected to come to save His people, than the Son of David or the Suffering Servant of God." John the Baptist, his forerunner, in fulfillment of prophecy, prepares the way of "the Lord." What else can this mean, Warfield asks, but that Jesus Christ is very God and, therefore, that Messiah is divine? It is precisely on this ground that Messiah is named "Jesus"—"precisely because 'it is He that shall save His people from their sins'—He, that is, Jesus, shall save His people, that is, Jesus' people,—in fulfilment of the promise of the saving Jehovah."[8]

Isaiah 9:6

Isaiah 9:6 challenges our attention in this regard "with the same insistency" as Psalm 45:6. Messiah is here designated, "the Mighty God, the Everlasting Father, the Prince of Peace." The "obvious meaning" is that the promised Messiah is divine. Warfield cites J. A. Alexander (1809–1860), who argues that attempts to

---

[7]W, 3:19, 22–25.
[8]W, 3:27–28.

refer this designation to Hezekiah are compelled by theological necessity and not the exegesis of the text.

> The doctrine that this prophecy relates to the Messiah was not disputed even by the Jews, until the virulence of the anti-Christian controversy drove them from the ground which their own progenitors had steadfastly maintained. In this departure from the truth they have been followed by some learned writers who are Christians only in name, and to whom may be applied with little alteration, what one of them (Gesenius) has said with respect to the ancient versions of this very text, viz., that the general meaning put upon it may be viewed as the criterion of a Christian and an anti-Christian writer.[9]

Of particular interest in this verse is the expression גִּבּוֹר אֵל, "mighty God," which as Hengstenberg remarks, "can only signify God-Hero, a Hero who is infinitely exalted above all human heroes by the circumstance that he is *God*." Warfield argues that the phrase is defined by its use again in Isaiah 10:21, where it refers to Jehovah; "that is to say, the Messiah is declared to be God in the same sense in which Jehovah is God." Warfield acknowledges that the Messiah is represented in the Old Testament as a human king, the offspring of David. But as with his interpretation of Psalm 45, he will not take either side of the equation for the whole: Messiah is represented as *both* God and man. "In such passages the Old Testament revelation falls into a self-contradiction, from which only a miracle has been able to deliver us, the Incarnation of the Son of God." Isaiah's language goes well beyond what would be appropriate for any mere human being, however unique. The child to be born will be much more than a mighty man and more than a mighty king. He will be mighty אֵל, God. Nor will it do to impute the God-king notions of Israel's neighbors to Israel herself. The theory "requires too many assumptions, and these assumptions receive no support from the facts. As we have already seen, the ancient orient knows nothing of an eschatological king, and Israel knows as little of a deified King." Attempts to "explain away" Isaiah's language are both futile and "absurd."[10]

Warfield contends that "the prophets do attribute a divine nature and do ascribe divine functions to the Messiah," and he seems glad to announce that the "entire body of 'results' of the 'Old Liberal' criticism concerning the development of the Messianic hope—which it tended to relegate more and more completely to post-exilic times—has been hopelessly broken up." This hope "was aboriginal in Israel, and formed, indeed, in all ages the heart of Israelitish religion." It was

---

[9]*W*, 3:28–29.
[10]*W*, 3:29–30, 35, 38 (Hengstenberg's emphasis).

not, as the old liberalism alleged, the creation of postexilic times. Warfield cites Herman Bavinck in support.

> In place of the feverish efforts which were more and more ruling in the dominant school of literary criticism to remove all Messianic prediction to post-exilic times, it is now acknowledged that the pre-exilic prophets, not only themselves cherished such Messianic expectations, but also presuppose them among the people; nor have they themselves excogitated them and proclaimed them as novelties to the people; but they have received them from the past and are building on expectations which have existed from ancient times and have been current in Israel.[11]

Daniel 7:13-14: The Son of Man

Daniel 7:13–14, with its depiction of the Son of Man, has been recognized as messianic by all sides until modern times, and for Warfield it is perhaps the leading Old Testament passage to demonstrate that the expected Messiah was divine.[12]

Some have attempted to limit this Son of Man to mere humanity and interpret the language that goes beyond the human as identifying this figure as a divine representative. To do this, however, is to dissever this prophecy from "the entire course of Messianic expectation," which presents the Messiah as coming both from Israel and from heaven. But in this instance Warfield is willing to go the next step: this prophecy is somewhat novel in that it so stresses the heavenly origin and, thus, "the transcendental element of the Messianic figure" himself, that it can appear "to neglect, if not quite to obscure, its human side." This figure is a heavenly being. He comes on the clouds. He stands before God's throne. It is "hopeless" to represent such a figure as "wholly human." It is Jehovah, the Creator and Lord of nature, who can ride on clouds. More to the point, this Son of Man is not described as coming from heaven to earth or, for that matter, from earth to heaven. He comes "out of obscurity into manifestation" and as "simply drawing nigh to the throne." The emphasis is clearly on the "immediate vicinity of God" into which he comes for "coronation." Nor is this being a mere angel. He is "the Lord-Messiah, the Lord of the new world, to whom is to be given the dominion of the world, and all the peoples and all the times."[13]

The Son of Man is certainly God's representative, but he is himself a heavenly, divine being. Yet he stands "in direct relation to the people." "Though he thus belongs to the category of man, he is not, however, forthwith to be assigned to the earthly sphere. He comes from heaven." Daniel's Son of Man bears virtually no

---

[11] W, 3:38–39.
[12] W, 3:40.
[13] W, 3:41–42, 44.

"this-world traits" whatever. In short, we have here a sampling of the Old Testament hope of a coming Messiah who is himself God. This is "a superhuman figure, a figure to whose super-human character justice is not done until it is recognized as expressly divine." And it was so understood by students of Scripture throughout Israel's ancient history. This was further the understanding Christ displayed "by applying it to Himself to present Himself as a heavenly Being who had come forth from heaven and descended to earth on a mission of mercy to lost men."[14]

Other Old Testament Passages

Warfield mentions, in passing, Psalms 2 and 100; Micah 5:2; Jeremiah 23:6; Zechariah 13:7; and Malachi 3:1 as other passages that could as well have been chosen for his examination of the question of the deity of the Messiah in the Old Testament, and he cautions us not to think that the question depends only upon the passages he has selected.

> The salient fact regarding it [the deity of the Messiah] is that it is an essential element in the eschatological system of the Old Testament and is inseparably imbedded in the hope of the coming of God to His kingdom which formed the heart of Israelitish religion from its origin. We have only to free ourselves from the notion that the Messianic hope was the product of the monarchy and to realize that, however closely it becomes attached to the Davidic dynasty in one of its modes of expression, it was an aboriginal element in the religion of Israel, to understand how little it can be summed up in the expectation of the coming of an earthly king.

The idea of the divine Messiah, Warfield insists, is "the soul of the entire Old Testament." This was the long hope of Israel. "The appearance of the Messiah presents itself more and more clearly to the view of the prophets as the perfect theophany, the final coming of Jehovah." We cannot read the Old Testament without sensing that the Messiah it promises is one in whom God himself will come to his people.[15]

THE MESSIAH IN THE NEW TESTAMENT

The Lord of Glory, Warfield's most extensive defense of the deity of Christ—also among his earliest, thus laying the groundwork for arguments found in his later christological writings—commences from the conviction that the whole purpose of the New Testament is to tell of Christ. He is its "proper subject," and "every

---

[14]W, 3:44, 46–47.
[15]W, 3:25, 47–49.

line" of it makes its own contribution to the overall portrait of him. Moreover, every detail of this portrait must be considered as we form our estimate of the writers' conception of Christ's person—both the primary and subsidiary evidence, the direct and the more incidental—and it is often the more incidental evidence that appears most convincing. That the deity of Christ is "taken for granted" throughout the New Testament writings is perhaps the most impressive, even if not the most obvious, of all the evidence for this conviction on the part of the apostles and early church.[16]

The specific lines of evidence Warfield examines in *The Lord of Glory* concern primarily the various titles and designations of Christ that the New Testament writers employ. From the use of these various designations, Warfield seeks to ascertain the attitude toward Christ and "the loftiness of the estimate placed upon His person by these writers, and by those whom they represent." What Warfield finds is that this evidence, running through the entire New Testament, testifies to "the profound conviction cherished by our Lord's first followers that He was of divine origin and nature."[17] We will trace Warfield's approach as he develops it in this work and supplement it with his fuller comments on selected passages elsewhere in his writings.

The Synoptic Gospels: Mark

In this quest Warfield surveys the entire New Testament, but the bulk of his attention is given to the Gospel records, and of these primarily the Synoptics. A few samplings here will suffice to illustrate Warfield's approach. He acknowledges that the term "lord" is often used as a generally honorific title similar to our "sir." Yet, he argues, among the Gospel writers its significance seems to "grow in richness and in content" and "expand in significance until it ends by implying supreme authority." Similarly, the term "messiah" is an official designation that could possibly refer to anyone solemnly designated and commissioned to God's work. "But when applied to Jesus it takes on fuller and fuller significance until it ends by assimilating Him to the Divine Being Himself." By this designation Jesus is clearly not conceived of merely as a divine representative "but as Himself a superhuman person." "When, for example, Jesus is quoted as declaring that 'the Son of Man is Lord even of the Sabbath' (or, perhaps, 'of the Sabbath, too'), the implication is that He is Lord of much more than the Sabbath." "It is no doubt sometimes very difficult to determine whether in a given instance it ["lord"] refers to God or to Jesus, a fact which has its significance." He is David's Lord,

---

[16]*LG*, 1; cf. *W*, 2:189.
[17]*LG*, 2–3.

greater than David and greater than Solomon. He is "the Lord" (Jehovah) whose way was to be prepared by John the Baptist in fulfillment of prophetic hope. The implications of Jesus' own use of "Lord" are those of supremacy and sovereignty. He claims for himself (Mark 2:28; 12:36–37; 13:35; 11:3) and is recognized by his disciples (Mark 11:3) as possessing

> supreme sovereignty,—a sovereignty superior to that of the typical king himself (12:36–37), extending over the divinely ordained religious enactments of the chosen people (7:28, cf. 7:15–19), and entitling Him to dispose of the possessions (11:3) and the very destinies of men (13:35). There is here asserted not only Messianic dignity and authority, but dignity and authority which transcend those ordinarily attributed even to the Messiah (12:36–37), and are comparable only to those of God Himself (1:3).[18]

This superior dignity was immediately (εὐθυς) attributed to Jesus even by the demons he confronted: "What have you to do with us, Jesus of Nazareth? Have you come to destroy us? I know who you are—the Holy One of God" (Mark 1:23–24). This recognition at first sight presupposes that there was "something about Jesus which betrayed to an eye which saw beneath the surface His super-human nature—whether this were thought of as His supreme holiness or as His unapproachable majesty."[19]

Jesus' constant use of "the Son of Man," clearly his preferred self-designation, is likewise charged—by Jesus' own usage of it and its original context in Daniel—with unmistakable implications of a superhuman figure of heavenly origin, one who is to return on the clouds and "clothed in glory" and "sitting at the right hand of power," indeed, a "heavenly being." Jesus' very use of the title at all, "with its obvious reference to the vision of Daniel, necessarily carried with it the assertion of heavenly origination and nature."[20]

Even in that enigmatic passage where Jesus confesses ignorance as to the time of his return, he plainly ranks himself above the angels. In his statement, "Concerning that day or hour, no one knows, not even the angels in heaven, nor the Son, but only the Father" (Mark 13:32), there is clearly a gradation of rank in which he, "the Son," stands "as definitely and as incomparably above the category of angels," and as belonging to a "superior class." He accordingly claims that the angels are "his angels" and that in that great day they will obey his command as he sends them to gather his elect (13:27). To Mark, Jesus is

---

[18]*LG*, 36, 9–12.
[19]*LG*, 20.
[20]*LG*, 29–30, 39.

more than superhuman; he is superangelic, "and the question at once obtrudes itself whether a superangelic person is not by that very fact removed from the category of creatures."[21]

Similarly, Jesus' use of the terms "Son of God" and "the Son" is so freighted with supernatural implications that even apart from such a passage as Mark 13:32, where his superangelic nature is expressly stated, we are forced to the conclusion, particularly in light of passages such as 12:6; 14:62; and 15:39, that "a supernatural personality as well as a supernatural office is intended to be understood by it." And if this is so, Warfield continues,

> in view of the nature of the term itself, it is difficult to doubt that this supernatural-ness of personality is intended to be taken at the height of the Divine. What can the Son, the unique and "beloved" Son of God, who also is God's heir, in contradistinction from all His servants, even the angels, be—but God Himself?[22]

Beyond this, Jesus is presented as the "bridegroom" (Mark 2:19–20), a designation unmistakably reminiscent of those Old Testament passages in which Jehovah presents himself in that light (e.g., Hos. 2:19). Put simply, "The use of 'the Bridegroom' as a designation of our Lord assimilates His relation to the people of God to that which in the Old Testament is exclusively, even jealously, occupied by Jehovah Himself," and raises the question whether Jesus is not thereby, at least in some sense, identified with Jehovah. Warfield answers the question affirmatively. And this, in turn, he argues, sheds light on passages such as Mark 12:35, in which, citing Psalm 110, Jesus refers to himself as "David's Lord"—a term that, in this context at least, can scarcely fall short of being David's God.[23]

Warfield summarizes his study of the presentation of Christ in the Gospel of Mark:

> It is idle to speak of Mark presenting us in his account of Jesus with the picture of a purely human life. It belongs to the very essence of his undertaking to portray this life as supernatural; and, from beginning to end, he sets it forth as thoroughly supernatural. . . . Whatever else this life was, it certainly was not, in view of any observer, a "natural" one. . . . We should not misrepresent Mark if we said that his whole Gospel is devoted to making the impression that Jesus' life and manifestation were supernatural through and through.[24]

---

[21]*LG*, 37; *SSW*, 1:153–54.
[22]*LG*, 45.
[23]*LG*, 45–47, 50.
[24]*LG*, 32–34.

The Synoptic Gospels: Matthew and Luke

Matthew and Luke begin their accounts with a record of the supernatural birth of the supernatural Jesus. Matthew highlights the deity of Christ in the names given to him: both "Immanuel" (Isa. 7:14; Matt. 1:23) and "Jesus" declare him to be Jehovah himself come to save his people from all their sins (Ps. 130:8; Matt. 1:21). Luke introduces him as "Savior," who is "Christ the Lord" (Luke 2:11). Warfield assumes that the term "the Lord" here is intended to add significance to the term "the Christ"—"else why is it added?" But he wonders in what way can "Lord" add climax to "Christ," when in "Christ" itself "the Anointed King, there is already expressed the height of sovereignty and authority as the delegate of Jehovah." He surmises that the addition of "Lord" is intended to convey the idea that the "Christ" now born is a divine Christ. This notion is greatly strengthened by the contextual notes of Christ's supernatural birth and another title of supreme dignity, "Son of the Most High" (Luke 1:32). Again, also in Matthew, Jesus presents himself as the mighty "Son of Man" who will send "his angels" to weed out sinners from "his kingdom" and who will himself "reward" and judge (Matt. 13:41; 16:27; 24:31; Luke 9:26). "Who is this Son of Man," Warfield asks pointedly, "surrounded by his angels, in whose hands are the issues of life? . . . Who is this Son of Man at whose behest his angels winnow men?" In Luke 15, Jesus speaks three parables that purport to reveal the emotions of heaven and the heart of God in receiving sinners. His claim is that he must receive sinners, "because this is heaven's way," and that in him, therefore, heaven is "manifested."[25]

Beyond this, the evidence for Christ's deity that Warfield finds in Matthew and Luke runs largely along similar lines as that in Mark, but with some important additions, most notably Matthew 11:27 (with Luke 10:22) and Matthew 28:19. In Matthew 11:27, Jesus claims as "the Son" "a relation of practical equality" with the Father, who, Warfield notes, is himself described in the loftiest of terms, "Lord of heaven and earth" (v. 25). This relation Jesus expresses in terms of exclusive "mutual perfect knowledge" and exclusive revelation. The Son, in the very same way as the Father, is unknowable, beyond the grasp of the creaturely mind. Only the Father can know the Son, and only the Son can know the Father. "The Father and the Son, and all that is in the Father and the Son, lie mutually open to each other's gaze." "The knowledge which the Father has of the Son is a specifically divine knowledge. Therefore also the knowledge which the Son has of the Father is also a specifically divine knowledge." This assertion of reciprocal knowledge "rises far above the merely mediatorial function of the Son, although it underlies His mediatorial mission: it carries us back into the region of metaphysical rela-

---

[25]LG, 144; SSW, 1:153–54.

tions." The Father and the Son are "mutually intercommunicative." "The depths of the Son's being, we are told, can be fathomed by none but a divine knowledge, while the knowledge of the Son compasses all that God is; from both points of view, the Son appears thus as 'equal with God.'" Accordingly, the Son alone can make the Father known. Further, the mutual knowledge of Father and Son is put on equal par.

> The Son can be known only by the Father in all that He is, as if His being were infinite and as such inscrutable to the finite intelligence; and His knowledge alone—again as if He were infinite in His attributes—is competent to compass the depths of the Father's infinite being. He who holds this relation to the Father cannot conceivably be a creature.

Simply put, this is Jesus' "culminating assertion" of his own essential deity. Clearly, Jesus possessed more than a merely human self-consciousness.[26]

Luke's version is slightly different but in essence the same. He does not say that the Father and Son know each other but that each knows "'what the other is,' that is to say, all that each is." Even so, "it would be difficult to frame a statement which could more sharply assert the essential deity of the 'Son.'" "In this great passage we have what must be considered the culminating assertion on our Lord's part of His essential deity."[27]

An assertion such as this leaves little room for surprise when Jesus as "the Son" claims openly to share fully, with the Father and the Holy Spirit, in the name of God: "All authority in heaven and on earth has been given to me. Go therefore and make disciples of all nations, baptizing them into the name of the Father and of the Son and of the Holy Spirit" (Matt. 28:18–19 ESV mg.). If in Matthew 11:27 Jesus declares his intercommunion with the Father, here he asserts that

> all authority in heaven and earth has been given Him, and [he] asserts a place for Himself in the precincts of the ineffable Name. Here is a claim not merely to a deity in some sense equivalent to and as it were alongside of the deity of the Father, but to a deity in some high sense one with the deity of the Father.[28]

The note of Christ's deity is resounded throughout the Gospel of Matthew as Matthew attributes to Jesus divine prerogatives, divine power, and a divine nature. Jesus holds men's destinies in his own hands. He shares the glory and the name of God. He is the inaugurator of God's kingdom. He is the judge of all the

---

[26] *LG*, 92–93, 82–83, 155; *PTR* 11, no. 4 (1913): 660–64; *SSW*, 1:154–55; cf. *W*, 10:396–97.
[27] *LG*, 119, 155.
[28] *LG*, 83; *W*, 3:162.

earth. Matthew's general representation of Jesus, Warfield argues, "necessitates a doctrine of His nature and relations with God" as expressed in the great claims of Jesus in Matthew 11:27 and 28:19. "It were impossible for Matthew to paint Jesus as he has painted Him" without such a conception of him. "So far from these passages offending the reader as they stand in Matthew's Gospel, therefore, and raising doubts of their genuineness, we should have had to postulate something like them for Matthew, had they not stood in his Gospel."[29]

Thus, Warfield concludes, the Synoptic writers "unite" in their representation of Jesus as a person "of the highest exaltation." The designations used of him are "obviously" employed "with the highest implications these appellatives are capable of bearing." "Nothing is left unsaid which could be said in simple and straightforward narratives to make it clear to the reader that Jesus is the Messiah: and nothing is lacking in what is said to make it clear that this Messiah is more than a human, even a divine, person." He is not merely the Davidic king who reigns over the kingdom and people of God; he is Jehovah himself come to visit his people with redemption. "The essential deity of the Son could not receive more absolute expression." "It is abundantly clear that the Synoptists conceived Jesus, whom they identify with the Messiah, as a divine person; and represent Him as exercising divine prerogatives and asserting for Himself a divine personality and participation in the divine Name."[30]

The Synoptic Gospels and Jesus' Mission

In his lengthy "Jesus' Mission, According to His Own Testimony (Synoptics)," War-field draws out the meaning and implications of Jesus' statements as to his reason for coming into the world. The study centers on the "I came" (and equivalent) sayings of Jesus in the Synoptic Gospels, which shed light on Jesus' "divine mission." The passages are as follows: Mark 1:38 = Luke 4:43; Matthew 5:17; Mark 2:17 = Matthew 9:13 = Luke 5:32; Matthew 10:34f.; Matthew 15:24; Luke 12:49ff.; Mark 10:45 = Matthew 20:28; and Luke 19:10. We will take the first as an example. In Mark 1:38 (= Luke 4:43) Jesus calls his disciples to go to the next towns "in order [ἵνα] to preach." He then adds the explanatory clause, "because for this purpose I came out [ἐξῆλθον]" (BBW). In Luke's account he speaks similarly but in terms of the necessity (δεῖ) of his going to preach because (ὅτι) to this he "was sent [ἀπεστάλην]." Jesus came to preach the gospel of the kingdom—the messianic proclamation. This preaching, in turn, as the narrative and parallels bear out, was verified by the accompanying miracles—yet another of Jesus' messianic credentials. Jesus "came" and "was sent"

---

[29]*LG*, 95–96.
[30]*LG*, 125, 127, 133, 140, 145.

for this purpose. His words reflect a consciousness of a divine mission. Moreover, the specific word ἐξῆλθον, "I came out," is significant. He "came out" from where? And from where was he "sent"? The terminology, reminiscent of Jesus' similar sayings in the Gospel of John, are reflective of a preexistence and heavenly origin and, taken all together, Jesus' own affirmation of his divine nature.[31]

The Gospels and the Foresight of Jesus

In "The Foresight of Jesus," Warfield develops the Gospels' presentation of Jesus as one who knew in detail why he had come and what he was to do. This "prevision" determined all that Jesus did. He knew his life ahead of time. There were no surprises and no compulsions. Jesus was not "influenced" by anyone to become what he was—his entire life was governed by the divine δεῖ, which he continuously recognized. His life was therefore a supernatural life lived out under the direction of his own omniscience.

The bulk of the Gospels' mention of Jesus' foresight surrounds his many predictions of his death (e.g., Matt. 12:40; 17:17, 22–23; 20:28; 26:28; Luke 12:49–50; John 2:19; 10:11, 15; etc.), resurrection (e.g., Matt. 12:40; 16:21; 17:9, 23; 20:19; John 2:19; 10:18; etc.), and his return to the Father and then to the earth (e.g., Matt. 10:23; 16:27; 19:28; Mark 10:40; Luke 17:22; Matt. 24:34–37, 44; 25:31; 26:64; etc.). Jesus knew his life, and he knew the whole sweep of history and his relation to it. But his foresight was not limited to his own career as such. He reads men's hearts (Matt. 9:4; Mark 2:5, 8; 8:17; 12:15, 44; Luke 5:22; 7:39; John 1:47; 2:24–25; 4:17–19; 6:64, 70; 13:11; 21:17). He knew when and where Peter must cast his net in order to catch fish (Luke 5:4; cf. John 21:6). He knew that the first fish Peter would catch, this time fishing with a hook, would be one that had swallowed a coin (Matt. 17:27). He knew where his disciples would find an ass and its colt and that the owners would allow Jesus to use it (Matt. 21:2). He knew that upon entering the city they would meet a man with a pitcher of water and prepare to serve the master (Mark 14:13). He knew the coming denials of Peter (Matt. 26:31). He knew the career of his followers (Matt. 4:19) and the persecutions they would face (Matt. 10:17, 21; 24:9; John 16:1). He knew the entire history of God's kingdom in the world (Matt. 16:18; 24:5, 24). And so on.[32]

The examples seem endless. "In the Gospel presentation, foresight is made the principle of our Lord's career." It is evident that "the Evangelists designed to represent Jesus as endowed with the absolute and unlimited foresight consonant with His Divine nature." The life of Jesus that the Gospel writers present to

---

[31] *W*, 2:255–324.
[32] *W*, 2:71–97; cf. his earlier "Jesus' Foreknowledge of His Death," *TBS*, new series, 3, no. 1 (January 1901): 57–58; cf. Warfield, "The Independence of our Lord," *The Herald and Presbyter* 44, no. 21 (1884): i.

us "is distinctly a supernatural life . . . ; and the human aspect of it is treated by each alike as an incident in something more exalted." It is clear that they were representing Jesus in such a way that expressed their conviction "that in Jesus Christ dwelt the fulness of the knowledge of God" (Matt. 11:27; Luke 10:22; John 8:38; 16:15; 17:10).[33]

The Synoptic Jesus—the Historical Jesus

Ever the polemic theologian, Warfield is well aware of the advances of New Testament criticism of his day, and so before he leaves his discussion of the Synoptic Gospels, he turns his attention to answering the critical claims as they bear on the question of the deity of Christ. In his eighth chapter of *The Lord of Glory*, entitled "The Jesus of the Synoptics the Primitive Jesus," Warfield demonstrates at length that the Synoptic estimate of Christ as divine is not merely the opinion of the three writers; it is also very evidently the estimate held by the original Christian community they represent and for whom they wrote. That is, "We have here the conception of Jesus which prevailed in the primitive age of the Christian propaganda." "Certain extremists," Warfield remarks, "largely in order to escape this very conclusion," attempted to assign the composition of these books to the late second century. But Warfield dismisses these "extremists" with the conviction, shared by "most reasonable men today," that the Synoptics were all written before AD 80. This assures us that the witness of the Synoptics to Jesus, expressed with such simplicity and unstudied emphasis, is a witness to the "aboriginal faith of Christians," for it would be impossible that such a conception of Jesus falsely grew among Christians within only a "short generation" from the death of Jesus.[34]

Nor do the findings of literary criticism weaken this conclusion. Grant the appeal to the yet earlier documents underlying the Synoptic Gospels, and the portrait of Jesus presented in them is the very same "supernatural Son of God."[35] Warfield demonstrates at length that the hypothetical sources that the several schools of criticism reconstruct for the Synoptics all yield a witness to the deity of Christ that is ten or perhaps twenty years earlier and closer to the church's faith of the AD 30s. "The assurance that our Gospels rest on earlier documentary sources becomes thus an additional assurance that the conception of the person of Jesus

---

[33]*W*, 2:93, 79–84.

[34]*LG*, 146–47.

[35]The argument presented here in *The Lord of Glory* Warfield presents again in the first major section of his article, "Jesus Christ," published originally in *NSHERK* 1910 (*W*, 3:149–69; this quotation is from 156). See also his treatment of this in "The 'Two Natures' and Recent Christological Speculation," in *W*, 3:286ff. Warfield stresses this point again in "The Question of Miracles," in *SSW*, 2:185–88.

which they present in concert is the conception which held the mind and heart of the Church from the very beginning." Those documents which,

> even in the view of the most unreasonable criticism, are supposed to underlie the structure of our present Synoptics are freighted with the same teaching which these Gospels themselves embody as to the person of our Lord. Literary criticism cannot penetrate to any stratum of belief more primitive than this. We may sink our trial shafts down through the soil of the Gospel tradition at any point we please; it is only conformable strata that we pierce. So far as the tradition goes, it gives consentient testimony to an aboriginal faith in the deity of the founder of the religion of Christianity.[36]

Likewise the resort to historical criticism is of no help in the attempt to escape the divine Christ of the primitive church. Historical criticism, seeking to ascertain not simply the older and/or later documentary strata or what the Synoptists and their community thought of Jesus but also what Jesus himself taught, bears witness to the very same supernatural Jesus. His repeated claims to be "Lord," the heavenly "Son of Man," "the Son," one who fully participates in the divine name and who alone is known by and has exclusive knowledge of the Father, "only bring home to us with peculiar poignancy" the testimony of Jesus' own self-witness. The witness of the Synoptics, however examined, is consistently and exclusively to the divine Christ.[37]

But are these documents trustworthy? Or do they still represent a Jesus of the Evangelists' own making? Assuming that Jesus could not have made such claims for himself, critics allege that the Gospel writers have evidently put their own words on Jesus' lips, that they have read back their own ideas into his teaching. What we must do, therefore, they insist, is distinguish between their words and the words of Jesus. The Evangelists' love for Jesus—intentionally or not—has skewed their representation of him, and we must now penetrate behind them in order to discover the real Jesus of history.

But why must we distrust the Synoptists so? Love for Jesus is hardly evidence of fraud and deceit, particularly on the part of men concerned—indeed, even willing to die—for truth. And even so, how shall we get behind their report? Suppose Jesus did actually lay claim to deity. How else could we know it but from those who write of him? On what grounds can we affirm that unsympathetic reporters alone are trustworthy? Yet these are the underlying canons of the critical reconstruction of the historical Jesus—we must search for *contrary* statements and fragments,

---

[36]*LG*, 148, 155.
[37]*LG*, 157; *W*, 3:253–55.

those which would suggest a purely human Jesus, in order to find the Jesus of history. Faced with this, Warfield remarks:

> Surely we do not need to pause to point out that the procedure we are here invited to adopt is a prescription for historical investigation which must always issue in reversing the portraiture of the historical characters to the records of whose lives it is applied. The result of its universal application would be, so to speak, the writing of all history backwards and the adornment of its annals with a series of portraits which would have this only to recommend them, that they represent every historical character as the exact contrast to what each was thought to be by all who knew and esteemed him.

Warfield calls this "the apotheosis of topsytervydom" and adds that the "absurdity" of such an approach is heightened by the fact that, as virtually all sides allow, the writings in view and the documents on which they rest all come from such an early date as to certainly reflect the universal conviction of those first-generation Christians.[38]

It is not surprising, given the unanimity of the early church in its view of Jesus, that these critics have a very difficult time discovering the data they demand, and so Warfield observes that "the groundlessness of this assault on the trustworthiness of the portrait of Jesus presented in our Synoptics may fairly be said, therefore, to be matched by its resultlessness." There is simply no "naturalistic Christ" to be found anywhere but in the assertions of the critics themselves. The Gospel records provide no material whatever out of which such a naturalistic Christ can be created. The method is "purely subjective" and altogether unreliable, and Warfield finds more sympathy for those who resort to saying that the Jesus of history is now hopelessly lost and hidden beneath "the incrustations with which faith has enveloped it" and for those even bolder critics who take the next logical step and ask why there is need of assuming a real Jesus at all. How could such a naturalistic Jesus account for the rise of Christianity in the first place? And if a supernatural Jesus is not needed, why do we need any Jesus at all?[39]

If Warfield shows disdain, he also shows some amusement with the critics as they take up the role of Christian apologist against the more radical of their disciples. The "fatal subjectivity" that rules the so-called historical method comes back to haunt them and leaves them without defense against extremists. To allow such subjective grounds of inquiry leaves wide open the possibility of eliminating the figure of

---

[38]*LG*, 161; Warfield, "Convinced against His Will," *TBS*, new series, 3, no. 5 (May 1901): 246–47; cf. *W*, 3:286–310.
[39]*LG*, 162–63.

Jesus from history altogether, and the only way to save itself from such an extreme is to impose "arbitrary limitations upon the application of its subjective principle," a move that renders the principle itself worthless. What keeps one from going the distance of the other is not a matter of principle or evidence, "but only of temperament." "There is just as little reason in a sound historical criticism to discover the Jesus of Bousset behind the Jesus of the Evangelists, as there is for discovering with Kalthoff that there was no real Jesus at all behind the Jesus of the Evangelists." The problem, Warfield surmises, is not one of historical evidence but one of bias.[40]

> The plain fact is that the Evangelists give us the primitive Jesus, behind which there is none other; and the attempt to set the Jesus they give us aside in favor of an assumed more primitive Jesus can mean nothing but the confounding of all historical sequences. The real impulse for the whole assault upon the trustworthiness of the portrait of Jesus drawn in the Gospels lies not in the region of historical investigation but in that of dogmatic prejudice.

Settled disbelief will not be overcome even by the facts. But Warfield insists that the facts remain.

> The plain fact, however, is that this supernatural Jesus is the only Jesus historically witnessed to us; the only Jesus historically discoverable by us; the only Jesus historically tolerable. We can rid ourselves of Him only by doing violence to the whole historical testimony and to the whole historical development as well. Not only is there no other Jesus witnessed in the documents, but no other Jesus can have formed the starting point of the great movement which, springing from Him, has conquered to itself the civilized world.[41]

And so Warfield says mockingly, "It makes very entertaining reading to observe Bousset, for example, grudgingly conceding the fact, and then nervously endeavoring to save himself from the consequences of the damaging acknowledgment." And again:

> Their position is certainly a hard one between these extremes from which they recoil and the portrait of the Evangelists toward which their recoil brings them back. In endeavoring to avoid conclusions recognized by them as intolerable they are compelled to give recognition to facts as to the claims of the real Jesus which are fatal to their whole elaborately argued position.[42]

---

[40]*LG*, 171–72; *W*, 3:313–67.
[41]*LG*, 163–64.
[42]*LG*, 165–66.

And again:

> Why should sane people take part in such a "theological mill" in which "as-yet Chris-
> tians" and "no-longer Christians" struggle together in the arena with nothing at
> stake,—for certainly the difference between the reduced Jesus of the one and the no
> Jesus of the other is not worth contending about? . . . It is only the conservative, secure
> in the possession of the real Jesus, who can look serenely upon this shameful folly
> and with undisturbed detachment watch the wretched comedy play itself out.[43]

Warfield then cites a number of Synoptic passages that trouble the critics, passages that they must admit as genuine, yet with implications they are not willing
to accept. The famous passage in which Jesus admits ignorance as to the time of
his return, for example, must on critical assumptions be accepted as a genuine
saying of Christ, for no mere "hero worship" would have attributed ignorance to
one believed to be the omniscient God. The passage has the "ineradicable stamp
of genuineness" and enjoys the acceptance of critics such as Paul W. Schmiedel
(1851–1935) as "absolutely credible." Yet, as observed earlier, in this passage Jesus
proclaims himself superior to the angels and separate "from the entire category
of creaturely existence, and assimilated to the divine." "The critics indeed are left
in a great quandary." Similarly, Warfield points out that in his "woes" pronounced
on Bethsaida and Chorazin (Matt. 11:21; Luke 10:13) and his reply to John the
Baptist's inquiry (Matt. 11:5; Luke 7:22)—both of which sayings are well attested
and admitted by all sides as genuine—Jesus himself claims to have performed
miracles. The supernatural Jesus is precisely the claim of the historical Jesus. We
are left to decide the matter on *his* word, and the focus of the question becomes
one of the veracity of Jesus himself.[44]

Warfield acknowledges that this is embarrassing and even offensive to an
"anti-supernaturalistic age," and so it is not surprising to him that scholars of
the previous half century labored to separate the supernatural from the life of
Jesus. But he is amused at the "great difficulty" they have experienced "in the
attempt to construct a historical sieve which will strain out miracles and yet let
Jesus through." Warfield understands, then, why some have preferred to "take
refuge in the counsel of desperation which affirms that there never was such a
person as Jesus, that Christianity had no founder, and that not merely the portrait
of Jesus, but Jesus Himself, is a pure projection of later ideals into the past." The
problem, again, is not one of evidence but of bias. In the entire flawed process it is
"pure subjectivity which rules, and the investigator gets out as results only what

---

[43] *W*, 3:315.
[44] *LG*, 168–69; *PTR* 12, no. 4 (1914): 580.

he puts in as premises. And even when the desired result has thus been wrested from the unwilling documents, he discovers that he has only brought himself into the most extreme historical embarrassment."[45]

Warfield finds the whole endeavor—both the attempt to desupernaturalize Jesus and the resulting desperate attempt to be rid of him altogether—nothing short of ridiculous.

> No progress whatever has been made in eliminating the divine Jesus and His super-natural accompaniment of mighty works. . . . It admits of no doubt, and it is not doubted, that supernaturalistic Christianity is the only historical Christianity. . . . It is the desupernaturalized Jesus which is the mythical Jesus, who never had any existence, the postulation of the existence of whom explains nothing and leaves the whole historical development hanging in the air.[46]

The retention of the Christ of the Gospels in any recognizable form necessarily entails the retention of the supernatural Christ. Warfield confidently concludes that the "real Jesus" is the supernaturalistic Jesus of the Synoptics and that there is no other. The Synoptists testify to the deity of Christ, and the Jesus whom they report testifies the same. But it is not only the Jesus of the Synoptists that so testifies; it is the only Jesus of history who so testifies. "On the basis of the Synoptic record, in other words, we can be fully assured that Jesus not only was believed to have taught that He was a divine person, but actually did so teach." The assumed conviction of the deity of Christ is coeval with Christianity itself. "There never was a Christianity, neither in the times of the apostles nor since, of which this was not a prime tenet."[47]

In another place Warfield summarizes the matter passionately, revealing his ultimate concerns:

> What justification is there derivable from history for calling the new Christ, Christ, the new Christianity, Christianity? The new "interpretation" stands out of all relation to fact,—whether the facts of history or the facts of experience. The Christ which it offers is not the Christ of the historical tradition; the Christianity it teaches is not the Christianity which has conquered the world; nor can the Christ and the Chris-tianity it provides meet the needs of sinful men. Its idea of sin must be deepened, its idea of salvation must be heightened, its conception of the function of Christ in salvation must be illimitably enlarged, before this "Christianity" can possess the

---

[45]W, 3:163, 165.
[46]W, 3:164–66.
[47]LG, 172–73; SSW, 1:153.

slightest historical claim to that name, or become in the slightest degree glad-tidings to a sin-cursed race.[48]

The Gospel of John

John's Gospel is widely recognized as the Gospel of the divine Christ, and, accordingly, many—perhaps most—studies of Christ's deity have laid great stress on John's testimony. Warfield does not deny the obvious, of course, but he begins his examination of John's display of the deity of Christ convinced that the Evangelist can go no higher than the Synoptists have already taken us. What can be more than Jesus' assertion of Matthew 11:27 or 28:19? John may lead us to such high christology more often, but he can certainly take us no higher. There is, however, a difference in method and relative emphasis.

> In the Synoptists it is the Messiahship of Jesus which receives the primary emphasis, while His proper deity is introduced incidentally in the course of making clear the greatness of His Messianic dignity. In John, on the contrary, it is the deity of our Lord which takes the first place, and His Messiahship is treated subsidiarily as the appropriate instrumentality through which this divine Being works in bringing life to the dead world.[49]

It is in this sense only that John's Gospel is the Gospel of the deity of Christ.

This difference in point of view is evident in the opening narratives of each of the Gospels. Luke begins with a statement of assurance as to the accuracy of his research and trustworthiness of his account of the life and work of the Redeemer. Mark very quickly introduces Jesus in order to associate him with the early beginnings of Christianity. Matthew commences with a glance backward to the development of the people of God in order to introduce Jesus as "the culminating act of the God of Israel in establishing His Kingdom." These all subsequently advance toward their own exhibition of the divine majesty of this man, Jesus. John, by contrast, takes as his starting point the eternal divine being who, becoming flesh, entered the world on a mission of salvation. "The others begin on the plane of human life. John begins in the inter-relations of the divine persons in eternity. . . . This Jesus, say the others, is God. This God, says John, became Jesus."[50]

"The Word" is John's unique designation for Jesus, and in reference to this name the Evangelist calmly makes three declarations—so calmly, in fact, that we may miss their significance though each is of utmost importance. The three

---

[48]*PTR* 11, no. 2 (1913): 307.
[49]*LG*, 175–76; *SSW*, 2:642–46.
[50]*LG*, 176; *SSW*, 1:148–49.

declarations affirm, respectively, his eternal subsistence, his eternal intercommunion with God, and his eternal identity with God. Concerning Christ's eternal subsistence, John writes, "In the beginning was the Word." "The verb 'was' . . . is not a mere copula, but a strong assertion of existence." The verb is in the imperfect tense, which Warfield describes here as "the imperfect of continuous existence." And so he translates for emphasis, "In the beginning the Word *was*." John does not say that the Word was "from the beginning" but that in the beginning the Word already was. His assertion is that of absolute eternity. At creation, when things began to be, the Word was already in existence. And so we are not surprised when John explains "that 'all things' without exception 'were made by Him, and apart from Him there was not one thing made which has been made.' The Word was not made; He always *was*. All that has been made was made by Him."[51]

Concerning the Word's eternal intercommunion with God, John continues, ". . . and the Word was with God." Warfield reminds us that these words are still governed by the words "in the beginning" and declare "the eternal mode of existence of this eternally existent Word." Warfield goes on to explain that the specific mode of existence that John declares for the Word places him "in an ineffable immediacy of relation to God." The phrase "with God" is not the common expression translated such, "but a more pregnant one. It intimates not merely co-existence, or some sort of local relation, but an active relation of intercourse. The Word, existing from all eternity, exists from all eternity in intercommunion with God." He has existed eternally but not alone—"a relation is asserted; and a relation implies a duality." Further, the relation is an "intimate" one and distinctly personal. "There can be intercourse only between persons." The distinct personality of the Word is here asserted and said to have been eternally in communion with God.[52]

Finally, John identifies the Word with God. He is not only "with God." He is God himself—"the Word was God." "Eternally subsisting alongside of and in communion with God, the Word is yet not a separate Being over against God. In some deep sense distinct from God, He is at the same time in some high sense identical with God." John therefore clarifies his previous statement in order to preserve it from misunderstanding. The Word always was in communion with God, and yet he always was God himself. We have here the fundamental ingredients of the doctrine of the Trinity. "We are but expressing John's meaning, then—in other words, but nevertheless nothing but his meaning—when we declare that Jesus Christ is the Second Person of the Adorable Trinity."[53]

---

[51]*FL*, 83, 87–88; *SSW*, 1:148–50.
[52]*FL*, 88–89.
[53]*FL*, 89–90, 92.

John's narrative then moves throughout to reaffirm Christ's divine nature and climaxes with Thomas's worshipful exclamation, "My Lord and my God!" (John 20:28). Warfield conjectures that there may be a heightening in reverence from "my Lord" to "my God," but he adds that "Lord" can in this context "fall little short of 'God' in significance." Likely both terms are meant to imply deity, only "the former with the emphasis upon the subjection, and the latter with the emphasis on awe, due to deity." At any rate, the two terms joined together express as strongly as possible the deity of Christ, and this worship Jesus welcomes. This passage therefore not only provides the estimate of Christ held by John and Thomas, and presumably those for whom John was writing, but further provides the witness of Jesus himself.[54]

Throughout the narrative John often emphasizes the deity of Christ in ways similar to those of the Synoptics ("Christ," "King," "Son of Man," "sent," "came," etc.). And Warfield reminds us that it is Matthew who tells us of Jesus' unique oneness with the Father (Matt. 11:27; 28:19). But it is John who elaborates on the idea of Jesus' relation to God most fully. Jesus and God the Father "are one" (10:30; cf. 5:18). Jesus is in the Father, and the Father is in him (10:38). To have seen Christ is to have seen the Father (14:9; cf. 8:19; 10:15; 14:7). To honor the Father one must give equal honor to the Son (5:23). And so on it goes. This all comes to bear, in turn, on John 17:3, where in his "high priestly prayer" Jesus vividly associates himself with "the only true God": "This is eternal life, that they know you the only true God, and Jesus Christ whom you have sent" (17:3). Eternal life consists in the knowledge of God and of Jesus Christ. That God and Christ are in some deep sense joined as the co-source of eternal life is unmistakable. Yet God is "the only true God." Further, Christ is one who is "sent" from God and so in some real sense is distinct from him. Still further—a familiar emphasis in the Gospel of John—although Jesus is "sent" on this mission of salvation, he must come from heaven to earth to carry it out. He is therefore of heavenly origin. The matter is complex. "How He can be the true God and yet the sent of God raises the deeper questions of the Trinity and the Covenant and the Two Natures which are alluded to us in the text." As "Son of God," his own self-designation (5:25; 9:35 KJV; 10:36; 11:4), Jesus "claims for Himself not only miraculous powers (9:35; 11:4), but the divine prerogative of judgment (5:25; cf. 5:27); and that He was understood, in employing [this term] of Himself, to 'make Himself equal with God,' and therefore to blaspheme (10:33, 36)."[55]

---

[54]*LG*, 182.
[55]*LG*, 187, 196; cf. *SW*, 217–44.

Although perhaps some twenty years later than the Synoptists and in some ways unique in his mode of expression, John is at one with them in his representation of Christ as God himself come in the flesh. This is John's testimony to Jesus, and it is Jesus' own self-witness.

Elsewhere Warfield summarizes this analysis of the Gospels: "We may reject, if we please, the Christology of the evangelists, and, rejecting it, insist that Christ was not a divine-human, but simply a human being. But we can get no support for this private, and possibly pious opinion of our own, from the writings of the evangelists."[56]

The Acts of the Apostles

Warfield emphasizes that the book of Acts reflects the testimony of the Christian community to Christ's deity at a time earlier than John and, indeed, earlier than some of the writing of the Synoptics. John's high christology is by no means new. Acts demonstrates that the deity of Christ was aboriginal in the church, even if often expressed in different terminology. Jesus is regularly addressed by "the supreme honorific 'Lord'" (1:6, 24; 7:59–60; 9:5, 10, 13; 22:8, 10, 19; 26:15), which in all cases is employed "with the profoundest reverence." As such he is the object of prayer and characterized as "the possessor of divine powers and the exerciser of divine functions." He is appealed to as One who "know[s] the hearts of all" (1:24), as the forgiver of sin (7:60), and as the receiver of the spirits of the dying saints (7:59). Curiously, the title "Lord" is used interchangeably both of Christ and of God the Father, so frequently so that it is "often extremely difficult to determine whether by 'Lord' Jesus or God is meant. That is to say, so clearly is Jesus 'God' to this writer [Luke] and those whose speech he reports that the common term 'Lord' vibrates between the two and leaves the reader often uncertain which is intended."[57] Peter designates Jesus "Lord of all" (10:36), a phrase strikingly reminiscent of Paul's "God over all" (Rom. 9:5). Indeed, in Acts 20:28, Paul speaks of Jesus in terms of precise deity.

Finally, Acts witnesses "the usurpation" of the Old Testament designation of God as "the Name" exclusively in reference to Christ. Salvation is found in "no other name" but his (4:12). The disciples rejoiced in that they were counted worthy to suffer for "the name" (5:41). This unguarded use of the divine "name" in reference to Jesus provides conclusive evidence that Jesus is so exalted in the

---

[56]*W*, 3:296–97.
[57]*LG*, 207–8, 210–11.

minds of Christians that they tend naturally "to substitute Him in their religious outlook for Jehovah."[58]

The Pauline Epistles

Turning from Acts to the Pauline Epistles does not take us to a later, more developed witness to the Christian conception of Jesus. Paul's letters all date earlier than the composition of Acts, and some before the Gospels. Nor is the christology of his epistles different from that of the Gospels and Acts. Rather, Paul gives us merely a different—a specifically didactic rather than narrative—approach, which yields often more direct and precise statements of the primitive estimate of Jesus.

As in Acts but more so in Paul's epistles, the narrative name "Jesus" falls into the background while "Lord" comes noticeably forward. The constant reference of this title to Jesus is much more than a formal mark of respect. "It is the definite ascription to Him of universal absolute dominion not only over men, but over the whole universe of created beings (Phil. 2:11; Rom. 10:12)." Nor is this lordship grounded merely in Jesus' exaltation and postresurrection glory. On the contrary, for Paul it was "the Lord of glory" who was crucified (1 Cor. 2:8). Even in the days of his flesh, glory belonged to Jesus as his "native right." Underlying this understanding of Christ's lordship is his title "the Son of God" (Rom. 1:4), which indicates not what Christ is to us but what he is in himself. With Paul,

> the maxim rules that whatever the father is, that the son is also: every father begets his son in his own likeness. The Son of God is necessarily to him just God, and he does not scruple to declare this Son of God all that God is (Phil. 2:6; Col. 2:9) and even to give him the supreme name of "God over all" (Rom. 9:5).

"Son" is a metaphysical term indicating that "in His being of being" he is just what God is. Thus, Christ's lordship is rooted not in his work but in his person: because he is the Son of God, he is our Lord. Warfield seems to miss altogether any notion of Christ's earned or achieved mediatorial lordship gained in reward for the successful completion of his earthly work. New Testament statements to this effect (e.g., Matt. 28:18; Acts 2:36; Rom. 14:9; Phil. 2:9; Heb. 2:9) are consistently taken by Warfield to refer merely to Christ's reclaiming of his original and eternal glory.[59] He also misses the redemptive-historical implications—expounded by his close friend and younger Princeton colleague Geerhardus Vos—of passages that present Christ in his resurrection state as having passed into the new order of the age to

---

[58]*LG*, 219; cf. *SW*, 37–65.
[59]*LG*, 223–25; *W*, 2:239–40.

come.[60] In Romans 1:4, for example, Warfield seems to struggle somewhat with his exegesis as he understands Christ's resurrection exclusively in terms of a display of his deity. However, he does not miss Paul's regular witness to Christ's inherent lordship. Before coming to this earth in poverty, Christ was "rich" (2 Cor. 8:9) and bearing "the form of God" (Phil. 2:6). For Paul, Warfield asserts, Christ's lordship was not a matter of promotion or elevation of status, except as understood as his "return," following his humiliation, to his original glory. For Paul, Warfield argues, Christ's lordship was a matter of inherent eternal divine majesty.[61]

Accordingly, the recognition that "Jesus is Lord" expresses for Paul the very "essence of Christianity." Here Warfield cites several passages (Rom. 10:9; 2 Cor. 4:5; 1 Cor. 12:3; Phil. 2:11). This formula, "Jesus is Lord," sums up the gospel proclamation (2 Cor. 4:5); to confess Jesus as Lord is to find salvation (Rom. 10:9), for no one can say this except by the enabling of God's Spirit (1 Cor. 12:3); and so "serving the Lord Christ" is the distinctive mark of the Christian (Col. 3:24).

This conviction of Christ's essential lordship is strengthened by the constant employment of the term "Lord" in the Septuagint in reference to Jehovah, and Paul's regular referencing of these passages to Christ (e.g., 2 Thess. 1:9; 1 Cor. 1:31; 10:9, 26; 2 Cor. 3:16; 10:17; Rom. 10:13; Eph. 6:4; 2 Tim. 2:19; 4:14). Warfield cites Isaiah 45:23 as a particularly vivid example, since it is cited in reference to God in Romans 14:11 and with reference to Jesus in Philippians 2:10. "Under the influence of these passages the title 'Lord' becomes in Paul's hands almost a proper name, the specific designation for Jesus conceived as a divine person in distinction from God the Father." He further notes that Paul uses this term "Lord" in reference to Christ not only regularly but almost exclusively. Warfield questions whether this term is ever once employed in reference to God the Father other than in a few citations from the Old Testament. "And in any case such employment is very exceptional. It is accordingly in point of fact the determinate title for Jesus as distinguished from God the Father."[62]

Warfield notices further, therefore, that Paul regularly couples "the Lord Jesus Christ" with "God our Father" and "the Father" as the "co-source" of grace and peace and all divine saving blessings and, thus, the object of prayer. Similarly, throughout the Pauline corpus, while "Lord" and "God" are kept as distinct persons, they are yet joined as the common objects of Christian worship and reverence. In both circumstances, it is God who is in view, yet he is spoken of as "God our

---

[60]See, for example, Geerhardus Vos, "Our Lord's Doctrine of the Resurrection," 1901; reprinted in *Redemptive History and Biblical Interpretation*, ed. Richard B. Gaffin (Phillipsburg, NJ: Presbyterian and Reformed, 1980), 317–23.

[61]See *LG*, 248–50; *W*, 2:238–49.

[62]*LG*, 226–27.

Father and Lord Jesus Christ."[63] There is a distinction between them, yet they are in some profound sense one. For Paul, then, "Lord" is the Trinitarian name for Christ. "God, Lord, and Spirit" is his regular language for the Trinity. And if this is so, then "Lord" is not simply a general term of respect because he recognizes Jesus as supreme. "It is to him the specific title of divinity by which he indicates to himself the relation in which Jesus stands to Deity." Warfield explains that Jesus is Paul's "Lord" not merely because he has been given universal dominion but because "he is 'Lord,' who with the Father and the Spirit is to be served and worshiped, and from whom all that the Christian longs for is to be expected. . . . He is 'Lord' because He is in His own person the Jehovah who was to visit His people and save them from their sins." In short, "Nothing could exceed the clearness and emphasis with which Paul represents Jesus' divine majesty not as an attainment but as an aboriginal possession."[64]

In support of this interpretation of Christ's lordship and against those who would make distinction between "God" and "Lord" as a lesser, subordinate deity, Warfield marshals emphatic statements of the apostle that exclude any such notion. Christ is from eternity "in the form of God" and equal with God (Phil. 2:6), the former expression meaning "nothing less than to have and hold in possession all those characterizing attributes which make God God: having which He could not but be equal with God, because He was just God." He is "the Lord of glory" (1 Cor. 2:8). "In him the whole fullness of deity dwells bodily" (Col. 2:9). He is "God over all, blessed forever" (Rom. 9:5). He is "our great God and Savior" (Titus 2:13), an expression that Warfield describes as "one of the most solemn ascriptions of proper deity to Jesus Christ discoverable in the whole compass of the New Testament." But in a similar way, Paul says in Romans 5:8 that "God commends [as it is more emphatically translated] *his* own love to us" (BBW). How, Warfield asks: "by dying for us while we were yet sinners? No—by *Christ's* dying for us while we were sinners!" But what is this but a declaration of Christ's oneness with God? "How does God commend His *own* love for us—by someone else's dying for us?" Warfield answers, "Obviously the relation between Christ and God is thought of as so intimate that Christ's dying is equivalent to God Himself dying." Christ is himself God (Col. 2:2–3). And he is "the image of God" (2 Cor. 4:4; Col. 1:15), which can only mean that we may see in Christ all that God is. He is "just the invisible God made visible." In all these Warfield finds indisputable evidence that the Lord Jesus is in no way inferior to God the Father but equal and in fact a sharer with him in the divine fulness.[65]

---

[63]For a fuller explanation of these points, see the discussion in chapter 5 on the doctrine of the Trinity.
[64]*LG*, 231–32, 235.
[65]*LG*, 245, 252 (emphasis original), 254; *W*, 10:282.

Warfield therefore argues that Pauline statements reflective of Christ's subordination to the Father are only to be understood economically, in terms of Christ's humiliation and saving mission. In treating these humiliation passages Warfield vigorously maintains Christ's uninterrupted deity. He "became poor," but in a deeper sense he maintains his eternal riches. He was and "ever remains 'in the form of God.'" He subjects himself to great humiliation for the purpose of redemption but forever maintains his essential deity. Only on the presupposition, not only of the doctrines of the Trinity and the incarnation, but of the covenant of redemption also, "in accordance with which the Persons of the Godhead carry on each His own part of the work of redemption," can we possibly understand and can the apostle "speak of our Lord now as 'in the form of God,' 'on an equality with God,' nay, as 'God over all,' and now as subject to God as His Head and His God with reference to whom He performs all His work." And only on this presupposition can he "speak of 'God the Father' and 'Jesus Christ our Lord' as each 'God over all,' and yet declare that there is but one Being who is God."[66]

The letters of the apostle Paul, Warfield reminds us, come to us from the sixth and seventh decades of the first century and reflect, then, that even in those days of the primitive church Christ was understood in the Christian community as "in His essential Being just God Himself." It is therefore impossible to believe, Warfield argues, that "there ever was a different conception of Jesus prevalent in the Church: the mark of Christians from the beginning was obviously that they looked to Jesus as their 'Lord' and 'called on His name' in their worship." Nor can this conclusion be escaped by a denial of Pauline authorship to any of the letters that bear his name, for they all with seamless consistency attribute the same deity to Christ. Admit any of Paul's epistles to the discussion, which even the most radical of the critics are forced to do, "discard any number of them you choose," Warfield challenges, and "the conception of Jesus in those that remain is not altered thereby." Paul's letters do not even show a chronological development in his christological thought. From his earliest to his latest letters, the Christ he represents is

> the divine "Lord," whose right it is to rule: the "Son of God," consubstantial with the Father: the "great God and Saviour" of sinners: "God over all, blessed forever." And in their consentient testimony to the deity of Christ they make it clear to us that upon this point, at least, the whole primitive Church was of one unvarying mind.[67]

---

[66]*LG*, 237–38.
[67]*LG*, 255–61.

The General Epistles

Turning to the General Epistles, Warfield finds "corroborative evidence" for his previous conclusions regarding the "absolute harmony of early Christianity" in its "lofty conception" of Jesus as Lord. Here also "Jesus appears fundamentally as the divine object of the reverential service of Christians."[68]

Of special interest are the epistles of James and Jude, who, although (half) brothers of Christ, remained unbelieving during the days of his earthly life (John 7:5). James is still more significant in that his epistle appears at such an early date (AD 45), earlier in fact than any other canonical New Testament book. James and Jude each identifies himself as a "bondservant" of Jesus Christ (James 1:1; Jude 1), but James's remark is more suggestive for our purposes: he calls himself "a bondservant of God and of the Lord Jesus Christ," thus in the Pauline fashion explicitly attributing supreme lordship to Christ in a sense that acknowledges him as equal with God. Like Paul, James also uses "the name" in reference to "the Lord" Jesus (5:14), thereby substituting the name of Jesus for that of Jehovah. He also employs the unique designation "our Lord Jesus Christ, the Glory" (2:1 BBW). Warfield takes "the glory" (τῆς δόξης) as an appositional genitive, which further defines Christ in his majesty. The meaning, Warfield argues, is that Jesus is the One "to whom glory belongs," the realization of the prophetic hope of Jehovah residing in glory among his people (cf. Zech. 2:5). "He is, in a word, the Glory of God, the Shekinah: God manifest to men." Jude continues in the same vein. For him, Jesus is his "Despotic Master and Lord" (δεσπότης, v. 4 BBW), an epithet entirely fitting from one who is his bondslave. Warfield argues that the overtones of deity are unmistakable.[69]

Peter's designations for Christ are simple—"Christ," "Jesus Christ," "Lord"—but no less profound, particularly as Peter uses "Lord" in applying to Jesus Old Testament passages that speak of Jehovah (e.g., 1 Pet. 3:15), "and thus assimilates [Christ] to the divine Being." Peter names him "the chief Shepherd" (1 Pet. 5:4) and the "Overseer of [our] souls" (1 Pet. 2:25), titles that Warfield acknowledges are more soteriological than ontological but in which the notion of deity remains. "Savior" rings with overtones of deity also, particularly in Peter's phrasing, "our Lord and Savior Jesus Christ" (2 Pet. 1:11; 2:20; 3:18) and "our God and Savior Jesus Christ" (2 Pet. 1:1). And as does Jude, Peter also owns him as his "Master" (δεσπότης).[70]

John is still more pronounced in his reminders of Christ's deity. Unlike elsewhere in the General Epistles, John refers regularly to Christ as "the Son of God,"

---

[68]*LG*, 262–63.
[69]*LG*, 264–65.
[70]*LG*, 267–68.

"the Son," and "the Son of the Father," titles unmistakably reflecting divine dignity and the very closest association with the Father. For John, Jesus is so closely
associated with God the Father that to deny him is to deny the Father (1 John
2:23), to confess him is to confess the Father (2:23; 4:15), and to abide in him is to
abide in the Father (2:24). "Obviously to John, the 'Son of God' is Himself God,"
something which John himself explicitly affirms in 5:20: "This is the true God
and eternal life." We are "in him," and if in him then in God, for he is himself this
God who is true.[71]

The General Epistles, written by close associates of Jesus, provide corroborative
testimony to Warfield's thesis that according to all evidence available, "it did not
occur to anyone in the primitive Christian community to put a lower estimate"
upon Christ than that of absolute deity. There is "absolutely no trace" of any lower
view of him than this. The evidence all suggests that from its very beginning the
church has had no opinion of Jesus other than that he is her divine Lord.[72]

The Epistle to the Hebrews

Warfield traces the many titles of Christ that appear in Hebrews and notes that
the terms "Son" and "priest" "form respectively the favorite ontological and the
favorite soteriological designations of Christ in this Epistle." It is primarily by the
use of the term "Son"—his "more excellent name"—that the writer expresses his
conception of Jesus' person. While not at all denying the humanity of Christ—
indeed, this epistle uniquely enlarges on Christ's humanity—it is Christ as "the
Son of God," given the supreme names and "clothed with all the attributes of
God, that gives its whole tone to the Epistle." This emphasis begins in the opening verses of the letter. The "Son" is set above the prophets and the angels, God's
highest representatives on earth and highest creatures in heaven. As "Son" who
is "the effulgence of God's glory and the very image of his substance," Christ
reveals God and is uniquely qualified as God's "fellow," the "reduplication" and
"repetition of God's glory" and "reiteration" of God's substance. As "Son" he is
called "God" and "Lord" (1:8, 10), designations that appear to be "explications"
of that more excellent name. "The 'Son' is just God over again in the glory of His
majesty." Christ is all that God is, in "His whole nature, with all its attributes.
. . . The 'Son' of God in no single trait in the least differs from God." This "Son" is
addressed as God by God himself (1:8; cf. Ps. 45:6). Christ stands separate from and
above every creature "just because He is 'God' Himself," one who is "not merely
transcendent but sheerly Divine." His priestly work likewise finds its value in

---

[71] *LG*, 272–73.
[72] *LG*, 274–75.

this unique status of representing both God and man. Throughout the epistle the aim ultimately is soteriological, granted, but everywhere this soteriology is grounded in the highest christology—redemption is the work of the God-man and Son-priest Jesus Christ.[73]

In his *The Lord of Glory*, Warfield gives little more than passing mention to the phrase χαρακτὴρ τῆς ὑποστάσεως αὐτοῦ (Heb. 1:3), which he translates, "the very image of his substance." But in his "Calvin's Doctrine of the Trinity" he argues at a bit more length, against Calvin, that ὑποστάσεως must indicate not "person" but "essence." Christ is not the image of the Father's person, for it is in just this, their personality, that they are distinct. "What we sum up under this 'Fatherhood' and 'Sonship' is just the distinguishing 'properties' by which the two are differentiated from each other." The Son shares the likeness of the Father and is thus his "image" in that "each is sharer in the identical essence. After all, therefore, the reason why the Son is the express image of the Father is because, sharing the divine essence, He is in His essence all that the Father is." That is to say, as to the essential deity of the Son, "He is all that God is, the perfect reflection of God." The intent of the writer to the Hebrews is to assert that Christ "differs in no single particular from 'God': He is God in the full height of the conception of God."[74]

The Apocalypse

That Christ in the book of Revelation is presented in the highest terms of divine dignity is recognized by all sides. Here Jesus is "the living one" who is eternal (1:18), omniscient (1:14; 2:18; 19:12), the One who searches men's hearts (2:23), and whose hands possess the keys of death and hell (1:18). If God is "the Alpha and the Omega, the beginning and the end" (21:6; cf. 1:8 and Isa. 44:6), Christ can say also, "I am the first and the last, and the living one" (1:17–18; cf. 2:8), "I am the Alpha and the Omega, the first and the last, the beginning and the end" (22:13). The opening address (1:4–5) presents Christ in his Trinitarian relation: "Grace to you and peace from him who is and who was and who is to come, and from the seven spirits who are before his throne, and from Jesus Christ." Like the prayers of Paul, John calls for divine, soteric blessings equally from God, from his Holy Spirit, and from Jesus Christ. Differing only in form from the other New Testament writings, the book of Revelation presents the same Christ and reflects the same lofty conception of him.[75]

---

[73] *LG*, 277–80; *W*, 3:5.
[74] *W*, 5:213–15.
[75] *LG*, 286–97.

Conclusion and Supporting Arguments

Warfield concludes succinctly, that the deity of Christ "is the presupposition of every word of the New Testament." He is the supernatural Savior who entered supernaturally into this world to accomplish his work. Moreover, "It is impossible to select words out of the New Testament from which to construct earlier documents in which the deity of Christ shall not be assumed." Nor does the New Testament provide any data whatever that would support an inference that the Christian community ever held a different view. Warfield concludes his study with the affirmation that "the whole Christian community, and that from the very beginning, was firmly convinced that Jesus Christ was God manifest in the flesh," and he challenges, "There really can be found no place for doubt of this fact."[76]

How can we account for this universal and unquestioned conviction, Warfield asks, except on the assumption that Christ really was a divine person? Surely, the first Christians did not hold such an opinion "without evidence—without much evidence—without convincing evidence." And what is this convincing evidence? The primary evidence is obviously that which comes from Jesus himself. It is in Christ's own teaching that this notion was heard most convincingly. But the evidence must go further, for men do not naively believe such claims simply because they are made. "Our Lord's life, His teachings, His character, must have been consonant" with his great claims. "His deeds as well as His words must have born Him witness." This we must acknowledge by the nature of the case. Such startling claims just cannot be embraced apart from a life that equaled them.

> We can understand how His followers could believe Him divine, if in point of fact He not only asserted Himself to be divine but lived as became a God, taught as befitted a divine Instructor, in all His conversation in the world manifested a perfection such as obviously was not human: and if dying, He rose again from the dead. If He did none of these things can their firm and passionate faith in His deity be explained?

For Warfield, it is difficult to believe that the whole Christian community embraced their Lord as divine from the beginning and that Jesus himself taught that he was divine unless Jesus was, in fact, divine.[77]

Warfield pushes the question further by explaining the difficulty involved in believing the claim. How else can we account for universal acceptance of such high claims from a young man whose public life lasted but three years, and that largely under a scorn and hatred that grew steadily until finally he was put to death as a criminal in the most disgraceful manner known? Yet he left behind

---

[76]*SSW*, 1:153; *W*, 3:298; *LG*, 298–99.
[77]*LG*, 299–300.

him the germ of a worldwide community, whose very existence is grounded in a common belief in his absolute deity. Without the most convincing evidence of these great claims—indeed, without unquestionable proof—Christianity itself is unexplained, particularly a Christianity that universally and unquestioningly held to Jesus' deity. Clearly, for those first Christians, Christ had provided that proof. His teaching, his life, and—the crowning act of all—his resurrection settled the matter conclusively. And, Warfield challenges, "This very faith itself becomes thus a proof of the truth of His claims."[78]

Those who heard Jesus were thus forced into a dilemma. Supposing Christ's claims were false, how can they be accounted for? Was Jesus then a wicked man to make such claims falsely? Or was he a wild fanatic? A liar? Insane? None of these options explains the case. Yet, "These are the alternatives: grossly deceiving; grossly deceived; or else neither deceiving nor deceived, but speaking the words of soberness and truth." And so Warfield concludes:

> Neither Jesus nor His followers could have invented the claims to deity which Jesus is reported to have made for Himself: for the truth of these claims is needed to account both for Jesus and for His followers. . . . Grant that Jesus was really God, in a word, and everything falls orderly into its place. Deny it, and you have a Jesus and a Christianity on your hands both equally unaccountable. And that is as much as to say that the ultimate proof of the deity of Christ is just—Jesus and Christianity. If Christ were not God, we should have a very different Jesus and a very different Christianity. And that is the reason that modern unbelief bends all its energies in a vain effort to abolish the historical Jesus and to destroy historical Christianity. Its instinct is right: but its task is hopeless. We need the Jesus of history to account for the Christianity of history. . . . But so long as we have either the Jesus of history or the Christianity of history we shall have a divine Jesus.[79]

We cannot assume that such a conception of him arose from his later followers. Not only does this testimony reach back to the very inception of the Christian church, but a naturalistic Jesus could never have risen to the stature that this testimony bears of him, particularly in such a brief time. "The miracle of the invention of such a portraiture, whether by the conscious effort of art, or by the unconscious working of the mythopoeic fancy would be as great as the actual existence of such a person." Moreover, Warfield continues,

> the attempt vitally to realize and reproduce it results inevitably in its reduction. A portraiture which cannot even be interpreted by men without suffering serious loss

---

[78]*LG*, 301; *W*, 3:388–89.
[79]*LG*, 302–4.

cannot be the invention of the first simple followers of Jesus. Its very existence in their unsophisticated narratives is the sufficient proof of its faithfulness to a great reality.

Warfield states, "The conception of the God-man which is embodied in the portrait which the sources draw of Christ, and which is dramatized by them through such a history as they depict, can be accounted for only on the assumption that such a God-man actually lived, was seen of men, and was painted from the life."[80]

Pushing the matter still further, Warfield frequently argues that only by the deity of Christ can we explain Christianity itself. "The plain fact is that the supernatural Jesus is needed to account for the supernatural Christianity which is grounded in him." This is a point Warfield is willing to press. "Whatever else may be said of it, this must be said—that out of the Jesus into which the naturalistic criticism has issued—in its best or in its worst estate—the Christianity which has conquered the world could never have come."[81] It was precisely Jesus' supernaturalism that captured the attention of his contemporaries and gave rise to the Christian movement, and apart from his supernaturalism, it becomes impossible to explain its very origin and subsequent advance. "The revolution which Christ has wrought in the world," Warfield argues, cannot be explained apart from this. "The new life he has brought into the world; the new creation which he has produced by his life and work in the world; here are at least his most palpable credentials."

Take it objectively. Read such a book as Harnack's "The Expansion of Christianity," or such an one as Von Dobschutz's "Christian Life in the Primitive Church"—neither of which allows the deity of Christ—and then ask, Could these things have been wrought by power less than divine? And then remember that these things were not only wrought in that heathen world two thousand years ago, but have been wrought over again every generation since; for Christianity has reconquered the world to itself each generation. Think of how the Christian proclamation spread, eating its way over the world like fire in the grass of a prairie. Think how, as it spread, it transformed lives. The thing, whether in its objective or in its subjective aspect, were incredible, had it not actually occurred. . . .

Or take it subjectively. Every Christian has within himself the proof of the transforming power of Christ, and can repeat the blind man's syllogism: Why herein is the marvel that ye know not whence He is, and yet He opened my eyes. . . . The transformed hearts of Christians, registering themselves "in gentle tempers, in noble motives, in lives visibly lived under the empire of great aspirations"—these

---

[80]W, 3:160.
[81]W, 3:166, 169.

are the ever-present proofs of the divinity of the Person from whom their inspiration is drawn.[82]

"The supreme proof to every Christian of the deity of his Lord," Warfield concludes, "is then his own inner experience of the transforming power of his Lord upon the heart and life." He is speaking here not objectively but of the Christian's own awareness and inner compulsion to acknowledge Christ's lordship. "The supreme proof *to every Christian*," he says. His point has to do with that which every Christian intuitively knows and must instinctively acknowledge. In his own heart of hearts the Christian knows this is something he cannot deny. "Not more surely does he who feels the present warmth of the sun know that the sun exists, than he who has experienced the re-creative power of the Lord know Him to be his Lord and his God." Warfield continues:

> Here is, perhaps we may say the proper, certainly we must say the most convincing, proof to every Christian of the deity of Christ; a proof which he cannot escape, and to which, whether he is capable of analyzing it or drawing it out in logical statement or not, he cannot fail to yield his sincere and unassailable conviction. Whatever else he may or may not be assured of, he knows that his Redeemer lives. Because He lives, we shall live also—that was the Lord's own assurance. Because we live, He lives also—that is the ineradicable conviction of every Christian heart.[83]

It is doubtful that Warfield thought that this line of argument—the supernatural effects of the message about Christ—would prove significantly persuasive as an apologetic aimed toward unbelievers; it is, after all, an argument the force of which rests on ground that is common only to those who already believe it. But it is nonetheless one of Warfield's favorites, and the argument, somewhat reminiscent of 1 Corinthians 1:18–31 and not altogether subjective, crops up often in his works. For him, there is no explanation for the transforming effects of Christ other than that Christ was and is capable of this supernatural work. And there is no other explanation for the unmistakable record of transformed lives wherever the gospel of Christ has gone. What cause could sufficiently explain this effect? he asks. The Jesus of his critics simply cannot, and it is a "standing wonder" to him how they can miss this obvious fact. "No matter what Jesus criticism extracts from the sources, the Jesus which actually was is the Jesus which is required to account for His effects in the world." Warfield explains:

---

[82]*SSW*, 1:155–56.
[83]*SSW*, 1:156–57.

It is undeniable, that the Jesus which lies on the face of the sources is the very Jesus who appears in these effects. It will not do to attempt to account for the presence of the Divine Jesus in the historical records on the ground that it is a natural creation of those who have felt the effects of Jesus, and to substitute for Him another Jesus who stands in no recognizable relation to these effects. What needs to be accounted for is not the rise of the Divine Jesus in the consciousness of His first followers, but the fading of the Divine Jesus out of the consciousness of so many of His later followers. It is this last estimate of Him which stands in contradiction with the observed effects He has left in the world.[84]

Finally, Warfield asks what kind of a Jesus is needful for sinners. Will the Jesus of liberal criticism do? Is this Jesus of modern rationalism equipped to address our needs? "Though 'pure reason' be sufficient for the religion of pure nature, what warrants the assumption that its sufficiency is unimpaired when nature is no longer pure?" And what about that "inexpugnable sense of guilt" that is common to all men? "Shall we hope to soothe it to sleep with platitudes about the goodness of God; assurances that God is love, and that love will not reckon with sin?" Warfield answers, "That deep moral self-condemnation which is present as a primary factor in all truly religious experience protests against all attempts merely to appease it." How can we deal with this matter of our sin? Where can we find one who can make satisfaction?[85]

The real question at issue, Warfield insists, is not the historicity of Jesus or, specifically, his deity. The question has to do with the human condition and the very nature of Christianity itself. Indeed, so long as we can feel ourselves competent to save ourselves, we will not see any need for a supernatural, divine Savior. But when we find ourselves in the throes of self-condemnation for sin against God, only a divine Redeemer will do. Similarly, only after we have ceased to view the essence of Christianity as a redemptive religion can we entertain alternative notions about the historicity and identity of Christ. But so long as propitiation is necessary and so long as Christianity is a religion for sinners, history must know a Redeemer, and that Redeemer must not merely be one of us—he must also be divine.

POLEMICS: THE DEITY OF CHRIST UNDER ATTACK

Warfield wrote three primary articles answering specific attacks on the deity of Christ, and at least brief mention should be made of them here.[86] These articles

---

[84]*W*, 10:300.

[85]*W*, 3:339–40.

[86]"Concerning Schmiedel's 'Pillar Passages'" (1913) in *W*, 3:181–255; "Misconception of Jesus, and Blasphemy of the Son of Man" (1914) in *W*, 3:53–94; "Jesus' Alleged Confession of Sin" (1914) in *W*, 3:97–145. See also "May We Trust Our Gospels," *TBS*, new series, 4, no. 4 (October 1901): 239–40.

focus on the attempts of Paul W. Schmiedel and others to find in the Gospels remnants of the true "historical" Jesus. The Jesus of history, it is assumed, could not have been supernatural or divine, and it was claimed that some traditions to this effect survive in the Gospel records. These passages purportedly reflect an original Jesus who was understood in purely naturalistic terms, terms that are exclusive of any notion of supernaturalism and/or divinity. The passages in question are as follows: Mark 3:20–22 (where his family considers him to be out of his mind and the scribes ascribe his miracles to the power of Satan); Matthew 19:16–17 (and parallels; Jesus' alleged confession of sin); Matthew 12:31–32, Mark 3:28–30, and Luke 12:10 (Jesus' alleged confession of exclusive humanity and subordination to the Holy Spirit); Mark 13:32 (Jesus' confessed ignorance of the time of his return); Mark 15:34 and Matthew 27:46 (Jesus' forsakenness of God); Mark 8:12 (Jesus' refusal to work a sign); Mark 6:5ff. (Jesus' inability to perform miracles); Mark 8:14–21 ("the leaven of the Pharisees" referring not to bread but to teaching); Matthew 11:5 and Luke 7:22 (the signs of the Messiah seen as only figuratively miraculous).

Mark 3:20–22: Jesus Allegedly Out of His Mind, or of Satanic Power

In Mark 3:20–22, Jesus' relatives heard of his growing influence in Galilee and, perhaps somewhat embarrassed, determined that Jesus was beside himself— out of his mind. The scribes, people who themselves had heard his words and witnessed his works and therefore could not deny the supernatural power present with him, were unwilling to attribute his power to God and thus ascribed it to a satanic source. The two judgments are entirely opposed in character and in emotion: the one a judgment of pity, the other of anger. But they are alike in their unfavorable assessment of Jesus and the movement he created. It is thus alleged that such assessments provide disproof of the supernaturalness of Jesus and his ministry. Those who saw him did not, evidently, consider him divine.

It is not without significance, however, that in both cases this negative judgment was formed by people settled in their unbelief. Jesus' brothers were themselves still relatively uninformed of the work he had begun in Galilee and did not come to believe in him until after the resurrection. And the scribes were settled in their opposition to him. Warfield finds all this illustrative of the dilemma that inevitably confronts every person who hears about Jesus. Jesus' career and teaching were not that of any ordinary man, and we are thereby forced to decide whether he was "something more than a normal man or something less." Does the difference about him indicate that he was supernatural or subnormal? Divine or "out of his mind"? This is what every man must answer. Is Jesus from God? Or is he evil? Possessed by the Evil One? Out of his mind? These are the options. We must worship him, or we must condemn him. He either makes or mars the world. And in the end, it is not Jesus but we ourselves who stand trial in the question, for our answer reveals more about us than it does about Jesus. Men who judge Jesus negatively do not thereby degrade him.[87]

Matthew 12:31–32: Jesus' Alleged Subordination to the Holy Spirit

The attribution of Jesus' work to the power of Satan (Matt. 12:31–32; Mark 3:28–30; Luke 12:10) prompts Jesus to warn of blasphemy against the Holy Spirit, the lone sin that can find no forgiveness. But in his shaping of this warning, it is alleged, Jesus ranks himself beneath the Holy Spirit in his essential nature. Blasphemy against him may be forgiven, but blasphemy against the Holy Spirit cannot. Does not this constitute Jesus' own confession that he is less than God? Warfield objects that this assumes no such subordination at all. There is a subordination of the offense—blasphemy against the Son of Man is forgivable, but blasphemy against the Holy Spirit is not. But there is no subordination at all in terms of comparative dignity. Jesus' claim that he could be the object of "blasphemy" seems, in fact, to assume deity. The very possibility of "blaspheming" the Son of Man reflects a sense of his deity. Indeed, it would appear presumptuous otherwise for him to assume the need to clarify that blasphemy against him is forgivable. Warfield finds support for this understanding in the intensive or ascensive καί in Matthew 12:32: "Every blasphemy shall be forgiven; yea if one blaspheme the Son of Man" (BBW). There is a heightening. Jesus refers to blasphemy against him not simply as *an* instance but as *the* instance above all others that illustrates the "incredible reach" of God's grace in forgiveness. Even blasphemy against the Son of Man shall be forgiven! The necessary implication here, Warfield insists, is that Jesus is divine. For that matter, Jesus here no more distances himself, in terms of dignity, from the Holy Spirit than he does from God the Father. "Every sin and blasphemy shall be forgiven." Blasphemy against God the Father and against the Son of Man are forgivable; only that against the Holy Spirit is not. Jesus here does not in any way subordinate himself or indicate for himself nondeity; he only emphasizes the particular heinousness of the sin of blasphemy against the Holy Spirit. This particular sin, in contrast to all other blasphemies against God, is unforgivable.[88]

---

[87] W, 3:54–72. Later Warfield adds, "At bottom, however, disbelief, when it works itself out, must not merely neglect Jesus but condemn Him." We must acknowledge him as having come from God, or we must declare him out of his mind or possessed of the Devil (94); cf. LG, 33–34.

[88] W, 3:75–76, 84–85.

As to the specific identity of this sin of blasphemy against the Holy Spirit, Warfield offers no fixed definition. He surveys many of the attempts to classify it but notes that sufficient information is lacking to provide certainty. It may be that attributing his power to the Devil is not itself the sin he has in view. It may be that this sin has only been approached and so has prompted his warning. It is impossible to know, and Warfield declines conjecture. But this difficulty allows no reason whatever "for cutting the knot by representing Jesus as definitely subordinating Himself—and God also—in dignity of person to the Holy Spirit." Such a reading is not only alien to the Gospels but entirely at odds with their whole drift. The Evangelists saw no such implication, and no reason can be found, other than bias, to find one at all. "He who authoritatively makes this great declaration of the relative heinousness of sins, and calmly announces what sins shall and what sins shall not be forgiven, whether in this world or in that which is to come, does not mean to proclaim Himself a mere man."[89]

Matthew 19:16–17: Jesus' Alleged Confession of Sin

To the rich young man who asks Jesus, "Good master, what good thing may I do in order that I may have eternal life?" Jesus responds, "Why do you call me good? Only one is good" (Matt. 19:16–17 BBW). Thus, it is alleged, Jesus confesses the great distance between himself and God in terms of inherent goodness and thereby acknowledges himself to be merely a man. Against this, Warfield argues, first, that such an interpretation places more weight on the enclitic με ("me") than it can bear. No contrast between Jesus and God is in view but only a distinction between the "good thing" about which the young man inquires and the known commands of God. Matthew's wording is clear: "Why do you ask me concerning [περί] that which is good?" Warfield offers this paraphrase: "Why dost thou inquire about the good as if that were a matter still in doubt? God, who is goodness itself, has published the eternal rule of righteousness." The εἷς ("one") implies no such contrast between Jesus and God, and to read it as such immediately places more weight on the enclitic με than it is capable of bearing. Rather than contrasting himself with God, here, Jesus is "only in the most emphatic way pointing to God and His published law as the unique source of the law of life. His own relation to God is completely out of sight."[90]

Mark's and Luke's accounts read more simply, "Why do you call me good? No one is good except God alone." The general drift is the same as in Matthew. To understand this as something along the lines of "You are wrong in calling me

---

[89] W, 3:90, 93.
[90] W, 3:105–8.

good; this predicate belongs to no one but God alone!" again places too much weight on the enclitic με. The emphasis in the statement falls rather on ἀγαθόν ("good"). What is significant is not that the young man called *Jesus* good but that he had called Jesus *good*. "This is the fundamental fact regarding the passage which must rule its whole interpretation." In this case, the sense of Jesus' reply falls along these lines: "There is a great deal involved, if only you appreciated it, in calling me good; for there is no one that is good but one, that is God." The contrast is not between Jesus and God but between God and all others, and calling Jesus "good," therefore, carries great significance. Whether or not this is specific acknowledgment of deity on Jesus' part—something that Warfield doubts—it provides no ground for admission of nondeity. Jesus is merely bidding the man to look nowhere for prescriptions for eternal life except in God's revealed will. "The search for a master good enough to lead men to life finds its end in God and His commandments." In sum, Jesus directs the young man's attention to God, and in so doing his concern

> is not to glorify Himself but God: it is not to give any instruction concerning His own person whatever, but to indicate the published will of God as the sole and perfect prescription for the pleasing of God. In proportion as we wander away from this central thought, we wander away from the real meaning of the passage and misunderstand and misinterpret it.[91]

Warfield dismisses altogether further arguments to the effect that Matthew borrowed this story from Mark and "improved" the more objectionable wording. Mark obviously saw nothing objectionable in his record. There is no reason whatever to consider Matthew so dishonest as to wrest the words of Christ to a contrary purpose, and he is not so bungling as to attempt such a feat while allowing some objectionable material to remain. An interpretation that rests entirely on the presumed dishonesty of Matthew and on the stupidity of both Matthew and Mark is hardly worth serious consideration.

Miscellaneous Objections

Mark 13:32 (Jesus' confession of ignorance) we have considered above. Warfield remarks that this passage must have troubled Schmiedel himself, given that in it Jesus, although he admits one point of ignorance, ranks himself above the angels and on the side of God in contrast with even the highest of his creatures. Similarly, it is only the most devious exegesis that would reduce Jesus' feedings

---

[91] *W*, 3:106–8, 139.

of the five thousand and the four thousand to mere parables. And even if they were parables, that would hardly prove that he did no miracles at all. Again, when Jesus points to his miracles in reply to the inquiry of the disciples of John the Baptist (Matt. 11:5; Luke 7:22), it is by no means a natural interpretation that reduces these to figurative statements of spiritual accomplishments—although, again, even if they were, that could hardly be offered as proof that Jesus worked no miracles at all. Similarly "unreasonable" is the attempt to take Jesus' refusal to give a "sign" (Mark 8:12; cf. Matt. 16:4; 12:39; Luke 11:29) as a confession of his inability to work miracles altogether. Likewise his failure to work miracles in Nazareth (Mark 6:5) can scarcely be made to indicate that he could work no miracles at all and that his supposed healings were but "faith cures." The language suggests merely the inappropriateness of his miracles in that place. And his cry of dereliction on the cross (Mark 15:34) certainly reflects Jesus' human consciousness, but why this must demand that Jesus had *only* a human consciousness is not at all evident.[92]

Conclusion

In short, if these passages demonstrate that Jesus was exclusively human and not divine, it is striking that the Synoptists themselves are "strangely unaware of it." Warfield characterizes all these critical arguments as but the last desperate attempts of frustrated scholars to deny the evidence and prove what is unprovable. That many of these passages conclusively prove that Jesus was human is not doubted, but that they demonstrate that he was exclusively human is entirely beyond the evidence. The critics are simply unwilling to entertain the notion that the Jesus consistently presented in the Gospels is both God and man—truly God but not exclusively God. And so Warfield insists again, as he does frequently throughout his writings, that at the end of the day we are forced to see that "no stratum of tradition has been reached by [Gospel criticism] in which the portrait of Jesus differs in any essential respect from that presented in the Synoptic Gospels," whose objective was "to present before adoring eyes the figure of a divine, miraculous Jesus." All the data that can be found points to a supernatural Jesus who was worshiped as divine by his very first followers. If the supernatural Jesus is displaced, it cannot be on historical grounds. One may conclude that Jesus was merely human, but he must do so apart from any warrant from all available evidence.[93]

---

[92] *W*, 3:237–40.
[93] *W*, 3:183, 240–55.

In this same vein Warfield maintains that the only way for the critics to have a merely human Jesus is to "write history backwards." The new canon of historical criticism is that "whatever may be found in the historical document inconsistent with the point of view of the author of that document evinces itself as more original than the document itself." The canon is exactly backwards, Warfield argues, "simply a neat receipt for obtaining as a result of 'criticism' precisely the opposite view of the history from that presented in all the sources!" Never mind what those who knew Jesus wanted to say about him. Let the critic find hints of contrary views that may have slipped in through them, and then let him represent these "findings" as the remnants of a more reliable and "original" history. Here he finds a Jesus not at all like the one described by actual eyewitnesses and acquaintances, a Jesus not found in any of the actual historical sources. But in this way, by "*reversing* the whole historic testimony," the critic will at last have the purely human Jesus he set out to find.[94]

The Humanity of Christ

Warfield devotes considerably less attention to a defense of Christ's humanity than he does to Christ's deity, most likely because Christ's real humanity was not a matter of dispute. Yet the emphasis he gives to Christ's humanity, when he does treat it, is equally strong, and he will not allow the needed reaffirmation of Christ's deity to minimize in any way the importance of his humanity. Indeed, it would be difficult to find in other theologians a doctrine of the humanity of Christ more deeply considered and more fully developed than Warfield's. Warfield addresses the subject in perhaps more length under his treatments of the two natures and the incarnation, and we will examine that in due course. But he also addresses the subject itself in ways that merit specific attention.

THE REAL MAN

In "The Revelation of Man," an exposition of Hebrews 2:6–9, Warfield carefully notes the emphasis that the inspired writer places on the "perfect identification of Christ with man." He was made a little lower than the angels. He suffered even death. In every way he was made like his brethren. Since we are made of blood and flesh, so he in like manner partook of the same.

---

[94]"Convinced against His Will," 246–47 (emphasis original); cf. *W*, 3:286–310.

> The emphasis is upon the completeness of the identification of the Son of God with the sons of men. . . . The perfection of His identification with us consisted just in this, that He did not . . . assume merely the appearance of man or even merely the position and destiny of man, but the reality of humanity.[95]

He was made what we are, blood and flesh. He assumed our physical nature. He suffered being tempted. Christ is presented to us here as possessing "every faculty and capacity that belongs to the essence of our nature."

In a virtually unprecedented study, "The Emotional Life of Our Lord," Warfield investigates one aspect of Christ's humanity that is largely overlooked. Beginning from the premise that "it belongs to the truth of our Lord's humanity, that he was subject to all sinless human emotions,"[96] Warfield investigates the information that the Gospels provide concerning this aspect of Jesus' humanity. He notes the tendency either to minimize or magnify Jesus' emotions and, thus, to leave us either with a cold and remote Jesus who is virtually incapable of sympathizing with us in all our weaknesses or with a Jesus so crassly human that he is hardly worthy of our reverence. But Warfield is convinced that an honest examination is nonetheless possible and of value. Tracing the relevant data, he observes that the emotions most frequently attributed to Jesus in his earthly life are compassion (Matt. 9:36; 14:14; 15:32; 20:34; Mark 1:41; 6:34; 8:2; Luke 7:13; etc.), love (Mark 10:21; John 11:3, 5, 36; 13:1, 34; 14:21; 15:8–12), indignation and anger (Matt. 9:30; 12:16; Mark 3:5, 12; 10:14; Luke 18:15; John 2:17; 11:33, 38), joy and gladness (Luke 10:21; John 15:11; 17:13), and the mental anguish and despair associated with and in view of his coming death (Matt. 26:37; Mark 14:33; Luke 12:50; 22:44; John 12:27; 13:21). All these, as well as others that Warfield discovers, not only highlight but serve to confirm the truth and reality of Christ's human nature. The Lord Jesus hungered, thirsted, endured physical pain, experienced pleasure, wept, wailed, sighed, groaned, became angry, chided angrily, rejoiced—he experienced the full range of human emotion, guilt excepted (save as our sin-bearing substitute), and showed himself in daily life to have a human nature and even his own individuality and what we call temperament.

But nowhere is Warfield's understanding of Christ's humanity more clearly pronounced than in "The Human Development of Jesus."[97] Here Warfield examines the implications of Luke's unique characterizations of Jesus in his early life. Luke presents Jesus' human development successively as "infant" (βρέφος, 2:16), "child" (παιδίον, 2:40), and "boy" (παῖς, 2:43). The Evangelist also rather

---

[95]*PGS*, 5, 10.
[96]*PWC*, 93.
[97]*SSW*, 1:158–66.

formally summarizes Jesus' entire growth and development from childhood to manhood: "And the child grew and waxed strong, becoming (more and more) filled with wisdom, and the grace of God was upon him" (2:40 BBW). Again, "And Jesus increased in wisdom and in stature and in favor with God and man" (2:52). While the passage is charged with suggestions that Jesus was an extraordinary child, still this language expresses a normal human development. Luke draws attention to Jesus' physical, intellectual, and even moral or spiritual progress. Daily he grew and became strong, and as he grew in stature, he correspondingly increased not only in knowledge but also in skill in the practical use of knowledge—"wisdom" and moral and spiritual insight. God's grace was upon him as he advanced "in favor with God." As he grew, he advanced more and more in wisdom, and as the grace of God was given him, he increased also in character such that God looked on him with increasing favor. He was, in turn, a good child, a good boy, a good youth, and a good man; and with each new stage of development there was an accompanying increase in wisdom and in moral and spiritual power. "In a word, Jesus grew as steadily and rapidly in character and in holiness as he grew in wisdom, and as steadily and rapidly in wisdom as he grew in stature."[98] He advanced continually in favor with both men and God.

There is much to be derived from all this, and Warfield notes some implications in passing. But "quite the most fundamental gain" we derive from this portrait is "the assurance it gives us of the truth and reality of our Lord's humanity." The Lord Jesus did not seem one thing while being another. It is impossible to read Luke's portrait and doubt that the One he is describing is a real man, one who advances to manhood in every respect alike—physically, intellectually, and spiritually. His was a remarkable development in that the passage seems to suggest a steady and unbroken progress, and in this sense Jesus was an exceptional child. His was nonetheless a truly human development—one without sin and therefore the only truly "normal" human development, but a truly human development nonetheless.[99]

This attribution of a "complete and real humanity" to Jesus continues not only through Luke but through all the Gospel narratives alike. In them all, Jesus remains truly human, with all the attending limitations. Accordingly, Jesus himself tells of his ignorance of the day of judgment, and he is repeatedly represented as seeking knowledge through questions and expressing surprise.

There are no human traits lacking to the picture that is drawn of him: he was open to temptation; he was conscious of dependence on God; he was a man of prayer; he

---

[98]*SSW*, I:159.
[99]*SSW*, I:160.

knew a "will" within him that might conceivably be opposed to the will of God; he exercised faith; he learned obedience by the things he suffered. It was not merely the mind of a man that was in him, but the heart of a man as well, and the spirit of a man. In a word, he was all that a man—a man without error and sin—is, and must be conceived to have grown, as it is proper for a man to grow, not only during his youth, but continuously through life, not alone in knowledge, but in wisdom, and not alone in wisdom, but "in reverence and charity"—in moral strength and in beauty of holiness alike.[100]

Warfield goes still further. He is unreserved in his willingness to ascribe to Jesus exactly all the attributes of humanity, including its limitations. Indeed, he insists that to do less would be to deny that Christ's was, in fact, a true humanity. And so he takes issue with one writer who remarks that Jesus' growth in wisdom continued until his death. This does not suffice. If Jesus' humanity is a real humanity, Warfield reasons, then why should we assume that his growth in wisdom ceased upon his death? Should we not expect that our learning and growing in wisdom will not cease at death but will continue in heaven through eternity? And if so for us, then so also for our Lord. All this must be "not only with reference to his wisdom, but also with reference to all the traits of his blessed humanity. For Christ, just because he is the *risen* Christ, is man and true man—all that man is, with all that is involved in being man—through all the ages and into the eternity of the eternities."[101]

"We need not fear," Warfield exhorts, "that we may emphasize too strongly the true, the complete humanity of Christ. It is gain and nothing but gain, that we should realize it with an acuteness that may bear the term of poignant. All that man as man is, that Christ is to eternity." It is, indeed, the inheritance of our Reformed tradition that we do not hesitate "to face the fact and rejoice in it, with all its implications." If as a man Christ has finite knowledge, then his finite knowledge continues forever. Human nature can never be infinite. In our Reformed tradition we have "no reserves" of confessing Jesus' limitations as a man and "no fear of overstating the perfection and completeness of his humanity." There can be "no danger" at all in recognizing "the fullest meaning" of Luke's account of Jesus' early development, "and the descriptions of his human traits provided for us by all the evangelists."[102]

Warfield's treatment of the humanity of Christ does not follow the more common lines of evidence—his death, his thirst and hunger, his bleeding, and such.

---

[100]*SSW*, 1:161–62; cf. "The Faith of Jesus and Faith in Jesus," *TBS*, new series, 2, no. 6 (December 1900): 354.
[101]*SSW*, 1:162 (emphasis original).
[102]*SSW*, 1:162–63.

Following Luke, he speaks instead in sweeping terms of all the limitations of humanity and attributes these human limitations to Jesus. Whatever it is to be human is true of Jesus, fully and completely.

THE SINLESS MODEL

Although sin is common to all humanity, it is not essential to true humanity, and Warfield adoringly points out that Jesus stands as the exception. True man he is, but sinful man he is not. He is the model and pattern of ideal humanity.

Psalm 8 presents man in his creaturely glory as having dominion over all God's creation. Yet as Hebrews 2 points out, it is a dominion still not fully realized. Man has fallen. "But we see . . . Jesus" (Heb. 2:9), and in him we see "man as man, man in the possession and use of all those faculties, powers, dignities for which he was destined by his Creator." He is "the pattern, the ideal, the realization of man." In Jesus we have revealed to us man as he was intended to be.[103]

Jesus' human development as recorded in Luke is a normal human development, as we have just seen. It was nonetheless an exceptional development in that, as a young child, Jesus grew and improved steadily and without interruption. He progressed at equal pace in moral and spiritual character as well as in stature, spiritually as well as physically, in favor with God as well as with men. As he grew physically, he correspondingly grew in moral depth and character—extraordinary human development indeed! Yet it is "normal"—in fact,

> the only strictly normal human development, from birth to manhood, the world has ever seen. For this child is the only child who has ever been born into the world without the fatal entail of sin, and the only child that has ever grown into manhood without having his walk and speech marred at every step by the destructive influences of sin and error.

This perfection has significance as far as humanity itself is concerned. "This is how men ought to grow up; how, were men not sinners, men would grow up." It is a great thing, Warfield goes on to explain, that human history has seen one such man, for it serves as an example for us. There has been one man who has reached his creaturely ideal, and this life stands before us "as an incitement and an inspiration." As we observe his perfect human development, we see that the Lord Jesus Christ provides, further, the model "for every age and for every condition of man." He is the model child, the model youth, and the model man.

---

[103]*PGS*, 8–9.

From him we learn what humanity was meant to be and what humanity now ought to be.[104]

What we see, specifically, in Christ's humanity, Warfield says, is "perfection." There was no sin in him. He was without moral blemish or spot. Those who accompanied him testified to his sinlessness, and even his enemies were frustrated by their inability to find fault with him. With him there was no confession of sin, no twinge of conscience, not the "slightest hint of inner conflict with sinful impulses." To be sure, such was the excellence of his perfection that we are unable to characterize it adequately. The excellences of the best of men, by contrast, are usually condensed to a most outstanding virtue by which he is specially known. "Thus we speak of the faith of Abraham, the meekness of Moses, the patience of Job, the boldness of Elijah, the love of John." But, by contrast,

> the perfection of Jesus defies such particularizing characterization. All the beauties of character which exhibit themselves singly in the world's saints and heroes, assemble in Him, each in its perfection and all in perfect balance and harmonious combination. If we ask what manner of man He was, we can only respond, No manner of man, but rather, by way of eminence, *the* man, the only perfect man that ever existed on earth, to whom gathered all the perfections proper to man and possible for man, that they might find a fitting home in His heart and that they might play brightly about His person. If you would know what man is, in the height of his divine idea, look at Jesus Christ.[105]

So also Jesus manifested the full range of human emotions, but never in excess and never in any manner that would belie other virtues. His anger, for example, did not inhibit his compassion. Nor did his love keep him from feelings of indignation against evil. And his joy was such that even in his sorrow he did not give way to despair. In every emotion and in every virtue he is the model. "The mark of his individuality was harmonious completeness: of him alone of men, it may be truly said that nothing that is human was alien to him, and that all that is human manifested itself in him in perfect proportion and balance." Whether in pity or grief or joy or even rage he remained always in control. He teaches us not to eradicate our affections but to sanctify them.[106]

In Jesus we have the perfect embodiment of God's law, the measure of what humanity was intended to be. What a straightedge is to a carpenter's board, Jesus is to the human soul. He is the standard. In the passion narratives, for example, the shameful character of Pilate, the hypocrisies of the priests, and the fickle-

---

[104]*SSW*, 1:160.
[105]*PGS*, 12–14 (emphasis original).
[106]*PWC*, 141–43.

ness of the mob are all thrown into prominence precisely because they are in the presence of perfection, humanity in its ideal. It is Jesus who shows us what we ought to be in contrast to what we are. Indeed, "No man ever so feels his utter depravity as when he thinks of himself as standing by the side of Jesus. In this presence even what we had haply looked upon as our virtues hide their faces in shame and cry, 'Depart from us, for we are sinful men, O Lord.'" In Jesus' life as it is recorded in the Gospels we see "the ever-growing glory" of his perfect life in contrast to the "ever-increasing horror" of human weakness and sin he exposes. Next to him all classes of humanity are seen in contrast to what they ought to be. Jesus Christ alone is what man ought to be, and it is therefore to him that we are to look if we would see man as he was designed to be. Jesus is "the pattern, the ideal, the realization of man. Looking upon Him, we have man revealed to us." In that he was made one of us, "He reveals to us in His own life and conduct what man was intended to be in the plan of God." "When we turn our eyes toward Him, we see in the quality of His humanity God's ideal of man." In short, Jesus Christ "exhibits to us what man is in the idea of his Maker," and to look on him is to elevate our ideals and raise our expectations.[107]

THE FORERUNNER

But Christ in his humanity stands as more than an example for us. If he were only our example, we would cry in despair and in utter frustration, for an example alone falls short of changing the heart and imparting new life. As an example alone he would show us what we ought to be but what we could never become. We thank God for Christ as our example, but "we thank Him that He is much more than our example." He is our Redeemer, and he is our life. He became all that we are in order to become our sin-bearer, and as perfect man he died in place of sinners and has purchased the sanctifying Spirit for us. So in Jesus we see not only what we should be but what we shall be. As our forerunner he has run the race ahead of us and shown us what we shall become by his work for us and in us. "We shall be like him."[108]

The Two Natures of Christ

COMPETING CLAIMS

Warfield enthusiastically embraces and vividly expounds both the deity and the humanity of Christ, and he laments that it is "one of the most portentous

---

[107]*SSW*, 2:688–92; *PGS*, 9, 11, 12, 15, 16–20.
[108]*PGS*, 22–23.

symptoms of the decay" of vital, historic, biblical Christianity in his day that these truths were being denied. Various theories of *kenosis*, devised in German theology over the previous century and then in English, left the church with a Christ divested of deity.[109] This notion Warfield finds intolerable. Only a Christ who is both divine and human will do, and anything less empties Christianity itself of its significance. Without the doctrine of the two natures of Christ there is no real incarnation, and without a real incarnation there is no Christianity "in any distinctive sense." This is "the hinge" on which the Christian system, a religion of redemption, turns.[110]

Emphasis in the discussion of the two natures of Christ necessarily gravitates to his divine nature. Apart from a few ancient influences, such as the Gnostics, Apollinarians, Monophysites, and a tendency in confessional Lutheran *commu- nicatio idiomatum* (communication of properties or attributes), there is no com- plete "divinitising" of the whole Christ to be found in the history of the church. The revolt of kenoticism against the two natures, therefore, was "nothing more or less than the explanation of Christ in terms of mere humanity." Attempting to ground their view in Philippians 2:7, kenotic theologians presented a Christ who in the incarnation "emptied" (ἐκένωσεν) himself of deity and became a mere man. Opposite the tendency of Lutheran christology, kenoticism was somewhat an attempt "to secure a purely human Christ" while paying lip service to his deity. The result is a Christ of one nature—human, "shrunken deity" though it may be. Warfield agrees with Albrecht Ritschl's description of kenoticism as *verschämter Socinianismus*—Socinianism indeed, but a Socinianism less bold—and he deplores it as stealing away the divine Christ and even God himself. For what kind of God is it who is alternately God and then not God as he chooses?[111]

The kenotic theologians labored to explain away all notions of Christ's deity in the New Testament; Warfield, ever the polemicist, labored to expose their attempts as futile. He addressed a considerable number of kenotic theologians and later kenotic types. He also gave extensive attention to the "purely humani- tarian" christologies of his day and, turning the tables, exposed the "reduced Jesus" as a pure myth.

Warfield perceives kenoticism as a bald rationalism that finds its corresponding motive in pure subjectivity and previously held philosophical presuppositions. It is driven by a settled determination to see in the earthly Christ nothing more than a human being. Johannes Weiss (1864–1914), for example, simply asserts

---

[109]Warfield traces the historical development of kenoticism in his "Late Discussions of Kenosis," a lengthy review of three recent titles on the subject (*PRR* 10, no. 40 [1899]: 701–4).
[110]*W*, 3:259.
[111]*W*, 3:373–76.

that the idea of two natures residing in one person is "unthinkable." Schmiedel pronounces it "simply impossible." And William Adams Brown just declares that such a notion is unsatisfying to the human mind. Such subjectivity scarcely deserves comment.[112]

Kenoticism also misrepresents history. Warfield cites Albert Schweitzer's (1875–1965) contention that the two natures doctrine was the invention of the Chalcedonian fathers and demonstrates at length his wresting of the historical facts. The Chalcedonian fathers invented nothing, and the doctrine they formulated "had no single new element in it." The doctrine (of the two natures) itself was not new. Indeed, Warfield argues,

> No one of the disputants in the long series of controversies which led up to Chalcedon . . . cherished the least doubt of this doctrine—not even Arius, and certainly not Apollinaris, or Nestorius, or Eutyches, or any of the great Monophysite or Monothelite leaders, or any of their opponents. The doctrine of the Two Natures formed the common basis on which all alike stood; their differences concerned only the quality or integrity of the two natures united in the one person, or the character or effects of the union by which they were brought together. It was the adjustment of these points of difference alone with which the council was concerned, or rather, to speak more precisely, the authoritative determination of the range within which such attempted adjustments might be tolerated in a church calling itself Christian.

Warfield goes on to argue that "there was never a time" when the two natures of Christ were not "the universal presupposition," both intellectually and devotionally, of Christians. There is no one-natured Christ to be found anywhere but in "the outlawed sects of the Docetists on the one hand, and the Ebionites with their successors, the Dynamistic Montanists, on the other." As the church emerged from the apostolic age, it brought the doctrine of the two natures of Christ with it. This doctrine was common to all Christians in its earliest, indeed, its very formative stage. Everywhere Christianity has traveled its adherents have been recognized as worshipers of Jesus Christ. This doctrine was so settled in the consciousness of Christians that it could not be unsettled until the rise of "radical" Socinianism and the eighteenth-century Enlightenment. Not until then was this doctrine considered "impossible."[113]

BIBLICAL STATEMENTS

That the doctrine of the two natures of Christ was held by the church so constantly is explained only by the fact that it is "intrenched [sic] in the teaching of the New

---

[112] W, 10:156–57, 316; W, 3:165, 254–55, 259–60, 288–89.
[113] W, 3:261–63.

Testament" itself. Warfield therefore remarks of the kenoticists that "the Bible has fallen to pieces in their hands." H. R. Mackintosh (1870–1936) wrote that "the life and consciousness of Jesus" are represented in the New Testament as "in form completely human." Warfield responds, simply, "The oddest thing about Prof. Mackintosh's Kenoticism, however, is that he seems to think he has a Biblical basis for it," and Warfield wonders how Mackintosh can so characterize the one who said, "Before Abraham was, I am." And so he remarks with a touch of sarcasm, "We cannot withhold the expression of our sympathy for Prof. Mackintosh in the difficulties he experiences in attempting to impose his *a priori* schematization of the Person of our Lord on a New Testament text obviously so impatient of it."[114] Warfield is thoroughly persuaded that biblical support for kenotic theories is wholly lacking. They are built on philosophical presuppositions only and against all the relevant biblical—and historical—data. For his part, Warfield finds in the New Testament extensive and unanimous support of the two-nature christology of historic Christianity. This doctrine is in the New Testament everywhere presupposed.

Philippians 2:5–11

On several occasions Warfield provides careful analysis of the critical passage on *kenosis*, Philippians 2:6–7.[115] Here Christ is plainly asserted to be "on an equality with God" ($\check{\iota}\sigma\alpha\ \theta\epsilon\dot{\omega}$), a statement that shouts of the highest christology. The language means nothing less than that Christ held in possession all that makes God God. That "in the form of God" ($\dot{\epsilon}\nu\ \mu o\rho\phi\hat{\eta}\ \theta\epsilon o\hat{\upsilon}\ \dot{\upsilon}\pi\dot{\alpha}\rho\chi\omega\nu$) asserts as much is evident not only by the fact that it stands parallel to "equal with God" but also by the very connotations of the terms themselves. "Form" indicates "those qualities which make anything the particular thing it is," that is, its character and intrinsic nature. The apostle therefore does not say, simply, that Jesus is God; he says more. To say that Christ is "in the form of God" is to emphasize more precisely and "in the most express manner possible" that he has in his own possession "the whole fulness of attributes" and all "those characterizing qualities" which make God God. Paul intends to stress to his readers that Christ is all that God is.[116]

Nor is the apostle making a mere historical statement, as if he were describing merely what our Lord was before the incarnation but is no longer. The verb tense is important. He says "*being* [$\dot{\upsilon}\pi\dot{\alpha}\rho\chi\omega\nu$, existing, subsisting] in the form of God." There is no indication of cessation of his deity. "Paul is not telling us here, then,

---

[114]W, 3:263; W, 10:260, 308, 318.
[115]W, 10:162–65; LG (1907), 225–26, 232–33, 237–38, 248–50; W, 3:270–72; W, 2:175–209; SW, 247–70.
[116]W, 3:270–72; W, 2:177.

what our Lord was once, but rather what He already was, or, better, what in His intrinsic nature He is." He is throwing into prominence the essential nature of this one who came and lived as a man, that we will better appreciate the greatness of his work for us.[117]

The strong adversative ἀλλά is important in this respect also. Paul is introducing a contrast. Christ "took no account of himself" *despite* who he was and the rights he retained as God. He was God and in full possession of all that it is to be God; *nevertheless*, he made himself of no reputation. So far from intimating that Christ laid aside his deity in his incarnation, Paul is asserting that he fully retained his deity throughout his earthly life. Jesus humbled himself "until death" (μέχρι θανάτου). Throughout the entire course of his life he was "consciously ever exercising self-abnegation, living a life which did not by nature belong to him, which stood in fact in direct contradiction to the life which was naturally His." He was made "not man, but 'in the likeness of a man.'" He was truly man, but "Paul would not have his readers imagine that He had become merely man." His assertion is not "that our Lord was once God but had become instead man; he teaches that though He was God, He had become also man." The "unbroken continuance of our Lord 'in the form of God,'" Warfield insists, is "the very essence" of Paul's assertion and the governing consideration throughout the passage.[118]

Next Warfield takes up the clause οὐχ ἁρπαγμὸν ἡγήσατο τὸ εἶναι ἴσα θεῷ ἀλλὰ ἑαυτὸν ἐκένωσεν, which he renders, "he did not look greedily upon his being on an equality with God but took no account of himself." Warfield argues at some length to demonstrate that κενόω, in all its occurrences in the New Testament (Rom. 4:14; I Cor. 1:17; 9:15; 2 Cor. 9:3), is constantly and exclusively used in a metaphorical sense "and cannot here be taken literally." This is clear, in context, in that the "emptying" is described as a "taking (λαβών) the form of a servant." Warfield comments simply, "You cannot 'empty' by 'taking'—*adding*." There is no exchange of one nature for another; there is a *taking*, an adding of another. He also observes that this verb is often used without a genitive either expressed or implied in the context. For example, a physician might speak of "emptying" the digestive tract without ever suggesting "of what" it was emptied. So also here. Moreover, "himself" (ἑαυτὸν) appears in a prior position, thus receiving greater emphasis. Paul's point is not that Christ "*emptied* himself" but that he "emptied *himself*." Noting this lends still more weight to the contention that κενόω must be taken in a metaphorical sense, as it is in its other New Testament occurrences. In other words, "if the language may be pardoned," Christ emptied himself of

---

[117] W, 2:178.
[118] W, 2:178–79; W, 10:162–63.

himself; that is, "he made no account of himself." "He humbled himself." He acted in self-abnegation. He "was not self-regarding" but instead had regard for others. His entire life, therefore, and every act he performed as a man, "He did voluntarily, by an ever fresh act of voluntary self-abnegation."[119]

Precisely what Christ did in making no account of himself is explained in the following clauses: he "took upon him the form [μορφὴν] of a servant, and was made in the likeness of men: and being found in fashion as a man, he . . . became obedient" (KJV). That is, he took to himself all that it is to be human, indeed, an actual "servant." As the ecclesiastical language has well stated, Christ "assumed" (λαβών) humanity, a real human nature. He did not merely enter into a man; he "took a human nature up into personal union with Himself"—God assuming humanity. Therefore, on his becoming "in the likeness of men," Warfield comments, "He remained much more than He seemed." He was real man, truly human. But all the while he remained also "in the form of God." "The Lord of the world became a servant in the world; He whose right it was to rule took obedience as His life-characteristic." The apostle is reminding his readers that Christ Jesus is "both God and man, God who has 'assumed' man into personal union with Himself, and has in His assumed manhood lived out a human life on the earth."[120]

In summary, "the two most obvious theological implications" of Philippians 2:6ff. are "that of the unbroken persistence of the Son of God 'in the form of God' after His incarnation, and that of the consequent coexistence in the incarnate Son of 'two natures.'" The passage shows Christ to have lived on earth as a man, but that life was a life that was "alien to his intrinsic nature, and assumed only in the performance of an unselfish purpose."[121]

Romans 1

Warfield claims that the opening verses of Romans provide the most exact description of "the Christ that Paul preached" to be found anywhere in Paul's writings. It is Christ as "Lord" (v. 4) that Paul has in view, and he correspondingly refers to himself as his "slave" (v. 1). Paul conceives of Christ's lordship in the very highest sense and of himself as Christ's property, with no rights of his own. Paul further couples "the Lord Jesus Christ" with "God our Father" as the common source of the soteric blessings of grace and peace (v. 7). While remaining distinct, Christ and the Father are together the single object of Paul's prayerful address and are the conjoint benefactor of divine blessing. They are alike addressed in terms of

---

[119]W, 2:178–79; W, 10:162–63.
[120]W, 2:179–82; W, 10:163, 265; PRR 10, no. 40 (1899): 717–18.
[121]W, 10:162; W, 2:177.

highest reverence—"God" and "Lord"—and are for Paul the common object of worship. And this comes from the same apostle who elsewhere writes, in effect, "You know perfectly well that there is no God but one" (1 Cor. 8:4, 6).[122]

Paul further calls Christ "the Son of God" (Rom. 1:4), a designation reflecting not what Christ is to us but what he is in himself. "The Son of God" is equal with God (cf. Mark 14:61; John 10:31–39). Christ is the Son of God in himself and is therefore our Lord. Christ's lordship, Warfield remarks, is rooted ultimately not in historical events or in the conference of supernatural powers or dignity but in his own metaphysical nature. Clearly, in Paul's mind, Christ possesses divine dignity, and it is this divine person, "the Son of God . . . Jesus Christ our Lord," which Paul says he has been sent to preach.[123]

But this is not all that Paul preached about Christ. Besides these two designations ("Son of God" and "Lord"), the apostle also describes the subject of his preaching as one "who became of the seed of David according to the flesh, and who was marked out as the Son of God in power according to the Spirit of holiness by the resurrection of the dead" (Rom. 1:3–4 BBW). As announced by the prophets (v. 2) Christ "became" of the seed of David, and Warfield notes the intimation of preexistence. Following J. B. Lightfoot he comments that he who always was the Son of God now "became" of the seed of David. He came into the world as the promised Messiah and departed "as the demonstrated Son of God." But it is not as though he ceased to be the Son of God when he became the seed of David. "It was rather just because He was the Son of God that He became of the seed of David." He was qualified for the office of messiahship "by being the Son of God."[124]

Warfield understands the phrase "demonstrated to be the Son of God by the resurrection" to indicate that by his resurrection Christ was marked out as divine, and this, he repeats, explains the chronological progression from "became the seed of David" to "declared to be the Son of God." He was the divine Son before becoming Messiah, but he was demonstrated to be the divine Son of God in his resurrection. He continues now as both. As noted above, Warfield misses the redemptive-historical significance of "declared to be the Son of God *with power*" that was articulated by Vos. Vos would not deny the accuracy of Warfield's exposition, as far as it goes. But Warfield was evidently completely unaware of Vos's exposition of the implications of the passage to the effect that Christ by his resurrection passed from life in this age into the new order of the age to come. He understands the statement exclusively in terms of a declaration of Christ's deity and misses entirely any significance of the temporal succession of *states* to which

---

[122] W, 2:235–38.
[123] W, 2:238–40.
[124] W, 2:240–50.

Christ had passed. Still, Warfield does not miss the fact that the clauses "do not express two essentially different modes of being through which Christ successively passed," from human to divine. He was the divine Son who came and who, remaining the divine Son all along, became also the seed of David, the messianic King. Warfield is justified in finding evidence here for the two natures of Christ, even if he is mistaken in limiting it to that.[125]

Hebrews

In Hebrews 1–2, Warfield explores the same theme as it is drawn out with broader strokes. The author of Hebrews exhausts himself in the first chapter as he attempts to exhibit adequately the "divine dignity" of Christ. High above the prophets, men through whom God spoke directly, Christ is "Son." He is the Creator and Sustainer of all that is. He is the effulgence of God's glory and the very impression of God's substance. He is even higher than the angels, the most exalted of God's creatures, for he has a more excellent name. Indeed, he is the object of the angels' worship. "Nay, He is given the name of the almighty and righteous God Himself, of the eternal Lord, who in the beginning laid the foundations of the earth and framed the heavens, and who shall abide the same when heaven and earth wax old and pass away." "To the author of this epistle our Lord is above all else the Son of God in the most eminent sense of that word." Yet in the second chapter the author takes a startling turn. This one whom angels worship "was made a little lower than the angels," thus stooping to that which for man's part is a most exalted dignity. "He descended an infinite distance to reach man's highest conceivable exaltation." He took "our blood and flesh" and was made like us in every way. Such are the depths of his humiliation. Yet he did not cease to be God during the days of his flesh—throughout his life he remains "a Son." This is the wonder of it all, that "although he was a son, he learned obedience" (Heb. 5:8). Here is one who is two in nature. He is God, and he is man—two natures in one person.[126]

The Epistles

Warfield refers briefly but pointedly also to several other New Testament passages that in one way or another lend support to the doctrine of the two natures of Christ. In 2 Corinthians 8:9, Paul speaks of Christ, though rich, becoming poor for the salvation of his people. In Galatians 4:4 the birth of Christ is described specifically as an incarnation: the Son of God is born of a woman. He who is the

---

[125]W, 2:235–52; cf. Geerhardus Vos, "The Eschatological Aspect of the Pauline Conception of the Spirit," 1912; reprinted in Gaffin, *Redemptive History*, 103–5.
[126]*PGS*, 3–4, 10; W, 2:185–88.

Son of God is sent by God to save, and to save he becomes what man is—human and under law. In Romans 8:3, Paul speaks of Christ as the Son of God come in the flesh. The high christology of Romans 9:5 is unmistakable—Christ is "the God over all, blessed forever"—but kenotic theologians are not deterred by it, even if they must amend the text. Weiss finds it "inconceivable" that Paul should speak this way of Christ and so assumes a textual corruption. Warfield mocks such biased subjectivity, pointing out that "there is not a scintilla of evidence of textual corruption" in Romans 9:5 and that Weiss's assumption rests solely on his own lower christology, which he is determined to impute to the apostle. That Paul here explicitly refers to Christ as God is a "plain fact" to which honest christological theories must adjust. In Colossians 2:9 the apostle declares that in Christ "the whole fullness of deity dwells bodily" (cf. Col. 1:19). This is to say, simply, that "Christ is an incarnation of the Godhead in all its fulness." The incarnate Christ was fully divine. This is impossible to reconcile with a lower christology. On 1 Timothy 3:16, "He was manifested in the flesh," Warfield notes an unmistakable implication of Christ's preexistence and, thus, his deity. Before his birth he was something other than flesh. Though previously hidden from human eyes, in his fleshly, earthly life he "was manifested." This is the Pauline equivalent of the Johannean "the Word became flesh." A change of state is implied, "a change by virtue of which what was hidden is now brought to light, and it is brought to light because brought into flesh." In 2 Timothy 1:10, Christ's appearance on earth is described as an "'epiphany,' which is the technical term for manifestations on earth of a God." He is "our great God" (Titus 2:13). Beyond these Warfield cites that seemingly endless list of passages in which Christ is spoken of as having lived out his life as a man yet is described "with the supreme reverence which is due to God alone" and is even designated specifically as "God," "the true God," "our great God," and the like.[127]

Christ as "Lord"

Warfield further points to "that whole series of passages" in which Christ is designated "Lord" (κύριος). He will not allow the contention of Weiss and others that speaking of Christ as "Lord" places him on a lower plane than God, but he insists that the terminology is expressly equivalent. As "Lord," Christ is recognized as having in full possession all divine attributes and prerogatives. As "Lord," he is worshiped. "Lord" is Paul's divine name for Christ. He refers to the triune God not as "Father, Son, and Spirit" but as "God, Lord, and Spirit." There is no distinction in dignity between the terms "Lord" and "God." "God" is a term of "pure exaltation,"

---

[127] W, 2:182–90; W, 3:267–68, 272; FL, 382.

but "Lord" connotes "more expressly the idea of sovereign rulership in actual exercise." Warfield conjectures further that Paul employs the designation "Lord" for Christ in part because of his conviction that Christ,

> as the God-man, has become the God of providence in whose hand is the kingdom, to "reign until he hath put all his enemies under his feet." . . . In a word, the term "Lord" seems to have been specifically appropriated to Christ not because it is a term of function rather than of dignity, but because along with the dignity it emphasizes function.[128]

The Synoptic Gospels

When Warfield turns to the Synoptic Gospels, he looks incredulously upon the kenotic theologians who think they find there a purely human Christ. The Christ of the Gospels is so evidently divine, although human also, that it would seem impossible to deny. The earthly life of Jesus as portrayed in the Gospels would more accurately be described as "a human episode in the divine life." Warfield is very willing to let the reader decide for himself. Can anyone read the Gospels and honestly come away with the impression that "Jesus' life and acts were determined for him by the necessary limits of a well-meaning but weak humanity"? Are we not driven by the Gospel writers, rather, to see a Christ whose life, actions, and limitations were altogether voluntary and chosen? Warfield predicts that "no simple reader of the Gospels will be easily persuaded" that the life of Jesus in the Gospels reflects the life of one who had lost the capacity for acting with supernatural power. His refusal to turn the stones to bread was not due to a lack of power but due to a determination of will—"else where was the temptation?" Likewise his refusal to come down from the cross when challenged to do so by the mocking crowd, we are assured, was due to the determinations of his own will and not a lack of ability. But once we have seen this—that the limitations of Jesus' life were voluntary and not a necessary limitation that had befallen him in consequence of his incarnation—"we have cut up the kenotic theory by the roots." And so Warfield condescendingly remarks, "The advocate of the kenotic theory who, under the condemnation of the Epistles, seeks comfort from the Gospels, certainly has a claim upon our pity."[129]

The Gospel of John

The affirmations of the apostle John in the prologue to his Gospel are vivid and to the point. At the outset he declares Christ's eternal subsistence, his eternal

---

[128]W, 3:274–76.
[129]W, 3:163; W, 10:165–66.

intercommunion with God, and his eternal identity with God: "In the beginning was the Word, and the Word was with God, and the Word was God" (John 1:1). John's language could scarcely be plainer. Christ was God from all eternity. Yet John declares that this, the eternal God, became man: "The Word was made flesh" (1:14). He assumed real humanity. But not leaving us to question whether he continued in his deity, John adds, "and dwelt among us, (and we beheld his glory, the glory as of the only begotten of the Father,) full of grace and truth" (KJV). His glory was not merely inferred—it was open to sight and observed. The invisible God, whom no one has seen, has been made known by Christ, who is "only begotten God" (μονογενὴς θεὸς, 1:18 BBW). Warfield notes that "only begotten" stands without the article, which points up the idea of quality rather than individuality. He reminds us further that "only begotten" does not convey the idea of subordination or derivation but of uniqueness and consubstantiality: "Jesus is all that God is, and He alone is this." Further, of this "only begotten God" John affirms that he "is" in the bosom of the Father. His former relationship "with God" (1:1) is still unbroken and did not change in his incarnate state. It is on this ground that John declares that Christ is able to "interpret" (ἐξηγέομαι) God to men. Warfield summarizes, "In this remarkable sentence there is asserted in the most direct manner the full Deity of the incarnate Word, and the continuity of His life as such in His incarnate life; thus He is fitted to be the absolute revelation of God." As noted above, this is how John contrasts with the Synoptics. "The others begin on the plane of human life. John begins in the inter-relations of the divine persons in eternity. . . . This Jesus, say the others, is God. This God, says John, became Jesus." It is thus that John prepares his readers for the famous narrative that follows—a portrait of a divine Christ walking as man among men.[130]

The Teaching of Christ Himself

Finally, Warfield surveys the teaching of Christ himself and finds there the source of the doctrine that is common to the New Testament writers. In the Gospel of John, Jesus says that he is "from above" and "not of this world" (8:23; 17:16), that he "descended from heaven" (3:13), that he is "one" with the Father (10:30), that to see him is to see the Father (14:9), and that he is coeternal and of equal glory with the Father (17:5). He claims for himself "the timeless present of eternity as His mode of existence" (8:58). But for all his glory, still he is "descended" to earth, and to some extent his glory was obscured. "There was a sense, then, in which, because He had 'descended,' He was no longer equal with the Father." Hence, he can affirm, "the Father is greater than I" (14:28), which "obviously means" that

---

[130]W, 2:190–94; SSW, 1:148–49.

there is "a sense" in which he was no longer equal to the Father. He was God, and he was man.[131]

Jesus' assertions of deity in the Synoptics were surveyed above in consideration of Christ's deity, and Warfield travels much of the same ground in this context also. Christ takes his place above angels, declares the kingdom of God to be his own kingdom and God's elect to be his elect, claims that he is the glorious Son of Man and Son of God, and so on. The contrast between the disciples' "Jesus Christ makes you whole" or "In the name of Jesus of Nazareth, walk!" and Jesus' own "I will, be clean" or "I say to you, arise!" is stunning. Not only is he a worker of his own miracles, but he is the worker of the disciples' miracles as well. He claims unique knowledge of God (Matt. 11:27) and ranks himself not in equality with God merely but in a place "of absolute reciprocity and interpenetration of knowledge with the Father." He commands converts to be baptized "in the name of the Father and of the Son and of the Holy Spirit," thus placing himself in the triune Godhead. Warfield lays particular stress, in this context, on Jesus' statement recorded in Mark 13:32 (cf. Matt. 24:36): "But of that day or hour no one knows, not even the angels in heaven, nor the Son, but the Father alone." Warfield observes the "ascending scale of being" inherent in the statement "not even the angels, nor even the Son" and notes that Jesus places himself above the angels, the highest of God's creatures. There is no one higher than the angels but God. Yet, at the same time, Jesus claims ignorance: even he does not know "that hour." For both attributes (supreme, divine dignity and ignorance) to be present in one person, that person must be both God and man. As to his deity, Christ is above the angels. As to his humanity, his knowledge is limited. If this sounds contradictory, Warfield reminds us that it is only apparently so. It is substantively no different from Paul's statements that the Jews "crucified the Lord of glory" (1 Cor. 2:8) and that God has purchased the church "with his own blood" (Acts 20:28). This is nothing more than the mystery of the two natures.[132]

SUMMARY CONCLUSION

Kenotic theories rest neither on exegetical nor on historical grounds but on philosophical presuppositions, particularly the gratuitous assumption that two natures could not possibly reside in one person. Such theories proceed accordingly with an exclusive focus on Christ's human nature and with the preconviction that the whole of his life can be explained in such terms. "The beginning question seems to be: 'How much of Christ's life on earth can be accounted for on the Kenotic

---

[131] W, 2:197–200.
[132] W, 2:200–206; W, 10:169–70.

assumption?'" Warfield insists that the method is flawed. "When we begin by begging the whole question . . . we can scarcely avoid arriving at the predestined goal." But other questions must be allowed to guide the discussion:

> How much of Christ's life can be accounted for without the Kenotic assumption? . . . How much of the phenomena of Christ's life on earth as recorded in the Gospels cannot be accounted for on the Kenotic assumptions? . . . How far does the Kenotic assumption accord with the conceptions of Christ's person held by Himself and His accredited apostles?

Allowing these necessary questions, Warfield argues, the kenotic theories all fail. In summary, the kenotic doctrine stands in conflict with (1) the didactic teachings of the christological passages of Scripture, (2) the life of Christ as displayed in the Gospel narratives, (3) the Bible's explicit presentation of the two natures of Christ, (4) its presentation of Christ as the revelation of God, (5) its doctrine of the Trinity, (6) its doctrine of the immutability of God, (7) the common tenets of sound philosophy according to which being cannot be separated from attributes, (8) the dictates of common sense, which cannot allow that a being can be essentially omnipresent and yet not everywhere or essentially omniscient yet ignorant, (9) the historical faith of the church, and (10) the ineradicable demands of the Christian heart.[133]

Any notion of a "historical," purely human Christ lying in or behind the New Testament writings, Warfield finds impossible. It is "a pure invention" and exists nowhere "except in the imaginations" of biased theologians. The Gospel writers themselves know nothing of such a Jesus, "nor does He lurk anywhere in the background of their narratives." To the New Testament writers all and to Jesus himself, such a perception of Christ is patently "nonsense." So overwhelming is the biblical evidence that in 1907, Warfield can describe kenoticism as having "lost respect," and then in 1911 as virtually dead; and in 1914 he can express sympathy with Biedermann's caustic remark concerning the kenotic theories that "only one who has himself suffered a kenosis of his understanding can possibly accord them welcome." The only Christ to be found anywhere in the Scriptures, Warfield confidently and repeatedly asserts, is one who is both divine and human.[134]

"It is undeniable that the Christ of the whole body of New Testament writers, without exception, is a Two-Natured Person—divine and human." That this doctrine was held by the church so constantly is explained only by the fact that

---

[133]*PRR* 10, no. 40 (1899): 710–12, 723–25.
[134]*W*, 3:283, 298–303, 376; *W*, 10:159; cf. "The Synoptic Jesus—the Historical Jesus" in the discussion of the deity of Christ, above.

it is deeply "intrenched [sic] in the teaching of the New Testament" itself. Warfield argues, further, that this doctrine is not merely a synthesis of all the varying
strands of data found in the New Testament; it is the doctrine of Christ taught in
the New Testament collectively and by each of the authors individually. Whatever
differences there may be between the various books and authors, the two natures
they hold in common. This conception of Christ underlies them all. The church
has universally presupposed the two natures because the New Testament itself
rests on that presupposition. "When Christian literature begins, this is already
the common assumption of the entire church." The various theories of "divergent
Christologies" within the New Testament have all been so thoroughly discredited
that no one can possibly hold them any longer.[135]

WARFIELD IN TRANSITION?

In his review of *The Person and Work of Christ*, a collection of Warfield's christological writings published in 1950 by Presbyterian and Reformed, John Murray
(1898–1975) surprisingly alleges that Warfield's christology underwent a significant change around 1914. For evidence, he points to Warfield's article "The
Person of Jesus Christ" (1915) and his earlier sermon "Imitating the Incarnation"
(1913). Murray gives high commendation of Warfield's exegetical, theological,
and homiletical expertise, but he claims that in his earlier (1913) treatment of the
famous *kenosis* passage, Philippians 2:5–12, Warfield allowed that in the incarnation, the Son "divested himself of his equality with God." Murray contends that
in Warfield's 1915 article, by contrast, he made no such concession but argued
most thoroughly that in his humiliation, Christ retained his equality with God.
Murray found Warfield's earlier and later discussions to be conflicting—"quite
opposed"—and reflective of a radical transformation in his thinking.

The language in Warfield's 1913 sermon that Murray finds objectionable reads,
"It was although He was in the form of God, that Christ Jesus did not consider His
being on an equality with God so precious a possession that He could not lay it
aside, but rather made no account of Himself." Warfield later asks rhetorically,
"Did Christ stand upon His unquestioned right of retaining His equality with
God?" Murray alleges that the "obvious implication" of this is that in Warfield's
judgment, "Christ divested Himself of His equality with God."[136]

If Murray's observation were accurate, it would reflect a startlingly abrupt and
monumental shift toward orthodoxy in Warfield's thinking, a shift made all the
more remarkable by its occurrence at such a late date in his distinguished career.

---

[135]*W*, 3:263, 266, 283, 285.
[136]*Collected Writings of John Murray*, vol. 3 (Carlisle, PA: Banner of Truth, 1982), 358–61.

To be sure, Murray speaks of this shift generously in terms of Warfield's own christological development, but it is a dramatic change nonetheless.

Murray is mistaken, however, and the evidence against him is overwhelming.[137] First, the very language that he finds objectionable in Warfield's sermon is found in his later article, which Murray thinks contradicts it, and of which he approves. In the 1915 article, which Murray holds to be the more mature Warfield, Warfield writes of Christ's glory, which "had been left behind" during his earthly sojourn. "There was a sense, then, in which, because He had 'descended,' He was no longer equal with the Father." Again he writes, "There was a sense in which He had ceased to be equal with the Father, because of the humiliation of His present condition, and in so far as this humiliation involved entrance into a status lower than that which belonged to Him by nature."[138] His language here is at least as explicit as that of 1913. We can only guess why Murray would find the 1913 language objectionable and this language acceptable; it would seem that he did not read the 1915 article carefully enough. What is clear is that Warfield himself did not consider his language self-contradictory. So far as Warfield was concerned, there had been no "development" in his christological thinking on this point.

Second, as providing possible explanation, Murray, the consummate systematician, evidently could not appreciate Warfield's willingness, as an exceptionally rigorous exegetical theologian, to stretch theological (even Chalcedonian) concepts in keeping with the language of inspired Scripture. In the passage in question (Phil. 2:5ff.), the apostle Paul does stretch our thinking to the limits. He emphatically affirms Christ's continued deity throughout his incarnational state, as Warfield insists. However, Warfield wants to do justice to the apostle's words— Christ "did not consider equality with God something to be grasped but emptied himself." This language, taken alone, is open to various understandings. Warfield is willing to use the language as is, and when he affirms that Christ "did not consider His being on an equality with God so precious a possession that He could not lay it aside, but rather made no account of Himself," and when he asks, "Did Christ stand upon His unquestioned right of retaining His equality with God?" he is merely echoing the inspired apostle. And so he concludes that there is "a sense" in which Christ was no longer equal to the Father. The precise "sense" in which he was no longer equal, in Warfield's thinking, is economic—that Christ was now a man with human limitations, born under law, and (economically) subordinate to the Father. The miracle of the incarnation—the depths of humiliation coupled

---

[137]Carl Trueman makes brief note of this also in his 2001 lecture, "The Glory of Christ: B. B. Warfield on Jesus of Nazareth," *The Evangelical Library Bulletin*, no. 106 (Autumn 2001): 8–9; cf. Trueman, *The Wages of Spin* (Fearn Ross-shire: Mentor, 2007), 114–18.

[138]*W*, 2:199.

simultaneously with eternal dignity—strains the mind and stretches the ability of human language to describe it. This is the nature of the case. But Warfield is determined to give full weight to the biblical text. He apparently seeks to employ biblical language that does justice to both sides of the equation, and he is willing to live with a tension that makes Murray uncomfortable.[139]

Finally, and most tellingly, it is evident that Warfield maintains this same emphasis (on the full deity of Christ in his incarnate state) consistently at all points of his career. In our earliest known published statements of Warfield—his 1876 sermon preached in Dayton, Ohio—he glories in the mystery of Christ's two natures. "In the person of Christ two natures are united to form one person. He is both truly God and truly man, two complete and separate natures 'united without confusion, without conversion, eternally and inseparably.'" Mystery though this is, "yet we have the clear declaration of God's word that it is true, and we accept it as simply and absolutely true on its testimony." In 1887, Warfield describes the incarnate Christ as a "divine person" who lived a "divine life" on earth, and as One who, by reason of his majesty, is incomprehensible and of "immeasurable distance" from us. In 1888, he refers to the Jesus of the Gospels as "the perfect God-man" and stresses that Jesus is God *manifested* in the flesh. In 1891, he writes that "all the Gospels are written out of devout adoration of the divine Savior, and portray our Lord as divine." He notes Jesus' "self-witness to his oneness with God" and repeatedly describes the earthly Jesus of the Gospels as "the divine Messiah, the divine Benefactor, the divine savior . . . the infinite God." Still more explicitly, in his 1893 sermon titled "Incarnate Truth," Warfield not only speaks of the incarnate Christ as "the God of love manifest in the flesh," "the manifested Jehovah," "the God-man," having "oneness with God," and possessing divine omniscience; he specifically deplores the kenotic theories, which suggest that when God became man he "surrendered the attributes of divinity"—theories that leave us with a God who "had shrunk to the capacity of a man" and lived a "purely human life." He laments kenoticism as a theory that, if true, would leave the sorrowing world "like Mary standing weeping in the garden and crying, 'They have taken away my Lord.'" In 1895, Warfield exults in the salvation that could be accomplished by none but the "God-man" himself. In 1896, he asserts emphatically that in light of Jesus' resurrection we have ground to believe the claims of this One who "made himself equal with God." In his 1898 "Recent Reconstructions of Theology" he deplores

---

[139]Warfield's teacher and predecessor Charles Hodge expresses the same tension when he says, speaking of the hypostatic union, that "we may say of Christ . . . that he is less than God and equal with God." *Systematic Theology*, 3 vols. (1871; repr., Grand Rapids: Eerdmans, 1952), 2:392. He speaks similarly of Christ in his comments on 2 Cor. 8:9, that Christ "so far laid aside the glory of his divine majesty." *1 & 2 Corinthians* (1859; repr., Edinburgh: Banner of Truth, 1978), 577.

the prevailing tendency in "Christian" theology that "deprecates" the person of Christ and will not allow the biblical and historic doctrine of the God-man. Here he describes the kenotic doctrine disparagingly as "a new Socinian defection," and as a mere "happy expedient by which we may lull our reverence to sleep by still speaking of Jesus as God, while we yet find nothing but what is purely human in his speech or action; by which we may decline his authority while offering him an empty homage." In two reviews—1899 and 1900—he severely criticizes the kenotic theories of Thomas Adamson and others and insists that a "humanized Jesus" is entirely unacceptable to the Christian. And in his classroom lectures on christology at the turn of the century he presents clearly the orthodox understanding of Christ's two natures, refutes all alternatives, and insists that only as the God-man could Jesus make satisfaction for sin.[140]

In "The Human Development of Jesus" (1900), Warfield provides his fullest treatment of Jesus' humanity and humiliation. He shows a zealousness to do full justice to the Scripture's presentation of Christ as all that man is. He points out that as a man, Jesus "increased in wisdom and knowledge," was open to temptation, was conscious of dependence upon God, was a man of prayer, exercised faith, "learned obedience by the things which he suffered," and so on. And he emphasizes that "the Reformed theology which it is our happiness to inherit, has never hesitated to face the fact [of Jesus' complete humanity] and rejoice in it, with all its implications." Jesus was a man with a fully human mind, heart, and spirit. He was whatever it is to be a man—a man without error and without sin, but a man. Warfield is zealous to acknowledge that Jesus' humanity was the very same as our own, in all our creaturely weakness and limitations. But Warfield is equally zealous to clarify that Jesus, even in his state of humiliation, was fully God. "Alongside of these clear declarations and rich indications of his true and complete humanity, there runs an equally pervasive attribution to him of all that belongs to deity. . . . If all that man is is attributed to him, no less is all that God is attributed to him." And he further exhorts us to resist the tendency to "pare down" either side of this equation. Jesus was both fully man and fully God, and the attributes of both his "perfect deity" and his "perfect humanity" were always in his "constant possession." All through his humbled state, Jesus, according to Warfield in 1900, possessed "all that belongs to deity" and remained "all that God is." That is to say, simply, his equality with God was unbroken and undiminished.

---

[140]*The Dayton Daily Democrat*, July 25, 1876, 4; *SSW*, 2:127–28 (emphasis added), 296–98, 639–45, 458–61, 151; *SSW*, 1:199; *PRR* 10, no. 40 (1899): 701–25 and *PRR* 11, no. 42 (1900): 370–71; N. W. Harkness, unpublished class notes from Warfield's lectures on systematic theology, 1899–1901 (Princeton Seminary library archives), 34–40; *W*, 10:166, 260.

The glory of the Incarnation is that it presents to our adoring gaze, not a humanized God or a deified man, but a true God-man—one who is all that God is and at the
same time all that man is: on whose mighty arm we can rest, and to whose human
sympathy we can appeal. We cannot afford to lose either the God in the man or the
man in the God; our hearts cry out for the complete God-man whom the Scriptures
offer us.[141]

To continue, in his 1903 "The Question of Miracles," Warfield reasons that
we should expect to witness the miraculous in Jesus' earthly ministry, and he
grounds this presumption in Jesus' divine character. He says, rather poetically,
"One might as well expect a lamp to burn without rays extending from it into the
surrounding darkness, as the Son of God to descend from heaven without trailing
clouds of glory as he came." Again, his reasoning seems clearly to be grounded
in a recognition of Jesus' deity even in his incarnate state. More explicitly, in his
brief 1906 article "The Supernatural Birth of Jesus," Warfield vigorously argues for
the Christian necessity of faith in a supernatural Savior—one who is "a true God-
man." In his 1907 review of David W. Forrest's *Authority of Christ*, Warfield affirms
pointedly that the "two most obvious theological implications" of Philippians
2:6ff. are "that of the unbroken persistence of the Son of God 'in the form of God'
after His incarnation, and that of the consequent coexistence in the incarnate
Son of 'two natures.'" He emphasizes at length throughout his review that Jesus'
divine nature was not transmuted into humanity, that even artificial exegesis
cannot drive from the passage its insistent declaration that Christ, in becoming
man, retained "in full possession all that characterizes God as God," and that "the
controlling factor" in Christ's life of humiliation was therefore a "continuous act
of voluntary self-abnegation"—by which assertion Paul "sets aside at one stroke
the whole kenotic contention."[142]

Warfield's major 1907 work on christology, *The Lord of Glory*, was given precisely
to a defense of the deity of Christ. He asserts repeatedly the unqualified deity of
Christ in his incarnate state and argues at length that this was the conviction of
the primitive church. He uses the language of "equality" with God and goes still
further, insisting that Jesus unbrokenly maintained his divine "identity." Here
he declares that Jesus' lordship, not merely in his exaltation but throughout his
earthly career also, is "the essence of Christianity." And in this, his earliest discussion of the passage in question (Phil. 2:5–11), even the paragraph headings reveal
Warfield's orthodoxy—"Jesus the Man . . . But Not Merely Man . . . The Two Sides of
Christ's Being." He plainly asserts that Christ "remained unbrokenly 'in the form

---

[141]*SSW*, 1:162–66.
[142]*SSW*, 2:192; *W*, 3:455; *W*, 10:162–65.

of God.' . . . It cannot be denied that there underlies this whole mode of conception the idea of 'the two natures' of Christ, on the basis of which alone can this duplex method of speaking of Him be defended or even comprehended." Indeed, throughout this 1907 work he draws out at considerable length this point that it was the conviction of the earliest Christians that Jesus was the divine Messiah. It is no minor issue but a matter of fundamental significance for Warfield that Christ, in the state of his humiliation, was all that God is and was in every sense, economic considerations only excepted, equal to him. In his own 1908 review of this work, he describes it as an exposition and argument that "to our Lord's first followers as a whole, and to Himself as well, He was nothing other than God manifest in the flesh."[143]

The evidence continues. Writing in 1908, Warfield specifically argues against the idea that Christ ceased to be God in his incarnate state. He insists that Jesus Christ "is all that God is, yet God as manifested," and that "only by so recognizing him as God in the flesh . . . can we understand the life he lived and the work he did." Christ is "God manifested, fully manifested, in the flesh." In 1909, he emphasizes primarily the claims of the incarnate Christ himself as to his own deity, and that "the assumed conviction of the deity of Christ is coeval with Christianity itself. There never was a Christianity, neither in the times of the apostles nor since, of which this was not a prime tenet."[144] In 1910, he repeatedly refers to the incarnate Jesus as "divine," "the supernatural Son of God," "deity," having "intrinsic divine powers," "the God-man," and so on. This, he argues, is the only Jesus of history. In 1911, he insistently argues that Christ in his incarnate state was "not merely the most perfectly God-indwelt man who ever was. . . . He is God as well" and that Christianity is "rooted" in this very truth. His lengthy 1911 article "The 'Two Natures' and Recent Christological Speculation" is given entirely to establishing "the two natures" of the incarnate Christ, a doctrine that Warfield insists self-consciously belonged to the church from its very first days. The same "two natures" terminology is found in his 1912 article "The Emotional Life of Our Lord."[145]

Early in 1913, Warfield published a rather lengthy review of H. R. Mackintosh's kenotic *The Doctrine of the Person of Jesus Christ*. With sarcasm he insists that the theory has no biblical support whatever and that "no resting place can be found in a half-way house between Socinianism and orthodoxy." And he insists that no Christian heart can consent to surrender either the divine or the human nature of Jesus Christ.[146] Later in the same year, Warfield published a lengthy rebuttal

---

[143]*LG*, 225, 248; *PTR* 6, no. 1 (1908): 128.
[144]*SSW*, 1:153.
[145]*SSW*, 1:148–57; *W*, 3:149–77, 259–310; *W*, 10:259–60; *BTSp*, 35–90.
[146]*W*, 10:318–19.

of Schmiedel's famous "pillar passages." Schmiedel alleged that these pillar passages from the Gospels presented a purely human Christ and thus represented the original Jesus tradition. Warfield argued in detail that Schmiedel had done violence to the passages in question and that the only Jesus known to history is the "supernatural" and "divine" Jesus. "No stratum of tradition has been reached ... in which the portrait of Jesus differs in any essential respect" from that of the Gospels. The "aboriginal church" was a community of people who worshiped Jesus; this was not a later development. The Jesus of the Gospels and of the first Christians "claimed our worship" as one who was "truly God."[147]

Similar statements are also found throughout his 1914 article "The Twentieth Century Christ." Here Warfield highlights the particulars of various kenotic approaches and condemns their "vain attempts" to ground their christology in Philippians 2:8. "No Christian heart will be satisfied with a Christ in whom ... there was no Godhead at all while He was on earth, and in whom ... there may be no manhood at all now that he has gone to heaven." The "reduced" Jesus and "shrivelled God" of kenoticism, Warfield argues, is not the Jesus of the Bible, of history, or of salvation and eternal life. The true Jesus is the God-man.[148]

Warfield's obvious orthodox christology in these 1913–1914 articles is particularly noteworthy, given Murray's impression that Warfield underwent a theological change in 1914. Murray erroneously dated Warfield's allegedly defective sermon as 1913, but this sermon was first published in 1914. Murray may simply have surmised that the sermon was preached in 1913, but it must be assumed that the sermon reflects the views Warfield held in 1914 when he published them. This mistake on Murray's part makes his allegation still more difficult to sustain in that the time frame for Warfield's alleged "shift" becomes impossibly narrow, particularly in light of the fact that at the very same time Warfield was publishing other articles in defense of orthodox christology. It would seem evident that Murray simply misunderstood Warfield's 1913/1914 sermon.

Evidence mounts seemingly without end. Warfield's orthodox christological convictions did not begin around 1915, as Murray's charge would have us believe. Nor did they waver around 1913–1914. Nothing could be clearer in Warfield than that all through his christology, from the beginning to the end of his career, he consistently, emphatically, and enthusiastically—even passionately—affirms the miracle of Christ that although he was God from eternity, he, remaining all that God is, was manifested as a man. Indeed, throughout all Warfield's writing, this is not only a prominent but a most cherished theme.

---

[147] W, 3:181–255; citations from 183 and 244.
[148] W, 3:371–89.

One would have expected Murray, who was a great admirer of Warfield and in some respects the heir of Warfield's theological chair,[149] to have been more familiar with Warfield and the overall character of his christological writings. Murray clearly held Warfield in the highest regard, and his unwitting misrepresentation of him can only be attributed to his lack of acquaintance with him.[150] He evidently misunderstood Warfield's 1914 sermon, but this misunderstanding would have been cleared away quickly had he read Warfield more widely and the 1915 article more carefully.

THEOLOGICAL FORMULATION

Warfield's doctrine of the person of Christ is summed up in the term "incarnation." Christ is not a man inhabited by God. He is not a humanized God or a deified man. He is truly God and truly man. Warfield insists that we give full justice to both strands of scriptural data—Christ's deity and his humanity. On the one hand he will acknowledge with his opponent Paul Wernle that in the days of his flesh Christ is seen to be profoundly humble before God and unreservedly casts himself on the Father in utter dependence upon him for all things. This Warfield will not deny but in fact is eager to stress. He who possessed a truly human soul not simply might but *must* have been, in respect to that soul, subjected to ignorance (Mark 13:32) and the sense of mortal agony when rejected by God (Mark 15:34). But Warfield is not willing to let this strand of evidence stand for the whole, for on the other hand Christ is seen also in the days of his flesh as "sharer of the whole extent of the divine knowledge," as making high claims which reach "to the supreme deity itself." He alone "knows the Father," and the Father alone knows him. He alone has authority to forgive sin, to judge, to raise the dead. He is above the angels. God's kingdom is *his own* kingdom, and he rules over it. He is uniquely "one" with the Father. He shares the glory and honor of the Father. All this must be given full weight also. "Such a combination of mental states within the limits of a single nature," Warfield says, is "inconceivable." "It is inconceivable that the same soul could have produced two such contradictory states of mind contemporaneously." The only conclusion that can be drawn from the evidence

[149]Murray was instructor in systematic theology at Princeton, 1929–1930, and then professor of systematic theology at Westminster Seminary, established by J. Gresham Machen in 1929 as the new "Old Princeton," 1930–1967.

[150]Murray arrived at Princeton three years after the death of Warfield and was a student of J. Gresham Machen and Geerhardus Vos. Princeton historian David B. Calhoun notes that Murray had a particularly high regard for Vos as "the most penetrating exegete it has been my privilege to know" (David B. Calhoun, *Princeton Seminary*, vol. 2, *The Majestic Testimony 1869-1929* [Carlisle, PA: Banner of Truth, 1996], 353). This enthusiasm for Vos is evident in Murray's work and may explain, at least in part, his comparative neglect of Warfield.

is that "the self-consciousness of Jesus is, in other words, duplex, and necessarily implies dual centers of self-consciousness," "two minds." Thus, Jesus learns from others that Lazarus is sick but knows apart from any further message that he is dead. He weeps at the grave yet calmly gives thanks for the miracle of resurrection before it takes place. At points throughout the Gospels he expresses utter dependence upon God, and at others he announces his own mighty "I will." The difficulty is not with the biblical evidence but only with our understanding. And Warfield recognizes the difficulty in grasping just how two such diverse natures can exist and function in a single person—even if the difficulty is "more theoretical than practical." He is not surprised, therefore, at the serious deviations that appeared in history as attempts were made to state the doctrine systematically. If one side or another receives unequal emphasis, or if incomplete statements are formulated, error inevitably results. But he is thoroughly persuaded that this conception of the person of Christ must be carefully guarded—that in him two complete natures unite, inseparably and without conversion or confusion—for only this understanding brings harmony to what otherwise is full of perplexity. There is mystery, to be sure. But this is but the mystery of the incarnation, and without this mystery there could be no incarnation at all. If this is not the solution to the puzzle—two natures in one person—the puzzle is insoluble. Only in this understanding of Christ's person "can the mind rest." This is the presupposition of all the biblical writers in their portrait of Jesus.[151]

Another word Warfield offers to express this doctrine is "assumption." In the incarnation, God did not merely enter into a man, and Jesus was not merely "the most perfectly God-indwelt man who ever was." He was that, but "he is God as well." He is the God-man. In the incarnation, God did not merely enter into a man. Rather, he

> took a human nature up into personal union with Himself. Accordingly "assumption" is the theological term to describe the act; and it would be truer to speak of the human nature of Christ as existing in God than of God as existing in it. Jesus Christ is primarily not a man in whom God dwells, but God who has assumed into personal union with Himself a human nature as an organ through which He acts.[152]

Warfield argues, therefore, that Chalcedonian christology is but a "very perfect synthesis of the biblical data." The biblical data is complex and at times seemingly divergent, but it finds its harmonious statement in the affirmation of Chalcedon,

---

[151] *W*, 3:250, 263–65, 305, 309–10; *W*, 10:164, 168–69, 260–61; *W*, 2:195, 208, 308; *PWC*, 95; *PRR* 10, no. 40 (1899): 715; *SSW*, 1:164–66.
[152] *W*, 10:259–60, 264–65.

that the two natures are united in the person of Christ "without confusion, without conversion, eternally and inseparably"—perfect humanity and perfect deity. Warfield avows that the statement of Chalcedon is nothing more than "a careful statement in systematic form of the pure teaching of the Scriptures." It takes in all the relevant biblical data and, thus, has stood ever since as the christological norm for all the major branches of the church. Moreover, if this is not the solution, then "the mystery of His personality passes over into a mere mass of crass contradictions which cannot all be believed."

> There can scarcely be imagined a better proof of the truth of a doctrine than its power completely to harmonize a multitude of statements which without it would present to our view only a mass of confused inconsistencies. A key which perfectly fits a lock of very complicated wards can scarcely fail to be the true key.

We may deny one or the other, but we cannot allow both sets of claims in a merely one-natured Christ. Warfield therefore insists that neither strand of truth be trimmed or ignored. He will allow neither Docetism nor Ebionism nor Appolinarianism nor Monothelitism. The Christ of the New Testament is a Christ who is man, with all the limitations of humanity, and who is God, with all the dignity and prerogatives of deity. "In him dwells all the fullness of the Godhead bodily."[153]

Christ as the Revelation of God

It is in this vein that Warfield speaks of Christ as the revelation of God to men. Much more than an interpreter of God like the prophets and much more than a messenger of God like the angels, being "the very effulgence of God's glory and the very impress of his substance," Christ is truly a divine manifestation— "both a *manifestation* and a manifestation of *what is divine*." According to the Evangelists, "Jesus' perfection is the manifestation of the τελείωσις of the absolute God." Warfield clearly relishes speaking of Christ in these terms. In him we behold the glory of God's "grace and truth" (John 1:14), and he is the One who "interprets" God to us (John 1:18)—not merely by what he says but in his very person.[154]

In his lengthy essay "The Emotional Life of Our Lord," Warfield not only examines the emotions of Jesus, per se, but also by them what we learn about God. Granted, some emotions are purely human, such as the feeling of lack or deprivation or pain. Here we see the Son of God in real humanity. But Christ is divine

---

[153] W, 2:207–8; W, 3:263–65; cf. SSW, 1:165.
[154] W, 10:166–67 (emphasis original).

also. Thus, we are not surprised to see in his "compassion" toward the sick and needy—expressed even in tears, deep groans, and sighs, such as his wailing over Jerusalem—a revelation of divine mercy, the heart of the God who pities his creatures. Probing deeper, we see in the Lord Jesus a heart of "love," a love that intends good, a love of benevolence; and in this love we see what God is like. The love of Christ in self-sacrifice for sinners is a demonstration of the heart of God. He loves and receives sinners, and in this, God is manifest. Likewise, "indignation" and "anger" are not merely the self-expression of a moral being generally, but viewing the indignation and anger of Christ we see the response of God toward evil and toward the miserable effects of sin upon humanity. Still, our Lord's anger did not inhibit the expression of his compassion, as our anger often does. Both emotions appear in perfect harmony: he loves and has pity toward the weak, yet he rebukes in anger and resentment all that is evil. The same could be said of his "gladness" and of other emotions also. Paying close attention to Christ, we learn of God himself.[155]

The Two Natures a Gospel Essential

Finally, Warfield sees the two natures of Christ as essential to the gospel itself. This is not a "negligible speculation" attached to Paul's gospel. The Jesus Paul preached was a divine-human Savior. There is "no half-way house" between the options that Christ is both God and man and that he is a mere man, and "no Christian heart will be satisfied" with a Christ who is not both divine and human. No Christian heart can consent to give up either.[156]

The various *kenosis* theories devised in Warfield's day left the church with a Christ divested of deity, and this was a notion Warfield could not allow to go unchecked. Apart from a real incarnation of the second person of the Godhead, there is no Christianity at all in any meaningful sense. Indeed, this is the hinge on which the Christian system turns, its very center and core. Only a Christ who is both divine and human will do. This is so simply because Christianity is above all else a sinner's religion—it is a religion of redemption. There was no intrinsic need for God the Son to become incarnate—there was nothing lacking in him, no need unfulfilled. Nor was it necessary for him to save sinners. But given his gracious purpose to save, "it was necessary" for him to be made like us in every way so that he could stand as our substitute and make propitiation for our sins (Heb. 2:17).

---

[155] *PWC*, 93–145; *SSW*, 1:154.
[156] *W*, 2:251–52; *W*, 3:376; *W*, 10:319.

This is the whole rationale of the incarnation, and this is its glory: "Christ Jesus came into the world to save sinners" (1 Tim. 1:15). Its entire motive was one of grace. Human sin was its occasion, and human redemption was its goal. This is the linchpin of the gospel—the glorious Son of God stooped to become all that we are in order to bring us rescue. Only in recognition of this great condescension of grace do we learn the love of God for us. Only here are our faith and love drawn out to their full height. And only here can we find a Savior "on whose mighty arm we can rest, and to whose human sympathy we can appeal." Our Savior must be both God and man. "We cannot afford to lose either the God in the man or the man in the God; our hearts cry out for the complete God-man whom the Scriptures offer us." In nothing less could we find ground for hope.[157]

---

[157]*SSW*, 1:146–47, 166; cf. *PGS*, 29–53.

There is no one of the titles of Christ which is more precious to Christian hearts than "Redeemer." There are others, it is true, which are more often on the lips of Christians. The acknowledgment of our submission to Christ as our Lord, the recognition of what we owe to Him as our Saviour,—these things, naturally, are most frequently expressed in the names we call Him by. "Redeemer," however, is a title of more intimate revelation than either "Lord" or "Saviour." It gives expression not merely to our sense that we have received salvation from Him, but also to our appreciation of what it cost Him to procure this salvation for us. It is the name specifically of the Christ of the cross. Whenever we pronounce it, the cross is placarded before our eyes and our hearts are filled with loving remembrance not only that Christ has given us salvation, but that He paid a mighty price for it.

It is a name, therefore, which is charged with deep emotion, and is to be found particularly in the language of devotion. Christian song is vocal with it. . . .

W, 2:375.

The Satisfaction of Christ

The Resurrection of Christ

7

CHRISTOLOGY 2: THE WORK OF CHRIST

We have said that B. B. Warfield was, at heart, a christologian, but we have not reached his heart of hearts until we note that, for him, christology is soteriology.[1] We might say as accurately that for Warfield soteriology is christology. The point is that Warfield perceives Christianity as fundamentally a redemptive religion—indeed, for him Christianity *means* redemption—and the significance of Christ, so far as sinners are concerned, is that he is the divine Redeemer. He is the Lord from heaven, to be sure. He is the glorious second person of the triune Godhead. He is αὐτοθεότης. But it is the *suffering* Messiah that is "the nerve of the whole New Testament presentation" of Christ. Although the cross and the theology of substitution had fallen on bad times and was being rejected with increasing disdain, Warfield insists that it is only "when we see in Him [Christ] a slaughtered lamb, lying on a smoking altar, from which ascends the sweet savour of an acceptable sacrifice to God for sin, that we can rise to anything like a true sense of the glory of Jesus Christ." For this reason, Warfield remarks, it is Christ as "Redeemer"—"the name specifically of the Christ of the cross"—that most endears the heart of every Christian to him. Christ crucified is the hinge on which the Christian gospel turns, and it is this settled conviction that moves Warfield to expend much energy both

---

[1]Significant Warfield titles treating the work of Christ include the following: "Jesus' Mission, According to His Own Testimony," in *W*, 2:255–324; "The New Testament Terminology of Redemption," in *W*, 2:327–72; "'Redeemer' and 'Redemption,'" in *W*, 2:375–98; "Redemption," in James Hastings, *Dictionary of the Apostolic Church*, 2 vols. (New York: Scribners, 1918), 2:302–9; "Christ Our Sacrifice," in *W*, 2:401–35; "The Essence of Christianity and the Cross of Christ," in *W*, 3:393–444; "Atonement," in *W*, 9:261–80; "Modern Theories of the Atonement," in *W*, 9:283–97; "Imputation," in *W*, 9:301–9; "Jesus Christ the Propitiation for the Whole World," in *SSW*, 1:167–77; "The Resurrection of Christ an Historical Fact," in *SSW*, 1:178–92; "The Resurrection of Christ a Fundamental Doctrine," in *SSW*, 1:193–202; plus the many sermons published in his *The Power of God unto Salvation*, *Faith and Life*, and *The Savior of the World*, as well as many significant reviews of books.

discrediting the "Christless Christianity" of his day, which played down the cross, and expounding the necessity and nature of Christ's saving work.[2]

The Satisfaction of Christ

Warfield stresses repeatedly throughout his writings that "in the centre of its centre, in the heart of its heart, salvation is deliverance from sin."[3] It is not merely a new ethic, though it is surely that. It is not merely a transformed life, although it is certainly that. Warfield himself makes much of that *to* which we are saved as well as that *from* which we are saved. But this is secondary. Christian salvation, first and foremost, is rescue from sin and sin particularly in its aspect of guilt. "Deliverance from guilt stands first"[4] in the New Testament conception of Christ's redemptive work. There is also emancipation from sin's power and "the removal of all the ills of life constitutes its final issue," but "all this is conditioned upon" Christ's bearing the penalty of our sins in his own body on the tree.[5]

Warfield feels very deeply that this fact of human sin and guilt renders the redemptive character of Christianity so essential, and he insists that this is what gives the gospel its meaning. "The core of the gospel is assuredly that Christ Jesus came to save *sinners*."[6] Warfield, therefore, is in settled opposition to those who, although clinging to the old terminology of "redemption," interpret it merely as "reformation." Theirs is not the Christianity of Christ, he insists. Christianity is a sinner's religion, and it is a religion of deliverance.

Accordingly, when Warfield attacks the "Christless Christianity" of his day, his burden is not merely that it is Christ, considered by himself, who is essential to Christianity. Repeatedly throughout his writings he remarks that the gospel is a message "not only of Christ *simpliciter*, but of Christ as crucified." "Christianity, in the core of the matter, consists in just this, 'Jesus Christ and Him as crucified.'" Other religions point a way to God, but Christ presents himself as that way, and that way is the way of his cross. Indeed, to remove the cross of Christ is to abolish Christianity itself. "Christianity is the cross; and he who makes the cross of none

---

[2]*SW*, 80, 100; *W*, 2:375; *W*, 3:393–444. Warfield notes, curiously, that although this designation "Redeemer" has been a favorite in Christian verse and song, in the New Testament it is used only of Moses as a type of Christ, never of Christ directly (Acts 7:35) (*W*, 2:365, 378–79).

[3]*SW*, 46.

[4]Warfield evidently means "first" in the sense of the most fundamental need.

[5]*W*, 9:262. Warfield here seems clearly to be reacting to the denials of this aspect of Christ's work so common in his day. It would be easy to sense that his treatments of the positive aspects of salvation (that *to* which we are saved) are somewhat neglected, but this is due, at least in large part, to the climate of debate and the pressures he feels from it.

[6]*PGS*, 47 (his emphasis).

effect eviscerates Christianity." "The theology of the writers of the New Testament is very distinctly a 'blood theology.'"[7]

> A Christless cross no refuge for me;
> A Crossless Christ my Savior may not be;
> But, O Christ crucified! I rest in thee![8]

HISTORICAL SUMMARY

What, precisely, is this "blood theology," and what is the significance of Christ's cross? The early church did not involve itself in precise discussions of the nature of Christ's death. This is in part because the minds of the early teachers were engrossed in more immediately pressing issues, such as the person of Christ and the Trinity. This is also, Warfield remarks, because of the clarity of the New Testament presentation of Christ's death as a piacular sacrifice. Christians simply employed the language of Scripture and therefore understood the cross as expiatory.

Very early on, Christians began to emphasize prominently one aspect of Christ's death presented in the New Testament; namely, that it was a ransom that delivered us from Satan. It was Anselm (d. 1109) who in his *Cur Deus Homo?* gave the atonement its first thorough discussion, representing it in terms of Roman law as a "satisfaction" of divine justice and laying out its relations to the two natures of Christ and to the magnitude of human guilt. Anselm's discussion "determined the outlines of the doctrine for all subsequent thought." But it was not "until the Reformation doctrine of justification by faith threw its light back upon the 'satisfaction' which provided its basis, that that doctrine came fully to its rights." Luther first articulated with clarity, breadth, and depth the nature of Christ's death as a deliverance from guilt and all the consequences of sin. Then, finally, in the Protestant scholastics "the complete doctrine of 'satisfaction' was formulated with a thoroughness and comprehensiveness of grasp which has made it the permanent possession of the Church." Warfield describes this final stage as "its developed form," which represents Christ as making penal satisfaction for sinners "by his blood and righteousness," and that with a dual reference—"to the justice of God, outraged by human sin, in bearing the penalty due to our guilt in His own sacrificial death," and "to the demands of the law of God requiring perfect obedience, in fulfilling in His immaculate life on earth as the second Adam the probation which Adam failed to keep."[9]

---

[7] *SW*, 88; *W*, 3:367; *SSW*, 1:47; *W*, 2:433; *PGS*, 202.
[8] A hymn Warfield cites at the conclusion of his article, "The Dogmatic Spirit," in *SSW*, 2:667.
[9] *W*, 9:263–64.

LEADING THEORIES OF THE ATONEMENT

This doctrine of "the satisfaction of Christ" has held sway but not without controversy. Various theories have risen, each stressing this or that aspect of the biblical teaching and often to the neglect or denial of others, particularly the "ordinarily central matter" of the expiation of guilt. Warfield provides five categories of theories (in ascending order), grouped according to the person or persons on whom the theory perceives the work of Christ as terminating.[10]

Theories That View the Work of Christ as Terminating on Satan

First, there are the theories that conceive of the work of Christ as terminating on Satan so as to secure the release of those held in bondage. These "triumphantorial" views, somewhat common in the Patristic age, passed out of vogue as the doctrine of satisfaction became better known. This group of theories has taken several forms—whether as buying off or overcoming or even outwitting Satan—and reflects one aspect of the biblical representation. Even Luther utilized this conception to some degree. These theories generally were not held to be the whole of the scriptural representation of the work of Christ; they merely reflected a profound sense of the bondage in which sinners are held and the rescue gained in Christ (Heb. 2:14).

Theories That View the Work of Christ as Terminating Physically on Man

Second, there are "mystical" theories that stress not the death but the incarnation of Christ, and not what Christ did but what he was. God the Son assumed a fallen human nature and by the power of his divine nature purified it from sin and presented it perfect before God as the firstfruits of humanity. Men are saved as they partake of this purified humanity by faith and "become leavened by this new leaven." These theories have been described as "salvation by sample" or "salvation by gradually extirpated depravity." Some versions of this theory conceive of the blood of Christ—his life—being offered in heaven "that it might vitalize ours, as it were by transfusion." Tendencies to this kind of theory, present in the Platonizing fathers and more developed in Neoplatonism, were represented in the Reformation age by men like Andreas Osiander (1498–1552) and Caspar Schwenckfeld (1489–1561), and in the modern church by Friedrich Schleiermacher in Europe and by the Mercersburg school in America.[11]

---

[10]W, 9:266–78.
[11]W, 9:269.

Theories That View the Work of Christ as Terminating on Man, Inducing Him to Action

A third variety, "moral influence theories," transfer actual work of atonement from the work of Christ to "the response of the human soul to influences or appeals proceeding from the work of Christ." Christ's work, then, has its immediate effect not on God but on man, who is led by it to a state of mind and heart—repentance and faith—that will be acceptable to God. God, in turn, is affected by the work of Christ, but only secondarily, as through the medium of repentance and faith. In this school of thought, faith and repentance are the work that atones for sin, and the work of Christ is understood in terms of his teaching and/or his example and/or his influence and/or the removal of false conceptions of God. Christ is the first Christian in that he realizes and proclaims the love of God and his willing-ness to forgive sin on the sole condition of abandonment of sin and obedience. He reveals God's hatred of sin and love for souls, and this revelation leads men to repentance. Some views present Christ as offering a perfect sorrow and "sym-pathetic repentance" for our imperfect repentance. The moral influence theory presents Christ as delivering sinners not primarily from guilt but from the power of sin. "The nerve" of the theory is "the reaction of Christ's personality on the lives of His fellow men. The actual atoning fact appears to be discovered not in what Christ does, nor even in what He is—but in what men do under the inspiration of His life among them." Variations of this theory have been held by Peter Abelard (1079–1142), the Socinians, Horace Bushnell (1802–1876), and, in Warfield's day, Albrecht Ritschl and Auguste Sabatier (1839–1901).[12]

Theories That View the Work of Christ as Terminating Primarily on Man and Secondarily on God

Fourth, "rectoral" or "governmental" theories present the suffering of Christ as so affecting man that it deters from sin and leads to repentance. Thus, God is enabled to forgive sin with safety to his moral government in the world. According to this theory, moral law is a product of the divine will and is therefore capable of being relaxed by that will. Punishment is a necessary act of justice only insofar as it effects greater good, that is, the moral reformation of the sinner and the restraint of sin. In God's saving purpose, therefore, God relaxes his demand by forgiving man on the basis of his repentance and reformation,

> while as an administrative precaution he makes an exhibition of severe suffering in the person of his Son, in order that all other subjects of his moral government

---

[12]*W*, 9:269; *W*, 10:466.

may be deterred from making the impunity of repentant men as an encouragement to disobedience. The atonement, therefore, was an exhibition solely of the divine benevolence, but not of justice in the ordinary sense of that word.[13]

In these theories the death of Christ finally becomes of cardinal importance, but the atoning fact here also lies in man's own reformation. Man's opposition to God is broken down not by the manifestation of the love of God in Christ but by the crucifixion "inducing in man a horror for sin, through the spectacle of God's hatred of sin afforded by the sufferings of Christ." Through a contemplation of Christ's death, and of God's willingness to inflict such sufferings on his Son so that he might thus be enabled to forgive sin, man is led to repentance. This theory, developed by Hugo Grotius (1583–1645) and standard fare among evangelical Arminians, presents the work of Christ "not as supplying the ground on which God forgives sin, but only as supplying the ground on which He may safely forgive sin on the sole ground of His compassion." This view purports to hold to an objective atonement. Christ's death shows how greatly God hates sin and stands as the symbol of the consequences of sin. But it is not a payment for sin. The crucifixion has "no other effect on God than to render it safe for Him to forgive sin," not by affecting God himself but by affecting men "by awaking in them such a poignant sense of the evil of sin as to cause them to hate it soundly and to turn decisively away from it"—that is, to repent.[14]

Theories That View the Work of Christ as Terminating Primarily on God and Secondarily on Man

The fifth group of theories, in its "lowest form," views Christ as entering sympathetically into our condition, such that he "keenly felt our sins as His own, that He could confess and adequately repent of them before God." This, then, is all that justice requires. This theory rises higher than the ones already mentioned in that it looks on Christ "as really a Saviour, who performs a really saving work, terminating immediately on God." The so-called "middle theory," as this descriptive term implies, finds its position between the moral influence theories on the one hand and the doctrine of satisfaction on the other. This theory, which has held a very wide influence, is rooted in a view of sacrifices as mere gifts offered to the king in order to secure his favor. It sees the work of Christ "as consisting in the offering to God of Christ's perfect obedience even to death, and by it purchasing God's favor and the right to do as He would with those whom God gave Him

---

[13]SSW, 2:421; cf. 315–20.
[14]W, 9:273, 288–89; cf. W, 8:162–65.

as a reward." The Arminian version of this theory allows that Christ's work was an expiatory sacrifice, but it does not allow that his blood, any more than that of bulls or goats, "had intrinsic value equivalent to the fault for which it was graciously accepted by God as an atonement." This theory preserves the "sacrificial form" of the biblical teaching, and it understands redemption as accomplished by Christ for sinners. But it falls short of the biblical doctrine of satisfaction, which, rising still higher, understands Christ as dying in the sinner's place as substitutional payment for his sin. Our Lord's redeeming work "at its core" is a "true and perfect sacrifice" offered to God in our place. This is the doctrine that has been acknowledged by all the great branches of the church, Greek, Latin, Lutheran, and Reformed.[15]

Summary Observations

Warfield observes that of these theories, three remain dominant. They gather around the names Abelard, Grotius, and Anselm. Warfield enthusiastically embraces the Anselmic doctrine, and he provides three general criticisms of the alternatives. First, they show no real appreciation of divine justice, in that no real satisfaction is offered, and thus the blood of Christ is rendered virtually irrelevant. God forgives on the basis of his good will or his love, or on the basis of repentance. But it would be neither reasonable nor moral for God to forgive on these grounds.[16] There must be a satisfaction of divine justice, and sin must be expiated.

Second, the alternative theories distort the love of God. God *is* love, but it does not follow that he is nothing but love. The distinguishing characteristic of Christianity is not that it preaches a God of love but that it preaches a God of conscience. This is the God of the Bible. While he is love, he is also righteous and thoroughly honest, "a God who deals honestly with Himself and us." "In this fact lies, perhaps, the deepest ground of the necessity of an expiatory atonement."[17]

Third, these theories do not adequately appreciate how sin subjectively affects the human heart, "deadening it to the appeal of motives to right action however powerful, and requiring therefore an internal action of the Spirit of God upon it before it can repent: or of the purchase of such a gift of the Spirit by the sacrifice of Christ." "It does not go to the root of matters as presented either in Scripture or in the throes of our awakened heart." In order to validate these alternative theories one would need to demonstrate (1) that repentance and faith constitute a sufficient ground for acceptance with God; (2) that such a repentance and faith

---

[15]*W*, 9:276–78.
[16]*W*, 10:467; *PTR* 13, no. 1 (1915): 120.
[17]*W*, 9:296.

can be exercised by sinful men; and (3) that the work of Christ was designed and able to produce in sinful men this faith and repentance that are necessary to avail with God. Warfield is convinced that these form an impossible task.[18]

Warfield remarks that the popularity of these alternative theories is due to the fact that a deep sense of sin is quickly vanishing from the conscience of modern men and that where there is no deep sense of sin, there can be little perceived need of atonement. It was of little surprise to Warfield that the doctrine of penal satisfaction was losing ground in his day, given the lost sense of sin. "But if we are sinners, and in proportion as we know ourselves to be sinners, and appreciate what it means to be sinners, we will cry out for that Savior who only after He was perfected by suffering could become the Author of eternal salvation."[19] That is to say, sinners need an atonement that expiates sin, that delivers them from sin, and that reconciles them to God.

WARFIELD'S FORMULATIONS

Of first significance is that the death of Christ was a substitutionary sacrifice offered to deliver sinners from the penal consequences of God's broken law. Warfield argues that "satisfaction" best captures the whole meaning and significance of Christ's work, a term that emphasizes the full payment of a debt and, hence, the sufficiency of Christ's work judicially. "Atonement" is a common rendering of the Hebrew כפר and has the sense of "propitiation" or "expiation." This representation of the work of Christ is correct, but it does not take in the entirety of the significance of Christ's work as unfolded in the New Testament. The work of Christ did indeed cancel guilt, but it also provided righteousness. Even so, Warfield argues, it is undeniable that the New Testament writers "enshrine at the center of this work its efficacy as a piacular sacrifice, securing the forgiveness of sins." "The heart of the heart" of the Bible's plan of salvation "is expiation," and the biblical writers "represent God as sheerly unable to forgive sin on any other grounds whatever."[20]

This theology of substitutional sacrifice Warfield draws out at length everywhere he touches the subject of Christ's death and largely under the language of "sacrifice" and "redemption."

Christ Our Substitute

Throughout his expositions of the work of Christ, Warfield stresses the centrality of substitution.

---

[18] W, 9:290; W, 10:204.
[19] W, 9:297.
[20] W, 9:261–62; W, 8:165.

> We do not get to the heart of Paul's doctrine of reconciliation until we bring clearly
> before us what he teaches of the way in which it has been accomplished. That
> way is, briefly, by a great act of substitution. . . . If Paul's doctrine of reconcili-
> ation is the heart of his Gospel, his doctrine of substitution is the heart of the
> heart of his Gospel.[21]

Moreover, Warfield insists that substitution must be understood in its strictest
sense: Christ took our law-place. Our law-place was made his. He assumed our
place, our responsibility before God the judge, and made satisfaction for sin as
though it was his own. The gospel culminates and finds its true significance here.
"One has died for all, therefore, all have died" (2 Cor. 5:14). He "who knew no sin"
was made sin for us (2 Cor. 5:21). Christ took our law-place and satisfied—paid in
full—the judicial debt incurred by our sin.[22]

Warfield argues that only substitution could satisfy the demands of God's
vindicatory justice. Christ's sacrifice was made not to "public" justice, as the
Arminian and governmental theory of the atonement argues, but to God's "judicial"
justice, to satisfy the demands of a righteous and offended God. In the "public"
or governmental view, God relaxes his justice, inflicting less punishment than
what is deserved. In the biblical view, Warfield argues, God acts as a judge, not
merely as a ruler or governor. The justice he administrates is not distributive or
public but judicial and vindicatory. In order to maintain order, a commanding
officer may execute one of every ten men who mutinied. A judge, however, must
execute justice on each. God as a truthful, righteous judge cannot look upon a
sinner as anything but a sinner. He cannot pretend that the sinner is not guilty.
Nor can he accept a sinner into his fellowship. Nor can he forego punishment.
Nor can the punishment be less than what is demanded by the offense. Thus to
save sinners, God offered his Son as their substitute, imputing their sins to him
and making expiation by his death. Christ did not pay fifty cents on the dollar but,
suffering in our place, made full payment for our sins. God forgives, therefore,
not out of hand but on the ground of justice, in keeping with a law whose demand
has been fully satisfied by Christ the substitute, who out of infinite love provided
himself as the substitute.[23]

Warfield cautions that while the preposition "for" is very significant in phrases
such as "one died for all" and "he . . . was made sin for us," we must not lose ourselves in pedantic discussions of it. Most often the biblical writers employ the

---

[21]*SW*, 152.
[22]N. W. Harkness, unpublished class notes from Warfield's lectures on systematic theology, 1899–1901
(Princeton Seminary library archives), 39–43.
[23]Ibid., 31, 38–42.

word ὑπέρ, "for the sake of, for the benefit of." Christ died for our sake, for our benefit. The more precise term, ἀντί (Matt. 20:28), is used less frequently, but this is due, no doubt, to its more technical sense. The New Testament writers were not writing textbooks of systematic theology. "They were giving expression to their deepest religious convictions, and they could not but choose language charged with their profound emotions." But the sense is the same in either case. When the apostle says that Christ was "made sin on our behalf," the meaning is clearly that he has paid the penalty of our sin by dying in our stead and in our place. The more precise terminology is used often enough to show that the biblical writers had in mind the fact of his dying in their place, even though more commonly the biblical writers speak instinctively and with emotion in terms of the benefits they have received. "That Christ died instead of them was the exact truth, analytically stated; that He died for their sake was the broad fact which suffused their hearts with loving emotion."[24]

Jesus emphasizes this aspect of his work in Matthew 20:28, and "it is embedded" in every part of the New Testament: Hebrews 2:17; 1 Peter 3:18; 1 John 2:2; Romans 8:3; 1 Corinthians 5:7; Ephesians 5:2. Biblical writers freely and frequently describe Christ's work under the category of substitution, involving the idea of imputation or transference of sin and legal standing. This is the "center" of the teaching of the New Testament writers regarding the work of Christ, and it is from this viewpoint that they speak of the death of Christ as efficacious (Rom. 3:25; 5:9; 1 Cor. 10:16; Eph. 1:7; 2:13; Col. 1:20; Heb. 9:12, 14; 1 Pet. 1:2, 19; 1 John 1:7; 5:6–8; Rev. 1:5).[25]

Warfield argues in a climate that is hostile to the notion of substitution. He cites one author as declaring it "inconceivable" that Christ's death could at the same time be both a terrible crime and a means of satisfying divine justice. Warfield responds:

> What can the astonished reader do but pause in wonder and ask, Why? Why does not the philosophy of Gen. 50:20—"And as for you, ye meant evil against me; but God meant it for good, to bring to pass, as it is this day, to save much people alive"—apply here as it applies throughout God's dealings with men?[26]

This is the heart of the heart of Warfield's soteriology, and he never fails to emphasize it—Christ in the sinner's place, dying for his benefit, and by this great injustice satisfying all the demands of divine justice and thus supplying our only rescue.

---

[24]SW, 154; W, 2:379.
[25]W, 9:262.
[26]W, 10:201.

Christ Our Sacrifice

Warfield finds it startling that theologians of his day could argue that the New Testament writers made very little of the idea of Christ's death as a sacrifice. After surveying such arguments he concludes, "The reader will scarcely escape the impression that a great deal of unavailing trouble is being expended here in an effort to remove unwelcome facts out of the way." The notion of Christ's work as a sacrifice is in fact deeply embedded in the New Testament. It is reflected in the frequent New Testament terminology of blood: to say that Christ redeems us "by his blood" is to speak in terms of ritual sacrifice. Jesus himself spoke in these terms (Matt. 26:28; cf. 20:28), and this blood language is echoed in the apostle Paul (1 Cor. 11:25). But it is not only on allusions such as these that this doctrine rests. The New Testament writers "work out the correspondence" between Christ's death and that of the various Old Testament sacrifices and show that the old sacrifices anticipated and are repeated in the death of Christ. Further, the writers "ascribe the specific effects of sacrifice"—expiation, pardon—to Christ's death (Matt. 26:28; Acts 5:30–31; 1 Cor. 15:3; 2 Cor. 5:21; Eph. 1:7; Col. 1:14, 20; Titus 2:14; Heb. 1:3; 9:28; 10:12; 1 Pet. 2:24; 3:18; 1 John 2:2; 4:10; Rev. 1:5). And "they dwell particularly, in truly sacrificial wise, on the saving efficacy of His out-poured blood" (Rom. 3:25; 5:9; 1 Cor. 10:16; Eph. 1:7; 2:13; Col. 1:20; Heb. 9:12, 14; 1 Pet. 1:2, 18–19; 1 John 1:7; 5:6, 8; Rev. 1:5). It would be difficult indeed to read the Bible and not notice the sacrificial connotations of Christ's death.[27]

For obvious reasons, it is rarely doubted that the Jews of Jesus' day and the biblical writers themselves understood sacrifice as distinctly piacular. From the beginning this was its consistent focus and significance. Warfield argues in detail that Abel's offering is to be understood in these terms also. It is difficult to believe, he says, that the difference between the acceptability of the offerings of Cain and Abel "hung on the different characters of the two offerers." Scripture states that God looked with favor not merely to Abel and not to Cain but to Abel's offering itself and not to Cain's (Gen. 4:4–5). The writer to the Hebrews likewise states that Abel's was a "more acceptable sacrifice" than Cain's (Heb. 11:4). "The different characters of the two men seem rather to be represented as expressing themselves in differing conceptions of man's actual relation to God and of the conditions of approval by Him and the proper means of seeking His favor." Warfield argues that it is not reading too much into the Genesis narrative to understand it as "intended" both to present the origin of sacrificial worship and to specify which kind of offering pleases God. Cain and Abel represent what have become known as the symbolical theory and the expiatory theory respec-

---

[27]W, 2:401–2, 427–28.

tively. It was "by faith" that Abel presented his sacrifice to God (Heb. 11:4), which seems to imply

> that Cain's offering was an act of mere homage; Abel's embodied a sense of sin, an act of contrition, a cry for succor, a plea for pardon. In a word, Cain came to the Lord with an offering in his hand and the Homage theory of sacrifice in his mind: Abel with an offering in his hand and the Piacular theory of sacrifice in his heart.

It was for this reason that God looked favorably to Abel's offering and not to Cain's.

> The one was a reach by man to God; the other was a stooping down of God to man. The fundamental difference is that in the one case sacrifice rests upon consciousness of sin and has its reference to the restoration of a guilty human being to the favor of a condemning God: in the other it stands outside of all relation to sin and has its reference only to the expression of the proper attitude of deference which a creature should preserve towards his Maker and Ruler.

In short, Cain positioned himself as a creature; Abel positioned himself as a sinner. Cain offered himself to God; Abel offered a substitute.[28]

That the sacrifices of Israel's cultus were also expiatory Warfield finds impossible to deny.[29] He entertains the suggestions of Ritschl and others who see them as gifts of homage or as bribes or fines but can find no biblical support for them. He does not question that elements of adoration are involved, but he insists that anything less than expiation falls short of the ancient Jewish understanding. The whole ritual of confessing sin over the animal before its slaughter points in the direction of expiation. This is especially clear in the ritual of the annual Day of Atonement, with its substitutive bearing away of sin made so explicit. Warfield notes also that the alternative theories allow little significance to the slaughter of the victim. "This circumstance alone is probably fatal to the validity of these theories," he argues, and particularly as viewed in light of the New Testament writers' explanation of Christ as a sacrifice.

> There is reason to believe that the slaughter of the victim or destruction of the offering constitutes the essential act of sacrifice; and certainly in the New Testament it is

---

[28] W, 2:405–11. In a footnote Warfield quotes another author in defense of the interpretation that the phrase "the blood of Abel" in Heb. 12:24 should be understood as the blood of Abel's sacrifice. Given the rather long quotation that he provides, Warfield seems to favor this understanding. But he does not explicitly commit (W, 2:407).

[29] Warfield finds this same significance, at least generally, in pagan sacrifices also. The Levitical legislations are not innovative in this sense (W, 2:410–20).

precisely in the blood of Christ or in His cross, symbols of His death, that the essence of His sacrificial character is found.

Christ's death was not an especially bloody event; indeed, the Evangelists make relatively no mention of his blood in their narrative of his crucifixion. The apostolic emphasis on Christ's blood can be explained only in terms of its expiatory import. There is further the New Testament presentation of Christ as "our Passover, sacrificed for us," "making peace by his blood," making "propitiation" in his blood, and so on. "Christ loved us and gave himself up for us, an offering and a sacrifice to God for an odor of a sweet smell." Certainly, any attempt to escape the notion of expiation is but "an effort to remove unwelcome facts out of the way."[30]

Warfield summarizes the idea of sacrifice briefly: "In all sacrifices there is a thing offered—the victim, we may call it for brevity's sake. This victim is an intermediary. When we say intermediary, however, we say representative. And when we say representative, we say broadly, substitute." That is, in expiatory sacrifices the offerer approaches God "burdened with a sense of sin and seeking to expiate its guilt." The victim he presents is viewed as the substitute, an intermediary or representative, to whom has been transferred the sin of the worshiper and who bears the penalty of the sins thus transferred to him. The penalty having been vicariously borne, the worshiper receives forgiveness. It belongs to the nature of a sacrificial offering, then, that it terminates on God. That is, the sacrifice affects God, first of all, and not the worshiper. There is benefit derived to the worshiper, to be sure, but the immediate effect and the first importance has to do with God—he is propitiated (ἱλάσκομαι, Heb. 2:17) by the removal of sin. The very purpose of the sacrifices is to influence God so as to secure his favor. "Every time the writers of the New Testament speak of the work of Christ under the rubric of a sacrifice, therefore, they bear witness . . . that they conceive of His work as directed Godward and as intended directly to affect God, not man."[31]

The book of Hebrews is given in large part to the exposition of this theme. Here not only is Christ's death explicitly described as a sacrifice, "but all the sacrificial language is gathered about it in the repeated allusions which are made to it as such." The sustained references to the Levitical sacrifices, which themselves were undeniably conceived as expiatory, are represented as prospective of Christ's death, which, in turn, is characterized as a *propitiatory* work (ἱλάσκομαι, Heb. 2:17; cf. ἱλαστήριον, Rom. 3:25; ἱλασμός, 1 John 2:2; 4:10). The notion of sacrifice as expiatory is unmistakable in the book of Hebrews. But Warfield contends further that other than in terms of the relative degree of attention given to the matter,

---

[30] W, 2:414, 428.
[31] W, 2:416–20.

Hebrews does not stand apart from the other New Testament books in this regard. All the many passages that emphasize Christ's blood are to this point exactly.[32] In fact, it is our Lord himself who said that he came "to give his life a ransom for many" (Matt. 20:28) and to establish the new covenant "in his blood" (Matt. 26:28). Indeed, the prophets John the Baptist (John 1:29) and Isaiah (chap. 53) speak to this in advance. Nothing can be clearer than that "the theology of the writers of the New Testament is very distinctly a 'blood theology.'" When they employ this language of blood and "giving up his life," "they intended to represent that death as performing the functions of an expiatory sacrifice; wished to be understood as so representing it; and could not but be so understood by their first readers who were wonted to sacrificial worship."[33]

In short, when the New Testament writers—as they so often do—connect forgiveness with the "death" or "blood" of Christ, they remind us again that our release from sin and guilt came only by the propitiatory and expiatory sacrifice of our Redeemer. "The blood of Jesus,—O, the blood of Jesus!—when we have reached it, we have attained not merely the heart, but the heart of the heart of the Gospel." This doctrine of the sacrificial death of Christ is not only essential to Christianity,

> but in a very real sense it constitutes Christianity. It is this which differentiates Christianity from other religions. Christianity did not come into the world to proclaim a new morality and, sweeping away all the supernatural props by which men were wont to support their trembling, guilt-stricken souls, to throw them back on their own strong right arms to conquer a standing before God for themselves. It came to proclaim the real sacrifice for sin which God had provided in order to supersede all the poor fumbling efforts which men had made and were making to provide a sacrifice for sin for themselves; and, planting men's feet on this, to bid them go forward. It was in this sign that Christianity conquered, and it is in this sign alone that it continues to conquer. We may think what we will of such a religion. What cannot be denied is that Christianity is such a religion.[34]

Christ Our Redeemer

Within this larger framework of vicarious sacrifice offered for expiation, the significance of "redemption" becomes the more clear. Warfield argues extensively that

---

[32] W, 2:429–30. In a footnote Warfield lists (1) general passages, Heb. 9:14, 20; 10:29; 12:24; 1 Pet. 1:19; 1 John 1:7; (2) eucharistic passages, Matt. 26:28; Mark 14:24; Luke 22:20; 1 Cor. 11:25; John 6:53–56; 1 Cor. 10:16; (3) the formula διὰ τῆ αἵματό (or its equivalent), Acts 20:28; Eph. 1:7; Col. 1:20; Heb. 9:12; 13:12 (1 John 5:6); Rev. 12:11; and (4) the formula ἐν τῇ αἵματι (or its equivalent), Rom. 3:25; 5:9; 1 Cor. 11:25 (27); Eph. 2:13; Heb. 10:19 (Heb. 13:25); 1 John 5:6; Rev. 1:5; 5:9; 7:14.
[33] W, 2:429–34. Warfield offers further proof in Harnack's observation that wherever Christianity went, blood sacrifices ceased to be offered.
[34] W, 2:434–35; SW, 88.

"redeem" does not indicate deliverance merely but specifically deliverance upon payment of ransom. "Ransoming" or "release by payment of ransom" is the consistent significance of the λύτρον word group in secular Greek, the Septuagint, and the New Testament. If mere deliverance were the intended meaning, λύειν would easily be the word of choice. But "no Greek lips could frame it [the word λύτρον], no Greek ear could hear it, in any of its derivatives," without a consciousness of this its intrinsic meaning. "It is safe to say that no Greek . . . could write down any word, the center of which was λύτρον, without consciousness of ransoming as the mode of deliverance of which he was speaking." Even in the Septuagint where the redemption of God's people is in view, it is accomplished by a great expenditure of God's almighty power, and thus "there is an abiding implication that the redemption has cost something." "The word is essentially a modal word" and emphasizes that the deliverance spoken of has come only at the payment of a cost. Our favored terminology—"to redeem," "redeemed," and "redeemer"—has come to us from the Latin *redimo* and is less precise; the word has suffered considerable attrition in our usage. We might have done better, in order to preserve the significance of the doctrine, had we reflected the Greek terminology and used instead the language of "ransom," "to ransom," "ransomed," and "ransomer."[35]

Warfield acknowledges that the English words "redeem," "redemption," and "redeemer" have come to be used more loosely and have lost any necessary connotations of "buying out"—"buying back" is often all that is implied, and sometimes mere deliverance with no connotation of purchase at all is in view. But he denies that the λύτρον word group has suffered any such decay in its New Testament usage; rather, the contexts in which this word is used clearly indicate otherwise. In a number of instances the payment of a price for deliverance is prominent, and the idea of ransoming is unmistakable. "In the remaining instances this intimation becomes no doubt rather an assumption, grounded in their form and their usage elsewhere." In some cases the idea of ransoming is specifically prominent, the means of deliverance. In other instances the deliverance itself is more prominent, the consequence of the ransom. "In neither case, however, is either element of thought really suppressed entirely"—Christ delivers his people by ransoming them (cf. Heb. 9:15; Eph. 1:7; Rom. 3:24).

It is Christ himself who first assigned to his death the meaning of ransoming. In Mark 10:45 and Matthew 20:28 he declares that "the Son of Man came not to be served but to serve, and to give his life as a ransom for many" (λύτρον ἀντὶ πολλῶν). The significance of this, Warfield notes, is elucidated and enforced in those passages in John that speak of his laying down his life for the sheep

---

[35]*W*, 2:327–72, 340–41, 351–52, 380, 385; "Redemption," in Hastings, *Dictionary of the Apostolic Church*, 2:303.

(John 10:11) and for his friends (15:13), and of his giving his flesh for the life of the world (6:51). In this declaration (Mark 10:45 = Matt. 20:28), Jesus speaks of himself as the supreme example of service in a way that is somewhat parallel to Philippians 2:5ff. He the heavenly Son of Man (Dan. 7:13) has come to serve others, and the capstone of his service is the giving of his life in death, purchasing the deliverance of his people. His purpose in coming was simply to perform this service. He thus describes his ransoming death as a voluntary gift—"giving his life." The ransoming nature of his death is pointedly highlighted in his use of the most exact wording the Greek language affords (λύτρον). And with the preposition ἀντί—"in the place of" or "instead of"—he emphasizes the idea of exchange, or substitution.

> In this declaration, then, our Lord Himself sets forth in language as precise as possible His work of service for man as culminating in the vicarious payment by His voluntary death of a ransom price for them. This is what He came to do; and in this, therefore, is summed up briefly the nature of His work for men.[36]

As would be expected, this declaration of our Lord finds echoes in the teaching of the apostles after him. In 1 Timothy 2:6, for example, Paul affirms of the man Christ Jesus, the sole Mediator between God and men, that "he gave himself a ransom for all." Here he uses the strengthened form (ἀντίλυτρον), emphasizing the ideas of both ransoming and exchange-substitution. The voluntary nature of the offering is emphasized again in the phrase "gave himself," the full significance of which may be gathered from Galatians 1:4: "who gave himself for our sins" (cf. Gal. 2:20; Eph. 5:2, 25). And the addition of ὑπέρ describes those for whom the ransom is made as beneficiaries of it. The entire substance of our Lord's declaration in Matthew 20:28 (= Mark 10:45) is repeated here, and what our Lord declares to be the substance of his mission, Paul declares to be the sum of the gospel committed to him to preach (1 Tim. 2:7).[37]

In Titus 2:14 the apostle repeats the same emphasis. Jesus Christ, our great God and Savior, the epiphany of whose glory is the object of our blessed hope, "gave himself for us to redeem us from all lawlessness and to purify for himself a people for his own possession who are zealous for good works." The assertion is the same as that of 1 Timothy 2:6. Christ's work is described as a voluntary ransom given in behalf of his people. Only here, as in Galatians 1:4, the emphasis is on the effects of Christ's ransoming work. His death effected our purification and

---

[36]"Redemption," 303–4; W, 2:361–62.
[37]"Redemption," 304; W, 2:361.

holiness of life and conduct. That is to say, in his death Christ purchased for us "not only relief from the guilt but also release from the power of sin."[38]

The apostle Peter reminds his readers, "You were ransomed from the futile ways inherited from your forefathers, not with perishable things such as silver or gold, but with the precious blood of Christ, like that of a lamb without blemish or spot" (1 Pet. 1:18–19). Clearly, Peter is as concerned with conduct as Paul, and he too sees this as a consequence of Christ's ransoming death. But he is even more explicit in emphasizing the idea of purchasing and the price of that purchase. Paul was content to say that Christ "gave himself for us" (Titus 2:14). Peter specifies that the price of our redemption is the precious blood of Christ. Deliverance by means of the payment of a ransom is distinctly the meaning in view. Peter further relates this blood to that of the sacrificial lambs of the Mosaic offerings and thereby blends the ideas of ransom and sacrifice. "The blood which Christ shed as a sacrifice is the blood by which we are ransomed. The two modes of representation express a single fact."[39]

The notions of sacrifice and ransom are linked again in Hebrews 9:12, where the writer tells us that Christ "entered once for all into the holy places, not by means of the blood of goats and calves but by means of his own blood, thus securing an eternal redemption." Christ both "entered the holy place" and "obtained eternal ransoming" by the one shedding of his blood. The "once for all" in the former clause and the "eternal" in the latter assimilate the two assertions in one another. Unlike the Levitical priests, Christ entered the holy place just once, because unlike their offerings, which were only temporary in effect, the effect of his offering is eternal.[40]

In Ephesians 1:7 Paul speaks very specifically to the notion of Christ's death as a deliverance by ransom: "In him we have redemption through his blood, the forgiveness of our trespasses" (cf. Col. 1:14). Here again Paul specifies Christ's blood as the ransom price. What is peculiar to these passages is that in both, Paul immediately identifies the ransoming with "the forgiveness of our trespasses" (Eph. 1:7) or "sins" (Col. 1:14). In the Colossians passage especially the context is that of a larger deliverance from the powers of darkness (Col. 1:13), and Paul expressly asserts that this deliverance is accomplished by means of the ransoming for the forgiveness of sins. That is, it is only because Christ's ransoming blood purchased our forgiveness that we have deliverance from the tyranny of darkness and are transferred into his kingdom.

---

[38]"Redemption," 304; W, 2:361.
[39]"Redemption," 304–5; W, 2:361–62.
[40]"Redemption," 305.

We thus reach a very close determination of the exact point at which the ransoming act of Christ operates, and of the exact evil from which it immediately relieves us. It relieves us of the guilt and the penal consequences of our sins; and only through that relief does it secure to us other blessings. It is, at its very centre, just "the remission of our sins" that we have in Christ when we have in Him our ransoming.[41]

The nature of our ransoming is unfolded for us in Romans 3:24 more than in any other passage. "Nearly all the scattered intimations of its essential nature found here and there in other passages are gathered together in one comprehensive statement." The point at hand is justification, and Paul's emphasis is that we are justified before God "only gratuitously, by an act of pure grace on God's part"; however, God can so justify only on the ground of the ransoming work of Christ in his sacrificial death. This alone is the ground of God's forgiveness of our sins, and this forgiveness is identified with the justification God gratuitously gives. We are "justified by his grace as a gift, through the redemption that is in Christ Jesus." This and the next verse blend the ideas of ransoming and expiation—the blood of Christ effects both. God justifies us freely but only because Christ has offered himself in our place and wiped away our sin.

> God has set [Christ] forth as an expiatory sacrifice through faith in His blood, for the manifestation of His righteousness in the forgiveness of sins. Christ, then, has been offered as an expiatory sacrifice: this enables God to forgive sins righteously; those thus forgiven are justified gratuitously; and this justification has taken place in view of, and that is as much as to say by means of, the ransoming which has resulted from the shedding of the blood of Christ. The ransoming provided by Christ is, in a word, the means by which God is rendered gracious; and in this His grace, thus secured for us, He gratuitously justifies us, although we, as sinners, have no claim upon this justification.[42]

In one New Testament passage, Hebrews 11:35, the use of ἀπολύτρωσις may seem at first glance to speak of deliverance without the idea of ransom. This verse describes those faithful who, in order to obtain a better resurrection, would "not accept the ransoming." But Warfield replies that this word by itself is enough to carry the intimation. Moreover, although there is nothing else in the immediate context to suggest the idea of ransom, it is not difficult at all to understand this statement as reflecting a refusal on the part of these faithful ones, under threat of death, to renounce their faith in order to be given the promised ransoming. The price was too great. They would not recant even in order to be given deliverance

---

41 Ibid.
42 Ibid., 305–6.

from their persecutors. Indeed, the writer's reference here may well be to 2 Maccabees 6–7 where this language is used in just such a case. The condition of release was too great, and so it was refused. In such a context the use of ἀπολύτρωσις as "deliverance on payment of a ransom" is entirely fitting. And, finally, it must be kept in mind that elsewhere in this epistle (9:12, 15) this is clearly the intended meaning of the word.[43]

Paul's use of "ransoming" in passages such as Romans 8:23; 1 Corinthians 1:30; and Ephesians 1:14 might be thought an exception to this meaning also, where "ransoming" is spoken of in an eschatological context. But Warfield insists that this in no way eviscerates the word of its normal meaning but rather speaks of redemption consummated. In the very context of Ephesians 1:14, for example, there is explicit confirmation of this meaning (Eph. 1:7). There is no reason to think that the idea of ransoming is absent.[44]

So the notion of payment as a means to deliverance is essential to the terminology of redemption. The ransom price was the Lord himself, his life, his blood given on the altar of the cross. "No subtlety of interpretation can rid such passages of their implication of ransoming." The upshot of all this is that emphasis is thrown on sin, the fundamental presupposition, and on the cost of our deliverance. Sin demanded a penalty. The sinner was indebted to divine justice. Giving his life in sacrifice, our Lord offered himself as payment, thus making satisfaction for sin. Our deliverance came at the cost of his blood.[45]

This is the distinctive character of Christianity—Christ's dying in place of his people, securing their deliverance by the sacrifice of himself in payment for their sin. In "The Essence of Christianity and the Cross of Christ," Warfield takes sharp issue with Professor Clyde Macintosh of Yale Divinity School concerning his view of the cross as unessential for modern Christians. Warfield remarks that Macintosh's rejection of the cross is nothing new, for "Christianity had not grown very old before it discovered that the preaching of Christ crucified was unto the Jews a stumbling-block and unto the Greeks foolishness." The novel feature of Macintosh's position, Warfield observes, is that it seeks to retain the name "Christian." Warfield makes this point often, that Christianity is precisely a redemptive religion, and apart from this there is no Christianity at all. A religion without redemption by whatever name is "a specifically different religion." From the very beginning—indeed, as defined by its Founder—redemption has always belonged to the very essence of the Christian faith. It is precisely this that sets Christians apart from all others. "A Christianity without redemption—redemption in the blood of

---

[43]Ibid., 308.
[44]Ibid., 308; W, 2:363–65.
[45]W, 2:362. Curiously, Warfield nowhere treats the ἀγοράζω word group.

Jesus Christ as a sacrifice for sin—is nothing less than a contradiction in terms. Precisely what Christianity means is redemption in the blood of Jesus."[46]

Reconciliation

The sacrifice has been offered, and the ransom has been paid. Sin has therefore been removed, and as a result the sinner is reconciled to God. Because sin is the point at issue between the sinner and God, the gospel "finds its key-note in a doctrine of reconciliation. The core of Paul's Gospel is indeed expressed in this one word, Reconciliation"—a reconciliation secured by expiation.[47] The apostle Paul therefore characterizes his ministry as "the ministry of reconciliation" and his gospel as "the message of reconciliation" (2 Cor. 5:18–19).

The whole presupposition in all this, again, is "a deep and keen sense of human sin and that in the aspect of guilt." Man has rebelled against God and is at enmity with him. More seriously, God is at enmity with man. His wrath is being revealed from heaven against their abounding unrighteousness. We are enemies of God, and "God looks upon us as such." Further, as a display of this enmity, "we cherish the feelings appropriate to that condition—being enemies in our minds by wicked works, and because of a carnal mind necessarily at enmity with the Holy God." But what gives joy to the apostle Paul and what gives him the great missionary zeal he has is that in Christ's death this enmity has been removed. "In Christ God was reconciling the world to himself, not counting their trespasses against them" (2 Cor. 5:19, 21). The enmity has been "abolished" by Christ's cross (Eph. 2:16), and as a result of his propitiation, peace has been established. Christ is therefore called "our peace" (Eph. 2:14), and his gospel "the gospel of peace" (Eph. 6:15; cf. Acts 10:36). In the Old Testament prophecy, Christ is promised as the "Prince of Peace" (Isa. 9:6), a designation, Warfield observes, that must be informed by Isaiah 53:5, which says of the Messiah that "the chastisement of our peace was upon him" (KJV)—that is, "because that punishment by which our sins are expiated and we are reconciled with God should be borne by Him." In short, "We are at enmity with God and can have peace with Him only in the blood of Christ."[48]

SUMMARY

The necessity of expiation is as evident as the fact of human sin. Platitudes about divine benevolence will not suffice. Sin must be reckoned with. Warfield is willing to argue the necessity of expiation even on the ground of natural revelation. There

---

[46]W, 3:357–58, 442, 444.
[47]SW, 147; Harkness, class notes, 38.
[48]FL, 327; SW, 148–49.

is within us an "inexpugnable sense of guilt" that cannot be soothed to sleep with assurances of God's goodness and love. Love, we know, by itself cannot reckon with sin. "That deep sense of moral self-condemnation which is present as a primary factor in all truly religious experience protests against all attempts merely to appease it. It cries out for satisfaction." Our conscience can never fully be persuaded that God somehow must distribute forgiveness generally and indiscriminately, that it is necessary for him to forgive us. We understand intuitively that such would subvert moral order. We know, in other words, that forgiveness can only be accomplished by an actual expiation. "No appeal to general metaphysical or moral truths concerning God can serve here." No appeal to his goodness or his love or his kinship to us who are created in his image will do. No, "the sinful soul, in throes of self-condemnation, is concerned with the law of righteousness ingrained in his very nature as a moral being, and cannot be satisfied with goodness, or love, or mercy, or pardon. He cries out for expiation." It is therefore to be expected that "the essence of Christianity has always been to its adherents the sinner's experience of reconciliation with God through the propitiatory sacrifice of Jesus Christ."[49]

At the conclusion of his article, "Atonement," in which he examines the chief theories of the atonement that have been offered in the history of the church, Warfield summarizes his own thinking on the subject crisply.

> The Biblical doctrine of the sacrifice of Christ finds full recognition in no other con-
> struction than that of the established church-doctrine of satisfaction. According to it,
> our Lord's redeeming work is at its core a true and perfect sacrifice offered to God, of
> intrinsic value ample for the expiation of our guilt; and at the same time is a true and
> perfect righteousness offered to God in fulfillment of the demands of His law; both
> the one and the other being accepted by God, accruing to their benefit; so that by this
> satisfaction they are relieved at once from the curse of their guilt as breakers of the law,
> and from the burden of the law as a condition of life; and this by a work of such kind and
> performed in such a manner, as to carry home to the hearts of men a profound sense
> of the indefectible righteousness of God and to make to them a perfect revelation of
> His love; so that, by this one and indivisible work, both God is reconciled to us, and we,
> under the quickening influence of the Spirit bought for us by it, are reconciled to God,
> so making peace—external peace between an angry God and sinful men, and internal
> peace in the response of the human conscience to the restored smile of God.[50]

THE EXTENT OF ATONEMENT

Warfield nowhere treats the doctrine of the extent of the atonement at length. He treats it descriptively in *The Plan of Salvation*, but he nowhere provides an in-

---

[49] *W*, 3:339–40, 355.
[50] *W*, 9:278.

depth treatment of it. He does touch the issue often, however, in his expositions of various passages thought by others to teach a universal atonement. Beyond this, his Reformed sympathies are evident virtually everywhere he treats the substitutive and efficacious nature of Christ's death. A sketch of his thinking on this matter follows.

Discussion

Warfield not only acknowledges but insists that Christ's vicarious sacrifice was of infinite value. "The value of the suffering is dependent on the dignity of the person." Here he notes that a right understanding of the person of Christ is prerequisite to a right understanding of his work. By virtue of his true humanity Christ offered himself as a genuine substitute. And by virtue of his deity the sacrifice he offered was of infinite value. Hence, Warfield acknowledges an infinite sufficiency to Christ's work. Its efficacy, however, "we can all see by looking around us."[51]

First, Warfield argues that particularism is a necessary outworking of theistic supernaturalism. He traces this out in *The Plan of Salvation*. All supernaturalists believe that salvation is a work of God; and theists, by definition, believe that God, being a person, acts according to purpose. Working out from these premises, Warfield argues that since God himself does the saving, supernaturally and purposefully, it follows that he works individually in the human heart. A divine, supernatural salvation is not doled out at the will of an institution but is wrought immediately in the human heart by God himself. This leaves us with particularism. That this particularism in divine intent matches up with the saving work of Christ, the Son, is a given. Warfield does not quite say it in these words, but the drift of his argument seems simply to be that if the Son offered himself in sacrifice for a different people other than those whom the Father had chosen to save and whom the Spirit would quicken, then he would be out of step with the triune purpose. Such disharmony within the Godhead is inconceivable. The Son comes to save those whom the Father has given him, and to these alone the Spirit ministers regenerating grace. As in all his works, the triune God is of a single purpose.

Second, the nature of the atonement defines its extent. Warfield here argues simply from the nature of Christ's death as a substitutional sacrifice that actually makes satisfaction to God and expiates sin. Given this definition of the work of Christ—a meaning Warfield argues vigorously and at great length to sustain—a universal atonement would demand a universal salvation. An atonement that makes satisfaction cannot by the nature of it be conditional but must be efficacious. And given the reality of a populated hell, therefore, there must be a particular

---

[51]Harkness, class notes, 38–40.

design and intent to Christ's saving work. The death of Christ was not designed merely to make an opportunity of salvation; it is everywhere in the Scriptures described as designed to save. The New Testament writers "enshrine at the center" of Christ's work "its efficacy as a piacular sacrifice, securing the forgiveness of sins." That is to say, all those for whom Christ died are thereby redeemed—not provisionally but actually. The saving efficacy lies not in the sinner's response to Christ but in what Christ himself does. Often Warfield stresses this efficacious nature of Christ's substitutional work. "The New Testament writers ascribe the saving efficacy of Christ's work specifically to His death, or His blood, or His cross" (see Rom. 3:25; 5:9; 1 Cor. 10:16; Eph. 1:7; 2:13; Heb. 9:12, 14; 1 Pet. 1:2, 19; 1 John 1:7; 5:6–8; Rev. 1:5).[52]

This issue crops up in a critical review where Warfield marvels at J. Gibson Smith's inability to reconcile the doctrine of penal substitution with the doctrine of the coming judgment. That is, "If Jesus satisfied the divine justice on the Cross, then there can remain no more remembrance of sin, and accordingly there can be left no place for a Coming Judgment." The answer is so obvious that Warfield finds it nearly incredible that any could miss it—Christ rendered satisfaction for his people, and judgment remains for those who are lost. This truth can only be missed by a blinded zeal for a so-called universal atonement. Warfield agrees that "a universal satisfaction for sin on the Cross would have abolished all impending judgment." This is precisely the dilemma that faces any doctrine of universal atonement. The only alternative is a view of the atonement that does not see it as substitutional and expiatory and that transfers the actual saving work to the sinner's repentance and faith—a view Warfield condemns as failing to take sin and the justice of God seriously.[53]

This second argument is where Warfield would rest the matter, and in light of this truth of the efficacy of Christ's work, he would claim as teaching "particular redemption" all those biblical passages which present Christ as the substitute bearing the sinner's curse. Substitutional atonement is necessarily particular, for, as Warfield explains, "that men could perish for whom Christ died, Paul never imagined that human minds could conceive." In this context Warfield turns the tables on the universalists and insists that they, not the particularists, are those who limit the atonement. In their view the atonement merely "renders men salvable" and actually saves no one. The particularist asserts with full conviction that it is the work of Christ that actually saves. He will go further and assert that it lays the groundwork for a free offer of salvation to all. But it is the universalist

---

[52] W, 9:261–62; SSW, 2:315–20; Harkness, class notes, 44–45.
[53] W, 10:202–3, 197–98; SSW, 2:317–19.

who places severe limits on the atoning work of Christ, and this by defining it in such a way that it is stripped of its very essence. An atonement that does nothing for anyone that it does not do for everyone obviously saves no one. "There is, in a word, no issue between the parties as to the extent of the atonement. Their issue is as to its nature."[54]

Biblical Universalism

This understanding of the efficacy of Christ's work also guides Warfield in his interpretation of passages that speak of Christ's work in universal terms. In commenting on 1 John 2:2, Warfield focuses on the word "propitiation," a term that describes actual salvation, not a mere "opportunity" for salvation. The saving, propitiatory work of Christ, the apostle John says, is not for "our" sins only but "for the sins of the whole world." Warfield departs from Calvin and others who view "the whole world" as "the churches of the elect dispersed through the whole world" and insists that the passages speak of universal salvation—Christ is propitiation "for the whole world." But given the fact of eternal punishment, neither can this passage teach universal atonement, else the word "propitiation" would be emptied of its soteric content. Yet, the passage plainly indicates that "the John who places the world and Christian in directly contrary relations to Christ, nevertheless in the present passage places them in precisely the same relation to Christ." Warfield insists, then, that John is looking ahead to the final completion of Christ's saving work in the eschaton, at which time "the whole world" will be saved. Warfield stresses repeatedly in these types of passages that Christ's work is completed in stages and that in the eschaton it will not be individuals only but the world that is brought savingly to Christ. John, therefore, "is not an 'each and every' universalist: he is an 'eschatological' universalist. He teaches the salvation of the world through a process," a process that may be very long in reaching its goal, but a process that infallibly shall reach its goal.[55]

Warfield looks toward a latter day of glory and finds warrant for such an anticipation in universalistic passages such as these. He treats John 1:29 after the same fashion. Christ, the sacrificial lamb, says John the Baptist, "takes away the sin of the world!" It is the language of expiation, and we cannot empty such language of its soteric content. And "world," he insists, must be understood in broad terms—it is "pure universalism." "Not many nations, but the whole world, is what he bids us see redeemed in Christ: the Jesus he proclaims as the God-provided sacrifice bears upon His broad and mighty shoulders nothing less than the world's sin."

---

[54]*SW*, 141; *SSW*, 2:318–20; *PS*, 95–96.
[55]*SSW*, 1:167–77.

The Baptist is "fixing his eyes upon the ultimate goal which . . . shall at length be attained."[56]

So also in John 3:16, Warfield emphasizes again that the "love" spoken of is clearly a saving love. The express statement of the passage is that God loved the world and so sent his Son to save it. "But neither will the text allow us to suppose that God grants His immeasurable love only to a few, abstracted from the world, while the world itself He permits to fall away to its destruction." No, to understand the statement aright "we must rise to the height of this divine universalism" and see in it the glorious prospect of a redeemed world.[57]

Similarly in 2 Corinthians 5:14–15, 18–19, where the apostle Paul speaks of Christ's death "for all" and of God through Christ "reconciling the world to himself," we cannot miss the soteric content. It is not opportunity for salvation that is in view but salvation itself. "To eviscerate Paul's whole Gospel for the sake of gratuitously imposing on his language an inoperative universalism of redemption which does not save" would be a great mistake. "The very nerve of his great declaration that 'Christ died for all; therefore all died,' is that participation in the death of Christ is salvation." To die with Christ is to live with him; there are "no half-measures" here. All those for whom Christ died, died with him and consequently rose with him and became a new creation in him. Everyone who has been made the object of Christ's love in his death finds himself constrained by that love to live for him as a "new creation." The verse cannot be broadened to include the lost but describes the saving effects of the atonement in the experience of all for whom it was intended. When the apostle extends this saving efficacy to "the world," then, "he is proclaiming the world-wide reach, the world-wide destiny of God's salvation."[58]

In the case of Hebrews 2:9, which speaks of Christ as "tast[ing] death for everyone," Warfield cautions us again not to attach a meaning to the passage that the author did not intend. The author speaks of salvation, but "his interest is not in asserting that each and every man who lives in the world, or has lived or will live in it," shall be saved. The writer to the Hebrews knows very well that not all men shall be saved, for he himself warns vigorously against neglecting this great salvation and thus incurring the fate of the lost. "He is speaking in our text moreover not of the intention with which Christ died, but of the realization of that intention through the power of the ascended Christ." He is intent on showing that what Christ did in dying, he did not for himself but for others, that by it he will lead many sons to glory. "And therefore the 'every one' of this verse is

---

[56]SW, 69–100.
[57]SW, 103–30.
[58]SW, 137–47, 155–57.

immediately translated into the 'many sons' of the next." There is then a narrowing of the reference, a more precise definition. Even so Warfield affirms "the racial effect of our Lord's work," and looks ahead to a saved humanity.[59]

The Resurrection of Christ

Warfield comments that it was characteristic of liberalism's attack on the supernatural to represent the historical miracles that lie at the foundation of the Christian faith as unimportant. So the New Testament teaching of the resurrection of Jesus,[60] for example, need not be taken at face value. What is important is that Jesus' immortal spirit lives beyond the grave. It is not important to our faith that Jesus continues to live physically—only that he lives. Visions of him after the crucifixion were spiritual apparitions, not physical appearances, so liberals argue. Warfield says of such liberals, "They are ready enough to believe in the continued existence of Jesus after death. When it comes to a 'resurrection' they mock. In other words they wish to eliminate from the religion of Jesus all that distinguishes it from natural religion, and still to call themselves Christians." And so Warfield cautions, "It is the essence of distinctive Christianity that is at stake in the controversy they raise." Warfield championed Christian supernaturalism generally, but he understood the resurrection of Christ as especially central. "Around the two great facts, of the expiatory death of the Son of God and his rising again, Paul's whole teaching circles. Jesus Christ as crucified, Christ risen from the dead as the first fruits of those that sleep—here is Paul's whole Gospel in summary." Warfield does not expend quite the effort in defense or exposition of the resurrection that he does in reference to Christ's atoning death, but in the few places where he does treat the doctrine, he demonstrates his earnest concern for it and his appreciation of its fundamental place in the Christian gospel. The resurrection of Christ is to Warfield "the great central fact" of the apostolic preaching, faith, and life, "the hinge" on which turn all the Christian's hopes and his confidence in life and in death. Once again, in this question "it is the essence of distinctive Christianity that is at stake."[61]

---

[59]*SW*, 177–82.

[60]Warfield's primary treatments of the doctrine are found in but two articles—"The Resurrection of Christ an Historical Fact," in *SSW*, 1:178–92, and "The Resurrection of Christ a Fundamental Doctrine," in *SSW*, 1:193–202. A third article, "Christianity and the Resurrection of Christ," *TBS*, new series, 8, no. 4 (April 1908): 277–83, and a sermon on 2 Tim. 2:8, "The Risen Jesus," in *SW*, 191–213, are both very similar to "The Resurrection of Christ a Fundamental Doctrine."

[61]*W*, 3:151; *SW*, 192, 195; "The Present Day Depreciation of Christ's Resurrection," *TBS*, new series, 2, no. 6 (December 1900): 357–59.

A HISTORICAL FACT

Warfield distinguishes between Christian doctrines and facts. The two are not mutually exclusive, of course—Christian doctrines are such only because they are facts, and the historical facts of Christianity are its foundational doctrines. But there is something of a difference. The incarnation, for example, is a Christian dogma, and Christians must believe its factual occurrence. But the descent of God the Son to human estate was unobserved and unobservable to any human eye. The resurrection, on the other hand, "is a fact, an external occurrence within the cognizance of men to be established by their testimony." Moreover, it was the same body that was laid in the tomb that was resurrected. Doubtless there was some change, as Paul describes of the resurrection body in 1 Corinthians 15. But the risen body of Jesus "was in such a sense the same body that was laid in the sepulchre, that when it came forth *the tomb was left empty.*"[62]

David Hume (1711–1776) contended that no testimony to the miraculous can be accepted as credible unless the falsehood of the testimony would itself be more miraculous than the miracle it endeavors to establish. Modern skepticism follows in step and allows no room for the supernatural or the miraculous. It "must," therefore, be rid of the resurrection of Christ. Jesus' resurrection is central, and "on it all other doctrines hang." Warfield responds that the factuality of the resurrection of Christ rests on "a mass of proof" such that turns David Hume's famous dilemma on its own head. The eyewitness testimony of the historical books of the New Testament, Warfield insists, establish the "absolutely crushing fact" of Christ's resurrection.[63]

The Usual Lines of Evidence

The testimony of eyewitnesses is solid, but skeptics must set it all aside on the ground that such an event is clearly impossible. Further, skeptics claim that the historical books that record the resurrection of Christ are late compositions and so do not present reliable, firsthand testimony. These critics may be answered in two ways, Warfield suggests, one of which would be to prove the authenticity of the New Testament books. This was done repeatedly over the previous half century, and Warfield is confident of the resulting "triumphant vindication" of the credibility of the Gospel records. He does not argue along these lines himself, at length, but he remarks only broadly on the compelling character of both the internal and the external evidences of the credibility of the Gospel records.

---

[62]*SSW*, 1:178; "Present Day Depreciation of Christ's Resurrection," 357 (emphasis original).
[63]*SSW*, 1:178–79.

The Gospels proclaim the original faith of the Christian community, and though simple peasants, their authors present a biography of Christ that no man or body of men—whether mythologists or philosophers—could ever have concocted. The divine-human personality of Jesus exhibited in such exact proportions and then dramatized through such a long course of teaching and action without a single inconsistency "can be accounted for only on the hypothesis that they [the Evangelists] were simply detailing the facts." Similarly, there are many "undesigned coincidences in minute points" concerning the resurrection between the book of Acts and the admittedly genuine epistles of Paul. The historicity of Acts, and that of the Gospel of Luke which it brings with it, is self-evident and well established. Likewise, the immediate successors of the apostles universally accepted their works as authoritative "Scripture" and "Holy Books." There is no ground left for denying the genuineness of the Gospels and Acts, and, therefore, there is "no room left for denying the fact of the Resurrection."[64]

Answering the Critics on Their Own Ground

These arguments are well used and well established, and so Warfield assaults the critics from another angle. He waives all references to disputed books and takes only the New Testament books that even the most radical of the critics acknowledge as genuinely apostolic—John's Revelation and Paul's Romans, 1 and 2 Corinthians, and Galatians—in order to demonstrate from them the historicity of the resurrection. John is an eyewitness of the resurrection and speaks of it in his Revelation (1:5, 2:8), but Warfield is willing even to dismiss John, for the sake of the argument, accept only Paul's undisputed books, and draw from them "the evidential value of their references" to Christ's resurrection.[65]

First, there is the testimony of Paul himself. He not only states that Christ rose from the dead but claims himself to have seen the risen Christ (1 Cor. 15:8). More than claiming to have seen the risen Christ, he bases his apostleship on this sight (1 Cor. 9:1). This sight of the risen Christ followed that of the other apostles (1 Cor. 15:8), and it was a sight that constituted his call and appointment to that apostleship. Paul's claim was of a true "sight" of Christ in his resurrected state. It will not do to reduce his sight of Christ to a mere theophany or his living spirit. Paul's claim and whole argument throughout 1 Corinthians 15 concerns *bodily resurrection*, and it was this sight of the bodily resurrected Christ that produced his conversion and call to the apostleship (simultaneously, Gal. 1:16)

---

[64]*SSW*, 1:179–81.
[65]*SSW*, 1:181.

and figured heavily in his very argument concerning the bodily resurrection of believers.[66]

Because Paul's apostleship rests on the resurrection of Christ, it is no surprise that his epistles bristle "with marks of his intense conviction of the fact of the resurrection" (Rom. 1:4; 4:24–25; 5:10; 6:4–5, 8–11, 13; 7:4; 8:11, 34; 10:7, 9; 14:9). It would be foolish, then, to deny that Paul was himself "thoroughly convinced that he had seen the risen Jesus," and Warfield notes that "the sceptics themselves feel forced to admit this fact."[67]

Did Paul then simply see a deceiving vision? Was he of an overly enthusiastic spiritual temperament that left him unable to distinguish between vivid subjective ideas and external facts? Paul received visions (2 Cor. 12) but was not a visionary and certainly knew the difference between them and sight. The time reference "last of all" (1 Cor. 15:8) points to objective fact, a real sight of Christ on the level of that of the other apostles. Recognizing this, Baur and others have tried to characterize Paul as hurting with conscience, doubting, sickly, thirsty, tired, then struck by the sun on the Damascus road or perhaps by a storm, which induced an imaginary vision. Such a distraction of mind is contradicted by the apostle Paul himself (Gal. 1:13ff.). Warfield responds, simply, that this whole line of argument assumes the historical reliability of Acts, which is the very point these critics are unwilling to concede. If Acts is unreliable historically, then these facts from it cannot be so used. But if Acts *is* historically reliable, then Paul's conversion is nothing like this critical portrayal. Moreover, if Acts is reliable, then so also is Luke—in which case the resurrection of Christ is well attested, and the case is won.[68]

There is a further problem with the visionary scheme. Even if such a portrayal of Paul's Damascus road experience were more plausible than it actually is, still it would have to be discounted, for it is not Paul alone who has seen the risen Christ but others also. Paul introduces us to other eyewitnesses and founds his gospel on this fact. Indeed, he tells us in Galatians 2:6ff. that the gospel he preaches is the same as that preached by Peter, James, and John, who believe with the same intensity in the fact of the risen Christ. In 1 Corinthians 15:3ff. Paul declares that the risen Jesus was seen not only by him but also by Cephas, James, and all the apostles—and that more than once—and in fact by more than five hundred others, most of whom were still living when Paul wrote his letter, and to whose witness bearing he appeals.

Warfield then draws some observations. There were many witnesses, not only a few. These witnesses were not unknown but were men to whom appeal could be

---

[66]*SSW*, 1:181–82.
[67]*SSW*, 1:182.
[68]*SSW*, 1:183–84.

made for testimony. There is then a multitude of (something at least more than two hundred and fifty) individual testimonies. "Paul is admitted to be a sober and trustworthy writer; this Epistle is admitted to be genuinely his; and he here in a contemporary document challenges an appeal to living eye-witnesses." Further, the witnesses included the original apostles, and from this two other facts follow: the original disciples believed they had seen the risen Lord, and they claimed to have seen him on the third day after his burial (1 Cor. 15:4).[69]

Further, this testimony was not only convincing to Paul, but it was convincing to the whole body of Christians. Paul is not the only one who based his conversion on the resurrection of Christ; so also did all Christians. His letters reflect that his readers were as convinced as he that Jesus had risen from the dead. "To the Corinthians, Galatians, Romans—this is *the* dogma of Christianity." Further, Paul is not afraid to rest his apostleship on it (1 Cor. 9:1; Gal. 1:1). He even rests our justification on it (Rom. 4:24–25).

> These are but specimens of his practice. Both purposed and incidental allusions are made to the Resurrection through all four of these Epistles of such character as to prove that it was felt by Paul that he could count on it above all other facts as the starting-point of Christianity in the minds of his readers.[70]

The force of this is considerable, particularly given that in some of these churches there were rifts and parties antagonistic not only to one another but to the apostle himself. These people were not all naively willing to accept just anything the apostle said. Yet, with all these parties, the resurrection of Jesus was common ground, and Paul could enforce any doctrine that is grounded on it. Even to his bitterest opponents he would prove his apostleship by claiming to have seen the risen Lord. And one of these letters (Romans) was written to a church with which Paul had had no previous personal dealings; even so, this was the common faith. "It is plain, then, that the resurrection of Christ was in Paul's day deemed a primordial, universal, and essential doctrine of Christianity." It was not an outgrowth of a later Christian community, nor did it have its origin in Paul. It was always, from the very first, the common aboriginal faith of the entire Christian community.[71]

Gathering up the results of all this, Warfield offers the following summary. First, the resurrection of Christ was a doctrine common to all Christians at the time these epistles were written. Second, the original followers of Christ, includ-

---

[69] *SSW*, 1:185.
[70] *SSW*, 1:185 (emphasis original).
[71] *SSW*, 1:186.

ing the apostles, claimed to be eyewitnesses of his resurrection; therefore, from the very beginning the entire church was thoroughly convinced of it. Third, the entire church, from the beginning, believed that it owed its life and continued existence and growth to its firm belief in this doctrine. What has to be accounted for, then, is (1) the faith not of one man only but of a multitude of eyewitnesses; (2) the faith not of a particular party but of the entire church; (3) the effect of this faith in thoroughly transforming the characters and enthusiasm of its first adherents; and (4) "their power in propagating their faith, in building up on this strange dogma a large and fast growing communion, all devoted to it as the first and ground element of their faith."[72]

We can account for all this only in one of the following ways. Either the original disciples of Christ were deceivers who deliberately contrived the story; or they were terribly deluded, believing a fantastic but untrue story; or the belief was grounded in fact, and Christ did indeed rise from the dead. The first of these alternatives is very old (Matthew 28), but is admitted by all sides to be ridiculous. Christ's burial is well attested (1 Cor. 15:4), and the enemies of Christianity, if they had stolen the body, would have produced it so as to destroy Christianity at its very beginning. The disciples, even if they had desired to steal the body in order to promote a hoax, clearly had no courage to attempt it. And the very idea of Christianity owing its life to such a hoax is absurd. The second theory cannot be true, for again what about the body? And why was it not produced? And how could a whole body of men be so confused and deluded? The grave was empty. How could so many believe it to be empty if it were not? Did Jesus really not die, as Schleiermacher hypothesized, but only swoon, and then creep out of the tomb unnoticed? Then what of the eyewitnesses? Did they, in seeing a weak, frail, wounded, half-dead man mistake him for the risen, conquering Lord? Does the death-defying courage of the apostles really trace back to a half-dead Jesus in hiding? And how would this reflect on the character of Jesus himself? And if the grave were lost, or if the disciples merely had seen a vision, then, again, why did not the enemies of Christ simply produce the body? Moreover, there was no expectation of resurrection, there was no time for such a belief mythically to grow, and above five hundred visionaries are simply too many. Or "was all Palestine inhabited by Francises of Assisi?"[73] The facts of the case leave us to the third alternative only—Jesus Christ actually rose from the dead.

There are other lines of proof that could be examined, such as the *results* of the resurrection in transforming those who believed it, in the founding of a church,

---

[72]*SSW*, I:187.
[73]*SSW*, I:190–91.

and in the vindication of the genuineness and historicity of the historical records of the Gospels and Acts. "Taking all lines of proof together, it is by no means extravagant to assert that no fact in the history of the world is so well authenticated as the fact of Christ's resurrection." And when this fact is established, Christianity itself—with its essential supernatural character—is established also. So also is the gospel and every Christian's hope in Christ.[74]

A FUNDAMENTAL DOCTRINE

This fundamental significance of Christ's resurrection is difficult to overstate. Christians and their enemies alike have in the past agreed that the resurrection of Christ from the dead is "the very citadel of the Christian position"; so long as it stands, Christianity itself stands also.[75]

Its Primary Place

According to the liberalism of Warfield's day, however, this is all mistaken. Harnack, for example, allows that the disciples and their followers believed that the resurrection of Christ is, in fact, the mightiest power by which the gospel has won the world. But he also asserts that the question is a matter of indifference. Whether it was a sound conviction or a delusion is of no moment, for faith is not and must not be grounded in history or in facts. Faith must be independent of all facts. That Jesus is the living Lord is enough, whatever state of existence he now has.

The attempt in all this, purportedly, is to render Christianity immune to the onslaughts of historical science. "If it is independent of all details of history it cannot be wounded through the critical reconstruction of the historical events which accompanied its origin." But the actual effect, obviously, is "to destroy altogether all that has hitherto been known as Christianity; the entire detachment of Christianity from the realm of fact simply dismisses it into the realm of unreality." The original Christianity was preeminently rooted in historical events, and this is particularly so in regard to the resurrection of Jesus. "If Christianity is entirely indifferent to the reality of this fact, then 'Christianity' is something wholly different from what it was conceived to be by its founders." That is to say, with the reality of the resurrection, Christianity itself is at stake. If its doctrines are not facts grounded in history, it is not the religion it professes to be.[76]

What cannot be denied is that the reality of the resurrection of Christ "formed the center of the faith of the founders of Christianity." Jesus himself staked his

---

[74]*SSW*, 1:191–92.
[75]*SSW*, 1:193.
[76]*SSW*, 1:194–95.

whole claim upon it, and this was the single and sufficient "sign" or credential he agreed to give (Matt. 12:40; John 2:19). And not Jesus only but his earliest follow-ers understood their primary task as that of bearing witness to his resurrection (Acts 1:22; 2:32; 4:33; 10:41; 17:18), and they attributed their steadfast faith to its power (1 Pet. 1:3, 21; 3:21). "Paul's whole gospel was the gospel of the risen Savior." There are particularly two passages in Paul's letters that reveal the supreme place he gave to the resurrection. The first is 1 Corinthians 15, in which he explicitly suspends the entire credibility of the gospel and of the entire apostolic witness on the bodily resurrection of Christ. If Christ did not rise, then the apostles are all liars, the gospel is a myth, and no salvation of sinners has yet been accomplished. In some ways even more striking is Philippians 3:10, where Paul "represents the very essence of the saving knowledge of Christ to reside in knowing 'the power of his resurrection.'" That is, Paul finds the center of gravity of the Christian life and of the Christian faith in the fact of Christ's resurrection.[77]

Its Primary Significance

It would be impossible, then, to assign the resurrection of Christ a more fun-damental place, and Warfield outlines some of the reasons for giving it such prominence. First, from an apologetic point of view, this is "the fundamental fact" of Christianity. If Christ had not risen from the dead, the supernatural character of the Christian religion might be debated, and the validity of his claims would be left in serious doubt. Contrariwise, once his resurrection is established, the supernatural character of Christianity, the validity of Christ's claim as the Son of God, and the trustworthiness of his teaching are all beyond all doubt. We may hesitate to believe the reports of his supernatural life, but when his resurrection is established, we can hesitate no longer. The entire Christian religion, in fact, is stamped as divine, and so long as the resurrection of Christ stands, "Christianity, too, must stand as the one supernatural religion."[78]

Second, the resurrection of Christ is fundamental to "the revelation of life and immortality which Christianity brings to a dying world." That is, by Christ's resur-rection believers are brought to taste the age to come. Here Warfield inches very close to the redemptive-historical significance of the resurrection expounded by Geerhardus Vos. He states that by the resurrection of Christ believers are "permit-ted to experience the reality of that other world to which we are all journeying." He does not quite speak in terms of experiencing that world to come in Christ today; he speaks only in terms of hope. He seems to think the believer's experi-

---

[77]*SSW*, 1:195–96.
[78]*SSW*, 1:197–98; "Christianity and the Resurrection of Christ," 282.

ence of Christ's resurrection is captured wholly in terms of regeneration and the eschaton. But this hope, born by Christ's resurrection, is for Warfield nonetheless an invigorating hope that enlivens and revolutionizes the Christian conscious-ness and begets steadfast faithfulness in service for Christ.[79]

Third, the resurrection of Christ yields "confidence in his claims, his teach-ings, and his promises." By his resurrection all he taught was given indisputable credibility. He claimed to be equal with God; he proclaimed the forgiveness of sins; he offered eternal rest. If he had not risen, these would all lack credibility. But given his resurrection, all he taught is rendered trustworthy.

Closely related to all this is the simple fact that Christ's resurrection is essen-tial to the fact of Jesus himself. Warfield complains at several points, as well as in this connection specifically, of the line of thought stemming from Albrecht Ritschl that the reality (or unreality) of Jesus' resurrection is not a question of importance.

> The main fact, we are told, is not whether that body that was laid in the tomb was resuscitated. Of what religious value, we are asked, can that purely physical fact be to any man? The main fact is that Jesus—that Jesus who lived in the world a life of such transcendent attractiveness, going about doing good, and by His unshaken and unshakable faith in providence revealed to men the love of a Father God; this Jesus, though He underwent the inevitable experience of change which men call death— yet still lives. Lives! Lives in His Church; or at least lives in that heaven to which He pointed us as the home of our Father, and to which we may all follow Him from the evils of this life; or at least lives in the influence which His beautiful and inspiring life still exerts on His followers and through them on the world. This, this, we are told, is the fact of real religious value.

The beauty of such language and sentiments renders the argument compelling indeed. The fact of *Jesus* is enough! History and fact are not essential to religious belief—Jesus is enough! But, Warfield asks, which Jesus? The Jesus of history? Who is this "Jesus" who is to be our inspiration? Did he really live on earth? And did he manifest faithful reliance upon divine providence? Which Jesus is it that reveals to us the love of God? Is it the Jesus who actually lived and died? If it is the simple fact of *Jesus* that is important, then history and fact are essential after all. Christianity stands or falls with historical facts, and it is these historical facts that give it its form as a religion. The only Jesus known to history is the Jesus who said he would die and rise again, a supernatural, miraculous Jesus. Remove the

---

[79]*SSW*, 1:198–99.

supernatural, and there is no Jesus left at all, much less a Jesus who can inspire and teach us.[80]

Next, "The resurrection of Christ is fundamental to the Christian's assurance that Christ's work is complete and redemption is accomplished." He claimed to give his life a ransom for his people. He claimed that the new covenant was established in his blood. It is said of him that "he was delivered up on account of our trespasses." Is there warrant to believe this? On what ground can we be assured that his sacrifice for sins was, in fact, successful and effective? On what ground can we be assured that he did, in fact, exhaust the curse for his people? Warfield answers, "That he died manifests his love, and his willingness to save. That he rose again manifests his power, and his ability to save." In this way Christ can be said to have been both "delivered up on account of our trespasses" and "raised on account of our justification." If he paid the penalty of our sin, then the curse of that sin cannot have broken him; he must have broken it. "To save, He must pass not merely to but through death. If the penalty was fully paid, it can not have broken Him, it must needs have been broken upon Him. . . . It is only because He rose from the dead that we know that the ransom He offered was sufficient, the sacrifice was accepted, and that we are His purchased possession." In short, "Had he not emerged from the tomb, all our hopes, all our salvation would be lying dead with him unto this day."[81]

Again, the resurrection of Christ is fundamental also to our own hope of rising from the dead. His resurrection from the dead "drags ours in its train." He accomplished a reversal of the curse for those for whom he died and rose. When he rose, the resurrection of the dead had come, the beginning of a great harvest. We do not sorrow as those who have no hope; our hearts swell with glad anticipation, "for if we believe that Jesus died and rose again, even so them also that are fallen asleep in Jesus will he bring with him." If Christ did not rise from the dead, could we nourish so great a hope as this? Apart from Christ's resurrection we have no hope of resurrection ourselves.[82]

Finally, by Christ's resurrection we are assured of his universal lordship. This is the implication of 2 Timothy 2:8: "Remember Jesus Christ, risen from the dead, the offspring of David." Apart from his resurrection we might believe in Jesus' love, and we might believe in the continued existence of his soul. But how could we be assured of his Davidic kingship or his rule and triumph over evil? How could death be subject to him if he did not rise? It is by his resurrection that Christ is enthroned over heaven and earth, Lord and King over all.[83]

---

[80]"Christianity and the Resurrection of Christ," 279–81.
[81]*SSW*, 1:200; "Christianity and the Resurrection of Christ," 283.
[82]*SSW*, 1:200–201; "Christianity and the Resurrection of Christ," 283.
[83]"Christianity and the Resurrection of Christ," 283.

Warfield elsewhere briefly expands on this general theme where he states that had Christ "only died for us, perhaps salvation might have consisted solely in relief from this penalty of sin which He bore for us. That He ascended out of death to the throne, conquers the throne itself for us." His point in context is to show that by his resurrection—alluded to cryptically in Hebrews 2:9, "crowned with glory and honor"—Christ acted not alone but as the representative of his people, accomplishing the glory intended for them but lost in Adam. In his resurrection to glory, Warfield argues, Christ leads "many sons to glory" also.[84]

In these ways the resurrection of Christ is fundamental to Christianity. If we can do without the resurrection of Christ, then we have no need of Christianity at all. A Christianity without the resurrection has nothing to offer the sin-stricken human soul, for all of Christianity's hopes rest on the empty tomb. By his resurrection we are assured that every enemy, even death, has been put under his feet, and we can say with confidence now "that nothing can separate us from the love of God which is in Christ Jesus our Lord,—yes, not even death itself,—and that nothing can harm us and nothing take away our peace." In short, the fact of the resurrection of Christ is "certainly fundamental to a Christianity that saves." Surely it is good for us, Warfield counsels in light of the apostle Paul's charge to Timothy, "to remember Jesus Christ, risen from the dead, of the seed of David."[85]

> O the comfort, O the joy, O the courage, that dwells in the great fact that Jesus is the Risen One, of the seed of David; that as the Risen One He has become Head over all things; and that He must reign until He shall have put all things under His feet. Our brother, who has like us been acquainted with death,—He it is who rules over the ages, the ages that are past, and the ages that are passing, and the ages that are yet to come. If our hearts should fail us as we stand over against the hosts of wickedness which surround us, let us encourage ourselves and one another with the great reminder: Remember Jesus Christ, risen from the dead, of the seed of David![86]

---

[84]*SW*, 166.
[85]*SSW*, 1:202; "Christianity and the Resurrection of Christ," 283.
[86]*SW*, 212–13.

"But I tell you the truth"—none of you has asked me,
but I lovingly volunteer to tell you,—"It is good for you that I go
away." This departure is not a forced one, by way of defeat
and loss; it was planned from the beginning and is part of the great
plan by which I am to redeem not only Israel but the world.
Note the emphatic "I": "It is good for you that I go away." Why this
emphasis? Because there is another to whom this work
has been committed and whose offices are necessary for the
consummation of the work, "Because unless I go, the Helper will
not come to you; but if I go, I will send Him to you."

FL, 119 (emphasis original).

PNEUMATOLOGY

8

The doctrine of the Holy Spirit[1] has no separate chapter in the Westminster Confession of Faith, and those who criticize the confession on this score, Warfield says, have missed the obvious: the confession is itself "a treatise on the work of the Spirit." That is, the confession has so much to say about the Holy Spirit that it treats the subject throughout. It is no deficiency that it does not include a chapter on the Holy Spirit, Warfield contends, "because it prefers to give *nine* chapters to it." A separate chapter on the topic would simply collate teachings already stated throughout the confession and present a "meager summary" of the other nine chapters. So pervasively important did Warfield view the doctrine of the Holy Spirit.[2]

Warfield's observations regarding the Westminster Confession parallel in some degree his own theological work. In terms of numbers of pages, Warfield did not have the output directly on this area of study that he did on some others—although his work in this regard was by no means lacking! Yet in his introductory note to Abraham Kuyper's *Work of the Holy Spirit*, Warfield displayed a comprehensive grasp not only of the subject itself but also of all the literature on the subject throughout the history of the church—Latin, German, French, Dutch, and English. More importantly, his was not merely a thorough grasp of the subject, but the work of the Spirit was a prominent and recurring theme throughout his works and a frequent topic of choice in his published sermons. Of course Warfield is most famous for his treatment of the Spirit's work in the inspiration of the Scriptures, and this concentrated emphasis was due in greatest measure to the need of the hour. Yet everywhere in Warfield's

---

[1] Primary titles in which Warfield treats this subject include the following: "The Spirit of God in the Old Testament," in *W*, 2:101–29; *SSW*, 2:711–17); "On the Biblical Notion of 'Renewal,'" in *W*, 2:439–63; "On the Doctrine of the Holy Spirit," in *SSW*, 1:203–19; "New Testament Terms Descriptive of the Great Change," in *SSW*, 1:267–77; "The Love of the Holy Ghost," in *SSW*, 2:718–24; *PGS*, 121–48; "The Leading of the Spirit," in *PGS*, 151–79; "The Conviction of the Holy Spirit," in *FL*, 116–27; "The Outpouring of the Spirit," in *FL*, 135–45; "The Spirit's Testimony to Our Sonship," in *FL*, 179–92; "The Spirit's Help in Our Praying," in *FL*, 193–201; "Spiritual Strengthening," in *FL*, 267–78; "The Sealing of the Holy Spirit," in *FL*, 289–97; and *Counterfeit Miracles*.

[2] *SSW*, 1:205 (emphasis original).

writings he reflects a similar concern for the work of the Spirit in its every dimension. Perhaps it would be better to say that he everywhere reflects a deep sense of dependence on and appreciation for the work of the Spirit, and this is a major part of his concern in his continual and vigorous defense of Christian supernaturalism and his commitment to the Reformation principle of *soli Deo gloria*. Former students recall his unrelenting emphasis on salvation as a divine work. O. T. Allis, for example, reports his declaring to the class with a twinkle in his eye, "Gentlemen, I like the supernatural!" At the heart of his doctrine of "the great change"—both in regeneration and in progressive sanctification—was this prominent emphasis on the work of the sovereign Spirit. If for Warfield religion in its purest form is Calvinism, and if religion is at its height expressed in humble and adoring dependence upon God, then informing it throughout is a robust understanding of the person and work of the Holy Spirit. To see all this in Warfield we must look to his treatments of themes such as the Trinity, inspiration, regeneration and effectual calling, sanctification, perfectionism, and so on. For this chapter, however, reflecting somewhat his own description of the Westminster Confession, we will restrict our attention primarily to his more specific titles treating this doctrine, leaving his treatments of related themes to their respective contexts.[3]

In his "Brief and Untechnical Statement of the Reformed Faith," Warfield provides a broadly stated summary of his doctrine of the Holy Spirit:

> I believe that the redemption wrought by the Lord Jesus Christ is effectually applied to all his people by the Holy Spirit, who works faith in me and thereby unites me to Christ, renews me in the whole man after the image of God, and enables me more and more to die unto sin and to live unto righteousness; until, this gracious work having been completed in me, I shall be received into glory; in which great hope abiding, I must ever strive to perfect holiness in the fear of God.[4]

Characteristic of Warfield and in keeping with his larger conception of Scripture and the Christian faith, the statement is shaped in soteric terms. It is not meant to be exhaustive, and in previous paragraphs of this "Statement" he speaks also of the Spirit's place in the Trinity and his work of inspiration in the production of the Scriptures. But the Spirit's saving role in the life of the Christian is clearly the focus of Warfield's understanding and attention. The human race, by sin, forfeited

---

[3]*W*, 2:43–44; *SSW*, 1:218; Oswald T. Allis, "Personal Impressions of Dr Warfield," *BT* 89 (Fall 1971): 11.
[4]*SSW*, 1:408.

the right to the Spirit's work, but in grace God has taken steps to restore the work of the Spirit to humanity, and in Christ has made it just and righteous to do so.[5]

Certainly this redemptive focus informs Warfield's conviction that the work of the Spirit is "a theme higher than which none can occupy the attention of the Christian man." But more fully Warfield describes the Holy Spirit as the "Executor of the Godhead," the One by whom the will of the triune God is carried out, "not only in the creation and upholding of the worlds and in the inspiration of the prophets and apostles, but also in the regenerating and sanctifying of the soul." This further explains Warfield's observation regarding the Westminster Confession as consisting of nine chapters on the work of the Holy Spirit: as the executor of the Godhead he is necessarily the subject of study in all the works of God, such as creation and providence, as well as salvation. Once again, for Warfield the study of the work of the Spirit, "this greatest of all Christian subjects," is by the nature of the case of pervasive significance and redemptive focus.[6]

Historical Perspective

REFORMED CONTRIBUTION

In his understanding of the person and work of the Holy Spirit, Warfield was self-consciously a grateful heir of the Reformed tradition. The first to designate Calvin as "the theologian of the Holy Spirit,"[7] Warfield saw the Reformer as the watershed interpreter of this doctrine: for all practical purposes, this doctrine enjoyed no full exposition until Calvin. Speaking of Calvin, Warfield writes,

> Above all he gave to the Church the entire doctrine of the Work of the Holy Spirit, profoundly conceived and wrought out in its details, with its fruitful distinctions of common and efficacious grace, of noetic, aisthetic, and thelematic effects,—a gift, we venture to think, so great, so pregnant with benefit to the Church as fairly to give him a place by the side of Augustine and Anselm and Luther, as the Theologian of the Holy Spirit, as they were respectively the Theologian of Grace, of the Atonement, and of Justification.[8]

In Warfield's day great attention had been given to the subject, yet in his view only the Reformed had done it justice. This Reformation gift to Christian theology was advanced in the English-speaking world specifically by way of the Puritans

---

[5]*FL*, 137.
[6]*SSW*, 1:204; *W*, 2:105; *W*, 5:229; *PR* 10, no. 38 (1889): 334.
[7]*W*, 5:107.
[8]*W*, 5:21; cf. *SSW*, 1:213.

and certain of their successors. Only in English does one find such an "immense literature" on the doctrine of the Holy Spirit. Warfield reasons that the Westminster Confession, as a Puritan document, "was sure to be" in its very essence a treatise on the Holy Spirit. For other examples of Puritan emphasis and contribution to the study, Warfield lists John Owen (1616–1683), Thomas Goodwin (1600–1680), and Stephen Charnock (1628–1680) as "only the best known examples among a multitude which have fallen out of memory in the lapse of years." He further observes that this doctrine formed the "hinge" of the theologizing of the English nonconformists for a century and a half, and he sees this emphasis as carried forward only in "those who have the best right to be looked upon as the successors of the Puritans."[9]

Warfield emphasizes that this all is unique to the English-speaking world. Throughout the history of the church and in all other places, nothing like this "copious stream of literature" on the Holy Spirit has ever been produced. He describes the "poverty of Continental theology" in this regard as "depressing" and cites but two small French and a couple of Dutch authors as exceptions. Warfield mentions several German works but describes them as largely "only very formal" and so dominated by mistaken theological presuppositions as making scarcely a contribution to the discussion. Only the work by the German K. A. Kahnis provides a truly worthy exception to this dearth, and in Warfield's estimation the comprehensive treatment of the work of the Holy Spirit by Abraham Kuyper is the high-water mark of Continental literature on the subject.[10]

All this leads to the conclusion that "the doctrine of the Holy Spirit was only slowly brought to the explicit consciousness of the Church, and has even yet taken a firm hold on the mind and consciousness of only a small section of the Church." The early church busied itself with an investigation of the *person* of the Holy Spirit—his deity and personality, and so, his place in the Trinity—and of his one function in the inspiration of Scripture. The doctrine of the *work* of the Holy Spirit is the gift of the Reformation, advanced only in Reformed theology and particularly in Puritanism. This for Warfield is not surprising, for it is in Reformed theology that the Christian is thrown back to a necessary dependence upon the grace of God administered sovereignly by the Spirit. Thus, the seeds of this doctrine are spread over the pages of Augustine. Luther grasped it, and Zwingli shows at times that he did also. But it was Calvin who gave us the doctrine in its full and systematic form, and only in his wake has the doctrine made advance.[11]

---

[9]*SSW*, 1:205–7.
[10]*SSW*, 1:206–12.
[11]*SSW*, 1:212–14.

EXPLANATION

Warfield demonstrates that this course of development is to be expected, for the full development and apprehension of the doctrinal system of Christianity necessarily followed a logical process. Attention must first be given to the "objective elements" of the Christian faith before its "subjective elements" can be fully grasped. And so first there was the development of the Christian doctrine of God, which was not complete until it had assimilated the various strands of truth regarding the Trinity, among which the two natures of Christ was prominent. Moreover, it was not until the church had grasped the doctrine of the person of Christ that its attention could be driven poignantly to the doctrine of sin—"man's need and helplessness." And only then could the nature of the work of Christ be fully understood. And only then could the church come to grips with "the subjective provision to meet [man's] needs in the work of the Spirit." Warfield observes that "this is the logical order of development, and it is the actual order in which the Church has slowly and amid the throes of all sorts of conflicts . . . worked its way into the whole truth revealed to it in the Word." Thus, the order is theology proper, christology, anthropology (hamartiology), the accomplishing of redemption, and the application of redemption. Or, to describe this development in biographical terms, the process has led from Athanasius to Augustine, then to Anselm, and then to the Reformation "capstone" in Luther and in Calvin. All along, the various elements of the doctrine of the person and work of the Spirit were being gathered, but only in the successive outworking of each stage was the full harvest gathered.[12]

Warfield notes two "antagonistic forces" that have, through the centuries, hindered the full development and appreciation of the doctrine of the work of the Spirit. Wherever sacerdotal or libertarian tendencies were entrenched, the need for the work of the Spirit was suppressed. In the Roman Catholic system, from which the Reformers emerged, the church itself is deemed the depository of grace. Saving grace is dispensed by the church in its sacraments. And in such an environment there is little need for a doctrine of the work of the Spirit. The claim may be that the Spirit stands behind the church's distribution of the sacraments, but the reality in such an atmosphere is that prominence and attention are given to the sacraments and the church, not to the Holy Spirit. Efficacy in the distribution of grace belongs to the church and its priesthood, and in such a case the Spirit may be effectively ignored.[13]

---

[12] *SSW*, 1:214–17.
[13] *SSW*, 1:217.

Just as Luther rightly saw Erasmus's *Freedom of the Will* as striking at the foundation of the whole notion of salvation by grace, so also a robust doctrine of the work of the Spirit is inevitably suppressed wherever the will of man is considered "the decisive factor in the subjective reception of salvation." In proportion to the emphasis placed on the "freedom" of the human will, the doctrine of the work of the Holy Spirit necessarily languishes. Even where this may not be formally the case, it is the practical effect.[14]

Where either of these tendencies exists—sacramentalism or libertarianism—the doctrine of the Holy Spirit inevitably falls into neglect.

> Engagement with this doctrine has been intense only along the banks of that narrow stream of religious life and thought the keynote of which has been the *soli Deo gloria* in all its fulness of meaning. With this key in hand the mysteries of the history of this doctrine in the Church are at once solved for us.[15]

Again, the soteric focus of Warfield's conception of the doctrine of the Holy Spirit is evident.

The Holy Spirit in the Old Testament

Warfield emphasizes that like the doctrine of the Trinity, the doctrine of the Spirit of God is an "exclusively Biblical doctrine." It is an idea entirely foreign to all pagan thought and came into the world by way of Christianity. Its essentials are latent in the Old Testament revelation, and in this sense, at least, the fundamentals of the doctrine are common to both Testaments. The name the Spirit of God is familiar to both, even if it is more frequently the subject of New Testament writers. The Spirit of God is mentioned in about half of the Old Testament books, but all New Testament books refer to him except for three brief personal letters (Philemon, 2 and 3 John). Unevenness in references to the Spirit can be observed within the New Testament as well as the Old. In the Old Testament the Spirit of God may receive no mention at all in, say, Leviticus, Joshua, Ruth, and Ezra; but in Genesis, Judges, Nehemiah, and the Prophets he is a familiar theme. And even

---

[14] *W*, 9:472; *SSW*, 1:217–18. In 1920 Warfield wrote an article in *The Presbyterian* expressing his opposition to the proposed "plan of union for evangelical churches." Not surprisingly, his opposition was grounded partly in the statement on the Holy Spirit in the union's proposed creed. Warfield's redemptive focus on and the accompanying *need* for a robust doctrine of the Holy Spirit informed his complaint: the creed spoke of the Spirit merely "as guide and comforter," which in Warfield's view was a woefully inadequate depiction of the Spirit's great work. With such a creed all the progress since Augustine and the Reformers "goes out of the window." *SSW*, 1:386.
[15] *SSW*, 1:218.

if mention of him is more pervasive throughout the New Testament, there is a striking unevenness, say, between Matthew and John or Paul, or for that matter between the earlier and latter chapters of Romans.[16]

IDENTIFICATION: THE SPIRIT OF GOD AND THE HOLY SPIRIT

More importantly, Warfield stresses that from the Old Testament to the New, no discontinuity in the conception of the Spirit is noticeable. There is an increased frequency of mention, but again, unevenness is observable within the New Testament itself. And there is an increased clarity and fulness of understanding, but again this is noticeable as we pass from the Pentateuch to Isaiah or from Matthew to John or Paul. What is more significant than any of these differences is the marked continuity between the two Testaments' revelation of the Spirit. The apostles speak with a fuller understanding and clarity, but there is no hint of radical discontinuity, no evidence of a surprising turn in their understanding of God on this score. "If there be any fundamental difference between the Old and the New Testament conceptions of the Spirit of God, it escapes us in our ordinary reading of the Bible." Indeed, "We naturally and without conscious straining read our New Testament conceptions into the Old Testament passages."[17]

The New Testament writers very naturally encourage this identification in that their "Holy Spirit" is none other than the "Spirit of God" of the Old Testament. Over and again the New Testament writers equate the two. For them it was the Holy Spirit who guided Israel and whom Israel resisted (Acts 7:51). It was in the Holy Spirit that Christ (through Noah) preached to the antideluvians (1 Pet. 3:18–20). Just as in the New Testament, so in the Old, the Holy Spirit was the author of faith (2 Cor. 4:13). It was the Holy Spirit who spoke through the prophets (Matt. 22:43; Mark 12:36; Acts 1:16; 28:25; Heb. 3:7; 10:15). Zechariah (7:12) and Nehemiah (9:20) tell us that God sent his word by his Spirit. And Peter affirms that the descent of the Spirit on Pentecost was the accomplishment of God's promise through Joel (Joel 2:27–28; Acts 2:16). And so on, the identifications continue. The New Testament writers make it very plain that "the Spirit of God" (Old Testament) and "the Holy Spirit" (New Testament) are one and the same person.[18]

CONTRAST: DEGREES OF REVELATION

It is one thing to establish this identification, but it is quite another to discern the degree of revelation—and thus the degree of understanding—concerning the

---

[16]*W*, 2:101–2.
[17]*W*, 2:102–3; *SSW*, 2:711–12.
[18]*W*, 2:103–4; *SSW*, 2:712.

Spirit in the old dispensation without the fuller commentary given in the new. Given the established principle of progressive revelation, on the one hand, and the deep unity that exists between the Testaments, on the other, we should expect that while no inconsistencies would exist between them on this doctrine, there would be a difference in completeness. This question turns on what the two Testaments say about the Spirit as a distinct person who performs distinct activities.[19]

His Person

The Spirit of God in the Old Testament is certainly presented both as God himself and as a person who acts as a free, willing, intelligent being. He is said to be sent from God; thus, he is in some sense distinct from God. There is God, who is one, and there is the Spirit of God—God the giver and God the given, God the source and God the executor of his will. This objectifying of the Spirit as distinct from God begins as early as Genesis 1:2. And throughout the Old Testament record the Spirit is presented both as God himself at work, acting *sua sponte* ("of its own will"), and as sent from God to execute his will.

These facts collectively require the conclusions that are finally given with clarity in the New Testament—that while God is one in essence, this essence is shared among a multiplicity of persons. But these conclusions are never drawn in the Old Testament revelation, and in this sense the Old Testament revelation of God was never fully developed. There are hints that find ready explanation in the New Testament, anticipations that only later are brought to the light of a fuller understanding. The Spirit is objectified personally, in some way distinct from the "I" of God who stands as the cause of all that is, yet everywhere identified with God. But he is never quite hypostatized. There is this "tendency" in the Old Testament presentation of the Spirit, and by this a "preparation" is made for the full revelation of the Trinity in the New Testament. The points of connection are such that when the fuller revelation comes, it coalesces with the earlier revelation so easily that Christians, reading their Old Testament with this fuller understanding, scarcely notice the difference.[20]

More than this could hardly be expected in the Old Testament revelation of God. To keep Israel from the idolatries around her, it was essential that she learn well that God is a person and that he is one. Premature revelation of God's three-in-oneness, Warfield surmises, may have done them harm. First God's unity and personhood must be firmly established in their minds. And so God reveals himself truly and fully, but not all at once. Then Warfield exhorts,

---

[19]*W*, 2:104–5; *SSW*, 2:712–13.
[20]*SSW*, 2:713–15; *W*, 2:124–26.

What we need wonder over is not that the hypostatical distinctness of the Spirit is not more clearly revealed in the Old Testament, but that the approaches to it are laid so skilfully [sic] that the doctrine of the hypostatical Holy Spirit of the New Testament finds so many and such striking points of attachment in the Old Testament, and yet no Israelite had ever been disturbed in repeating with hearty faith his great Sch'ma, "Hear, O Israel, the Lord our God is one Lord" (Deut. 6:4).[21]

His Work

In both Testaments the Spirit of God "appears distinctly as *the executive of the Godhead*": it belongs to him to carry out the common purpose of the triune Godhead. In the Old Testament this work builds on the ruins of the old creation in preparation of the coming of the Messiah and the eventual establishing of the new creation. Broadly speaking, the Old Testament presents the Holy Spirit at work, first, in the world and then in the theocracy; and within the latter his work is both national and individual. These three spheres of his work—the cosmical, the theocratic, and the individual—are roughly, in that order, the successive presentation of the Spirit's work in the Old Testament.[22]

I. *The cosmical Spirit.* From the opening verses of the Old Testament where the Spirit of God is portrayed as hovering in creative power over the deep (Gen. 1:2), bringing order from nothingness, he appears as the "source of all order, life and light . . . , the divine principle of all movement, of all life and of all thought in the world." He is, in a word, immanent, and as such "is set over against God transcendent." God speaks the world into existence, and it is by means of his Spirit that his will and word are carried out. The Spirit is the very ground of the existence and persistence of all things, "the source and originating cause of all movement and order and life." God is over the world, creating and ordering its existence, and by his Spirit he is in the world, executing his will through it.[23]

This broad conception is represented in any number of references to specific cosmic processes. By the Spirit of God the heavens are garnished (Job 26:13), for example. He gives life (Pss. 36:9; 104:30), and only because of him does life continue (Job 12:10; 27:3; 33:4; 34:14–15). Not just physical life, but he is the source of intellectual life (Job 32:8) and ethical life also (Gen. 6:3 KJV).[24]

This portrayal of the Spirit of God as immanent alongside the high doctrine of the transcendence of God serves as a corrective both to deism, on the one hand,

---

[21] *SSW*, 2:715; cf. *W*, 2:127–28.
[22] *W*, 2:105–7 (emphasis original).
[23] *W*, 2:107–8.
[24] *W*, 2:109–10.

and to pantheism or other cosmotheistic conceptions, on the other. The immanence is not such that it entangles God in creation as a physical world spirit.
From the beginning he is held as distinct from the created order. Hence, he hov-
ers over it (Gen. 1:2) and is sent by God to it as Creator (Ps. 104:29–30) and giver
of life (Isa. 43:5). Although he penetrates all things (Ps. 139:7), he is nevertheless
"the *personal* cause of physical, psychical and ethical activities" and, exercising
choice, determines even the *differences* that exist among men and among the
entire created order (Job 32:8; Isa. 40:7; Gen. 6:3). Both natural and supernatural
activities are traceable to him (1 Kings 18:12; 2 Kings 2:16; 19:7; Isa. 37:7). He is at
once the great transcendent God, who alone is to be worshiped, and the personal
immanent Spirit, who pervades all space and is the immediate source of all being
and life. He is not apart from but one with the great almighty God of the heavens,
yet immanent and personally active in the world.[25]

As the Creator, upholder, and governor of all things, the immanent agent in
all the changes and movements of the world, the Spirit of God is therefore the
ground of the Christian doctrine of providence—"God in the world and in history,
leading all things to their destined goal." Warfield adds, "If without God there
was not anything made that has been made, so without God's Spirit there has not
anything occurred that has occurred."[26]

2. *The theocratic Spirit.* The Spirit of God works predominantly, in the Old
Testament, in relation to the theocracy, the kingdom of God in the nation of
Israel—what Warfield also refers to as the "second creation." In its broader aspect
this work concerns the kingdom generally, and in its narrower aspect it concerns
individuals in that kingdom (see below).

As "the theocratic Spirit" the Spirit of God is primarily "the source of all the
supernatural powers and activities which are directed to the foundation and
preservation and development of the kingdom of God in the midst of the wicked
world." Specifically, in this connection, the Spirit of God endows chosen "organs"
of the theocracy with the abilities necessary for the fulfillment of their calling.
Among these supernatural works are gifts of miraculous strength, resolution,
energy, courage in battle (Othniel, Judg. 3:10; Gideon, 6:34; Jephthah, 11:29; Samson,
13:25; 14:6, 19; 15:14; Saul, 1 Sam. 11:6; David, 1 Sam. 16:13), the supernatural gifts
of skill in constructing a worthy sanctuary for the worship of God (Ex. 28:3; 31:3f.;
35:31; 1 Chron. 28:12 KJV), and the gift of wisdom for administering judgment and

---

[25] *W*, 2:110–11 (emphasis original).
[26] *W*, 2:111–12.

government (Moses and the seventy elders, Num. 11:17, 25; Joshua, Num. 27:18; Deut. 34:9;Saul, 1 Sam. 10:1; David, 16:13).[27]

More prominent was "this greatest gift" of "supernatural knowledge and insight, culminating in the great gift of Prophecy." This was given to the seventy elders (Num. 11:25), Saul (1 Sam. 10:6; 11:6), and of course the prophets (cf. Num. 24:2; 1 Sam. 16:13; 2 Chron. 15:1; 20:14; Hos. 9:7 ["the man of the Spirit" = "the prophet"]; Isa. 48:16; Mic. 3:8). In Nehemiah 9:20, 30 and Zechariah 7:12 the prophets are portrayed as "a body of official messengers, through whom the Spirit of God made known His will to His people through all the ages." That is, they were "official mouthpieces of the Spirit of God, serving the people of God as His organs."[28]

These manifestations of the Spirit have an official character as the instruments through which God revealed himself, and through them the Spirit made God's presence among his people evident. These manifestations laid the foundation for the Christian doctrine of "God in the Church, leading and guiding it, and supplying it with all needed instruction, powers and graces for its preservation in the world."[29]

Warfield emphasizes that the Spirit of God empowers people for service always in a way that makes it impossible to confuse his official gifts with the native powers of his chosen organs. Just as in the lower sphere (his work in the world) he is not submerged in matter but always distinct and acting upon it, so in his theocratic ministrations he acts from without. God "gives" his Spirit, "puts the Spirit on" chosen men, and "fills" them with his Spirit (Num. 11:25, 29; Isa. 42:1; Ex. 31:3). The Spirit "comes" and "comes mightily" upon men (Judg. 3:10; 11:29; 14:6, 19; 1 Sam. 11:6; etc.), "falls" on them (Ezek. 11:5), breaks in upon them, seizes them, and puts them on like a garment (Judg. 6:34). The prophets and all the organs of the Spirit's theocratic work are simply the instruments of his mighty power, a power sometimes referred to by the equivalent phrase, "the hand of the LORD" (2 Kings 3:15; Ezek. 1:3; 3:14, 22; 33:22; 37:1; 40:1). The temporariness and intermittent character of the theocratic gifts further serve to demonstrate that they are given for the Spirit's purposive work. These gifts were not the possession of the organs themselves, and the men so gifted were not able to exercise these gifts merely at their own will: the gifts "came and went according to the divine gift." They are everywhere represented as given specially by God for his own given purpose, his chosen means of working through men.[30]

---

[27]W, 2:112.
[28]W, 2:114–15.
[29]W, 2:116.
[30]W, 2:117–18.

Finally, Warfield cites Isaiah 11:1–5; 42:1–8; and 61:1–3 to show that "the representations concerning the official theocratic Spirit culminate in Isaiah's prophetic descriptions of the Spirit-endowed Messiah." The endowments of the Spirit that had been given separately to others unite in him, "so that all previous organs of the Spirit appear but as partial types of Him to whom as we are told in the New Testament, God 'giveth not the Spirit by measure' (John 3:34)." To others the Spirit was "measured" (Isa. 40:13) in keeping with the role assigned them. But in Christ the kingdom is consummated, and thus the Spirit is poured out upon him without measure. In turn, because the Spirit was the source of his graces also, Christ becomes "the type not only of the theocratic work of the Spirit, but also of His work upon the individual soul, perfecting it after the image of God."[31]

3. The individual Spirit. Just as the Spirit of God was actively preparing God's kingdom for his people on a national level, as the theocratic Spirit, so also he was active in the individual human soul, preparing and fitting his people for the kingdom. In this respect the Spirit of God is distinctly the Spirit of grace. "As he is the source of all cosmical life, and of all theocratic life, so is He also the source of all spiritual life," upholding and governing the soul and conforming it to his own ideal, to make it share in the blessings intended for his theocratic people.[32]

> In a word, the Spirit of God, in the Old Testament, is not merely the immanent Spirit, the source of all the world's life and all the world's movement; and not merely the inspiring Spirit, the source of His church's strength and safety and of its development in accordance with its special mission; He is as well the indwelling Spirit of holiness in the hearts of God's children.[33]

In this connection Paul speaks of the "Spirit of faith" empowering the saints of the Old Testament (2 Cor. 4:13 BBW)—an expression that must refer to the Spirit of God as the source of their faith. Similarly, the impulses to live a life pleasing to God are not the product of the man himself or his environment; they are nothing other than the work of the Spirit within, shaping his children to conform to his will. This point was made more generally in connection with Genesis 6:3, where the Spirit is said to be active in promoting ethical behavior. Similarly, God's "good Spirit" was given to instruct the people in the person of Moses (Neh. 9:20). And Samuel said to Saul that the Spirit given to him would change him into a different person (1 Sam. 10:6; cf. v. 9). This ethical transformation coming as a consequence

---

[31] *W*, 2:118–19.
[32] *W*, 2:119–20.
[33] *W*, 2:120.

of the Spirit's work may lie behind Peter's remark that the writers of the Old Testament were "holy men of God" (2 Pet. 1:21 KJV).[34]

The leading passage in this connection is Psalm 51, David's cry of repentance and prayer for mercy following his sin with Bathsheba. Here he prays for the creation of a new heart and the renewal of a right spirit within him (v. 10), and the ground of his hope for this inner transformation is the continuance of God's "Holy Spirit" within him (v. 11)—an expression that seems to reflect David's understanding of the Spirit of God as the author and source of personal holiness. David's prayer for the "creation" of a "new heart" and the renewal of his spirit reflects further his hope for "total rebegetting" and thorough inward and outward transformation. His continuance in this transformation and "joy of salvation" is altogether dependent upon the continuance of the Spirit of God within him. Warfield refers to all this in Psalm 51 as "the high-water mark of Old Testament revelation" in regard to the saints' recognition of sin and the work of God in personal salvation.[35] These twin conceptions of grace and holiness find echo also in Psalm 143:10 and Isaiah 63:10–11, where the thought of the Spirit of God leading in the ways of holiness is prominent.

This presentation of the Spirit of God as the Spirit of grace and holiness climaxes in the Old Testament prophecies of the coming messianic age—an age that is to be marked distinctly as the age of the Spirit. It will be a day in which God will gather his people to his kingdom so that none will be missing (Isa. 34:16), a day in which righteousness will prevail (Isa. 32:15) and the knowledge of the Lord will be pervasive (Isa. 44:3–5). The abiding presence of the Spirit will constitute the crowning blessing of the new covenant promises (Isa. 59:21; Ezek. 11:19; 18:31; 36:26) and effect the conversion of God's people (Ezek. 37:14; 39:29; Zech. 12:10) over all the world (Joel 2:28–32). Warfield observes that this series of passages brings obviously before us "the indwelling God, author of all holiness and of all salvation," and lays the groundwork for the Christian doctrines of regeneration and sanctification, wherein God quickens the soul and develops it in holiness.[36]

DISTINCTIVE NEW COVENANT MINISTRY

Warfield sees all this as establishing "the fundamental unity" of the doctrine of the Spirit in the Old Testament with that in the New. In both Testaments the Spirit of God performs all the same functions and bears all the same characteristics. "They are conceived alike both in their nature and in their operations." And once

---

[34]*FL*, 236–39; *W*, 2:120–21.
[35]*W*, 2:121; *FL*, 20–22.
[36]*W*, 2:122–23.

again, "If there be any fundamental difference between the Old and the New Testament conceptions of the Spirit of God, it escapes us in our ordinary reading of the Bible, and we naturally and without conscious straining read our New Testament conceptions into the Old Testament passages."[37]

Even so, Warfield recognizes that the age of the new covenant is marked distinctly as the dispensation of the Spirit. This was the promise of the new covenant. The apostle John apparently reflects this in his comment that "the Spirit had not been given" (John 7:39). Jesus himself said that the Comforter could not come until he, Jesus, went away and sent him (John 16:7), and in seeming anticipation of this, Jesus breathed on his disciples and said, "Receive the Holy Spirit" (John 20:22). Surely all this marks the significance of Pentecost (Acts 2). So the question remains to be answered, what is the difference between the work of the Spirit in the Old and New Testaments? "What is meant by calling the new dispensation the dispensation of the Spirit?"

Warfield begins by eliminating the alternative: it cannot mean that the Spirit of God was not active in the old dispensation. It has already been demonstrated that the New Testament writers themselves represent the Holy Spirit as active previously in all the same ways he is active in this new era. Warfield concludes that the question turns on "the preparatory nature of the Old Testament dispensation." Its blessings came as a prelibation, a foretaste of what would be given in days to come.

> The Spirit worked in Providence no less universally then than now. He abode in the Church not less really then than now. He wrought in the hearts of God's people not less prevalently then than now. All the good that was in the world was then as now due to Him. All the hope of God's Church then as now depended on Him. Every grace of the godly life then as now was a fruit of His working.

All of this, Warfield argues, was the same. The difference lies in the *purpose* for which the respective dispensations were designed. "The object of the [old] dispensation was only to prepare for the outpouring of the Spirit upon all flesh. He kept the remnant safe and pure; but it was primarily only in order that the seed might be preserved."[38]

As Warfield explains this point, he takes a next step and speaks in terms of a new global outpouring of the Spirit that was only anticipated before. Through centuries the Spirit of God had seen fit to confine the workings of grace to one people. He preserved the mustard seed, but now it is planted and is by his workings "grow-

---

[37] W, 2:124; SSW, 2:711–12.
[38] W, 2:128–29; SSW, 2:715–16; cf. FL, 135–36.

ing up to a great tree which shades the whole earth." This was the significance of the gift of tongues at Pentecost—the now global nature of the Spirit's work. But Warfield returns and says that this universality is not in itself what explains the difference between the work of the Spirit in the Old and New Testaments. The difference "is that it is directed to a different end," by which he means that the Spirit's purpose is no longer to preserve the seed, merely, but to plant and perfect it until the gathering of the full harvest. Then again he speaks in terms of a grow-ing fulness of the Spirit's work, as a pent-in stream that has overrun its banks. And he concludes accordingly: "In one word, that was a day in which the Spirit restrained His power. Now the great day of the Spirit is come." That is to say, the old dispensation was designed specifically as preparation for the fuller work of the Spirit that has come in the new, and this new and fuller work Warfield conceives in terms of the *extent* of the Spirit's work throughout the world.[39]

All this Warfield argued in his articles published in 1895. The difference between the work of the Spirit in the two Testaments is to be understood in terms of its purpose, and this purpose is to be understood in terms of the extent of his work in the earth. But in the final point of his 1916 sermon on Acts 2:16–17, "The Outpouring of the Spirit," Warfield carries the thought a step further. We are "compelled" by the language of the new covenant promise (e.g., Ezek. 36:26) to conclude that in this new dispensation the work of the Spirit has come with "a more prevailing and a more pervading force." The difference is not simply one of extent after all. There is a qualitative difference, a difference in intensity. David marks the high point of religious experience in the old dispensation (see above). But even so, that was a day in which sanctification "lagged behind." The work of the Spirit was in every way the same. But in this age we have "the promise of a holy Church." And this Warfield sees as being fulfilled progressively, on both the individual and the corporate levels. Throughout the centuries the church has wept over her backslidings, but in the end Christ, by this powerful working of the Spirit, will see his bride perfected in holiness, without spot or wrinkle or any such thing.[40]

The difference, then, is to be understood in terms of both extent and intensity. As Warfield summarizes:

> Because we live under this dispensation, we are freed from the outward pres-
> sure of law and have love shed abroad in our hearts, and, being led by the Spirit
> of God, are His Sons, yielding a willing obedience and by instinct doing what is
> conformable to His will. Because this is the dispensation of the Spirit we are in

---

[39]*W*, 2:129; *SSW*, 2:716–17; *FL*, 139–43.
[40]*FL*, 144–45.

the hands of the loving Spirit of God whose work in us cannot fail; and the world is in His powerful guidance and shall roll on in a steady development until it knows the Lord and His will is done on earth as in heaven. It is because this is the dispensation of the Spirit that missions shall make their triumphant progress until earth passes at last into heaven. It is because this is the dispensation of the Spirit that it is an age of ever-increasing righteousness and it is because it is the dispensation of the Spirit that this righteousness shall wax and wax until it is perfect. Blessed be God that He has given it to our eyes to see this His glory in the process of its coming.[41]

The Ministries of the Spirit

As was mentioned at the outset of this chapter, Warfield's understanding and treatment of the work of the Spirit is found throughout his writings. The work of the Spirit in illumination and the giving of faith in particular are common points of emphasis for Warfield, reflected in our chapters on apologetics, theology proper (the knowledge of God), bibliology (the *testimonium*), and soteriology (which treats also of Warfield's understanding of the work of the Spirit in regeneration and sanctification). Other areas of emphasis on the Spirit's work found among his published sermons will be surveyed here.

CONVICTION

In his "Upper Room Discourse" our Lord describes his disciples as in continuous union and communion with him, as purchased by his death for them, and, in their lofty position, as his "friends" from whom he withholds nothing, not even his own life. In contrast he describes their condition in the world as hated, persecuted, and even martyred. Jesus says that in the midst of this difficulty they are to bear witness of him. Sad as they are (John 16:6), this picture is not all dark and gloom, nor does it hold the prospect of inevitable failure and defeat: Jesus also promises that, having gone away, he will send them the Holy Spirit, because of whom victory will belong to Christ. Indeed, "it is good" that he is going away, for, he says, "unless I go the helper will not come to you; but if I go, I will send him to you; and it is he who, on his coming, will convict the world as to sin, and as to righteousness and as to judgment." Jesus' comfort to his disciples in his absence lies in his provision of the Holy Spirit, and with him, his program for success in the gospel enterprise.[42]

---

[41]*FL*, 145.
[42]*FL*, 116–20.

The Spirit's work as the agent of Christ's victory consists in the application of Christ's work in the saving pursuit of sinners. Christ's disciples will be persecuted and even slain, but they will nonetheless win, for they do not strive single-handedly but by the power of the Spirit sent to them for just this purpose: he will convict the world (John 16:8). And although the disciples cannot at this point appreciate the greatness of this provision their Lord is making for them, after his resurrection they will, and they themselves will then speak of the great power of the Holy Spirit that will accompany their ministry.

The Spirit's work of conviction focuses on three specific issues: sin, righteousness, and judgment. First, he convicts of sin. The world by itself does not truly know its sin and accompanying guilt, but the Holy Spirit is come to bring home this realization to them. This element of concern—conviction of sin—is mentioned first and in a sense underlies the others. It is the first step to the recovery of the world. The world's sin is epitomized in its rejection of Christ; this is the touchstone, and there is no revelation of character so telling as that which refuses Christ, as is implied by the simple question, "What do you think of Christ?" And so Jesus says that the Spirit convicts of sin "because they do not believe in me" (v. 9). Second, the Spirit convicts of righteousness—of what genuine righteousness is, of what is required to attain a true righteousness, and therefore of the world's helpless need for righteousness. This righteousness is attainable only because Christ's saving work is complete, and so Jesus says that the Spirit convicts of righteousness "because I go to the Father" (v. 10). And third, the Spirit convicts of "overhanging judgment"—of the nature and unavoidability of divine judgment because of sin and the absence of the required righteousness. In his death and resurrection Christ rendered defeat to the world's prince, Satan, and thereby declared the impending judgment on the world also. But because the world is blind to its fate, the Holy Spirit is given to bring conviction.[43]

In all this our Lord provides exposition of the manner in which he will conquer the world. His conquest is assured, for the conviction of sin, righteousness, and judgment—so necessary to salvation—is ensured by the work of the sovereign Spirit. In short, Christ has sent his Spirit to give success to his atoning work and to bring about the completion of the redemption of the world that he secured in his blood.[44]

---

[43]*FL*, 122–26.
[44]*FL*, 117–20, 126–27. In this connection Warfield often speaks also of the Holy Spirit as the giver of life and the author of faith. See chapter 10, "Soteriology," below.

...E SEALING OF THE HOLY SPIRIT

In Ephesians 4:30 the apostle Paul writes, "And do not grieve the Holy Spirit of God, by whom you were sealed for the day of redemption." Warfield comments that "sealing expresses authentication or security, or, perhaps, we may say, authentication and security." The focus is on the security of the believer, who is marked out, authenticated as one who is redeemed and "made secure as to the completion of the redemption." The same emphasis is evident in Ephesians 1:13, where the apostle writes that we were "sealed with the holy Spirit of promise" (KJV), who is "the pledge" or "earnest" of our inheritance. That is, it is the ministry of the Spirit to work out all the promises to us and bring them to fruition. He is himself the down payment and guarantee of our full realization of redemption.

We are God's purchased possession, bought with the precious blood of Christ. But this redemption is not yet complete—the "day of redemption" awaits us in the future to which we who are purchased are to be safely brought. And for this great realization we have been sealed, "the Holy Spirit of promise" being both the foretaste and the pledge of it. This is a most emphatic assertion that those who are bought by Christ will be kept to experience the fulness of salvation promised them. The Spirit of God, having convicted us of sin, having drawn us to Christ in faith, and having come to us himself as a pledge of final salvation, will bring us safely to our appointed end.[45]

THE SPIRIT'S TESTIMONY TO OUR SONSHIP

Not only is the Holy Spirit our guarantee of coming glory, but he has also come to us in order to assure us of and bring us to experience our present sonship. Warfield cites Romans 8:16 as the verse on which the great Protestant doctrine of assurance is grounded and the verse that most clearly expresses the ministry of the Holy Spirit in that assurance: "The Spirit himself bears witness with our spirit that we are children of God." This doctrine of assurance holds that every Christian "may and should be assured that he is a child of God—that it is possible for him to attain this assurance and that to seek and find it is accordingly his duty." This very simply is the affirmation of Romans 8:16, and it further affirms that the Holy Spirit himself actively ministers this assurance of "childship" to God. The verse is clearly designed to encourage the believer—engender confidence in the heart of the believer—with a testimony to our sonship by none less than the Holy Spirit himself. We are not left to doubt and gloom; nor are we left to our own uncertain

---

[45]*FL*, 289–94; cf. "The Holy Spirit Our Pledge," *TBS*, new series, 4, no. 6 (December 1901): 360.

conjectures or imaginations. "The Spirit himself" bears testimony that we belong to God as his children. This is the plain and emphatic affirmation of the verse.[46]

It is equally clear that this verse would caution us not to confound the testimony of the Spirit with the testimony of our own consciousness. Whether we understand the dative to be translated "with our spirit" or "to our spirit," the Holy Spirit is clearly distinguished from our own spirit, and his testimony from ours. Indeed, this is the very nerve of the statement—that the Christian is encouraged to realize the *divine* witness to his sonship.[47]

However, Warfield emphasizes, "Distinctness in the source of this testimony from that of our own consciousness is not the same as separateness from it in its delivery." Indeed, although the apostle clearly distinguishes these two, he at the same time seems to suggest that the witness of the Spirit to our sonship is indeed given in conjunction with the testimony of our own spirit. That is, it seems most natural to translate the phrase "bears witness *with* our spirit," in which case the idea of bearing witness in conjunction with the testimony of our own consciousness is as emphatically asserted as is the distinction between the Holy Spirit and our own spirit. Both ideas are present. In fact, Warfield argues, even if we were to translate "bears witness *to* our spirit," it would seem still to convey the idea of the Spirit's witness consenting to our spirit's witness—a conjoined witness of both spirits in which the one gives confirmation to the other. In this case the emphasis on the conjunction may be lost, but the idea of conjunction would remain. Once more, this understanding of a conjoined witness seems to be demanded from the context, in which Paul affirms that by him we cry "Abba" (v. 15). Verse 16 is practically a subordinate clause to verse 15, and they combine to teach us that the testimony to our sonship comes distinctly from the Spirit of God but confluently with the testimony of our own consciousness. It is not the one without the other.[48]

This distinction is important, Warfield argues, for it will keep us from the abuse of the verse that too many have given it. Too many have grasped the teaching of this verse regarding the Spirit's witness when in fact they have no other credible ground for assurance, subjective or objective. But the fact is there are signs that accompany genuine conversion—hatred of sin, love for the brethren, and so on. But the Spirit of God does not work in a vacuum, and the assurance of sonship he gives is not a blind assurance grounded in nothing. He ministers assurance concurrently with our spirit, which would imply the presences of a reasonably well-grounded assurance—evidence of grace. The testimony of the

---

[46]*FL*, 179–82.
[47]*FL*, 182–83.
[48]*FL*, 179–86.

it is intended to serve not as a substitute for the testimony of our own spirit but "as an enhancement of it." As Warfield explains:

> Its object is not to assure a man who has "no signs" that he is a child of God, but to assure him who has "signs," but is too timid to draw so great an inference from so small a premise, that he is a child of God and to give him thus not merely a human but a Divine basis for his assurance. It is, in a word, not a substitute for the proper evidence of our childship; but a Divine enhancement of that evidence.[49]

Those who argue that assurance should be grounded either syllogistically (the promise is sure to those who believe the gospel; I believe the gospel; hence, I am a child of God) or mystically, in the witness of the Spirit, present a false antithesis, and to debate the question in this way is fruitless. Both considerations play into the proper grounding of Christian assurance. The Spirit is the "efficient cause" of our assurance, but he is not the "formal ground" of it.[50]

Warfield then cautions that in all this concerning the mode in which the Spirit delivers assurance, we should not lose sight of the reality of the divine witness itself. The affirmation is that the Holy Spirit assures believers of their sonship. He does not work this sense of assurance in our hearts without reason but by giving "true weight and validity to the reasons that exist and so leading to the true conclusion, with Divine assurance." He continues:

> The function of the witness of the Spirit of God is, therefore, to give to our halting conclusions the weight of His Divine certitude. It may be our reasoning by which the conclusion is reached. It is the testimony of the Spirit which gives to a conclusion thus reached indefectible certainty. We have grounds, good grounds, for believing that we are in Christ, apart from His witness. Through His witness these good grounds produce their full effect in our minds and hearts.[51]

THE LOVE OF THE HOLY SPIRIT

Twice in his published works Warfield provides an exposition of James 4:5 entitled "The Love of the Holy Ghost."[52] The translation he prefers for this verse is a marginal reading from the Revised Version: "Or think ye that the Scripture saith in vain, That Spirit which He made to dwell in us yearneth for us even unto jealous envy?" In the context James is addressing the problem of quarrels that marred the fellowship of that infant church, and he traces the problem back to such unseemly

---

[49]*FL*, 187; cf. 179–81, 185–87.
[50]*FL*, 187–89; *PRR* 5, no. 19 (1894): 549.
[51]*FL*, 191–92.
[52]*SSW*, 2:718–24; *PGS*, 121–48, a sermon some twenty-seven pages in length.

and worldly vices as hedonism and greed and selfishness. Verse 5 constitutes James's rebuke against all this, a rebuke grounded in a reminder of God's love. Warfield summarizes the teaching of the verse as "a declaration, on the basis of Old Testament Teaching, of the deep yearning which the Holy Spirit, which God has caused to dwell in us, feels for our undivided and unwavering devotion."[53]

The imagery involved is not new to James: it is the figure of marriage describing the relation of the Christian to God. Because Christians are "married" to God, any love for the world is a breach of our vows. Hence, in verse 4 James condemns adultery. Dallying with the rival lover is unfaithfulness to God, our husband. For his part, God loves his bride deeply. And because he loves her, he pursues her and longs for her faithful affection.

Nor is there anything new in this teaching of God's love for his people. Indeed, James, writing the very first of the New Testament books, Warfield says, grounds his rebuke in the teaching of the Old Testament Scriptures as something of which his readers are already aware. James does not cite a particular passage from the Old Testament but seems to summarize its teaching on the subject. The prophets in particular are replete with passages that depict God as the loving husband chasing after the affection and loyalty of his unfaithful people (Jer. 3:20; Ezek. 16:38, 60–63; Hos. 2:18–20). This much is familiar biblical teaching, both for James and for his readers.

What James seeks to stress is the intensity of this divine love for us: he "yearns for us, even unto jealous envy." This again is not entirely new and reflects many Old Testament passages that speak of God as jealous for the love and faithfulness of his people (Ex. 34:14; Nah. 1:2; Zech. 8:2). But James does advance the notion not only with the use of the verb, which appears also in Psalm 42:1, but also with the adverb, which expresses "the feeling which one is apt to cherish toward a rival." It is with "sickening envy," Warfield summarizes, that

> God contemplates our dallying with the world and the world's pleasures. He envies the world our love—the love due Him, pledged to Him, but basely withdrawn from Him and squandered upon the world. The combined expression is, you will see, astonishingly intense. God is represented as panting, yearning, after us, even unto not merely jealousy, but jealous envy. Such vehemence of feeling in God is almost incredible.[54]

Warfield insists this is no mere anthropomorphism but a blessed revelation of the heart of God toward us who belong to him. However difficult it may be to

---

[53]*PGS*, 121.
[54]*PGS*, 128–29.

believe that God loves us with such passion, we must believe it, for he tells us that he does.

> What can we do but admiringly cry, Oh, the breadth and the length and height and depth of the love of God which passes knowledge. . . . Strain the capacity of words to the utmost and still they fall short of expressing the jealous envy with which He contemplates the love of His people for the world, the yearning desire which possesses Him to turn them back to their duty to Him. It is this inexpressibly precious assurance which the text gives us; let us, without doubting, embrace it with hearty faith.[55]

Warfield points out further that his text makes it clear that this love of God for his people is to be considered not in corporate terms only but in individual terms also. Commonly in Scripture it is the larger body of God's people who are under consideration as the objects of his love—the house of Israel in the Old Testament and the church, his bride, the Lamb's wife, in the New Testament. And in such passages individuals, of course, share in God's love but only as they are part of the larger body: with some noted exceptions (Ps. 73:27; Rom. 7:4), the notion of love for the individual is generally not as prominent. But here the reference is explicitly individual—it is the individual believer who is warned of the stirrings of God's loving jealousy in view of the believer's unfaithfulness to him.

The primary contribution of this text, however, is that it directly attributes this love of God for his people to the Holy Spirit. In this respect, the text is almost unique. In the Old Testament it is the Lord, the covenant God, who stands in covenant marriage union with his people Israel and who is jealous over their loyalty. In the New Testament it is Christ the Lamb who loves and cherishes the church and has taken her to be his bride. But in this passage it is God the Holy Spirit who is said to love with yearning affection. God has given his Spirit to dwell within, and he dwells within in passionate love for us and with jealousy for our loyal affection.

On the one hand, this should not surprise us, for the persons of the triune God cannot be divided but always act in concert with one another. To say "God is love" is necessarily to confess the same each of Father, Son, and Spirit. But this particular emphasis is immensely useful in that it forces to our attention the love of the Holy Spirit for us—a notion that is not commonly given due consideration. We often give thanks to the Father for sending his Son in love to save us (John 3:16–17; 1 John 4:10; Rom. 5:10) and for loving us such that we are given the privilege of being his children (1 John 3:1). And we commonly rejoice in the great love of Christ in giving himself for us (Eph. 5:2; 1 John 3:16). These glorious truths we

---

[55]*PGS*, 129–30.

never let escape us. But to draw comfort from this clearly revealed truth, tha
Holy Spirit, who dwells within us, loves us also—this is too seldom the experience of the believer. Yet here it is for us, Warfield exclaims, intended for our use
in just this way (cf. Rom. 15:30). And what a glorious thought it is,

> that the Spirit of all holiness is willing to visit such polluted hearts as ours, and
> even to dwell in them, to make them His home, to work ceaselessly and patiently
> with them, gradually wooing them—through many groanings and many trials—to
> slow and tentative efforts toward good; and never leaving them until, through His
> constant grace, they have been won entirely to put off the old man and put on the
> new man and to stand new creatures before the face of their Father God and their
> Redeemer Christ. Surely herein is love! . . . [and] what immense riches of comfort
> and joy this great truth has in it for our souls![56]

What but his love for us could explain the Spirit's constant pursuit of us even in
our most determined unfaithfulness? What love this is that outlives our shameful
disregard and backslidings. "It is only because the Spirit which He hath caused
to dwell in us yearneth for us even unto jealous envy, that He is able to continue
His gracious work of drawing our souls to God amid the incredible oppositions
we give to His holy work." And, in turn, what a great incentive to holiness this is.
How could we "dally with sin" and "forget our covenanted duties to God" when
we know that God the Spirit, dwelling within, lovingly pursues us with jealous
envy?[57]

From here Warfield proceeds to explore this love more fully in light of the fact
that the Spirit is given to "indwell" us. "See how close the love of God is brought
to us. It is made to throb in our very hearts; to be shed abroad within us; and to
work subtly upon us, drawing us to itself, from within." In light of this we may
understand more clearly Paul's declaration that the flesh wars against the Spirit
and the Spirit against the flesh (Gal. 5:17). Paul portrays the Spirit as part of our
own very being, striving from within to keep us to himself and from sin. Again,
this enables us better to understand Paul's declaration in Romans 8:26 that the
Spirit of God makes intercession for us with groanings of love, when we do not
know what to pray for.[58] The Spirit's coming to us is not a temporary sojourn. He
has not come to visit but to abide with us, to make his home within us, to settle in
and make us his permanent dwelling. God has not covenanted with us halfheart-
edly. He takes us as his wife in permanent and not merely temporary union. He

[56]*PGS*, 138.
[57]*PGS*, 139–40; *SSW*, 2:723.
[58]*PGS*, 140–41.

has come to abide in us forever, and his love for us is so great that from within he continuously pursues us, even through our sin. Though we run from him at times, he does not abandon us to ourselves, but remaining with us he strives within to woo us back to himself. His jealous love is undying and relentless. Indeed, it is precisely because we have fallen into such loving hands as these that we have hope for life and for eternity. He will not let us go but will always strive longingly and persistently from within us to keep us for himself.

This is the love of God the Spirit for us. "Could there be given us a higher incentive to faithfulness to God than is contained in this revelation of the love of the Spirit for us?" Warfield asks rhetorically. "Could there be afforded us a deeper ground of encouragement in our Christian life than is contained in this revelation of the love of the Spirit for us? . . . Could there, then, be granted us a firmer foundation for the holy joy of Christian assurance?"[59] That is to say, the love of the Holy Spirit for us is an exhilarating love, a sanctifying love, an enduring love, and therefore an assuring love.

THE LEADING OF THE SPIRIT

Warfield complains that while the doctrine of the leading of the Spirit has been much spoken of, it seems to be little understood. Too often it is understood to refer to a supposed mystical guiding of the Spirit in matters of, say, business, decision making, and the like. But none of this approximates the biblical description of this ministry of the Holy Spirit. Romans 8:14 is the sole passage that speaks directly to the issue: "For all who are led by the Spirit of God are sons of God." The verse is almost without parallel in the New Testament, the only other being Galatians 5:18, where in a similar context Paul again employs the same phrase: "But if you are led by the Spirit, you are not under the law." These two passages, almost entirely alone, provide definition of this doctrine.

First of all, Warfield points out, Romans 8:14 makes it pointedly clear that this "leading of the Spirit" is not a ministry reserved for eminent saints only. It is a ministry of the Spirit that is common to all God's children: "All who are led by the Spirit of God are sons of God." This, indeed, is what differentiates the children of God from all others, which is the apostle's point in verse 9: "Anyone who does not have the Spirit of Christ does not belong to him." It is entirely mistaken to refer this ministry to special sanctity or such. This ministry "is not the reward of special spiritual attainment; it is the condition of all spiritual attainment."

---

[59] *PGS*, 147–48.

Without it we would remain hopelessly the children of the Devil, and only by this are we enabled to cry, "Abba, Father."[60]

Next, the purpose of this leading is not to escape difficulties or sufferings but specifically to enable us to overcome sin. In the previous passage Paul describes our inherent sin and its effects in us, and he answers this problem by pointing us to the Spirit of God dwelling within, giving new life, freeing us from bondage to sin, and bringing us to live no longer as debtors to the flesh. He implants a new principle of life, which becomes a new ruling power over us, leading us to holiness. This "leading of the Spirit," then, is simply a synonym for the process of sanctification. Far from a leading of eminent saints in business and other such decisions, this ministry is given to all God's children in order to transform them and lead them in the paths of holiness and truth.[61]

Finally, this leading of the Spirit, Paul says, is not sporadic, given on special occasions of special need or direction, but continuously affecting the Christian throughout the whole of his life. Its only object is the eradication of sin, leading to holiness, and therefore it has bearing on every activity of every kind—physical, intellectual, and spiritual. It is simply the power of God unto salvation at work in the believer, constantly leading to the goal of sanctification.[62]

Warfield expands, or rather, more carefully defines the matter with the following observations: First, he stresses the "extraneousness" of this influence. Something can be "led" only by an influence distinct from itself, and Paul's language here emphasizes this distinction. It is the Spirit of God, he says, who "leads" God's children. It is not merely the success of our higher, regenerate powers over the remnants of the old man yet lingering in us. Nothing other than the Spirit of God brings the heart into subjection. This is the significance of the corresponding terms "natural" or "self-led" man, and "spiritual" or "Spirit-led" man. Our progress in godliness, the apostle affirms, is due specifically to the supernatural influence of the Holy Spirit.[63]

Second, Romans 8:14 emphasizes the "controlling power" of the Spirit's influence on the children of God. The Spirit is not a mere guide, pointing the way in which we should go. Nor is he a mere leader, going before us in the way or even commanding the way. Nor does he merely uphold us as we ourselves determine the way in which we should go. The language speaks of controlling influence. The word "led," which the apostle uses here, is used also of leading animals (Matt. 21:2), leading the helplessly sick (Luke 10:34; 18:40), and of leading prisoners

---

[60]*PGS*, 153–55; *W*, 8:122–24.
[61]*PGS*, 155–58.
[62]*PGS*, 158–60.
[63]*PGS*, 160–62.

18:28; Acts 6:12; 9:2). The term may be used in such a way that the idea of force retires somewhat into the background (Acts 9:2; John 1:42). "Yet the proper meaning of the word includes the idea of control, and the implication of prevailing determination of action never wholly leaves it." That is to say, the "leading" influence of the Spirit in the lives of God's children is a controlling influence. An outside power has come to our hearts to bring us to the attainment of holiness. He does not merely suggest this way to go. Nor does he merely point the way we ought to go. Nor does he merely rouse in our minds certain inducements toward righteousness. Rather he has taken the helm to bring us to holiness. We were formerly slaves to sin, but a new power has come upon us and broken that bondage— not that we should now be left to make the way ourselves, but that we should be "powerfully directed" on the course set for us. Accordingly, the apostle tells us that although we have been emancipated from bondage, we are still bound—not to the flesh but to the Spirit—to live after the Spirit. In brief, the believer is under a new power, a new and beneficent control. There is One dwelling within us who has come to rule, to lead us in the way God would have us go.[64]

Apparently out of concern to avoid certain "higher life" teachings, Warfield cautions that this new power is not a substitute for our power: it is merely a new ruling, dominating power. To be "led" is not to be carried. The Holy Spirit "carried along" the prophets in their writing of Scripture (2 Pet. 1:21), but in "leading" his children he controls their action, "yet it is by their effort they advance to the determined end." The believer is not purely passive. Rather, under the controlling influence of the Spirit the believer strives to attain the goal while the controlling and sanctifying Spirit "supplies the entire directing impulse." The prophets could not be exhorted to "work out their own messages with fear and trembling"—the Spirit of God "carried" them along for exactly this purpose. But the child of God is commanded to work out his own salvation with fear and trembling precisely because the Spirit of God within is influencing him to that end (Phil. 2:12–13). Under his control we walk the path he has set for us. "It is His part to keep us in the path and to bring us at length to the goal. But it is we who tread every step of the way." Weary and faint as we may become along the way, we continue under the Spirit's enabling control.[65]

Warfield concludes with a note of joy and praise for the "strong consolation" that is found for us in this "gracious assurance." It is designed to minister comfort and encouragement. Poor and weak as we are, we may fear that sin is too powerful for us. But the Holy Spirit is more powerful, and we need not despair,

---

[64]*PGS*, 162–67.
[65]*PGS*, 167–72.

for he leads us. "If God be for us, who can be against us." "Sin has a dreadful grasp upon us; we have no power to withstand it. But there enters our hearts a power not ourselves making for righteousness. This power is the Spirit of the most high God." We must then move forward not in despair but in hope and in expectation of triumph, for the victory is assured. "The Holy Spirit within us cannot fail us," however rough may be the way we must tread. Under his influence the holiness God demands of us will be realized.[66]

SPIRITUAL STRENGTHENING

Very closely related to this is the notion of "spiritual strengthening" of which the apostle Paul speaks in Ephesians 3:16. This ministry of the Spirit includes both the idea of "spiritual" as distinguished from physical strengthening and the idea of strengthening by the Holy Spirit as distinguished from any earthly agency. Paul's prayer here is for divine inner strengthening ministered by the Spirit of God.

This spiritual strengthening, Warfield explains, "is identical with" the abiding of Christ in our hearts by faith (v. 17).[67] Of emphasis here is not the coming or arrival of Christ in the heart but his abiding. Christ has already arrived in believers' hearts, and Paul is praying that he will abide. Paul is not praying that his readers will be converted; assuming they are, he prays for their spiritual strengthening, and this he describes in terms of Christ's abiding in their hearts. More precisely, their spiritual strengthening is dependent on the abiding of Christ in their hearts by faith—this is its source. Anyone who has read his New Testament, however, understands immediately that Paul is here speaking of the Holy Spirit. It is by the Spirit, the executive of the Godhead, that Christ indwells the heart, and the two, in this sense, are "one and the same great fact." But Paul's point is that Christ is the ultimate source and ground of the believer's spiritual strength. Still it is the Spirit himself who strengthens us (v. 16). So Warfield summarizes, "He so strengthens us that He gives us 'might' in our inner man. The way He does this is by forming Christ within us."[68]

This strengthening, in turn, is accomplished as the Spirit increases our apprehension of spiritual things (vv. 17–19). Enlarging our grasp of the immeasurable love of Christ for us, the Spirit brings us to greater levels of spiritual attainment. By increasing our apprehension of Christ's love, he pours a sense of his love into our hearts, and thus—having grounded us firmly in this widening grasp of the love of Christ—he increases our spiritual strength. This strength enables us to

---

[66]*PGS*, 172–79.
[67]Or "issues in" the abiding of Christ in the heart by faith, depending on how the infinitive clause is to be understood. In either case, Warfield argues, the point to be noted is the abiding of Christ in the heart.
[68]*FL*, 268–70.

grasp spiritual truth by which, in turn, he gives us increased spiritual strength until finally we are made like him—"filled with all the fullness of God" (v. 19).[69]

THE SPIRIT'S HELP IN OUR PRAYING

In the eighth chapter of Romans the apostle Paul is addressing the difficulty that attends the Christian life in a world of sin and curse, a difficulty made still more difficult by reason of our own weaknesses. Yet the exhortation is to persever-ance, and the apostle's object in large part is to encourage the saints by means of a reminder of the ever-continuing help of the Spirit of God within them. One example of this help is his role in our praying:

> Likewise the Spirit helps us in our weakness. For we do not know what to pray for as we ought, but the Spirit himself intercedes for us with groanings too deep for words. And he who searches hearts knows what is the mind of the Spirit, because the Spirit intercedes for the saints according to the will of God. (Rom. 8:26–27)

Prayer is the "vital breath" of the Christian. Indeed, in such fallen conditions as these days of distress the Christian must "live by prayer." The encouragement Paul offers is the affirmation that the Holy Spirit puts words to our prayers that are fitting and thus effective. He works within us to ensure that we ask God for what we really need so that we will obtain what we ask. In our weakness we do not know what we should rightly pray for, nor do we pray with due fervency. Even in our sincerity we fail and do not know how to pray. Besides our mere "weaknesses," we also have our remaining sin with all its recalcitrance. But by the Spirit of God working in our hearts, we are led to pray aright "in matter and manner" so that our petitions "are rendered acceptable to God, as being according to His will."[70]

The Spirit helps us in praying by making this "intercession for us with groan-ings that cannot be uttered." This intercession, Warfield argues, is not an objec-tive intercession made in heaven for us, as Christ intercedes—the intercession "is known to God not as God in heaven, but as 'searcher of hearts.'" Again, it is "not an intercession through us as conduits" who are ourselves unengaged. "It is an intercession made by the Spirit as our helper and not as our substitute." This groaning intercession is made by the Spirit "over and above" our own praying. That is, he works within so as to bring us to see rightly what we need and to shape our prayers accordingly. "They are our desires, and our groans. But not apart from the Spirit. They are His; wrought in us by Him." And thus by his hidden, inner

---

[69] FL, 270–78.
[70] FL, 193, 197–99; SSW, 2:706.

working in us, to frame our thoughts, we are brought to pray according to the will of God.[71]

Warfield asks in conclusion, "Is not this a very present help in time of trouble?"[72] Surely, in the ministry of the Holy Spirit, God has given a fulness of provision for all that he requires of us.

The Miraculous Gifts of the Spirit

SUPERNATURAL GIFTS AS APOSTOLIC CREDENTIALS

In regard to miracles Warfield perceived error on several fronts. The rise of modernism in his day had led to a widespread doubt and even outright denial of the supernatural in the New Testament, including its claims to Jesus' miracles. And Warfield opposed this surrender to naturalism vigorously. On another side was the growing influence of Roman Catholicism and its claims to the miraculous. And on yet another side was the recent arrival and rise of Pentecostalism and its accompanying gifts of faith healing and tongues speaking, a debate that spilled into Warfield's own Presbyterian Church, as highlighted in a series of articles in the *Princeton Review*.[73] Against the first, Warfield argues that their position is grounded in a naturalistic presupposition that is contravened by the historical evidence.[74] He devotes attention to the latter two in his book discussing the question of the continuation of the miraculous gifts, and the title he gives the book, *Counterfeit Miracles*, reveals immediately the answer he gives the question.[75]

In *Counterfeit Miracles*, originally a series of lectures presented at Columbia Theological Seminary (South Carolina) in 1917, during one of Warfield's rare appearances away from Princeton, Warfield makes a distinction between the "ordinary" and "extraordinary" gifts, or the nonmiraculous and miraculous gifts respectively. His purpose is to trace out at length the claims to miraculous gifts through the decades and then the centuries following the apostles in order to demonstrate that the extraordinary gifts ceased in the apostolic age. To underline the point, Warfield focuses not on biblical or apostolic miracles but on specifically postapostolic or postbiblical miracles. His argument is essentially twofold. Foundationally but

---

[71]*FL*, 199–201.

[72]*FL*, 200.

[73]Marvin R. Vincent, "Modern Miracles," *PRR* 4, no. 15 (1883): 473–502; Dr. R. L. Stanton, "Healing Through Faith," *PRR* 5, no. 17 (1884): 49–79; Marvin R. Vincent, "Dr. Stanton on 'Healing Through Faith,'" *PRR* 5, no. 18 (1884): 305–29.

[74]*SSW*, 2:167–204.

[75]In some later (posthumous) publications of *Counterfeit Miracles*, the title was changed to *Miracles: Yesterday and Today, True and False.*

only briefly he argues from the New Testament that the miraculous gifts, though themselves revelatory, were primarily apostolic credentials, signs of the apostles' office given to establish their authority and credibility.[76] He does not argue that only the apostles possessed such gifts; to the contrary, Warfield contends that the exercise of such gifts was the norm in the apostolic churches. But he insists that these gifts were apostolic or apostolically given and that in either case they serve as apostolic credentials (2 Cor. 12:12; Heb. 2:4; cf. Acts 2:43; Gal. 3:5). Second, his book is primarily a historical study in which he surveys the time following the apostles to demonstrate that history indeed testifies to this point of doctrine, that immediately following the time of the apostles these gifts died out, and that subsequent claims were either mistaken or fraudulent.

By way of clarification it is helpful to recognize that Warfield does not argue that *miracles* have ceased. His argument is that the miraculous *gifts* have ceased. As he summarizes:

> And now let us very briefly sum up from our own point of view what it seems that we ought to think of Faith Healing. First of all, as regards the *status quaestionis*, let it be remembered that the question is not: (1) Whether God answers prayer; nor (2) whether, in answer to prayer, He heals the sick; nor (3) whether His action in healing the sick is a supernatural act; nor (4) whether the supernaturalness of the act may be so apparent as to demonstrate God's activity in it to all right thinking minds conversant with the facts. All this we all believe.[77]

"We believe in a wonder-working God; but not in a wonder-working church," Warfield asserts. And again, "All Christians believe in healing in answer to prayer." He agrees heartily that God still may intervene in human affairs and that he may do so miraculously. But this is not to say that God still gives this power to his people as he did to the apostles, and it is this that Warfield denies.[78]

The general consensus in Warfield's day, arising especially within Anglicanism, was that the miraculous gifts died out gradually over the succeeding decades after the apostles, finally becoming extinct at or about the time of Constantine (c. 313) once the church was established. These gifts, under this view, were given in order to aid in the advance of the gospel and the extension of the church during its infancy. But Warfield argues that there is not a word of support for this view in the New Testament. And this view has no principled explanation for the cessation of the gifts in the fourth century, for if their purpose was to aid in the

---

[76]CM, 21, 24–25; "Miracle," in *Davis Bible Dictionary* (Philadelphia: Westminster Press, 1917), 505; "The Christian Doctrine of Revelation," *The New York Observer* 73 (July 4, 1895): 4–5; W, 1:47.
[77]CM, 192.
[78]CM, 58, 187, 192–93.

establishment of the church in the Roman Empire, then why would they not continue today as the church makes its advance in other places? Warfield argues that this view is grounded in assumption and the bias of previous teaching, and the facts of history militate against it absolutely. The historical facts demonstrate that the miraculous gifts, so far from dying out gradually, died out in the time immediately following the apostles, and this adds historical confirmation to the New Testament teaching that they were given specifically as apostolic credentials. Historical sources further establish, Warfield argues, that soon after this period of "silence," claims to the miraculous did not gradually decline but began to increase—in number and in extravagance—as the years passed.

> There is little or no evidence at all for miracle working during the first fifty years of the post-Apostolic church; it is slight and unimportant for the next fifty years; it grows more abundant during the next century (the third); and it becomes abundant and precise only in the fourth century, to increase still further in the fifth and beyond.

Warfield explains further:

> The writings of the so-called Apostolic Fathers contain no clear and certain allusions to miracle working or to the exercise of the charismatic gifts, contemporaneously with themselves. These writers inculcate the elements of Christian living in a spirit so simple and sober as to be worthy of their place as the immediate followers of the Apostles. Their anxiety with reference to themselves seems to be lest they should be esteemed overmuch and confounded in their pretensions with the Apostles, rather than to press claims to station, dignity, or powers similar to theirs. So characteristic is this sobriety of attitude of their age, that the occurrence of accounts of miracles in the letter of the church of Smyrna narrating the story of the martyrdom of Polycarp is a recognized difficulty in the way of admitting the genuineness of that letter.[79]

Examining these earliest claims to miracles, Warfield finds problems of credibility. Some of these claims are merely broad assertions without reference to specific cases and for which no other witness exists (Justin Martyr).[80] Sometimes even the given writer making the claim acknowledges that he was only repeating hearsay (Irenaeus). And there are reports of failure, on the part of claimants, to

---

[79]CM, 10–11, 35–36.
[80]Both Colin Brown and L. Philip Barnes, following him, find a weakness in this point of Warfield's argument. If, with Warfield, we are to reject a claim to the miraculous because it lacks many corroborative witnesses, then the resurrection of Lazarus, for example, must be rejected also, for it has only one witness—the apostle John (Colin Brown, *Miracles and the Critical Mind* [Grand Rapids: Eerdmans, 1984], 200–201; L. Philip Barnes, "Miracles, Charismata and Benjamin B. Warfield," *EQ* 67, no. 3 [1995]: 229–30). But of course this objection would not have carried much weight with Warfield, for John's witness comes to us by inspiration of God.

produce an instance or show evidence when challenged to do so (Theophilus of Antioch). And then as the decades pass, claims increase. "And so we pass on to the fourth century in an ever increasing stream, but without a single writer having claimed himself to have wrought a miracle of any kind or having ascribed miracle working to any known name in the church, and without a single instance having been recorded in detail." If these claims are to be accepted, it will only be on the ground of general and unsupported assertions. Warfield argues that some of the claims to miracles beyond the third century are in fact claims not concerning present miracles but past, referring to apostolic times (Eusebius). Indeed, Tertullian and Irenaeus at times speak of miracles as past and as distinctively apostolic. Throughout the years the language of Christian writers reflects a distinct recognition of the apostles in this regard, a tone that indicates an understanding that the apostolic period was unique.[81]

Returning to his foundational point, Warfield finds a ready explanation for this historical observation that the miraculous gifts died out in the years immediately following the apostles. These gifts were apostolic credentials, gifts designed to authenticate them in their capacity as spokesmen for God. This was the purpose of miracles throughout Scripture. The miraculous gifts had not been given continuously but only sporadically in biblical history, and they should not be expected to be given either indiscriminately or continuously. To be sure, others besides the apostles possessed these gifts also, but only those to whom they were communicated by the apostles (cf. Acts 6:8, Stephen; and Acts 8:5–7, Philip). The miraculous gifts "belonged, in a true sense, to the Apostles, and constituted one of the signs of an Apostle" (2 Cor. 12:12; Heb. 2:4; cf. Acts 2:43; Gal. 3:5).[82] And so it should not be surprising that within the generation following the apostles these gifts were noticed to have ceased and came to be spoken of in the past tense (Heb. 2:4).

Warfield acknowledges the exceptions of Acts 2 and Acts 11. "Only in the two great initial instances of the descent of the Spirit at Pentecost and the reception of Cornelius are charismata recorded as conferred without the laying on of the hands of Apostles."[83] But he argues that the case of the Samaritans in Acts 8 is normative and evidently intended by Luke to teach that the miraculous gifts were apostolic in nature and not common to all. The Samaritans were brought into the church by the witness of nonapostles. In other places adding people to the church was the result of apostolic work, and apparently miraculous gifts had

---

[81]*CM*, 12–16.

[82]*CM*, 21, 24–25; "Miracle," 505; "The Christian Doctrine of Revelation," 4–5.

[83]*CM*, 21–22. Warfield notes that Acts 9:12–17 is not an exception, as is sometimes assumed: "Ananias worked a miracle on Paul but did not confer miracle-working powers. Paul's own power of miracle-working was original with him as an Apostle, and not conferred by any one" (*CM*, 245n48).

been conferred by the apostles. But in Acts 8 there was no such apparent presence of the Spirit's miraculous gifts until the apostles came and conferred them. The passage seems intended to make plain that "it was through the laying on of the hands of the Apostles that the Spirit was given" (cf. v. 18). So pronounced was this as an apostolic function that when Simon the sorcerer saw it, he was jealous of the power and offered to purchase it from the apostles (vv. 18–19).

> It could not be more emphatically stated that the Holy Spirit was conferred by the laying on of the hands, specifically of the Apostles, and of the Apostles alone; what Simon is said to have seen is precisely that it was through the laying on of the hands of just the Apostles that the Holy Spirit was given. And there can be no question that it was specifically the extraordinary gifts of the Spirit that were in discussion; no doubt is thrown upon the genuineness of the conversion of the Samaritans; on the contrary, this is taken as a matter of course, and its assumption underlies the whole narrative; it constitutes in fact the very point of the narrative.[84]

Warfield summarizes that this case of the Samaritans is important in three ways. First, it enabled men "to distinguish between the gifts of grace and the gifts of power," without which there would have been a danger of considering as genuinely Christian only those with the miraculous gifts. Second, it emphasizes that the source of the powers was apostolic, apart from whom these gifts could not have been conferred. And third, it further highlights the role of these gifts as authenticating marks of the apostles as founders of the church. Warfield notes that the apostle Paul possessed these same gifts and the authority to confer them, and he stresses again "that in the entire New Testament we meet with no instance of the gifts showing themselves—after the initial instances of Pentecost and Cornelius—where an Apostle had not conveyed them." This connection of the miraculous gifts to the apostles is so obvious that one wonders how it could ever be overlooked. Warfield states his conclusion in a quote from Bishop John Kaye (1783–1853):

> My conclusion then is, that the power of working miracles was not extended beyond the disciples upon whom the Apostles conferred it by the imposition of their hands. As the number of these disciples gradually diminished, the instances of the exercise of miraculous powers became continually less frequent, and ceased entirely at the death of the last individual on whom the hands of the Apostles had been laid. That event would, in the natural course of things, take place before the middle of the second century—at a time when Christianity, having obtained a footing in all

---

[84]CM, 22; W, 9:622–23.

the provinces of the Roman Empire, the miraculous gifts conferred upon the first teachers had performed their appropriate office—that of proving to the world that a new revelation had been given from heaven.[85]

SUPERNATURAL GIFTS AND REVELATION

Pressing further, Warfield contends that the apostolic *charismata* are but an illustration of a yet deeper principle, one that is connected with divine revelation. The miraculous gifts are not a constant fixture in biblical history. Nor do they appear here and there vagrantly or without discernable purpose. Rather, these gifts appear at revelatory periods of redemptive history "when God is speaking to His people through accredited messengers." These periods of miracles are witnessed with (1) Moses and Joshua, in the exodus and entrance into the Promised Land; (2) Elijah and Elisha, in the struggle for the survival of true religion against false; (3) Daniel and his companions, when God confirms the faith of his people while they are in heathen exile; and (4) Christ and his apostles, in the attesting of Christ and the establishing of the Christian faith.[86] That is, miracles serve to vindicate the messenger, and that in order to validate the message he gives. This is just the pattern of the miraculous in Scripture.

Jon Ruthven subjects Warfield's cessationism to an extended critique from a Pentecostal perspective,[87] and while it is not our purpose here to defend either Warfield or Ruthven, it may be helpful to point out that at several points Ruthven seems to confuse Warfield's denial of the continuance of the miraculous *gifts* with a denial of postbiblical miracles altogether. Ruthven's failure to grasp this distinction is evident, for example, when he cites Jeremiah 32:20 to refute Warfield's claim that miracle workers appear only occasionally and in certain periods of biblical history. The prophet says, "You [God] performed miraculous signs and wonders in Egypt and *have continued them to this day*, both in Israel and among all mankind and have gained the renown that is *still yours*." But this verse does not speak to Warfield's argument, and in citing it as he does Ruthven misses a critical distinction. Warfield's point is that *the ability to perform* miraculous signs—as seen in Moses, Elijah, the apostles—is given only occasionally in the biblical record, and that for the purpose of accrediting God's appointed spokesmen and thus establishing the revelation he gives through them.[88]

---

[85]*CM*, 23–24. Cited in John Kaye, *The Ecclesiastical History of the Second and Third Centuries, Illustrated from the Writings of Tertullian*, 3rd ed. (London: F. and J. Rivington, 1845), 98ff.

[86]*CM*, 25–26; "Miracle," 505.

[87]Jon Ruthven, *On the Cessation of the Charismata: The Protestant Polemic on Postbiblical Miracles* (Sheffield: Sheffield Academic, 1993).

[88]Ibid., 73 (his emphasis). Barnes misses this distinction also in "Miracles, Charismata and Benjamin B. Warfield," 233–35.

This being the case, the rich abundance of the miraculous in the apostolic period displays that age as one marked prominently by revelation from God. In turn, one would expect that when this period of revelation closed, its accompanying signs would also cease. Though one might assume, with the mystic, that God would reveal himself atomistically to each individual throughout the course of history, this simply has not been God's way. "He has chosen rather to deal with the race in its entirety, and to give to this race His complete revelation of Himself in an organic whole." And once this revelation was made, further revelation was no longer needed. Citing John Calvin, Warfield asserts that it would be unreasonable to seek miracles where there is no new gospel. And he enlists the support of Abraham Kuyper and Herman Bavinck to the same effect: once this new revelation was given and then attested to by supernatural gifts, its attesting gifts were withdrawn as the one complete and vindicated revelation was left to be disseminated throughout the world.[89]

What is important for Warfield is that in Christ (and by extension, his apostles) there is a final completeness to divine revelation. Borrowing from Bavinck, he presses the point further.

> Had any miracles perchance occurred beyond the Apostolic age they would be without significance; mere occurrences with no universal meaning. What is important is that "the Holy Scriptures teach clearly that the complete revelation of God is given in Christ, and that the Holy Spirit who is poured out on the people of God has come solely in order to glorify Christ and to take of the things of Christ." Because Christ is all in all, and all revelation and redemption alike are summed up in Him, it would be inconceivable that either revelation or its accompanying signs should continue after the completion of that great revelation with its accrediting works, by which Christ has been established in His rightful place as the culmination and climax and all inclusive summary of the saving revelation of God, the sole and sufficient redeemer of His people.[90]

CHRISTIAN CLAIMS TO THE MIRACULOUS

Next Warfield turns to miraculous claims from all the following centuries of the church. A brief summary of this largely historical analysis will suffice here. As he analyzes the claims to the miraculous in the Middle Ages and the Roman Catholic Church, Warfield finds, first, that the claims are never made by the (supposed) miracle worker himself. They are made by others. This silence on the part of purported miracle workers is strange in light of the biblical precedent in which Jesus and Paul pointed to their works as attesting to their veracity. It is also strange in

---

[89]*CM*, 25–27.
[90]*CM*, 27–28. Citation from Bavinck's *Gereformeerde Dogmatiek*.

that some of the alleged miracle workers themselves speak of miracles on the part of others, still making no mention of their own and leaving us to learn of them only from later writers. Second, Warfield finds that some, such as Augustine, claim miracles for others, but this only years after the fact and after denying the same in the intervening years. Third, Warfield finds that in this period the miracles stories unmistakably represent heathen modes of miracle working and seem certainly to have arisen from pagan notions and practices infused into Christianity. Fourth, the supposed miracles entail ridiculous and self-contradictory notions, many of which stories are clearly lifted out of paganism and given a Christian name. And finally, Warfield argues that many claims must be dismissed on other doctrinal grounds—involving as they do notions that are clearly inconsistent with biblical teaching. All this renders the historical claims to miraculous gifts distinctly unreliable.[91] Warfield treats the Irvingite claims and those of the faith healers in a similar way, often pointing out how the outlandishness of their claims discredited them within the experience and lifetime of their adherents.[92]

BIBLICAL QUESTIONS

Ruthven faults Warfield for the paucity of specifically biblical argument in defense of the thesis of his lectures recorded in *Counterfeit Miracles*. This may indeed be a weakness of the book when considered in light of the larger argument. It would certainly be helpful for our purposes to have extended exposition from Warfield of the related biblical passages. But the purpose of Warfield's lectures was primarily historical, and so it would seem unfair to fault him for following his intent.[93] And in his fifth lecture ("Faith Healing"), Warfield does take up several lines of biblical argument, if only briefly.

In *The Ministry of Healing, or Miracles of Cure in All Ages*, A. J. Gordon (1836–1895) appeals to three primary biblical passages in support of the continuance of the gift of healing. The first, Mark 16:17–18, Warfield rules out of court at the outset on grounds that the passage is spurious. Still the authority in textual criticism, Warfield speaks with complete confidence on this score: "The passage is uncanonical and of uninspired origin." He adds further that it is a good thing for us that these verses are not genuine, for if they were, they would raise serious questions as to the faith of virtually all Christians. "These signs" of tongues, healing, and drinking poison innocuously are said here to accompany *all* believers. "I should

---

[91]*CM*, 35–69, 73–124.
[92]*CM*, 127–53, 157–96.
[93]Ruthven, *On the Cessation of the Charismata*, 92–93. Ironically, although Warfield's focus is historical, and although this occupies the largest part of Warfield's work, Ruthven provides no analysis of Warfield on this score.

not like to have the genuineness of my faith made dependent" on these things, Warfield remarks. Moreover, he points to a resulting contradiction: other biblical teaching makes it plain that "these signs" follow not believers, merely, but those on whom the apostles laid their hands.[94]

The next passage Warfield takes from Gordon's biblical defense is James 5:14–15, which Warfield immediately dismisses as irrelevant to the discussion. The passage merely exhorts Christians to be Christian in their sickness as well as in their health. There is little if anything in the passage that is exceptional to ordinary Christian experience—prayer for healing, church involvement, the care of the elders, and so on—and this with the accompanying promise that God heals in response to the prayers of his people. The emphasis in the passage is not on the anointing with oil—"that is a mere circumstantial detail, thrown in by the way." Rather, "The emphasis falls wholly on the sick man's getting himself prayed for officially by the elders of the church, and the promise is suspended wholly on their prayer, on the supposition that it is offered in faith." And the anointing with oil Warfield takes in a medicinal sense. Oil was a universal medicine in the day, and the word for anointing is not the ceremonial term but the term meaning "to rub." The exhortation is to offer medical help while looking to the Lord for healing. But even if the oil is symbolic of the Holy Spirit and the anointing a ceremonial rite, there is no exclusion here of the ordinary medical attention. More to the point, there is nothing of miraculous gifts. God heals in answer to prayer, and that is the promise this passage makes.[95]

Elsewhere Warfield speaks more specifically in regard to "the prayer of faith." He emphasizes that faith is the only subjective condition for answer to this prayer for healing. "He that prays in faith shall surely receive. For faith can no more fail in prayer than in salvation." This of course demands clarification, and so Warfield continues: "If any one is puzzled by so unlimited a promise, let him reflect what faith is and whence faith comes. If faith is the gift of God in this sphere, too—as assuredly it is—then faith can no more fail than the God who gives it can fail." Surely God will not mock us by working faith in us by his Spirit, only to refuse its request. But the prayer that is offered in this God-wrought faith is what is promised to be effective. "Man-made faith" of course may fail, "for that is no faith at all." But this prayer of "God-inspired faith" will infallibly be heard. Warfield likens this to Romans 8:26 and the Spirit's intercession in prayer. And he suggests a further hint of it here, paraphrasing James's assurance, that it is "energized prayer" that is

---

[94]*CM*, 167–69. Cf. Warfield, "The Genuineness of Mark 16:9–20," *Sunday School Times* 24, no. 48 (1882): 755–56; "Inspiration and the Spurious Verses at the End of Mark," *Sunday School Times* 25, no. 3 (1883): 36–37; "Are the Last Twelve Verses of Mark Part of 'The Word of God'?" *The Presbyterian* 53, no. 3 (1883): 8–9.
[95]*CM*, 169–73.

effective. The gist of the whole matter is that "there is no condition of successful prayer but faith," and effective prayer is only God given.[96]

Warfield does not bother with those biblical passages that speak to instantaneous miraculous cures, because there is no argument from either side on this question. "The question at issue is, whether such miraculous works may still be performed, now that the period of revelation has gone by." The list of gifts in I Corinthians 12 he dismisses as likewise irrelevant, for the question at issue is precisely whether the miraculous gifts are ordinary and to be continued in the church or extraordinary and therefore connected to the apostles. And Warfield finds it surprising that any faith-healer would appeal to John 14:12, in which Christ promises that "greater works" will be witnessed by his followers, for surely no one can claim to have surpassed Christ in miracle working. The promise undoubtedly refers to the promise of the Spirit, fulfilled at Pentecost, by whose power Christ's followers have gone to "conquer the world" in the gospel's advance.[97]

Warfield devotes more attention to Matthew 8:17, where Matthew says that Christ performed miracles of healing "to fulfill what was spoken by the prophet Isaiah: 'He took our illnesses and bore our diseases.'" This verse, Warfield begins, has no direct bearing on the discussion of the continuance or cessation of miraculous gifts. It speaks only of the miracles that Christ performed in the days of his earthly ministry, and it makes not even a hint of miracles his followers might or might not perform. Still, the verse is made by some to bear indirectly on the question by the doctrine it is supposed to teach; namely, that here Christ is presented as not just our sin bearer but also our sickness bearer—that he bore our sicknesses vicariously, as he did our sins, and that he bore them so that we would not ourselves have to bear them. Simply put, Christ is said here to atone for and bear away our illnesses. Warfield finds all this confused. Surely the suggestion is not that disease is a fault for which we are responsible. And if not a fault, then how can it be atoned for? The term used in Isaiah 53 does not mean to "bear away" our sicknesses but to endure them. If it means that he has taken away our sicknesses as our sin, can we now say that there is no disease to them who are in Christ Jesus? And if so, must not we infer, given the inevitability of our eventual demise and decay, that none of us is in Christ Jesus after all? All this Warfield points out as the confusions of this interpretation.[98]

The error of this interpretation does not lie in its supposition that Christ's atoning work entails physical restoration and freedom from disease and suffering, the fruit of sin. This supposition is quite correct. The error lies in confusing

---

[96]*FL*, 435–36.
[97]*CM*, 173–74, 306–7n29.
[98]*CM*, 174–76.

the objective accomplishing of redemption and the subjective effects it has on us, and in failing "to recognize that these subjective effects of redemption are wrought in us gradually and in a definite order."

> Ideally all of Christ's children were saved before the foundation of the world, when they were set upon by God's love, and given by the Father to the Son to be saved by Him. Objectively they were saved when Christ died for them on the tree, purchasing them to Himself by His own precious blood. This salvation was made their personal possession in principle when they were regenerated by the Holy Spirit, purchased for them by the death of Christ in their behalf. It was made over to them judicially on their believing in Christ, in the power of the Holy Spirit thus given to them. But it is completed in them in its full effects only when at the Judgment Day they stand, sanctified souls, clothed in glorified bodies, before the throne of God, meet for the inheritance of the saints in light. Here, you perceive, is a process. Even after we have believed in Christ, and have a title as justified men to the benefits bought for us by His blood and righteousness, entrance into the actual enjoyment of these several benefits remains a process, and a long process, to be completed in a definite order.[99]

That is to say, just as our struggle with sin is ongoing throughout this life, only to be complete in the next life, so also our struggle with diseases and all the fruits of sin. Moreover, we live under the faithful providence of God in a world established by him, a world that is governed, under his providence, by certain forces. And just as we are subject here to the law of gravity, so also we are subject to the sufferings and sicknesses that are common to all men. At any rate, Matthew 8:17 does not in any way offer relief from sickness in this life. "We trust in Him and He keeps us. There is no specific promise that He will keep us otherwise than by His providence and grace. Do not these suffice for all our needs?"[100]

Gordon continues with arguments that are not exegetical in nature but, he believes, grounded in biblically informed reason. He argues first that "if miracles should cease, they would form quite a distinct exception to everything else which the Lord introduced by His ministry." The error here, Warfield argues, lies in the hidden assumptions. If the miraculous gifts were, like baptism and the Lord's Supper, instituted in the church as ordinances of the Christian religion, then they would be expected to continue throughout the church age. But of course they were never so instituted by Christ, and this assumption is unwarranted. Second, Gordon argues that it would seem that if miracles are "signs," it would be expected that they continue. But Warfield points out that this argument proves too much:

---

[99]CM, 176.
[100]CM, 176–80.

all of Christ's miracles were signs; should not then all his miracles, even nature miracles, be the permanent possession of the church? Few would go this far.[101]

Warfield summarizes this section of his argument with a series of assertions:

(1) No promise of such miraculous action on God's part exists in Scripture. (2) No facts have been adduced which will compel the assumption that such miraculous healing takes place. (3) Such a miraculous method of action on God's part would be wholly unnecessary for the production of the effect desired; God can heal the bodily hurt of His people without miracle. (4) The employment of such a method of working would be contrary to the analogy of God's mode of working in other spheres of His activity. (5) It would be contrary to the very purpose of miracle, which would be defeated by it. If miracles are to be common, every day occurrences, normal and not extraordinary, they cease to attract attention, and lose their very reason of existence. What is normal is according to law. If miracles are the law of the Christian life they cease to serve their chief end.[102]

The remaining assertions Warfield expands more fully. (6) He criticizes the continuationist view for overlooking several important related biblical facts, of which Warfield cites two. First is the previously established teaching that the miraculous gifts were apostolic credentials, and if so, the presumption is that the miracles would not continue beyond the apostolic age. Second, the continuationist view fails to account for the cases of sickness in the New Testament that were not healed—Trophimus (2 Tim. 4:20) and Timothy (1 Tim. 5:23). To this Warfield comments that "it seems quite clear that Paul did not share the views of our modern Faith-Healers." (7) He criticizes the faith-healing doctrine for spawning other false doctrines such as the unscriptural equation of sickness and sin, and perfectionism. More to the point, faith healers overlook and at times contradict a biblical view of suffering. Sickness and suffering are often a tool in the hands of God, displaying his favor in chastening and improving the Christian. (8) Warfield criticizes the continuationist view of the gift of miraculous healing as running contrary to God's normal appointed means. And (9), his final proposition criticizes the miracle workers as "professionals" with a priestly function, standing between the believer and God—a fault that in turn leads to spiritual pride and autocracy.[103]

---

[101]CM, 180.
[102]CM, 193.
[103]CM, 194–95.

It [Heb. 2:6–9] begins . . . by adducing the language of the eighth Psalm, in which God is adoringly praised for His goodness to man in endowing him, despite his comparative insignificance, with dominion over the creatures. The psalmist is contemplating the mighty expanse of the evening sky, studded with its orbs of light, among which the moon marches in splendor; and he is filled with a sense of the greatness of the God the work of whose hands all this glory is. "O Lord, our Lord, how excellent is Thy name in all the earth, who hast set Thy glory upon the heavens!" He is lost in wonder that such a God can bear in mind so weak a thing as man. "When I consider Thy heavens, the work of Thy fingers, the moon and the stars, which Thou hast ordained; what is man, that Thou art mindful of him, and the son of man, that Thou visitest him?" But his wonder and adoration reach their climax as he recounts how the Author of all this magnificent universe has not only considered man, but made him lord of it all. In an inextinguishable burst of amazed praise he declares: "Thou hast made him but little lower than the angels, and crownedst him with glory and honor. Thou madest him to have dominion over the works of Thy hands; Thou hast put all things under his feet." . . . So the praise returns upon itself and the Psalm closes with the repeated and now justified exclamation, "O Lord, our Lord, how excellent is Thy name in all the earth!" It is a hymn, you observe, of man's dignity and honor and dominion. God is praised that He has dealt in so wondrous a fashion with mortal man, born from men, that He has elevated him to a position but little lower than that of the angels, crowned him with glory and honor, and given him dominion over all the works of His hands.

PGS, 6–8.

9

ANTHROPOLOGY AND HAMARTIOLOGY

Warfield's writings are not often directed formally to the doctrines of man and sin. The theological context of his day took his attention elsewhere. But there are two leading exceptions to this broad generalization. The first is in reference to the doctrine of sin and, specifically, what Warfield saw as a resurgence of Pelagianism in both liberalism and the perfectionist teachings of otherwise evangelical writers. This concerned him deeply, and he addressed Pelagian thought often, but nearly always in the context of grace and the doctrine of salvation; hence, his thought in this regard will be explored more fully in chapter 10 (soteriology). The other exception is in reference to the question of creation and evolution. The 1859 publication of Darwin's *On the Origin of Species* had brought a revolution of sorts, and its impact on Christian theology was a matter of considerable interest and debate. Warfield maintained a keen interest in the question his entire life and kept himself thoroughly abreast of the literature, both scientific and theological. With some frequency he addressed the subject himself in his lectures, various published articles, and most often in book reviews. Because some have argued that Warfield's position on evolution changed over the years, the dates of his works and respective statements warrant notice here. Matters otherwise related to the doctrines of man and sin are treated here in proportion to the attention Warfield gave them.

The Origin of Man[1]

HISTORICAL CONTEXT

Thoroughly convinced of the supernatural character of Christianity, Warfield was always alert to expose theories with naturalistic tendencies. His interest in the topic

---

[1] Mark Noll and David Livingstone have provided a helpful service to Warfield studies in the collection of Warfield's writings on this theme in their *Evolution, Science, and Scripture*.

of evolution seems to have begun while he was breeding cattle with his father in Kentucky, but his concern for supernaturalism was the driving concern behind his continuing interest in the subject. The Darwinian philosophy was sharply on the rise in Warfield's day, and it increasingly demanded hearing. But its essential naturalism—"atheism," as Warfield's mentor Charles Hodge had famously characterized it—was blatantly anti-Christian. Warfield often stated that it may be possible to hold to biblical Christianity and some form of evolution, but he complained that evolutionism had become more a philosophy than a science, a philosophy that was presuppositionally antisupernaturalistic and explained the whole of existence in specifically naturalistic terms.[2] This would never do. The physical universe, the animals, and man himself were all the result of the creative work of God.

> "In the beginning God created the heaven and the earth." That is the first sentence in the Christian revelation. That God alone is the first and the last, who changes not; that all that exists is the work of his hands and depends on his power for both its existence and its continuance in existence—this is the unvarying teaching of the whole Bible. It is part of the very essence of Christianity, therefore, that the explanation of the universe is found in God; and its fundamental word is, accordingly, "creation."

Whatever common ground might be discoverable between Scripture and the various scientific hypotheses of the day, this much Warfield insisted on throughout his career: "I believe in God almighty, maker of heaven and earth." "The fundamental assertion of the Biblical doctrine of the origin of man is that he owes his being to a creative act of God." By contrast, he remarks:

> Over against the Christian conception there has arisen in our day, however, a movement which has undertaken to explain the world and all that it contains without God, without any reference to any unseen, supernatural, spiritual element. The watchword of this movement is "evolution." And its confession of faith runs, "I believe in an eternal flux and the production of all things out of their precedent conditions through the natural inter-workings of the forces intrinsic to the changing material."[3]

Warfield takes opportunity on several occasions to expose and even scorn this note of naturalism. One of his favorite themes is the folly of assigning to chance what only can be accomplished by cause and design. In 1903 he writes sarcastically:

> Aimless movement in time will produce an ordered world! You might as well suppose that if you stir up a mass of type with a stick long enough, the letters will be found

---

[2]*ESS*, 159–63; cf. *W*, 9:27–29.
[3]*ESS*, 198; *W*, 9:235.

to have arranged themselves in the order in which they stand on the printed pages of Dante's *Inferno*. It will never happen—though you stir for an eternity. And the reason is that such effects do not happen, but are produced only by a cause adequate to them and directed to the end in view. . . . Assuredly, what chance cannot begin to produce in a moment, chance cannot complete the production of in an eternity. . . . What is needed is not time, but cause.

In a 1908 review, after examining the need of the Darwinian hypothesis "to allow time for the evolution of living things," Warfield remarks with ridicule, "When men catch at straws like this to buttress their theories, it becomes clear what a strawy foundation they are building on."[4]

In 1911 he borrows from his 1903 sarcasm and complains that

men seemed to imagine that, if only time enough were given for it, effects, for which no adequate cause could be assigned, might be supposed to come gradually of themselves. Aimless movement was supposed, if time enough were allowed for it, to produce an ordered world. It might as well be supposed that if a box full of printers' types were stirred up long enough with a stick, they could be counted on to arrange themselves in time in the order in which they stand, say, in Kant's "Critique of Pure Reason." They will never do so, though they be stirred to eternity.[5]

At bottom the debate over origins was for Warfield the struggle of naturalism versus supernaturalism. That God is the Maker of all that exists is the fundamental postulate of biblical Christianity. And what is meant by "God" is "a *super*natural God" who is above and beyond nature and not entangled in it, one who is not just "another name for nature in its coordinated activities, or for that mystery which lies beneath and throbs through the All." The Christian God is immanent indeed, but before all else he is the transcendent God who rules and directs as God above all. This God, "the *super*natural God," is our Maker.[6]

Curiously, in Warfield's personal copy of Charles Hodge's *What Is Darwinism?* he (presumably Warfield) has pencil markings highlighting Hodge's remarks as to the naturalistic character of Darwinism, including Hodge's famous conclusion that Darwinism is atheism. Whether Hodge was instrumental in formulating this conviction in Warfield cannot be known, of course, but it was an emphasis in Hodge that Warfield noted and an emphasis that he himself maintained throughout his career.

---

[4]*ESS*, 228–29, 243; *W*, 10:183.
[5]*ESS*, 228–29, 243; *W*, 9:247.
[6]*W*, 9:27–29, 31–33 (emphasis original).

CREATION AND EVOLUTION MUTUALLY EXCLUSIVE

Throughout his career, Warfield sought to clarify that, on the face of it, creation and evolution are mutually exclusive concepts. That is, creation connotes the bringing into existence of something new, something that is not already "in" previously existing forms. Evolution, by contrast, speaks of a development and improvement of previously existing matter. Evolution, by definition, originates nothing; it only modifies. To say "evolution" is to deny creation, and to say "creation" is necessarily to deny evolution. These are "contradictory processes," and "whatever comes by the one process by that very fact does not come by the other. Whatever comes by evolution is not created; whatever is created is not evolved." To speak as some do of evolution as "creation by gradualism" or "creative evolution" is nonsense. Each excludes the other. "You cannot modify by originating; you cannot originate by modifying." This is not to say that there cannot have been both creation *and* (subsequent) evolution, Warfield often concedes, but it is to say that evolution by the very nature of it cannot explain origins. Warfield at times expresses frustration that this basic distinction is not recognized. Evolution, if it occurred at all, is a secondary and later phenomenon. These two issues must not be confused. Evolutionists often completely overlook this fundamental distinction and problem. Even the theistic evolutionist cannot explain ultimate origins in terms of evolution: evolution originates nothing. So far as Christian theology is concerned, Warfield insists that man is not merely improved organic matter. He is a new being resulting from the creative power of God.[7] At these points there is no middle ground between evolution and the Christian faith.

> Christianity demands and must demand also the direct supernatural interference and immediate production by which something new is introduced which the existing matter and forces are incompetent to produce. At this point there is absolute conflict which cannot be compromised. One or the other must be overcome, and in being overcome must be so far discredited.[8]

CREATION, MEDIATE CREATION, AND EVOLUTION

It is important, for Warfield, that we carefully distinguish the concept of mediate creation from both immediate creation and evolution. Immediate creation differs from evolution in that it speaks of origination *ex nihilo*. It is an altogether

---

[7]*ESS*, 201–4; *W*, 10:380; N. W. Harkness, unpublished class notes from Warfield's lectures on systematic theology, 1899–1901 (Princeton Seminary library archives), 2. In his review of Darwin's biography Warfield highlighted Darwin's own frustration on this point, that evolution cannot account for origins. See *ESS*, 103–6.
[8]*ESS*, 125, 200–204, 214–15.

miraculous act of God in which he brings the universe into existence from nothing. "That the act of creation was an immediate operation of God's power without all means is inherent in the very nature of the case."[9] Mediate creation differs from both alternatives in that it speaks of God's miraculously bringing about something *new* out of previously existing matter. In mediate creation God does not merely guide a process of development in such a way that new forms emerge out of the potential already inherent in older forms; that is evolution—modification pure and simple, or perhaps providential guidance. Mediate creation is

> the truly creative acts of God occurring in the course of his providential govern-
> ment by virtue of which something absolutely new is inserted into the complex of
> nature—something for the production of which all that was previously existent in
> nature is inadequate, however wisely and powerfully the course taken may be led and
> governed—something for the production of which there is requisite the immediate
> "flash of the will that can."

These are the three means by which God may have brought about the world order: creation from nothing, mediate creation, and evolution.[10]

THE CHRISTIAN ATTITUDE TOWARD EVOLUTION

With these distinctions held in mind, Warfield advises us concerning the Christian attitude toward evolution. First, he must insist strenuously that evolution cannot explain origins. Evolution can only speak of subsequent modification. He must with equal vigor deny that evolution can take the place of mediate creation. Evolution cannot account for the arrival of matter; within matter it cannot account for the arrival of living beings; it cannot account for the human soul, the human mind, self-consciousness, sin, or the afterlife; and it cannot account for the incarnation of Christ. All of these require a supernatural act of God producing something absolutely new. But with this said, Warfield allows that a Christian as such has "no quarrel with evolution when confined to its own sphere as a suggested account of the method of the divine providence." It should be noted here that Warfield speaks of the Christian's accepting evolution as a "suggested" account of the divine providence. This is the position he maintained throughout his career. Kept in its own place, evolution is not necessarily incompatible with Scripture, *if* at some point it might be demonstrated to be true. He continues his counsel: what the Christian must insist on "is that providence cannot do the work

---

[9] *SSW*, 2:201.
[10] *ESS*, 204–9.

of creation and is not to be permitted to intrude itself into the sphere of creation, much less to crowd creation out of the recognition of man, merely because it puts itself forward under the new name of evolution."[11]

THE ORIGIN OF MAN

Within these options—immediate creation, mediate creation, and evolution—how are we to understand the origin of man? On this question Warfield observes, simply, that the Scriptures teach, and in seemingly more ways than we can count, that man owes his being to the creative act of God. Moreover, this is "the constant presupposition of every portion of Scripture," as well as the express assertion of so many passages. He points for examples to Psalms 8; 89:47; and 119:73. But of course it is in the opening chapters of Genesis that this teaching is presented most plainly.

> So God created man in his own image,
>   in the image of God he created him;
>   male and female he created them. (Gen. 1:27)

"The LORD God formed the man of dust from the ground and breathed into his nostrils the breath of life, and the man became a living creature" (Gen. 2:7). That we owe our existence to God is one of the most basic presuppositions of Scripture and one of the most intimate convictions of our own consciousness. Warfield speaks often and at length of this "ineradicable sense of dependence" we have on God as a result of our creation in his image. Man is not self-created, as modern speculation would have us believe. He is created by God.[12]

But Warfield is willing still to find room for the evolutionist to acknowledge creation, and he reasons that the evolutionist should not need to press his theory so far as to exclude divine, creative activity in the production of something new. That is, even within an evolutionary framework there should be room for mediate creation. Indeed, the biblicist does not require that God's activity in the creation of man is such that excludes all process or interaction with natural factors. Psalm 89:47, for example, declares that God "created all the children of man," and Psalm 119:73 that he fashioned the psalmist himself. "But surely no individual since Adam has been fashioned by the mere fiat of God to the complete exclusion of the interaction of natural forces of reproduction." From this and Genesis 2:7, Warfield concludes, "It does not appear that the emphasis of the biblical assertion that man

---

[11]*ESS*, 209–10; *W*, 10:380–85.
[12]*ESS*, 212.

owes his existence to the creative act of God need therefore exclude the recognition of the interaction of other forces in the process of his formation."[13] Again, this is the position Warfield consistently maintained throughout his career. Whether he himself accepted evolution is a separate question, but he did specifically allow it as a Christian option.

Warfield is careful to say, however, that this option is allowable only so long as one maintains that man originated as the result of God's supernatural creative activity. The Genesis account insists on this. In the creation of man God does not say, "Let the waters or the earth bring forth" as he had said previously. There is no secondary production here. Rather, he says, "Let us make." In the preceding days there is reproduction "after its kind," but "man is set forth as created after the kind of God—'God created man after his own image.'" Man did not arise from below. There was a double act and a double result: man was formed "from the dust of the ground, but he was not so left; rather, God also breathed into his nostrils a breath of life," signaling that there is something about man that comes from above also. No purely evolutionary scheme will suffice here. And having reaffirmed this, Warfield once again allows that "if"—and he always stresses this "if"—the facts demonstrate the reality of an evolutionary process, then it may only be understood within this framework. No evolutionary scheme can find common ground with Scripture until it recognizes that in the arrival of man, God, supernaturally intruding, has created something new.[14]

THE CREDIBILITY OF EVOLUTION

In his classroom lecture on evolution, "Evolution or Development," prepared originally in December 1888 and used repeatedly thereafter, Warfield describes three general positions that can be taken in reference to the question. First, we may take evolution as "an adequate philosophy of being" and "as supplying a complete account of the origin and present state of the universe." That is, we may take the evolutionary theories at face value as an explanation of the facts. This position is tantamount to atheism with a new form of expression. Second, "We may consider the evolutionary hypothesis as a discovery by science of the order and conditions under which the various living forms have as a matter of fact come into existence" and by which forms have been produced. In this way theism is presupposed, and evolution is viewed only in terms of second causes. This was the position of Warfield's earlier mentor at Princeton College, James McCosh—evolution is thoroughly consistent with Christian theism and in fact

---

[13]*ESS*, 213–14.
[14]*ESS*, 215–16.

constitutes the method through which God accomplished the creation. This was evidently the view Warfield held in the days of his undergraduate work. Looking back to the arrival of McCosh at Princeton, Warfield claims to have already been "a Darwinian of the purest water."[15]

Third, we can view the evolutionary hypothesis "as a more or less probable, or a more or less improbable, conjecture of scientific workers as to the method of creation," waiting final verdict on the question while scientists continue to test the theory against the facts. This is the position Warfield takes for himself and recommends to others, and he further advises that we not make any adjustments to our theology to accommodate "what is as yet a more or less doubtful conjecture." Evolution is still on trial, and Warfield says that when McCosh claims that we have the same proof for evolution that we have for Newton's theory of gravitation, "he has allowed his enthusiasm to run away with his judgment." As of yet evolution cannot give account of the facts, and thus it is not yet a scientific theory but a hypothesis. Moreover, if evolution can finally give an account of the facts, it will still be left to determine whether it gives a true accounting of the facts. "I do not assert that [evolution] cannot account for [the facts], but anyone who asserts that it can has certainly overstepped the boundary line of determined fact and made overdue use of his scientific imagination." So much has yet to be demonstrated in this theory that we simply cannot build any theology around it.[16]

Warfield refers to himself as a layman in scientific matters, but throughout his life he maintained a more than curious level of interest in the subject. He had clearly read very widely and carefully, and he was able to speak freely of the varying evolutionary theories, analyzing their differing claims and weighing their respective merits. It is not necessary to survey all his thinking in this regard, but we should note that he did criticize evolution on grounds of the geological record, which, "when taken in its whole scope and in its mass of details is confessed as yet irreconcilable with the theory of development by descent." Likewise he finds the appeal to embryology unable to account for the fact that supposed later stages of development retain a transcript of previous stages. Similarly, Warfield makes much over the seemingly limitless and impossible demands the evolutionary theory makes on time. This, he notes, is becoming more a problem recognized within the evolutionary-scientific community itself. "The matter of time that was a menace to Darwinism at the beginning thus bids fair to become its Waterloo." So also the evolutionist faces difficulty with the "limits to the amount of variation to which any organism is liable." Warfield concludes, "On these and similar

---

[15]*ESS*, 115–16; B. B. Warfield, "Personal Recollections of Princeton Undergraduate Life IV—The Coming of Dr. McCosh," *Princeton Alumni Weekly* 16, no. 28 (1916): 652.
[16]*ESS*, 67, 115–22, 164–69.

grounds I should therefore venture to say that any form of evolution which rests ultimately on the Darwinian idea is very improbable as an account of how God has wrought in producing species."[17]

Warfield speaks often in this vein, insisting throughout his career that evolution remains an unproven hypothesis. But is it not likely that it will be proven? "Is it not at least *probable?*" he asks rhetorically. Cannot prescient minds expect that proof will be forthcoming? He responds: "Many think so; many more would like to think so; but for myself, I am bound to confess that I have not such prescience. Evolution has not yet made the first step" toward explaining many things. "In an unprejudiced way, looking over the proofs evolution has offered, I am bound to say that none of them is at all, to my mind, stringent." Laymen have the right to affirm with confidence that the evolutionary hypothesis remains "far from justified by the reasoning with which it has been supported." If the facts are with the evolutionist, they "have themselves to thank for the impression of unreality and fancifulness which they make on the earnest inquirer." In another place he cautions, "We would not willingly drag behind the evidence, indeed—nor would we willingly run ahead of it." Again, "Most men today know the evolutionary construction of the origin of man; there are many of us who would like to be better instructed as to its proofs."[18] In 1895 he writes mockingly:

Students of logic might obtain some very entertaining examples of fallacy by following the processes of reasoning by which evolutionists sometimes commend their findings to a docile world. . . . Because a possible genealogy can be constructed for a number of forms, chiefly in the upper strata, for which evolution might possibly supply an account, it does not follow that evolution is shown to be the true account of the whole series of forms presented to us in the crust of the earth.[19]

In 1898 he says of evolutionists under review:

If their writers did not put evolution into their premises, they would hardly find so much of it in their conclusions. They all start out with the assumption of evolution as a thing "as universally acknowledged as is gravitation" (p. 2), and supplied long since with "demonstrative evidence" (p. 4); but they oddly enough appear to be still on the outlook for evidence for it, and cannot avoid speaking now and again of valuable material for its establishment (p. 4). This varied attitude toward their fundamental assumption seems to the lay reader not altogether unaccountable. He gets an impres-

---

[17] *ESS*, 122–25; cf. 165–69; *W*, 9:245–51.
[18] *ESS*, 121–22 (emphasis original), 143, 152, 171.
[19] *ESS*, 168.

sion that as greater and greater masses of fact are accumulated, the load is becoming a little too heavy for the original assumption of evolution to carry.[20]

He further writes that laymen

who are more concerned to learn what is true than to adjust an old theory to fit the new facts which may from time to time be brought forward, will not fail to observe that every eon in the infinite past back into which the origin of man is pushed, and every step toward making the lines of descent of the various animal forms more parallel, raises a new difficulty in the path of the prevalent assumptions of evolution. . . . The time has already fully come when the adherents of evolution should do something to make it clear to the lay mind that a full accumulation of facts to prove their case can never come—or else abate a little of the confidence of their primary assumption.[21]

Similarly, he writes in 1908:

What most impresses the layman as he surveys the whole body of these evolutionary theories in the mass is their highly speculative character. If what is called science means careful observation and collection of facts and strict induction from them of the principles governing them, none of these theories have much obvious claim to be scientific. They are speculative hypotheses set forth as possible or conceivable explanations of the facts. . . . For ourselves we confess frankly that the whole body of evolutionary constructions prevalent today impresses us simply as a vast mass of speculation which may or may not prove to have a kernel of truth in it. . . . This looks amazingly like basing facts on theory rather than theory on facts.[22]

Once more, in a 1916 review Warfield speaks optimistically of evolution as demonstrating teleology, design. "Imbedded in the very conception of evolution, therefore, is the conception of end." Here he seems to be more open to evolution. But later in this same review he writes more critically of the woeful lack of proof for it.

The discrediting of [Darwin's] doctrine of natural selection as the sufficient cause of evolution leaves the idea of evolution without proof, so far as he is concerned— leaves it, in a word, just where it was before he took the matter up. And there, speaking broadly, it remains until the present day. . . . Evolution is, then, if a fact, not a triumph of the scientist but one of his toughest problems. He does not know how it

---

[20]ESS, 184–85.
[21]ESS, 186–87.
[22]ESS, 244–46.

has taken place; every guess he makes as to how it has taken place proves inadequate to account for it. His main theories have to be supported by subsidiary theories to make them work at all, and these subsidiary theories by yet more far-reaching subsidiary theories of the second rank—until the whole chart is, like the Ptolemaic chart of the heavens, written over with cycle and epicycle and appears ready to break down by its own weight.[23]

This said, Warfield does not deny but specifically affirms that holding to an evolutionary scheme is not necessarily inconsistent with theism. In "Evolution or Development," Warfield argues that a theist may hold a higher view of the evolutionary process than the deist and see in it all the everywhere-present God accomplishing his will. "But to be a theist and a Christian are different things." This is a distinction Warfield often makes. It is one thing to reason as a theist that God is at work through evolution. It is quite another matter to say that this is consonant with Scripture and with Christian doctrine. Certainly, a thoroughgoing evolutionism is impossible to reconcile with Christianity and its frank supernaturalism. Certainly evolution cannot account for the immaterial human soul, its substantiality, and its persistence in life after the dissolution of the body. So also evolution cannot account for the fact that man is a moral being with a conscience—these are matters inevitably tied up with creation in God's image. Evolution completely reverses the biblical teaching in regard to humanity's fall into sin and posits a moral development. Similarly, evolution cannot address the question of ultimate origins, and it cannot account for the incarnation of Christ. On all these matters evolutionary theories undermine Christian doctrine.[24]

So Warfield cautions that it is not enough to ask whether evolution may be consistent with theism. "The test point," he insists, is whether it is consistent with the Bible in its specific statements and in its related doctrines. He further insists on the priority of God's written Word over the "discoveries" of science.

All statements will find their test in facts, but it does not thence follow that revelation will find its test in science. Science is not fact, but human reading of fact; and any human reading of fact may well bow humbly before the reading given by God. In the conflict between the infallible Word and the "infallible science," it is the part of reason to prefer the word-statement sufficiently authenticated as divine to the word-statement which is obviously very human indeed.[25]

---

[23]*ESS*, 319–20.
[24]*ESS*, 125–29.
[25]*ESS*, 130, 174.

It is God's written Word that provides the touchstone of truth, and all else must be judged by it.

The next question, therefore, is whether evolution may be compatible with Scripture. On this point Warfield says, "The sole passage which appears to bar the way is the very detailed account of the creation of Eve. . . . We may as well admit that the account of the creation of Eve is a very serious bar in the way of a doctrine of creation by evolution." We should note here that Warfield's words are a bit of an overstatement. Perhaps he was thinking of exegetical versus theological barriers, for the account of the creation of Eve was not, in fact, the only bar to evolution that Warfield could see for the Christian. In the previous paragraphs he noted problems such as the origin of the human soul and the afterlife. These matters likewise are irreconcilable with evolution, in Warfield's view. But this only qualifies a bit his next assertion, "that there is no *necessary* antagonism of Christianity to evolution, *provided that* we do not hold to too extreme a form of evolution." He continues:

> To adopt any form that does not permit God freely to work apart from law and that does not allow *miraculous* intervention (in the giving of the soul, in creating Eve, etc.) will entail a great reconstruction of Christian doctrine, and a very great lowering of the detailed authority of the Bible. But if we condition the theory by allowing the constant oversight of God in the whole process, and his occasional supernatural interference for the production of *new* beginnings by an actual output of creative force, producing something *new*, i.e., something not included even *in posse* in the preceding conditions, we may hold to the modified theory of evolution and be Christians in the ordinary orthodox sense.

But just as important to us in discerning Warfield's own view is his next statement: "I say we may do this. Whether we ought to accept evolution, even in this modified sense, is another matter, and I leave it purposely an open question."[26]

CONCLUSION

What then is Warfield's view of the evolution question? We know for certain that he consistently rejects any *purely* evolutionary explanation for the arrival of man, and by this he means especially the human soul. He also rejects as "exegetically untenable" the understanding of the "days" of Genesis 1 as twenty-four-hour days standing at the climax of successive ages of development. With this he also rejects the understanding that the Genesis account concerns the origin only of

---

[26]*ESS*, 130–31 (emphasis original).

those things which man can see, leaving unaddressed the long ages of development previous to man.[27] And in an 1897 review of Methodist theologian Luther Tracy Townsend (1838–1922), Warfield enthusiastically commends the author for rejecting "not merely the naturalistic but also the timidly supernaturalistic answers" as to the origin of man and for insisting "that man came into the world just as the Bible says he did. Prof. Townsend has his feet planted here on the rock." Then Warfield explains his support further:

> When it is a question of scriptural declaration versus human conjecture dignified by any name, whether that of philosophy or that of science, the Christian man will know where his belief is due. . . . [Prof. Townsend's] trust in the affirmations of the Word of God as the end of all strife will commend itself to every Christian heart.[28]

Warfield's adherence to Scripture is obvious.

Although there was an openness on Warfield's part to allowing evolution within a Christian framework, David N. Livingstone misstates the matter in a 1986 article when he says that Warfield "had been a key advocate of evolutionary theory at least since his student days at Princeton."[29] As noted above, Warfield does claim that in his first year at Princeton College, when theistic evolutionist McCosh arrived there as president, Warfield was already "a Darwinian of the purest water." But to allege that Warfield remained a "key advocate" of evolutionism throughout his life is to ignore his own later claims on the subject. Livingstone further claims that Warfield "remained enthusiastic" about the Darwinian theory. But it was particularly the Darwinian theory of evolution that received Warfield's sharpest attacks, and Warfield repeatedly noted that much of the Darwinian theory was being abandoned by scientists of his own day. These claims by Livingstone in 1986 are unwarranted, and it appears that by the time of his later work with Mark A. Noll his enthusiasm for Warfield's supposed continued evolutionism had softened somewhat.[30]

In their later works, Noll and Livingstone argue instead that over the course of his career Warfield came increasingly *again* to embrace the doctrine of evolution. The title of their article published in *The Journal of Presbyterian History* asserts their conclusion with confidence: "B. B. Warfield (1851–1921): A Biblical Inerrantist as Evolutionist." The article begins with the same confident note: "One of the best-kept secrets in American intellectual history is that B. B. Warfield, the foremost modern defender of the theologically conservative doctrine of the inerrancy of

---

[27]*ESS*, 145.
[28]*ESS*, 177–78.
[29]"B. B. Warfield, the Theory of Evolution, and Early Fundamentalism," *EQ* 58, no. 1 (1986): 78–79.
[30]E.g., *ESS*, 26, 29, 34, 41, 66, 183, 237.

the Bible, was also an evolutionist." In an earlier version of the article they imply that the reconciliation of evolution with biblical Calvinism was a "constant goal" of Warfield's throughout his time at Princeton. Uncritically leaning on Livingstone and Noll, Nancy Pearcey also portrays Warfield as an evolutionist without any qualification whatever. Leaning on Noll and Bamberg, Douglas Kelly writes similarly.[31] These representations of Warfield have become commonplace, but they appear to go beyond the evidence. Noll and Livingstone also affirm (rightly) that Warfield allowed the "possibility" of evolution within a Christian framework. They also state that other than in the narrative of Eve's creation, Warfield saw no necessary conflict between evolutionary development and Scripture. But if Warfield allowed for the *possibility* of evolution, and if he did see the narrative of the creation of Eve as standing in the way, on what ground can they say with confidence that Warfield did, in fact, accept evolution as true? Certainly, Warfield did acknowledge on repeated occasions throughout his career that Christian theism is not necessarily incompatible with some kind of evolutionary theory. But he never expressed that he did indeed accept an evolutionary hypothesis as a true accounting of the facts.

The confidence with which Noll and Livingstone speak stems primarily from two considerations. First, in a 1906 review of James Orr's *God's Image in Man*, Warfield notes Orr's argument that disparate development of mind and body is impossible, that it would be absurd to suggest an evolutionary development of the human body from a brutish source and a sudden creation of the soul by divine fiat. Warfield commends Orr's grasp of man as body and soul in unity and refers to this as "the hinge of the biblical anthropology." But always aware that a weak argument never helps a case, Warfield also comments that Orr's argument would lose its force against a theory of evolution *per saltum*—evolution by leaps under the directing hand of God propagating a human body from brutish parents while at the same time creating a soul for that body. In this instance, Warfield argues, God would be understood not as directing organic material to produce something the seeds of which are already in the earlier forms, but as directing an evolution *and* creating something new. Orr's argument did not take into account this possibility, and so it is not as persuasive as Orr seemed to think. But what is important here is that Warfield does not commit himself to the alternative he presents to Orr. He allows it as a possibility in order to demonstrate that Orr's argument fell short,

[31]David Livingstone and Mark Noll, "B. B. Warfield (1851–1921): A Biblical Inerrantist as Evolutionist," *JPH* 80, no. 3 (2002): 153–71; *ESS*, 14; Nancy Pearcey, *Total Truth: Liberating Christianity from Its Cultural Captivity* (Wheaton, IL: Crossway, 2004), 309; *Isis* 91 (2000): 291; Douglas F. Kelly, *Creation and Change* (Fearn Rossshire: Christian Focus, 1997), 140; cf. Stanley Bamberg, "Our Image of Warfield Must Go," *JETS* 34, no. 2 (1991): 230–42; Mark Noll, ed., *The Princeton Theology, 1812–1921* (Grand Rapids: Baker, 1983), 293–94.

but he does not embrace it himself. Neither does he express disagreement with Orr's position. This is how Warfield argues consistently over the course of his career—he allows the possibility of evolution, but he remains noncommittal. Noll and Livingstone overstate the case when they allege that Warfield here "proposed again his combination of evolution and some form of creation to account for the origin of humanity" and that he "had clearly accepted the theological legitimacy of an evolutionary account of the human body." Warfield pointed out a weakness in Orr's argument, and he allowed the possibility of an alternative, but he did not reveal his own commitments. Earlier in the same review, Warfield praised Orr for his "courage to recognize and assert the irreconcilableness of the two views and the impossibility of a compromise between them; he also undertakes the task of showing that the Christian view is the only tenable one in the forum of science itself." Warfield follows this with his evaluative comment: "That he accomplishes this task with distinguished success is the significance of the volume." Certainly these remarks read by themselves would have led Noll and Livingstone to a very different conclusion. The fact is that Warfield did not commit himself here to any evolutionary scheme.[32]

Indeed, at the conclusion of the same review Warfield raises yet another problem with evolution. Orr had remarked that "there is not a word in Scripture to suggest that animals . . . came under the law of death for man's sin." Warfield finds this statement surprising, and he advises that Orr has not thought through the implications of the issue well enough. "The problem of the reign of death in that creation which was cursed for man's sake and which is to be with man delivered from the bondage of corruption, presses on some with a somewhat greater weight than seems here to be recognized."[33] Warfield does not comment further, but he evidently sees the biblical account of death as an obstacle to evolution. Evolutionary theories depend on death in seemingly endless successions prior to man, yet the biblical account is that death has entered the creation only by means of human sin. Interestingly, if Orr was more decidedly opposed to evolution than Warfield, here Warfield provides Orr with more ammunition!

Finally, Warfield closes his review with a broad endorsement of Orr's work.

The book is a distinct contribution to the settlement of the questions with which it deals, and to their settlement in a sane and stable manner. It will come as a boon to

---

[32]*ESS*, 29, 37, 231–33; *W*, 10:136–41. Interestingly, Heslam argues from this quote that this indication of Warfield's increasing *unwillingness* to accept the evolutionary theory was due to the influence of his esteemed friend, the Dutch theologian Abraham Kuyper. Peter S. Heslam, "Architects of Evangelical Intellectual Thought: Abraham Kuyper and Benjamin Warfield," *Themelios* 24, no. 2 (1999): 13–15; also Heslam, *Creating a Christian Worldview: Abraham Kuyper's Lectures on Calvinism* (Grand Rapids: Eerdmans, 1998), 255–56.
[33]*ESS*, 235–36.

many who are oppressed by the persistent pressure upon them of the modern point of view [evolution]. It cannot help producing in the mind of its readers a notable clearing of the air.[34]

It would not seem that this 1906 review provides demonstration of Warfield's supposed acceptance of evolution.

The confidence of Noll and Livingstone in naming Warfield an evolutionist stems, second, from Warfield's 1915 essay on Calvin's doctrine of creation. Warfield surveys Calvin's emphasis that God created by means of second causes. In the beginning he created *ex nihilo*, but in the following days the already existing matter is commanded to "bring forth." Calvin did not teach a doctrine of mediate creation, Warfield argues. He taught, rather, that after the initial creation God brought subsequent things into existence from the previously created matter. This reflects Calvin's high doctrine of providence, the doctrine of *concursus*, which in this context means simply that God created by means of second causes. Warfield concludes that "Calvin's doctrine of creation is . . . for all except the souls of men, an evolutionary one." He goes on to acknowledge that "Calvin doubtless had no theory whatever of evolution; but he teaches a doctrine of evolution. . . . All that is not immediately produced out of nothing is therefore not created—but evolved." Calvin's doctrine was not simply evolutionism but "pure evolutionism."[35]

Warfield's work in all aspects of Calvin studies was exhaustive, and he has been hailed as Calvin's "incomparable American interpreter."[36] But that he represents Calvin accurately at this point is open to question. Indeed, John Murray fairly discredits Warfield on this point.[37] What is significant here, however, is not Warfield's accuracy or inaccuracy in interpreting Calvin. What is significant for our purposes is that whether accurately or not, Warfield does represent Calvin as teaching a doctrine of evolution, and it is quite tempting to see in this a reflection of Warfield's own leanings. To be sure, he never states agreement with Calvin that evolution was the means God used. In fact he asserts plainly that Calvin's position is inadequate within a framework of six natural days. Calvin's view would require these days to be ages, something Calvin does not allow. So Warfield sees inconsistency in Calvin's teaching at this point, as he understands it. Still, it is tempting to see in this interpretation of Calvin at least a possible reflection of Warfield's own evolutionary leanings, even if he does not quite say so. Gundlach suggests that Warfield may have wanted to establish evolution as within the

---

[34]*ESS*, 236.

[35]*W*, 5:303–5.

[36]E.g., *BSac* 92, no. 367 (1935): 358.

[37]John Murray, "Calvin's Doctrine of Creation," *WTJ* 17, no. 1 (1954): 28–42.

bounds of Calvinist orthodoxy, anticipating the possibility that evolution might one day be proven.[38] But Noll and Livingstone are on better ground here. Noll is right to describe this as "Warfield's strongest assertion of evolution."[39] But even so, this is not much.

In another place Warfield might appear to tip his hand in favor of evolution, but the remarks are so brief it is impossible to make much of them. In a review of *Christianity and Evolution* by Scottish theologian James Iverach, Warfield demurs that Iverach has made too much of evolution and too little of God. "Christ is no doubt the great exception" to evolution, Warfield says in agreement, "but," he adds by way of clarification, "he is not the sole exception." He continues, "'Evolution' can in no case be accepted as the formula of all that is; we must in any case rise above it to the higher formula of 'God'—who is more than evolution, who indeed works in evolution, but also out of it." This much sounds as if Warfield is granting evolution as a point of agreement. But these remarks are in 1895, much too early to fit Livingstone and Noll's thesis. Moreover, in the same review Warfield seems to indicate that he grants this merely for the sake of argument: "We say this is true 'in any case'; we intend to leave the impression that we are by no means as sure as is Dr. Iverach of the reality of evolution in the wide range which he gives it. We would not willingly drag behind the evidence, indeed—nor would we willingly run ahead of it."[40]

Something should be noted of the significance of Warfield's lecture "Evolution or Development," first prepared in 1888 for classroom use. Noll and Livingstone have referred to this lecture several times as representing Warfield's most skeptical period concerning evolution, for as cited above, here he perceives it as a "very improbable" theory. Their thesis is that from this most critical point he, through the years, came increasingly to embrace evolution. But it is not likely that this 1888 lecture can be so easily dismissed. Noll and Livingstone themselves point out that Warfield used this lecture repeatedly over the years, making minor adjustments along the way. Some of these later adjustments were additional remarks critical of evolution,[41] as for example a lengthy four paragraphs entitled "Evolution Not Yet Proven."[42] We do not know at what point this addition was made, but it was presumably later than 1888, and it indicates not a waning but a strengthening conviction against evolution. Moreover, although we cannot know how long this lecture was in use, it is the only Warfield lecture on the subject we have. It

---

[38]Bradley John Gundlach, "The Evolution Question at Princeton: 1845–1929" (PhD diss., University of Rochester, 1995), 296.
[39]*Modern Reformation* 7, no. 3 (1998).
[40]*ESS*, 152.
[41]E.g., *ESS*, 125.
[42]*ESS*, 117–18.

was evidently never replaced by another with differing views. Its substance is repeated in subsequent articles, and there is no evidence that leads us to think that Warfield ever abandoned the position outlined in this lecture, as Noll and Livingstone's thesis would lead us to think.

That Warfield actually committed himself to a doctrine of evolution is difficult if not impossible to affirm, simply because, although there are some indications that he entertained the idea, he never admitted to accepting it. More to the point, what he expressly claims is a critical agnosticism on the subject, and it would seem this is where the matter must rest. His agnosticism on the subject is what he states in his lecture prepared in 1888 and given repeatedly over the years, and the same agnosticism is reflected in his student's class notes at the turn of the century. Indeed, these class notes preserve one of Warfield's regular descriptions of evolution—"speculation." This expressed agnosticism is what we find repeated in various reviews over the years and in his more in-depth 1895 article, adapted from his 1888 lecture. In his 1901 and 1903 articles he expresses doubts and is expressly noncommittal. Continuously he speaks of the acceptability of evolution only "if" it were to be demonstrated as true—and that with the emphasis that it has not, in fact, been so demonstrated. He mocks the evolutionist's need for seemingly infinite time as though time were a magic wand to perform the impossible, and he speaks increasingly over the years of various evolutionary theories as losing support even within the scientific community. Granted, it is easiest to read his 1915 article on Calvin as reflecting his own leanings toward evolution, and there are other times also when he seems more open than his critical comments suggest. But as noted above, he lends broad endorsement to Orr's opposition to evolution. And in the 1916 review cited above he specifically and almost mockingly stresses evolution's lack of support. In the same year, he also reports an earlier conversation with McCosh in which McCosh insisted that all biologists under the age of thirty were evolutionists. "I was never quite sure that he understood what I was driving at when I replied that I was the last man in the world to wonder at that, since I was about that old myself before I outgrew it."[43] Warfield's own claim in 1916 is that he had rejected evolutionism by the early 1880s, and significantly, his remark seems to reflect his thinking still in 1916. That is, we are left to think that having outgrown his earlier evolutionism, Warfield claims still to reject it, although remaining open to it. Ironically, Livingstone confidently asserts that "Warfield left the matter an 'open question' in 1888, but there is no mistaking his increasing acceptance of evolutionary theory

---

[43]"Personal Recollections of Princeton Undergraduate Life," 652.

over the years."[44] It would not appear that the evidence supports Livingstone's enthusiasm.

The fact is that Warfield never overtly acknowledges evolution as true. The picture we have of him on this subject is continuously one of noncommittal. What he allows as a possibility both theologically and theoretically—that the Christian as such has "no quarrel with evolution when confined to its own sphere as a suggested account of the method of the divine providence"—he never explicitly endorses. He is not opposed in principle to some kind of evolution, but neither does he explicitly embrace it. He seems intrigued with evolution, and at times he seems willing to embrace it. But at the same time what he says is that he is undecided. And there is at least the hint in his 1916 comments—a year after his Calvin article—that he still has not returned to his earlier evolutionism. Indeed, his failure explicitly to embrace it may well be due to the fact that, as Noll and Livingstone acknowledge, as a "Biblicist," Warfield saw the Eve creation narrative as standing in its way; it would seem that this and related concerns surveyed above continued to stand in its way. This much is clear: although speaking with allowance of evolution at times, Warfield never expressly affirms it. What he explicitly affirms is that he rejected it sometime about age thirty and that he remains unconvinced.

The Antiquity of the Human Race

For all of the dispute theologians may have with evolution regarding man's origin, Warfield contends that the question of the age of man is of no biblical interest or theological consequence. Because the biblical narrative "seems" to convey a relatively short duration of human history, and because a tremendously long period of time is demanded "by certain schools of scientific speculation," the question seems to be of relevance. This appearance of conflict between biblical statements and scientific investigators made it necessary for theologians to investigate the matter. But this conflict is more imaginary than real, for the Bible does not assign a brief span of time to human history, and, Warfield observes, scientists (in his day) are increasingly recognizing that the time of human history cannot be as open-ended as some have thought. The conflict is an illusion.

Warfield concedes that a first reading of the genealogies of Genesis 5 and 11 would leave the impression of a short span of history for mankind. But this is only because we misunderstand them. Relying heavily on the work of his older

---

[44]David N. Livingstone, *Darwin's Forgotten Defenders* (Grand Rapids: Eerdmans, 1984), 119.

colleague Dr. William Henry Green, Warfield demonstrates that these genealogies are compressed accounts of a much longer line of descent. The genealogies from Abraham to Christ are demonstrably complete, but for the whole period from creation to Abraham we are left entirely to "inferences" drawn from the genealogies of Genesis 5 and 11. These, Warfield contends, provide no basis for chronological calculations, and if this is so, then "it is clear that we are left without Scriptural data for forming an estimate of the duration of these ages," and they may easily reflect an immense length of time.[45]

Not to be misunderstood, Warfield affirms that the genealogies, as God's word, are entirely reliable and trustworthy, but only "for the purposes for which they are recorded." These purposes did not require a complete record of each generation exhaustively, but only a representative line to establish descent. Hence, the ancient genealogies are "freely compressed," and it is often obvious that a large number of generations are omitted. "There is no reason inherent in the nature of the Scriptural genealogies why a genealogy of ten recorded links, as each of those in Genesis 5 and 11 is, may not represent an actual descent of a hundred or a thousand or ten thousand links." This is so because the purpose of the genealogies is not to provide exact and exhaustive chronology. The point is simply to establish the line of descent from one point to another.[46]

Warfield illustrates his point with the genealogy of Matthew, which he demonstrates is not one but two genealogies. Matthew 1:1 gives us the first: "The book of the genealogy of Jesus Christ, the son of David, the son of Abraham." This is obviously a very compressed genealogy with many generations skipped, but it sufficiently highlights the point at hand—namely, that Jesus is the promised Messiah of the famous Abrahamic and Davidic promises. The second genealogy (Matt. 1:2–17) is expanded considerably into forty-two links, divided symmetrically, doubtless for aid in memorization, into three groups of fourteen. But Warfield notes that this genealogy is also incomplete, skipping as it does the three kings Ahaziah, Joash, and Amaziah (cf. Matt. 1:8 and 2 Kings 8:25; 11:2; 14:1, 21; and 1 Chron. 3:11–12). This is typical of biblical genealogies, and lest we misunderstand and misuse them, we must keep in mind that their purpose was not to provide an exhaustive list for chronological purposes. Moreover, Matthew's divisions of the genealogy of Christ into three lists of fourteen "generations" each should alert us to the reduction of the patriarchal genealogies of Genesis 5 and 11 to two lists of ten each. This is adequate in order to accomplish the purpose at hand, but it is not exhaustive.

---

[45]W, 9:236–37; ESS, 217–19, 270–71; cf. William Henry Green, "Primeval Chronology," BSac 47, no. 189 (April 1890).
[46]W, 9:237–38; ESS, 219–20.

Next Warfield explains the purpose of what otherwise seems to be chronological detail. Why does Moses attach to each name in the list the age of the father at the birth of his son? The account does not read, merely, "Adam begat Seth" but "Adam lived a hundred and thirty years and begat Seth." The impression is easily left that this information is provided for chronological purposes, and it would seem that we need merely to add up these ages of the fathers at the birth of their sons to calculate the entire amount of time covered. Again Warfield borrows from Green and demonstrates that we are left with this impression only when we do not consider all of the details given in each generation. Moses does not provide only the age at which the father begat the son. There is also a statement of how long the father lived afterwards and how long his life span was altogether. We read not merely that "Adam lived one hundred and thirty years and begat Seth" but also that "the days of Adam after he begat Seth were eight hundred years, and he begat sons and daughters. And all the days that Adam lived were nine hundred and thirty years, and he died." Clearly, the information provided by these details contributes nothing to chronological considerations, and as such demonstrates that the purpose is not chronological at all. And if this is true of each listed generation individually, it is also true of the genealogy considered as a whole.

What, then, is the purpose of all this detail? Warfield answers:

> When we are told of any man that he was a hundred and thirty years old when he begat his heir, and lived after that eight hundred years begetting sons and daughters, dying only at the age of nine hundred and thirty years, all these items cooperate to make a vivid impression upon us of the vigor and grandeur of humanity in those old days of the world's prime. In a sense different indeed from that which the words bear in Genesis 6, but full of meaning to us, we exclaim, "Surely there were giants in those days!" This is the impression which the items of information inevitably make on us; and it is the impression they were intended to make on us, as is proved by the simple fact that they are adapted in all their items to make this impression, while only a small portion of them can be utilized for the purpose of chronological calculation.

Warfield thus advises that having found a purpose that accounts for all the information provided, we find no warrant to assume another reason that might account for only *some* of that information. That is to say, we have no warrant to interpret these genealogies as though they were given to provide exhaustive chronological data.[47]

---

[47] *W*, 9:239–41; *ESS*, 221–22.

This conclusion is strengthened when we observe that were we to isolate any of these links and read the information provided, we would not in that case immediately understand it in chronological terms. We would very naturally read the information as describing the strength and vigor of humanity in those ancient days. It is only when the number of links are brought together in a list that they create the illusion of providing chronological data. And if this is so, then we ought to conclude that these genealogies, like the other genealogies of Scripture, are compressed and not exhaustive. Hence, they provide no information of use for chronological calculations. "In a word, the Scriptural data leave us wholly without guidance in estimating the time which elapsed" between the creation of the world and the call of Abraham. "So far as the Scripture assertions are concerned, we may suppose any length of time to have intervened between these events which may otherwise appear reasonable."[48]

Thus, the question of the antiquity of man is a purely scientific one, and Warfield is willing to leave it there. However, drawing again on his acquaintance with scientific literature, he also notes, first, that science has yet to provide any solid data as to the length of human history; and, second, that the "tremendous drafts on time" that were customarily made in the earlier days of Darwinism have now (in his day) been discredited. He reports, illustrating at length and detail, that scientists in his day were becoming generally agreed "that man cannot have existed on the earth more than some ten thousand to twenty thousand years."[49] Thus Warfield demonstrates not only that the question of man's antiquity is of no theological import but also that the supposed conflict between Scripture and science on this score is more apparent than real, given that the Bible does not require a brief history and that science does not require a terribly long one.

The Unity of the Human Race

Warfield notes happily that unlike the question of its antiquity, the *unity* of the human race is no longer a matter of dispute. The advent of evolutionism has removed the motive for denying a common origin to humanity, "and rendered it natural to look upon the differences which exist among the various types of man as differentiations of a common stock." Consequently, the evidences of human unity have enjoyed full hearing. In the past various opposing theories have enjoyed a degree of notice. Co-Adamitism taught that several chief racial types have each descended independently of the others. Pre-Adamitism taught that man is a single

---

[48] *W*, 9:241–44; *ESS*, 221–22.
[49] *W*, 9:245–51; *ESS*, 222–28, 272–80.

species derived from a common stock, but it understood Adam not as the root of the human stock but as one of its shoots, the ancestor of the Jewish and the white races only. And even some early evolutionists suggested multiple times and places of human origins. Racial pride continues to exist among us, but with the exception of very few proponents, these theories lie in the past. The physiological unity of the race and its psychological unity in phenomena such as speech and common tradition speak compellingly to the fact of common origin.[50]

In contrast to the question of its antiquity, the *unity* of the human race is a matter of central importance to Scripture and Christian theology. It is built into the very structure of the Genesis account of man's origin in which humanity is begun with a single pair who, newly created and constituting "humanity in its germ," were commanded to multiply and fill the earth (Gen. 1:26–28). The first man was named Adam, "Man," and the first woman was named Eve, "because she was the mother of all living" (Gen. 3:20). All people are referred to as "sons of Adam," or "man" (Deut. 32:8 KJV; Ps. 8:4; 1 Sam. 26:19; 1 Kings 8:39; Ps. 145:12, etc.). The unity of the human race in a single pair is emphasized again in the flood account, in which all humanity is destroyed except the family of Noah, humanity's second father, by whose descendants again "was the whole earth overspread" (Gen. 9:19 KJV), as illustrated in the table of nations (Genesis 10). The differentiation of people is described in Genesis 11, and the narrative of the tower of Babel has profound religious-ethical significance: the divisions of mankind are the result of human rebellion and divine judgment. "What God had joined together men themselves pulled asunder." Throughout the Scriptures all mankind is treated as a unit, and humanity "shares not only in a common nature but in a common sinfulness, not only in a common need but in a common redemption." Indeed, the entire structure of biblical teaching regarding sin and salvation is built upon the assumption of the unity of the human race.[51]

Accordingly, Israel's privilege among the nations was not due to any difference in itself. Built into Moses' law, with its provisions for aliens and slaves, there was the reminder of their common humanity. Israel's privilege was due to divine mercy and God's purpose to save not Israel only but through Israel the whole world. Our Lord affirmed the origin of the human race in a single pair (Matt. 19:4), and the apostle Paul "explicitly declaring that 'God has made of one every nation of men' and having for His own good ends appointed to each its separate habitation, is now dealing with them all alike in offering them a common salvation" (Acts 17:26ff.). Moreover, "The whole New Testament is instinct with the

---

[50] *W*, 9:252–56; *ESS*, 280–85.
[51] *W*, 9:256–57; *ESS*, 285–87.

brotherhood of mankind as one in origin and in nature, one in need and one in the provision of redemption." Still more to the point, Warfield observes, "the fact of racial sin" is basic to the entire Pauline teaching of redemption (Rom. 5:12ff.; 1 Cor. 15:21f.), and basic to the fact of racial sin is the fact of racial unity. All men share in Adam's sin and his punishment only because all men were constituted in Adam. "And it is only because the sin of man is thus one in origin and therefore of the same nature and quality, that the redemption which is suitable and may be made available for one is equally suitable and may be made available for all." Jew and Gentile alike are under sin, and they are alike in the matter of redemption by the same God who is Lord of all and who by his grace in Christ will justify the circumcision and the uncircumcision alike by faith alone (Rom. 9:22–24, 28ff.; 10:12). Jesus Christ is presented to us as the last Adam, and he is therefore the Savior not of the Jews only but of the whole world (John 3:16; 4:42; 1 Tim. 4:10; 1 John 4:14). "The unity of the old man in Adam is the postulate of the unity of the new man in Christ."[52]

Thus for Warfield the doctrine of the unity of the human race carries with it implications that are of central importance to Christian theology and to Christianity itself. And coupled with all this is a corresponding ethical obligation.

> The unity of the human race is therefore made in Scripture not merely the basis of a demand that we shall recognize the dignity of humanity in all its representatives, of however lowly estate or family, since all bear alike the image of God in which man was created and the image of God is deeper than sin and cannot be eradicated by sin (Gen. 5:3; 9:6; 1 Cor. 11:7; Heb. 2:5ff.); but the basis also of the entire scheme of restoration devised by the divine love for the salvation of a lost race.[53]

That is to say, our understanding of the essential unity of humanity must show itself in our behavior toward others. Warfield was deeply committed to this biblical teaching, and he was far ahead of his time in the matter of condemning racial pride. He came from a prestigious line of outspoken abolitionists, and he was himself eager to take up the cause of blacks at a time when it was most unpopular to do so. In 1885 while still at Western Seminary he became a member of the Presbyterian Board of Missions to Freedmen, and in 1887 and 1888 he published two articles lamenting the plight of the freedmen and their children, and pleading for Christians to consider more seriously the doctrine they profess to believe. In "A Calm View of the Freedman's Case" and "Drawing the Color Line,"[54] Warfield

---

[52]*W*, 9:257–58.
[53]*W*, 9:258.
[54]*SSW*, 2:735–50.

stressed the great work that needed to be done in "the elevation and civilization" of the seven million out of America's fifty million souls who have finally been given freedom, only to face a vicious caste system—and he insisted it could be called nothing less—in which freedmen struggled under the debilitating burden of hopelessness with no prospect ever of improving their standing. Under the former system the slave was dehumanized, with no will of his own and owned by another, and with "emancipation," Warfield charged, the ex-slave was made not a free man but only a free Negro. Himself a son of the South, Warfield decried in his own Presbyterian church what he condemned in society at large. He argued that the Christian understanding that "God has made of one blood all the nations of the earth" must work its way out in real life.[55]

Predictably, Warfield's call for racial equality drew both support and criticism. One minister responded with fears of what would come if Warfield's counsel were followed—equality of black and white ministers, equal respect to black and white women, and, worst of all, probable intermarriage between the races. Referencing passages such as James 2:1–13 and Ephesians 3:1, Warfield responded simply that

> all this is no concern of yours & mine. For, just because the Church is the pillar & ground of the Truth by which the world is to be saved, the Lord has not left its advising to us but has given us instruction as to how it ought to be behaved in the Church of the Living God. . . . I cannot help believing that there is no line so wise or well or so loyal as simply to let God order his own house in his own way & gladly range ourselves by his side. Let us beware lest, in arranging things for oneself & so as to fit our personal prejudices, we build up a kingdom indeed, but not to God or one which He will neither own nor bless.[56]

Some years later, in 1907, Warfield published his views in poetical form under the title "Wanted—A Samaritan."

Prone in the road he lay,
Wounded and sore bested:
Priests, Levites passed that way
    And turned aside the head.

They were not hardened men
In human service slack:

---

[55]SSW, 2:740.
[56]For this and a fuller treatment of the same, see Bradley Gundlach, "Warfield, Biblical Authority, and Jim Crow," in BBW, 136–68.

His need was great: but then,
His face, you see, was black.[57]

Of further interest in this regard, in 1913, while acting president of the seminary and against the protest of his younger colleague J. Gresham Machen, who argued that whites and blacks should remain socially separate, Warfield championed the institution's recent decision to allow a black student to live in the student dormitory at Alexander Hall.[58]

The Constitution of Man

Material on Warfield's understanding of the constitution of man—dichotomy versus trichotomy—is rather thin, but it is sufficient to trace out the primary lines of his thinking. In his handwritten lecture notes[59] he traces out the various New Testament uses of σάρξ, πνεῦμα, and ψυχή, and draws some conclusions. Σάρξ can refer to the material flesh (James 5:3; Luke 24:39). It can also indicate the corporeal part of man, his body, so called as being made of flesh (Eph. 5:31; cf. v. 28; Acts 2:31; 2 Cor. 4:11; 10:3a; Phil. 1:22, 24; Col. 2:1). In this sense it is equivalent to σῶμα (1 Cor. 5:3). The New Testament writers also use σάρξ to refer to human nature, or "the whole of man," body and soul, "so called because the flesh (body) is his most apparent part" (John 1:14; Heb. 10:20; Rom. 4:1; 6:19; Phil. 3:4). Closely related to this, σάρξ can refer to humanity in general (John 3:6; Rom. 9:3; Matt. 24:22; Mark 13:20; Rom. 3:20). Σάρξ can also indicate human nature in its weakness, contrasted with God's strength; that is, weak human nature (Matt. 26:41). Finally, this term can refer to human nature in its impurity as contrasted with God's purity; that is, impure and sinful humanity (Rom. 7:5; 1 John 2:16).

The New Testament writers employ πνεῦμα in a variety of senses also. It refers to that which is spirit in essence and has no primary or necessary reference to the human soul. It can mean "wind" (John 3:8), "breath" (2 Thess. 2:8), purely physical life (Rev. 13:15), or the psychological (not physical) living principle in man (Luke 8:55; James 2:26; 1 Cor. 2:11; Col. 2:5). It also indicates spirit in essence, as opposed to material or body, whether of man's spirit as embodied (Luke 23:46) or as disembodied (Luke 24:39); angelic spirits whether good (Heb. 1:14) or bad

---

[57]Published in *Independent* (New York), January 31, 1907; also, B. B. Warfield, *Four Hymns and Some Religious Verses* (Philadelphia: Westminster Press, 1910), 11.

[58]David B. Calhoun, *Princeton Seminary*, vol. 2, *The Majestic Testimony 1869–1929* (Carlisle, PA: Banner of Truth, 1996), 505.

[59]Archives, Princeton Theological Seminary; see also Harkness, class notes, 2.

(Eph. 2:2); the divine Spirit, God the Creator (John 4:24); or the third person of the Trinity (Rom. 8:9; 1 Cor. 2:12).

In his lecture notes Warfield argues that the New Testament uses of ψυχή are largely parallel to πνεῦμα and that the two terms are used interchangeably. He cites as examples John 12:27; 13:21; Matthew 27:50; John 10:15, 17; and Luke 1:47. Πνεῦμα, like רוּחַ, simply denotes "spirit," and ψυχή, like נֶפֶשׁ, denotes "soul." The relation of these two terms in each language is the same; that is, they designate the same thing from differing points of view. "Spirit" describes the human spirit from the standpoint of its essence—it is not body but spirit. "Soul" describes that same "spirit" only from the point of view of its relation to body, embodied spirit. The Greek and Hebrew terms are equivalent in usage to that of the English. Genesis 2:7 expresses this exactly: God breathed πνεῦμα of life into man, and the man becomes a ψυχή. English has a third word, "ghost," which usually refers to a disembodied (formerly embodied) spirit, and the Greek has some equivalent to this also, for example, in Luke 24:37 (πνεῦμα); Acts 12:15 (ἄγγελος); and Revelation 20:4 (ψυχή).

Following this survey of the uses of these terms Warfield concludes that the New Testament "is no more trichotomous than the English language." The two terms πνεῦμα and ψυχή are used interchangeably, and πνεῦμα is used of animals (Eccles. 3:21; Ps. 104:29; Rev. 13:15), as is ψυχή. "Spirit" has reference to essence, as God and angels are said to be "spirit" beings. "Soul" simply speaks in reference to the human spirit's relation to the body. "All the uses of πνεῦμα and ψυχή are readily explainable from this distinction," just as the English terms. To introduce a trichotomous theory would run against the usage of the New Testament terminology, just as it would run counter to the human consciousness. Neither the New Testament nor our own consciousness gives warrant to regarding humans as comprising three parts. Man is constituted as body and soul/spirit.

Warfield then explains that any attribution of "body, soul, and spirit" to man, such as in 1 Thessalonians 5:23, is purely rhetorical in nature. This is evident, first, from the coexistence of such a reference with dichotomous passages, which speak of "body and soul/spirit" (Matt. 6:25; 10:28; Rom. 8:10; 1 Cor. 5:3; 7:34). These descriptions of human beings as having two parts are evidently intended to be taken as exhaustive, a description of the whole man. And if this is so, then the trichotomous descriptions must be understood accordingly. James 2:26 speaks to this point exactly—"the body apart from the spirit [πνεῦμα] is dead"—and does not allow for any third part (ψυχή) as the supposed seat of animal life in man, as the trichotomous view supposes.

Moreover, parallel expressions such as Matthew 22:37—"love the Lord your God with all your heart, and with all your soul and with all your mind"—even more formally distinguish καρδία, ψυχή, and διανοία. Yet we are not to understand the heart and the mind as separate in substance from the soul or, for that matter, from the spirit.[60]

Third, Warfield points out that the rabbis used נֶפֶשׁ to speak of the will, the faculty of choice, and πνεῦμα/רוּחַ to speak of the true reason. This may offer explanation to Paul's understanding of the nature of man as expressed in 1 Thessalonians 5:23.

Finally, Warfield simply points out that the early church fathers reading Paul's words in their own language certainly did not understand him to be speaking of man as having three parts. Their understanding was that of dichotomy.

Πνευμάτικος and Its Opposites

In an 1880 article in the Princeton Review, "Πνευμάτικος and Its Opposites," Warfield investigates the meaning of πνευματικός and the related or contrasting terms σαρκικός, σάρκινος, and ψυχικός, and their significance in describing man.[61] The -ικός ending on the adjective signifies "belonging to," or "determined by." Πνευματικός then indicates belonging to or determined by the πνεῦμα, whether πνεῦμα in a given context may indicate "breath" or "wind" or "the human spirit" or "the Holy Spirit." In its classical Greek usage, which can be traced to Aristotle, the term occurs infrequently and only in the three senses of "wind," "breath," and "soul"—and in this last sense as the contrast of σωματικός. But in Christian usage πνευματικός passes immediately out of this "lower sphere" and suggests something much higher than anything human. Of the twenty-five instances in which this word appears in the New Testament "in no single case does it sink even as low in its reference as the human spirit." In one instance it refers to the supernatural demonic powers (Eph. 6:12), and in all other instances to the Holy Spirit. To the Christian ear πνευματικός indicated "belonging to, or determined by, the Holy Spirit." And so Warfield suggests the proper translation as "Spirit-given," or "Spirit-led," or "Spirit-determined." Thus πνευματικός stands in contrast to σαρκικός (Rom. 15:27; 1 Cor. 9:11), σάρκινος (Rom. 7:14; 1 Cor. 3:1), and ψυχικός (1 Cor. 2:15; 15:44, 46).[62]

The term σαρκικός first comes into common use in the New Testament and indicates belonging to or determined by the σάρξ, that is, "fleshish" or "fleshly." Σάρξ in the New Testament regularly indicates what is human, especially with

---

[60]This paragraph of Warfield's handwritten lecture notes is extremely difficult to decipher completely, but this seems to be the gist of this second argument.
[61]"Πνευματικός and Its Opposites," PR 1, no. 3 (1880): 561–65.
[62]Ibid., 561.

the implication of *weak* humanity, whether physical or moral. Σαρκικός therefore quite naturally indicates *human* (Rom. 15:27), *weak* (2 Cor. 1:12; 10:4), or *impure* (1 Pet. 2:11; 1 Cor. 3:3, 4). Σάρξ, then, is simply the functional equivalent of the common phrase κατὰ σαρκά and possesses the same range of meanings.[63]

The related term σάρκινος occurs only four times in the New Testament (Rom. 7:14; 1 Cor. 3:1; 2 Cor. 3:3; Heb. 7:16). Warfield notes that the -ινος class of adjectives indicates the material out of which something is made.[64] Thus, σάρκινος connotes "made of flesh." From this primary meaning the word has taken on the secondary senses of either "fleshy" or abounding with flesh, or "bodily." The meaning "made of flesh" fits very well with 2 Corinthians 3:3, but none of these alternatives is possible in the other passages. And so Warfield offers the analogy of ἀδαμάντινος, which from "made of iron" came to indicate, simply, "hard." Similarly, σάρκινος, "made of flesh," given the New Testament connotations of σάρξ, may indicate "weak." This conclusion is strengthened when we compare the connotations of other -ινος adjectives, such as ἀνθρώπινος. So Warfield concludes that this term in its other three New Testament occurrences indicates "weak" and "impure."[65]

Next Warfield seeks to establish any distinction between σαρκικός and σάρκινος. On this question three opinions have been offered: (1) that there is no distinction at all between these terms (Shedd); (2) that σάρκινος is the stronger word (Meyer, Cremer); and (3) that σάρκινος is the weaker word (Delitzsch, Lange, Trench). Although the words are very close in meaning, Warfield argues that σάρκινος should be recognized as slightly weaker in force than σαρκικός. In Hebrews 7:16 σάρκινος describes the divine law as humanly weak only, with no connotation of impurity. In 1 Corinthians 3:1 the term is explained by ὡς νήπιοι, "which points more to a lack than to an active opposition." And in Romans 7:14, "unless violence is done to the whole context," the regenerate man is described as σάρκινος. Citing Trench, Warfield concludes that σάρκινος indicates "unspiritual," while σαρκικός indicates "anti-spiritual." Likewise Delitzsch explains σάρκινος as "one who has in himself the bodily nature and the sinful tendency inherited with it," and σαρκικός as "one whose personal fundamental tendency is this sinful impulse of the flesh."[66]

Ψυχικός describes man as being essentially "psychic" or "soulish." In the classics it expresses either what pertains to life or, more properly, what pertains

---

[63]Ibid., 561–62.

[64]Warfield here is likely leaning on Joseph Henry Thayer, *The New Thayer's Greek-English Lexicon of the New Testament* (1886; repr., Lafayette, IN: AP&A, 1879), 569.

[65]"Πνευματικός," 562–63.

[66]Ibid., 563.

to the soul. In this latter sense it is used frequently in contrast with σωματικιός, indicating that which pertains to the highest element in man's twofold constitution. In its usage, then, ψυχικός becomes interchangeable with the highest classical usage of πνευματικός. The point of reference is the highest or the spiritual part of man. When we turn to its New Testament usage, however, we find that the term has "fallen from its proud position" in secular Greek, for in every one of its occurrences there is "a very strong implication of dishonor" associated with it. In the classics ψυχικός stands in constant contrast to σωματικός, a word lower than itself, but in the New Testament, whether stated expressly or implied, it stands in contrast to πνευματικός, "a word infinitely higher than itself." Warfield explains, "The highest that heathen philosophy knew was the soul of man; but revelation had to set over against that the Spirit of God." And so while in the classics a ψυκικός thing is the most noble, in the New Testament it shrank to nothing in contrast to πνευματικός, "informed, led, or given by the infinite God." For example, Jude describes ψυκικοὶ as πνεῦμα μὴ ἔχοντες (Jude 19). So also in 1 Corinthians 2:14 the ψυχικός is described as those who cannot know the things of the Spirit of God, *because* they are πνευματικῶς. "The word means, then, that which pertains to, or is led or determined by, simple humanity, that is, usually unregenerate humanity; and the ψυχικοὶ are, shortly, the natural men, that is, the unregenerate."[67]

In contrast to σαρκικός and σάρκινος, however, ψυκικός is plainly the stronger term, for it references the higher part of man. Even so, all three terms refer to that which is human, human as considered in its weak and sinful state. "Thus, all that is in man, his highest and his lowest, is alike opposed to what is divine in its origin and action." But not equally so—there are degrees. A man cannot in any sense be both πνευματικός, led by the Spirit, and ψυκικός. The ψυκικός man is still opposed to all that is good and is still in his sins, unregenerate. Warfield summarizes:

> But his soul may be regenerated and yet be not yet wholly cleansed from sin; he may be νοῖ the servant of God's law while still σαρκί the slave of the law of sin (Rom. 7:25). Hence he may still be even σαρκικός and yet not *wholly* estranged from the Holy Ghost. So were the Corinthian Christians of 1 Cor. 3:3 and 4. But how terrible was their condition and in what words of power does Paul rebuke them for daring to remain in it! Even he, himself, however, was σάρκινος (Rom. 7:14). Even he, the great apostle in Christ Jesus (8:1), and having the Spirit (8:1ff.), was still of the flesh, fleshy; and so long as the imperfectly sanctified σάρξ clung to him was he groaning in spirit, awaiting the redemption of the body. Because human (σάρξ) and so long as he carried his unglori-

---

[67]Ibid., 563–64.

fied body, so long he continued to bear "remainders of sin" clinging to him, and hence was σάρκινος. Ψυχικός no Christian can be; σαρκικός scarcely; but σάρκινος, all must be until they, with renewed soul and body, enter into God's glory.[68]

From all this Warfield draws two final conclusions. First, when Paul uses σάρκινος in Romans 7:14, it cannot be argued, against the first and easiest reading of the passage, that he is here describing the experience of the unregenerate man. And second, there is no ground left for any trichotomist theory based on the New Testament usage of ψυχικός and πνευματικός, since the one bears reference to the human soul and the other to the Holy Spirit of God.[69]

The Origin of the Soul

Much as Warfield argued for creation over against evolution as the only adequate explanation for the origin of the human soul, so also he affirmed that every human soul is the immediate creation of God given to each child at birth. He published nothing on this subject, but a student's notes confirm that he held to the creationist and not the traducianist position. The creationist view of course was the position espoused by Warfield's teacher, Charles Hodge, whose *Systematic Theology* Warfield's students were required to read. This was also the majority position of Reformed theologians,[70] and like them all, Warfield acknowledged that Scripture only scarcely addresses the subject and never directly. And so like theologians on both sides of this fence prior to the contemporary abortion crisis, Warfield held his position but with generous allowance for the other, acknowledging that on this matter the Bible does not speak with clarity and that certainty is impossible. But for him the great difficulty with traducianism is the simplicity of the soul. Traducianism implies that the soul is material and hence divisible.[71]

The Original State of Man

Warfield speaks often of man as created in God's image but nearly always in connection with man's unshakable sense of dependence on and obligation to God. That is, he primarily treats the *imago Dei* within the context of theology proper as noted in chapter 3. He also speaks of it in connection with the unity of humanity,

---

[68]Ibid., 564–65 (emphasis original).
[69]Ibid., 565.
[70]Warfield's esteemed friend William G. T. Shedd of Union Seminary was the noted exception.
[71]Harkness, class notes, 3–4.

particularly as it applies to race relations, as noted earlier in this chapter. According to a student's class notes Warfield seems to define the image of God traditionally in terms of knowledge, righteousness, and holiness, and in this respect he presents man as differing from the animals and as the culmination of God's creative work. "Adam was like God in his person, an intellectual, moral, voluntary being different from beasts. Man was put at the culmination of the Creation, a self-conscious being, a spiritua [sic] self-governing and self-determining. Like God in character, in knowledge, righteous and holiness."[72]

Class notes at this point turn to a discussion of the covenant of works, a subject Warfield almost never addressed in print. He did produce a fourteen-page article on the translation of Hosea 6:7, which, after an exhaustive survey of others' translations (whether "Adam" or simply "man"), he takes to read, "They like Adam have broken my covenant." He notes that this was the translation accepted by A. A. Hodge but not by Charles Hodge, and not by some other Reformed interpreters; but he argues briefly that this translation ("like Adam" rather than "like man"), understood as a historical reference to Adam's infamous rebellion, better captures the force of Hosea's rebuke of Israel for her disobedience. The purpose of Warfield's article is to establish this translation; he does not at all address the significance of the "covenant" that Adam is then said to have transgressed. The class notes show an emphasis on Warfield's part that in this covenant agreement with Adam the point is not that a great penalty was made to hang on a small sin, but that a great promise was made to hang on a small condition of obedience, and that this displays God as gracious in his treatment of the race.[73]

Sin

Warfield's published remarks on the doctrine of sin are quite often—perhaps most often—made in connection with grace and the doctrine of salvation. He treats the doctrine of indwelling sin in connection with his critiques of perfectionism. The treatment here will primarily survey his views under a different arrangement and note any teaching not covered in chapter 10 (soteriology).

THE ORIGIN OF SIN

The Bible was written not merely to make us wise in speculation but to make us wise to salvation in Christ, and it therefore is not concerned to tell us much of

---

[72]Ibid., 4.
[73]*SSW*, 1:116–29; Harkness, class notes, 6.

the origins of evil, but merely of the origins of evil in humanity. And in this also there is mystery. Adam was created righteous, and yet he rebelled. Evil existed previously and came to Adam in powerful temptation, but temptation alone does not account for sin. Sin by its very nature is irrational and perverse, and as such necessarily entails mystery.[74]

That Adam's sin was imputed to all his posterity is the declaration of Romans 5:12ff. and 1 Corinthians 15:21. On the ground of federal headship, Adam's act is ours, and on the ground of imputation, his sin is given to us. There are actually three acts of imputation the Bible speaks of. Adam's sin is imputed to us, our sin is imputed to Christ, and Christ's righteousness is imputed to us. "In each case the transaction is identical," and the imputation is "immediate." Further, just as in justification the legal transaction carries along with it the gift of the Spirit and sanctification, so also Adam's sin brings with it not only guilt and punishment but also depravity and corruption. The doctrine of mediate imputation, the teaching that sin is transmitted by heredity, faces two difficulties. First, it cannot account for the biblical emphasis that it is specifically Adam's first sin that is imputed to us. And so Warfield asks rhetorically, "Why not Eve's? and why not the sins of all our ancestors?" Second, it cannot account for our Lord's failure to inherit sin. Warfield does not expand here, but he simply emphasizes that the doctrine of immediate imputation avoids both of these problems, fully accounts for the biblical data, and preserves the parallel of justification and the imputation of Christ's righteousness.[75]

This doctrine of imputed sin provides the only explanation of the universality of sin. Warfield chides the Pelagians on this score. Everyone, without exception, sins. On the Pelagian assumption of the neutrality of the human will, surely there would be in the history of humanity someone who pursued righteousness and not sin. Universal sin simply cannot be explained in terms of free will and Adam's bad example. In this connection Warfield references also the tendency to evil that is evident in all children from their youngest days. The only possible explanation for all this is that in consequence of the fall, all were made sinners.[76]

This doctrine also explains man's universal discontent and fear. In his sermon "Peace With God" (Phil. 4:7), Warfield expounds at some length on the lack of peace in the man without Christ. "How utterly out of joint he is—at war, in fact—with even his physical environment." Then comparing man with the ani-

---

[74]Harkness, class notes, 7.

[75]*ESS*, 257–58, 234–35; W, 10:140; Harkness, class notes, 14–15. According to a student's class notes, Warfield offered the following biblical passages in this connection: Jer. 17:9; Eccles. 8:11; Gen. 6:5; 8:21; Matt. 7:16–19; 12:33; Ps. 51:5; Job 14:4; 15:14; John 3:6; Eph. 2:3. He also emphasized spiritual "death" as the natural condition of all men: Eph. 2:1, 4; 4:17–18.

[76]Harkness, class notes, 14–15; W, 7:4, 10, 14; W, 10:381.

world around him, he notes that man is more helpless than them all. "Every other creature finds a place for itself in nature; nature cares for them all." But man has no place in nature where he is safe. He has "no natural covering to keep him warm, with no natural weapons to protect himself, with no speed for escape, and no cunning for hiding. The sun burns him and the winter freezes him." In brief, "Man knows himself to be at war with the world." Further, having obtained his food, man, unlike the animals, is still not satisfied. He is at odds not only with nature but with himself also. There is a "deep unrest" about him, so that if he like the animals lies in the pasture well fed and safe, he unlike them is not happy. There is a deeper need that he senses and that nothing external can satisfy. "He is out of joint with himself." He has a conscience and therefore knows both what is right and what is not right, "and this sense of sin, an ineradicable instinct in every soul, is the source of a restless uneasiness which knows and can know no peace." For this reason he is terrified of nature. All its forces and upheavals frighten him as "avenging furies" and as "tools of God's anger." He is out of sorts in every dimension. Worst of all, the terrors of conscience, the war in the heart, are due to the fact that he senses his alienation from and enmity with God. And all this inner conflict continues just so long as he knows he is a sinner, and "so long as it abides, he cannot be other than miserable." Revelation gives account for all this, simply, by the fall.[77]

This doctrine also supplies a solution for the so-called problem of evil. In 1908, Warfield contributed to a published "Symposium on the Problem of Natural Evils," in which he was asked to respond specifically to a question regarding the logic of the flood and other such catastrophes. How can they be considered "punishment for sin" when they involve the suffering of the innocent? "What logical connection can there be between the catastrophes in nature and man's sin?"

In his response Warfield appeals to Luke 13:4–5: "Those eighteen on whom the tower in Siloam fell and killed them: do you think that they were worse offenders than all the others who lived in Jerusalem? No, I tell you; but unless you repent, you will all likewise perish." Warfield points out that Jesus did not by this indicate that calamities are no proof of sin. He did not ask, merely, "Do you think these were sinners?" but rather, "Do you think these were sinners *more than others*?" Then Warfield draws the application: "This is to say clearly that no tower ever falls on any but sinners. We are all sinners, and are all alike, therefore, liable to be caught by falling towers, and we must not argue that we are not sinners because no tower has *as yet* fallen on us. It certainly will fall on us if we do not repent." Our Lord's point here is built on the same assumption as that of the

---

[77]*FL*, 330–33.

Old Testament—"all calamity is the proof of sin, and all sin will bring calamity." These two—calamity and sin—are inextricably bound together, except that the temporal distribution of the calamity lies in the hands of a sovereign God and is employed for his own ends. The questioner "seems to suppose that calamity can fall when there is no sin," but he overlooks the fact of the fall. Apart from the fall there would be no calamity, for God does not smite unjustly. But the Bible plainly tells us that "the whole world lies in wickedness," and only with this key can we unlock the mysteries of the divine purpose in calamity.[78] All this is to say that Adam's sin, passed along to all humanity, has brought its consequences to the whole world. And this forms the supposition on which the biblical teaching of salvation in Christ is grounded.

INABILITY AND FREE WILL

Inability is but a corollary of the fact of sin. There are three stages in treating this subject of sin, each of which depends on and is built upon the preceding. First is the doctrine of the imputation of Adam's sin, in which the guilt, punishment, and defilement of Adam are passed to all his posterity. Next, and consequently, is the doctrine of original sin, the inherent depravity of every child of Adam. Third, and again consequently, is the doctrine of inability. Inability has both a negative and a positive side: in our state of sin we are disinclined to good and inclined to evil. The denial of inability is virtually the denial of original sin and depravity.[79]

In order for a good work to be, in fact, good, it must be good in motive and intent, as well as in external act. And unless a good work is rendered "unto the Lord," it cannot be good. There is a distinction between social good and spiritual good. A sinner may well do what is "good" in meeting needs of his neighbor and of society. But because we are sinners, to do something that is truly good, good in reference to God, would be to act out of character. The heart is not good, and the heart cannot be cleansed by an act of the will. We do and act only in accordance with what we are; therefore, all our acts are corrupt (Gen. 6:5). This is inability. We cannot do anything truly good apart from the enablement of the Holy Spirit. Similarly, "The doctrine of inability does not affirm that we cannot believe, but only that we cannot believe in our own strength."[80]

Warfield emphasizes that this inability does not rise out of our nature as God made it. God made man good, but man has fallen from his original state into sin and corruption. Nor does it arise out of any loss of the faculties of the

---

[78]"A Symposium on the Problem of Natural Evils," *Biblical World* 31 (January–June, 1908): 123–24 (emphasis original).
[79]Harkness, class notes, 19.
[80]Ibid.; *SSW*, 2:726.

soul. Man does not lack the intellect or the freedom to act. These faculties, though in one sense still sound, are the faculties of a depraved creature and cannot but follow accordingly. Nor does inability arise from any loss of free agency. Freedom and ability are not synonymous. The will is *free* to move in any direction it chooses, but it is subject to the currents of the soul. The will is free, but it is dominated by a depraved being. Man is free to choose what he wants, but his "want" is precisely the problem. In the natural man, "sin reigns." This is inability.[81]

There are two operations of the Holy Spirit: common grace and special grace. We all resist the former, often successfully, and by it alone we could never be saved. If there had never been the fall, common grace would forever have sufficed to give us knowledge of God. But given the fall, a new power has entered the field—the power of sin. Herein lies our inability, and to overcome this a special grace is required. Special grace is "special" simply because it is efficacious to remove our sinful disposition and give new life. And thus it is never successfully resisted—this is the creative work of the Holy Spirit in regeneration.[82]

In his sermon on the rich young ruler entitled "The Paradox of Omnipotence" (Mark 10:27), Warfield explores briefly the inability that Jesus describes when he says that salvation is "impossible" for man. What held this young man back was not any lack of human faculty. He possessed the intelligence and the freedom necessary to keep God's commands. His "fatal lack" lay not in his constitution as a man "but in his ingrained disposition by which he was the man he was." Because he was the man he was, he could not rightly perceive values. Warfield continues:

> And like him, every son of man, though possessed of treasures of knowledge and crowned with the most striking virtues, will be found to lack the power to put in their relatively proper places the things of God and the things of this world. With one it is riches, with another it is pride, with another it is ease, with another ambition, that has taken possession of the soul. With all there is this real inability to rid themselves of "whatsoever they have" and turn single-heartedly to God.

Probing more deeply, Warfield concludes that the root of this inability is found in sin—"a sin-distorted vision, feeling, judgment—in a word, in a sin-deformed soul." The human problem lies in "a true inability rooted in a heart too corrupt to appreciate, desire or go out in an active inclination toward 'the good.'" It is

---

[81]Harkness, class notes, 20–21; *SSW*, 1:286; *W*, 10:448; cf. A. A. Hodge, "Free Will, or Freedom of the Will," rev. B. B. Warfield, in *Johnson's Universal Encyclopedia*, new edition, ed. Charles Kendall Adams, vol. 3 (New York: D. Appleton and Company, 1899), 575.
[82]Harkness, class notes, 19–20.

precisely because of this inability that man is left but to cast himself entirely upon divine mercy.[83]

In brief, "Inability is a sinful condition of the will, and the sole reason why a man cannot believe is that he is so exceedingly sinful that such a one as he cannot use his will for believing. He cannot will to do it because he loves sin too much."[84]

All this serves to shape the biblical teaching on the freedom of the will. Man is free to do what he wants to do. "Every Calvinist holds devoutly to the free self-determination of the soul in every moral action, and is at liberty to give whatever psychological explanation of that fact may seem to him most reasonable." But the Bible also teaches original sin, the inheritance of the corruption of Adam. The problem is that man's will is itself corrupt, and "freedom" does not entail ability. Freedom is a relative term. God is free also, but he is not able to sin, for that would be out of character and contrary to what he is. So also man is free, but he is not able not to sin, for that too would be out of character and contrary to what he is. Man's will is free, and he may do as he pleases without external compulsion. But given the distortions of the soul due to natural depravity, he is unable to do good.[85]

Warfield sums all this up with three basic propositions. First, "the organ of volition" is not the will only but the entire soul. Second, this same soul "possesses the inalienable property of self-determination," but the moral character of that determination depends entirely upon the moral character of the soul that guides it. And third, for that same soul to be holy and disposed to what is right it is wholly dependent upon the indwelling of the Holy Spirit. The soul does not possess a power to the contrary, to act other than in accordance with its own character and disposition. God is holy and thus is not able to sin (*non posse peccare*). Adam was created upright and thus had the ability not to sin (*posse non peccare*), but for the time of his probation he possessed also the power to sin (*posse peccare*). He did sin, and as punishment both "he and his descendants lost the *posse non peccare* and retained only the *posse peccare*, which thus became the fatal *non posse non peccare*."[86]

Pelagius defined free will in terms of an absolutely unconditioned power to choose between good and evil, and, denying natural depravity and original sin, he defined evil merely in terms of choices made. This strikes at the roots of the Christian faith. Speaking often of Pelagianism, Warfield is eager to expose it as specifically an anti-Christian religion, simply dressed up paganism and "essen-

[83]*PGS*, 102–3.
[84]*SSW*, 2:725.
[85]*SSW*, 2:423–24; Harkness, class notes, 23–27.
[86]*SSW*, 2:423.

tially heathen." Its insistence on human freedom renders salvation a self-work, "autosoterism," and thereby strips salvation of the supernatural and precludes any notion of grace. Augustine's struggle against Pelagius was "a struggle for the very foundations of Christianity." Indeed, "The real question at issue was whether there was any need for Christianity at all." It is precisely because of man's inherent guilt and depravity that salvation requires divine grace.[87]

Semi-Pelagianism admits to human injury in the fall such that man can do nothing morally good in his own strength. But it also contends that man is able of himself to incline himself to good with the result of obtaining divine cooperation. Thus, semi-Pelagians deny prevenient grace and affirm cooperating grace. Arminians admit original sin but deny original guilt, and for them Adam's descendants, "although corrupt and prone to sin from birth, are neither responsible nor punishable until there has first been bestowed upon them redemptively a gracious ability to the right." The Arminian reasons that there was therefore just one option open to divine justice: "either that Adam should be punished at once without issue, or that he should be allowed to generate seed in his own moral likeness, when equity required that an adequate redemption should be provided for all." This Christ did in his death, providing by it sufficient grace (both prevenient and cooperating grace) for all men. For the Arminian this grace is essential and must be provided equally for all in order to render all men responsible, and only by the abuse of this grace do men become guilty. People are guilty not because of Adam's sin but only by reason of their own sins. Stated simply, for the Arminian, ability underlies responsibility. To all this Warfield observes,

> Thus while Calvinism exalts the redemption of Christ, in its execution and in each moment of its application, as an adorable act of transcendent grace to the ill-deserving, Arminianism, in its last analysis, makes it a compensation brought in by the equitable Governor of the world to balance the disabilities brought upon men, without their fault, by the apostasy of Adam.

This is the difference between Calvinism and Arminianism. And that the Calvinistic understanding accords with the biblical teaching of divine grace and with the believer's experience in that grace is something Warfield scarcely sees need to argue. "This difference is the practical reason that Calvinism has such a strong hold upon the religious experience of Christians" as expressed so frequently in the hymns and prayers even of the evangelical Arminian.[88]

---

[87]W, 4:289–307, 317, 329; PS, 33–51; SSW, 2:422–23.
[88]SSW, 2:422–27.

REPENTANCE AND ORIGINAL SIN

In an 1899 article for *Union Seminary Magazine*, Warfield takes up the question, must we repent of original sin? He notes that the question is often asked triumphantly by those who oppose the doctrine, assuming that the question itself demonstrates the absurdity of the doctrine—the only sin we are conscious of is our own transgressions, and these alone demand repentance. But the question is sometimes asked also by earnest Christians seeking to perform their whole duty to the Lord. If all sin must be repented of, then in order to obtain forgiveness must I not repent of the sin inherited from Adam? And if not, am I not being frivolous with my sin?

Warfield advises that the answer must begin with a careful understanding of the terms "repentance" and "original sin." If repentance simply means sorrow, we will answer the question in quite a different way than if repentance means amendment of life. Similarly, if by "original sin" we mean Adam's personal sin made ours by an external act of imputation, our conclusion will be quite different than if by it we mean our own inborn depravity. And so Warfield counsels that we define the terms in their broadest possible way. Repentance must mean "not merely sorrow for and hatred of sin, but also the inward turning away from it to God, with full purpose of new obedience." And by "original sin" we must indicate "not merely adherent but also inherent sin, not merely the sinful act of Adam imputed to us, but also the sinful state of our own souls conveyed to us by the just judgment of God."[89]

With this understanding of these terms in mind it seems clear that we must indeed "repent of original sin." To be sure, we cannot repent of that first sinful act of Adam, but in fact our sympathies are with him. What we call original sin, "the corruption that is derived by us from our first parents," not only comes to us as a penalty but also "abides in us as sin." And surely, not only God but our enlightened conscience also must view this as sin and as abhorrent. God cannot look on it but with righteous indignation. The Arminians are wrong to speak of original sin merely in terms of "uncondemnable vitiosity," for "whatever is vicious is by that very token condemnable." In proportion, then, that our conscience is quickened and enlightened by the Holy Spirit and his Word, we will estimate our sinfulness as God estimates it and abhor and condemn it for the abhorrent corruption that it is.[90]

This is precisely the self-arraignment we witness of Paul in Romans 7. Enlivened by the Spirit of God, he is in deep contrition not only for what he has done but

---

[89]*SSW*, 1:278–79.
[90]*SSW*, 1:279–82.

...hat he is. For such a man, "the very core of his repentance will be his firm determination not only to *do* better but to *be* better." And so Warfield concludes that, "so far from its being impossible to repent of original sin, repentance, considered in its normative sense—not as an act of turning away from this sin or that sin, but of turning from sin as such to God—is fundamentally just repentance of 'original sin.'" Warfield adds, "Until we repent of original sin, we have not, properly speaking, repented in the Christian sense at all." It is essentially heathen to view sin atomistically, in terms only of specific transgressions. The Christian view "probes deeper" until he "finds behind the acts of sin the sinful nature." Indeed, we have not truly repented until we have recognized "and felt the filthiness and odiousness" of our depraved nature and turned away from it "to God with a full purpose of being hereafter more conformed to his image as revealed in the face of Jesus Christ," who alone never needed repentance.[91]

Looking Forward

The picture of humanity given us in Scripture is that of a great failure. Created with high dignity, only a little lower than the angels, we have rebelled, have fallen, and have not attained the glory for which we were created as God's vice-regents over creation. It is the testimony of Psalm 8 that God made man to have and exercise dominion over all of creation. He has crowned man "with glory and honor and put everything under his feet" and "put everything in subjection to him" (Ps. 8:5–6; Heb. 2:6–7). Surely, for bestowing this honor and dignity, God is deserving of great praise. But amid this wonder at God's goodness there is the sad note of human failure: "But now"—the contrast—"we do not yet see all things subjected to him" (Heb. 2:8). Humanity has failed and has yet to live up to its intended glory.[92]

Yet this is not the end of the story. The writer of the epistle to the Hebrews continues: we do not yet see man in his intended dignity, but we see Jesus who also was "made a little lower than the angels" (Heb. 2:9). Such was the depth of his gracious humiliation. He stooped "to reach the exalted heights of man's as yet unattained glory." The glorious Son has become man—truly all that we are as men—and in him we are enabled to see what man was intended to be. Warfield entitles his sermon on Psalm 8 and Hebrews 2, "The Revelation of Man." Here, in Jesus, we see what man was created to be. Here is One who needs no repentance, One who has not fallen, One who has never sinned. Here is One who displays every virtue in perfect proportion and degree. Here is "the pattern, the ideal, the

---

[91] *SSW*, 1:279–82 (emphasis original).
[92] *PGS*, 3–8.

realization of man. Looking upon Him, we have man revealed to us." Here is a man who, according to the testimony of those who accompanied him, was "without blemish and without spot." "He did no sin, neither was guile found in his mouth." Here is a man who was "separate from sinners" and altogether "without sin." Here in Jesus Christ the world has witnessed—just this once—humanity as it ought to be, just what it was created to be. In his youth he was subject to his parents, and as he grew in stature he increased also in favor with God as well as with men. That is to say, he demonstrated at each stage of his life the perfect model of what every man should be at each of those stages of life. Unlike Adam and unlike us, when faced with temptation he remained faithful. Here, once in the history of all the world, we have the one man who displayed for us all dignity and honor that humanity was created to attain—but a dignity forfeited in the fall.[93]

And so it is significant that the author of the epistle to the Hebrews writes, "not yet." We do "not yet" see all things subjected to man. "But we see Jesus," who having become like us and having suffered for us was crowned with glory and honor. And as he entered through suffering into glory, it was not for his own sake merely but "in the process of bringing many sons to glory." "He is the sanctifier, they are the sanctified; and He is not ashamed to call them brethren." He came to be one of us in order to make propitiation for us and to deliver us from bondage. That is to say, "We are to look upon Jesus in His perfect manhood as our forerunner. In his perfection we are to see the revelation of what we too shall be when He shall have perfected His work in us as He has already perfected it for us." He is our example, but he is more than our example. He is our forerunner. If he were our example only, how desperate we would be as we see in him only what we ought to be. "What hopeless gloom would inevitably settle upon our souls." But with him as our forerunner, as our life, as the One who having died has purchased the sanctifying Spirit for us, we see in him much more than a perfect man. Indeed, we see in his perfect manhood what we ourselves will become. "Beloved, now we are the children of God, and it is not yet made manifest what we shall be. We know that, if He shall be manifested, we shall be like Him." Here is the Christian hope. "'We shall be like Him.' Our hearts take courage, and we rest on this word. We shall be like Him!" Here is the glory that is in store for us. "In the strength of this hope let us live our life out here below, and in its joyful assurance let us, when our time comes to go, enter eagerly into our glory." Man has fallen indeed, but in Jesus Christ he will be raised again to be all he was created to be and all that he ought to be.[94]

---

[93]*PGS*, 8–20; *SSW*, 1:158–63.
[94]*PGS*, 20–26.

O the Love of God Almighty,
O His ceaseless love!
Piercing through the depths beneath us,
Through the heights above;
Wider than the boundless spaces
Where the stars do dwell;
Kindling Heaven with its brightness,
Reaching down to hell.

Yea, our mother may forget us;
Yea, our father fail;
Yea, the bridegroom may grow careless,—
Other thoughts prevail;
We may change, and all the whiteness
Of our souls may blot:
O the Love of God Almighty,
Lo, it changes not.

Holy is the Lord Almighty,
Righteous past compare:
We are sinners,—who among us
Can his vengeance bear?
Lo the Cross! and One upon it
Coming from above!
O the Love of God Almighty,
O His saving love!

Poem by Warfield, published in the *New York Observer* 79
(December 19, 1901); also in, *Four Hymns and Some Religious Verses*
(Philadelphia: Westminster Press, 1910), 3.

10

SOTERIOLOGY

Warfield speaks often of the fundamental redemptive character of Christianity—a "sinner's religion"—and takes great delight at seemingly every opportunity in expounding matters related to God's powerful and gracious rescue of guilty sinners through Christ. God has revealed himself progressively with a redemptive purpose, and that revelation has reached its apex in the person and work of Jesus Christ, whose incarnation Warfield always describes in salvific terms. He glories in the truth that through Christ sinners are made right with God, renewed, and secured to final glory. Salvation is accomplished for us in time by the workings of the triune God, whose purpose to save runs from eternity to eternity.

The Plan of Salvation

In *The Plan of Salvation*, Warfield examines the various views offered within Christendom regarding the order and outworking of the decrees of God concerning human salvation. That God acts in salvation according to a plan is a given in theism, for purpose is essential to personhood. Even the deist must acknowledge that God acts according to plan, even if in that system God's plan is carried out in a mere mechanical fashion. In the deist conception salvation is not by chance, but neither is it by the immediate workings of a personal Deity. But if we grant the theistic conception of God—that he is a personal being who maintains immediate control over his creation—then we are forced to acknowledge that he acts according to plan in human salvation. The question here has to do with the nature of this plan. On this there are widely differing opinions within professing Christendom.

NATURALISM (AUTOSOTERISM) VERSUS SUPERNATURALISM

As was pointed out in chapter 1, the question of naturalism versus supernaturalism was in many respects the defining question of the day, and Warfield saw this

principle at work not only in such discussions as inspiration and the incarnation. He saw it as the defining issue in soteriology also: either God saves us, or
we save ourselves. That salvation is from God is the belief universally held by all
professing Christians; that salvation comes from ourselves is the universal doctrine of heathenism. It is this understanding that prompted Jerome to describe
Pelagianism, the first autosoteric scheme to arise in the church, as the "heresy
of Pythagoras and Zeno." Pelagius built his system on the assumption of the full
ability of the unaided human will to do what God requires—the principle that
human obligation implies human ability—so that, in the end, man has saved
himself. He has within him all the necessary powers. The effect of Adam's fall
was but that of a bad example—humanity is not itself scarred from it. "Man is
able to be without sin," and "he is able to keep the commandments of God," said
Pelagius. At every moment, every man is fully able to cease from all sinning and
to continue on in perfection. For the Pelagian, "grace" is merely the endowment
to man of this inalienable freedom of will and the divine inducements to use
his freedom for good. Additionally, God has given the law and the gospel for
illumination and persuasion. And he has given Christ "to supply an expiation for
past sins for all who will do righteousness, and especially to set a good example."
Those who submit to these inducements and exercise their freedom to cease from
sinning and do right are accepted by God as righteous and will be rewarded for
their good works.[1]

Such a system, which "casts man back upon his native powers," Warfield insists,
is not, properly, religion at all but a system of ethics, "fitted only for the righteous
who need no salvation."[2] Augustinianism triumphed over Pelagianism and its
stepchild, semi-Pelagianism, and insisted that it is God alone who saves. Not some
but all the power exerted in saving the human soul is from God. But Augustine's
triumph was only formal, for while the church officially acknowledged both the
necessity and the prevenience of grace, it refused to acknowledge, and in fact
denied, the efficacy of grace. Thus, the downward pull of synergism prevailed, and,
despite its official condemnation by the church, semi-Pelagianism dominated
the church of the Middle Ages.

In Luther and in Calvin, Augustinianism found new champions. To Luther,
Pelagianism was the heresy of heresies, equal to unbelief itself. To Luther and
Calvin alike it was but the fodder that fed human pride, filling men "with an
over-weening opinion of their own virtue, swelling them out with vanity, and
leaving no room for the grace and assistance of the Holy Spirit." But in Luther's

---

[1] *PS*, 33–35; *SSW*, 2:422–23.
[2] *PS*, 17, 36.

very successor, Philip Melanchthon (1497–1560), "the old leaven of self-salvat began to make its way back. In time, even Reformed churches began to draw back, and rationalistic notions of freedom of the will and human independence began to gain precedence. God saves, but he does so merely by keeping the way of salvation open for those who exercise their free will aright. Warfield wonders if such can properly be called salvation at all. He further wonders whether a gospel that is contingent on the human will can be good news to anyone, for the will is precisely the problem—it is diseased and hostile against God. Indeed, it is dead. "For the sinner who knows himself to be a sinner, and knows what it is to be a sinner," not a "whoever will" gospel but "only a 'God will' gospel will suffice." If the only gospel that can be given to men with dead and sinful wills is merely a "whoever will" gospel, "who then can be saved?"[3]

Autosoterism is but a dream that cannot save at all. Warfield cites Spurgeon approvingly: "If there be but one stitch in the celestial garment of our righteousness which we ourselves are to put in it, we are lost."[4] It is *God* who saves sinners.

SACERDOTALISM VERSUS EVANGELICALISM

Among supernaturalists, significant differences of opinion remain, most fundamentally the division between sacerdotalism and evangelicalism. Both are supernaturalists in that they both acknowledge that all the power exerted in saving the soul is from God. The difference between them lies in the manner in which this divine power is brought to the human soul, whether immediately or by means of supernaturally endowed instrumentalities—the church and sacraments. The point at issue is the immediacy of God's saving activity: "Does God save men by immediate operations of his grace upon their souls, or does he act upon them only through the medium of instrumentalities established for that purpose?"[5]

Evangelicalism preserves the notion of "pure" and "consistent supernaturalism." It "sweeps away every intermediary between the soul and its God, and leaves the soul dependent for its salvation on God alone, operating upon it by his immediate grace." The evangelical directs the sinner, in need of salvation, to look to God himself for grace rather than to any means of grace. His whole hope is that God the Holy Spirit is "actually operative where and when and how he will." It is God alone who saves. This "evangelicalism" is, simply, Protestantism.[6]

The greatest defect in the sacerdotal conception of salvation, best represented by the Church of Rome, is that it places sinners in the hands of men rather than

---

[3] *PS*, 39, 45, 49.
[4] *PS*, 51.
[5] *PS*, 18.
[6] *PS*, 19.

a merciful God. Instead of being directed to God, we are "referred to an institution." According to the sacerdotal scheme, God desires the salvation of all men
and has made adequate provision for the salvation of all via the church and its
sacraments; but the actual distribution of grace is performed at the hands of the
church, and apart from the church there can be no salvation at all. All this is a
very small step away from naturalism; it is still salvation at the hands of men. By
this system, "direct contact with and immediate dependence upon God the Holy
Spirit" is replaced by a "body of instrumentalities" on which the soul is tempted
to depend. The sacerdotal system "thus betrays the soul into a mechanical conception of salvation."[7]

To understand sacerdotalism aright, three observations must be kept in
view. First, the church has taken the place of the Holy Spirit, and the Christian
therefore

> loses all the joy and power which come from conscious direct communion with God.
> It makes every difference to the religious life, and every difference to the comfort
> and assurance of the religious hope, whether we are consciously dependent upon
> instrumentalities of grace, or upon God the Lord himself, experienced as personally
> present to our souls, working salvation in his loving grace.

We have here, clearly, two very different types of piety—one fostered by dependence on instrumentalities of grace and one fostered by a conscious communion
with God as a personal Savior. The Protestant rejection of sacerdotalism is in the
interest of vital religion, "and this repudiation constitutes the very essence of
evangelicalism. Precisely what evangelical religion means is immediate dependence of the soul on God and on God alone for salvation."[8]

Second, sacerdotalism neglects the personality of God the Holy Spirit and
treats him as if he were a mere force. The church describes itself as "the store-
house of salvation," as though salvation were a commodity that could be stored
and dispensed at its will.

> It would probably be no exaggeration to say that no heresy could be more gross than
> that heresy which conceives the operations of God the Holy Spirit under the forms
> of the action of an impersonal, natural force. And yet it is quite obvious that at bot-
> tom this is the conception which underlies the sacerdotal system. The Church, the
> means of grace, contain in them the Holy Spirit as a salvation-working power which
> operates whenever and wherever it, we can scarcely say he, is applied.[9]

---

[7]*PS*, 55, 66.
[8]*PS*, 66; cf. *W*, 7:113–15.
[9]*PS*, 67.

Third, this system subjects the Holy Spirit in his gracious operations of salvation to the control of men. Rather than viewing the means of grace as instruments that the Holy Spirit uses in working salvation, the Holy Spirit is made an instrument of the church—an instrument that the church, the means of grace, puts to use in working salvation.[10] The initiative belongs to the church, and the Holy Spirit is placed at the church's disposal. Until the church puts him to work, he waits for its permission. This "degrading" concept of the Spirit of God and his saving work is not worthy of "religion," and Warfield dismisses it out of hand.

Pure sacerdotalism is most clearly represented in the Roman Catholic Church, which presents itself as "the institution of salvation, through which alone is salvation conveyed to men." Saving grace is exclusively administered by the church. "Where the church is, there is the Spirit; outside the church there is no salvation." But sacerdotal theology is not restricted to the Church of Rome. The Church of England teaches in strikingly similar terms, and confessional Lutheranism continues it in a modified form. Still there is something standing between the sinner and his saving God. The evangelical contradiction of sacerdotalism is merely a consistent denial of naturalism. An insistence on supernaturalism drives evangelicals to put their sole trust in God alone and refuse "to admit any intermediaries between the soul and God, as the sole source of salvation." It is only a true evangelicalism that "sounds clearly the double confession that all the power exerted in saving the soul is from God, and that God in his saving operations acts directly upon the soul."[11]

UNIVERSALISM VERSUS PARTICULARISM

The evangelical note of individual and immediate dependence upon God alone for salvation is formally sounded by the whole of Protestantism, and it is this note that shapes its piety. Protestant piety is "individualistic to the core, and depends for its support on an intense conviction that God the Lord deals with each sinful soul directly and for itself."[12] In odd yet obvious contradiction to this basic conviction, however, there exists within Protestantism a widespread tendency to explain God's saving activities in universal, rather than in individual, terms. The work that God does in salvation, according to these universalistic interpretations, he does equally for all men alike, making no distinctions. This is the position of evangelical Arminianism, evangelical Lutheranism, and others.

---

[10]*PS*, 67.
[11]*PS*, 18–20.
[12]*PS*, 69.

It would seem that if these two premises are held—that God and God alone saves by the workings of his grace immediately upon the human heart, and that he works equally in all men alike—then all men alike will be saved, without exception. The conclusion is unavoidable unless one or the other of the premises is relaxed in some way. Scripture speaking so plainly on this matter, precious few evangelicals have been willing to claim that all men are, in fact, saved. Instead, they draw back to a position that allows for a universalistic work on God's part yet issues in a particularistic result. God alone works in salvation, according to this view, but all that he does is directed indiscriminately to all men. It would seem necessary, therefore, either to affirm that the critical and decisive move in salvation belongs not to God but to man—in which case we have fallen from evangelicalism to naturalistic autosoterism—or to affirm that the operations of God's saving grace are not universal but individual. We cannot affirm both unless we are willing to embrace outright universalism. "Consistent evangelicalism and consistent universalism can coexist only if we are prepared to assert the salvation by God's almighty grace of all men without exception."[13]

The hesitancy on the part of some evangelicals to ascribe a thoroughgoing particularism to God in the distribution of his saving grace is widespread. Evangelical Arminianism affirms that salvation ultimately depends on the exercise of the human will. Evangelical Lutheranism affirms the efficacy of baptism in communicating regenerating grace, a grace that is left to the individual to take advantage of, cooperate with, and act upon. The naturalistic ("semi-semi-Pelagian") and sacerdotal tendencies are evident. In neither of these cases is salvation construed as monergistic. Further, in neither is salvation *given*—it is only made available. Salvation is made available and left to man either to resist or not, to take advantage of or not. It is the *opportunity* of salvation that is given freely to all. The result, then, is that God does not save all men—he saves none. He only opens a way of salvation to all, "and if any are saved they must save themselves." What God does *toward* the salvation of one he does for all. He does not actually save by himself alone, nor is his work individualistic. Warfield asks, "Where then is our evangelicalism?"[14]

Universalistic notions seem to be driven by the assumptions that God "owes" salvation equally to all men, that it would be unfair for him to favor a few, and that sin is not really sin deserving of wrath but rather misfortune deserving of pity—that is, a low view of sin. Warfield illustrates the matter by comparing a doctor and a judge. We might fault a doctor who, although able to relieve a sickness

---

[13]*PS*, 70.
[14]*PS*, 21, 79.

in all, actually relieves only some. Yet we may wonder how a judge could release any guilty offender at all. God in his love does pity and save, but he is righteous as well as loving. Accordingly, God in love saves only as many "as he can get the consent of his whole nature to save." God "will not permit even his ineffable love to betray him into any action which is not right." We might sympathize with the "leveling" tendencies of politics—freedom for all, rights for all, education for all, and so on. The cry from a nation's citizens to its government to give all "an equal chance" is one thing. But the turbulent self-assertion of convicted criminals demanding clemency is quite another. We must fix it firmly in our minds, Warfield insists, that salvation is the right of no one and that a "chance" to save oneself is no chance of salvation for any, and that if anyone at all is saved, it must be by a miracle of divine grace on which no one has any claim whatever. All this is so designed that any who are saved can only be "filled with wondering adoration of the marvels of the inexplicable love of God." Indeed, Warfield continues, "To demand that all criminals shall be given a 'chance' of escaping their penalties, and that all shall be given an 'equal chance,' is simply to mock at the very idea of justice, and no less, at the very idea of love."[15]

In all resistance to particularism the decisive factor in salvation is transferred from God to man—whether naturalistically or sacerdotally—and the evangelical principle of dependence upon God alone for salvation is lost. The parting of the ways remains here. "Certainly, only he can claim to be evangelical who with full consciousness rests entirely and directly on God and on God alone for his salvation." Calvinists contend that supernaturalism in salvation, the immediacy of the divine work, and the evangelical ascription *soli Deo gloria* all demand particularism. At bottom, what divides particularists from inconsistent universalists is "just whether the saving grace of God, in which alone is salvation, actually saves. Does its presence mean salvation, or may it be present, and yet salvation fail?" If it is God himself who acts to save individual men apart from any intermediaries, and if all the glory must be ascribed to him for it, then we are left to see that he is selective in his saving work.[16]

DIFFERENCES AMONG PARTICULARISTS

The Extent of the Atonement

Still, among particularists some differences remain. Some hold that God has only some men in view—that is, those who are actually saved—in *all* his saving operations, while others discriminate in this matter and assign some of his saving

---

[15]*PS*, 74, 80–81.
[16]*PS*, 86, 23.

operations a particularistic reference and some a universal reference. This latter view seeks to mediate between the two (universalistic and particularistic) conceptions and maintains particularism in the process as well as in the final issue of salvation but yields to universalism in the actual redemption of the sinner by Christ's death. According to this view, the death of Christ has, in the plan of God, a hypothetical reference to all men indiscriminately but a particular reference in the actual application of it to the soul. Christ died for all men if they believe, but it is left to the Spirit of God sovereignly to work faith in the heart; hence, a modified particularism. This scheme, which conceives that God's elective decree logically follows his decree of redemption, is known historically as Amyraldianism and descriptively as postredemptionism, hypothetical redemptionism, or hypothetical universalism. The question at issue is whether the death of Christ has universal or particular design, and, therefore, the precise point reduces to whether or not the death of Christ *actually* saves those for whom Christ died or only makes that salvation possible. The genuine validity that Amyraldianism gives to the principle of particularism renders it a "recognizable form of Calvinism,"[17] but the particularism to which it gives assent is only inconsistently applied.

The debate settles on not the extent, exactly, but the nature and meaning of Christ's redemptive work. Does the death of Christ save, or does it merely make salvation possible? If Christ's death were designed to save all, then, clearly, given the fact that not all men are saved, its efficacious value would be lost. Particularists emphasize that "whatever is added to [the atonement] extensively is taken from it intensively." Hence, the issue remains here the same as in the debate with general universalism of the evangelical Lutherans and Arminians—do the saving operations actually save? If the work of Christ actually saves, we are left with a consistent particularism. If on the other hand Christ's redemptive work has universal intent, then it is itself not efficacious. Christ did not die, truly, as the sinner's substitute, bearing the penalties of his sins and securing eternal life for him; he died only to "open the way" of salvation and make salvation possible. He died, in this case, merely to "remove all the obstacles" that stand in the sinner's way to salvation. "But what obstacle stands in the way of the salvation of sinners, except just their sin?" And if Christ's death did not, in fact, remove the obstacle of sin, then the atonement lays no real foundation for the salvation of sinners, and its redemptive value is evaporated. It does nothing for any man that it does not do for all men; it therefore (given the Scripture's clear denial of universalism) saves no one. Such an altered atonement wounds Christianity at its very heart. We are left to choose between an atonement of high, efficacious

---

[17]*PS*, 93.

value and an atonement of wide intentions. The two notions cannot coexist. Only the consistent application of the principle of particularism does justice to the nature of Christ's death.[18]

Lapsarianism

Among consistent particularists themselves, however, a difference remains. The point at issue between them is not the actual work of God in saving sinners. The question behind all this is whether God, in election and preterition, contemplated men as merely men or as sinful men. The former alternative is known to history as supralapsarianism and the latter as sub- or infralapsarianism. Warfield insists, simply, that merely to ask the question is to provide the answer, for whether we speak of election or preterition, the underlying assumption is sin and/or salvation. In either case men as sinners in need of salvation are in view. Even in Romans 9, where God is said sovereignly both to hate and to love, to elect and to reprobate, his basic assumption throughout is that all men stand already condemned before an angry God. He has in view "a world of lost sinners." If men were not sinners, then God's sovereign rejection of them would not be to their destruction; it would be to some other destiny fitting for them. But because they are sinners, their rejection is to punishment. Both election and reprobation have men as sinners in view.[19]

CONCLUSIONS

In summary, if we acknowledge theism, then we must acknowledge supernaturalism in salvation. If supernaturalism, then evangelicalism. And if evangelicalism, then particularism.

And particularism is Calvinism. Calvinism is the consistent application of the evangelical principle that God alone saves, that he saves according to purpose, and that his saving operations are applied immediately to the individuals who are saved. "Calvinism is only another name for consistent supernaturalism in religion."[20] The naturalist denies a God of providence and sees the universe

---

[18]*SSW*, 2:320; *PS*, 94–95.

[19]*W*, 2:54. Warfield elsewhere positions infralapsarianism within the general mainstream of the Reformed tradition, but he acknowledges that it is not the only Reformed position. In his lengthy study, "Predestination in the Reformed Confessions," he demonstrates that none of the historic Reformed symbols are explicitly supralapsarian (or Salmurian), and yet "none are polemically directed against it." And some leave the question open. However, some are explicitly infralapsarian, and none oppose infralapsarianism. It goes too far, he admits, to speak of the Reformed creeds at large as "distinctly Infralapsarian," but he agrees with Philip Schaff's assessment that "all the Reformed Confessions . . . keep within the limits of infralapsarianism" (*W*, 9:228–30; cf. *SSW*, 2:429–32).

[20]*CA*, 502.

directed simply by "the laws of nature." The sacerdotalist conceives the grace of God in salvation distributed mechanically by means of the sacraments. The Arminian sees God's activity in salvation as spread evenly over the entire world, a general, universal force acting uniformly in all cases. Hence, "The fundamental principle of Arminianism is that salvation hangs upon a free, intelligent choice of the individual will; that salvation is, in fact, the result of the acceptance of God by man, rather than of the acceptance of man by God."[21] The Calvinist, by contrast, recognizes

> the pure theistic conception of a personal God—a God who, just because he is a person, must in all things act, not as an amorphic force by a uniform pressure made effectual here, there, or elsewhere by differences in the object on which it impinges, but in accordance with his own free purpose, the product of his own intellect, affections, and will.[22]

Particularism in the processes of salvation, therefore, becomes the mark of Calvinism. "As supernaturalism is the mark of Christianity at large, and evangelicalism the mark of Protestantism, so particularism is the mark of Calvinism."[23] Christian supernaturalism, consistently applied, ultimately demands particularism. Supernaturalism leads us away from sacerdotalism to the immediacy of the divine operations of saving grace (i.e., evangelicalism) and on to particularism. To deny particularism is, ultimately, to reject Christianity.

Election

Warfield argues that the doctrine of predestination was "the central doctrine of the Reformation" and "the hinge" on which "their whole religious consciousness and teaching turned," and he cites Luther himself as witness. Luther viewed his dispute with Erasmus over the freedom of the will and the sovereignty of grace as "the top of the question" (summam caussae) involved in the Protestant revolt against Rome. "You and you alone," Luther says to Erasmus, "have seen the hinge of things and have aimed at the throat." "The whole substance of Luther's fundamental theology was summed up in the antithesis of sin and grace: sin conceived as absolutely disabling to good; grace as absolutely recreative in effect." Warfield notes that Luther was not alone in this but was at one with all the great Reformers in it. "In one word, this doctrine was Protestantism itself. All else that Protestant-

---

[21]"Children in the Hands of the Arminians," Union Seminary Magazine 17, no. 3 (1906): 167.
[22]SSW, 1:94.
[23]PS, 87.

ism stood for, in comparison with this, must be relegated to the second rank." This "revival of Augustinianism," with its fundamental antithesis of sin and grace, is "the soul of the whole Reformation movement."[24]

ELECTION A SOVEREIGN DECREE

As noted in chapter 5, Warfield views the doctrine of soteriological predestination against the larger backdrop of God's all-inclusive decree and views it as a specific application of that decree. That God acts according to purpose is the fundamental postulate of theism. To affirm that God has ordained all that comes to pass is simply consistent theism. Moreover, to affirm God's foreordination of all things is already to have affirmed that he has determined the destinies of all men. God "works *all things* according to the counsel of his will" and elects to salvation accordingly (Eph. 1:11). Election, like the whole course of all events, is due not "to chance, nor to necessity, nor yet to an abstract or arbitrary will," but only to "the almighty, all-wise, all-holy, all-righteous, faithful, loving God," who predetermines all that is. It is not God in bare sovereignty who orders all things, or God in sovereign wisdom only, but God "in his completeness as an infinite moral Person." Election, as the larger decree itself, is therefore eternal, absolute, immutable, independent, free, unconditional, and effective. In the actual presentation of the doctrine, Scripture particularly stresses the idea of the sovereignty of God's elective choice.

> The very essence of the doctrine is made, indeed, to consist in the fact that, in the whole administration of His grace, God is moved by no consideration derived from the special recipients of His saving mercy, but the entire account of its distribution is to be found hidden in the free counsels of his own will.[25]

Scripture makes it very plain that God does not bestow his saving operations equally either in space or in time. "His sovereignty shows itself not only in passing by one individual and granting His grace to another; but also in passing by one nation, or one age, and granting His grace to another." The consistent witness of the whole Scripture is that sinners are saved not in any measure as a result of their wills but as a result of God's. Salvation is his sovereign bestowal of mercy, the supreme act of his inconceivable love and glorious grace. Warfield says of Paul that his soteriology was predestinarian because, first and foremost, he was a consistent theist, but also because man is a sinner and as a sinner, condemned

[24]"Is It Restatement That We Need?" *The Presbyterian* 70, no. 33 (1900): 8; *W*, 9:117–18, 472, 476–77.
[25]*SSW*, 1:97; *W*, 2:60–62.

and without means or even the right to approach God. Salvation, therefore, must be wholly of grace, and every initiative God's.[26]

ELECTION OF GRACE

There is nothing about the doctrine of election that is "more steadily empha-sized" in Scripture than that it is due only to God's grace sovereignly distributed, and so it is with this broader subject of grace that Warfield begins his exposition of the doctrine. Taking Ephesians 2:5, 8 as his starting point he observes that Paul's intention is not to remind the Ephesian believers that they are saved. He is intent, rather, on reminding them of *how* they were saved. The manner in which they were saved, he reminds them twice over, is by pure grace. God came to them when they were lying helpless in their sins and spiritual death, and he saved them by *grace*. Grace is "the heart of the heart" of the gospel, the hinge on which the gospel turns.[27]

Warfield then analyzes the nature of saving grace and stresses its three lead-ing characteristics. First, grace is *power*. Grace is not simply a good disposition. It is active power, which of course is precisely what the human condition, bound in sin, requires. "Dead men cannot do anything. They need not instruction but life; not good counsel but power." It is because grace is power that sin "no longer has dominion" over us (Rom. 6:14). Grace does not merely instruct; it energizes. Indeed, it raises the dead. Second, grace is *love*. This is the fundamental implication of the word—favor, love. Grace is not bare power but power directed by love and exerted in kindness. It is the love of God in action and therefore has the character of mercy. When the apostle says we are saved "by grace," therefore, he says that our salvation is solely the result of the love of God. Third, grace is *gratuitous*. It is "the love of benevolence." Grace is not God's response to anything in us that merits his favor. It is pure, undeserved kindness given to us, in fact, contrary to our ill deserts. It is "kindness to the ill-deserving." Salvation is "a pure gratuity from God." Warfield observes that "the body out of which believers are chosen by God . . . is the mass of justly condemned sinners," and he concludes from this that God's discrimination among men in election is an act of mercy alone. Draw-ing all this together Warfield insists that we know nothing about salvation at all until we understand well that we are saved by pure grace, the powerful workings of God's unmerited, loving favor. And again he stresses that grace is "the heart of the heart of the gospel."[28]

---

[26]*FL*, 139; *W*, 2:45–46.
[27]*W*, 2:23; *SSW*, 1:285–86.
[28]*SSW*, 1:286–89; *W*, 2:64; cf. *W*, 4:401–5.

That God saves by grace, then, clarifies for us the nature of election. Grace is the manner in which God saves us; election is simply God's purpose or intention to save us by grace. This is why the apostle can describe it as "the election of grace" (Rom. 11:5 KJV). God did not save us by grace inadvertently, apart from any intention to do so. He saved us on purpose, and this purpose is called election. The purpose preceded the action and even the first manifestations of his love to lost sinners. The doctrine of election, then, reminds us with great emphasis that our salvation is wholly of God's good favor and is such that it leaves us only with "adoring wonder." Our election, our salvation, does not trace back to anything in us or about us. Nothing about us could ever have attracted God's "favorable notice," for God is no "respecter of persons" (Acts 10:34 KJV). By the nature of the case, Warfield says, apparently citing Puritan John Arrowsmith, we are predestined "according to the counsel of his own will, not after the good inclinations of ours." Those of us who are saved were, like all others, objects of God's just wrath and vengeance. Like all others, our wills were disinclined. We are chosen in order that we may *become* holy, not because of our holiness. Everything good about us hangs on God's gracious election, and election itself hangs "on God alone."[29]

ELECTION IN THE BIBLICAL RECORD

This gracious character of God's election was made necessary from the very hour of man's first sin. "God savingly intervenes *sua sponte* with a gratuitous promise of deliverance." At every stage it is God's sovereign and gracious initiative that advances the redemptive purpose. From Adam through Seth to Noah to Shem to Abraham, Isaac, Jacob, and the nation of Israel it is continually God's own initiative, God's own promise, God's intervention, God's covenant—all founded entirely on his unmerited love and directed to his own self-gratification in the manifestation of his saving mercy. God "knows" his people (ידע, Amos 3:2), "chooses" them sovereignly for his own purpose (בחר, Deut. 7:6–7), and "separates" them from all other peoples for himself and his own sake (בדל, Lev. 20:24, 26). His choice of Israel

> is an absolutely sovereign one, founded solely in His unmerited love, and looking to nothing ultimately but the gratification of His own holy and loving impulses, and the manifestation of His grace through the formation of a heritage for Himself out of the mass of sinful men, by means of whom His saving mercy should advance to the whole world.[30]

---

[29]*SSW*, 1:290–92, 298.
[30]*W*, 2:24–25.

That is to say, God's election is entirely of grace.

In the New Testament all this is brought into sharper focus still. In the Gospels his eternal purpose centers on the establishing of his kingdom, prepared for those so blessed to be a part of it. Entrance to the kingdom is given to God's elect by means of a "constraining call" (Luke 14:23), he reveals his kingdom according to his own good pleasure (Luke 10:21; Matt. 11:25–26), and his grace is distributed independently of merit (Matt. 20:1–16). To be sure, sinful men, "condemned already" (John 3:18), unwilling, and unable of themselves to come to Christ for life, must be sovereignly "drawn" by the Father in order to be saved (John 6:44, 65). Christ has come to save "the world" (John 3:16–17), and in the end the world indeed shall be saved. But in the meantime, since the coming of Christ into the world, there is a sifting of those who are "of the world" from those who are "of God"—in the world but not of it—by divine choice (John 15:19; 17:14). For these chosen ones only, Christ is the intercessory high priest (John 17:9), and to them only he grants eternal life (John 17:2). Accordingly, the Spirit of God works sovereignly in giving the new birth (John 3:1–8). All this demonstrates that God's elective decree is not conditioned on the foreseen activities of men and cannot be frustrated by men.[31]

The book of Acts continues in the same vein. Salvation (Acts 11:23) and even saving faith (Acts 18:27) are traced solely to the grace of God. Luke similarly speaks of faith as the results of God's own activity (Acts 2:47; 11:21; 14:27; 16:14) and the outworking of his eternal decree (Acts 13:48). And what is thus written large across the pages of the history of Acts is fully expressed in the epistles and especially the apostle Paul, whose predestinarian roots grow primarily out of his general doctrine of God who orders all that comes to pass, but also from his understanding of the nature of salvation as a gift of free grace, and of man, who in sin has neither rights nor means nor ability to lay claim on God's favor.[32]

Warfield offers three primary Pauline passages in which the apostle expounds soteriological predestination: Romans 8:29–30; Romans 9–11; and Ephesians 1:1–12. In Romans 8:29–30, Paul's intent is to encourage believers who find themselves in afflictions and suffering. He does this first by an appeal to God's universal government in directing all things to his good purpose (v. 28) and, secondarily, by a reminder of God's gracious purpose for them (vv. 29–39). This purpose of grace runs from eternity to eternity—from "foreknown" to "glorified." "Foreknown" carries the significance of electing love (as Amos 3:2), not simply "knowing ahead of time." This "pregnant" use of the term in both Peter and Paul conveys "the sense

---

[31]W, 2:32–40.
[32]W, 2:40–41, 45.

of a loving, distinguishing regard," which "assimilates to the idea of election." Passages such as Romans 8:29 and 11:2 exhibit the "impossibility" of understanding the term as mere "prevision." Hence, those foreknown are predestined to be conformed to the image of Christ. Those so predestined are called. Those called are justified. And those justified are glorified. All five steps are described in the past tense to emphasize that where any one of these is present, all are present with it. Still, the order in which they are stated reveals that in Paul's thought glorification rests on justification, which in turn rests on calling, and calling on predestination, and predestination on foreknowledge. The strict predestinarianism is obvious and can be avoided only by defining "foreknowledge" in a way that is inconsistent with its ordinary usage, with this context, and with the purpose for which this declaration is made. Paul's intent is to support his contention that we are more than lovers of God, merely, but that "God is for us" in such a way that none can stand against us. He is keen to ground our confidence in the fact that all saving benefits have come to us from his own hands. "It would seem little short of absurd," he argues, to hang all this "on the merely contemplative foresight of God." Rather, the apostle assures us, salvation in its entire process is suspended on divine predestination.[33]

Romans 9–11 follows with a perhaps even sharper assertion of the doctrine but treats it not on the individual plain, primarily, but on the historical plain in regard to the development and success of the kingdom of God. God chose Isaac and Jacob and rejected Ishmael and Esau before their births and before they had done good or evil. The impetus of salvation is not of the one who wills but of a sovereign and merciful God who determines these things sovereignly beforehand in order to establish his own purpose. God has mercy on whom he wills. He "shuts up all in disobedience" in order that he may distribute his mercy sovereignly (Rom. 11:32). When the apostle says that "it is not the children of the flesh that are the children of God but the children of the promise" (Rom. 9:8), he makes it plain that the inclusion of any individual in God's kingdom is due only to God's sovereign choice.[34]

That this passage (Romans 9–11) is speaking of salvation and not simply higher privilege is indisputable. The very epistle is given to expound at length "the power of God for salvation to everyone who believes, to the Jew first and also to the Greek" (Rom. 1:16). This passage was sparked by the apostle's discussion at the end of chapter 8 of the believer's soteric hope, it concludes with a praise to God for his generous distribution of mercy, and throughout its steady focus is the

---

[33]W, 2:42, 48–49.
[34]W, 2:49–54.

same. "Vessels of mercy" versus "vessels of wrath"—"if such language has no reference to salvation, there is no language in the New Testament that need be interpreted of final destiny."[35]

In Ephesians 1:1–12 the apostle Paul traces the history of salvation consecutively from eternity to eternity—from its preparation (vv. 4–5) to its execution (vv. 6–7), its publication (vv. 8–10), and its application (vv. 11–14). Salvation has come to us in fulfillment of God's eternal purpose; that is, we are saved only because before the world began, we were chosen out of the mass of sinful men and predestined to adoption through Jesus Christ—all this according to the good purpose of God's own will and to the praise of the glory of his grace. God's eternal decree is all-embracing. The cosmos itself, the kingdom of God, the individuals who constitute that kingdom—are all destined, according to God's own purpose and will, to be summed up in Christ.

INDIVIDUAL OBJECTS OF ELECTION

Scripture further emphasizes the individual particularity of God's elective choice. Election is not "the designation of a mere class to be filled up by undetermined individuals in the exercise of their own determinations," whether foreseen or unforeseen. Nor has God merely established that there would be in the end these two destinies of life and condemnation. God, in the words of the confession, ordains "whatever comes to pass," even the death of a sparrow and the falling of a single hair from our heads. His purpose is universal and all-inclusive. "The Biblical writers take special pains to carry home to the heart of each individual believer the assurance that he himself has been from all eternity the particular object of the Divine choice, and that he owes it to this Divine choice alone that he is a member of the class of the chosen ones" and therefore made able to fulfill the conditions of salvation. Indeed, it is "the very nerve" of the doctrine that each individual believer has from eternity been the particular object of the divine favor.[36]

In his sermon "The Eternal Gospel," Warfield expounds this point from the implications of 2 Timothy 1:9–10. Here the apostle Paul emphasizes "with a tremendous energy" that our calling to salvation was "not according to works of ours but according to His own purpose and grace"—a purpose and grace "given to us in Christ Jesus before times eternal." Warfield notes that this grace was not merely promised to us before times eternal. Nor does Paul say merely that we were destined for it. Rather, this grace was "actually and finally and unequivocally given" to us before times eternal. What has now been "manifested" or "made visible"

---

[35] W, 2:53.
[36] SSW, 1:100–101; W, 2:63–64.

(φανερόω) is but the outworking in time of "what was already done, concluded, accomplished in eternity." Our experience of saving grace is, of course, an experience within time; but it was nonetheless ours—"given us"—eternally.[37]

"PROBLEMS"

Warfield is careful to note that in their presentation of the doctrine of election the biblical writers do not feel themselves in the constraints of an antinomy. God's sovereign predestination serves both as a ground of assurance and "the highest motive of moral effort." Those "twin bases of religion and morality—the ineradicable feelings of dependence and responsibility"—are not "antagonistic sentiments of a hopelessly divided heart" but "the same profound conviction operating in a double sphere." In Paul's view, God works in *concursus*, in all things accomplishing his own will "in entire consistency with the action of second causes, necessary and free." Nor is it "dehumanizing" to man to work through him this way, but "an act of God's almighty power, removing old inabilities and creating new abilities of living, loving action" and "energizing man in a new direction of his powers."[38]

The biblical writers are not embarrassed by negative or unpleasant implications of the doctrine but rather themselves make these a part of their teaching. Preterition, for example, is not obscured but implicit in the very word ἐκλέγομαι, which, says Warfield (citing Meyer), "*always* has, and must *of logical necessity* have, a reference to *others* to whom the chosen would, without the ἐκλογή, still belong." It is simply impossible to choose *some* men to be saved without passing by ("preteriting") others. The "elect" are chosen not merely from condemnation but "out of a company of the condemned—a company on whom the grace of God has no saving effect and who are therefore left without hope in their sins" and left to the just punishment of those sins. There is no acceptable alternative to preterition, as Warfield summarizes:

> If God passes no man by in the distribution of his grace, then either all men must be saved or else the grace that is denied to none but given equally to all, cannot be effectual to salvation, cannot be irresistible. To deny sovereign preterition must thus logically lead either to Universalism or Arminianism.[39]

Warfield counsels that the difficulties we feel with regard to predestination are not problems that rise from Scripture, for Scripture is full of the doctrine. And

---

[37]*FL*, 407–9.
[38]*W*, 2:59–60.
[39]*W*, 2:64 (emphasis original); "Dr. Schaff and the Calvinistic System," *PJ* 17, no. 19 (1892): 290–91.

Scripture is full of predestination simply because "it is full of God, and when we say God and mean God—God in all that God is—we have said Predestination." Our difficulties with the doctrine arise, rather, from our natural feelings of independence and self-sufficiency. We are not willing to consider ourselves as "wholly at the disposal of another." In the words of the hymn, "we would not be controlled." Perhaps better, we are not willing to admit that we *are* controlled. But to admit that we are *not* controlled would be to assert that there is no God.[40]

Why does God elect only some and not all? And why does he send his saving grace only to those whom he has chosen to save? Warfield advises, simply, that these are not wise questions to ask. No doubt, God has his reasons, but he has not explained them to us. Why did our Lord raise only Lazarus that day in Bethany? We do not know. We may imagine. We may guess. But we can only know that he had his reasons. So with his sovereign election, we are best to leave it to him and content ourselves, like the apostle Paul, with a humble worship of our incomprehensible God (Rom. 11:33–36). Jesus' statement "even so, Father: for so it seemed good in thy sight" (Matt. 11:26 KJV; Luke 10:21 KJV) is to him—and so ought to be for us—"an all-sufficient theodicy" in the face of all God's discriminating and diverse dealings with men. But Warfield counsels further, that the question that should impress our minds is not why God chose some and not others, but why he chose any at all. The real difficulty is here—"how the holy God could get the consent of his nature to save a single sinner." Or again, "It is not difficult to understand why a just God does not save all sinners; the difficulty is to understand how a just God saves any sinners." An honest assessment of the matter will leave us here with wonder and, indeed, drive us to still more adoring wonder that God has chosen "me, even me, sunk in my sin and misery." Citing Bernard, Warfield writes, "God deserveth love from such as he hath loved long before they could deserve it. . . . His love will be without end, who knoweth that God's love to him was without any beginning."[41]

PASTORAL USES

For the weak soul who despairs that he may not be one of the elect, Warfield exhorts that we should not expend strength "prying into God's secrets," but we should instead simply "take him at his word." God does not lay out election as a requirement to the sinner, nor is his offer of grace an offer of predestination. No, "He offers you not predestination, but Christ; and He requires of you not election, but faith." The requirement for salvation is not election but repentance and faith, and the promise is that if you will come to Christ, you will be saved. Election is

[40]*SSW*, 1:103.
[41]*SSW*, 1:297–98; *W*, 2:39; *PTR* 11, no. 4 (1913): 702.

intended as a ground not of doubt and despair but of assurance and joy for the one who believes.[42]

Warfield stresses with urgency that there are evidences that we are chosen of God to salvation apart from which, we may be sure, there is no salvation. Our faith itself, of course, is one. But there is also the evidence of good works and holiness—faith, virtue, knowledge, temperance, patience, godliness, love of the brethren, and so on. These are the marks of God's elect. Those who are saved "certainly shall be holy," Warfield insists. "This is what he has chosen them to— that they shall be holy" (Eph. 1:4–5), that they shall be conformed to the image of Christ (Rom. 8:29). We are created in Christ Jesus "for good works" (Eph. 2:10). We can—we must—expect that God's elect are a holy people. "God has not chosen us to sloth." This is what we are called to. "We are not elected in order to dispense us from the necessity of being good. We are elected to make it possible for us to be good, yea, rather, to make it certain that we shall be good, not apart from but through our own efforts." The elect, then, are cautioned to "be careful to maintain good works" (Titus 3:8, 14) and "work out their own salvation with fear and trembling" (Phil. 2:12), to "make their calling and election sure" (2 Pet. 1:10). "We need not, we must not, seek elsewhere for proof of our election: if we believe in Christ and obey him, we are his elect children."[43]

But just as carefully and with as much certainty Warfield reminds us that this holiness required of the elect is not left to the elect to produce on their own. No, holiness is certain precisely because, "having chosen them to be holy, [God] has not left them to themselves, but, in his infinite grace, has taken them in hand to make them holy." God gives his elect the faith he requires of them; he also works in them the holiness he requires.

> We are not elected that we may not have to fight the good fight, but to secure that we shall fight it to the end, fight it successfully, and so finish the course; not that we may not require to keep the faith, but that we may, that we shall keep it triumphantly and receive the crown. We are not released by our election from the duties and struggles and strifes, not even from the trials and sufferings, of life: we are elected to be sustained in them and carried safely through them all.

The holiness to which God calls us, then, is a holiness that shall certainly be achieved, progressively in this life and perfectly in the next. "We shall be like him, because we shall see him as he is" (1 John 3:2).[44]

---

[42]*SW*, 240.
[43]*SSW*, 1:292–97.
[44]*SSW*, 1:292–97.

Accordingly, there is another pastoral interest in which the biblical writers zealously present this doctrine. It is useful not only as an incentive to holiness but also as a ground of confident assurance. An understanding of this truth should make believers keenly aware of "their eternal safety in the faithful hands of God." It is a frequent theme in the Pauline letters that our salvation is not committed to our own weak hands but to God; it rests securely in the faithfulness of the God who chose and called us according to his own eternal purpose (I Thess. 5:24; I Cor. 1:8f.; 10:13; Phil. 1:6). Although our act of faith, consequent on hearing the gospel, marked the beginning of our appropriation of salvation, both of these were but the outworking of God's sovereign purpose. At the beginning of the Christian life and all throughout, it is God's willing and energizing operations at work in us that move us to faith and good works (Phil. 2:12–13). The hope of the Christian, and that of the church generally, is in the mercy of a freely electing God. Our destiny has been left not to our weak arms but on the everlasting arms of the almighty God. With this as a benefit of the doctrine of election, who would want to believe otherwise?[45]

That this note of worship is, for Warfield, where the issue comes down, is illustrated in his response to those of his day who were moving to alter the confessional doctrine of the decree (WCF 3). To excise from the confession its doctrine of the divine decree we must first excise from the Scriptures "all that gives us a right as individuals to trust in the saving grace of God alone for the inception, continuance, and completion of our salvation," as well as all the many passages that present him as the author and governor of all things. "The real issue that is at stake," Warfield insists, is "whether we are still prepared to preserve in its purity and in its strength our fundamental confession of 'soli Deo gloria.' So long as that confession sounds in our hearts, so long must we confess all that our Confession sets forth in the opening four sections of its third chapter."[46]

That is to say, an understanding of God's elective decree serves to promote in us a "deep sense of grateful dependence" upon God. Warfield is convinced that his Calvinistic doctrine of election is of the essence of pure religion. Pure religion is expressed in utter dependence[47] upon God and trust in his mercy alone. It is the religion that is left remaining when all self-trust is driven out and leaves behind only trust in God. Pure religion is illustrated in the attitude of mind and heart when we pray, "when we kneel before God, not with the body merely, but with

---

[45]W, 2:57; SSW, 1:101.

[46]SSW, 1:102.

[47]Although Warfield opposed so much about Schleiermacher he seemed to have an appreciation for his notion of "absolute dependence" on God. But unlike Schleiermacher, for Warfield this was the necessary entailment of supernaturalism and particularism in soteriology.

the mind and heart" in humble acknowledgment of his supremacy and our utter helplessness apart from his grace. It is here that religion comes to its rights. In short, this doctrine promotes true worship.[48]

Divine Calling

EXPOSITION OF THE DOCTRINE

Throughout all his discussions touching soteriology Warfield reflects a firm sense of utter dependence on God alone, and he is zealous above all other considerations to magnify the "pure" and "unalloyed" grace of God the Savior. His conviction that he himself is a helpless sinner—a "miserable sinner," to use the historic language he is wont to keep alive—rescued sheerly by divine mercy alone, runs through virtually every page. At every turn he is unalterably opposed to every trace of Pelagianism, which currently shows itself in that "reduced Christianity" calling itself "modern Liberalism."[49] Salvation is deliverance, rescue, in every sense of the term, a rescue to which the sinner contributes precisely nothing but the sin from which he is saved, and Warfield will not countenance any human impingement on the divine glory in any part of the process. Grace—"pure grace," "sheer mercy," "monergism"—is the note resounding everywhere in Warfield's soteriology.

These twin convictions of sin and helplessness, on the one hand, and dependence and grace, on the other, are captured vividly in his careful treatment of those Synoptic passages in which Jesus blesses the little children or otherwise refers to them as illustrative of salvation (Matt. 18:1–4; 19:13–15; Mark 10:13–16; Luke 18:15–17).[50] Warfield demonstrates that these references have nothing to do with infants per se or with infant baptism or with infant salvation. Rather, Jesus uses the incident as a graphic illustration designed to stress that unless we "become as little children," we cannot be saved. What is it to become as a little child? Warfield argues that it cannot be humility, simply, for this is hardly the leading characteristic of little children. "Childlikeness" is to be understood in more objective terms. What is it that characterizes little children? Warfield answers: they are helpless. They have nothing to contribute. They can lay claim to nothing but are utterly dependent on the goodness of another. All of Christ's disciples are but "nursing infants" (Matt. 21:16)—helpless and utterly dependent. The incident of Jesus' blessing the children is intended distinctly to instruct us

---

[48]*SSW*, 1:95, 389–92.
[49]*W*, 10:452.
[50]This was clearly a favorite of Warfield's, receiving repeated attention in *SSW*, 1:234–52 (1904), 223–33 (1908); *W*, 2:449–50 (1911); *W*, 3:97–103 (1914); *FL*, 65–80 (1916).

regarding "the constitution of the Kingdom of God," which "is made up, not of children, but of the childlike." "The Kingdom of heaven is made up of those who are helplessly dependent on the King of Heavens."

> The upshot of all this is, then, this: that the Kingdom of God is not taken—acquired—laid hold of; it is just "received." It comes to men, men do not come to it. And when it comes to men, they merely "receive" it, "as"—"like"—"a little child." That is to say, they bring nothing to it and have nothing to recommend them to it except their helplessness. They depend wholly on the King. Only they who so receive it can enter it; no disposition or act of their own commends them to it. Accordingly the Kingdom of God is "of such as little children." The helpless baby on the mother's breast, then, now we can say it with new meaning, is the true type of the Christian in his relation to God. It is of the very essence of salvation that it is supernatural. It is purely a gift, a gift of God's; and they who receive it must receive it purely as a gift. He who will not humble himself and enter it as a little child enters the world, in utter nakedness and complete dependence, shall never see it.

The problem with the rich young ruler (Matt. 19:16–22 = Mark 10:17–22 = Luke 18:18–23) was precisely this. He had many possessions and "could not divest himself of everything and come into the Kingdom naked."[51]

Warfield notes that the pericope of the rich young ruler in all three Synoptics immediately follows the account of Jesus' blessing the little children. In Luke, these are immediately preceded by the parable of the Pharisee and tax collector (Luke 18:9–14). In Matthew they are immediately succeeded by the parable of the laborers in the vineyard (Matt. 20:1–16), "who were surprised that their rewards were not nicely adjusted to what they deemed their relative services." All of this is designed to stress that "the Kingdom of God is a gratuity, not an acquisition; and the effect of bringing them together is to throw a great emphasis upon this, their common teaching." Accordingly, Warfield refers to Jesus' conversation with the rich young ruler as the Synoptic parallel to Jesus' conversation with Nicodemus in John 3, where again Jesus stresses that just as the precondition of entrance to the kingdom of God is that radical transformation wrought by the Spirit of God, so this is precisely what the Spirit sovereignly gives in the new birth. Saving life is a gift divinely bestowed.[52]

This is a most familiar theme in Warfield.[53] In his sermon on 1 John 3:1 he comments that John marvels at the grace sovereignly bestowed on us that we should be called God's children. He remarks that John's language is not analytical but emotional,

---

[51]*FL*, 68–69.
[52]*W*, 3:97; *W*, 2:446–50.
[53]See also the discussions above (chaps. 2 and 3) on revelation and the knowledge of God and apologetics.

while nonetheless reflective of a settled conviction that God saves gratuitously. "'Behold! What manner of love is this!' 'To seek us out and make us the sons of God!' Language could not convey more clearly, more powerfully, the conception of the absolute sovereignty of the gift." Childship to God is a favor "bestowed"—graciously conferred—on us. We do not earn it. The Father has given it to us freely.[54]

Warfield treats this theme at considerable length in his sermon on Titus 3:4–7, in which the apostle Paul traces our salvation purely to God's kindness and grace, his benignity and philanthropy. The passage is "a psalm of praise to God for his saving love" and sings "not only 'Gloria Deo' but 'Soli Deo Gloria.'" Nor does this song of praise ascribe salvation to God generally or even in its root. It ascribes salvation "in every one of its details to God's loving activities and to them alone; it ascribes its beginning and middle and end to Him and to Him only." The apostle does not even see the need to mention faith, the condition we must perform in order to obtain salvation. "It is God alone who saves, 'not by means of any works in righteousness which we have done ourselves but in consequence of his mercy' and of that alone." The whole force of the passage is to assert that

> if we are saved at all, it is because—not that we have worked, not that we have believed,—but that God has manifested His benignity and philanthropy in saving us out of His mere mercy. He has, through Jesus Christ, shed down His Holy Spirit to regenerate and renovate us that we might be justified "by His grace,"—in other words, gratuitously, not on the ground of our faith,—and so be made heirs of eternal life.[55]

The attitude of trust and dependence on God, Warfield says repeatedly, is "the very essence of religion," apart from which there is no religion at all,[56] and it is this attitude of utter dependence upon God that he is eager to promote. Everywhere in his works, divine grace—with a corresponding utter dependence upon God—is a theme that dominates. It is out of sheer grace that God works, from beginning to end, to accomplish our salvation. Salvation is in every way a gratuity, and the sinner is left only in utter dependence upon God. The very wonder of salvation is that God has taken pity on rebel sinners and from his own side alone has rescued them and transformed them.

HUMAN INABILITY AND DIVINE INITIATIVE

That salvation is by grace is evident from man's condition in sin. According to the biblical view, the human problem goes much deeper than so many individual

---

[54]*FL*, 450–53.
[55]*FL*, 395–97.
[56]*PGS*, 213.

acts of sin. Our depravity is essentially "a great ocean of sin within us, whose waves merely break in sinful acts." Sin is "inborn, ingrained in nature itself" and leaves man altogether helpless. For remedy, it requires nothing less than a new creation. "An entire making over again can alone suffice," and it is from this understanding that David cries, "create in me a clean heart" (Ps. 51:10). Warfield finds human inability implied in Acts 26:18, where the apostle Paul is commissioned "to open their eyes and turn them from darkness to light, and from the power of Satan to God." The express statement is that men are in darkness, requiring that their eyes "be opened." Foolish minds are darkened and "they cannot know God," for they are in "bondage to Satan." Warfield considers it self-evident "that men cannot turn from darkness to light, from the tyranny of Satan to God, in their own strength" but need "the immanent work of the Holy Spirit." These are feats that God alone can accomplish. It is required that the apostle preach the gospel, and it is required that his hearers be converted. Even so, God alone can give the increase (1 Cor. 3:6–7).[57]

In a similar vein Warfield expounds Christ's affirmation in Mark 10:27 that salvation is "impossible" for men. He rejects out of hand all explanations of "the camel passing through the eye of the needle" that mitigate the difficulty of the task. The impossibility is absolute. Jesus does not say that salvation, for man, is difficult but not impossible. He says straightforwardly that it is impossible. Salvation can only be had by the workings of the omnipotent God, with whom "all things are possible." "Here is then the sharpest possible enunciation of the doctrine of 'inability.'" But Warfield points out that this inability on the part of man does not lie in any lack of human endowment. The rich young ruler, in reference to whom this affirmation of inability was made, did not lack either the intelligence to know the commands of God or the freedom to keep them. He had a relatively upright life and character. The Evangelist records, indeed, that "Jesus loved him." "Surely here is one, who, were it possible to man at all, might be expected to do what was necessary to inherit eternal life." No, his inability did not lie in any lack of human endowment. He possessed all the necessary faculties. His inability lay, rather, in his "ingrained disposition" of sin. The root of his inability was "a sin-distorted vision, feeling, judgment—in a word, in a sin-deformed soul, to which it is just as impossible 'to be perfect' as it is for the lame leg not to limp." Human inability, he summarizes, is "rooted in a heart too corrupt to appreciate, desire or go out in an active inclination toward 'the good.' What is in itself corrupt cannot but be corrupted in all its activities." Sin has had a "paralyzing" effect that cripples "all activities toward God," including even faith.

---

[57]*FL*, 19–20, 175–76.

"Inability is a sinful condition of the will," and the sinner is unable to use his will for believing "because he loves sin too much."[58]

Warfield finds the doctrine of inability summarized in John 5:44, where Jesus asks his opponents, "How can you believe, when you receive glory from one another and do not seek the glory that comes from the only God?" Here Jesus exposes "the grounds of men's unbelief as rooted in an essentially self-seeking and worldly spirit." Jesus has miraculously healed an impotent man, and from this incident grows his discourse intended to demonstrate the impotence of sinners to believe in him as the Savior of the world. The Jewish religious leaders are enraged with Jesus and seek to slay him, and Jesus simply observes that their eye is toward man and not God: "You accept praise from one another, yet make no effort to obtain the praise that comes from the only God." And so Jesus asks rhetorically, "How could you believe?" From this Warfield draws the following observations: (1) Jesus asserts that the Jews are unable to believe—there is a true inability of faith. (2) He traces this inability to its source in their misguided disposition. Their condition of mind and heart prevents them from believing. (3) The special sin that blinds them from seeing in Jesus a worthy object of faith is the sin of living for the world's approval instead of God's. (4) It follows from this that inability does not negate responsibility, for it is their own sinful motives that render them unable to believe. "They could not believe, but it was because of their wicked hearts."[59]

But in Mark 10:27, where Jesus pointedly affirms the inability of man to obtain salvation, this inability is not in itself the point he is seeking to stress. The "great lesson" of his declaration is not human inability but divine ability: "All things are possible with God." Jesus' purpose is to "detach their hearts from trust in themselves and cast them on God." In this discrimination between what men do and what God does for men lies "the totality of the gospel. . . . The Gospel, to Paul, consists precisely in this: that we do nothing to earn our salvation or to secure it for ourselves. God in Christ does it all."[60]

In 2 Corinthians 5:14–21 the apostle Paul speaks in absolute terms of the inevitable effects of Christ's death. Those for whom he died, died with him, and just as surely as they died with him, they live with him. The saving grace secured by Christ's death is infallibly effective in the experience of those for whom he died. Those for whom Christ died are actually saved, a salvation that affects the whole of their lives. Warfield finds it, then, one of "the most astonishing curiosities of exposition" that Christians could teach that the decisive act of salvation is

---

[58]*PGS*, 100, 102–3, 200–201; *SSW*, 2:725. Warfield adds that "for such a 'cannot' he is certainly responsible."
[59]*FL*, 94–99; cf. *W*, 9:341.
[60]*PGS*, 103–4; *FL*, 322.

supplied by an action of the human will. Such would imply that all that God has done in salvation is outside of us, a notion everywhere contradicted by the biblical writers. It is God who makes men "differ in their spiritual endowments," and it is God who "worketh in you both to will and to do of his good pleasure" (Phil. 2:13 KJV). God "works our very willing as well as our doing." "It is not of him that willeth, nor of him that runneth, but of God that sheweth mercy" (Rom. 9:16 KJV). Everywhere salvation in its every step is said to be "of God."[61]

In Romans 6–7 the apostle Paul alludes to this divine omnipotence which conquers human inability. On the one hand he declares that man is "of the flesh, sold under sin" (Rom. 7:14). On the other hand he writes that under grace "sin shall not rule over you" (Rom. 6:14 BBW). Certainly the apostle allows room here for the voluntary activities of men, "but as certainly he presents grace that comes to them gratuitously as both 'infallible' and 'irresistible.'" Paul's statement in Romans 6:14 is not one of potential but one of fact: "Sin *shall not* rule over you." And the reason for sin's broken rule is plainly stated: "*for* you are under grace." Clearly, then, "grace is a power which irresistibly brings the result"; it is "the almighty power of God which creatively works its effect" in us.[62] This is how sinners become believers—the irresistible grace of God.

Warfield considers irresistible grace necessary to a purely supernatural salvation and "the very heart of the doctrine of 'renewal.'" It is "the hinge" and "distinguishing principle" of the Calvinistic soteriology, which, at its very heart, is concerned to exclude all creaturely elements in the initiation of the saving process so as to magnify the pure grace of God.[63]

Warfield was a soteriological exclusivist in that he admitted salvation to none but those who believe (except infants). He is convinced that the reception of salvation depends on hearing and believing the gospel of Christ.[64] And he is confident that those whom in grace God has chosen will in God's providence hear the gospel so that they may believe. But this only leads him to emphasize grace again—neither the hearing nor the believing is left merely to the abilities of man. God's providence is over all, and he directs the gospel witness to those whom he has appointed to life. Likewise, the faith he requires of those who are to be saved is not left to their own native abilities to produce. That any sinner ever accepts the gospel proclamation is due only to a "call" from God working effectively in

---

[61]*SW*, 144–46.

[62]*W*, 10:448–49.

[63]*W*, 2:461; *W*, 5:359; *SSW*, 2:415.

[64]He specifically expresses disagreement on this point with William G. T. Shedd, who allowed that many would be saved apart from the gospel. *BTS*, 350; cf. *SSW*, 1:113–15; *PRR* 1, no. 1 (1890): 157; "How Shall We Escape?" in *Lile's Golden Lamp*, ed. R. M. Offord (New York: *New York Observer*, 1889): n.p. (devotional entry for January 13); cf. *SW*, 37–65.

him and enabling him to do so. God calls sinners to "his own kingdom and glory" (1 Thess. 2:12), and, Warfield asks, "Who else can have the power to dispose of these but He?" He answers, "He who calls you is faithful; he will surely do it" (1 Thess. 5:24). In Paul's understanding, the caller is emphatically also the performer.[65]

Accordingly, there is in Warfield a dominant emphasis on the role of the Holy Spirit who works powerfully and sovereignly in bringing sinners to Christ. He notes, for example, in 2 Corinthians 4:13 that the apostle Paul attributes his faith, like that of the Old Testament saints, to the workings of the Holy Spirit. He has the "same Spirit of faith."

> That the Spirit is called the "Spirit of faith" means that faith does not exist except as His gift; its very existence is bound up in His working. Just as we call Him the Spirit of life, the Spirit of holiness, and the like, because all life comes from Him and all holiness is of His making, so, when Paul calls Him the Spirit of faith, it is the evidence that in Paul's conception all faith comes from Him.

The apostle's expressed confidence—"With that same Spirit of faith . . . we also believe, and therefore speak" (BBW)—is not merely in his faith but in the Spirit of God who gave him faith. The apostle Paul understands faith to be the result of the operations of the Spirit in us.[66] Faith is the fruit of the Spirit (Gal. 5:22), a gift that he sovereignly distributes to men (1 Cor. 12:7).

Warfield supports this further in the *ordo salutis*, which he finds spelled out in Titus 3:4–7. Here the apostle tells us that God saves us by sheer mercy "through the renovating work of the Holy Spirit," which in turn is "founded on the redeeming work of Christ." We are told further that the renovating work of the Spirit is "in order that we might be justified and so become heirs." Hence, the purchase by the death of Christ is the condition that precedes the regenerating work of the Spirit, and the work of the Spirit is the condition that precedes justification and adoption. In the application of salvation, "the Spirit works by first regenerating the soul, next justifying it, next adopting it into the family of God, and next sanctifying it."[67]

In its every step it is the powerful working of God's grace that makes a man a Christian. The righteousness required of him is wrought for him by another and

---

[65]*SSW*, 1:113–15; cf. WCF 10; *PGS*, 209. Warfield notes the difference between the Synoptics and the Epistles (especially Paul) in the meaning given to the divine "call." In the Synoptics the call has the ordinary meaning of "invitation." In the Epistles, however, it is used in connection with divine election, "or, more precisely, as expressive of the temporal act of the Divine efficiency by which effect is given to the electing decree." Warfield cites Matt. 9:13; Mark 2:17; Luke 5:32 as examples of the former and Rom. 1:6–7; 1 Cor. 1:2; Rom. 8:28; 1 Cor. 1:24; Jude 1; Rev. 17:14 as examples of the latter.
[66]*FL*, 236–40.
[67]*FL*, 399; cf. *SSW*, 2:321–24.

credited to him freely. It is received only by faith—trust—but even this faith is given as a free gift. So also in sanctification, it is "God who works in you, both to will and to work for his good pleasure" (Phil. 2:13). "Every saving work of God actifies the soul, but no saving work of God waits on the soul's activities."[68]

All this yields great assurance to the Christian in his witness for Christ. We have not been sent to the world to tell it of things it already believes or even things it will readily accept. God "has sent us to preach unpalatable truths to a world lying in wickedness; apparently absurd truths to men, proud of their intellects; mysterious truths to men who are carnal and cannot receive the things of the Spirit of God." Should this lead us to despair? "Certainly," Warfield replies, "if it is left to us not only to plant and to water but also to give the increase. Certainly not, if we appeal to and depend upon the Spirit of faith. Let Him but move on our hearts and we will believe these truths."[69]

Justification by Faith

Although Warfield never produced a single in-depth exposition of the doctrine of justification, he did address the matter frequently in preaching, and here and there in his other works. He everywhere reflects his deep-seated appreciation for and ever-hearty embrace of the Reformed doctrine of justification by faith alone, which, for him, reflects the heart of the gospel. He acknowledges that Paul's statement of the doctrine of justification by grace through faith alone was stated in the context of his "ineradicable conflict" with the Judaizers, but he insists that this does not affect the substance of his teaching, only its form. It is, after all, not merely Paul's personal opinion that he proclaims but revealed truth. Paul's first concern was not the Judaizers. His first concern was the gospel, and it is this that brought him into conflict with the Judaizers. "He did not hold this doctrine of salvation because he polemicized the Judaizers, but he polemicized the Judaizers because he held this doctrine of salvation." Nor was this doctrine attained in controversy with his opponents. Rather, "he controverted the Judaizers because their teaching impinged on this precious doctrine."[70]

THE NATURE OF JUSTIFICATION

Warfield understands the apostle Paul to be concerned over the Judaizing tendency to admit human works or merit into the ground of justification. This, for

---

[68]W, 10:464.
[69]FL, 242.
[70]FL, 316–17.

him, was unthinkable. The work of Christ alone constitutes the whole ground of our acceptance before God. The gospel, Warfield says, "is not *good advice*, but *good news*. It does not come to us to make known to us what we must do to earn salvation for ourselves, but proclaiming to us what Jesus has done to save us. It is salvation, a completed salvation, that it announces to us." This is the crux of the matter, and this must be reflected in our doctrine of justification—our standing before God is given to us gratuitously in Christ; there is nothing at all the sinner contributes to it.[71]

In his classroom lecture Warfield asserts that in justification God acts as judge. In justification God does not merely pardon, as a sovereign ruler may pardon a subject. A pardoned man remains guilty. In justification the man is declared righteous. This declaration, in turn, is grounded in the imputation of Christ's righteousness to us and received by us through faith alone, apart from works of any kind. Warfield specifies further that faith is in Scripture always viewed as the instrument and never the ground of justification, as though it were a work for which we are rewarded. The dative is never used. The ground of justification is the righteousness of Christ. "Therefore, as one trespass led to condemnation for all men, so one act of righteousness leads to justification and life for all men" (Rom. 5:18).[72]

In Philippians 3:9 the apostle Paul's ambition is to be "found in him, not having a righteousness of my own that comes from the law, but that which comes through faith in Christ, the righteousness from God that depends on faith." The plain statement is that "every item and degree" of our own righteousness is specifically excluded from the saving equation. Even faith, though demanded, is not allowed a place in the ground of our justification. "According to his express statements, at least, we are saved entirely on the ground of an alien righteousness and not at all on the ground of anything we are or have done, or can do,—be it even so small a matter as believing." The apostle's whole point is to lay stress on the truth that "Christ Jesus is all." "The contrast is absolute," and the alternatives are mutually exclusive. Paul holds all personal efforts in contempt. All that we are and have, all that men can appeal to, the apostle counts not merely useless, but loss—"all one mass of loss, to be cast away and buried in the sea"—so that we may instead gain Christ and be found in him. "On the one side stand all human works—they are all loss. On the other hand stands Christ—He is all in all. That is the contrast." "The Gospel, to Paul, consists precisely in this: that we do nothing to earn our salvation or to secure it for ourselves. God in Christ does it all." There is never

---

[71]*PGS*, 50 (emphasis original).
[72]N. W. Harkness, unpublished class notes from Warfield's lectures on systematic theology, 1899–1901 (Princeton Seminary library archives), 45–47.

anything "in us or done by us, at any stage of our earthy development, because of which we are acceptable to God." We are accepted always and only "for Christ's sake, or we cannot ever be accepted at all." It is on this ground that the apostle exhorts the Philippians to "rejoice in the Lord." He is eager that their worship of God will be truly "spiritual worship," and spiritual worship can only be worship that is marked by a "boasting in Christ Jesus alone and the withdrawal of all confidence from the flesh." They must rejoice *in the Lord* and could rejoice *in the Lord* precisely because it was the Lord's own righteousness in which they stood. They were, after all, "saved—not self-saving souls." This "alien righteousness," the righteousness of Christ freely imputed to us, is the whole ground of our confidence before God.[73]

That is to say, what God requires of us—righteousness—he gives us in Christ. Here the term "imputation" is essential. Imputation is "simply the act of setting to one's account." Just as Adam's sin was imputed to his posterity, and just as our sin was imputed to Christ, so also Christ's righteousness is imputed to us. The grounds may differ in each, and the thing imputed may differ. "The consequent treatment of the person or persons to which the imputation is made may and will differ as the things imputed to them differ." But the act of imputation is the same in each case. It is not that God has merely smiled and agreed to let bygones be bygones. Nor has he relaxed the standard and determined no longer to require righteousness. Nor is it a fictional righteousness that is imputed. No, what he requires he provides. "The righteousness on the ground of which God accepts a sinner . . . is an absolutely real, and absolutely perfect righteousness. . . . It is the righteousness of Christ, provided by God in and through Christ." Christ performed the work required of us, and his merit is "imputed" to us—credited, "set to our account." This—the righteousness provided for us by God in Christ—is "the sole ground of our acceptance" before God. And thus imputation is "the hinge" on which turn the doctrines of human sin, the satisfaction of Christ, and justification by faith.[74]

This gift of righteousness comes to us freely but not without cost. Thus the apostle Paul argues in Romans 3:24–25 that God justifies only on the ground of the ransoming work of Christ. He does not—indeed, God cannot—justify a sinner arbitrarily but only on the ground of the satisfaction of his justice. In Christ's sacrificial and substitutional death God's justice is satisfied in his payment for sin.

> What Paul says is, that the ransoming that is in Christ Jesus is the means by which men, being sinners, are brought by God into a justification which they cannot secure

[73]*FL*, 316–25; *W*, 7:113–16.
[74]"The Hibbert Journal," *TBS*, new series, 7, no. 1 (January 1903): 57; *W*, 9:302, 305; *FL*, 316.

for themselves. If the ransoming that is in Christ Jesus is the means by which alone they can be justified, that is only another way of saying that God, who gratuitously justifies them in His grace, proceeds in this act in view of nothing in them, but solely in view of the ransoming that is in Christ Jesus.[75]

THE BENEFITS OF JUSTIFICATION

Warfield analyzes Romans 5:1–2 and characterizes it as "Paul's argument from experience." Paul takes as his point of reference not a declaration of doctrine but an experience common to all believers: "Therefore, since we have been justified by faith, we have peace with God." His point is that as a result of seeking justification from God not by works but by faith in Jesus Christ, all believers experience the peace of a quieted conscience and acceptance with God. His point is not that all believers ought to have this peace, but that all believers already have this peace. And it is on this universally acknowledged and undeniable fact that the apostle grounds his argument: you (believer) know in your own heart by the peace you experience that justification before God has come through faith.[76]

This argument from experience does not form the entire ground of the apostle's argument that justification is by faith. Just prior to this passage he establishes his argument on exegetical grounds: "Abraham *believed* God, and it was accounted to him unto righteousness" (Gen. 15:6; Rom. 4:3 BBW). Then, in the following passage, he appeals to the pattern of God's dealings with men in other matters: both sin and righteousness are imputed by a single representative man (Rom. 5:12ff.). But between these two passages he appeals to the universal Christian consciousness that peace with God has been established by faith: the fact that upon believing in Christ all Christians experience peace with God demonstrates that justification is indeed by faith. That is, "If the presence of the fruits of justification proves we are justified, the presence of the justification, thus proved, proves that justification is found on the road by which we reached it."[77]

Warfield then draws from this its primary implication; namely, that justification by faith is naturally adapted to produce peace and joy in the believing sinner. It is not without objective warrant that the believer enjoys this peace. Certainly, it is the Holy Spirit who produces this peace in us, but it is not an ungrounded emotion that he gives. It is, rather, a peace that rests on the nature of the transaction. Warfield explains at length that after we all have tried other means by which to find God's favor—self-efforts of various kinds, feverishly sincere though they

---

[75]"Redemption," 305–6; cf. chapter 7 above on redemption.
[76]*PGS*, 57–90; *SSW*, 2:142–51.
[77]*PGS*, 64; *SSW*, 2:147.

may be—we still do not experience the peace we seek. We may give ourselves entirely to the service of God, but this alone does not clear the conscience. There yet remains that gnawing sense of sin, a realization that we have not made the required grade. But in being justified *by faith* the result is different—"peace and joy are the natural, or, indeed, the necessary fruits" of seeking salvation by faith alone.[78] This method of justification is perfectly suited to quiet our conscience; indeed, it is calculated to satisfy the conscience and allay all feelings of guilt, for it rests on God's provision of a substitute—who supplies for us all the righteousness God requires of us and in whose blood perfect expiation of sin is made—and his gracious promise of full forgiveness in him. This method of justification does not leave us hoping that we have done well enough. It faces our unrighteousness squarely and makes full acknowledgment of it. It offers a substitute who does for us all that God requires of us. In Warfield's words, this method of justification "empties us of all righteousness which we may claim," and then it

> turns and points to a wonderful spectacle of the Son of God, become man, taking His place at the head of His people, presenting an infinite sacrifice for their sins in His own body on the tree, working out a perfect righteousness in their stead in the myriad deeds of love and right that filled His short but active life; and offering this righteousness, this righteousness of God, provided by God and acceptable to God, to the acceptance of the world.

And immediately Warfield says again, "Here is a mode of salvation which is indeed calculated to still the gnawing sense of guilt and quiet the fear of wrath." Here is an approach to God, a means of finding his favor, in which the conscience can safely rest. "We gaze on Christ and His sacrifice, and we know that God also sees it, and seeing it cannot condemn him who is in Christ."[79]

THE NEED OF JUSTIFICATION

In his brief 1911 article "Justification by Faith, Out of Date," Warfield considers the question of the relevance of this doctrine to modern man and argues passionately that if justification by faith is out of date, then salvation itself is out of date. For if justification means "to pronounce righteous," then "there is no justification for sinful men except by faith." The works of sinners are sinful, and these works can only condemn. Where then, except from a substitute, can the sinner obtain works on the basis of which he can be justified? This is precisely what is offered

---

[78] *PGS*, 69; *SSW*, 2:147–49.
[79] *PGS*, 76, 89; cf. *SSW*, 2:142–51.

the sinner in justification by faith—the works of Christ in exchange for his own sinful works. Justification by faith "does not mean salvation by believing things instead of by doing right. It means pleading the merits of Christ before the throne of grace instead of our own merits." It is certainly right to believe right things, but we cannot plead our own merits before God; we simply have no merits of our own to plead. "If we are to be justified at all, it must be on the ground of the merits of Another, whose merits can be made ours by faith." This is the reason God sent his Son into the world, "that whoever believes in him should not perish but have everlasting life."[80]

Paul's deep antagonism against his Judaizing opponents, then, is due to the damaging—indeed, the damning (Gal. 1:8)—consequences of attempting to admit works as a ground of salvation. Such teachers are "dogs" (Phil. 3:2), and they are deservedly called such, for their teaching precludes that attitude which Paul everywhere impresses on his readers—that attitude "in which the whole Gospel consisted for him—the attitude of entire dependence on Christ to the exclusion of everything in themselves."[81]

Faith

This notion—that the gospel consists in an attitude of entire dependence on Christ to the exclusion of everything else—defines Christianity emphatically and necessarily as a religion of faith, a gospel of trust. The whole of salvation, "in each of its steps and stages, runs back to God as its author and furtherer," and because of this, "a continual sense of humble dependence on God and of loving trust in Him is by it formed and fostered in every heart into which it makes entrance. Under the teachings of this gospel the eye is withdrawn from self and the face turned upward in loving gratitude to God, the great giver." "It must needs be by faith" that we receive all saving blessings, "for what is faith but a looking to God for blessings?"[82]

THE NATURE OF FAITH

Warfield describes faith variously as "trust," "a confident entrusting of ourselves to Christ," "looking to God for blessing," "casting" oneself upon God, "utter dependence" or "resting" or "reposing" on God, and simply "the instrument of reception to which salvation comes." It is therefore "the very essence of Christianity." It is

[80]SSW, 1:283–84.
[81]FL, 320.
[82]PGS, 213; FL, 170.

the "fundamental element of religion" on the human side, just as grace is the fundamental element of religion on God's side. Faith as "an attitude of dependence on God" is likewise "just the very essence" of true religion. "In proportion as any sense of self-sufficiency or any dependence on self enters the heart, in that proportion religion is driven from it." This is the only attitude becoming or even possible in weak and sinful man. If we are to be saved at all, it must be God who saves us. "Every sinner, when once aroused to the sense of his sin, knows this for himself—knows it in the times of his clearest vision and deepest comprehension with a poignancy that drives him to despair." And this despair is relieved only when he rests in God alone.[83]

That faith entails not only knowledge and assent but also trust Warfield finds illustrated in the faith of Abraham (Gen. 15:1, 6). The object of his faith was not the promise of God but God himself, "and that not merely as the giver of the promise here recorded, but as His servant's shield and exceeding great reward. It is therefore not the assentive but the fiducial element of faith which is here emphasized." He "put his trust in God" (Rom. 4:3, BBW trans. of ἐπίστευσεν τῷ θεῷ). To believe in God is to "rest in security and trustfulness upon Him." This sense of faith as trust is expressed in the New Testament primarily by the use of πιστεύω with one of several prepositions. Πιστεύω + ἐν seems to indicate confidence in the object of trust. Πιστεύω + ἐπί is somewhat parallel to this and expresses "steady, resting repose, reliance upon the object." Πιστεύω + εἰς, the leading New Testament expression, expresses "'an absolute transference of trust from ourselves to another,' a complete self-surrender to Christ." Following a survey of the various passages in which πιστεύω and πίστις occur, Warfield concludes again that faith, in the New Testament sense, is "self-abandoning trust," a "self-commitment of the soul to Jesus as the Son of God, the Saviour of the world."[84]

In short, given man's sin and consequent unworthiness on the one hand and God's gracious promise of rescue on the other, faith—faith as trust, reliance, dependence—is the only possible approach to God.

THE PSYCHOLOGY OF FAITH

In his 1911 article "On Faith in its Psychological Aspects," Warfield analyzes the notion of faith and how it is formed in the human mind. He stresses that "faith" or "belief" focuses on the grounds of the conviction expressed. It refers to a mental act or state "to which we feel constrained" by certain relevant and authoritative

---

[83]W, 9:332; W, 10:460; FL, 397; FL, 170; W, 2:506; FL, 171; FL, 155; PGS, 213.
[84]W, 2:471, 476–83.

considerations. Faith is not an arbitrary act; it is a mental state or act "determined by sufficient reasons." The Greek root meaning of πίστις is that of "binding," and the Hebrew האמי, אמונה go back to the idea of "holding." These ideas remain in our idea of faith. That which "holds" us or that which we discover to be "binding" on us is the object of "faith." There is an element of constraint, "bindingness" in faith that distinguishes it from an act of the will. Consent of belief is not the same as consent of the will. The consent of belief is a "forced consent" driven by compelling evidence. Belief is neither arbitrary nor voluntary but a necessary consent of the mind to what it perceives to be sufficient reasons or evidence.[85]

Although faith is forced consent, the product of evidence and not of volition, it nonetheless can be mistaken. Our beliefs may not, in fact, correspond with reality. We can be misinformed or misunderstand the evidence and thus believe what is in fact not true. Our minds may mistake weak evidence as strong or strong evidence as weak, and believe or not believe accordingly. Faith "does not follow evidence itself, in other words, but the judgment of the intellect on the evidence." And this judgment will vary according to intellect, states of mind, and disposition. But what evidence the mind judges to be true based on objectively adequate evidence is therefore necessarily believed. Even so, the will is not the determining element. Warfield agrees with Augustine that faith, then, rests on authority, not reason alone. Reason underlies faith, to be sure, but there is involved also a judgment as to the authority of the evidence, its credibility. Faith, therefore, entails "trust" as one of its prominent components. In fact, it seems evident that the notion of "trust" is the implication that rules the usage of the term "faith, belief" and "determines its applications throughout the whole course of its development."[86]

THE SOURCE OF FAITH

All this serves to demonstrate that the source of saving faith is found in God. Faith is not an act of the will. It is consent that is forced by our perception of that evidence and the object as trustworthy. Saving faith is not "inevitable" to the sinner merely because Christ is, in fact, trustworthy. The person's judgment of the worthiness of the object and the evidence will determine how compelling the evidence is. This, in turn, depends upon the person's capacity to appreciate the evidence rightly. Saving faith is not an arbitrary act of the will.[87]

---

[85] W, 9:313–17.
[86] W, 9:318–32.
[87] W, 9:319–34.

There are two factors in the production of faith. On the one hand, there is the evidence on the ground of which the faith is yielded. On the other hand, there is the subjective condition by virtue of which the evidence can take effect in the appropriate act of faith. There can be no belief, faith without evidence; it is on evidence that the mental exercise which we call belief, faith rests; and this exercise or state of mind cannot exist apart from its ground in evidence. But evidence cannot produce belief, faith, except in a mind open to this evidence, and capable of receiving, weighing, and responding to it. A mathematical demonstration is demonstrative proof of the proposition demonstrated. But even such a demonstration cannot produce conviction in a mind incapable of following the demonstration. Where musical taste is lacking, no evidence which derives its force from considerations of melody can work conviction. No conviction, whether of the order of what we call knowledge or of faith, can be produced by considerations to which the mind to be convinced is inhabile.[88]

There is then something more that is needed than evidence. Evidence is necessary, for it is on evidence that faith rests. But whether or not that evidence is compelling is determined by the subjective nature or condition of the person to whom it is presented. "This is the ground of responsibility for belief, faith; it is not merely a question of evidence but of subjectivity. . . . Our action under evidence is the touchstone by which is determined what we are." If the evidence presented is objectively adequate yet perceived subjectively to be inadequate, the fault is in us. This being the case, "it is easy to see that the sinful heart—which is enmity towards God—is incapable of that supreme act of trust in God." The sinner's heart is hostile against God. Sin has rendered trust impossible for him, and so the Scriptures represent faith as a gift of God. This gift, however, is not given in a way that violates our psychological constitution. Rather the Holy Spirit of God creates in us a "capacity for faith under the evidence submitted." He softens the heart and quickens the will "so that the man so affected may freely and must inevitably perceive the force and yield to the compelling power of the evidence of the trustworthiness of Jesus Christ as Saviour submitted to him in the gospel." In other words, there is renewal, regeneration, which issues in faith. There must before this be the atoning work of Christ, which cancels the guilt by which the sinner is kept under the wrath of God. Faith is truly man's own act, but it is just as truly God's gift to him so that he may so act. Stated briefly, our salvation is accomplished by Christ, and it therefore does not depend upon our faith—our faith depends upon it.[89]

---

[88] W, 9:335–36.
[89] W, 9:336–40; W, 7:336–37; W, 2:505–6.

For this reason Scripture consistently presents faith as "a gratuity from God in the prosecution of His saving work." Faith does not rise out of one's own strength or virtue but is given to those who are chosen (2 Thess. 2:13). It is God's gift (Eph. 6:23; cf. 2:8–9; Phil. 1:29), given through Christ (Acts 3:16; Phil. 1:29; 1 Pet. 1:21; Heb. 12:2), by the Spirit (2 Cor. 4:13; Gal. 5:5), by means of the preached Word (Rom. 10:17; Gal. 3:2, 5). Because faith is received from God (2 Pet. 1:1; Jude 3; 1 Pet. 1:21), thanks for it are to be returned to God (Col. 1:3–4; 2 Thess. 1:3). All ground of boasting is excluded, for even our faith is his gift to us. This sheds light, again, on the nature of faith. Warfield heartily endorses the scholastic term "instrumental cause" and says that everywhere in the Bible, faith

> is conceived as a boon from above which comes to men, no doubt through the channels of their own activities, but not as if it were an effect of their energies, but rather, as it has been finely phrased, as a gift which God lays in the lap of the soul. "With the heart," indeed, "man believeth unto righteousness"; but this believing does not arise of itself out of any heart indifferently, nor is it grounded in the heart's own potencies; it is grounded rather in the freely-giving goodness of God, and comes to man as a benefaction out of heaven.[90]

THE VALUE OF FAITH

Warfield is clearly a soteriological exclusivist in that he admits salvation to none but those who believe (except infants). He emphasizes this at length in his sermon "Jesus Only," based on Acts 4:12, and demonstrates with passion that throughout the history of the church this has always been the cutting edge of the Christian witness. "Participation in this salvation is certainly suspended on the proclamation and hearing of the gospel," and this thought served to drive the apostle Paul in his missionary endeavors. Even those who die never having heard of Christ, perish.[91]

Faith in Christ is the requisite channel through which salvation is received. Because man is a sinner, his faith terminates not on God immediately but on the Mediator, Jesus Christ, and through him on God. And this faith issues in justification. "He who humbly but confidently casts himself on the God of salvation has the assurance that he shall not be put to shame (Rom. 10:11; 9:33), but shall receive the end of his faith, even the salvation of his soul (1 Pet. 1:9)." By it we renounce our own righteousness and receive that righteousness "which comes through faith in Christ, the righteousness from God that depends on faith" (Phil.

---

[90]*W*, 2:505–6.
[91]*PGS*, 207ff.; *SSW*, 1:172; *SW*, 37–65.

3:9; cf. Rom. 3:22; 4:11; 9:30; 10:3, 10; 2 Cor. 5:21; Gal. 5:5; Heb. 11:7; 2 Pet. 1:1). On the ground of this substitute righteousness, credited by faith alone, without works, enmity is abolished (Rom. 5:1), and the one who believes in Christ, Warfield says, "is justified in God's sight, received into His favour, and made the recipient of the Holy Spirit" (John 7:39; Acts 5:32; Gal. 3:2). The immediate effect of faith is the possession, before the judgment day, of the righteousness wrought out by Christ; through this righteousness credited to the believer "the whole series of saving acts of God" and blessings of sonship follow.[92]

Yet it is not faith, itself considered, that possesses all this value. Warfield is careful to lay stress on the trustworthiness of faith's *object* and to emphasize that it is only from its object that faith derives its value. Justification is not said to come by repentance, for that would imply efforts on our part as ground for it. Justification comes through *faith as trust* precisely because it is accomplished solely by Christ. The saving power of faith resides in him. "It is not faith that saves, but faith in Jesus Christ." Faith in any other object than Christ crucified brings only a curse. "It is not, strictly speaking, even faith in Christ that saves, but Christ that saves through faith. The saving power resides exclusively, not in the act of faith or the attitude of faith or the nature of faith, but in the object of faith." It would be a radical misconception of the biblical presentation of faith to transfer even the smallest fraction of saving energy to faith. The Scriptures carefully attribute all the saving power "solely to Christ Himself." We must therefore "mind our prepositions," Warfield counsels—"'by' and 'through' convey the notification of different and not inconsistent relations," and they are instructive "with respect to passivity and activity. . . . The means by which God is reconciled to men is not their faith but the blood of Christ."[93]

Even so, because of the value of faith's object, faith is said to have certain important effects. It is the instrument through which we receive assurance of salvation and the justifying righteousness of Christ (2 Pet. 1:1). On the ground of this justification we are brought into God's favor and made the recipients of his Spirit, by whose indwelling we are constituted God's sons (Rom. 8:14) and heirs (Rom. 8:17; 1 Pet. 1:4–5). When we are justified by faith, a train of blessings follow. Enmity is removed and we have peace with God (Rom. 5:1–2), and we are given his Spirit by whom we overcome the world (1 John 5:4, 18–19). "In a word, because we are justified by faith, we are, through faith, endowed with all the privileges and supplied with all the graces of the children of God."[94]

---

[92] *W*, 9:340; *W*, 2:502–6.
[93] *SSW*, 2:148; *W*, 2:504; *W*, 10:461; *PTR* 1, no. 4 (1903): 674–75; *FL*, 397.
[94] *W*, 2:506–7.

INABILITY AND THE DEMAND OF FAITH

In his examination of the psychological aspects of faith Warfield demonstrates, as we have seen, that although faith rests on evidence, faith does not infallibly follow sufficient evidence. Disposition is the determining factor, and it is the ground of our responsibility.[95] But on a more pastoral level, in his "Inability and the Demand of Faith," Warfield offers counsel in dealing with the sinner who, genuinely seeking salvation, may yet despair of his inability to come to Christ. Warfield acknowledges the difficulty but counsels that in such a case progress might be made by gently yet faithfully pressing the following ideas.

First, it must be recognized that "the puzzle is a logical one, and concerns doctrine, not action; and it must not be permitted to stand as an obstacle to action." That is, we recognize our previous inability only after the fact, after regeneration and coming to Christ. Inability passes away in regeneration, but our consciousness of that great transformation, only after we have believed. "No man can know," Warfield counsels, "whether he is unable save by striving to act." We are obliged to believe, to turn to Christ. And we must be clear that "the doctrine of inability does not affirm that we cannot believe, but only that we cannot believe in our own strength. . . . We may believe . . . , but only in God's strength." Warfield finds illustration of this in the man with the withered hand (Mark 3:1–5). Jesus commanded the man to stretch out his hand, yet it was just that—stretch out his hand—that he was unable to do. This is the nature of the problem itself. "But Christ commanded, and he stretched it forth." Warfield surmises that what God commands, he in grace gives. The struggles of soul that we endure in the awareness of sin and need are themselves evidence of the workings of the Spirit of God. And so we have warrant to counsel men to believe: this is their responsibility.[96]

Next, Warfield reminds us that it is not man's responsibility to do what only God can do. It is not ours to give life; it is ours simply to believe. And "this very effort [to look to Christ] is already an exercise of the required faith." Indeed, the recognition of inability brings us to see how desperate our condition is, and seeing this we are reminded that "Christ is needed as a Savior all the more because we cannot do the least thing to save ourselves." Indeed, "Christ is not only a Savior to those who are naked and empty, and have no goodness to recommend themselves, but he is a Savior to those who are unable to give themselves to him." In this way the recognition of our inability serves to incite faith, for "you cannot be in too desperate a condition for Christ."[97]

[95] W, 9:336–37.
[96] W, 9:336–37; SSW, 2:726.
[97] SSW, 2:727.

Finally, Warfield suggests that the appeal should be driven home by our empha-sizing "the dangers of delay, and the roots of it in a sinful state." The sinner's professed "waiting for grace" is in reality a continued self-reliance and refusal of Christ. Many others before us, and as desperate, have come to Christ and found him able to save. He calls us to trust him, and unless we do, we will perish. This, Warfield suggests, is how to deal with such seeking souls: "They are not to be argued with but pressed to come at once to Jesus."[98]

SUMMARY

Faith, which comes to its rights only when there is a personal object, is primarily an "entrusting" of ourselves to God, an "adoring trust" in Christ. It has both passive and active aspects to it—surrender and consecration. And it involves the three elements of *notitia, assensus, fiducia* ("knowledge," "assent," "trust"). "No true faith has arisen unless there has been a perception of the object to be believed in, an assent to its worthiness to be believed or believed in, and a commitment of ourselves to it as true and trustworthy." There is no faith in a thing or person of which we have no knowledge. "Implicit faith" in this sense is an absurdity. And of course there is no faith in a thing or person to whose worthiness we do not give assent. There is also no faith "in that which we distrust too much to commit ourselves to it." In every movement of faith there is an intellectual, an emotional, and a volitional element. The whole man is involved in the entirety of his being. The central movement of faith is doubtless that of assent, but this assent always depends on a movement not of the will but of the intellect. "The *assensus* issues from the *notitia*." And "trust" is "the product of the assent." But the disposition to believe and the capacity for faith, being naturally contrary to man's fallen consti-tution, is given by God in the re-creative work of the Holy Spirit.[99]

Conversion: "The Great Change"

Salvation in Christ involves more than legal forgiveness. It involves "a radical and complete transformation" of the soul (Rom. 12:2; Eph. 4:23) by the Spirit of God (Titus 3:5) that constitutes the believer a "new man" (Eph. 4:24; Col. 3:10) who is "no longer conformed to this world" (Rom. 12:2; Eph. 4:22; Col. 3:9) but shaped in knowledge and holiness after the image of Christ (Eph. 4:24; Col. 3:10; Rom.

---

[98]*SSW*, 2:727–28.
[99]*W*, 2:505; *W*, 9:331–32, 340–42; *FL*, 155.

12:2). In Christ is provided not only an objective but also a subjective salvation from sin.

> It is uniformly taught in Scripture that by his sin man has not merely incurred the divine condemnation but also corrupted his own heart; that sin, in other words, is not merely guilt but depravity: and that there is needed for man's recovery from sin, therefore, not merely atonement but renewal; that salvation, that is to say, consists not merely in pardon but in purification. Great as is the stress laid in the Scriptures on the forgiveness of sins as the root of salvation, no less stress is laid throughout the Scriptures on the cleansing of the heart as the fruit of salvation. Nowhere is the sinner permitted to rest satisfied with pardon as the end of salvation; everywhere he is made poignantly to feel that salvation is realized only in a clean heart and a right spirit.[100]

"The great change" experienced by every believer upon entering the Christian life has both a Godward and a manward side. God "renews," "begets," "regenerates," and "creates"; man "repents" and "turns." God regenerates, "recreating the governing disposition" of the soul, and conversion instantly and inevitably follows. Warfield recognizes this personally transforming aspect of salvation as the fulfillment of God's new covenant promise (Jer. 31:33; 32:39; Ezek. 36:26; 37:14) in which he promises the powerful inner workings of his Spirit in giving new life (a "new heart") that manifests itself in inward and outward holiness. Growing out of this provision of the regenerating and sanctifying Spirit are all the New Testament exhortations to and descriptions of renewal, conversion, progressive sanctification, and glorification.[101]

Repentance indicates primarily a change of mind, and this change of mind is one that issues in an amended life. Hence, in Matthew 21:29, Jesus speaks of the previously disobedient son who "repented, and went" (KJV) as his father commanded him. So also in Jesus' application of the parable to the Jewish leaders, he scolds them for not "repenting and believing" John the Baptist. Repentance is a change of mind that issues in amendment of life. But in its largest view repentance also entails godly sorrow over sin. This is all stated succinctly in 2 Corinthians 7:8–11, particularly verse 10: "Godly grief produces a repentance that leads to salvation." Warfield summarizes that repentance is a turning

> from all wrong to all good, in which the trend of our life is altered, in which, in a word, we turn our backs on Satan and all the works of the flesh, and our face to God

---

[100]W, 2:439–40.
[101]SSW, 2:323; FL, 455; W, 2:439–62.

and his service. The repentance of the New Testament is a total change of mind and heart, not only from some sins but from sin itself.

Warfield finds this illustrated in the prodigal son, who "came to himself" and returned humbly to the father (Luke 15:17).[102]

True repentance, moreover, does not view sin merely atomistically, in terms of so many evil acts. If we are ourselves sinful and guilty, then true godly sorrow and change of mind will have in view not only what we do but what we are, our sins as well as our sinfulness. There will be a recognition of personal demerit and guilt. "He only has really repented who has perceived and felt the filthiness and odiousness of his depraved nature and has turned from it to God with a full purpose of being hereafter more conformed to his image as revealed in the face of Jesus Christ."[103]

Warfield notes the proper order in all this. There is godly sorrow, on which repentance rests; there is the change of mind in reference to sin, repentance; and there is the resulting alteration of life, "the fruits of repentance." Scripture says, "Godly grief produces a repentance that leads to salvation" (2 Cor. 7:10); "repent and believe" (Mark 1:15; Matt. 21:32); "repent and turn" (Acts 3:19, 26:20); "believe and turn" (Acts 11:21). "We need not press such phraseology beyond its capacity for bearing, but it seems at least to suggest the order *metanoia, pistis, epistrophe*; that there is first a change within, then faith, and then a corresponding change without." All this is man's responsibility and work. However, Warfield is quick to point out that repentance is declared to be the gift of God (Acts 5:31; 11:18; 2 Tim. 2:25). This suggests a divine side, a previous activity on God's part that leads to the change these words describe, and this divine activity leads him to a discussion of "a group of words which represent [God's side] as a renewing, a rebegetting, a quickening, a resurrection, and even as a re-creating," which produces, "in the highest sense of the term, a new man" (Col. 3:10; cf. 2 Cor. 5:17). Warfield characterizes this as a "repristination of man" wrought sovereignly and efficaciously by God the Holy Spirit, who awakens the soul and radically changes its disposition in reference both to sin and to God, thus enabling it to repent and believe.[104]

This "conversion" shows itself not only in faith and repentance but in all of life. Faith issues in newness of life (Col. 2:12) and is characterized by the instinctive response, "What shall I do, Lord?" (Acts 22:10). Dying with Christ we also rise with him to new life (Romans 6). In Christ we are a new creation in which the old has passed away and all things have become new (2 Cor. 5:17). Believers are men

---

[102]*SSW*, 1:270–71.
[103]*SSW*, 1:280.
[104]*SSW*, 1:271–77; cf. *SSW*, 2:321–24.

made new by the power of the Holy Spirit. Christ has died for us to this end—so that we, having died with him, will no longer live to ourselves but unto him (2 Cor. 5:14–15); and "the end can no more fail than the means." Those for whom Christ died find themselves living by the constraint of that love (v. 14), and all of life is adjusted and shaped accordingly. "You cannot die with Christ and not rise again with Him: it cannot be that He who knew no sin shall have been made sin for you, and you who have known no righteousness shall not be made the righteousness of God in Him." Stated in theological terms, there can be no justification that does not issue in sanctification. Our salvation is not only from the penalty but also from the power of sin.[105]

This transformation of life is described figuratively in the New Testament as a change of clothing (Eph. 4:24; Col. 3:9–10; cf. Gal. 3:27; Rom. 13:14); the old man is laid aside like dirty clothes, and the new man is put on like a clean garment. Sometimes conversion is described in terms of a metamorphosis (Rom. 12:2). It is also spoken of descriptively in terms of reanimation (John 5:21; Eph. 2:4–6; Col. 2:12–13; Rom. 6:3–4) or a re-creation (Eph. 2:10; 4:24; Col. 3:10). And sometimes it is referred to, more technically, as sanctification, a making holy (1 Thess. 4:3, 7; 5:23; Rom. 6:19, 22; 15:16; etc.). Sometimes, in more direct reference to its source, this new life is described as the "living" or "forming" of Christ in us (Gal. 2:20; Rom. 6:9–10; Eph. 3:17; Gal. 4:19; cf. 1 Cor. 2:16; 2 Cor. 3:8) and as the indwelling of Christ or his Spirit in us or being led by the Spirit (Rom. 8:14; Gal. 5:18). The subjects of this work are referred to as "spiritual men," men led of the Spirit (πνευματικοί, 1 Cor. 2:15; 3:1; Gal. 6:1; cf. 1 Pet. 2:5) as contrasted with "carnal men," "men dominated by their own weak, vicious selves" (ψυχικοί, 1 Cor. 2:14; Jude 19; σαρκικοί, 1 Cor. 3:3). All through the New Testament the great emphasis on God's "power" working in us is to this end. "It does not require an exercise of divine power to extend power; it does require it to endow and enable us with all the qualities, energies, and activities that make for, and that make holiness and life."[106]

It is important to Warfield to note that this change of life is not an optional extra to the Christian. Jesus taught Nicodemus that "the radical transformation of the Spirit of God" is "the precondition of entrance" to the kingdom of God. Heart and life transformation is part of the warp and woof of salvation itself. Justification by faith is the root of our salvation, but sanctification is "its substance." Salvation is never pardon only; it is also a cleansing and transformation. In opposition to perfectionist and higher life teachers such as Asa Mahan (1799–1889) and Andrew Murray (1828–1917), Warfield insists that there can be no separation of regeneration

---

[105]SW, 156–59; cf. FL, 455.
[106]W, 2:458–62; cf. PGS, 151–79.

from sanctification. He argues that "the essence" of Romans 8:29–30 "is to teach that God selects his children, chooses the goal to which he shall bring them, and brings them safely to that goal; and it justifies us in saying that without exception, 'whom he regenerates, them also he sanctifies.'" It was the ancient new covenant promise that God would write his law on his people's heart (Jer. 31:33), that he would take out the stony heart and replace it with a heart of flesh so that they would now walk in keeping with his commands (Ezek. 11:19). All this is the promised work of the Spirit of God in the lives of all of God's people. Salvation necessarily entails a changed life. God works in his people to renew them, and the response inevitably is that of repentance and conversion. God's work of salvation is such that "he who really is a child of God will necessarily possess marks and signs of being so."[107]

Perfectionism and the Doctrine of Sanctification

George Marsden observes retrospectively, "When the Keswick conferences came to Princeton, from 1916 to 1918, they were entering the lair of the aging lion of strict Presbyterian orthodoxy," and spotting this major doctrinal deviation, the lion pounced. Warfield's final published writings, the latest of which in the series were published posthumously, are his lengthy critical analyses of the varieties of Christian perfectionism and higher life teachings made popular in the previous century and prominent in Keswick theology. The subject held considerable interest and importance for Warfield, for his treatments of these perfectionists are thorough and reflect extensive and meticulous historical research, as well as a comprehensive acquaintance with the lives, experiences, and various doctrinal peculiarities of each representative. Totaling a thousand pages, these critical works comprise a significant percentage of Warfield's already massive literary output and constitute the most complete analysis of perfectionism yet to appear in English. Throughout this analysis Warfield remains prepared to affirm points of agreement with the perfectionist expositions he samples. Nevertheless, his critical comments are somewhat caustic at times as he detects arrogance and blasphemy among the more extreme proponents, and theological and logical inconsistencies among the more moderate—all of which detract, in Warfield's view, from the glories of biblical soteriology. In his analyses we are not left with a comprehensive or detailed view of Warfield's own doctrine of sanctification, but his larger theological framework is clear as he criticizes views he considers aber-

---

[107]W, 7:91; W, 2:440, 447, 461; PR 10, no. 38 (1889): 335; FL, 191.

rant. Thus, in his final published works, he provides us with his most complete exposition of the doctrine of the Christian life, the natural starting point in our examination of his understanding of Christian holiness.[108]

Warfield credits—or rather, blames—John Wesley as the leading source of perfectionist doctrine in modern Protestantism,[109] but he traces perfectionist tendencies to two more fundamental historic sources: mysticism and Pelagianism. Either of these streams, or even a combination of both, accounts for virtually all perfectionist teachings, but it is Pelagianism that lends itself to the doctrine particularly well. Wesley's perfectionism, for example, bears similarities to the mysticism of the Quakers, but it is from an essentially Pelagian libertarianism that his doctrine grows. Warfield states it categorically: "Wherever again men lapse into an essentially Pelagian mode of thinking concerning the endowments of human nature and the conditions of human action, a Perfectionism similar to that taught by Pelagius himself tends to repeat itself." The perfectionism may appear more or less "evangelical," depending upon the degree of supernaturalism admitted. But Pelagianism it remains, at least in degree.[110]

RITSCHLIAN (LIBERAL) PERFECTIONISM

The brand of perfectionism taught by Albrecht Ritschl is a "highly individualized example of Pelagianizing Perfectionism quite independent of all either Mystical or Wesleyan influences." For Ritschl, there is no natural bias toward evil in humanity; in fact, there is a bias toward good. Sin is admittedly universal, but

---

[108]George M. Marsden, *Fundamentalism and American Culture*, 98. The sheer number of pages Warfield devoted to this topic reflects, presumably, the strong sense of error he perceived in it. The attempt here is to ascertain with some degree of completeness his thinking concerning both the errors of the various brands of perfectionism and the biblically defined themes of sanctification and the Christian life as Warfield understood them. It must be kept in mind, however, that the summary provided here is still relatively brief, seeking in a few pages to account for more than a thousand in Warfield.

[109]Warfield says pejoratively, "It was John Wesley who infected the modern Protestant world with this notion of 'entire, instantaneous sanctification'" (*W*, 8:562).

[110]*W*, 7:3. Warfield traces several strains of perfectionist teachings that may be grouped generally as follows: (1) the liberal or rationalist perfectionism of Ritschl and others; (2) the Oberlin perfectionism, primarily of Charles Finney and Asa Mahan; (3) the mystical perfectionism of Thomas Cogswell Upham and others, including the embarrassingly antinomian "perfectionism" of John Humphrey Noyes, the "Bible Communist"; (4) the German holiness movement, particularly as expounded in "Pastor Paul" and its chief exponent Theodor Jellinghaus; (5) the higher life, victorious life, and Keswick movements of Britain and especially America in many of its leading exponents. Not all of these movements are organically related, but some influences among them are common. For example, Methodist lay teacher Phoebe Palmer (1807–1874) simplified and popularized the perfectionism of John Wesley and taught it to many others, such as Thomas Upham. Robert Pearsall Smith preached his holiness message in England, France, Germany, and Switzerland. The Oxford campaign was particularly successful, but his reception in Germany and Switzerland was even more enthusiastic. Of this campaign Smith said, "All Germany seemed to be aroused," and "all Europe is at my feet" (*W*, 7:321), and in the wake of these efforts others continued to reap the perfectionist harvest in Britain and Germany. It was at Oxford that Jellinghaus found the teachings and took them to Germany.

the explanation for its appearance in each individual is not to be found in the sinfulness of the individual. The cause is to be found rather in the circumstances into which each individual is born; the only "problem" on the individual's side is his ignorance or immaturity—his will is yet "uninformed." The evil bias to which each individual succumbs is the result of his own free self-determination. If the external inducements toward good had been stronger, we might have avoided the corruption to which we have all fallen. Still, however, each individual remains capable of transforming his character and, in conjunction with others who have likewise overthrown the kingdom of sin, building the kingdom of God in which he may be "perfect."[111]

For Ritschl, the will is moved by intentions and dispositions and impulses that he is not embarrassed to describe as "coercive." Yet he argues also that the will has the power of self-determination, if it so chooses, even in opposition to contrary influences. Warfield laments Ritschl's failure to explain *how* such self-determination can remain after one has fallen into sinful dispositions that must certainly have become ingrained: "It looks as if we were asked to believe that the will, which is at every step determined by dispositions, has in this instance first to create the dispositions by which it is determined, in opposition to the dispositions by which it is at every step determined." The freedom is absolute, even if irrational. Ritschl does not explain this independence of the human will. He merely asserts that any notion of moral responsibility demands it. Yet Warfield persists, "We wonder what has become of Ritschl's psychological determinism." He concludes that Ritschl "stands forth as fully fledged a Libertarian as Kant, or even as Pelagius himself."[112]

Yet Ritschl goes further than Pelagius and, Warfield argues, to yet another self-contradiction. Pelagius taught original innocence and asserted the neutrality of the human will. Ritschl argues for original goodness. "We cannot conceive of a will without definite direction to an end," he argues, and this end is not evil but good. But it seems Ritschl wants to eat his theological cake and have it too, for the ground on which he rejects original sin is that "it assumes that there is a will previous to individual acts," which of course is "the same assumption involved in the doctrine of original goodness." Ritschl wants it both ways—a will that is free absolutely, with no moral predisposition, and a will that is inclined to good. But these "are not only not the same thing; they are not even capable of conciliation."[113]

---

[111] W, 7:4, 14.
[112] W, 7:4–5, 7–8.
[113] W, 7:9–10, 13.

The irony continues: Ritschl offers infants and small children as evidence. Our attempts to educate our children, he argues, rest on the assumption of a general, even if indefinite, inclination to good. Warfield mockingly dismisses Ritschl's theory with an appeal to common human experience: "Such a theory does great honor to the children which Ritschl has seen grow up around him; we need to confess that those we have known do not confirm it."[114]

The difficulty for Ritschl goes still further: there is the stubborn fact of man's universal sinfulness. How can this be explained? We come into the world with an inclination to good, Ritschl would have us believe, and we are fully capable, by the free act of our own volition, of living a sinless life. Yet none of us has made such a choice, not even those of us born to Christian parents who from our infancy seek to train us to do good. Not most of us but every one of us chooses sin, and at some point this universal "will not" looks very much like a universal "cannot." How is it that there is no evidence in all of humanity of this boundless capacity for choosing goodness? On the question of how a child disposed to good chooses evil, Ritschl appeals to the arbitrary freedom of the will. But that will not do—evidence for the capacity to evil abounds; our question here is, where is the evidence for the power of the will to choose good? Surely, if such power exists, then in the history of all humanity there must be some evidence of it. The burden of proof rests on Ritschl to demonstrate how it is "that all men come into the world with a bias to good and yet all men without exception choose sin."[115]

Ritschl answers by arguing, in terms ironically reminiscent of the Calvinistic doctrine of inability, that sin is "inevitable" because of the general condition of man and the circumstances into which we are born. The as-yet uninformed will is biased toward good but insufficiently so, and thus the temptations that confront it are overwhelming. Warfield summarizes, "His formula for universal sin is just universal freedom plus universal temptation, with the decisive emphasis on the temptation." Our environment, this "kingdom of sin" into which we have been thrust, is the real culprit.[116]

But Ritschl's "diseased logic" has matters hopelessly reversed. How do we account for this "kingdom of sin"? Is it not itself the creation of human sin? Can it be both the creator and the creature of human sin?

Unless men had sinned before there was any kingdom of sin to infect them with its corruption, there never would have been any kingdom of sin. The kingdom of sin is simply the *congregatio peccatorum*, and sinners must exist before they can congre-

---

[114]Citing the words of Henri Schoen, *W*, 7:10.
[115]*W*, 7:11–12; *W*, 8:177.
[116]*W*, 7:15.

gate. They bring sin into the congregation, not take it out of it. And that means in the end that the cause of sin must be found in something in the sinner rather than in something in his environment.[117]

Ritschl's formula—universal freedom plus universal temptation—does not give sufficient account for the origin, much less the universality of human sin.

One final difficulty remains. For Ritschl, our character is just the state of our will at that point. We must exercise mastery over our predispositions, and we must govern them in the interests of a good end if we are to be good. But this is psychological nonsense: who is this "we" that must govern our will against our predisposition? "Do not these 'predispositions (*Anlagen*) of the soul' really constitute all the 'we' that exists? Must we not have another 'we,' with another equipment of dispositions, before we can form a purpose antagonistic to it and dominate it in its interests?"[118] Ritschl's irrational rationalism has caught him again. He cannot explain how "we" can exercise "our" will contrary to what "we" will.

Ritschl has a distinct need, however, to preserve the notion of human freedom, for "in his rigorous anti-supernaturalism, he has nothing to which sinners may appeal for their salvation from sin except their own wills."[119] In Augustinianism, the depths of human depravity are more than matched by the heights of divine grace. There is no need to preserve any degree of human dignity or merit if there is a Redeemer and a supernatural, re-creating Spirit. But for Ritschl, we do not need rescue; we need but to exercise our own will. What cannot be accomplished by the human will cannot be accomplished at all.

But here again we are met with difficulty. Living in this kingdom of sin, we sin "inevitably," from which we must infer that "the influences of evil in the kingdom of sin are stronger than those to good in the Kingdom of God." This leaves one wondering how men, now long accustomed to the evil "inevitably" thrust upon them and deeply affected by its influences, can now turn at will to the kingdom of God. Ritschl allows only the theoretic possibility that a man could be so caught up in his choice of sin that he loses all power to the contrary; such a condition could exist, but he cannot say when. The power to the contrary is possessed by all. Ritschl does not attempt explanation. He merely asserts this arbitrary power of the will. He thus reduces the new birth and the work of "the Holy Spirit" to so much human activity. This amounts to an essentially deistic thinking in that "the actual life of the believer is left by God wholly to

---

[117] W, 7:15; the Latin reads "congregation of sinners."
[118] W, 7:23.
[119] W, 7:20.

himself."[120] So far is Ritschl willing to go in his opposition to any kind of mysticism or supernaturalism.

Similarly, for sanctification we need only to will to do good. Self-sanctification is the order of the day. The "Holy Spirit" of which the Bible speaks is merely the "power of righteous conduct and of self-sanctification or moral character-formation" and the "knowledge of God" common to all Christians.[121] Our "knowledge of God" may serve as the inducement to our will, but it is our will alone that determines our state and our character. Nor does justification necessarily lead to sanctification. There is no divine factor. Supernaturalism is altogether excluded from Ritschl's rationalism.

Warfield critically highlights Ritschl's antisupernaturalistic "theology." For Ritschl, there is no human soul that objectively exists metaphysically, and therefore no hope of immortality. The "soul"—human nature itself—is but the will. The will *is* the nature. "Character" is but the condition of the will at the moment. The being of God also "is dissolved in the acid of Ritschl's non-substantial metaphysics. . . . As a matter of course Ritschl knows nothing of a Trinity in the Godhead. And where there is no Trinity, there can be no preexistent Christ, and no personal Holy Spirit." Any use of such phrases as "deity" or "divinity" in reference to Christ is explained in terms that rob them of their usual meaning. The Holy Spirit is not a person who objectively exists. Nor is he an action or a force by which God works in us. No, for Ritschl the Holy Spirit "is, in its real nature, just the 'knowledge' which is common to the Christian community, and under the influence of which as a motive, the individual Christian sanctifies *himself*." He is not to be thought of as the "Divine means" of regeneration or reformation. He is "just a 'knowledge': a knowledge *of God*, no doubt, but just a *knowledge* of God." He has no existence as a substantial entity. He is merely the spirit of the Christian community "conceived as an influence" but with no will or objective existence of his own.[122]

This "knowledge" held by the Christian community points up the true significance of Jesus. It is Jesus, the bearer of the complete revelation of God and therefore founder of the kingdom of God, who first taught us that God has no ill-will toward us and has no intention of condemning us for our sin. He will let bygones be bygones. He desires and purposes only to do us good, and it is this that we must understand. There is no such thing as guilt, only a *sense* of guilt wrongly assumed. Accordingly, justification is but a new attitude on man's part toward God. Ritschl has a light view of sin and no sense at all of divine holiness or judgment. Jesus' work as teacher is what establishes him as the "savior"—he

---

[120]*W*, 7:33, 35.

[121]*W*, 7:24–25.

[122]*W*, 7:21, 23, 24–26, 40 (emphasis original).

SOTERIOLOGY

taught us to be rid of our guilt and to understand God's love for us. Accordingly, his abiding value is found in the example of one who lives in this awareness of God's love. This knowledge which Jesus taught and which is communicated to us by the Christian community, in turn, moves us to love God in return and desire to please him; this is regeneration and justification (which for Ritschl are not distinguished). Faith itself is not a dependence upon God and Christ but exclusively the act of freedom in which one chooses good. "Christianity" is nothing more or less than the religion of Jesus, living by his example and teaching, and as we thus live, "we shall be as divine as He." There is nothing supernatural here, nothing miraculous. Nor is there anything of mysticism, or of the Spirit's influence on the human soul or the soul's communion with God. The whole Christian life, from beginning to end, is "natural" and psychological. There is nothing supernatural about it.[123]

This (antisupernaturalism) appears to be the driving force in Ritschl's perfectionist doctrine. Accordingly, while he claims to find in Paul a doctrine of perfectionism, he does not actually believe that such perfection objectively exists; "perfectly Christian," not "a perfect Christian," is all he is after. Indeed, true perfection would almost certainly entail supernaturalism and thus threaten Ritschl's whole construct.

Warfield judges Ritschl's doctrines of God and sin as "profoundly immoral."[124] And in his somewhat scathing "The Ritschlian School," Warfield condemns the Ritschlian system as

> merely the old Socinianism in a new garment, cut from the cloth of Neo-Kantian speculation. Its views of sin and grace were of the lowest; it knows, as on its doctrine of sin it needed, no atonement and no divine Savior; it denied all living relation to an exalted Christ, and, indeed, all vital communion with God; and like the disciples that Paul found at Ephesus, it "did not so much as hear whether there is a Holy Ghost."[125]

This summarizes the reasoning behind a harsh characterization of Ritschlianism that Warfield wrote several years earlier: "When we say Ritschlianism, however, we say not only Socinianism but Socinianism in a decadent form." Warfield finds that Ritschl's "camouflaged Rationalism" is but a system of ethics explained in almost exclusively naturalistic terms and is only "by a strange transmutation of meaning" still called "theology." It is, in the end, neither true perfectionism nor

---

[123]W, 7:26–27, 36, 40–42, 46, 55–63.
[124]W, 7:55–63.
[125]SSW, 2:449.

even real "theology" that Ritschl offers. It is a kind of pious moralism that neither allows divine aid nor achieves true holiness. It allows for no removal of guilt but seeks to erase all sense of guilt. It replaces a divine Redeemer with a human will and redemption with self-effort. For the measuring of this effort, it has as its standard not the law of God but the individual's own self-defined "calling." In place of sanctification it offers self-sanctification, in place of grace it offers nature, and in place of divine enablement it offers human freedom. The love of God is to influence us to good, but there is no divine intervention. Throughout it is a purely human endeavor. Ritschl wanted desperately to avoid any form of mysticism, and in this pursuit he surely succeeded. But what he offered in place of mysticism was neither perfection nor Christian. It is "a perfect network of illusions."[126]

> In his hatred of supernaturalism, he gives us no God to flee to, and no God to visit us. His total discarding of what he calls "mysticism" is really the total discarding of vital religion. His whole labor impresses the reader as a sustained effort to work out a religious system without real religion; or, with respect to our present subject, to make out an issue of justification into sanctification without any real justification to issue into sanctification and without any real sanctification for justification to issue into.[127]

Still, this criticism may be of little consequence for Ritschl, Warfield acknowledges, for Ritschl's "religion" truly is "at bottom less a system of theology than a system of ethics." It has to do, in the main, with Christian behavior, and "it lies at the very nature of a naturalistic system that it should lay all its stress on the activities of the Christian life. There is nothing else on which it could lay its stress."[128]

The level of "perfection" that satisfies the Ritschlian ethic is not surprising, given its larger naturalistic context. Ritschl's perfection is not absolute. Perfection is simply "the qualities which enter into the Christian ideal, however incomplete may be their quantitative realization in the individual." We now live under the inspiration of the love of God. The joy of this life is what constitutes "blessedness" and "eternal life." By this new understanding of God we are impelled to trust his "providence" in our lives and the world and to adopt his purpose as our own and to work toward it. Siding with God, we seek to live for the purpose for which he has created us. Realizing our "vocation" in living for the kingdom of God—"this is what Christianity is," and this is what constitutes Christian perfection.[129] Moral

---

[126] *W*, 10:406; *W*, 7:109, 55, 56.
[127] *W*, 7:109.
[128] *W*, 7:67, 55.
[129] *W*, 7:68–70, 78. Warfield notes that providence for Ritschl is merely the course of things. At most it is a deistic concept.

perfection as judged by the law of God is not what Ritschl has in view. Warfield summarizes:

> We are under no law but such as is evolved out of our moral disposition in the course of our activities themselves: and we evolve this law, of course, only as it is needed and fulfil it as it is made. . . . Emancipated from all externally imposed law, we are a law to ourselves, and we recognize no other law as having dominion over us.[130]

Citing Ritschl, he continues:

> Christian perfection, he says, consists . . . just in "freedom of action." In this freedom of action, the Christian, seeking the final end of the Kingdom of God, imposes on himself—"gives himself"—a "law." He gives himself this law "by the production of principles and judgments of duty." Thus the law which he follows, and by following which he manifests himself as what he ought to be, is his own product, developed, as means to its accomplishment, out of the aim which he is pursuing. Not only is no "statutory law" imposed on him from without, but no immanent law is written on his heart by the finger of God. He evolves his own rules of life.[131]

Thus, the Christian can be assured of his perfection even though he violates the law of God. To be sure, it is "a very imperfect perfection" that Ritschl extols. In his own words, "Alongside of the conviction of justification through faith, a consciousness of personal moral perfection, especially of perfect faithfulness in our vocation, is possible, which is disturbed by no twinges of conscience."[132]

All this Warfield condemns as both absurd and immoral. No self-defined yet poorly achieved morality can by any reasonable use of language be called "perfection," and no standard but the law of God itself is adequate to judge human morals. Ritschl's "perfectionism" fails on all counts: its philosophical-theological framework is grounded in illusions, its standard of morality and estimate of sin are intolerably low, and it justly deserves the label "antinomianism."[133]

Moreover, Warfield takes issue with Ritschl's complaint that "unless the possibility of attaining perfection be held before Christians all impulse to effort dies in them." The attainability of perfection, in other words, is a necessary incentive to the Christian's continued struggle for holiness. But Ritschl "forgets that dissatisfaction with their present condition supplies a much more powerful spur to effort." Further, should that perfection be reached, then

---

[130] W, 7:95.
[131] W, 7:96–97.
[132] W, 7:91–92.
[133] W, 7:92, 100, 94.

motive and exertion would at once be lost.... It is a much more powerful incitement to effort that he should know the evil of the case in which he is, the difficulty of the task which lies before him, the always increasing reward of the journey as it goes forward, and the supreme greatness of the final attainment.[134]

Moreover, in the words of Thomas Adam (1701–1784), which Warfield cites approvingly: "The moment we think that we have no sin, we shall desert Christ."[135]

In Warfield's judgment, neither in substance nor in motive does Ritschl's perfectionism promote true, biblical Christian holiness.

PERFECTIONIST AND HIGHER LIFE MOVEMENTS

Warfield carefully traces the influence of Ritschl's perfectionist doctrine in the writings of his disciples, analyzing their respective deviations from and/or additions to Ritschl's teaching and assessing each argument on exegetical and theological grounds as presented.[136] He gives extensive and detailed analysis also to the German higher life movement (*Die Heiligungsbewegung*[137]), various kinds of mystical perfectionism, and the higher life, victorious life, and Keswick movements. Warfield's treatment of these teachings is meticulous and precise, and it serves as a vivid sample of his thoroughness as a historical theologian. Particularly since there is so much overlap among these and with Ritschl, it is not necessary at this point to provide a detailed review of each of Warfield's critiques, whether historical or theological, but only to glean from them what is necessary toward a further understanding of his own doctrine of sanctification.[138]

Oberlin Perfectionism

The theology of Jonathan Edwards underwent significant modification by his heirs in New England. Timothy Dwight (1752–1817), Edwards's grandson, began the process of change for a better doctrinal statement in the nineteenth century, but it was Dwight's most outstanding pupil, Nathaniel William Taylor (1786–1858), who developed the "New Haven Theology" most extensively. In turn, it was Taylor's most noted pupil, evangelist Charles Grandison Finney (1792–1875), who shaped

---

[134] *W*, 7:105.
[135] *W*, 7:129. Thomas Adam was an evangelical minister in Britain. His *Private Thoughts on Religion* were his own private (not intended for publication) reflections on his personal soul struggles. The searching work was widely influential in various circles of theological persuasion. Warfield cites him several times and refers to him as "a man of no common power of analytic and speculative thought."
[136] *W*, 7:136–301.
[137] Warfield translates *Die Heiligungsbewegung* loosely, "the fellowship movement," according to its leading characteristic.
[138] Cf. *W*, 7 and *W*, 8. Much of Warfield's discussion throughout these sections is purely historical and biographical and need not detain us here.

this new theology—"Taylorism"—into revivalistic practice and followed it through to a doctrine of perfectionism. The Princetonians all opposed this "New Divinity," and John H. and Jonathan Neil Gerstner aptly observe that

> if Hodge was the nemesis of Taylor, the "fury" which pursued Finney was B. B. War-field. Of course, Finney had other Princeton theologians opposing him in his own lifetime and many another Calvinist as well. His definitive Princetonian opponent, however, was Warfield whose *Studies in Perfectionism* traced perfectionism from the Arminian root in John Wesley to its full Pelagian fruit in Charles Grandison Finney.[139]

Warfield devotes well over two hundred pages to an analysis of Finney, Asa Mahan, and the brand of perfectionism they propounded from their Oberlin College. Finney is widely revered by American evangelicals today as the father of modern revivalism, and in his own day wielded enormous influence, his converts reportedly numbering around a half million. Warfield judges Finney's revivalism as but "a Pelagian revival," specifically, of the Taylorite variety. Finney's theology and "new measures" rested on "a doctrine of plenary ability"—the notion that all that is obligated of us we are able to perform and that obligation is limited by ability.

It was Finney the educator who came to preach perfectionist theology, having been introduced to it by his Oberlin colleague Asa Mahan. Concerned over the generally low state of Christian living, Mahan earnestly sought a corrective in the teaching that sanctification, like justification, is received by a direct act of faith. As in justification so also in sanctification we must cease from all self-efforts and "trust Christ universally." There is an unconditional either-or: "either works or grace; either effort or trust." His preaching formerly had been marked by the Pelagianism of the new divinity variety, and in it Mahan allowed no place for faith in sanctification—sanctification was purely a matter of works. Now the tables had turned, and he allowed no place for effort in sanctification. Sanctification is attained neither by efforts nor by faith *and* effort. It is attained by faith alone, immediately and entirely. Learning and acting on this new discovery marked Mahan's "second conversion" or "baptism with the Holy Ghost," in which, he testifies, he was brought to a higher plane of living. This new discovery he took to Finney, and after seeking it for himself, Finney also came to experience the "second blessing." From here on, the preaching of both men was marked by this perfectionist note. Oberlin perfectionism was born.[140]

---

[139]"Edwardsean Preparation for Salvation," *WTJ* 42, no. 1 (1979): 62–63.
[140]*W*, 8:51–53; cf. 122–24.

The leading features of the Oberlin perfectionism are these: first, "the immediate attainment of entire sanctification by a special act of faith directed to this end";[141] second, that there are accordingly "two kinds of Christians, a lower kind who had received only justification, and a higher kind who had received also sanctification";[142] and third, a fluctuating scale by which the Christian's "perfection" is measured.

As to the first, Warfield agrees that sanctification is by faith, but in a very different sense. According to the New Testament, Warfield argues, faith is not related to sanctification in the same way it is related to justification. We do not believe in order to be justified and then believe in order to be sanctified, directing our faith first to the one and then to the other. Sanctification is related immediately not to faith but to justification, and "as faith is the instrumental cause of justification, so is justification the instrumental cause of sanctification. . . . Justification comes through faith; sanctification through justification, and only mediately, through justification, through faith." By the nature of the case the necessary order is faith, justification, sanctification. Sanctification, in other words, is obtained by "the fundamental act of faith by which we receive the forgiveness of our sins." Separate acts of faith are not required for justification and sanctification. "The Scriptures require of us not faiths but faith." "Here [in Oberlin perfectionism] is a doctrine of salvation," Warfield observes, "not by faith, but by faiths."[143]

Warfield also warns about the very notion of receiving justification and sanctification separately, for it necessarily destroys the unity of salvation, breaking it up to be received piecemeal. Mahan exclaims, "What a melancholy reflection it is . . . that most believers advance no further in the Christian life than 'the washing of regeneration,' are ignorant of Christ as the Mediator of the new covenant, and, consequently, have no experience of 'the renewing of the Holy Ghost.'" Warfield responds, "Is it not a more melancholy reflection still that a Christian teacher can so cut Christ's great salvation up into sections as to imagine that a sinner can sincerely repent of his sins, and cast himself in faith on Christ for salvation—and

---

[141]In Finney's message of "sanctification by faith," Warfield finds inconsistency. Finney is a Pelagian of the New School variety. He is not a quietist and therefore would not be expected to preach a message of "stop trying, and start trusting." The Pelagian demands effort from beginning to end. Yet as noted above, Finney learned from Mahan and preached a message of simple faith for sanctification. He even rebuked those who sought it by prayer and fasting. Warfield is puzzled by it: "We greatly wonder how 'faith' does all this and not only that it is faith that does it, not Christ: Christ supplies only the model to which faith conforms us. For light on this dark question, however, we shall have to go elsewhere." Still, it is a Pelagian sanctification in that it is a sanctification of works only and determined by the human will (W, 8:61).

[142]W, 8:67. These first two points may be referred to as the "original" or "early" version of the Oberlin perfectionism. Finney and his associates later abandoned both points and affirmed that all who are justified are entirely sanctified all by the same act of faith and at the same time, and that there is therefore only one kind of Christian, that is, entirely sanctified (W, 8:138–52).

[143]W, 7:363, 358; W, 8:100, 520.

then not receive it?" Warfield is insistent: we cannot have Christ as our justification without also having him as our sanctification. "We cannot take Him in one
of his offices as our Mediator, and reject Him in another."[144]

Warfield further denies both that sanctification is attained immediately and
that it is attained in its entirety in this life. Finney finds support for these notions
in familiar lines of thought: our perfection is the will of God; God promises us
perfection; the Holy Spirit is given to accomplish our perfection; and so on.
"Every one of these propositions is true," Warfield notes, "and none of them is to
the point." They miss the point simply because they fail to address the question
of timing, whether it involves a process or happens all at once. Finney forces a
dilemma—that either we are made perfect in this world, or Christ has failed to
sanctify us. But the dilemma is a false one. God's purpose will not fail, but exactly
when and *how* God will accomplish this purpose are separate questions entirely.
For Warfield, the complete enjoyment of the fulness of God's redemptive purpose,
for individuals and for the world itself, awaits the eschaton.[145]

As to the second feature of the Oberlin perfectionism, that there are two classes
of Christians, Warfield answers that there are, in fact, individual Christians at
virtually "every conceivable stage" of spiritual attainment. Given that sanctification is a process culminating only in glory, we should expect to see Christians at
virtually every point in the spectrum. But Warfield shudders to hear of a "Christian" who is yet an "unchanged sinner," nor will he countenance any notion of
Christians' differing in class or kind—one as justified only and another as both
justified and sanctified. Indeed, the very idea that a person may die justified but
not sanctified and "go to heaven a corrupt and polluted, though not guilty, wretch"
runs exactly contrary to "the fundamental principle that without holiness no man
shall see the Lord" (Heb. 12:14). All Christians are by very definition both justified
and sanctified, even if the degree of their sanctification may differ among them.
The New Testament is "absolutely impatient of their separation from one another,
and uniformly represents them as belonging together and entering as constituent
parts into the one, unitary salvation which is received by faith."[146] Warfield judges
that it is a "defective view of justification" that allows these conclusions.

> Corruption is the very penalty of sin from which we are freed in justification; holi-
> ness is the very reward which is granted us in justification. It is therefore absurd
> to suppose that sanctification can fail where justification has taken place. Sancti-
> fication is but the execution of the justifying decree. For it to fail would be for the

---

[144]*W*, 8:100, III, 99.
[145]*W*, 8:59.
[146]*W*, 8:119, 100; *W*, 7:363.

acquitted person not to be released in accordance with his acquittal. It is equally absurd to speak of a special "sanctifying faith" adjoined to "justifying faith"; "justifying faith" itself necessarily brings sanctification, because justification necessarily issues in sanctification—as the chains are necessarily knocked off of the limbs of the acquitted man.[147]

In short, "justification and sanctification are but successive steps, inseparably joined together by an immanent bond, in the realization of the one salvation which is received by faith."[148]

The third feature of the Oberlin perfectionism—its fluctuating scale by which the Christian's "perfection" is measured—Warfield finds particularly troubling. Finney's perfectionism defined sin exclusively in terms of voluntary action and maintained that we have no obligation beyond our ability to perform; what we ought to do we are able to do, and what we are unable to do, for whatever reason, we are no longer obliged to do. The result is "a perfection that consists in complete righteousness, but in righteousness which is adjusted to fluctuating ability." Perfectionism it is, but it is a perfectionism of action only and one that is fluctuating in degree, measured only by the person's ability and not by the law of God exclusively. On this point Warfield cannot resist criticizing Finney for pushing the principle "to such an extreme as to adjust them in detail to the moral capacity of each individual sinner, all the way down to moral idiocy; with the effect of making our sin the excuse for our sin, until we may cease to be sinners altogether by simply becoming sinful enough." Warfield judges the idea of measuring Christian "perfection" by a sliding scale as ridiculous, if not blasphemously antinomian.[149]

Warfield finds this "imperfect perfection" to be characteristic of all varieties of perfectionist teachings. The original perfectionist teacher was Pelagius himself, and rather cynically Warfield remarks, echoing Harnack, that there appears to be an inability on the part of Pelagius and his followers "to notice any appreciable difference between what they actually do and what they ought to do." The same was true of Ritschl and now of the higher life movements also—it is not an actual perfectionism after all. In some way or another, varying with each perfectionist teacher, not all sin is sin. Theodor Jellinghaus (1841–1913), has in view "conscious" and "premeditated and wilful" sinning.[150] This is a perfection

---

[147] W, 8:100.

[148] W, 7:370.

[149] W, 8:58, 71.

[150] PTR 1, no. 3 (1903): 457; W, 7:376. Jellinghaus was the theologian of *Die Heiligungsbewegung*, who converted to perfectionist theology by the efforts of Robert Pearsall Smith in 1874 at the Oxford campaign. Late in his life Jellinghaus reversed and condemned his earlier perfectionist teachings.

of acts only and not of nature. Nor is it therefore a state of confirmed perfection, for the sinfulness residing in the nature "lies there in the background so far affecting him that it is due to it that he can sin again." Further, it is a very subjective perfection at that, one measured by the Christian's "own subjective standard which is always imperfect and always changing"; it is not an objective perfection as measured by the law of God. It is a perfection that allows even for an accusing conscience and for

> sins of weakness, inadvertence, hastiness, ignorance, even if these sins are rooted in bad habits or bad judgment or bad conditions which have been created by his own former sins. . . . It is even possible for the perfect man to be very imperfect in his life-manifestations in the just view of his fellow-men. . . . Perfection with him is so little a matter of exact conformity to a perfect moral and religious standard that it is consistent with not only a fundamental evil nature lying in wait in the background of life, but with a multitude of actual sins . . . even when the commission of them is not unaccompanied with some sense of wrong-doing.[151]

Warfield then observes, "We think it must be admitted that the model from which he has painted his portrait of the perfect man was drawn rather from the ranks of what most of us would speak of as sincere Christians," and he wonders why Jellinghaus bothers to call such a man "perfect." For Jellinghaus a Christian may do a great deal of sinning and yet be "free from sin"; without blushing he can say of such Christians that they "do not sin."[152]

Warfield finds this a trait common to all brands of perfectionism. Not all sin is sin, and a great deal of imperfection can still be called perfect. Accordingly, some teachers speak of perfection simply in terms of *motive* or *intent*, others of actions only, others of conscious sinning ("living up to the light that is in us"); others speak in terms of voluntary versus instinctive acts, others of actions as measured by a relative scale in keeping with knowledge, and still others of eradicating "the sin nature." Often in such constructions what the Scriptures call sins become merely "errors," "infirmities," and "inadvertences," but still the believer is said to be "perfect." Whatever the equivocation, such "mitigated perfection" Warfield condemns as essentially antinomian.

> [It] not only lowers the standard of perfection and with it the height of our aspirations, but corrupts our hearts, dulls our discrimination of right and wrong, and betrays us into satisfaction with attainments which are very far from satisfactory. There is no more corrupting practice than the habit of calling right wrong

---

[151] W, 7:382–84.
[152] W, 7:384–85.

and wrong right. That is the essence of antinomianism. . . . And this is the real arraignment of all perfectionist theories. . . . They lull men to sleep with a sense of attainments not really made; cut the nerve of effort in the midst of the race; and tempt men to accept imperfection as perfection—which is no less than to say evil is good.[153]

Elsewhere he observes that "Christian perfection differs from all other kinds of perfection precisely in this, that it is not real perfection." Warfield dismisses this as "that Antinomian tendency which is the nemesis that follows on the heels of all forms of perfectionism." He adds, "In order to vindicate the perfection of the Christian the perfection of the perfection is sacrificed."[154]

Warfield gives similar criticism of the common perfectionist notion that love is regarded as the essence of perfect holiness. To love is to be holy. Warfield agrees that love will bring a man to fulfill the law of God (cf. Matt. 22:36–40); but he refuses to allow anything but the law of God itself to define holiness, and he views any alternative as morally destructive.

In assuming this attitude there is danger, of course, of conceiving of love as a substitute for holiness; and of supposing that if a man has love he has all the holiness he needs. And the double peril lurks in this path, of sentimentalizing the conception of the Christian life, on the one hand—fostering a tendency to conceive it in terms of emotion rather than of morality—and of directly relaxing the demands of righteousness, on the other.[155]

In short, perfectionism necessarily entails an inadequate estimate of sin and holiness. A deep sense of sin or a profound conception of sin renders all perfectionist teaching impossible.[156]

Finally, Warfield of course rejects the whole underlying Pelagian foundation of Finneyism. First, Finney contends that sanctification is the prerequisite of justification. Finney argues:

(1.) That present, full, and entire consecration of heart and life to God and His service, is an unalterable condition of present pardon of past sin, and of present acceptance with God. (2.) That the penitent soul remains justified no longer than this full-hearted consecration continues.[157]

---

[153] W, 8:525, 448, 458.
[154] W, 8:528–29.
[155] W, 8:442–43.
[156] W, 8:554.
[157] W, 8:148.

Finney's justification entails no imputed righteousness; it is rather a theology of personal merit throughout. Still more fundamentally, this requisite sanctification itself depends solely on the human will, which is fully capable of doing all we are commanded. All this Warfield dismisses out of hand on the grounds of the supernaturalism necessarily involved in Christian salvation.

> Let us remind ourselves moreover that the matters which fall under discussion here [the attainment of sanctification] are of the order of what the Bible calls "things of the Spirit," things which are not to be had at all except as imparted by the Holy Ghost; and that it is therefore peculiarly infelicitous to speak of them as "attainable," merely on the ground of "natural ability." In so speaking of them, we seem gravely in danger of forgetting the dreadful evil of sin as the corruption of our whole nature, and the absolute need of the Spirit's free action in recovering us from this corruption. The unregenerate man cannot believe; the regenerate man cannot be perfect; because these things are not the proper product of their efforts in any case but are conferred by the Spirit, and by the Spirit alone.[158]

Warfield characterizes Finney's Pelagian perfectionism much as he characterized that of Ritschl: "It is quite clear that what Finney gives us is less a theology than a system of morals. God might be eliminated from it entirely without essentially changing its character. All virtue, all holiness, is made to consist in an ethical determination of the will."[159]

Other perfectionist teachings come in several varieties, each with its own peculiar emphasis. Some lay stress on a "moment by moment deliverance" attained by a "moment by moment surrender" to Christ, by whose strength one is kept from sin. But this puts the cart before the horse and then again behind.

> The plain fact is that we cannot suspend a supernatural salvation on natural activities . . .—if it is wrought by Christ, it cannot be dependent on our "moment by moment" faith, but our "moment by moment" faith must be dependent upon it. We cannot teach both a supernatural and a natural salvation.[160]

The various strains of mystical perfectionism are grounded not in the motions of the human will, as is the case with Pelagian perfectionism, but in the experience of union with the divine, the inward formation of Christ in the heart, the new birth, communion with God, the indwelling of the Spirit of God, the "second blessing," the coalescing of our will with God's, and so on. It may be that perfec-

---

[158]W, 8:74–75.
[159]W, 8:193.
[160]W, 7:336–37.

tionism comes by faith, but this faith is generally understood in terms of a passive receptivity on the part of the empty soul that waits to be filled. The human part, if there is one, is to remain empty and await this divine work, to consent and abandon oneself to it. Beyond this there may be contemplation or meditation, but the will is absent. The believer must not strive for holiness but "let God do it" and wait to receive it. Accordingly, we must not be preoccupied with sin and how it is to be removed; we must seek rather to be removed of self and be filled and controlled by the divine. To be possessed by God is the experience of perfection. Among the mystical perfectionists there are variations of emphasis and modifications of detail, but some notion of absorption with or by God is an ideal they hold in common. All of this misses entirely the biblical requirement to mortify sin and to run and struggle and fight.[161]

The Higher Life Movements

The decline of soteriological Calvinism and the rise of Pelagian and semi-Pelagian theology among the American churches in the mid-nineteenth century provided the atmosphere for the rise of perfectionist teaching in evangelical groups. As valued as perfectionist theology was to many, however, it was (and is) claimed as an actual experience by only a relative few within evangelical churches. Neither John Wesley nor Francis Asbury (1745–1816), the two brightest lights of Methodism, claimed to have achieved perfection. From the eighteenth century onward, relatively few who have embraced the doctrine have actually owned the experience of it. The resistance it met from Warfield and others has held it back not only from Reformed churches but from evangelical churches generally. Still, perfectionist theology has remained alive and well in its stepchildren of the holiness movements in the nineteenth, twentieth, and now twenty-first centuries. The "kindred doctrines" of the higher life and victorious life and Keswick movements, and the doctrines of sanctification generally held in evangelical churches were spawned by the perfectionism that preceded it. Warfield chronicled and critiqued the "holiness" theology of the stepchildren just as he did the parents and was almost equally unimpressed by them.[162]

---

[161] W, 8:379. Warfield does not miss this strain of semi-Pelagian and even Pelagian influences in the mystical perfectionists (W, 8:431–36).

[162] W, 8:464. In his treatment of the higher life movement Warfield makes mention of Robert C. McQuilkin, a leader in the victorious life movement (W, 8:587). McQuilkin evidently felt that Warfield had misrepresented the victorious life advocates, and his son, J. Robertson McQuilkin, reports the following: "My father . . . told me that when this book [Warfield's *Studies in Perfectionism*] was published, he went to Warfield and discussed the matter of Keswick teaching and perfectionism at length. Afterwards Warfield admitted, 'If I had known these things, I would not have included the last chapter in my work'" ("The Keswick Perspective," in *Five Views of Sanctification*, ed. Stanley Gundry [Grand Rapids: Zondervan, 1987], 245n8). But interesting as this may be, the quote cannot be accurate. First, Warfield never saw the publication of

The higher life doctrine came in several varieties and is known by various labels. The German manifestation was *Die Heiligungsbewegung*, "the sanctification movement." The British and American versions are known as the Keswick, higher life movement, interior life, and victorious life movements. Some representatives of these movements were themselves perfectionists, and this Warfield does not find surprising. "The seeds of a consequent Perfectionism are sown, indeed, wherever the Higher Life doctrine is preached, and must produce their harvest whenever the artificial restraints of the Higher Life discreetness are relaxed." Some were given also to miracles, healings, and other extravagances.[163]

But with variations allowed, Warfield finds a common thread running through all, a thread of characteristic features spun in Wesleyan perfectionism.

> In all of them alike justification and sanctification are divided from one another as two separate gifts of God. In all of them alike sanctification is represented as obtained just like justification, by an act of simple faith, but not by the same act of faith by which justification is obtained, but by a new and separate act of faith, exercised for this specific purpose. In all of them alike the sanctification which comes on this act of faith, comes immediately on believing, and all at once, and in all of them alike this sanctification, thus received, is complete sanctification. In all of them alike, however, it is added, that this complete sanctification does not bring freedom from all sin; but only, say, freedom from sinning; or only freedom from conscious sinning; or from the commission of "known sins." And in all of them alike this sanctification is not a stable condition into which we enter once for all by faith, but a momentary attainment, which must be maintained moment by moment, and which may readily be lost and often is lost, but may also be repeatedly instantaneously recovered.[164]

Warfield finds "the very spirit of the Higher Christian Life" to lie in a sanctification received by a special act of faith distinct from that of justification, a sanctification that does not eradicate the sinful nature but leaves the old nature of sin unaffected. "All our sanctification is 'in Christ,' external to our self, and is drawn upon only for our daily need 'moment by moment,' that is to say, for our conduct solely, since it does not affect our nature." There must be not only trust but a continual

---

his book *Studies in Perfectionism*. This two-volume work is a collection of his essays that were originally published in various theological journals from 1918 to 1921, the last of which was published posthumously (1921); the two-volume work to which McQuilkin refers was not published until 1931–1932, some ten or eleven years after Warfield's death. Second, the "last chapter" of the book to which this McQuilkin quote refers is the chapter on the higher life, which was in fact not the last but the very first article of the series published (1918). As to the accuracy of the substance of the remark—that Warfield acknowledged a misunderstanding—we have no way of judging. We only know that while Warfield continued to write on the broader subject of holiness-perfectionism, he made no retractions.

[163] W, 7:25; W, 8:471.
[164] W, 8:563.

trusting, abandonment and continual abandonment, surrender and continual surrender, yielding and continual yielding at every successive moment, and so on. In this way the believer is not necessarily made more holy, but he is made more successful in overcoming sin. And this is the work of Christ or of the Spirit but not the work of the believer. The believer's duty is merely to "allow" God to work in him—to place the clay in the hands of the potter, something the potter cannot do himself—so that the potter can do his work of shaping and molding.[165] In the higher life doctrine,

> what we obtain by faith is Christ—as a Preserver from sinful acts. By continuous faith we obtain Him continuously—as Preserver from sinful acts; and only from those particular sinful acts with which we are for the moment threatened. We do not at any time obtain Him as Savior from all possible sins, but only as Savior from the particular sinful acts for protection from which we, from time to time, need Him. Thus we are never made "holy" in any substantial sense, so that we are ourselves holy beings. And also accordingly we are never made "holy" in any conclusive sense, so that, being holy in ourselves, naturally we continue holy.[166]

Warfield finds all this to be entirely inadequate on many counts. First, higher life theology shares with its perfectionist parents the mistaken implicit teaching that we are saved "not by faith but by faiths" and "Wesley's primary error"—the "crass separation of sanctification from justification" and with it "the creation of two different kinds of Christians, a lower and a higher variety." Higher life teachers speak of the "ordinary Christians," who are "ignorant of the fulness of the salvation which is in Christ," and who know only of salvation from the penalty but not from the power of sin. With a touch of sarcasm Warfield turns the tables: "Where they have met with these 'ordinary Christians' we have no power to conjecture. They are not the ordinary Christians with whom we are familiar." Nor, he remarks further, is such a teaching "the ordinary Christian teaching." The "ordinary" Christian teaching has never taught either that salvation in Christ is "exhausted in its objective benefits" or that a believer can receive justification without receiving sanctification also. This two-tier experience of Christianity is "indistinguishable" from the doctrine of a "second blessing" and "a second work of grace" of the Wesleyan-type perfectionism, which forgets that "it is to all Christians, not to some, that the great promise is given, 'Sin shall not have dominion over you'" (Rom. 6:14). This separation of sanctification from justification "forces from us the astonished cry, Is Christ divided? And it compels us to point afresh

---

[165] W, 8:548, 538–40.
[166] W, 7:387.

to the primary truth that we do not obtain the benefits of Christ apart from, but only in and with His Person; and that when we have Him we have all."[167]

Second, as this is merely an overcoming of conscious sinning, with "the old sin nature" remaining intact, this sanctification is of no real sanctifying value at all. Warfield says of Lewis Sperry Chafer (1871–1952) in this context:

> He does not seem to see that thus the man is not saved at all; a different, newly created, man is substituted for him. When the old man is got rid of—and that the old man has to be ultimately got rid of he does not doubt—the saved man that is left is not at all the old man that was to be saved but a new man that has never needed any saving.[168]

Warfield says of Robert Pearsall Smith (1827–1898), who espoused an entire yet increasing sanctification (in reference merely to known sins), "It seems to have escaped his mind that a Christian's growth is a progressive cleansing from imperfections and has not 'maturity' but 'cleansing' as its goal." "That is to say that *nothing* in the way of betterment has happened" to the Christian himself. This doctrine is costly. In it we "lose the elevating power of a high ideal. And we are to be satisfied with never being 'well-pleasing to God.'" By contrast, "What the Scriptures teach is that we shall be more and more transformed into Christ's image until at last, when we see Him as He is, we shall be like Him, and therefore in ourselves—as He has made us—well-pleasing to God."[169] Sanctification for Warfield transforms the Christian himself, not simply his actions.

> Whenever one-sidedness in the conception of Christ's salvation has shown itself in the history of Christian teaching, the tendency has been apt to be to emphasize its subjective at the expense of its objective side, rather than the objective at the expense of the subjective.... It is not the "ordinary Christians" who hold to a fatally deficient conception of salvation, but the advocates of the "Victorious Life"; and strange to say, the fatal deficiency of their conception of salvation lies on the subjective side. They teach a purely external salvation. All that they provide for is deliverance from the external penalties of sin and from the necessity of actually sinning.

In such a scheme of salvation as this, "deliverance from corruption has no place." It is "too poverty-stricken a conception of salvation to satisfy any Christian heart." In Warfield's judgment,

---

[167] W, 8:520, 567, 569–70, 575; PTR 17, no. 2 (1919): 322–27; W, 8:569; cf. PR 10, no. 38 (1889): 334.
[168] Review of *He That Is Spiritual*, by Lewis Sperry Chafer, PTR 17, no. 2 (1919): 325. Chafer was a popular Presbyterian evangelist and founder of Dallas Theological Seminary. He would later still refer to Warfield as "America's ablest theologian" (*BSac* 109, no. 434 [1952]: 183).
[169] W, 8:528; W, 7:388–89 (emphasis original).

to keep a sinner, remaining a sinner, free from actually sinning, would be but a poor salvation; and in point of fact that is not the way the Holy Spirit operates in saving the soul. . . . He cures our sinning precisely by curing our sinful nature; He makes the tree good that the fruit may be good. . . . We cannot be saved from sinning except as we are saved from sin.[170]

Third, the entire scheme rests on a Pelagian theology—a "fundamental naturalism" as Warfield calls it. The "whole process" of sanctification is suspended on the human will.

We say "the whole process" because it emerges that not only is God helpless to work on and in us unless and until we truly place ourselves in His hands for the purpose, but He is equally helpless to keep us in His hands when once He has undertaken the work on and in us that has been committed to Him. We must not only surrender ourselves to Him, but we must also "abide" in Him. . . . Very strange clay this, passive in the potter's hands, to which the potter can do nothing unless it lets him![171]

In higher life teaching, Christ does all the work, and we give him the freedom to work by our faith, surrender, or yieldedness. Warfield characterizes this as reducing Christ to a mere "instrument through which we perform" the work of sanctification ourselves. Criticizing the same view in Charles G. Trumbull (1872–1941), Warfield writes that this is to "place God at the disposal of man, and to encourage man to use Him in order to obtain results which he cannot attain for himself."[172]

This is not precisely the same as trusting God to do it. We must not entrust it to God to be done, as we assign a job to a workman and require him to do it according to specifications. We must trust God to do it—it, as all other things—in His own perfect way. The former attitude makes God our instrument to do our bidding.[173]

Smith declares: "Full faith gives the full deliverance; partial faith the partial victory. So much faith, then so much deliverance, no more, no less! . . . *If we would live up to the gospel standard of holiness, we must believe up to the gospel standard of faith.*" Warfield replies, "It is our faith, then, which regulates our grace; and that means that it is we and not God who save. . . . This is a dismal outlook for

---

[170] W, 8:575–76, 579–80.
[171] W, 8:550, 539.
[172] W, 8:516, 609. Trumbull was one-time editor of *The Sunday School Times*, a popular victorious life speaker, one of the founders of America's Keswick, biographer of C. I. Scofield.
[173] W, 8:537–38.

those of 'little faith,' and indeed is as complete a doctrine of work-salvation as Pelagius' own."[174]

Fourth, Warfield also detects in this "abandonment to Christ for sanctification" theology an impossible conundrum.

> If, when we "abandon" ourselves to Christ, we place ourselves in His Hands, so that He becomes responsible for all results, does He not become responsible for our continued "abiding" too? But Mr. Smith intends to remove precisely that out of His responsibility and to reserve precisely that to us as the condition of Christ's keeping us. This amounts in the end, of course, to saying that He will keep us, if we will only keep ourselves: He will keep us in the way if we will only keep ourselves in the Way. Mr. Smith is, to put it in one word, teaching Quietism, not Evangelicalism. It is our will, after all, not Christ's will, that governs our lives. Christ can keep us only if we let him keep us. We must first "abandon" ourselves to Him before He can take responsibility for our lives. He can maintain His control of our lives only if we "abide" in Him. And at any moment we can—are "liable" to—snatch their control out of His hands.[175]

That is to say, Christ will sanctify us so long as we allow him to do so, and he will keep us from falling so long as we do not fall.

Warfield uncovers this same doublespeak in Hannah Whitall Smith (1832–1911), the wife of Robert Pearsall Smith. In her words, "The indwelling presence of Christ destroys (or 'renders inert') the body of sin, and keeps it so; but the moment the soul lets go of Christ, or turns its eyes away from Him, that moment its old evil all returns."[176] Warfield responds:

> It is evident that Mrs. Smith is here at her wit's end. She is trying to teach at once that our old nature is expelled by Christ and that it is not expelled; that Christ keeps us permanently, and that His keeping is only moment by moment; that our abiding in our grace rests on Christ alone, and that it depends absolutely on ourselves. It is an impossible task. . . . The mind reels as it tries to imagine how this can be—if, for example, Christ not only "drives out His enemies," but "keeps them out." The cart is surely put before the horse. Surely we cannot "let go of Christ," "turn our eyes away from Him," unless the old evil has already returned. A pure heart—and we are told that Christ has made the heart pure and keeps it pure—cannot do these things. And this old evil, all of which returns, where has it been all the intervening time?[177]

---

[174] W, 8:520 (Smith's emphasis).
[175] W, 8:532.
[176] W, 8:549.
[177] W, 8:549–50.

Fifth, this essentially quietistic model conflicts with those passages of Scripture which present the Christian's advance in sanctification in terms of labor and exertion. This matter will be resumed shortly.

Sixth, in the "old nature/new nature" theory, so basic to the teaching of the victorious life, Warfield finds hopeless confusion. Somewhat condescendingly he writes in response to Robert McQuilkin:

> "A Christian possessed of the indwelling Spirit of God," we read with sad eyes, "may choose to walk after the flesh." That is no doubt because he is possessed of rather than by the Spirit of God. At any rate it belongs ineradicably to "the Christian" to turn on the old carnal nature, or the new Spiritual nature, as he may choose, and let it act for him. Who this "Christian" is who possesses this power it is a little puzzling to make out. He cannot be the old carnal nature, for that old carnal nature cannot do anything good—and presumably, therefore, would never turn on the Spirit in control. He cannot be the new Spiritual nature, for this new Spiritual nature cannot do anything evil—and this "Christian" "may choose to walk after the flesh." Is he possibly some third nature? We hope not, because two absolutely antagonistic and noncommunicating natures seem enough to be in one man. The only alternative seems, however, to be that he is no nature at all—just a nonentity: and then we do not see how he can turn on anything. Mr. McQuilkin is not wholly unaware of the difficulty to thought of the notion he is presenting. "That a Christian should possess two natures," he writes, "one wholly evil and incapable of doing good, the other wholly good and incapable of doing evil, is a mystery, and no words of man's wisdom can explain how these two natures exist in one personality." That surely is true.[178]

Similarly, Warfield finds the "overstrained doctrine of the Christ within us" to be "somewhat unintelligible mysticism" and self-contradictory. As we "let go and let God," Christ "takes over" our life in such a way that "our individuality has been abolished and Christ has taken its place." The Lord Jesus assumes our "body, mind, soul, and spirit." He has become us, and "we" no longer exist. We "have passed away and Christ has been substituted for us: we and He are not one and another—there is but one left and that one is Christ." Then Warfield quotes Trumbull as saying, "I need never again ask Him to help me, as though He were one and I another; but rather simply [ask Him] to do His work, His will, in me, and with me, and through me." To this Warfield wonders "how 'we' can ask 'Him' anything"![179] Unintelligible mysticism.

The problem becomes worse. Trumbull holds that it is our "ineradicable power to resist Christ"—the negative use of our free will—that accounts for our

---

[178] W, 8:587.
[179] W, 8:595–96.

sinning. Yet "Christ has become me as literally as the tree which furnishes the wood of which a desk has been made has become that desk." "Christ within us" is now our animating force. And so Warfield wonders how, then, it is that we sin at all? "How in the name of all that is rational, can I retain a power to resist Him when I retain no body or mind or soul or spirit of my own? . . . Where is the seat of this power to resist Him? And how can it act—successfully act—against the only agent that acts at all?" Warfield notes that Trumbull begs his readers "not to think that he is 'suggesting any mistaken unbalanced theory that, when a man receives Christ as the fulness of his life, he cannot sin again.'" But Warfield asks in return:

> How can we help thinking just that when we have been told that Christ has constituted Himself our very being, our body, mind, soul, and spirit; and, seizing the reins, has become the sole agent in all our activities—He who "cannot fail"? Can Christ, who has thus become our very life, living thus in us, sin through us? And if He cannot sin through us, how can "we" sin, when it is no longer we who live, but He that lives in us?

To speak of "free will" in this context is to deny the very thesis being put forward. The two ideas "destroy one another, and one must give way before the other." Much better, Warfield proposes, to speak of Christ's making the tree good so that the fruit also will be good. Christ dwells within us in order to make us good, "that our works, freely done by us, may under His continual leading, be good also. . . . Mr. Trumbull's attempt to perform the impossible feat of uniting in one system an express autosoterism and an equally express quietism naturally brings him into endless self contradictions."[180] Pelagian, self-contradictory mysticism is the characterization Warfield gives of the victorious life teaching.

Eighth, Warfield argues that the higher life doctrine fosters a defective view of sin and holiness, and, worse still, an unworthy concept of God.

> Corresponding to this defective outlook on sin and holiness was an equally defective attitude towards God and His relation to men. None of the high attributes of God were denied, but the practical effect of the teaching was to encourage men to look upon Him as a force existing for them and wholly at their command. . . . Nevertheless, the open teaching of the whole movement is to the effect that God acts—and can act—in the matter of sanctification, as in the whole matter of salvation, only as man, by his prior action, releases Him for action. This is not a wholesome attitude to take towards God. It tends to looking upon Him as the instrument which we use

---

[180] W, 8:600–602.

to secure our ends, and that is a magical rather than a religious attitude. In the end it inhibits religion which includes in its essence a sense of complete dependence upon God.[181]

Ninth, Warfield accuses higher life teachers of the sin of pride. The two classes of Christians created by this theology, "a lower and a higher variety," give preachers occasion to congratulate themselves "upon not being as other men are—'ordinary Christians,' 'average Christians.'" Warfield notes that "these 'ordinary' or 'average' Christians come in for a good deal of little-disguised scorn" and are told that "not more than one in a thousand" attain the level of "victory" that they have attained. It is ironic that such teachers of "holiness" should thus be compared to the Pharisee of Luke 18:11. Warfield also finds all this strikingly reminiscent of Matthew 20:20–24, and summarizes, "But it is not of humility that we especially are made to think as we read." Indeed, "spiritual pretension" and self-congratulation are the "inevitable" fruits of such a teaching as this. Warfield agrees with Charles H. Spurgeon that this kind of thinking is "deluded . . . vainglory," and he prefers as more realistic that self-estimate engendered by Reformed theology and expressed by Thomas Adam: sin is so deeply a part of who we are that not only do we sin inevitably, but "when we have done all we ever shall do, the very best state we ever shall arrive at, will be so far from meriting a reward, that it will need a pardon. . . . If I was to live to the world's end, and do all the good that man can do, I must still cry 'mercy!'"[182] The two theologies produce two corresponding fruits—one of more sin and the other of a humble recognition of it.

Finally, Warfield judges that the higher life theology is a hindrance rather than a help to the Christian life. Neither deep repentance nor ecstasy of aspiration finds room here. With the law of God marginalized, an adequate appreciation of grace is lost. The *summum bonum* of the Christian life becomes rest and peace. "God, as He is no longer greatly feared, neither is any longer greatly loved." Even trust itself, so prized by the teachers of the higher life, is misplaced—dependence is on our own trust rather than on God. "Pelagius, when he hung salvation on works, at least demanded perfect righteousness as its ground. In this teaching perfect righteousness is dispensed with, and the trust in favor of which it is dispensed with disappears with it. . . . If we are to depend upon our own trust it ceases to be trust."[183]

Warfield summarizes succinctly his own assessment of the higher life doctrine of the holiness movements:

---

[181] W, 8:554.
[182] W, 8:571; W, 7:127–28.
[183] W, 8:555.

A certain levity lies at the heart of "the Keswick Movement"; its zeal is to assure ourselves that we are actually and fully saved, rather than to give ourselves to the repentance which is due to our sins, to the working out of salvation with fear and trembling, to heavenly mindedness, and a life of prayer and a walk in love. It imagines that there can be faith without repentance and conquest of sin without moral struggle. The law, sin itself as evil desire in the regenerate, the determined fulfillment of the will of God in vital endeavor, are pushed into the background. It seeks, in a word, peace instead of righteousness, and the trail of a spiritual euthymia lies over it.[184]

In brief, "this is a fatally externalizing movement of thought, and brings with it a ruinous under-estimate of the baneful power of sin." This view will never survive "in the presence of a deep sense or a profound conception of sin." Neither will it survive where a worthy concept of God is faithfully maintained.[185]

THE SINNING CHRISTIAN

Warfield gives particular attention to the perfectionists' attempt to ground their teaching exegetically in the letters of apostles John and especially Paul and to position the apostles against the Reformers. In some cases Warfield merely dismisses the attempt as "absurd" with no need of further remark. In other cases Warfield demonstrates at some length that in pitting the apostle Paul against the Reformers, the perfectionist teaching has presented a lopsided view of each. With both Paul and the Reformers thus misrepresented, an "artificial antagonism has been produced, and, if you restore to each what has been omitted, the two melt into one another." Both the apostles and the Reformers, Warfield continues to insist, present us consistently with that "paradox" of "miserable-sinner Christianity."[186] Warfield devotes extensive space to Paul Wernle (1872–1939) and accuses him of "coming to the subject of study with a hypothesis already in hand, and 'verifying' that hypothesis by seeing how far it can be carried through." Wernle is guilty, Warfield accuses, of

> much twisting and turning in the effort to make the unwilling texts fit into the assumed hypothesis: and no one surely could have given us more twisting and turning than Wernle does. . . . It would be difficult to determine which Wernle thinks less well of—orthodox Protestantism or Paul. He stands apart from both, and from his superior position of critic speaks biting words of each.[187]

---

[184]W, 7:339–40.

[185]W, 8:554–55.

[186]W, 7:144, 151.

[187]W, 7:152–53. Wernle was a Swiss Protestant theologian and enthusiastic (yet independent) follower of Ritschl. Coming from a pietistic Moravian family background and having studied under Harnack

In rebuttal Warfield provides a display of "miserable-sinner Christianity" in Paul. A few samples will suffice. Where Wernle argues that the eschatological standpoint of Romans 6 shows the Christian to have already passed into resurrection life and that, therefore, the Christian cannot sin, Warfield sees Paul saying something much different. Warfield does not speak in terms of what was later designated "realized eschatology" but rather argues the "as if" notion that characterizes it: "it is '*as if* alive from the dead' that we are to walk (v. 13)." He then offers an observation that is "subversive to Wernle's whole point of view." The apostle Paul, Warfield notes,

> is speaking to a constituency among whom sinning has not automatically ceased on their believing.... Paul is contemplating a situation in which not only is it conceived that sins may occur in the life of Christians, but it is understood that, occurring in it, they receive the same treatment as the sins that are past—make drafts on the same grace, and thus "cause that grace to abound."[188]

Warfield argues that both sin and grace continue to be the experience of the believer, even if in increasingly contrasting proportion. Commenting on Romans 8:1, he remarks simply that the apostle "does not say, 'There is therefore now no sinning for those in Christ Jesus.' He says, 'There is therefore no condemnation to those in Christ Jesus'; and on the face of it this means . . . that those in Christ Jesus live in an atmosphere of perpetual forgiveness."[189] The issue involved in justification is not past sins only but continued sins. Again, both sin and grace continue to be the experience of the believer, even if, again, in increasingly contrasting proportion.

Romans 7 also provides for Warfield a grounding for "miserable-sinner Christianity." In verses 14–25, Paul "probes the human heart, and even uncovers his own soul for us," finding an as-yet imperfect Christian. Warfield takes the last verse of the chapter (v. 25) as a summary statement of the passage, that Paul serves Christ not in a sinless state but with a divided mind. This, in turn, further informs the meaning of the declaration of Romans 8:1. The believer has no condemnation despite the fact of his divided mind and resulting imperfect life.[190]

Similarly, when Paul warns of the problem of misbehavior at the Lord's Supper in Corinth (1 Cor. 11:17–34), he writes, "But if we judged ourselves truly, we would not be judged. But when we are judged by the Lord, we are disciplined so that we

---

(1851–1930), Wernle made his mark early with his *Der Christ und die Sünde bei Paulus* (1897), which Warfield here criticizes at length.

[188] W, 7:162–63 (emphasis original).

[189] W, 7:170.

[190] W, 7:135, 171–72; cf. 180–81.

may not be condemned along with the world" (vv. 31–32). What is significant here is that not only does the apostle rebuke the sins of the Corinthian believers in this matter specifically, but in his change from the second person ("you") to the first person ("we") he broadens the exhortation to all believers, himself included. His exhortation at this point applies to all Christians. The Corinthians had been guilty of the specific faults he rebukes. But all Christians are sinners, and thus all Christians alike—the apostle also—are responsible to "judge themselves."[191]

Still more striking is 2 Corinthians 12:20–21, where Paul specifies the horrible sins of which his converts in that church were capable and, in fact, guilty:

> For I fear that perhaps when I come I may find you not as I wish, and that you may find me not as you wish—that perhaps there may be quarreling, jealousy, anger, hostility, slander, gossip, conceit, and disorder. I fear that when I come again my God may humble me before you, and I may have to mourn over many of those who sinned earlier and have not repented of the impurity, sexual immorality, and sensuality that they have practiced.

Here Paul speaks not of preconversion sins, nor merely of sins possible to commit. He speaks of the sins of the believers at Corinth still not repented of, and for those sins he rebukes them.[192]

Likewise in Philippians 3:12 the apostle expressly declares that he has "not yet attained" and is "not yet perfect." Even elders in the church yet sin (1 Tim. 5:20). The repeated ethical imperatives of the New Testament (e.g., 2 Cor. 7:1) all assume that the transformation of Christians was not yet complete. Similarly in 1 Corinthians 9:27, Paul admits to his own need constantly to struggle against sin. All this is in obvious keeping with the New Testament commands to Christians to cease rendering evil for evil (1 Thess. 5:15; Rom. 12:17), Jesus' instruction to pray for forgiveness (Matt. 6:12, 14; Mark 11:25–26; Luke 11:4), the broader New Testament instruction for the treatment of the sinning brother (e.g., Gal. 6:1; Eph. 4:32; Col. 3:13; 1 Pet. 4:8; 1 John 5:16–18), and the general characterizations of Christians found throughout the New Testament (e.g., James 3:2; 4:8; 1 John 1:8). The whole tone of 1 John 1:8ff., Warfield argues, "is not that Christians are sinless men who may possibly, however, be overtaken in a rare fault; but that Christians are sinful men, seeking and obtaining in Christ purification from their sins and striving day by day to be more and more delivered from them." And so Warfield does not find it surprising that the apostle Paul speaks in the present tense of the forgiveness that believers enjoy: "we *have* . . . the forgiveness of sins" (Col.

---

[191] *W*, 7:258–59.
[192] *W*, 7:261–63.

1:14; Eph. 1:7). Passages such as these demonstrate at least "that the forgiveness of sins was a blessing enjoyed, alike by Paul and his Christians, as a continuous possession, and that this forgiveness must be taken sufficiently inclusively to embrace all the sins that existed for him and them." This may not quite show that Christians are continuously sinning, but it at least proves that "forgiveness was looked upon by them as the fundamental blessing on which they rested their whole lives long."[193]

Warfield appears stunned at the temerity of Finney "to 'challenge the world' to adduce any Scripture to support what he calls 'the doctrine of justification in sin, in any degree of present rebellion against God.'" Warfield argues, "Paul might seem to have written a great part of his epistles expressly to provide materials for meeting this challenge." Warfield proceeds to cite Romans 3:21ff.—with its pointed emphasis on the freeness of divine grace given only to believing yet ill-deserving sinners—as ample demonstration of the Pauline teaching that God justifies *sinful* believers.[194]

In another context Warfield summarizes:

> It is too clear to be denied, that the Scriptures are full of exhortations to men, assumed to be justified, to make advances in their holy walk, and therefore cannot mean to teach that every justified man is by the very act by which he received his justification also at once fully sanctified. It is also too clear to be denied that, in point of experience, not all who must be presumed to be justified are fully sanctified—unless we are prepared to refuse to recognize as a Christian at all any one who is not obviously perfect—a position to the intolerableness of which Jellinghaus shows himself to be keenly sensitive.[195]

"MISERABLE SINNER" CHRISTIANITY

Warfield sees clear reason why we sin: the fruit is corrupt only because the tree itself is corrupt, and given our sinfulness, our sins inevitably follow.

> There is no sinful nature which is not active. . . . So certainly as the *operari* follows the *esse*, so certain is it that as long as the *peccatum habituale* exists the *peccatum actuale* occurs. . . . As long as it [the *peccatum habituale*] lies in the background it must of necessity show itself in every act. Its existence in Paul makes him in the fullest sense of the word a "miserable sinner," incapable of not sinning, because incapable of being in his acts anything but himself.[196]

---

[193] W, 7:167, 218–19, 224, 261–62, 271, 277–78.
[194] W, 8:156–57.
[195] W, 7:372.
[196] W, 7:221.

For a perfectionist of any variety, the term "miserable sinner" cannot and must not be used in reference to the Christian. But Warfield is quite prepared to accept this as an accurate and appropriate characterization of himself and of every Christian. Following Luther's dictum that the Christian is *simul iustus et peccator* ("at the same time just and a sinner"), indeed, *semper* ("always") *iustus et peccator*, and in agreement with the traditional Reformed doctrine of remaining sin in the believer, Warfield glories in the fact that although he is a "miserable sinner" and this side of heaven will always be a "miserable sinner," he is nonetheless truly perfect in his status before God in Christ while awaiting his full transformation to perfection in the eschaton. He maintains no illusion that his transformation, although well under way, has yet been completed. He finds in the Scriptures, in the historic statements of the church, and in his own heart and life ample evidence that he is yet, to borrow Luther's words, a Christian "in the making." In short, our justification ensures both our sanctification and our glorification, but our sanctification is an ongoing process never completed in this life. Accordingly, the apostle Paul describes himself as "less than the least of all the saints" (Eph. 3:8 KJV) and the "chief" of sinners (1 Tim. 1:15 KJV).[197]

Moreover, this self-understanding is a necessary one—it "belongs to the very essence of the type of Christianity propagated by the Reformation." At the heart of the Christian gospel "lies the contrast of sin and grace," which drives the Christian to "feel himself continuously unworthy of the grace by which he lives." At no stage of Christian development are we acceptable to God by virtue of what we do.

> Our need of Christ does not cease with our believing; nor does the nature of our relation to Him or to God through Him ever alter, no matter what our attainments in Christian graces or our achievements in Christian behavior may be. It is always on His "blood and righteousness" alone that we can rest. . . . We are always unworthy, and all that we have or do of good is always of pure grace. Though blessed with every spiritual blessing in the heavenlies in Christ, we are still in ourselves just "miserable sinners": "miserable sinners" saved by grace to be sure, but "miserable sinners" still, deserving in ourselves nothing but everlasting wrath.[198]

We are always but pardoned criminals. "In fact and in act" we are continuously sinful and in need of "unbroken penitence throughout life." Our problem lies in what we are, not simply in what we do; sin, therefore, "is a quality which, entrenched in the heart, affects all of our actions without exception." It is not a

---

[197] W, 7:91, 220.
[198] W, 7:113–14.

question of which of our actions are sinful and which are not—everything we do is tainted. We will never be truly perfect "until our hearts are perfect."[199]

Given the indispensableness of this doctrine, it is not surprising that Warfield finds this aspect of Christian doctrine and devotion embedded in a long list of Protestant ecclesiastical formularies, both doctrinal and devotional: Luther's Large and Short Catechisms, the various branches (Prussian, American, German) of the Lutheran church; Calvin's Catechism, the Heidelberg Catechism, the Calvinistic liturgies; the Catechism of the Church of England and its articles and prayers; the Easter litany of the Moravian church, Zinzendorf, the English evangelicals—all "Christ-trusting Christianity . . . casts its orbit around that center."[200]

But we must not misunderstand. It would be a mistake to think that because the Christian is always sinful, he must therefore be marked by despair or depression and doubt. To the contrary, the Christian is marked by assurance and "overmastering exultation."[201] And for good reason.

> We are sinners and we know ourselves to be sinners, lost and helpless in ourselves. But we are saved sinners; and it is our salvation which gives the tone to our life, a tone of joy which swells in exact proportion to the sense we have of our ill-desert; for it is he to whom much is forgiven who loves much, and who, loving, rejoices much.[202]

Borrowing Harnack's phrase, Warfield speaks of "'solaced contrition'—affliction for sin, yes, the deepest and most poignant remorse for sin, but not unrelieved remorse, but appeased remorse. There is no other joy on earth like that of appeased remorse." The Christian life is marked by a recognition of sinfulness and a contrasting joy in the awareness of rescue by divine grace. This type of piety, fostered in the Scriptures and brought into sharp focus by Augustine, was soon lost due to ideas of human merit so prominent in the Middle Ages. But "Luther brought it back. His own experience fixed ineradicably in his heart the conviction that he was a 'miserable sinner,' deserving of death, and alive only through the inexplicable grace of God." He found that although he could not think highly of himself, he could not think too highly of Christ. And so "it became his joy to be a 'miserable sinner,' resting solely on the grace of Christ."[203]

The Christian's continued recognition of sin and grace is vitally important for Warfield, therefore, not only because it "belongs to the very essence" of the Chris-

---

[199] W, 7:114; W, 8:457.
[200] W, 7:126.
[201] W, 7:114.
[202] W, 7:114.
[203] W, 7:113–17; cf. W, 4:251–54; W, 9:494; W, 10:494–95; PS, 66, 69; FL, 149–51.

...an gospel itself but also because of its indispensable usefulness in Christian devotion and worship. This concept of sin and grace has "moulded the piety of all the Protestant generations."[204] It informs for us the significance of that needed petition, "Forgive us our debts" (Matt. 6:12). The Christian's recognition of his own sinfulness and consequent reliance upon divine grace are attitudes fostered and made necessary by the very gospel they have embraced and continue to embrace. Recognition of our sin is part and parcel of our continued reliance upon Christ.

> Sin and Christ; ill desert and no condemnation; we are sinners and saints all at once! That is the paradox of evangelicalism. The Antinomian and the Perfectionist would abolish the paradox—the one drowning the saint in the sinner, the other concealing the sinner in the saint. . . . [quoting Thomas Adam] "It is a great paradox, but glorious truth of Christianity . . . that a good conscience may consist with a consciousness of evil." Though we can have no satisfaction in ourselves, we may have perfect satisfaction in Christ. . . . It is clear that "miserable sinner Christianity" is a Christianity which thinks of pardon as holding the primary place in salvation.[205]

There is contrition because of "a life of continuous dissatisfaction with self," and there is corresponding joy in a "continuous looking afresh to Christ as the ground of all our hope." "Miserable sinner Christianity" is a necessary part of what drives the Christian to look continuously to Christ as the sole object of his faith. It incites continued appreciation for Christ as Savior and, therefore, a continued feeding upon him for life. "Thus in complete dependence on grace, and in never ceasing need of grace . . . the saint goes onward in his earthly work." Our "whole lives long" we rest on God's grace of forgiveness.[206]

Warfield summarizes with the words of Thomas Adam: "On earth it is the great exercise of faith . . . to see sin and Christ at the same time, or to be penetrated with a lively sense of our desert, and absolute freedom from condemnation; but the more we know of both, the nearer approach we shall make to the state of heaven."[207] *Simul iustus et peccator.*

THE NATURE OF SANCTIFICATION

Drawing on all this we can now develop more positively Warfield's doctrine of sanctification. For Warfield sanctification in the life of the believer is a progressive experience growing out of an initial radical transformation of heart and life

---

[204] W, 7:117; cf. SSW, 2:426–27; FL, 149–51.
[205] W, 7:130.
[206] W, 7:90, 219.
[207] W, 7:130.

in regeneration by the Holy Spirit and culminating in the glory of the eschaton. Warfield is insistent that the believer's sinfulness—extreme though it may be—is more than matched by the grace of God in Christ and by the creative work of the Holy Spirit. Borrowing from Jesus' parable of the sower, Warfield observes that what allows the seed to grow in one case and not another is the condition of the soil—and that soil is made good only by the preparations of divine grace. Accordingly, he regularly speaks of the Spirit's work of illumination or enlightenment in the darkness of the human heart. This creative work affects man's entire being—intellect, emotions, desires, will, and all that constitutes the human soul. The beginnings of the Christian life are grounded in the supernatural workings of God in grace immediately upon the human heart in which we are basically and radically transformed. Any talk of the role of the will in sanctification, therefore, must take into account this consideration that the will is shaped by the renewed heart. Here Warfield is at one with Jonathan Edwards and the older (as distinct from the new divinity) New England tradition. The affections are "a fount of moral character," and they, having been transformed by grace, "give character to the will."[208]

Initial Sanctification

David Cho argues that "Warfield's evaluation of perfectionism was wholly based on the progressive aspect of sanctification without any reference to the definitive aspect of sanctification" later articulated by John Murray, and that Warfield therefore "lacked a fully balanced approach in his evaluation of perfectionism."[209] John Walvoord seems to suggest the same in his brief review of *Perfectionism* when he warns that Warfield "does not properly distinguish between state and position in respect to Christians."[210] But this contention is at least overstated and appears to have missed some important considerations. First, it must be granted that Warfield nowhere uses the language of "definitive sanctification" as such. But then, Warfield nowhere develops the doctrine of sanctification *en toto*. Warfield's doctrine of sanctification must largely be gleaned from his criticisms of perfectionists who held that the Christian is without sin; he therefore had little occasion to address what Murray later designated "definitive sanctification." Almost the entire body of Warfield's writings on the doctrine of sanctification comes by way of analysis and critique of perfectionist and higher life theologies. The closest Warfield comes to presenting a comprehensive presentation of sanctification is

---

[208]*W*, 8:420–22; *SSW*, 2:325.
[209]David D. Cho, "The Old Princeton Presbyterian Response to the Holiness Movement in the Late Nineteenth and Twentieth Centuries in America" (PhD diss., Westminster Theological Seminary, 1994), 100–101. See John Murray, "Definitive Sanctification," 1967; reprinted in *Collected Writings of John Murray*, vol. 2 (Carlisle, PA: Banner of Truth, 1978), 277–93.
[210]*BSac* 116, no. 464 (1959): 359.

in his revision of a very brief article written originally by his predecessor, A. A. Hodge. In the main, then, Warfield's doctrine of sanctification must be gleaned from his criticisms of the errors of perfectionist and higher life teachers. Even so, the exercise is not as clean as it might seem, for Warfield's chief aim is not at all to provide detailed elaboration of the doctrine of sanctification. Indeed, he gives relatively little positive construction at all; at length he points out logical fallacies and faulty exegesis involved in the various perfectionist teachings and throughout seems to assume that his (Reformed) audience will understand the theological errors he highlights. In other words, Warfield simply never provides a thorough Reformed view of sanctification as such; he gives critique of the perfectionist or higher life teachers. It may be fair to say, therefore, that definitive sanctification evidently did not enjoy a prominent role in Warfield's writing. But it is not at all warranted to say that Warfield was unaware of it.

Indeed, there is good evidence to the contrary. The brief Hodge-Warfield article on sanctification includes the statement that sanctification involves "the cleansing of the soul from sin and emancipation from its power." Warfield does not expand on this point, but then almost nothing in this brief article receives much expansion of any kind. The progressive character of sanctification is more heavily emphasized, but the notion of purity and freedom from sin is explicitly highlighted. Further, in "The 'Higher Life' Movement," Warfield spends most of a page arguing similarly from the text and revision of Toplady's famous hymn "Rock of Ages." The end of the first stanza originally read,

> Be of sin the double cure,
> Cleanse me from its guilt and power.

But Warfield notes the more common wording, given by T. Cotterill in 1815:

> Be of sin the double cure,
> Save from wrath, and make me pure.

The original version, Warfield argues, is "fatally inadequate," and the revision is "more exact." Whether Cotterill's revision was intended to achieve greater exactness of rhyme or of theological expression, Warfield observes, he has improved the doctrinal statement of the hymn. "Christ's blood does something more for us than cleanse us from the guilt and power of sin: it cleanses us also from the corruption of sin." In Christ we enjoy imputed righteousness but also a basic holiness that has radically transformed the inner man. If this is not the fully developed "definitive sanctification" of Murray, it is at least the beginnings of it.[211]

But there is more. Murray grounds this doctrine in many passages of Scripture, but primarily in the sixth chapter of Romans, where he demonstrates at length from Paul's "death to sin" metaphor the absoluteness of sanctification. He summarizes his doctrine of definitive sanctification concisely: "This means that there is a decisive and definitive breach with the power and service of sin in the case of every one who has come under the control of the provisions of grace." Warfield argues along these lines exactly. Regularly he emphasizes that sanctification grows out of the creative work of the Holy Spirit by which the sinner is made holy—and wholly new; that is, sanctification entails a decisive break with sin. In his "On the Biblical Notion of Renewal" he employs terms such as "renovation" in conjunction with both regeneration and sanctification and stresses at great length that "salvation in Christ involves a radical and complete transformation wrought in the soul. . . . Nowhere is the sinner permitted to rest satisfied with pardon as the end of salvation; everywhere he is made poignantly to feel that salvation is realized only in a clean heart and a right spirit." This notion is essential to Warfield's argument that justification and sanctification cannot be separated and that there are not "two kinds" of Christians—all who are justified are also made holy in Christ.[212] The apostle Paul, Warfield notes, teaches "very explicitly" in Romans 6 that justification is necessarily accompanied by sanctification. "The whole sixth chapter of Romans, for example, was written for no other purpose than to assert and demonstrate that justification and sanctification are indissolubly bound together; that we cannot have the one without having the other." For that matter, the sharp disjunction between the "power" and the "penalty" of sin is overdrawn: "One asks in amazement, What is the penalty of sin? And what is salvation from it? Is not our sinfulness the penalty above all other penalties of sin, and is not holiness just salvation from sin?" Warfield insists that "holiness [realized and experienced] is the very reward which is granted us in justification." "We cannot divide Jesus and have Him as our righteousness while not at the same time having Him as our sanctification." Being "reckoned righteous" demands that we are also "made righteous." These statements in context all entail, in Warfield's understanding, a basic and decisive break with sin that is experienced by every believer. He argues at length that the "sanctification" of the holiness teachers, being a sanctification of acts only, is entirely inadequate, and it is their "fatal defect" that they provide no cleansing or deliverance from inward corruption.

---

[211]W, 8:477. Interestingly, at least at one point in his argument (*Collected Writings*, 286–87) Murray seems to follow exactly the argument of Warfield (W, 7:358, 363).

[212]Murray, *Collected Writings*, 2:280; W, 7:65; W, 2:439–40; cf. W, 8:481.

Biblical sanctification entails purifying the man himself. Indeed, Warfield's whole doctrine of progressive sanctification rests on the firm understanding that the believer has already undergone a radical and thorough transformation of heart and life, for "the process of transformation wrought out in our sanctification does only actualize in us what from the beginning we have trusted Christ for; it is a 'working out' of our salvation." That is to say, progressive sanctification depends for its very existence on definitive sanctification. To borrow (rather loosely) the language of the Presbyterian higher life exponent W. E. Boardman (1810–1886), for Warfield, the "first" and "second" conversions coalesce in the experience of every believer at the very inception of the Christian life.[213]

Warfield argues this most graphically in his criticism of the victorious life teachings of W. H. Griffith-Thomas (1861–1924),[214] who sought a mediating position between "eradication" and mere "suppression" and came up with what he called "counteraction" of the sinful nature. Warfield finds several logical and exegetical inconsistencies here, but in answer he provides a striking statement of the radical break with sin that all Christians have experienced. What the Scriptures teach, he argues forcefully, is "eradication."

> They [the Scriptures] propose to free us from sinning by freeing us from the "principle of sin." Of course, they teach that the Spirit dwells within us. But they teach that the Spirit dwells within us in order to affect us, not merely our acts; in order to eradicate our sinfulness and not merely to counteract its effects. The Scriptures' way of cleansing the stream is to cleanse the fountain; they are not content to attack the stream of our activities, they attack directly the heart out of which the issues of life flow. . . . Counteraction there is; and suppression there is; but most fundamentally of all there is eradication.[215]

To be sure, Warfield is careful to point out that this work is not completed in this life, but even so, this language is graphic in its insistence that there has been in the life of every believer a radical breach with sin.

Throughout Warfield's writings this is both assumed and argued. Sin's former power is broken in the experience of every believer. Every Christian has undergone a "repristination" of soul. This is more than sufficient to demonstrate that Warfield understood very well something of what Murray later called "definitive sanctification." Murray worked this out more "definitively" than did Warfield, particularly in terms of the New Testament use of ἁγιάζω and its cognates, and

---

[213] W, 8:100, 208, 475, 478, 551, 568, 570, 575.
[214] Griffith-Thomas was an English minister, scholar, teacher, popular conference speaker, and cofounder with Lewis Sperry Chafer of Dallas Theological Seminary.
[215] W, 8:583.

he gave fuller exposition to Romans 6 in this regard. But Warfield saw very well that sanctification begins in the supernatural re-creative work of regeneration and that it is rooted in our union with Christ in his death and resurrection.[216] The believer is one who has been made holy.

Accordingly, Warfield frequently offers the Christian himself as evidence of the truthfulness of Christianity and of the power of the gospel. Everywhere the gospel has gone, it has left transformed men and women behind. He speaks of "the regeneration of society" that has been effected "by the forces brought into the world by Christianity." In 1895 Warfield reviewed a new title that examined the character of early Christianity and that demonstrated that Christians are noted to be people of superior life and character. Warfield remarks with appreciation that this is always the case: "It was in this sign that Christianity conquered, and in it that it must ever conquer, when conquer it will and does." And in virtually every soteriological context, Warfield insists that "the great change" is not a matter of theory only but of experience, that in salvation the sinner is radically and thoroughly transformed and that this transformation is inevitably reflected in every believer.[217]

Progressive Sanctification

It is accurate, however, to say that Warfield speaks of sanctification *primarily* in terms of its progressive experience, a "constant advance toward sinlessness" that entails both the increasing emancipation from and eradication of sin (cleansing) and the progressive development of the newly "implanted spiritual life and infused habits of grace." Everywhere he speaks of salvation as in progress and as experienced in successive stages. And this experience, though it involves effort and struggle on the part of the believer, is nonetheless grounded in a thoroughgoing supernaturalism. He criticizes Mahan, whose later theology "operated with an unconditioned either-or: either works or grace; either effort or trust. As he had formerly allowed no place for faith in sanctification, so now he did not wish to allow any place for effort in sanctification." But Warfield comments, Mahan "seems not to be able to understand that we must both 'work and pray,' as the popular maxim puts it; both believe and labor; he wishes us to 'cast all the responsibility' on Christ after a fashion which smacks more of mysticism than the Gospel." In this revealing statement Warfield puts the lie to those who have characterized him as

---

[216]For that matter, Warfield would surely have noticed the idea prominently embedded in the Westminster Confession: "They who are once effectually called, and regenerated, having a new heart, and a new spirit created in them, are *further* sanctified, really and personally through the virtue of Christ's death and resurrection (I Cor. 6:11; Acts 20:32; Phil. 3:10; Rom. 6:5–6)" (13.1, emphasis added). W, 2:454.
[217]SSW, 1:223; W, 10:143.

ig "minimized the element of human responsibility by making sanctifica-
... almost exclusively the sovereign act of God." To the contrary, for Warfield, a
sanctification without effort is an unbiblical mysticism.

> We do not stop to point out the injustice of setting sanctification by effort and sanc-
> tification by faith in mutually exclusive opposition to one another. . . . [Believers']
> efforts to be holy are themselves part of the sanctifying effects of the faith by which
> they are united with Christ—not all of it nor even the main part of it, but a part of
> it. Effort and faith cannot in themselves be set in cross opposition to one another,
> as if where the one is the other cannot be. They rather go together in a matter like
> sanctification which consist in large part of action.[218]

Warfield's disapproval of the various mystical approaches to sanctification
lies largely in that they ignore the many biblical injunctions that demand mor-
tification of sin, running a race, struggle, fighting, strength in battle, and other
such exertion of energy. Similarly, he objects that the perfectionist and higher
life teachings often aim too low, in that they are "preoccupied with the pursuit of
happiness," and tend in many ways to subordinate everything else to this pursuit.
He cites perfectionist titles as proof: Hannah Whitall Smith's *The Christian's Secret
of a Happy Life* and Isaac See's *The Rest of Faith*. Warfield caustically remarks in
the words of Watts's famous hymn: "Men grow weary of serving the Lord; they do
not wish to fight to win the prize; they prefer to be carried to the skies on flowery
beds of ease." Sanctification entails a struggle against sinning and against the
remaining corruptions of the heart, an active engagement in the advancement
of the life of faith.[219]

By contrast, Warfield understands Romans 7 as the portrayal of the constant
struggle of the believer to "eradicate" sin. So far from "letting go," the Christian
must fight against sin, and the struggle is lifelong. Similarly, on 2 Peter 3:14–18
he notes that the apostle requires active engagement on the part of the believer
in the advancement of the Christian life. Peter does not allow simply that we
wait for God to give the increase. He commands us "to exert ourselves" (v. 14; cf.
1–10, 15) and teaches that in this effort we are engaged in struggle toward our own
sanctification. Warfield remarks sharply, "There is no Quietism here."[220]

Still further, the object of this struggle, Warfield demands, is nothing short of
complete moral perfection. As we have seen, one of his complaints of the various
perfectionist teachings is that their perfection is inevitably less than perfect. But

---

[218] W, 7:91; SSW, 2:325–27; Randall Gleason, "B. B. Warfield and Lewis S. Chafer on Sanctification," JETS 40,
no. 2 (1997): 255; W, 8:104–5; cf. SWW, 1:43; W, 8:52.
[219] W, 8:491–92, 553.
[220] W, 8:553; cf. W, 2:459–60.

Warfield will not allow that the Christian struggle is for anything less than entire ethical and moral purity. In 1 Peter 1:15, God's holiness is "the goal to which we must strive to attain." In his sermon on 2 Corinthians 6:11–7:1 entitled "New Testament Puritanism," Warfield emphasizes the extent of the apostle Paul's exhortation, "Let us cleanse ourselves from all filthiness of the flesh and spirit," to which he adds, "perfecting holiness in the fear of God" (2 Cor. 7:1 KJV):

> It is perfection, we perceive, that the Apostle is after for his followers; and he does not hesitate to raise this standard before the eyes of his readers as their greatest incitement to effort. They must not be content with a moderate attainment in the Christian life. They must not say to themselves, O, I guess I am Christian enough, although I'm not too good to do as other men do. They must, as they have begun in the Spirit, not finish in the flesh; but must go on unto perfection.

Warfield continues:

> What are they to cleanse themselves from? *Every* defilement—every *kind* of defilement—not only of the flesh but of the spirit. Aiming at what? At the completion of holiness in the fear of God! The Apostle does not tell them they are already holy—except in principle. They obviously were not already holy—except in principle.[221]

But in all this emphasis on the believer's effort Warfield will not have us dependent upon ourselves, and he does not fall guilty to the Pelagianism he everywhere condemns. His whole outlook is grounded in a thoroughgoing supernaturalism. This struggle is rooted in a union with Christ in his death and resurrection and in the creative power of the Holy Spirit in us. God has not worked in us by persuasion only but has made the tree good so that the fruit also can be good. Warfield criticizes Hannah Whitall Smith's contention that "God's working depends upon our co-operation"; for Warfield, it is the reverse—our cooperation depends wholly upon God's working in us. Nor is the believer's struggle merely to "yield" or "surrender" or "trust" but rather an active engagement in opposition to sin and all compromise—"evil in all its forms . . . every *kind* of defilement" of both flesh and spirit—in short, a struggle in the fear of God to achieve "perfect sanctification," for holiness is the very "substance" of our salvation. For Warfield, sanctification demands a "moment by moment" *struggle*, and given our state of weakness, this struggle must continue throughout this life. Yet in this struggle there is every encouragement offered, for as in all other aspects of salvation, God is the energizer of his people, himself bringing them both to will and to do according to his good

---

[221] *FL*, 255–56, 447 (emphasis original).

pleasure (Phil. 2:12–13). We must indeed "work out [our] own salvation," but we do so in clear view of the great fact that the power within us to bring us to practical, realized righteousness is none other than God himself.[222]

Warfield summarizes Paul's doctrine of sanctification as consisting in the following three propositions. First, in contradiction to the perfectionists, Paul insists that "to grace always belongs the initiative—it is grace that works the change." It is not in our turning to God, our trusting, or our "allowing" God to work that this work originates. It is of God. Second, "to grace always belongs the victory—grace is infinite power." There is no failure: whom God justifies he sanctifies. And third, "the working of grace is by process, and therefore reveals itself at any given point of observation as conflict." Sanctification is, in short, a work of God in all his people by which they are certainly—even though progressively—made holy.[223]

The Means of Sanctification: Scripture

In turn, success in this struggle stems from an acquaintance with divine truth. Ethics apart from revelation is hopeless. Warfield recognizes that there have been many whose learning has left them dry and with little evident transformation. But he has no time for a supposed Christianity that holds "no opinions" or holds an understanding of divine truth in low esteem. He insists that the Christian life from its very outset is driven by an awareness of revealed truth from and about God. Certain convictions are necessary from the start and are "absolutely determinative" of the whole of Christian living. "We cannot go one step without them. And what we call Christianity is bound up with a very definite" understanding of them. It is unfair to mock, as some have, at the controversy over "a mere diphthong" (*homoousios* vs. *homoiousios*), when that controversy involves the "whole substance" of Christianity. We are sanctified by the truth (John 17:17), and it is impossible for there to be true personal Christian advance apart from an appreciation of certain necessary truths. Warfield quotes John Wesley to illustrate the problem:

> No less a man than John Wesley is appealed to, however, to support this minimizing of the value of truth. . . . "I am sick of opinions," he writes; "I am weary to bear them; my soul loathes the frothy food. Give me solid substantial religion; give me a humble gentle lover of God and man, a man full of mercy and good fruits, a man laying himself out in the work of faith, the patience of hope, the labor of love. Let my soul be with those Christians wheresoever they be and whatsoever opinions they are of."

---

[222] *W*, 8:433, 538; *FL*, 243–58, 308, 312.
[223] *W*, 8:584; cf. *SSW*, 2:325–28.

Warfield grants that Wesley may well have been reacting against some who had nothing but "opinions" to show for their Christianity. But still he asks, "Did he ever see such a man as he here paints for us" who did not hold to and who was not possessed by certain essential opinions? How can there be such a man as he describes—full of faith and hope and love—who was not himself controlled by the opinion not only that God is but that God is love? What is the "work of faith" unless that faith has a defined object? "Solid substantial religion," Warfield insists, cannot exist "apart from the 'opinions' which lie at its basis." A man who is not of the opinion that God is or that Jesus lived or that he was the Son of God simply does not and cannot live as the one who holds these opinions. "This is the reason why Christianity is propagated by preaching. There may be other ways in which other religions are spread," but not Christianity. Christianity is fundamentally "faith," and faith implies something believed.

> Whatever we may say of a so-called Christianity which is nothing but "opinions," there is no Christianity which does not begin with opinions, which is not formed by opinions, and which is not the outworking of these opinions in life. Only we would better call them "convictions." Convictions are the root on which the tree of vital Christianity grows. No convictions, no Christianity. Scanty convictions, hunger-bitten Christianity. Profound convictions, solid and substantial religions. Let no man fancy it otherwise. Ignorance is not the mother of religion, but of irreligion.[224]

In his Princeton address, "The Religious Life of Theological Students," Warfield relates to the students the popular false dichotomy between the learning of theology and the practice of piety. "Sometimes we hear it said that ten minutes on your knees will give you a truer, deeper, more operative knowledge of God than ten hours over your books." He responds, "What! Than ten hours over your books on your knees?" His point is that learning is not antagonistic to godliness—indeed, if it is, then all learning must be abolished! "No mistake could be more gross." Rather, our learning must be a means by which godliness is advanced. And so he asks, "Are you, by this constant contact with divine things, growing in holiness, becoming every day more and more men of God?" As he would emphasize to his students on another occasion, "Religious knowledge and religious living go hand in hand."[225] Here Warfield reveals his own conviction that it is by means of increasing acquaintance with the Scriptures, divinely revealed truth, that God enables the Christian to progress in sanctification.

---

[224] *SSW*, 1:265–68; *SSW*, 2:281–88, 478–80, 483–86.
[225] *SSW*, 1:412, 417; *SSW*, 2:494.

The Means of Sanctification: Gospel Truth

More to the point, Warfield remarks, in agreement with the Reformers, that we must focus our attention on and increase our acquaintance with the great redemptive work of the triune God, for it is these truths "which minister to edification." This is clearly the focus of Warfield's thinking: it is not merely an acquaintance with divine truth generally but specifically an increased acquaintance with divine redeeming grace and its benefits that most effectively promotes Christian holiness. "The love of Christ constrains us." The source of our obedience to Christ is an apprehension of his love to us. Just as self-sacrificing love is "the essence of the Christian life," so also for its incentive we are referred to the self-sacrificing love of Christ. A clearer recognition of our privileges in Christ promotes our living up to those privileges. Moreover, for Warfield the key to Christian piety is a clear sense of dependence on God, fostered by Augustinian notions of sin and grace, as noted above. This theme dominates his writings, and he is convinced that nothing is more suited to the development of this sense of dependence, therefore, than a fuller acquaintance with these truths.[226]

Warfield elaborates on this point in his sermon on Ephesians 3:14–19, where the apostle Paul prays for spiritual strengthening, the building up of the inner man, by the Holy Spirit. This strengthening is for believers, those in whose hearts Christ already "abides" through faith. Christ, by the Spirit, is the source of our strength, received through faith. This strengthening is accomplished specifically by enlarging our apprehension of spiritual things. Specifically, God's Spirit ministers to us an increasing understanding of Christ's love and by this means gives increased spiritual strength. Warfield's point is simply that it is by a growing acquaintance with gospel truth—the love of Christ—that we progress to that great goal of divine likeness that awaits the children of God. The apostle, then, prays not only for this goal but "for the path that leads to this goal," which is knowledge of the gospel. To be sure, it is only by the Spirit of God that such knowledge can be truly appreciated, but it is by this knowledge nonetheless that love is enhanced and progress is attained.[227]

Warfield argues similarly from Ephesians 4:30, where the apostle grounds his appeal to refrain from sin in the blessings that have been supplied to us by divine grace. He emphasizes that the apostle's regular custom in his epistles was first to expound the blessings of grace and then to press that understanding of grace as the incentive to holiness. Ephesians 4:30 is but one example of this: "And do not grieve the Holy Spirit of God, by whom you were sealed for the day of redemp-

---

[226]W, 5:196; PWC, 104; PR 10, no. 38 (1889): 335; PS, 66; W, 7:115, 117.
[227]FL, 276–77, 282–84.

tion." Here the motivating power in the appeal to holiness is the keeping grace of God by means of the Holy Spirit. By him we are "sealed" forever, an assertion intended to emphasize the believer's security. Yet this reminder of grace, so far from serving as a license to sin, establishes "the high motive of gratitude" and provides powerful incentive to holiness.[228]

In two separate publications Warfield expands on the implications of James 4:5 under the title "The Love of the Holy Ghost." Here the apostle tells us that the Holy Spirit "intensely envies" for us. The figure, Warfield remarks, is that of marriage, and the assertion, plainly, is that the Holy Spirit of God loves us. It is because he loves us that he is jealous over us. And our knowledge of this love of God the Holy Spirit is unsurpassed as an incentive to increased faithfulness to God and moral cleansing.

> Could there be given us a higher incentive to faithfulness to God than is contained in this revelation of the love of the Spirit for us? . . . Could there be afforded us a deeper ground of encouragement in our Christian life than is contained in this revelation? . . . Could there, then, be granted us a firmer foundation for the holy joy of Christian assurance?

Similarly in his sermon on Acts 2:16–17 he emphasizes that, having been freed from the outward pressure of law and now enjoying the Spirit's ministry of filling us with a sense of God's love for us in Christ, we are thereby given great incentive to obedience and to become more conformed to his will. Clearly, for Warfield there was no means more suited to progress in holiness than an increased acquaintance with the loving grace of God our Redeemer. "The love of God for sinners is the main theme of the Bible, and forms the mainstay of the Christian."[229]

As another example, in "The Principle of the Incarnation," Warfield fervently expounds the divine motive or purpose of the incarnation. He emphasizes repeatedly that this motive was soteriological, that God became man specifically in order to rescue fallen sinners. This is the glory of the Christian faith, the very "center and core" of Christianity. He is eager to stress the love and grace of God in going to such lengths for our salvation. Winding up his study, he observes that from this fact alone we learn the true greatness of God's love for us. He cites Bonaventura as stating that nothing "more ardently kindles the affection of faith" than our apprehension of this great fact. Warfield agrees but takes the matter a step further and speaks in exclusive terms. It is "only" by our studied recognition of divine redeeming grace that the Christian's faith and love will grow. Indeed, "only" by

---

[228]*FL*, 289–97.
[229]*SSW*, 2:718–24; *PGS*, 121–48; *FL*, 145.

recognition will our love be "drawn out to its full height." For Warfield, our understanding of saving truth is the "only" fountain of Christian holiness.[230]

So also in his sermon on Titus 3:4–7, "The Way of Life," after expounding at length the graciousness and freeness of salvation in Christ by the triune God, he notes that it is by teaching these truths that believers are given incentive to maintain good works. It is the minister's privilege to remind believers that they are not their own saviors, that their salvation is not suspended on their own efforts. Rather, believers are to be reminded that God is their Savior, that Christ has suffered for their sins, that the Holy Spirit works faith in them—in short, that it is by mercy alone, apart from any works of their own, that they are saved. It is the minister's duty and privilege to proclaim these truths. But shall believers, then, because they recognize more clearly that they are saved out of God's mercy and apart from any works of their own, be careless to maintain good works? No, "because of this" they are now careful to maintain good works. This is the Christian's incentive to progress in godliness.[231]

Consistently Warfield reflects the conviction that reminders of God's mercy in salvation promote Christians to progress in holiness. Throughout his works this line of thought is prominent, that the Christian life is fueled by a growing appreciation of divine grace. This was his own practice in preaching also, for his sermons are marked by a clear emphasis on God's saving mercy. Warfield is convinced that the "highest" and "most powerful" motive to holiness is not law and fear but grace and assurance of the fulness of salvation in Christ.[232]

In all this Warfield is in strong sympathy with his esteemed Princeton predecessor, Archibald Alexander, who, in determining the source of diminished spiritual growth in Christians, traces the problem to a lack of acquaintance with the gospel of grace. We have a "defect in our belief in the freeness of divine grace," he writes. We fear that if the gospel of grace is preached in all its fulness, some will be tempted to take sin lightly; consequently, the gospel is not preached as freely as it should be. But it is only by faith that the Christian life can grow, and apart from a firm understanding of free grace, there is no possibility of faith. Thus, "the new convert lives upon his frames rather than on Christ, while the older Christian is still found struggling in his own strength and, failing in his expectations of success, he becomes discouraged first, and then he sinks into a gloomy despondency, or becomes in a measure careless." The only explanation for such a case, Alexander is convinced, is that preachers have failed to acquaint Christians properly with grace. "Until religious teachers inculcate clearly, fully, and

---

[230]*SSW*, 1:144–47.
[231]*FL*, 400–401.
[232]Cf. *FL*, 294–97.

practically, the grace of God as manifested in the Gospel, we shall have no vigorous growth of piety among professing Christians." The gospel must be "expounded in all its rich plenitude of mercy, and in all its absolute freeness."[233]

The Means of Sanctification: The Public Means of Grace

Warfield exhorts his ministerial students that in order to obtain spiritual progress they, like every Christian, must give themselves to the public means of grace that God has instituted for this purpose. He emphasizes specifically the opportunities afforded by the seminary itself—the Lord's Day morning service and afternoon "conference" in the Miller Chapel, the time of corporate (faculty and student) prayer at the close of each day accompanied by a brief meditation from Scripture, and the monthly "concert of prayer." He stresses both the spiritual value of these opportunities and the duty of the student to take advantage of them as a regular habit. Corporate prayer, worship, and hearing of the Word are, to Warfield, leading means of cultivating the inner man. "No richness of private religious life, no abundance of voluntary religious services on the part of members of the organism, can take the place of or supersede the necessity for the fullest, richest, and most fervent expression of this organic religious life through its appropriate channels." Warfield's caution that no private devotion can "supersede" this corporate means of grace reveals his understanding that the public means of grace are primary and universally obligatory and valuable. Moreover, precisely because of this value of corporate ministry, Warfield adds that classroom prayer and instruction are likewise intended and valuable not for academic advancement only but for spiritual enrichment. The occasions of Warfield's writing do not often lend themselves to addressing this theme. But when the occasion calls for it, he does address it, and in doing so he reveals that in his thinking, it is a matter of primary significance. The public means of grace are uniquely suited to the cultivation of the spiritual life.[234]

In a particularly poignant passage, Warfield emphasizes this point to his students by an appeal to the example of Christ.

> Surely, if ever there was one who might justly plead that the common worship of the community had nothing to offer him it was the Lord Jesus Christ. But every Sabbath found him seated in his place among the worshiping people, and there was no act of stated worship which he felt himself entitled to discard. Even in his most exalted moods, and after his most elevating experiences, he quietly took his place with the

---

[233]Archibald Alexander, *Thoughts on Religious Experience* (1844; repr., Carlisle, PA: Banner of Truth, 1998), 165–66.
[234]*SSW*, 2:476–78; *SSW*, 1:411–22.

rest of God's people, sharing with them in the common worship of the community. Returning from that great baptismal scene, when the heavens themselves were rent to bear him witness that he was well pleasing to God; from the searching trials of the wilderness, and from that first great tour in Galilee, prosecuted, as we are expressly told, "in the power of the Spirit"; he came back, as the record tells, "to Nazareth, where he had been brought up, and"—so proceeds the amazing narrative—"he entered, as his custom was, into the synagogue, on the Sabbath day." "As his custom was!" Jesus Christ made it his habitual practice to be found in his place on the Sabbath day at the stated place of worship to which he belonged. "It is a reminder," as Sir William Robertson Nicoll well insists, "of the truth which, in our fancied spirituality, we are apt to forget—that the holiest personal life can scarcely afford to dispense with stated forms of devotion, and that the regular public worship of the church, for all its local imperfections and dullness, is a divine provision for sustaining the individual soul." "We cannot afford to be wiser than our Lord in this matter. If any one could have pled that his spiritual experience was so lofty that it did not require public worship, if any one might have felt that the consecration and communion of his personal life exempted him from what ordinary mortals needed, it was Jesus. But he made no such plea. Sabbath by Sabbath even he was found in the place of worship, side by side with God's people, not for the mere sake of setting a good example, but for deeper reasons. Is it reasonable, then, that any of us should think we can safely afford to dispense with the pious custom of regular participation with the common worship of our locality?"

Warfield concludes with a plea: "Is it necessary for me to exhort those who would fain be like Christ, to see to it that they are imitators of him in this?"[235]

The Means of Sanctification: Prayer

Yet for Warfield the corporate means can never be sufficient in themselves but only as they are accompanied by and are expressions of inward grace. And so he emphasizes passionately that we have not gotten to the bottom of the matter until we penetrate beneath all this and consider our soul's private communion with God in prayer. "True devoutness is a plant that grows best in seclusion and the darkness of the closet; and we cannot reach the springs of our devout life until we penetrate into the sanctuary where the soul meets habitually with its God." This, he says, stands to reason. "If association with God's children powerfully quickens our spiritual life, how much more intimate communion with God himself." And so he exhorts "above all else that you strive after, cultivate the grace of private prayer." It is of course of utmost importance to remain always in a prayerful frame, and in

---

[235]*SSW*, I:421.

this way "pray without ceasing" (1 Thess. 5:17). This must be our goal, to cultivate a heart of continuous communion with God. But a prayerful habit of mind is not enough; nor will it be realized apart from setting aside specific seasons of formal prayer. This, Warfield insists, is "the foundation-stone of your piety," and for this there is no substitute. "There is no mistake more terrible than to suppose that activity in Christian work can take the place of depth of Christian affections." "We cannot get along without our Marthas," Warfield concedes. "But what shall we do when, through all the length and breadth of the land, we shall search in vain for a Mary?" That is to say, there can be no substitute to private devotion to God.[236]

In Acts 9:11, God instructs Ananias, "Rise and go to the street called Straight, and at the house of Judas look for a man of Tarsus named Saul, for behold, he is praying." The explanatory phrase "for he is praying" forms the basis of Warfield's sermon "Prayer as a Means of Grace."[237] The simple fact that Saul is praying is the reason God offers to Ananias that Saul is ready for his visit, "and the passage thus represents prayer as the state of preparedness for the reception of grace; and, therefore, in the strictest sense as a means of grace." Prayer by the nature of it is a confession of weakness, need, and dependence. It is a cry for help. And "no one can take this attitude once without an effect on his character," for in it we learn to look away from ourselves to one higher and greater and acknowledge our utter dependence on God.

> If there is a God who sits aloft and hears and answers, do we not see that the attitude into which prayer brings the soul is the appropriate attitude which the soul should occupy to Him, and is the truest and best preparation of the soul for the reception of His grace? The soul in the attitude of prayer is like the flower turned upwards towards the sky and opening for the reception of the life-giving rain. What is prayer but an adoring appearing before God with a confession of our need and helplessness and a petition for His strength and blessing? What is prayer but a recognition of our dependence and a proclamation that all that we dependent creatures need is found abundantly and to spare in God, who gives to all men liberally and upbraids not? What is prayer but the very adjustment of the heart for the influx of grace? Therefore it is that we look upon the prayerful attitude as above all others the true Christian attitude—just because it is the attitude of devout and hopeful dependence on God.[238]

More specifically, prayer is seen to be a means of grace, simply "because it is directed to God for grace." At its very core is petition for help, a means of obtain-

[236]*SSW*, 2:481–83; *SSW*, 1:422–24.
[237]*FL*, 146–53.
[238]*FL*, 149.

ing grace from God. Prayer is more than petition, of course, but it is at least petition. Considered in its broader aspects, as Paul indicates in 1 Timothy 2:1, prayer
includes supplication, intercession, and thanksgiving. That is to say, prayer at
bottom is communion with God. But what attitude can a man bring before God
except that of dependence for his favor? And so, again, we are made to see that
prayer is a means of grace.

> I think we may say, emphatically, that prayer is a means of grace above everything
> else because it is in all its forms conscious communion with God. This is the source
> of all grace. When the soul is in contact with God, in intercourse with God, in asso-
> ciation with Him, it is not only in an attitude to receive grace; it is not only actually
> seeking grace; it is already receiving and possessing grace.[239]

And so, Warfield concludes, "it is impossible to conceive of a praying man
... as destitute of grace." Prayer is a means of grace and, therefore, a means of
sanctification.

SUMMARY

Warfield was very self-consciously a theologian of the heart, and for him the spiritual life was "the most important subject which can engage our thought."[240] His
concern for a right understanding of theology was, in part, a concern with this
moral dimension, for a "looseness of belief" is inevitably the parent of "looseness
of practice."[241] He continuously placed heavy emphasis on the life-transforming
power of the gospel, the entailments of regeneration supernaturally wrought,
the powerful workings of the Spirit of God in every believer, conversion and "the
great change," Christian duty, prayer, the public and private means of grace, active
trust in divine providence, holiness of heart and life, and even social justice. He
preached and published many deeply affectionate sermons on such themes,
including two sermons directed specifically at the cultivation of the religious life
of ministers. The transformed life and its accompanying entailments of experienced communion with God were for Warfield of the very essence of God's saving
work in us.

In brief, Warfield rejects all forms of perfectionist and higher life teachings,
which either suspend sanctification on the will of man or deny the place of human

---

[239]*FL*, 152; cf. *FL*, 432.
[240]*SSW*, 1:411. John Walvoord represents a tradition more sympathetic to the higher life movements
criticized by Warfield, and so it is not surprising to find him expressing disagreement with him at certain
points. But it is nonetheless incredible that he should allege that "Warfield never seems to have adequately
distinguished spirituality from perfectionism." *BSac* 116, no. 464 (1959): 358.
[241]*W*, 1:393.

effort in it. Sanctification for Warfield is that holiness of heart and life to which believers are predestined and called. It is secured for them in the saving work of Christ, by which they are radically transformed in heart and in life. It is worked in them by the powerful operations of the Holy Spirit, marked by a keen sense of dependence on God, and cultivated further by attention to the appropriate means of grace. It entails a cleansing from and struggle against sin that continues progressively throughout this life and a growing experience of fellowship with the triune God.

Salvation Complete

Warfield's heaviest criticisms of the perfectionists are leveled, of course, at the extreme views of men such as John Humphrey Noyes, on the one hand, and the rationalism of Ritschl, on the other. But in regard to the doctrine of sanctification specifically, Warfield's criticisms of the perfectionists have to do primarily with the *ordo salutis*. Warfield notes repeatedly that the perfectionists' error does not lie in their insistence that the gospel promises entire sanctification. To the contrary, he joyfully agrees that perfect holiness is indeed the goal of Christian salvation. In this affirmation the perfectionists are quite right. For example, Warfield writes:

> What Jellinghaus has undertaken in the first part of his book he has accomplished with complete success. He has triumphantly shown from the Scriptures that there is complete deliverance in Christ Jesus for all who look to Him for it in simple faith. That is the teaching of Scripture, and Jellinghaus brings it out with great fulness, energy, and convincingness.[242]

The problem Warfield finds with this is one of timing. Speaking of Hannah Whitall Smith, he writes, "She wishes them [believers] to demand, like greedy children, all the feast prepared for them in the first course." It is good to be impatient with sin, but "it is a different matter to show impatience with God." A characteristic of the whole movement, he says, is that "they chafe under the delay and require all their inheritance at once. . . . All the Biblical assurances of salvation are assembled, and then the demand made, Give me all of it—now."[243]

Warfield is willing to be more patient. This interadvent period is marked by the accomplishment but not yet the full attaining of entire sanctification promised to us and secured for us in the death of Christ. In his sermon "Entire Sanctification,"

---

[242]W, 7:354.
[243]W, 8:537.

Warfield expounds the apostle Paul's prayer of 1 Thessalonians 5:23–24: "Now may the God of peace himself sanctify you completely, and may your whole spirit and soul and body be kept blameless at the coming of our Lord Jesus Christ. He who calls you is faithful; he will surely do it." For a full two-thirds of the sermon Warfield speaks pointedly of the high ethical demands of the Christian faith and its corresponding promise of perfection. He articulates at more length than any perfectionist the degree of perfection demanded by the gospel—it is "entire" sanctification that the apostle has in view. "Here we may say is 'Perfectionism' raised to its highest power, a blameless perfection, a perfection admitting of no failure to attain its end, in every department of our being alike, uniting to form a perfection of the whole, a complete attainment of our idea in the whole man." He adds:

> There is certainly no doctrine of "entire sanctification" that has been invented in these later days which can compare with Paul's doctrine in height or depth or length or breadth. His "perfectionism" . . . is real perfection. . . . A perfect perfection for a perfect man—an entire sanctification for the entire man—surely here is a perfection worth longing for.[244]

Moreover, Warfield stresses emphatically that this "entire sanctification" is an altogether attainable goal; indeed, it is something Christians *must* attain. Paul "treats it as distinctly attainable," not by our own doing but as the gift of God. "The accomplishment of this our perfection then does not hang on our weak endeavors. It does not hang even on Paul's strong prayer. It hangs only on God's almighty and unfailing faithfulness." At this point Warfield has out-perfected the perfectionists. But here, he points out, is the difference: the attaining of this perfection awaits the return of Christ.

> It [perfection] is not a matter of congratulation to them—as some Christian graces were, for the presence of which in their hearts he thanks God,—but a matter of prayer to God for them. It is a thing not yet in possession but in petition. It is yet to come to them. He does not permit us to suppose, then, that the Thessalonians had already attained—or should already have attained—it. . . . You see it is on the second advent of Christ . . . that the Apostle has his eyes set. There is the point of time to which he refers the completeness of our perfecting.

Entire sanctification is bound up with the blessed hope. "We shall be like Him" but not until "we see Him as He is." "Men here are not *comprehensores* but *viatores*; we are fighting the good fight; we are running the race. The prize is yonder."[245]

---

[244]*W*, 7:243–44; *FL*, 365.
[245]*PGS*, 24; *FL*, 366–71. The Latin contrasts the one who fully *comprehends* with the *traveler*.

Several times Warfield writes to the effect that "it belongs to the very essence of Christianity that we have not 'attained,'" which is to say, redemption demands complete and final sanctification—glorification. Perfection is not attained in this life but in the next. So he says:

> It belongs to the very essence of Christianity that we have not "attained"; and that this is the same as saying that sanctification is in progress and there is more to come. The Christian who has stopped growing is dead; or to put it better, the Christian does not stop growing because he is not dead. Luther rightly says that the Christian is not made but is in the making.[246]

This points up the perfectionists' mistaken assumption that salvation precludes sin altogether or that the admission of sin in the life of a believer is tantamount to a salvation that does not, in fact, save from sin. "Jesus would not seem to him [Jellinghaus] a complete Deliverer if we had to wait for the deliverance received in Him to be gradually accomplished in us through a long process of growth, especially if this prolonged itself throughout life."[247] And so for Warfield the pretended "perfections" of the perfectionists are both wrong and unnecessary; they stem from a misunderstanding of the nature of Christ's saving work in us—initially, progressively, and finally.

> Our wills, being the expression of our hearts, continually more and more dying to sin and more and more living to holiness, under the renewing action of the Christ dwelling within us by his Spirit, can never from the beginning of His gracious renewal of them resist Christ fatally, and will progressively resist Him less and less until, our hearts having been made through and through good, our wills will do only righteousness.[248]

And again, "What the Scriptures teach is that we shall be more and more transformed into Christ's image until at last, when we see Him as He is, we shall be like Him, and therefore in ourselves—as He has made us—well-pleasing to God."[249]

The perfectionists' mistake is one of timing. Full sanctification will come, and it will consist in a perfection more perfect than that of which the perfectionists speak. But not in this life. This goal will certainly be reached, but only in glory.

---

[246] W, 7:91.
[247] W, 7:372; cf. W, 8:96.
[248] W, 8:602.
[249] W, 7:389.

Concluding Observations

Reformed theology has occasionally been charged with an overemphasis on the objective and retrospective aspects of salvation and a comparative neglect of its subjective and prospective aspects. Warfield acknowledges that this is the impression easily left by the Reformers themselves, who out of enthusiasm for the newly rediscovered and fundamental doctrine of justification, "left its subjective side, which was not in dispute between them and their nearest opponents, in danger of falling temporarily somewhat out of sight." A selective reading of Warfield could leave this impression of him also. The theological abuses of the perfectionists, he felt, made it necessary to emphasize "miserable sinner Christianity" again. And he charged that their error was to emphasize the subjective at the expense of the objective side of salvation, taking the fruit while ignoring the root. Moreover, Warfield wrote polemically in a time when the penal aspect of Christ's death was denied outright. It is not surprising, then, that the objective and retrospective emphasis is more prominent in Warfield. Nevertheless, the subjective/prospective aspect of salvation is by no means overlooked. Nor is it merely assumed. Warfield does not grovel as a "miserable sinner," nor does he allow any notion of a Christian who remains unchanged. Rather, he glories in the lavish provisions of salvation in Christ. The Christian's privileged standing as a saint; his status as child of God in the realization of the Father's love and fellowship; his rich enjoyment of the Spirit; his freedom of conscience despite his sin; the fulness of righteousness imputed to him in justification; the new life, "repristination," purity, and inward and outward transformation all inevitably realized in renewal and in sanctification; the hope and final realization of glory with Christ—these all are common themes in Warfield. He sees salvation, fundamentally, as rescue from sin and the Christian as a rescued sinner. But this is by no means the whole picture of Warfield. To be sure, "Wherever personal Christianity exists there necessarily is also a radical break with sin."[250]

A former student at Princeton recalls that "it was a favorite classroom saying of the late Dr. B. B. Warfield that 'all theologies divide at one point—does God save men or do they save themselves?'"[251] It is not surprising that this was a favorite saying of his, for a high supernaturalism is perhaps the leading mark of his soteriology. "Salvation in every case of its accomplishment is nothing less than an authentic miracle of divine grace; always and everywhere in the strictest

---

[250]*W*, 2:460–61; *W*, 7:227; *W*, 8:119, 575–76.
[251]Rollin Thomas Chafer (1869–1939), brother of Lewis Sperry Chafer and professor of hermeneutics and apologetics at Dallas Theological Seminary. "A Syllabus of Studies in Hermeneutics Part I," *BSac* 91, no. 364 (1934): 460.

sense impossible with man, and possible only with God, with whom all things are possible." Along with the apostle Paul, Warfield is convinced, he proclaims a supernaturalistic gospel that supernaturally re-creates man in the image of God, gives him a new perception of Christ, rescues him from the eschatological divine wrath, takes the redeemed sinner "behind the veil" into heavenly places of fellowship with God, and gives him citizenship in the kingdom of God. The factual historicity of Jesus is all-important, for our faith is grounded in the events of the past. Yet what we need and what Christianity offers is not only a historical Jesus but "in Him a supernatural Christ, and in Him a supernatural redemption." A supernatural Savior accomplishing and granting a supernatural salvation to sinners is a favored theme repeated over and again throughout Warfield's works. He feels deeply that "the supernatural is the very breath of Christianity's nostrils," and that "an anti-supernaturalistic atmosphere is to it the deadliest miasma." He insists, "We cannot confess ourselves sinners—radically at breach with God and broken and deformed in our moral and spiritual being—and look to purely natural causes or to simply providential agencies . . . for our recovery to God and to moral and spiritual health." Everyone knows that the dead cannot, by nature, live, and unless the supernatural voice, "Lazarus, come forth!" had sounded, we would have remained lifeless. Apart from the supernatural influences of the Spirit of God, we have no hope. Man is not the architect of his fortunes.

> The Christian is not the product of the regenerative forces of nature under however divine a direction; he is not an "evolution" out of the natural man: he is a new creation. . . . We confess that it was God who made us men: let us confess with equal heartiness that it is God who makes us Christians.

Salvation in its whole process—"in its initiation and outworking alike"—is a work of God.[252]

Warfield enjoys citing the words of "that old revival hymn" (by James Proctor), which express in brief his understanding of the gospel:

> Cast your deadly "doing" down—
> Down at Jesus' feet;
> Stand in Him, in Him alone,
> Gloriously complete.

This, Warfield says, expresses the very *cor cordis* of the gospel. "The one antithesis of all the ages is that between the rival formulae: Do this and live, and, Live and

---

[252] *W*, 3:102; *PGS*, 204–12; *W*, 3:346; *W*, 9:29, 38, 44, 45; *SW*, 142–43.

do this; Do and be saved, and Be saved and do." It is this that determines whether we are ourselves trusting in God for salvation or not. If we, like the rich young ruler, feel that we must "do some good thing" in order to be saved, then we are not yet entrusting ourselves to Christ.

> Ethicism and solafideanism—these are the eternal contraries, mutually exclusive. It must be faith or works; it can never be faith and works. And the fundamental exhortation which we must ever be giving our souls is clearly expressed in the words of the hymn, "Cast your deadly doing down." Only when that is completely done is it really Christ Only, Christ All in All, with us; only then, do we obey fully Paul's final exhortation: "Let your joy be in the Lord." Only then do we renounce utterly "our own righteousness, that out of law," and rest solely on "that which is through faith in Christ, the righteousness of God on faith."[253]

Warfield's ultimate motive in this concern is clear. Man must be emptied "of all glory in the matter of salvation" so that all glory will return to God alone. He insists that we must be prepared to sing "not only 'Gloria Deo' but 'Soli Deo Gloria.'"[254]

---

[253]*FL*, 324–25.
[254]*FL*, 396.

[On 1 Tim. 3:14–15] There is a right way to order God's house; nay,
there is a way in which it must be ordered. That way is the way
which Paul has just laid down in his previous exhortations. And Paul
has written these exhortations in order that . . . Timothy might
know this right way, and act accordingly. . . .

In order that he might raise his reader's sense of this importance still
higher, the Apostle proceeds at once to enhance the reason
he has assigned for it. The Stress is laid on the words "God's house,"
and the succeeding ἥτις, in accordance with its character, assigns the
natural reason why it is important that God's house
should be properly ordered: "seeing that it is no less than the church
of the living God." No wonder one must be careful fitly to order
it! By "church" the Apostle means, in accordance with his teaching
elsewhere, a community belonging to God, and which as such
must receive its ordering from God alone (1 Cor 14:33); and the epithet
"living" is added still further to enhance its value in this context,
and thus still further to exhibit the importance of ordering it by God's
and not men's models. He now piles Pelion on Ossa, by adding
that this Church of the living God is "the pillar and ground of the
truth"—i.e., apparently the support and stay of the truth that
has been brought into the world with the opening of the new
covenant, without which it could not be retained in purity
or be spread abroad. The Church is thus described as God's
instrument for the preservation of the truth and for keeping it pure,
and His engine for propagating it in the world. The effect
of so describing it is still further to demonstrate its importance,
and the necessity of properly organizing it.

"Some Exegetical Notes on I Timothy,"
PR 8, no. 31 (1887): 507 (emphasis original).

The Character of the Church

Baptism
    BAPTISM AND SALVATION
    INFANT BAPTISM
    THE MODE OF BAPTISM

The Lord's Supper

Church Government

11

ECCLESIOLOGY

The doctrine of the church was not a leading point of dispute in Warfield's day, and so it follows, given his broader concerns for issues he considered more fundamental to the Christian faith, that he addresses this doctrine comparatively little in his writings. Warfield loved his own Presbyterian denomination deeply, and out of his concern for it he wrote extensively on contemporary questions of confessional change and even reunion with the Cumberland Presbyterians. But on matters of ecclesiology proper he did not devote a great deal of attention in writing.

Warfield did address the subject of baptism in a few articles and the Lord's Supper in a few others. From these we are able to discern both his specific understanding of the doctrines and some of his underlying reasoning. But such is not the case for other doctrines usually related to the church. From his widely varied writings we are able to glean Warfield's thoughts on this or that aspect of ecclesiology, and they will be noted below, but often he does not provide extensive supporting argument. For this head of theology, we will have to be content simply with a brief outline of his understanding.

The Character of the Church

Warfield nowhere elaborates at length on the nature of the church, but he does make reference to it in several places, highlighting his leading concerns. Most fundamentally, he repeatedly stresses that the church is a redeemed people. "The constitutive principle" of the Reformation, he remarks, was "its revised doctrine of the church," its discovery that "men and women are not constituted members of Christ through the Church, but members of the Church through Christ; they are not made the members of Christ by baptism which the Church gives, but by faith, the gift of God; and baptism is the Church's recognition of this inner fact." Or again, the "newly recovered Scriptural apprehension of the Church" by the Reformation was that the church is "essentially not an externally organized body but the people of God," and membership in the church is "mediated not by the external act of baptism but by the internal regeneration of the Holy Spirit." More pointedly, "only those already united to Christ have right within His house."[1]

Warfield expresses agreement with Augustine's emphasis that the church is essentially the *congregatio sanctorum*, but he laments that Augustine did not carry this thought through with consistency. This failure means that in a real sense Augustine is the father of Roman Catholicism. The identification of the church with the episcopacy and the understanding that the church is fundamentally a hierarchical institution, outside of which is no salvation, was a doctrine originated not by Augustine but Cyprian (d. 258). But Augustine perpetuated it. His mistake, Warfield observes, was his failure to distinguish between the "empirical" and the "ideal" church. Augustine often confused them and spoke of one in terms of the other. In the Donatist controversy his emphasis on the church as the sole sphere and distributor of salvation and the sole mediatrix of grace overly identified the church as the empirical church, and he thus betrayed his more fundamental and "profounder" conception of the church as the *congregatio sanctorum*. His better thinking was not brought to blossom until centuries later. Similarly, in another context Warfield writes, "The distinguishing doctrine" of the Reformed churches is the understanding that salvation is dependent on membership not in the visible church but in the invisible.[2]

In keeping with this fundamental understanding of the church as the people of God, Warfield emphasizes repeatedly its responsibility to maintain its purity faithfully. This, of course, is the defining struggle of his career, and he often presses this on the church as a whole. The unity for which Christ prayed (John 17) is not to be understood merely in terms of externals. Christian unity is in Christ and in Christian truth, and it is not a promotion but a betrayal of this unity to allow error to go unchecked or to foster a unity grounded merely in the lowest common denominator. Warfield found it deeply disturbing that many in his own denomination were eager to broaden the confession, unite with denominations holding aberrant theology, and allow membership to teachers of error. Repeatedly in his writings he stresses that the church, as the pillar and ground of the truth, is the guardian of the faith, "God's instrument for the preservation of the truth and for keeping it pure." It is the church's duty, therefore, both to teach and promote sound doctrine and to rebuke error and to silence, even exclude, those who oppose it. The gospel is both the ground of our unity and "the primary ground of righteous separation," and exclusion of false teaching and false teachers from

---

[1]*W*, 9:389, 422, 429–30.
[2]*W*, 4:121–22; *W*, 9:430. Here Warfield seems to identify the *congregatio sanctorum* ("assembly of saints") with the invisible church. Elsewhere, however, he identifies it as "the external manifestation" of the invisible church. See his "The Proposed Union with the Cumberland Presbyterians," *PTR* 2, no. 2 (1904): 300.

the church is but the application of the apostle's command, "Do not be unequally yoked with unbelievers" (2 Cor. 6:14). It is a mistaken notion of the church and of church unity that allows false teachers into its communion. "We cannot but think . . . that we should be as loyal to God's Word as charitable to our fellow-men." For Warfield, the church is the people of God marked out as "saintly" in matters pertaining to both faith and life.[3]

With regard to this emphasis on church purity Warfield offers a parable:

> Hear the parable of the thistles. Thistles certainly have beauties of their own, and many virtues, which nobody would care to deny. But they do seem out of place in a garden designed for roses, even though they proclaim themselves more beautiful than any roses in the garden. And the husbandman seems to have a duty towards thistles growing in the garden, which even their irritable *noli me tangere* ought not to deter him from executing, with all due kindness indeed, but with that firmness of touch which becomes one in dealing with thistles. Otherwise, what will he say to the Lord of the garden, whom even the more luxuriant growth of the thistles may not please, when they are tossing their bold heads in the bed intended for roses?[4]

This emphasis on the purity of the church, however, does not lead Warfield to a baptistic view of the church. As will be noted below, in connection with his discussion of infant baptism he remarks, "The Scriptures do not teach that the external Church is a company of regenerate persons—the parable of the tares for example declares the opposite: though they represent that Church as the company of those who are presumably regenerate."[5]

Baptism

Warfield laments that baptism is "a subject which can scarcely be touched without controversy," but it is a controversy from which he does not shy away. As noted

---

[3]*SSW*, 1:299–307; "The Proposed Union with the Cumberland Presbyterians," 300–301; "Christian Unity and Church Union: Some Primary Principles," *The Presbyterian Banner* 91 (1905): 103–4; "Some Exegetical Notes on 1 Timothy," 507–8. See also his *Acts and Pastoral Epistles and Philemon*, The Temple Bible series (1902; repr., London: J. M. Dent & Sons, 1930), xxxiii–xxxiv; "Revision or Reaffirmation," a letter from Warfield to the stated clerk of the General Assembly expressing his refusal to serve on the committee established in 1903 to discuss revision of the confession of faith; "Kikuyu, Clerical Veracity and Miracles," *PTR* 12, no. 4 (1914): 531, 533, 547, 585; "The Basis of the Proposed Union—Theoretical and Practical," *The Presbyterian* 75, no. 9 (1905): 8–9; "The Presbyterian Churches and the Westminster Confession," *PR* 10, no. 40 (1889): 654.
[4]*SSW*, 2:603. The Latin means, "Do not touch me."
[5]*W*, 9:393.

above, Warfield devotes comparatively little attention to doctrines of ecclesiology generally, but he does write on the subject of baptism.[6]

BAPTISM AND SALVATION

That baptism has no saving efficacy Warfield takes as virtually a given. The apostle Paul's vigorous defense of salvation by faith alone excluded any notion of the merit of either moral or religious acts. Abraham was justified before his circumcision— by faith alone and apart from all works (Rom. 4:9–12; cf. Gal. 3:7, 9). Salvation is dependent upon God's working in the individual heart, and it cannot be effected by any merely mechanical means.[7] That salvation is given individually and sovereignly by God is of the very essence of Protestantism. Whatever the significance of baptism, it is not the means of salvation.

At the same time, Warfield argues that the significance of baptism is not to be understood as merely representative and memorial. He acknowledges that baptism is indeed a "visible monument of the covenant," but he insists that it is more. He speaks of "the privileges and benefits conferred thereby," and he seems to allow the language of baptism "effecting" our union with Christ. More pointedly, he says, "If the individual, by accepting the rite, appropriates the offered covenant to himself, its performance becomes not only the seal of the covenant, but also the conveyance of its benefits, just as the signing and sealing of a deed conveys the property." Warfield distinguishes this from the "thaumaturgic" implications of the *opus operatum* theory, but he does not explain in detail.[8] In another context Warfield echoes the North African theologian Cyprian and encourages us to remember that the water of baptism "does not cleanse the flesh, but the soul." By this he means that it is not the precise mode of baptism that is important but the act itself, so long as it is done with "purity of intention and abundance of faith."[9] Again, Warfield does not provide detailed explanation, but his understanding is quite in keeping with the language of the Westminster Confession of Faith[10] and seems certainly to be that the sacrament is effective but only when accompanied by faith. Just how this understanding relates to his

---

[6]*W*, 10:158. The primary articles in which Warfield treats the subject of baptism are the following: "The Archaeology of the Mode of Baptism," in *W*, 9:345–86; "The Polemics of Infant Baptism," in *W*, 9:389–408; "Christian Baptism," in *SSW*, 1:325–31; "How Shall We Baptize?" in *SSW*, 2:329–50; and "IV. Discussion of Controverted Points [regarding the mode of baptism]" in the article entitled "Baptism," in *NSHEK*, 1:446–50.
[7]*SSW*, 1:325–26, 329; *W*, 9:444; *PS*, 52–68. Similarly, Warfield rejects the sacramental interpretation of John 3:5: "The axiom announced in verse 6 that all that is born of flesh is flesh and only what is born of the Spirit is spirit seems directly to negative such an interpretation by telling us flatly that we cannot obtain a spiritual effect from a physical action" (*W*, 2:456).
[8]*W*, 10:159; *SSW*, 1:330; *NSHERK*, 449.
[9]*SSW*, 2:333–34.
[10]WCF 28.1, 5–6.

insistence that salvation is received by faith alone, apart from either moral or religious works, he nowhere explores.

Abraham's circumcision was given to him, as a believer, as a sign and seal of the righteousness of the faith he possessed while still uncircumcised. Abraham received a righteousness from God by faith, and his circumcision was a sign and seal of that righteousness. His circumcision, then, was a visible sign that marked him out as one who belonged to the Lord as righteous, "and it sealed that righteousness to him under a covenant promise." In the transition from the old covenant to the new, the form of this rite has been changed to baptism, "the circumcision of Christ" (Col. 2:11). But the substance of this rite remains the same: it is a sign by which God marks out his people as his own. Baptism therefore is much more than our own profession of faith, although it is at least that. It is a sign and seal given by God, and it is thus his own witness that our faith is acceptable to him, and it is his own pledge that he has and always will treat us accordingly. "He who has been baptized bears in himself God's testimony and engagement to his salvation." It is his own "pledge" that he will "keep us as his own." In baptism our salvation "is not only symbolized for us but sealed to us, for baptism is given to us by God as an engagement on his part to bring us safely through to the end." "Having his mark upon us, and resting upon his pledge, we may go forward in joy and sure expectation of his gracious keeping in this life and his acceptance of us into his glory hereafter."[11]

It is in this way that the apostle Paul speaks of our being buried and risen with Christ in baptism (Col. 2:12; Rom. 6:4). His teaching is not that union with Christ is attained by means of baptism but rather that in baptism we declare that we are in Christ, participants in his saving death and resurrection, "and that these benefits are now sealed" to us by covenant promise.

> We are now like documents to which the seals have been attached. We may think that a signet ring with the name of the Lord upon it has been impressed upon us to authenticate us as his forever. What has happened to us is that we are called by the "honorable name" (James 2:7). The meaning of that is that we have been marked as the peculiar possession of our Lord, over whom he claims ownership, and to the protection and guidance of whom he pledges himself.

Baptism, in other words, "marks us out as sharers in all the benefits of Christ's redemption and pledges them to us."[12]

---

[11]*SSW*, 1:326–28, 330; *W*, 9:405–6.
[12]*SSW*, 1:327, 330.

By the nature of the case, therefore, this sign and seal is properly administered only to those who are saved. "Only those already united to Christ have right within His house and to its privileges." Stated more positively, this rite belongs to all who are Christ's. "Naturally, therefore, this sign and seal belongs only to those who are the Lord's." There is just this "one prerequisite—that we are the Lord's." This is what the sign means—that we belong to Christ.[13]

Warfield stresses this again in reference to the distinctive Reformation doctrine of the church as a people who belong to Christ. Growing out of this recognition that the church is the gathering of the elect is the understanding of the Reformed churches that men "are not saved because they are baptized, but they are baptized because they are saved." Baptism belongs to those who are in the church, those who are saved. Once more, Warfield emphasizes that baptism is for those who believe: "Men and women . . . are not made the members of Christ by baptism which the Church gives, but by faith, the gift of God; and baptism is the Church's recognition of this inner fact."[14] Baptism is the church's recognition of faith.

INFANT BAPTISM

None of this should be understood to call into question the validity of infant baptism, Warfield argues, for children of the covenant belong to the Lord also. Indeed, guided by the promise "for you and for your children" (Acts 2:39), believing parents must present—and may confidently present—their children to be baptized. It is not a profession of faith, which they are incapable of giving, but God's promise that assures us of their inclusion in Christ.

> We need not raise the question, then, whether infants are to be baptized. Of course they are, if infants, too, may be the Lord's. Naturally, as with adults, it is only the infants who are the Lord's who are to be baptized; but equally naturally as with adults, all infants that are the Lord's are to be baptized. Being the Lord's they have a right to the sign that they are the Lord's and to the pledge of the Lord's holy keeping. Circumcision, which held the place in the old covenant that baptism holds in the new, was to be given to all infants born within the covenant. Baptism must follow the same rule. This and this only can determine its conference: Is the recipient a child of the covenant, with a right therefore to the sign and seal of the covenant? We cannot withhold the sign and seal of the covenant from those who are of the covenant.[15]

---

[13] W, 9:389; SSW, 1:328.
[14] W, 9:443, 422, 429–30.
[15] SSW, 1:328; W, 9:430; cf. "Children in the Hands of the Arminians," The Union Seminary Magazine 17, no. 3 (1906): 169.

In Warfield's view covenant children may be presumed Christian, members of Christ.[16] Baptism is the church's recognition of faith. It is for the saved only, Warfield argues. Unbelievers should not be allowed in the church. He states categorically that "only Christ's children have a right to the ordinance of baptism." Baptism is God's pledge that he will sustain the salvation already given, and afterwards we "grow up" to an "assurance of pardon" previously received. Indeed, infant baptism itself is a testimony of God's gift of salvation already given. Warfield argues this pointedly. Infant baptism "presupposes that salvation is from the Lord." The infant is incapable of doing anything to make himself the Lord's, and if baptism must await something we do, then the infant has no right to the sacrament. But if salvation is entirely of the Lord, then infants can indeed be saved and, thus, receive the accompanying sign. As with Abraham, the signs and seals of salvation "do not precede [salvation] as its procuring cause or condition, but follow it as God's witness to its existence and promise to sustain it." Thus Warfield argues, "Every time we baptize an infant we bear witness that salvation is from God, that we cannot do any good thing to secure it, that we receive it from his hands as a sheer gift of his grace." Baptism does not precede but follows salvation, even in the case of infants. Just how this relates to the demand of faith, which infants at least cannot express, Warfield does not say. But for him it is a "fair" presumption, "the judgment of charity," that covenant children are saved, and, therefore, proper candidates for baptism.[17]

Interestingly, in another context Warfield chides an Arminian professor at length for teaching that children come into the world in a state of salvation. Warfield will not allow this even of the children of Christian parents, and he asserts that the majority of children born in Christendom, "even a considerable portion of the children of Christian parents," live to prove that they are, in fact, lost. And he concludes his discussion with a corresponding appeal: "It would be an infinitely sadder thing if any Christian parents anywhere should teach their children that they do not need salvation, and do not need to seek it diligently, and when they have found it to sell all that they have and purchase it." These conflicting ideas— that the children of Christians are presumably saved, that they need to be saved, and that most prove to be lost—were stated on separate occasions, and Warfield nowhere attempts to resolve them. Still, he nowhere argues that infants may be

---

[16]A former student recalls that in contrast to Charles Hodge, Warfield held that only the children of professing believers should be brought for baptism. Charles Brokenshire letter to John Meeter, June 25, 1942, p. 7.

[17]W, 9:389–90; SSW, 1:328–30. A student's class notes record Warfield as saying more pointedly, "We may be certain of salvation for infants who come in under the Covenant." N. W. Harkness, unpublished class notes from Warfield's lectures on systematic theology, 1899–1901 (Princeton Seminary library archives), 5.

baptized merely because their parents are believers; he argues that because of the covenant promise they themselves may be presumed Christian.[18]

"All Protestants should easily agree that only Christ's children have a right to the ordinance of baptism. The cleavage in their ranks enters in only when we inquire how the external Church is to hold itself relatively to the recognition of the children of Christ." The central "vice" of the Baptist position, Warfield alleges, is that "it attempts the impossible." That is, it baptizes only upon profession of faith even though none can ever infallibly judge such a profession. He understands "the field" in the parable of the tares to be the "external Church," in which case the parable teaches that the church is a company of those who are "presumably regenerate." And so, because such judgments cannot be made infallibly, the church must not be as restrictive and narrow as possible but "as inclusive as possible." And in the case of infants of believers, the church may "baptize on presumption and not knowledge"—thus being guided by the promise "to you and your children." Surely the divine promise is a "more solid basis" of judgment than a human profession, and since all baptism is made "on presumption," this presumption should be as broad as the promise. This, Warfield contends, is "solid proof" of the validity of infant baptism. He does not argue against Baptists that faith or salvation is unnecessary before baptism. His argument is that such should be presumed on the part of the children of believers.[19]

To this line of argument is added "the central and decisive point" in the controversy; namely, the continuity of the New Testament church with Israel of the old covenant, or, in his words, "the continuity of the Old and New Testament Church." If the church of the old covenant is the same as that of the new, and if the children of the old covenant were recognized members of the church via the rite of circumcision, then unless the New Testament Scriptures should indicate otherwise, children of today's church are members also. Children are included in the covenant by positive divine law, and they can only be removed by similar divine word. The lack of express warrant for infant baptism in the New Testament can in no way overthrow this warrant provided in the Old Testament. Citing Lightfoot, Warfield argues, "It is not forbidden in the New Testament to baptize infants,—therefore they are to be baptized." This "central proposition," Warfield contends, both establishes infant baptism and "cut[s] away at a stroke all of the arguments which are urged against" it.[20]

Warfield adds briefly that the history of the church and the prevalence of the practice of infant baptism still today argue for its validity. He does not expand on this point at all, but he does entertain the question of the meaning of infant

---

[18]"Children in the Hands of the Arminians," 167–76.
[19]W, 9:389–90, 393.
[20]W, 9:390, 400; W, 10:159; PR 10, no. 37 (1889): 159.

baptism in the earlier centuries. The earliest known records of infant baptism see baptism as having regenerating efficacy, but he argues that we must make distinction between the doctrine and the practice of infant baptism. That these early sources taught something aberrant in connection with the practice does not obscure the fact of their witness to the early practice itself.[21] The fact is that infant baptism has an ancient history.

This much is Warfield's "positive argument" in support of infant baptism. He devotes the large majority of "The Polemics of Infant Baptism," however, to a critical analysis of the arguments against infant baptism by the renowned Baptist theologian A. H. Strong (1839–1921). Here Warfield argues that Scripture passages that either command or describe adult baptism, or that presume credible faith, have no bearing on the issue; they simply do not address the question of infants. Moreover, passages such as Matthew 28:19; Acts 10:47; and Romans 6:2–5 do not demonstrate that a previous change of heart and life is necessary to baptism, although they do symbolize "the inner cleansing presumed to be already present." Most of the biblical passages Strong highlights are "occasional" in nature and cannot be stretched into universal norms. Certain passages do indeed address adults with the demand of faith and repentance before baptism, but this simply has nothing to do with the question of infants.[22]

Warfield acknowledges that there is no express New Testament command or example of infant baptism, but he insists that the passages that describe household baptisms (Acts 16:15, 33; 1 Cor. 1:16) cannot be ruled out of the discussion. They cannot by themselves establish the practice, for it cannot be known whether infants were present in these homes or not. But neither can their presence be disproven, and thus the question must be decided on other grounds. Warfield places 1 Corinthians 7:14 in this same category—its declaration that the children of a believer are "holy" is consistent with the practice of infant baptism, but it is capable of explanation otherwise and thus cannot settle the matter on its own. Similarly, the passages that speak of Jesus' blessing the children, while they may be consistent with the practice of infant baptism, merely allow a possible inference and can in no way establish the question on its own weight. "The message which the incident is made by our Lord to bring us, therefore,—and which, accordingly, the passage directly teaches us with no inferences of ours—does not concern either infant baptism or infant salvation, but distinctly the constitution of the Kingdom of God."[23]

Strong argues that since Scripture makes explicit requirement of faith before participation in the Lord's Supper (1 Cor. 11:29), the same must apply to baptism.

[21] W, 9:390–91, 402–3.
[22] W, 9:391–95, 400–401.
[23] W, 9:395–99; FL, 68–70.

But Warfield denies the argument outright. The one ordinance is an ongoing rite for those in the church, while the other is the initiatory rite. The restriction made explicit in the one case cannot legitimately be imposed on the other.[24]

Warfield can find no reason to exclude children of believers from the ordinance of baptism. There are compelling reasons to administer the ordinance to them and no compelling reasons to the contrary. Thus he concludes:

> The argument in a nutshell is simply this: God established His Church in the days of Abraham and put children into it. They must remain there until He puts them out. He has nowhere put them out. They are still then members of His Church and as such entitled to its ordinances. Among these ordinances is baptism, which standing in similar place in the New Dispensation to circumcision in the Old, is like it to be given to children.[25]

And as he summarizes elsewhere still more strongly:

> The Reformed Christian, suspending salvation for all alike upon the sovereign grace of God alone, operating in accordance with God's covenanted purposes of mercy, points with confidence to the terms of the promise, "To you and to your children." He enjoins parents who trust in the covenanted mercy of God, therefore, to present their children, on the credit of this promise, to the Lord in baptism, and to bring them up in His nurture and admonition. And he enjoins the Church to recognize them by means of this holy ordinance as God's children, heirs of all the promises; and to take order for their training as such, that they may adorn in life and conduct the Gospel by which they are saved. Failure to recognize them as the children of God would be to him treason against that very covenant in whose terms he finds all his own warrant for hope and peace.[26]

THE MODE OF BAPTISM

The question of the mode of baptism is to Warfield nothing more than a "curious question" that cannot possibly find an answer in the New Testament. We will search the New Testament in vain, he insists, if we are hoping to find any instruction as to how to perform the rite. The New Testament writers had "no care for such things." Indeed, it is a great understatement to say that the New Testament does not prescribe a mode of baptism. "It does not even suggest one mode as preferable." Nor does it describe how any particular instance of baptism in the New Testament was administered. "The New Testament nowhere either prescribes

---

[24]*W*, 9:401.
[25]*W*, 9:408.
[26]"Children in the Hands of the Arminians," 169.

or suggests to us how this rite is to be administered; and nowhere does it even allude to the rite in such a way as to supply ground for a confident inference as to its mode of administration." Doubtless the original readers of the New Testament knew how baptism was administered by the apostolic community. But the apostles themselves thought it a matter of unimportance and so remained completely silent concerning it. We are commanded to baptize, and we are commanded to do so with water. Beyond that we have precious little instruction or information. Such "mere externalities" simply are not a matter of concern. It would perhaps be easier for us if the New Testament writers prescribed a particular mode, but that would be at the cost of "evangelical freedom" and (echoing the apostle) entangle us again in a yoke of bondage.[27]

This is not to say that we are free to make of baptism anything we choose, Warfield cautions. "The law of decency and order" (1 Cor. 14:40) certainly imposes some limitations and would steer away from formalism, narrow legalism, and complete indifference alike. And so Warfield criticizes both those who demand, say, immersion, and those who take unseemly liberty, such as some who had reportedly been baptized *en masse* with water thrown on them by a priest with a brush or a tree branch, or water from a drinking cup smeared quickly and secretly on a child's face. But given Warfield's broad allowance, he cannot say that such abuses render such baptisms invalid, as much as he may like to in some cases. In fact, he concedes that even in such cases, if there was "purity of intention and abundance of faith" the baptism is valid.[28]

In defense of his agnostic position regarding the mode of baptism Warfield turns his attention to the arguments often advanced in support of any particular mode. Luke records that Philip and the Ethiopian "went down into the water" and "came up out of the water" (Acts 8:38–39), but these statements constitute no proof of immersion. Walking into and standing in shallow water is language very much in keeping with affusion, and in this context affusion is perhaps more probable than immersion, Warfield argues, although immersion is certainly possible. To demand immersion here, we would have to know on other grounds that this was the sole apostolic practice. Similarly, Luke records in Acts 10:47 that Peter asks if any can "withhold water" for baptism, a phrase that some have argued implies a small amount of water is all that is necessary, implying sprinkling. But this is not a necessary interpretation of the phrase, and immersion cannot be ruled out. Warfield argues similarly in reference to the Philippian jail, where it would be unlikely to find facilities for immersion, and Pentecost, where it would seem

---

[27]*SSW*, 1:329; *SSW*, 2:329–30, 334–35, 340; *NSHERK*, 447.
[28]*SSW*, 2:330–34.

difficult to have immersed so many—Luke simply does not record enough data
for us to draw any conclusions. Similarly, expressions such as "because water was
plentiful there" (John 3:23; cf. Luke 3:3), "baptized . . . in the Jordan" (Mark 1:9), or
"came up out of the water" (Mark 1:10; cf. Acts 8:36) should not be "overpressed"
to demand immersion, for the language is fitting also of other modes. There is
not enough information provided to draw any certain conclusions.[29]

Romans 6:3–4 and Colossians 2:12 each speak of "burial" with Christ in baptism,
and Warfield acknowledges that it is natural for those accustomed to thinking
of baptism as immersion to see that mode reflected in this language. Even so,
he insists that these passages, when understood rightly, provide not even an
allusion to immersion. Paul is speaking only of spiritual realities, the union of
the soul with Christ. Galatians 3:27 uses the figure of a change of clothing—"as
many of you as were baptized into Christ have put on Christ." But in neither case
is there reference to mode. Baptism is not intended to picture either burial or a
change of clothing. The focus is spiritual realities only. These passages do not tell
us that baptism for Paul was or was not immersion. They simply do not address
such questions.[30]

Nor does the word "baptize" itself indicate anything concerning mode. To be
sure, the primitive root word indicates "to be deep" and originally meant a dipping.
But in time it came to take on secondary ideas such as "moistening," "washing,"
"dyeing," "tempering," "imbuing," Warfield says, "without any implication of
'dipping.'" Moreover, it seems the New Testament, perhaps influenced by Jewish
usage of the term, employs the word in a specialized sense of "to cleanse" or "to
purify." From "dipping" to "dipping to cleanse," now the word had come merely
to mean "to cleanse." The single idea of purification is all that is in view, with no
connotations of mode whatever. In the New Testament writers it has become
a technical term to indicate ceremonial purification only. Any implications of
mode have been left entirely behind.

> In the Apocryphal books and in the New Testament—Ecclus. xxxiv. (xxxi) 25 (30);
> Mark vii. 4; Luke vi. 38; Heb. ix. 10—it is the standing term for the Jewish lustrations;
> and the designation of John's purificatory rite as a "baptizing," and of himself, its
> proclaimer, as, by way of eminence, "the baptizer," bears vivid testimony to the
> establishment of the term in its new sense. . . . The broad language of Heb. ix. 10
> in adverting to the lustrations of the law—"divers baptizings"—already brings us a
> suggestion of the width of the connotation of the term: however the Jewish lustra-
> tions were performed, they were all "baptizings."

---

[29] *SSW*, 2:337–38, 342–43; *NSHERK*, 447.
[30] *SSW*, 2:338–39; *NSHERK*, 448–49.

Warfield points for further support to Luke 11:38–39 and Mark 7:3ff., which he says indicate affusion or sprinkling. All this, he argues, leads us to conclude that the New Testament leaves us without any instruction whatever in regard to the mode of administering baptism.[31]

To decide the question, then, we are left to the nature of the ordinance itself under the guidance of the law of decency and order. What is most important, Warfield demands, is the symbolism of the rite. It is a washing, a cleansing. But for cleansing, a full immersion is not necessary. In the Old Testament, cleansing is symbolized by a bath and by sprinkling alike. And so in arriving at our individual determination of the matter, we may be influenced by Ezekiel 36:25 (sprinkling), Joel 2:28 (pouring), or the thought of fulness of cleansing (immersion). "Each of us may legitimately exercise his own preference" as guided by "the essential symbolism of cleansing," but no one is entitled to enforce his own preference on all. Indeed, Warfield considers it ironic that those who insist on a single mode (clearly a reference to immersionists) show no similar scruples in details regarding the Lord's Supper.[32]

Warfield gives considerable attention also to the history of the church and especially to its earliest centuries to examine the question. He concludes that there is not enough information available to decide the original mode on historical grounds. His own opinion is that the primitive mode was "probably by pouring water on the head of the recipient, standing, ordinarily perhaps, but apparently not invariably, in a greater or less depth of water." But he stresses that this is only an opinion and cannot be pressed. This mode can be traced back to the mid-second century, but immersion and trine immersion have similar early witness also. We cannot presume that any of these reflects the primitive practice. In short, the available historical and archaeological data do not provide a certain answer to the question.[33] What Warfield does learn from his historical investigation is that the "narrow attitude" toward baptism that demands one mode only is "a novelty of the modern Church."[34]

In brief, Warfield finds no indications that any importance at all should be attached to the issue of the mode of baptism. In fact he insists that even if it could be shown that the word "baptize" means to immerse or that the apostles and the early church practiced immersion, it would not follow that "so slender a circumstance as the mode of applying the water" could be so entailed in the essence of baptism that nothing could be baptism except immersion. "The New

---

[31]*SSW*, 2:344–47; *NSHERK*, 448.
[32]*SSW*, 2:348–50; *SSW*, 1:329; *W*, 10:160. Ironically, Warfield devotes an article of eighteen pages to the question of the posture of recipients at the Lord's Table (*SSW*, 2:351–69) and thus reflects some preoccupation with seeming nonessential details himself.
[33]*W*, 9:385–86; *NSHERK*, 449–50.
[34]*SSW*, 2:349–50; *NSHERK*, 447.

Testament considers it enough to establish it as the initiatory title of Christianity, outline its significance in broad touches, and let it go at that."[35]

The Lord's Supper

Both Christian ordinances symbolize salvation in its wholeness but under differing representations: salvation is a cleansing work, and salvation is a ransoming work.[36] It is of no minor significance that the Lord's Supper[37] was instituted in the midst of the Passover meal. That memorial of redemption from Egyptian slavery by means of a slain lamb pointed forward to the work of our Lord in delivering us from sin by the sacrifice of himself (John 1:29, 36; 1 Cor. 5:7; 1 Pet. 1:19; Rev. 5:6, 12; 7:14; 12:11; 13:8, etc.). That older lamb was but the "typical" representation of the Lamb that was slain before the world began. His body and blood according to his own declaration are represented in the bread and wine as the means of our redemption. Whatever there was about Jesus' words that may have been puzzling to his disciples, it was clear that he was identifying himself with the Paschal Lamb, the symbol of redemption. What it was to Israel, he is now for his people. This is the fundamental significance of the Lord's Supper—it is the Christian Passover, taking the place in the church that the former meal occupied in Israel. Here the type gives way to the antitype, and the feast of death becomes a feast of life. The celebration is not of his death, merely, but of the effects of his death.[38]

Although the Lord's Supper is a continuation of the Passover meal, the symbols have been changed. For Warfield this is the significance of the demonstrative "this"—"*This* is my body," he emphasizes. In the presence of the symbols of the older meal, Jesus passes by the lamb and takes the loaf, saying, "*This* is my body." And taking the cup he says, "*This* is my blood." No longer the lamb but the loaf and the cup—these are representative of him. The meal continues, but it has been transformed, and its symbols have been changed. He is the Paschal Lamb, only now we remember him with the bread and the cup. And the bread and the cup are not symbols of his body and blood only, but of his body and blood given in sacrifice for sin.[39]

Warfield emphasizes also that the supper is not the making of a sacrifice. It is a feast, a feast in celebration and commemoration of the Redeemer and his sav-

---

[35]*NSHERK*, 447, 449; *SSW*, 2:335.

[36]*SSW*, 1:330; *SSW*, 2:348–49.

[37]Warfield devoted only three titles to the subject of the Lord's Supper: "The Fundamental Significance of the Lord's Supper," in *SSW*, 1:332–38; "The Posture of the Recipients at the Lord's Supper: A Footnote to the History of Reformed Usages," in *SSW*, 2:351–69; "Communion in Christ's Body and Blood," in *FL*, 222–30.

[38]*SSW*, 1:332–36.

[39]*FL*, 228–29.

ing work. But it is not a memorial merely. It is an application of the sacrifice, a participation in the benefits attained by the sacrifice. This is what Paul indicates when he refers to those who eat a sacrifice as "participants in the altar" (1 Cor. 10:18). Symbolically we partake of his body and blood; that is, we profess ourselves beneficiaries of his sacrificial work. In one place, but without much comment, Warfield argues further that Christ is present in the sacrament, and by it the Holy Spirit binds Christ to the heart.[40]

The loaf has further symbolic significance as the one body of Christ. All who partake of Christ are bound together in internal unity, a unity in the common Redeemer. There is a real "communion" in Christ. Together we partake of him, and together we receive the benefits of his saving work. "The whole Christian world is a passover company gathered around the paschal lamb, and by their participation in it exhibiting their essential unity."[41]

Finally, in "The Posture of the Recipients at the Lord's Supper," Warfield takes up a historical inquiry of this practical question. His concern in the end is to preserve any necessary symbolism of the supper but also to make allowance for convenience. Most fundamentally the Lord's Supper is not an act of sacrificing and thus is not to be celebrated at an altar. It is a feast and thus is properly celebrated at a table. It is the Lord's Table. At the institution of this supper the original recipients sat recumbent, but this was merely the customary posture in that society and should not be considered essential to the celebration. Other possibilities adopted in various churches include standing, walking, sitting, and kneeling. All may be appropriate, but all are not equally desirable; and the association of kneeling with the idolatry of the mass renders it particularly unsuitable. Warfield suggests that the best option, considering symbolism and commodiousness, is the common practice of a table occupied on three sides with the fourth left open to the congregation.[42]

Church Government

Church government is a subject that Warfield seldom addresses.[43] In fact, nowhere, except for an article on the subject of deaconesses, does he address the matter in any depth at all. Still, the issue of church government is not a matter of indifference to him. At some points he laments that church polity is undervalued by

---

[40]*SSW*, 1:336–37; *SSW*, 2:351; *FL*, 226–29; *PTR* 5, no. 1 (1907): 160–61.
[41]*FL*, 229–30.
[42]*SSW*, 2:351–54, 368.
[43]Warfield devoted just three articles specifically to matters of church government: "Presbyterian Deaconesses," *PR* 10, no. 38 (1889): 283–93; a review of *The Form of the Christian Temple*, by Thomas Witherow, *PR* 10, no. 38 (1889): 330–33; and "The Relation of the Presbyterian Principle to the Historic Episcopate," *Methodist Review* 71 (1889): 845–50.

many, and he notes in 1 Timothy 3:13 the apostle's emphasis that precisely because "it is no less than the church of the living God" it "must" be well ordered and that careful attention must be given to the matter. The truth it guards is great, and the danger it faces is great also. Warfield adds his own emphasis, with a reminder that we today are still God's house, and we must treat its concerns with utmost diligence, faithfulness, and care.[44]

The church belongs to Christ, of course, and he is its Head. But his authority is mediated through the apostles and the Scriptures they "impose" upon the church. It follows that the church does not stand above the Scriptures, but the Scriptures above the church. The Scriptures are not a product of the church; rather they are "the authority which founded the church. The church certainly did not exist before the authority which Christ gave the apostles to found it, in virtue of which they have imposed the Scriptures on it as law."[45] Everywhere in his works Warfield emphasizes the authority of the apostles over the church. But he also notes that the apostle Paul was not merely a divinely appointed missionary but a kind of missionary-society of his own. That is, his authority over the churches was often exercised through his appointed agents and helpers. "Wherever they went they stood *in loco apostoli* and acted as his extended hand." Thus, he left Timothy in Ephesus and later recalled him and replaced him with Tychicus (2 Tim. 4:9, 12). And similarly he left Titus in Crete, later to replace him with Artemas, as he saw fit (Titus 3:12).[46]

Except in the apostles themselves, who were unique and whose office was limited to the lifetime of the original band, Warfield does not find explicit New Testament warrant for a church governing body above the local level. The fact that the apostles did not establish the church with a hierarchical structure establishes that hierarchicalism is not the best or the natural form of church government. Beyond this, matters such as the association of churches are consistent with the apostolically imposed order, but even they lack express warrant and were left to "human development." It would be unwarranted to assume, for example, that "the presbytery" of Timothy's ordination mentioned in 1 Timothy 4:14 is an association of elders from various churches, for there is no example of such in the New Testament; rather, ordination was a local church matter. Likewise the "council" of Acts 15 is unique and reflects a common apostolic authority only. "Let us confess that the New Testament gives us no example of other than congregational presbyteries; and rest our higher courts on the legitimate application in their

[44]*PR* 8, no. 31(1887): 507–8; *PR* 10, no. 38 (1889): 330; *Acts and Pastoral Epistles and Philemon*, The Temple Bible series (1902; repr., London: J. M. Dent & Sons, 1930), xxxii; *FL*, 375–78.
[45]*SSW*, 2:538.
[46]*PR* 10, no. 38 (1889): 333.

formation of the same principle of association which was divinely enacted in the congregational government."[47] Curiously, in all this Warfield does not follow the traditional Presbyterian understanding. As he summarizes:

> It is important to observe, however, that this unity was not organic, in the special sense of that word which would imply that it was founded on the inclusion of the whole Church under one universal government. The absence of such an organization is obvious on the face of the New Testament record, nor do its pages contain any clear promise of or prominent provision for it for the future. The churches are all organized locally, but no external bonds bind them together, except as this was here and there supplied to certain groups of churches by the common authority over them of the same apostolical founders. No central authority ruled over the whole Church. It is perfectly obvious that Jerusalem exercised no domination over Antioch, Antioch none over the churches founded by its missionaries. Nor were the churches associated in a common dominion of the whole over the parts. Even in the next generation the most powerful lever Rome could bring on Corinth was entreaty and advice. The apostles went forth to evangelize the world, not to rule it; they divided the work among themselves, and did not seek to control it as a "college"; they delegated their individual authority to the local officers and founded no dynasty, whether individual or collegiate.[48]

On the local level the apostles imposed the two offices of elder and deacon. Warfield understands the eldership as "an undifferentiated ruling-teaching office" and the diaconate as "an office of service" as distinguished from "ministry" in a higher sense. Each church was governed by a plurality of elders or presbyters (Acts 14:23; Titus 1:5), who are also referred to as bishops (Acts 20:17, 28; 1 Pet. 5:1–2; 1 Tim. 3:1–7; 5:17–19; Titus 1:5–7). Warfield designates "elder" as the title of dignity and "bishop" as that of function but understands them as referring to the same office. Earlier in Warfield's career he argued that Paul's reference in 1 Timothy 5:17—"the elders that rule well . . . especially those who labor in word and doctrine"—does not imply two distinct orders of presbyters. All elders rule, and all elders teach (1 Tim 3:2, 5; Titus 1:9), he said then, reasoning that Paul's words speak of degrees of honor and remuneration as determined by degrees of excellence in their respective works. But in a brief article that did not appear until after his death he argues differently: "All [presbyters] shared in the oversight of the church, and some of them labored *also* in word and doctrine" (emphasis added), and he adds that this gave rise to the later distinction between bishop and elder that became so common. Warfield seems also to find in James

---

[47] *PR* 10, no. 38 (1889): 332–33; "The Relation of the Presbyterian Principle," 848–49.
[48] *SSW*, 1:300–301.

warrant for a distinguishable pastoral office within the plurality of elders of the church in Jerusalem. He reasons briefly, "Jerusalem had differentiated for itself a 'bishop' out of its board of overseers, while as yet the separate pastoral office was unknown to the rest of the church; and even after it had spread to Syria and Asia it was still lacking in Philippi." This reference is clearly to Philippians 1:1, where Paul mentions "the overseers and deacons" of the church there, with no "bishop" or "pastor" outstanding among them.[49]

Warfield allows the office of deaconess, but he finds no reason to see it as part of the office described in 1 Timothy 3. Paul's discussion of the qualifications of deacons begins in verse 8, and it is very clear that in verses 12–13 he is still speaking of the same. It seems impossible, on this reading, to understand verse 11 as a separate discussion of deaconesses. The "women" of 1 Timothy 3:11 are better understood simply as the "wives" of the deacons. The only way around this understanding would be to assume that Paul is talking not about two distinct offices—deacons and deaconesses—but about a single office that consists of both. But Warfield objects, "We naturally recoil before so far-reaching an inference from so small a basis." Surprisingly, then, Warfield allows the office of deaconess solely on the presumed implication of Romans 16:1, with its mention of Phoebe "the servant" or "deaconess." He frankly admits that this interpretation rests on a "precarious foundation," that the term *diakonē* is capable of a broad range of connotations and need not mean "deaconess" in an official sense, and that there is no compelling reason in the context to understand this as a reference to the office of deaconess. Still he says that this "seems the more likely meaning." And for support he points to the postapostolic church, which did recognize the office. Curiously, Warfield does not allow the office of widow-servant (1 Timothy 5), even though it also came very quickly to be recognized as such in the ancient church.[50]

---

[49]*PR* 10, no. 38 (1889): 333; *PR* 8, no. 31 (1887): 707–8; *SSW*, 1:301; "Presbyter," in *A Dictionary of Religion and Ethics*, ed. Shailer Matthews and Gerald Birney Smith (New York: Macmillan, 1921), 348; cf. "Presbyterianism" in the same volume, 348–49.

[50]*PR* 8, no. 31 (1887): 505–6, 703–7; *PR* 10, no. 38 (1889): 283–84, 291–92. A student recalls that Warfield vigorously opposed the ordination of women as elders in the church (personal letter from Charles Brokenshire to John Meeter, June 25, 1942, p. 13).

I believe that as Jesus Christ has once come in grace, so also
is he to come a second time in glory, to judge the world in
righteousness and assign to each his eternal award; and I believe that
if I die in Christ, my soul shall be at death made perfect in holiness
and go home to the Lord; and when he shall return to his
majesty I shall be raised in glory and made perfectly blessed
in the full enjoyment of God to all eternity: encouraged by which
blessed hope it is required of me willingly to take my part in
suffering hardship here as a good soldier of Christ Jesus,
being assured that if I die with him I shall also live with him,
if I endure, I shall also reign with him.

SSW, 1:409–10.

12

ESCHATOLOGY

Compared to his treatment of other theological domains, Warfield's writings on eschatology were relatively few.[1] But the excerpt above represents the themes of his primary interest: the return of Christ to judge the world (with its attending concerns) and the Christian's hope of perfection in the presence of Christ in both the intermediate state and finally in the resurrection. On occasion Warfield touched on the more technical matter of the timing of end-time events, such as the relation of the coming of Christ to the climax of the kingdom (the millennial question), but his treatments of such questions were seldom lengthy or in great detail. And throughout all his discussions of eschatology, both personal and cosmic, he insisted that the purpose of all such study was ethical—the encouragement and edification of the Christian—and not purely academic. Clearly the most important points of eschatological concern and emphasis that recur in his writings have to do with the Christian's hope of perfection and bliss in the presence of Christ (the realized goal of individual salvation) and the eventual success of Christ in worldwide gospel advance—and this, at times, as it relates to the second advent of Christ. Both of these topics Warfield viewed in terms of a coming glory.

The Coming Glory: Cosmic Eschatology

Warfield nowhere treats the biblical teaching regarding end-time events in a systematic way;[2] he only treats major biblical passages that touch the theme

---

[1]Articles Warfield wrote specifically to address the theme of eschatology (personal or cosmic) are the following only: "The Prophecies of St. Paul," in *W*, 2:601–40; "The Millennium and the Apocalypse," in *W*, 2:643–64; "The Gospel and the Second Coming," in *SSW*, 1:348–55; "The Book of Revelation," in *SSW*, 2:80–92; "The Apocalypse," in *SSW*, 2:651–54; "Annihilationism,"in *W*, 9:447–57; "The Old Testament and Immortality," in *SSW*, 1:339–47; and "The Christian's Attitude Toward Death," in *PrS*, 316–37. These articles are generally brief, and some address matters of hermeneutics or historical definition more than issues of eschatology specifically. The major themes of eschatology mentioned below are touched frequently in other Warfield contexts but with little substantive addition to these.

[2]The closest to this would be his survey article, "The Prophecies of St. Paul."

and sometimes with a brief concluding summary. From these biblical studies, his broad eschatological outlook can be discerned.

THE SECOND ADVENT OF CHRIST AND JUDGMENT

Regarding the event of Christ's second coming, Warfield has relatively little directly to say by way of definition, but he emphasizes repeatedly that it will be an event marked primarily by universal judgment and resurrection. Warfield sees "the day of the Lord," prophesied by Joel, as a day in which the wicked and all who have refused Christ will be brought to "eternal destruction" (2 Thess. 1:6–10; cf. 1 Cor. 5:5). This is the note the apostle Paul pressed with special emphasis to his Gentile audiences. It is the "day on which [God] will judge the world in righteousness" (Acts 17:31), and in light of this he presents Christ not as judge only but as the One "who delivers us from the wrath to come" (1 Thess. 1:10). Hence, Paul views the day also with great anticipation, eagerly awaiting the glory and vindication of the saints that Christ will accomplish in that day (1 Thess. 1:10; 2:19; 3:13; 5:23; 1 Cor. 1:7–8). That is to say, the return of Christ will be a day of judgment in which there will be a just distribution both of punishment and reward (2 Tim. 4:8, 14; 1:16).[3] Terrible as that day will be for those who do not know Christ or obey his gospel, "it will be bliss unspeakable to those in Christ." The one will receive "eternal destruction, away from the presence of the Lord" (2 Thess. 1:9), but the other will be given "eternal dwelling with the Lord" (1 Thess. 4:17). "That day" is, for the believer, the object of eager and longing expectation (2 Tim. 4:8; Titus 2:13).

THE SECOND ADVENT OF CHRIST AND RESURRECTION

That the day of judgment associated with the return of Christ is marked by both reward and punishment presupposes a general resurrection, Warfield argues.[4] For example, in 2 Thessalonians 1:6–10 the apostle Paul specifies that both the eternal destruction of the wicked and the glory of the saints will be realized when Christ returns.[5] The judgment issuing in these divergent ends presupposes a resurrection that includes all the dead, both believing and unbelieving. Warfield asserts that Christ's resurrection is a first sampling and guarantee of the resurrection not only of the righteous but of all humanity. "All men that die rise again by virtue of Christ's conquest of death."[6] He argues emphatically that this can be the only right understanding of 1 Corinthians 15:20–22: "For as in Adam all die,

---

[3] W, 2:603–4.
[4] W, 2:604.
[5] W, 2:606.
[6] W, 2:604, cf. 621.

so in Christ shall all be made alive" (v. 22). Warfield will not countenance any possibility of such "strange misconceptions" as a selective resurrection, first of the just and then later of the unjust. Passages such as Acts 23:6; 24:15; 26:8, 23; 28:20; and Revelation 20:11–15, he insists, specify that the resurrection includes both the just and unjust. He argues that passages that affirm the resurrection of the just only (e.g., 1 Thess. 4:13–18; Phil. 3:11; 1 Cor. 15:23) have as their focus the encouragement of believers and make no specific mention of the unbelieving dead. He argues emphatically that these passages should be read not as implying a selective resurrection but rather with the understanding that the resurrection of the one class presupposes the resurrection of the other. Believers have not yet risen with Christ because, according to 1 Corinthians 15:26, death is the last enemy Christ will vanquish. It has been put off to "the end" (v. 24). Even the righteous, then, must wait "until all conquests are completed."[7]

THIS PRESENT AGE

This in turn, Warfield argues, serves to define the character of this present age (the time between the first and second advents of Christ) as "a period of advancing conquest on the part of Christ." The dead will be raised at his return (1 Cor. 15:23). This will mark "the end," a time when Christ will hand the fully consummated kingdom over to the Father (v. 24). But until then, Christ, now reigning in exalted universal dominion, is gaining conquest over all enemies (v. 25), the last of which is death (v. 26). This is an age of apostasy, false doctrine, persecution, conflict (1 Tim. 4:1ff.; 2 Tim. 3:1, 13), and antichrist (1 John 2:18, 22; 4:3; 2 John 7). Warfield argues that antichrist is not an eschatological but a present evil, not a person but a multitude of persons, and not merely persons but a heresy. Today is "the last hour" marked by antichrists and conflict with error. But all this is merely in the "first stages" of these last days, not the whole of it. Opposition to Christ will not grow ever greater. "The world is passing away" (1 John 2:17), and Warfield emphasizes that this period is one of conquest and not merely conflict: Christ is not merely striving against evil but "progressively overcoming" evil throughout this age. With the dawn of Christianity and the mighty forces within it, a "regeneration of society" has begun, and this age is not simply that of the church militant but also that of the triumphing church.[8]

---

[7]W, 2:605, 621–23. On 632–33 Warfield is particularly emphatic: "Nothing in the language suggests it . . . . Nothing in the context demands or even allows it. Nothing anywhere in Paul's writings justifies it. It is inconsistent with what we have found Paul saying about the Second Advent and its relation to the end. . . . And finally it is contradicted by his explicit statements concerning the general resurrection."
[8]W, 2:623, 637–38; SSW, 1:223, 356–62.

Warfield argues that this is the teaching of the apostle Paul also in Romans 11, which looks ahead to the ingathering of "the fullness of the Gentiles" (v. 25) and of "all Israel" (v. 26). So pervasive will be this gospel conquest that it will be as "life from the dead" (v. 15), which Warfield characterizes as "the universal Christianization of this world," by which he means "at least the nominal conversion of all the Gentiles and the real salvation of all the Jews." As such, this is the fulfillment of the prayer "Thy kingdom come, thy will be done in earth even as it is in heaven" (Matt. 6:10). It follows, then, that this age is characterized as "these last days" (Heb. 1:2) and "the end of the ages" (1 Cor. 10:11; cf. Acts 2:17; 1 Tim 4:1; 2 Tim. 3:1; James 5:3; 1 Pet. 1:20; 2 Pet. 3:3; 1 John 2:18; Jude 18), leading up to "the end" at Christ's return (1 Cor. 15:24).[9]

THE SECOND ADVENT OF CHRIST AND THE KINGDOM

Warfield does not share a particular liking for any of the standard terms describing the various millennial positions (a-, pre-, and postmillennialism).[10] This is due chiefly to his unusual understanding of Revelation 20, in which he interprets the "thousand years" as symbolic of the intermediate state (on which see below). But he agrees that the terms do focus on a significant question, and although not explicitly, he clearly opts for the postmillennial position, if only in general terms.[11] He understands 1 Corinthians 15:20–28 to describe Christ's reign as *culminating* in his return and the destruction of the last enemy. He views this as unquestionably "the uniform representation of the New Testament, which everywhere places Christ's kingdom before and God's after the Second Advent."[12]

Warfield specifies that it is by means of Christian witness that Christ's kingdom makes its advance. He may speak of the "evolution" of the kingdom, but it is an evolving that stems from specifically *gospel* advance. "Christians are His soldiers in this holy war, and it is through our victory that His victory is known."[13] Warfield understands Revelation 19 as symbolizing this also. The rider on the white horse is Christ, and he wins the victory by means of the sword that comes from his mouth—that is, by means of the spoken witness of his followers. Revelation 19

---

[9] *W*, 2:624; *SSW*, 1:348. But see *SSW*, 1:354, where Warfield speaks more confidently, affirming that Romans 11 must mean "nothing less than a world-wide salvation."

[10] *SSW*, 1:349, 351.

[11] In the 1880s Warfield sent letters to various premillennial theologians, including Samuel Kellogg, requesting recommended reading in defense of premillennialism (Warfield Collection, Special Collections, Princeton Theological Seminary Library). Not much premillennial literature was available in that day, and the responses offered very little overall. They did point to respected authors such as Frederic Godet, whom Warfield held in very high regard, but we have no way of judging the result of this exchange or the extent of Warfield's interest in premillennialism.

[12] *W*, 2:625, 662–63; *SSW*, 1:348–50.

[13] *W*, 2:631, 639; *SSW*, 1:361.

does not depict the return of Christ in glory and victory over enemies; it depicts the advance of his kingdom via the preaching of the gospel in this age. It is gospel advance, Christianizing the world, by which this kingdom is brought to its glorious culmination, and only then issuing in the return of Christ. This is the declaration of "the Great Commission" in which Christ commands his disciples to conquer the earth with the gospel empowered by his continued presence unto the end (Matt. 28:18–20). In Matthew 24:14, Jesus affirms the same, that "this gospel of the kingdom will be proclaimed throughout the whole world as a testimony to all nations, and then the end will come."[14] Warfield everywhere insists that the kingdom is advanced by means of the spread of the gospel, and he takes strong exception with W. G. T. Shedd, who allows that salvation may come to some apart from the gospel.[15] It is only by the gospel that Christ's kingdom is brought to its climax, and Warfield holds out every expectation that the gospel will, in fact, be successful in this task. It is, in turn, the character and purpose of the book of Acts to narrate this conquering mission of the church and the success of the risen Jesus in establishing the church in the world and fulfilling his promise to bring his church to final success.[16]

This is a theme Warfield returns to many times in his writing and preaching, and it is clearly a favorite. He sees in the individual Christian a microcosm of what God has set out to accomplish in the world. In the life and experience of the individual believer God is at work gradually to bring about a promised transformation until finally all his people are made perfectly and wholly to be like Christ; so also God has undertaken to transform the world over a process of extended time in which "the leaven of truth, thus brought into the world and applied by the Spirit in long process, shall in the end leaven the whole lump."[17] In sermon after sermon, with enthusiastic optimism, Warfield loves to point to passages that speak of the universal effects of the gospel: John 1:29, the Lamb that takes away the sin of the world; John 3:16–17, God's love reclaiming the world; 1 John 2:2, Christ the propitiation for the whole world; 2 Corinthians 5:14–15, 18–19, Christ's death "for all," God through Christ "reconciling the world to himself"; 2 Corinthians 6:2, this age as "the day of salvation," and so on.[18] Similarly, in his sermon on "The Outpouring of the Spirit" (Acts 2), he concludes with enthusiastic expectation that because this is the dispensation of the Spirit, it is a successful missionary age in which the gospel will make its "triumphant progress until earth passes at last

---

[14] W, 2:647–48; SSW, 1:351–53.
[15] BTS, 350.
[16] SSW, 2:46, 87.
[17] SSW, 1:43–44, 354.
[18] SSW, 1:148–77, 350; SW, 69–100, 103–30, 137–47, 155–57.

into heaven," an age that is therefore marked by ever-increasing righteousness "until it is perfect."[19] In "The Biblical Idea of Revelation," he observes this as God's purpose in history. Since the fall the earth has been marked by a curse (Genesis 3) and division (Gen. 11:1–9), but in the Abrahamic promise (Gen. 12:1–3) a hope is established that the curse will be reversed, and all the families of the earth restored under the glorious reign of God. For a time this hope was known to Israel only, but the promised salvation will extend "from the Jews" (John 4:22) to those who were far off (Eph. 2:13), and all the world will be blessed. God has made himself known for this very purpose.[20] In his in-depth article on predestination Warfield carefully notes God's cosmic purpose to reclaim the world by saving his elect and establishing his universal kingdom.[21]

In "Are They Few That Be Saved" he argues at length that the passages that speak of "few" finding salvation (Matt. 7:14; 20:16 KJV; 22:14; Luke 13:23) are not to be understood as describing the whole of this age. The parables of the mustard seed and of the leaven, and by implication the parable of the wheat and the tares also, plainly teach that there will be an eventual reversal.

> These small beginnings are to give way to great expansions. The grain of mustard seed when sowed in the field (which is the world) is not to remain less than all seeds: it is to become a tree in the branches of which the birds of heaven lodge. The speck of leaven is not to remain hidden in the mass of meal: it is to work through the meal until the *whole* of it is leavened.[22]

Warfield insists that both of these classes of passages must be examined together, and when they are, it becomes clear that in the end it will not be few but many—indeed, "the immensely greater part of the human race"—who will be saved. Christ is at work today putting his enemies down under his foot, and this surely must mean gospel advance.[23]

Again it should be noted that Warfield does not understand the "thousand years" of Revelation 20 as having any bearing on this discussion, and so the term "post*millennial*" does not fit him with exact precision. But the difference is linguistic only. He affirms that this interadvent age will be marked by growing

---

[19]*FL*, 145.
[20]*W*, 1:3–4.
[21]*W*, 2:36.
[22]*BTS*, 348 (emphasis original).
[23]*BTS*, 348; see more fully 334–50. As a side note of interest, on 336 in a footnote Warfield quotes his (premillennialist) grandfather, Robert J. Breckinridge, at length, from his *The Knowledge of God, Objectively Considered*. This is one of perhaps five times in his writings that Warfield mentions his grandfather, who was active in the Presbyterian Church as one of its leading pastors. But this is the only time Warfield cites him (and, as may be expected, with agreement).

gospel advance culminating in a latter-day glory, a "golden age" of a "Christianized" world just preceding the return of Christ. Warfield assures us that throughout this age evil will continuously wane "as conflict passes into victory." Certainly, this is postmillennialism.[24]

THE TIME OF CHRIST'S RETURN

Uncertain

Regarding the duration of this kingdom and the time of Christ's return, the New Testament writers everywhere reflect a decided uncertainty. They are assured that prior to Christ's return the kingdom will make full advance and all enemies will be made Christ's footstool (Acts 2:35; cf. Heb. 10:12–13; 1 Cor. 15:25). But the duration of this time of advance is not specified.

There is no doubt that the Thessalonian converts expected it within their own lifetime: their concerns about the departed believing loved ones is inexplicable otherwise. And significantly, Paul does not deny that Christ might return within their lifetime. He emphasizes that to die will not be to miss the glory of that day, but in 1 Thessalonians 4:15 and 17 ("we who are alive") he seems to leave open the possibility that he himself may live until that day also. This, however, is not to assert that he believes the Lord certainly will return so soon. He only leaves open the possibility. The difference between Paul and his young Thessalonian converts on this score is that while they believe that Christ certainly will come within their lifetime, Paul merely believes that he may. The time of Christ's return is a matter hidden in the secret purpose of God (1 Thess. 5:1). Paul on the one hand can command Timothy to keep the faith unto the coming of Christ (1 Tim. 6:14), reflecting the hope of a soon return, and he can on the other hand speak of his own impending death (2 Tim. 4:6) and that of others (2 Cor. 5:1–10). He is in fact altogether uncertain whether Christ will return before or after he and the present generation would pass on (1 Thess. 5:10, "whether we are awake or asleep"; cf. 1 Cor. 15:51, "we shall not all sleep, but we shall all be changed"; Phil. 1:21–22).[25] Echoing the teaching of Christ himself (Matt. 24:36), Paul makes it plain that of the time of Christ's return no one can be sure.

---

[24] W, 2:630, 662–64; SSW, 1:349. Walvoord mistakenly identifies Warfield as amillennial (BSac 100, no. 400 [1943]: 505–6), probably because of Warfield's interpretation of the thousand years of Revelation 20 as being fulfilled during this age. But this commonality with amillennialism is only superficial. Samuel Craig reports that Warfield's article in The Bible Magazine, "The Gospel and the Second Coming," was written specifically in answer to a request by the editor that he "set forth the post-millennial view"; BTS, xl.

[25] W, 2:606, 625, 634.

It is ours, therefore, to wait patiently (ἀναμένειν, I Thess. 1:10) and watch (I Thess. 5:6), for that day will come unexpectedly, like a thief in the night (I Thess. 5:2).[26]

What Must Come First

Still, the young Thessalonians were gullible and had been misled, persistent in their thinking that Christ's return must be immediate, and so in words echoing the Olivet Discourse (Matthew 24), Paul writes to the Thessalonians again with a correction, this time with details of things that must happen before that day (2 Thess. 2:1–12). The two major events that Paul insists must occur first are "the apostasy" and the revelation of "the man of sin," which, in turn, is now being held back by "the restrainer." Warfield notes that these events (the apostasy and the revelation of the man of sin) are not necessarily to be seen as associated in time with the coming of Christ. Paul stresses only that these two events must occur before that day, and that until these two events come to light, the return of Christ is not imminent. Further, Warfield argues, Paul seems clearly to have "a contemporary, or nearly contemporary phenomenon in mind," for the mystery of lawlessness and its corresponding restraint was already at work (2 Thess. 2:6–7). He notes further that since Paul is making obvious allusion to Jesus' Olivet Discourse (Matt. 24:15), it is clear that he, like Jesus, is referring to Daniel's prophecy of the abomination of desolations (Dan. 11:36). And since Jesus refers this prophecy to the siege and destruction of Jerusalem in AD 70, Paul's reference must be to the same. Warfield concludes, "We cannot go far wrong in identifying him with the Roman emperor," or, perhaps better, the line of emperors "considered as the embodiment of persecuting power." It was Titus who placed himself in the temple as divine and brought sacrilege to the Holy of Holies; this is the work of iniquity led by the man of sin.[27]

Warfield identifies the restrainer as the Jewish state, which provided umbrella-like protection and shelter for the nascent church in the Roman world, concealing it from notice. When the Jewish apostasy was complete, God deserted the temple and brought the destruction of Jerusalem. At that time Christianity was finally distinct from Judaism, and persecution then came to be directed against the church. "Thus the continued existence of Judaism was in the truest sense a restraint on the persecution of Christians, and its destruction gave the signal for the lawless one to be revealed in his time."[28] Warfield further suggests that if the

---

[26]W, 2:606.
[27]W, 2:609–11. Note that Warfield did not identify the man of sin with Antichrist (SSW, 1:356–62).
[28]W, 2:611.

masculine form of "the restrainer" must be pushed, it would refer to James, the apostle in Jerusalem, by whose witness the door of the gospel remained open to the Jews, thus restraining the growing apostasy and coming persecution. In either case, he affirms that "the apostasy" is clearly the turning away of the Jews from Christ and the gospel.[29]

The Coming Glory: Personal Eschatology
DEATH AND THE INTERMEDIATE STATE

Scripture views death never as natural but as an unnatural intrusion into humanity separating soul from body. The biblical view of humanity understands man as a unity of body and soul. Death, entering as the punishment for sin, has destroyed this unity. The apostle Paul, therefore, describes that state after death as one in which the soul is "naked"—a disembodied spirit only (2 Cor. 5:1; cf. James 2:26a). Death is therefore the dreaded enemy of humanity. Even though the Christian knows that death will not ultimately triumph, he still very naturally shrinks from it as a horrible foe.[30]

For the Christian, however, to die is to pass into the immediate presence of Christ (2 Cor. 5:6; Phil. 1:21). Death is the disruption of soul from body, not the extinction of the soul. After death the soul lives on. Warfield entertains the possibility that part of the confusion of the recent Thessalonian converts was a fear that those who had died had not only missed the momentous event of Christ's return but perhaps ceased to exist altogether. Warfield admits that this is not the most likely understanding of their confusion; but even if this was their fear, he reasons, they were mistaken; and so Paul writes clearly to correct them.[31] By implication, Warfield here seems himself again to deny any notion of soul sleep. The soul survives death, and for the Christian it is the event by which he is brought into the presence of Christ. So far as the soul itself, alone considered, is concerned, the intermediate state is a state of complete salvation—perfect in holiness, without sin, and with Christ. Unnatural and fearful as death may be and imperfect as that intermediate state may be, it is yet an infinitely desirable state for the believer. It is not that death is to be preferred to life but that perfected holiness in the pres-

---

[29]W, 2:612.

[30]SSW, 1:345; PrS, 319–21, 325, 326.

[31]W, 2:604–5, 634; cf. his review of two books on immortality, PTR 2, no. 3 (1904): 507–11. Warfield almost never makes reference to the state of the wicked dead. He speaks several times of the Christian's intermediate state, but more generally at one point he asks rhetorically, "Who does not live after death?" thus affirming his adherence to traditional Christian theology at this point ("Christianity and the Resurrection of Christ," TBS, new series, 8, no. 4 [April 1908]: 283).

ence of Christ, even in an as-yet imperfect state, is to be preferred to this body of death and sin. Imperfect yet "far better" (Phil. 1:21). Death itself is still repulsive, but what lies beyond it is infinitely better: "Christ is there."[32]

Warfield characterizes eschatological (millennial) interpretations of Revelation 20 as manipulative exegesis driven by preconceived notions of "eschatological dreaming." For him, Revelation 20 has to do with the intermediate state, not cosmic eschatology. Its symbolic portrait of blissful peace and safety, thrown up against the background of war, represents the souls of the righteous in heaven during this interadvent period. Here the saints are safe in the presence of Christ, and Satan is bound and unable to make assault. The dead in Christ are not the church militant on earth or the church triumphing through this age, but the church waiting—waiting yet living and reigning with Christ and at rest.[33]

Warfield presses this rather unusual interpretation in virtually all the exegetical details of the passage. The saints, he notes, have been "beheaded" and are described as "souls" (Rev. 20:4). Having passed through war and died in the Lord, they reign with him above the noise of war as disembodied spirits. Warfield connects this with Revelation 14:13—"Blessed are the dead who die in the Lord"—and Revelation 6:9—"the souls of those who had been slain for the word of God" resting underneath the altar—and sees Revelation 20 as merely an expansion of these two earlier passages. The "thousand years" is the symbol of completeness and represents paradise itself, heavenly blessedness in the intermediate state, safety from Satan's deception and attack; those outside the "thousand years" are still subject to those attacks. The "binding of Satan" is not for a period of time but in reference to that sphere (the intermediate state) represented by the symbol of the thousand years. The "thrones" given to the "souls" represent the shared reign of the righteous dead with Christ in his present kingly reign, the messianic period. These souls "come to life" in the "first resurrection," the intermediate state, as "saved souls" hidden with Christ in God. Warfield assures us that it is "scarcely possible" to read Revelation 20 without being struck repeatedly with this reminder "that the peace and security pictured is the peace and security of the blessed dead" sharing in the present reign of Christ. But he acknowledges that his interpretation cannot clearly identify "the nations"; he is left to say that it is a reference to the saints in heaven, but he admits that this is an odd use of the term. In short, Revelation 19–20 present a picture, concurrent with this age, of

---

[32]*PrS*, 327, 331–32, 335. To this Warfield adds, "The Romish invention of purgatory, by which for the great majority of the saved a period of purification of longer or shorter duration and of greater or less suffering is interposed between death and 'the going home to the Lord,' is not only a baseless but a wicked invention, at war with every statement of Scripture in the premises, and with every dictate of the truly Christian consciousness alike" (327).

[33]*SSW*, 1:348–49.

the toiling church on earth struggling to victory and the church above in peaceful rest and safety.[34]

RESURRECTION AND THE FINAL STATE

In the biblical view, the body may be spoken of as a "tent" of the soul (2 Cor. 5:1) but not as a prison house, as though the soul were captive in it and longing to be freed. The human soul was not created to exist "naked," apart from the body, and Christian salvation entails renewed and glorified body reunited with the soul. Even though in death God "saves the soul at once utterly," it still awaits "the perfecting of its old companion the body" and the final defeat of that last enemy, death, in resurrection.[35] This will happen, Warfield repeatedly reminds us, as a direct consequence of Christ's own resurrection, but not until he returns (I Cor. 15:22–23).[36]

In Matthew 22:31–32, Jesus offers a seemingly strange defense of the resurrection against the Sadducees: "Have you not read what was said to you by God: 'I am the God of Abraham, and the God of Isaac, and the God of Jacob'? He is not God of the dead, but of the living." It might seem at first glance that this line of argument would establish the doctrine of the continued conscious existence of the soul after death and not the doctrine of the resurrection. But Warfield cautions, "That is simply because we have preferred to be taught by Plato rather than by the Scriptures." In Scripture the departed souls are described as "dead." Consciously existing though they may be, they are referred to as in the realm of the dead. The realm of the "living," Warfield reminds us, refers to life of united body and soul. And so if God is the God of Abraham, and if Abraham is dead, then Abraham must rise again to partake of that life in which body and soul are again united.[37]

The nature of the resurrection body is a theme the apostle Paul takes up in I Corinthians 15:35–50. Paul implies in verse 12 that our resurrection body will be like that of Christ in his resurrection. His body was not only seen and handled, but it was also of real continuity with the body of his death—after all, after his resurrection his tomb was empty! In verses 35–50 the apostle makes clear that there will be a certain continuity of the new body with the old, but there will be certain differences also. The earthly body was suited to life on earth; the resurrection body will be suited to the powerful glories of heaven. Warfield summarizes that in the resurrection, God leaves our body "human but makes it perfect."[38] Accom-

---

[34]W, 2:648–58.
[35]PrS, 330–31.
[36]SSW, 1:200–201; W, 2:618.
[37]SSW, 1:346–47.
[38]W, 2:618–20.

panying the resurrection of the dead will be the transformation of the living, in which, sidestepping death, this mortal body will give way to incorruption and immortality (1 Thess. 4:16–17; 1 Cor. 15:51–55), and mortality will be "swallowed up by life" (2 Cor. 5:4).[39] This will be salvation realized in full—perfected in soul and in body. And this resurrection body, which Paul also describes as a "building from God, a house not made with hands, eternal in the heavens," dwelling with Christ and made like Christ, is the ultimate object of the believer's longing (2 Cor. 5:1–5; Phil. 3:21).

Warfield nowhere addresses the final destiny of the wicked at length. Passing comments, in appropriate contexts, of "condemnation" and such are the extent of his discussion of this topic. He indicates in one devotional passage that punishment is both universal and measured in degrees. Citing Jesus' woes against Bethsaida and Chorizin in Matthew 11:21–22, Warfield comments that all unbelievers are worthy of—and shall receive—judgment, but a much greater judgment will fall to those who have heard of Christ and yet rejected him. "How infinitely solemn a crisis the gospel brings to every city, household, life, to which it gains access! . . . God grant that we have not Chorazin hearts!"[40]

Warfield wrote one article on "Annihilationism," but it is a descriptive and historical study only and does not at all interact critically.[41] Why Wayne House in his *Charts of Christian Theology and Doctrine* classifies Warfield as an annihilationist is not at all clear,[42] but he certainly did not get his information from Warfield. Here and there in his writing, Warfield alludes to the doctrine of eternal punishment and always as a biblical truth. He acknowledges that the human mind recoils against it, but on the basis of Scripture he affirms it.[43] In his 1888 "The New Theology of the Antipodes," he criticizes the new rejection of the biblical doctrine of hell as incompatible with the teaching of Jesus.[44] In an 1895 review he writes, "We should dissent only from [John Miley's] difficulty in discovering rational grounds for the terrible indeed, but, as it seems to us, rationally reasonable, as well as Scripturally certain, doctrine of eternal punishment."[45] In 1888 he charges that the rejection of eternal punishment is rooted in a weak sense of divine justice and of the enormity of human sin, and he asserts that the loss of the doctrine would be too great a sacrifice to Christian theology. In 1890 he broadly refers to all forms of annihilationism as "in hopeless conflict with the

---

[39]W, 2:605, 620.
[40]"How Shall We Escape?" in *Lile's Golden Lamp*, ed. R. M. Offord (New York: *New York Observer*, 1889): n.p. (devotional entry for January 13).
[41]W, 9:447–57.
[42]H. Wayne House, *Charts of Christian Theology and Doctrine* (Grand Rapids: Zondervan, 1992), 139.
[43]W, 1:215 (1893).
[44]"The New Theology in the Antipodes," *The Independent* 40 (Aug 9, 1888): 1006.
[45]SSW, 2:316.

writers of the New Testament." And as late as 1904 he still refers to the lake of fire as "the eternal torment."[46] There is no evidence that Warfield ever wavered from this understanding.

Neither does he at any point address at length his thinking regarding the final state of the redeemed, although he frequently speaks of it in general descriptive terms.[47] Warfield sees it as a time of final inheritance, which he describes as a time of reward for service here (Col. 3:24) and of receiving the approval of Christ.[48] It is "the deposit of life" (2 Tim. 1:12), "the crown of righteousness" (2 Tim. 4:8), freedom from sin (Titus 2:14), and actual inheritance of eternal life (Titus 3:7). It is, in short, "the full realization of what is already enjoyed in its first fruits here or what comes in some abundance in the imperfect intermediate state."[49] Most often he speaks emotively in terms of completed redemption and the enjoyment of sinless perfection in the presence of Christ.[50] Describing that day in broad summary he says:

> That the blessed dead may be fitted to remain for ever with the Lord, He gives them each his own body, glorified and purified and rendered the willing organ of the Holy Ghost. Christ's living, though they die not, are "changed" to a like glory. Not only man, but all creation feels the renovation and shares in the revelation of the sons of God, and there is a new heaven and a new earth. And thus the work of the Redeemer is completed, the end has come, and it is visible to men and angels that through Him in whom it was His pleasure that all the fulness should dwell, God has at length reconciled all things unto Himself, having made peace through the blood of His cross—through Him, whether things upon the earth or things in the heavens— yea, even us, who were in times past alienated and enemies, hath He reconciled in the body of His flesh through death, to present us holy and without blemish and unreproachable before Him.[51]

Summary

Although eschatology is not a subject Warfield addressed at length, he did refer to its themes often and always in passionate terms of longing expectancy. For him, eschatology is soteriology, the culmination of Christ's saving work. He maintained

---

[46]*PR* 9, no. 35 (1888): 510; *ESS*, 62; *PRR* 1, no. 4 (1890): 695; *W*, 2:658–59. Although not explicitly, Warfield expresses similar disapproval with annihilationism in *PRR* 5, no. 19 (1894): 546.
[47]In his "The Revelation of Man" he muses at some length on what it will be, in the end, to be made like Christ, but he provides little explicit detail (*PGS*, 23–25).
[48]*W*, 2:630–31.
[49]*W*, 2:636.
[50]For example, see his "Entire Sanctification," in *FL*, 361–72.
[51]*W*, 2:640.

a deeply expectant optimism regarding the success of the gospel in this age, and he spoke of it often in terms of the culmination of Christ's saving work, whether personally or cosmically considered. He was obviously very deeply influenced by the prospect of the coming glory, particularly the anticipation of being with Christ and enjoying the fulness of promised—and long-awaited—salvation. These themes are common in Warfield even if he did not treat them specifically in detail.

> If you wish, as you lift your eyes to the far horizon of the future, to see looming on the edge of time the glory of a saved world, you can find warrant for so great a vision only in the high principles that it is God and God alone who saves men, that all their salvation is from him, and that in his own good time and way he will bring the world in its entirety to the feet of him whom he has not hesitated to present to our adoring love not merely as the Saviour of our own souls, but as the Saviour of the world; and of whom he has himself declared that he has made propitiation not for our sins only, but for the sins of the world.[52]

---

[52]*PS*, 99.

The truths concerning God and His relations are, above all comparison, in themselves the most worthy of all truths of study and examination. Yet we must vindicate a further goal for the advance of theology and thus contend for it that it is an eminently practical science. The contemplation and exhibition of Christianity as truth, is far from the end of the matter. This truth is specially communicated by God for a purpose, for which it is admirably adapted. That purpose is to save and sanctify the soul. And the discovery, study, and systematization of the truth is in order that, firmly grasping it and thoroughly comprehending it in all its reciprocal relations, we may be able to make the most efficient use of it for its holy purpose. Well worth our most laborious study, then, as it is, for its own sake as mere truth, it becomes not only absorbingly interesting, but inexpressibly precious to us when we bear in mind that the truth with which we thus deal constitutes, as a whole, the engrafted Word that is able to save our souls.

W, 9:79.

13

WARFIELD IN PERSPECTIVE

Warfield in Review

The theological labors of B. B. Warfield touch virtually every department of biblical and theological studies, and the depth and breadth of his grasp have been recognized from his own day to ours. Areas of particular emphasis stand out, however, due primarily to the needs of the day as he perceived them.

As we have seen, the character and authority of Scripture were the defining issue of Warfield's era. Although the bulk of his writings in this connection appeared in the earlier days of his career, it is a theme that reverberates throughout his work, and his contribution to the doctrine of inspiration is acknowledged by all sides. He provided what was to date the most extensive exegetical analysis of the primary passages relating to the doctrine (2 Tim. 3:16; 2 Pet. 1:21; John 10:34–35), thoroughly establishing Scripture as the very word of God. He bolstered this understanding with detailed analyses of the significance of such biblical terminology as "Scripture," "it is written," "it says," the prophetic "thus says the Lord," and of the parallel expressions "Scripture says" and "God says," emphasizing that this traditional view that he expounded was no novelty but in fact the gift of Christ and the apostles to the church. At the same time, he provided again the most thorough exposition of *concursus*, demonstrating that Scripture is *both* a thoroughly divine and a thoroughly human production.

His work on the canon of Scripture has not received as much notice, at least in part because much of it was not republished. But his accounting of the infant church's reception of the twenty-seven books of the New Testament as divine was extensive, and his insistence that the canon was determined by apostolicity deserves further recognition.

It is somewhat surprising that Warfield's doctrine of the Trinity has not received more notice, particularly his discussion of the order and relation of the three persons. Whether accurately or not he brought the notion of αὐτοθεότης to new light. Beyond this his detailed analysis of such expressions as "God our Father and the Lord Jesus Christ" provides solid exegetical grounding for the doctrine of the Trinity and goes a long way toward demonstrating a clearer understanding of the Trinity on the part of the apostolic church than is generally acknowledged.

It seems clear that Warfield's own primary concern was christology, and this as closely tied to soteriology. He roundly condemned and thoroughly discredited all forms of kenoticism, provided massive exegetical demonstration that the divine-human Christ is the only Jesus known to Scripture, and established that there is no other—that is, no nonsupernatural—Jesus known to history. All this was essential, he contended, for both a right worship of God and the accomplishing of our redemption. A supernatural Christ and a supernatural redemption were matters of heaviest concern to Warfield, and these make up the largest segment of his literary contribution.

Another area of recurring emphasis throughout his writings is the necessity of the divine initiative in salvation. Warfield provided sustained treatment of this theme in only a few places, but it is an often repeated emphasis nonetheless. He was eager at all times to preserve the supernaturalness of the Christian experience of grace. This discussion frequently bears also on Warfield's understanding and method of apologetics, another topic of repeated concern but formally in only a few places. There has been considerable misunderstanding of Warfield on this score, particularly in connection with his presumed dependence on the Scottish common sense philosophy and his understanding of the roles of reason and of the Holy Spirit. He has received much criticism on these matters, though more sympathetic interpretations are surely available. Similarly, more attention could be given to his continuity with Calvin along these lines. Warfield was confident that he had not departed from Calvin and that perceived differences were due to differing contexts, and his thinking deserves sympathetic investigation at least. However the details of these discussions may be perceived, Warfield's emphasis on the necessity of the sovereign work of the Spirit dominates.

Warfield's final major publications are given to exposing the errors of the various forms of perfectionist and higher life teachings. He saw these as altogether inconsistent with Reformed—and therefore biblical—theology, and he discounted them on exegetical, theological, and logical grounds. Sanctification, he insisted, is a work of God accomplished in stages. It is not to be accomplished apart from our cooperation in the means of grace. Our struggle with sin will continue as sin is only gradually eradicated in this life, and never fully this side of the grave.

These are the leading areas of emphasis in Warfield's work.

Warfield as a Polemic Theologian

POLEMIC AND SYSTEMATIC

In his memorial address regarding Warfield, Francis Patton remarks that Warfield "was a dogmatic rather than a systematic theologian, and was less interested in the system of doctrine than in the doctrines of the system. It was to the discussion of particular doctrines in connection with the most recent phases of thought that he gave the greater part of his attention."[1] Patton goes on to say that Warfield did not care much "how the materials that enter into a theological system are organized. He cared more about the separate blocks of doctrine than the shape of the building constructed out of them."[2] By contrast, J. I. Packer refers to Warfield's "The Idea of Systematic Theology" as "almost a benchmark account of the discipline."[3]

Patton was a long-time friend of Warfield's, and his observations must be taken seriously. But it is questionable that these remarks represent Warfield accurately. Though Patton was certainly acquainted with Warfield's writings, it does not seem he had read them closely. Warfield demonstrates at several points that he cared very much for the theological system to which his selected doctrinal studies were related. As we have seen, Warfield begins the theological task with apologetical theology, establishing the ground and material for the theologian in the corresponding truths of God and revelation. He makes much of the fact that the system itself is structured logically from apologetics to exegetical theology (culminating in biblical theology), to historical theology, to systematic theology, and finally to practical theology. And often he speaks in reference to the unity of truth, that all truth is God's truth and, because revealed by God, is necessarily unified and organically related. He emphasizes in several places that the perfect system of theology known now only to God shall one day be realized by the human mind also, and that meanwhile we must seek to build that edifice as carefully and as accurately as possible. And he often refers to the Calvinistic system as the purest expression and system of the Christian faith, a system he labored to keep intact throughout his career, discounting any notion that was inconsistent with it at any point. He often reflects also on the historical progress of the church's understanding of theology as a logical progression of the structure of the faith. He complains that Bible teachers such as R. A. Torrey, while teaching doctrines that are generally sound, relied too much on proof-texting and in the process missed

---

[1] Francis L. Patton, "Benjamin Breckinridge Warfield: A Memorial Address," *PTR* 19, no. 3 (1921): 386.
[2] Ibid., 387.
[3] J. I. Packer, "Is Systematic Theology a Mirage? An Introductory Discussion," in *Doing Theology in Today's World: Essays in Honor of Kenneth S. Kantzer*, ed. John D. Woodbridge and Thomas Edward McComiskey (Grand Rapids: Zondervan, 1991), 24.

the depth and the richness of Scripture's systematic presentation of these truths.[4] Often Warfield speaks of the relation of one doctrine to another and of its relation to the larger structure—for example, the appropriate relation of predestination to the doctrine of God and/or the doctrine of salvation, the relation of the doctrine of Scripture to the doctrine of God, the priority of christology to soteriology, and so on. He vindicates the traditional ordering of systematic theology with the doctrine of Scripture at its head, viewing it as the source of our knowledge of God and all related doctrines. He speaks often of the central redemptive nature of Christian faith as reflected in all its various theological branches. And although he heartily agrees with the fundamentalists in their defense of "the five fundamentals," he does not see this as a sufficient summary or defense of the Christian faith—which for him is nothing less than the Calvinistic system of theology. As Machen would say, it was Warfield who enabled him to "see with greater and greater clearness that consistent Christianity is the easiest Christianity to defend, and that consistent Christianity—the only thoroughly Biblical Christianity—is found in the Reformed Faith." Warfield doubtless had his blind spots, but to say that he did not care for the proper structuring of theology is mistaken. Warfield saw both the forest and the trees, and he cared very much to see them in right relation to each other.[5]

It would be interesting to see how Warfield would have arranged a systematic theology, had he written one, and whether it would have differed from Hodge's. He often seems to understand eschatology as a subset of soteriology and soteriology as a subset of christology, for example. That he understood all theology as organically related and interconnected we may be sure. In this volume we have followed Warfield's understanding as closely as possible, treating, in order, prolegomena, bibliology, theology proper, and so on, as is generally typical of Reformed theologies. Patton speculates that it was because of Warfield's (presumed) indifference to theological structure that he never produced a systematic theology of his own. His further remarks are more credible:

> But the strongest reason for Dr. Warfield's failure to write a system of theology is that being himself a pupil of Dr. Charles Hodge he made his *Systematic Theology* the basis of his own teaching. "Forty and six years was this temple in building," and Dr. Warfield was not the man to turn the key in the door of that temple and leave it to the moles and to the bats.[6]

Samuel Craig reports something similar:

---

[4]Review of *What the Bible Teaches*, by R. A. Torrey, *PRR* 10, no. 39 (1899): 562–64; *SSW*, 2:102–3, 674.
[5]David B. Calhoun, *Princeton Seminary*, vol. 2, *The Majestic Testimony 1869–1929* (Carlisle, PA: Banner of Truth, 1996), 226.
[6]Patton, "Memorial Address," 387.

When the writer once asked him why he did not write a Systematic Theology he replied that the time was not ripe for another effort in that direction because of the critical rather than constructive nature of the period in which we were living—a period in which all the principal doctrines of Christianity were being widely called in question if not openly denied. The implication of his reply was that the time would come for a more adequate systematic theology, but that that time had not yet arrived.[7]

Here we have it from Warfield himself that he was content with Hodge's work and did not feel that the time had come for a replacement. This view was not shared by all. Charles Brokenshire, for example, a former student of Warfield's, expressed his own disappointment that Warfield had not updated and replaced the work of Hodge.[8] And, of course, many since have expressed similar sentiments. But Warfield felt that Hodge needed no replacement in his day.

Craig's report, though, offers something that may vindicate Patton in some measure. Warfield was not unconcerned with the theological system, and Patton was mistaken to think otherwise. But Patton was obviously correct in saying that Warfield's attention was given *primarily* to contemporary critical thought. Warfield's remarks to Craig state this exactly, that the need of the day was to refute the critics in their various attacks. Hence, Warfield's works distinguish him as the *polemic* theologian.

That Warfield excelled in his task is obvious to all. His heart and his pen were ready always to give reason for faith, and he steadfastly refused ever to concede ground to naturalism and unbelief. He did not hesitate to oppose perceived theological error from any quarter, even if from his esteemed friends Kuyper and Bavinck. And for this task he came well equipped. Hugh Kerr, who served as Benjamin Breckinridge Warfield Professor of Theology at Princeton, 1950–1974, and who was not especially sympathetic with Warfield's theological position, stated that "Dr. Warfield had the finest mind ever to teach at Princeton Theological Seminary"; and Warfield's younger colleague at Princeton J. Gresham Machen once noted that Warfield "has done about as much work as ten ordinary men."[9] In terms of his range of scholarship and the depth and breadth of his theological grasp, Warfield was second to none. In his own day and still today Warfield is recognized as perhaps the most learned opponent of the old liberalism and of all that smacked of naturalistic tendencies in Christian theology. John Meeter summarizes:

---

[7]*BTS*, xlii.
[8]Brokenshire letter to John Meeter, July 25, 1942.
[9]Cited in *JGM*, 220.

Such is the style in which Warfield, in his writings, reached out from Princeton to the world of theological scholarship, with a mastery of all theological disciplines, surveying the whole range of Christian doctrine and all the changes of church history, responding to critics of the Bible with a learning that overmatched them.[10]

Wilber Wallis, having traced out in broad strokes the progression of Warfield's literary career, offers this summary:

> The major emphasis of Warfield's thought may be traced by decades: 1880–1890 emphasized Biblical foundations; 1890–1900 brought the clash with McGiffert over Christian origins; 1900–1910 was Christological; 1910–1920 logically was concerned with the application of redemption and the theology of the Holy Spirit. No doubt Warfield held the whole grand system from the beginning. It was only as the advance of rationalistic liberalism successively attacked first the Scriptures and then Christ and the salvation accomplished by Him, that Warfield responded with his masterly analysis.[11]

This may be a bit oversimplified, but it does provide a general frame of reference. We should note also that Warfield's earliest years of publication reflected his position as professor of New Testament. Riddlebarger observes:

> It appears to be quite significant that Warfield's first five major published works were in the field of New Testament, and all of them were specially oriented towards defending orthodoxy by using the "latest" critical methodology. Amazingly, between 1880 and 1886, the prolific young professor published at least 60 additional works in New Testament studies, the vast majority of these dealing with the latest developments in textual criticism, New Testament background, word studies and exegetical issues, as well as related Patristic studies.[12]

POLEMIC AND EXEGETICAL

When Warfield moved from the chair of New Testament at Western Theological Seminary to that of systematic theology at Princeton, many lamented the loss to New Testament studies. But his stint in New Testament proved foundational for him. For all his strengths and the breadth of his interests and grasp, perhaps his leading distinction is that he was first and foremost an exegetical theologian. His work and reputation as a polemicist and apologist may obscure this fact to those

---

[10]*SSW*, I:xiv.

[11]"Benjamin B. Warfield, Didactic and Polemic Theologian," part 2, *Covenant Seminary Review* 3 (1977): 90–91.

[12]Kim Riddlebarger, "The Lion of Princeton: Benjamin Breckinridge Warfield on Apologetics, Theological Method and Polemics" (PhD diss., Fuller Theological Seminary, 1997), 59.

who have not read him extensively, but all of Warfield's work was undergirded by a careful handling of the biblical text. Two outstanding examples of this are the massive exegetical undergirding he gave to the doctrine of the incarnation and two natures of Christ and to the doctrine of inspiration. In the history of both of these doctrines Warfield stands as the high-water mark, and his assault on kenoticism and the critical views of Scripture was exegetically profound and recognized as such by all sides.

A comparison of Warfield to his teacher Charles Hodge illustrates the point well. Warfield seemed to be aware of very little theological difference between him and his venerated predecessor and, as we have seen, saw no need to replace Hodge's textbook in systematic theology. He used the three volumes of Hodge happily. Yet when Warfield wrote his reminiscences of Hodge, he commented that although Hodge always comes to the right conclusions, his exegesis is not at all his strength. Warfield loved and revered his teacher deeply, and his comment reflects no disrespect of any kind. But it illustrates the difference between the two highly esteemed Princetonians. Hodge was first a theologian; Warfield was first an exegete. The one was a theologian who did exegesis; the other was an exegete who did theology. This, doubtless, is what Francis Patton intended to affirm when he remarked that Warfield "combined in rare degree the widely different attainments of Charles Hodge and Addison Alexander." John Mackay summarizes it well: "In all his dogmatics Dr. Warfield is supremely the exegete. His dogmatics is but exegesis of the superlative kind."[13]

Warfield's polemical work, however, entails more than biblical exegesis only, and historical theology is another of his obvious strengths. His universal grasp of the history of the doctrine of the Holy Spirit and its related literature, as we saw in chapter 8, illustrates his acquaintance with the history of doctrine. His works on Tertullian, Augustine, Calvin, the Westminster Assembly and divines, Finney, Edwards, inspiration, perfectionism, Pelagianism, infant salvation, and Ritschlian liberalism all display a similar interest in and grasp of the history of Christian thought.[14]

POLEMIC AND CONFIDENT

But it was more than his intellectual abilities and broad scholarship that brought Warfield to theological battle. Warfield's work begins with a settled conviction

---

[13]B. B. Warfield, "Charles Hodge as a Teacher of Exegesis," in A. A. Hodge, *The Life of Charles Hodge, D.D., LL.D.* (London: T. Nelson and Sons, 1881), 588–91; John Mackay, "Benjamin B. Warfield: A Bibliography," *The Expositor*, 24 (8th series, 1922): 33; *JGM*, 67.

[14]On Warfield's work in historical theology, see James McClanahan, "Benjamin B. Warfield: Historian of Doctrine in Defense of Orthodoxy" (PhD diss., Union Theological Seminary, 1988).

that God's Word is, in fact, true. And he insists that the only attitude appropriate toward a divinely revealed body of truth is that of confidence—indeed, even dogmatic confidence.[15] In language that anticipated the postmodern discussion, Warfield insists on the reality of objective truth and scorns those to whom the idea of truth is offensive. And he insists also that truth out of vogue is truth still. And for him truth centers in and is measured by God's Word. Even triumphantly at times he champions the doctrine that Scripture is true. Hugh Kerr characterizes Warfield's response to liberalism as that of "deadly fear" and "panic."[16] This not-so-subtle slur is typical of those who do not share his theological commitments and therefore do not understand his heart to contend for the faith or his utter confidence in it. But it is a complete misunderstanding of Warfield. The absolute truthfulness of Scripture is a theme Warfield emphasized since his very first publication in 1876. His battle for doctrine, he was deeply convinced, was a battle for truth—truth that, precisely because it is truth, will triumph in the end. Indeed, the advance of this truth will continue, Warfield often emphasized in keeping with his eschatological views, until by it the whole world is saved. Moreover, he argued, his resolved "dogmatism" was the only "appropriate attitude toward a body of truth given by revelation, and committed to men only to embrace, cherish, preserve, and propagate." The problem of his day, he complained, was that men "would discuss rather than receive truth." But for him, the Christian can take his stand in Scripture with complete confidence. "It may sometimes seem difficult to take our stand frankly by the side of Christ and his apostles," Warfield acknowledged. But he added, "It will always be found safe." The Christian must never concede the teachings of Scripture but rather "look out upon the seething thought of the world from the safe standpoint of the sure Word of God," which is "the only really solid basis of all . . . thinking." This is the ground, the basic presupposition, of which Warfield was deeply convinced: God's Word is truth, and adhering to its teaching we can never be proven wrong.[17]

It was this settled confidence that Christianity is "the truth" that undergirded Warfield's understanding of the role of apologetics and that guided his polemic career. Because Christianity is the truth exclusively revealed by God, it is not only reasonable but "the only reasonable religion." It is by its very nature an "aggressive religion," and its objective is by its exclusive "right reason" to "reason itself into the acceptance of the world." Engaging this inevitable controversy, "it

---

[15]SSW, 2:663.
[16]Hugh T. Kerr, "Warfield: The Person Behind the Theology," PSB 25, new series, no. 1 (1994): 88–89; cf. Lefferts A. Loetscher, The Broadening Church (Philadelphia: University of Pennsylvania Press, 1954), 10; SSW, 2:213–18.
[17]SSW, 2:109, 663–67; W, 1:73–74, 215–16, 421–23; cf. 180; SSW, 2:674–75.

stands calmly over against the world with its credentials in its hands, and fears no contention of men." Far from fearful, Christianity has every warrant to be on the offensive. It can never concede and cannot even be content with a defensive posture but must remain on the assault, inevitably progressing toward complete dominion. Precisely because Jesus is "incarnate truth," Warfield confidently affirms, no truth will ever contradict him or the religion he founded. Precisely because something is found to be true, it can never be found to be inconsistent with him. With a firm understanding of this, the Christian need never fear the tools of investigation that are brought against the faith but rather "cultivate an attitude of courage." None should be more confident and zealous with the new tools of research than we.[18]

Never fearful of scholarship, Warfield was very open both to progressive understanding of doctrine and to fresh expressions of it. He himself was unsurpassed in his learning of all the modern scholarly tools of investigation. He counsels that the Christian must never "assume an attitude of antagonism toward the truths of reason, or the truths of philosophy, or the truths of science, or the truths of history, or the truths of criticism. As children of the light, we must be careful to keep ourselves open to every ray of light." Warfield welcomed new investigations of truth and any new knowledge that came from them. But he would not allow "findings" that conflict with revealed doctrine to stand as true. New findings may drive us to reevaluate our beliefs, but we must not allow new "findings" to overthrow revealed truth. The faith of the church had been delivered to her "once for all" (Jude 3) by the apostles and prophets, and it is the solemn duty of the church to preserve that which had been committed to her and remain "the pillar and ground of the truth" (1 Tim. 3:15 KJV). Warfield was deeply convinced that the faith of the church had been given to her from her Lord via his apostles and that all her related doctrines are objectively true. New understanding of revealed truth we should pursue zealously and expect. But we can make no concessions to ideas that contradict the sure Word of God. "We may be sure that the old faith will be able not merely to live with, but to assimilate to itself all facts."[19]

> We do not say that people in glass houses shouldn't throw stones. We are glad they are throwing stones and we should be happy to encourage them in it. After all, the thing to do is to get the glass-houses all smashed; and this mutual stone-throwing is likely to accomplish that desirable end, and is therefore to be heartily welcomed

---

[18]*SSW*, 2:99–100, 119–21, 213–18, 463–64.
[19]*SSW*, 2:124–31, 213–18, 463–64, 672–79; *ESS*, 165.

by us. There is a house, not glass, built on the rock: when the stone throwing is all over it is likely that this house will be found standing alone.[20]

Illustrating this confidence, in his 1900 article surveying "The Century's Progress in Biblical Knowledge," Warfield makes reference to the fear of some Christians at the dawn of that century. But with a note of confident triumph he observes that in the wake of all the century's critical assaults on the faith, biblical knowledge has yet increased, and truth has made its greatest advance. It was the century of greatest attack on Scripture and yet the century of greatest progress of biblical knowledge.

> It [the nineteenth century] received the Bible from the dead hands of eighteenth century rationalism into hands that were cold with fear; it hands it on to the twentieth century with the courage of assured conviction. It has not been a century of quiet and undisturbed study of the Bible. Fierce controversies have raged throughout its whole length. But fierce controversies can rage only where strong convictions burn. And amid, or rather by means of, all these controversies knowledge has increased; and after them all we can only lay our hands on our mouths and say: "God fulfills himself in many ways." The very wrath of man has come to praise him in this sphere too; and the Bible has emerged from these fires, as out of all others, without so much as the smell of smoke upon its very garments.[21]

Similarly, in his 1898 article describing "Recent Reconstructions of Theology," Warfield laments the prevailing rejection of the authority of divine revelation in Scripture and the accompanying denigration of Christ in the popular kenotic theories of the day. But in his conclusion he emphasizes strongly that he is describing "tendencies" only; he is not predicting the future. To the contrary, he is assured that the truth of the historic faith will never be discredited. "I fall back gladly" on the assurances of the biblical writers, he says,

> that God will not permit his truth to perish out of the earth. . . . It is one thing to say that the current theologizing is in the direction of Rationalism, Naturalism, Socinianism; and another thing to say that Christianity is to sink in that slough. After all, the divine Christ is not abolished because men bid us cease to reverence him, or the Christian system of truth destroyed because men ask us no longer to believe it, or the divine Word robbed of its power because we are warned no longer to bow to its authority. Men may come and men may go, but these are things that abide forever.[22]

---

[20]"The Angel of Jehovah and Critical Views," *TBS* 8, no. 1 (July 1903): 60.
[21]*SSW*, 2:13.
[22]*SSW*, 2:103, 298–99.

In short, Warfield insisted that there is such a thing as truth and error, a. him it was simple: God's Word is truth, and all conflicting ideas are error. Thus, with the advance of knowledge, Warfield expected new criticisms and challenges of things previously held to be true. At several points in his writings he welcomes and champions the right of criticism as necessary to determining truth. But this is not to say that once a belief comes under criticism, it can no longer be held. "If we are of such sensitive disposition that we dare not assert or believe to be true what some acute or learned critic affirms to be impossible, we may as well strip off at once all our Christian garments. . . . There is nothing that has not been criticized." The problem with the prevailing biblical criticism is a flawed presupposition that determines ahead of time its supposed findings. It assumes the impossibility of that which it attempts to disprove. That is, the critics' attack on the supernatural is grounded on the assumption of invariable natural law, and it will not allow into consideration any evidence to the contrary. And so, Warfield observes, "With a truly Herod-like indifference they have murdered a host of innocent facts which stood in the way of their purposes." Yet after all this, Warfield insists, the supernaturalism of Scripture remains the more vindicated.[23] It was the exposing of these flaws and the vindication of Scripture's truth claims that characterized Warfield's career.

Warfield's Center

Warfield argued from the assumption that what Scripture teaches is demonstrably true. The next question has more to do with motive. What was Warfield seeking to accomplish in his polemic? Why were the chosen topics of importance to him? What was it about that truth that drove him to vindicate it not only with such scholarly rigor but with such persistence, vigor, and passion? Or, more simply, who was B. B. Warfield?

WARFIELD'S THEOLOGICAL COMMITMENTS

Warfield's theological commitments were, very simply, those of Westminster confessional Calvinism. This, he was convinced, was the purest expression of the Christian faith ever penned by human hand, "the ripened fruit of Reformed confession making."[24] This system of doctrine, he says,

---

[23]*SSW*, 2:9, 124–25, 127, 129–31, 595–96; cf. *SSW*, 2:167–204.
[24]*SSW*, 2:660; cf. *PRR* 8, no. 30 (1897): 355.

is the only system in which the whole order of the world is brought into a rational unity with the doctrine of grace. . . . It is only with such a universal conception of God, established in a living way, that we can face, with hope of complete conquest, all the spiritual dangers and terrors of our time. . . . But it is deep enough and large enough and divine enough, rightly understood, to confront them and do battle with them all in vindication of the Creator, Preserver, and Governor of the world, and of the Justice and Love of the Divine Personality.[25]

Warfield understands the formative idea of Calvinism to be its conception of God. The Calvinistic system of theology seeks first to give full recognition to God as God over all, the Lord almighty. This, Warfield loved to say, is but the essence of religion. Religion has to do with the relation of God and his creatures, and religion at its height is found in a due recognition of God as ruler over all and in our sense of utter dependence upon him. No system of theology better fosters this religious sense, Warfield says, than Calvinism. But all this is to imply a redemptive focus, and in fact Warfield describes Calvinism in soteriological terms. This God who is sovereign over all is no less sovereign in the salvation of sinners, and because of this distinct emphasis, this system of doctrine best serves to engender worship and a sense of humble dependence on him.[26]

Moreover, basic to the Calvinistic system, as we have seen, is the idea of supernaturalism. As he famously argues in his *Plan of Salvation*, if supernaturalism, then Christianity—Christianity in its biblical and historic expression and Christianity in its deepest evangelical and Reformed piety and most profound sense of dependence upon God.

The religion of the Bible is a frankly supernatural religion. By this is not meant merely that, according to it, all men, as creatures, live, move and have their being in God. It is meant that, according to it, God has intervened extraordinarily, in the course of the sinful world's development, for the salvation of men otherwise lost.[27]

WARFIELD'S UNDERSTANDING OF THE NATURE OF CHRISTIANITY

Probing deeper, Warfield understands Christianity as specifically a redemptive religion. At its very heart this is what Christianity means. This is a prominent theme in Warfield, but we will cite only a few samples.

---

[25]*W*, 5:366.
[26]*SSW*, 2:411–32.
[27]*W*, 1:3.

It is fundamental to the very conception of Christianity that it is a remedial scheme. Christ Jesus came to save sinners. The first Christians had no difficulty in under-standing and confessing that Christ had come into a world lost in sin to establish a kingdom of righteousness, citizenship in which is the condition of salvation.[28]

By "the fundamental theology of the Church" is meant especially the Church's con-fession of that series of the redemptive acts of God, by which he has supernaturally intervened in human history for the salvation of sinful man. . . . The message of Christianity concerns, not "the values of human life," but the grace of the saving God in Christ Jesus. And in proportion as the grace of the saving God in Christ Jesus is obscured or passes into the background, in that proportion does Christianity slip from our grasp. Christianity is summed up in the phrase: "God was in Christ, reconciling the world with himself." Where this great confession is contradicted or neglected, there is no Christianity.[29]

It belongs to the very essence of the type of Christianity propagated by the Reforma-tion that the believer should feel himself continuously unworthy of the grace by which he lives. At the center of this type of Christianity lies the contrast of sin and grace; and about this center everything else revolves.[30]

Again, he says crisply in summary, "A Christianity without redemption— redemption in the blood of Jesus Christ as a sacrifice for sin—is nothing less than a contradiction in terms. Precisely what Christianity means is redemption in the blood of Jesus." Elsewhere Warfield describes the incarnation as "the very core of Christianity," and this precisely because Christianity is first and foremost a redemptive religion. The incarnation has "sin as its occasion" and "salvation as its end"—"Christ came into the world to save sinners." Warfield insists that it is not Christ's prophetic or kingly office that is central but his priestly, his work of sacrifice.[31] And he argues at length in "The Essence of Christianity and the Cross of Christ" that no religious system that depreciates this redemptive focus is worthy of the name Christian. Accordingly, Warfield summarizes:

Were I asked to name the three pillars on which the structure of Christianity, as taught in the New Testament in its entirety, especially rests, I do not know that I could do better than point to these three things: the supernatural, the incarnation, redemption. In an important sense, these three things constitute the Christianity

---

[28]W, 9:411.
[29]SSW, 1:50.
[30]W, 7:113.
[31]W, 3:357–58; SSW, 1:140–41; Harkness, class notes, 38; cf. W, 3:435–40.

of the New Testament; proceeding from the more general to the more specific, they sum up in themselves its essence.[32]

Similarly, Warfield emphasizes that the study of the Trinity is but a study of God's self-revelation in the outworking of his redemptive purpose. That is to say, the revelation of the three-in-oneness of God is itself a gospel revelation made known only in the unfolding of his saving plan. Indeed, he understands divine revelation as itself a redemptive act and defines it as God's extraordinary intervention in human history "for the salvation of men otherwise lost."[33]

Warfield continues this theme in his discussion of the theological enterprise. He describes systematic theology as "the saving truth of God presented in systematic form." That is, Christian theology viewed as a whole is soteric. Systematic theology exists for this purpose, "to make wise unto salvation." The goal of the theological sciences, he says, is the knowledge of God. "No single Christian doctrine has been revealed to men merely as a tenet in philosophy, to make them wise; each and every one is sent to them as a piece of glad tidings that they may be made wise unto salvation." Thus, while on the one hand Warfield can describe systematic theology as having "the right to reign" or as being the "capstone," the "culminating department," and "queen" of the theological disciplines, he nonetheless insists that "doctrine is in order to life" and that, therefore, the theological enterprise finds its goal in practical theology. The systematic theologian, Warfield insists, is first and foremost "a preacher of the gospel."[34]

> If such be the value and use of doctrine, the systematic theologian is preeminently a preacher of the gospel; and the end of his work is obviously not merely the logical arrangement of the truths which come under his hand, but the moving of men, through their power, to love God with all their hearts and their neighbors as themselves; to choose their portion with the Saviour of their souls; to find and hold Him precious; and to recognize and yield to the sweet influences of the Holy Spirit whom He has sent. With such truth as this he will not dare to deal in a cold and merely scientific spirit, but will justly and necessarily permit its preciousness and its practical destination to determine the spirit in which he handles it, and to awaken the reverential love with which alone he should investigate its reciprocal relations.[35]

These kinds of examples from Warfield could continue at length. It was for him a regular point of emphasis that Christianity is in its very essence and meaning

---

[32] W, 3:450.
[33] SSW, 1:69–70; W, 1:3, 12–13.
[34] W, 9:5, 65, 74, 85–86, 91–92, 220–21; SSW, 2:209–11, 220, 258, 281, 288.
[35] W, 9:86.

a redemptive religion, a religion for sinners. The saving love of God for sinners is not only "the main theme of the Bible," and not only does God's self-revelation climax in the revelation of his saving grace, and not only does Christianity provide the only rescue for sinners, but Christianity is by definition a redemptive scheme divinely wrought. This is why Calvinism and supernaturalism must be maintained at all costs, because anything less deteriorates the redemptive character of the faith.[36]

WARFIELD THE CHRISTIAN

Warfield very clearly viewed himself in just these terms. He is well known as the great polemic theologian of Old Princeton Seminary. He is also well known as the great exponent of the inspiration and authority of Scripture. Accurate as these pieces of biographical data are, however, neither captures the heart of this Princetonian. Professionally, Warfield was first and foremost a christologian. Personally, he was above all else, a Christian. Theologically and experientially he knew himself to be a sinner rescued by a divine Savior, and this theme is the heartthrob that pulses through all his varied works. At his own theological center was the heart of a helpless sinner rescued by divine grace.

Samuel Craig, who was well acquainted with Warfield himself and his writings, alludes to this in passing:

> What most impresses the student of Warfield's writings apart from his deeply religious spirit, his sense of complete dependence on God for all things including especially his sense of indebtedness as a lost sinner to His free grace—is the breadth of his learning and the exactness of his scholarship.[37]

Mark Noll captures this well also:

> Although Warfield is today better known for his views on the Bible, a solid case can be constructed on the basis of his own works that his commitment to classic Protestantism was deeper and more comprehensive than even his commitment to biblical inerrancy as such. By this classic Protestantism, Warfield meant commitment to an Augustinian view of God, the sinful human condition, and salvation in Christ, but also a broadly open acceptance of the world as the arena of God's creative activity. For Warfield, the heart of both theology and active religion was the glory of God, who rescued sinful humans from self-imposed destruction and who

---

[36]*SSW*, 2:718; *SSW*, 1:82–87; *W*, 2:144.
[37]*BTS*, xvii.

enabled them to share his work of the kingdom in every sphere of life, including the natural world.[38]

Everywhere in Warfield's works is reflected not only his understanding of Christianity as a redemptive religion but also his own personal appreciation of that truth. Warfield saw himself first as one rescued by divine grace. He was no follower of Schleiermacher, of course, but he nonetheless loved to describe pure religion and Christian theology in terms of "absolute dependence" upon the mercy of God in Christ. This was a favorite Warfield theme.[39] At bottom, this is why supernaturalism was so important to Warfield: it meant redemption, the only redemption available to lost sinners. And ultimately this is what drove him in his polemic on every front. We learn from the example of the apostle Paul, he says, that "it is not a matter of small importance whether we preserve the purity of the gospel." The servant of Christ seeks to please not men but Christ. And the fact that we must keep before us is that the gospel must be maintained in its purity precisely because in Christ alone is salvation found. Apologetics is important in order to establish the grounds on which a sinner can be challenged to repent and believe the gospel. Naturalism must be discredited, because it ultimately destroys redemption and with it the foundation of the Christian's ground of hope. Likewise a "Christianity" so committed to naturalism that it rejects the resurrection of Christ is a Christianity we can "do very well without." It not only is foreign to Scripture but has nothing to offer sinners in need of salvation. The incarnation of the second person was only because of sin and in order to save, and the damage that is done by any of the ancient or modern christological heresies is that in one way or another they will render Christ disqualified as a redeeming substitute or otherwise leave us without a Savior. The doctrine of revelation is of redemptive importance also, for "how shall we be advantaged by a supernatural redemption of which we know nothing?" And who is competent to reveal and explain the meaning of God's redemptive acts but God himself?[40] Similarly, the doctrine of Scripture is important because the Christian owes his salvation to it.

> And may it not be fairly doubted whether you and I,—however it may have been with others,—would have had Christ had there been no Bible? . . . No: whatever might possibly have been had there been no Bible, it is actually to the Bible that you and I

---

[38]Introduction to *BBW*, 10.
[39]E.g., *PGS*, 238, 242–47; *PS*, 69–70; *W*, 2:240, 411; *W*, 4:128, 274, 304; *W*, 5:355–56, 357, 359; *W*, 7:119, *W*, 9:118, 263, 430, 465.
[40]*SSW*, 2:663–67; David P. Smith, "The Scientifically Constructive Scholarship of B. B. Warfield" (PhD diss., Trinity International University, 2009), 14; *SSW*, 1:201–2; *W*, 9:41–43.

owe it that we have a Christ,—a Christ to love, to trust and to follow, a Christ without us the ground of our salvation, a Christ within us the hope of glory.[41]

The inerrancy question, important as it is in itself, is further essential to a redemptive Christianity.

> The issue raised is whether we are to look upon the Bible as containing a divinely guaranteed and wholly trustworthy account of God's redemptive revelation . . . or as merely a mass of more or less trustworthy materials, out of which we are to sift the facts in order to put together a trustworthy account of God's redemptive revelation.[42]

To allow that biblical accounts of history are but legends will never do, for it will leave us with a mythical god also and, therefore, without a Savior.

> If indeed we can be satisfied with an imaginary God, legends will suffice for all our needs. But if we need a real God, who really intervenes in this sinful world, to save his people from their sins, we can never find him in any legend or learn from any legend how he has acted or may be expected to act. A legend can give us only what a legend contains—the imagination of a human heart. God—our real God—speaks to us out of a history, which is like himself, real.[43]

Warfield often took opportunity to discredit Pelagianism, but it was no mere party spirit that drove him to do so. His motive was shaped ultimately by this concern, that Pelagianism strips Christianity of its supernaturalism, ruins grace, destroys salvation, and robs God of the glory due him in redemption. Likewise, the evil of sacerdotalism is that it misdirects the person's sense of dependence to the church rather than immediately to God. Similarly, when he considered the contemporary opinion that justification by faith is "out of date," he cautioned that the real loss in such a case is that there is no gospel of salvation remaining at all, and if no gospel, no rescue for sinners. Warfield's extensive criticism of perfectionist teachings turned on this concern also: "The moment we think that we have no sin, we shall desert Christ." This concern is reflected in Warfield's eschatology also, for eschatology is nothing less than the study of the culmination of the saving work of Christ. Warfield saw the end times as a grand display

---

[41] W, 1:72–73.
[42] SSW, 2:581–82.
[43] "Fact or Fiction?" *The Presbyterian* 76, no. 37 (1906): 5.

of the success of the gospel in the host of individuals—humanity itself and the whole world with it—brought to glory.[44]

One more passage from Warfield should be mentioned to illustrate his motivation in his polemic against unbelief. In 1914, Robert Scott and George Gilmore edited a book in which over a hundred well-known theologians each contributed a chapter. Each man was asked if it would be helpful, in order to bring the disinterested and alienated back to the church, to follow Abraham Lincoln's suggestion that we establish as the "sole qualification for membership" the brief statement of Christ, "Thou shalt love the Lord thy God with all thy heart, and with all thy soul, and with all thy mind, and thy neighbor as thyself."[45] Harnack and Warfield were among the theologians who responded. Harnack's reply predictably expresses general agreement with Lincoln, as do others'. By contrast, Warfield's answer begins with a reminder that

> Christianity addresses itself only to sinners. Its Founder himself declared that he did not come to call the righteous but sinners; and its chief expounder declared with energetic emphasis that Christ Jesus came into the world to save sinners. . . . Christianity makes no appeal to men who do not feel the burden of sin.

Jesus' summary command to love, important as it is, Warfield insists, does not address Christianity's central concern.

> The moment a church took up such as position [as Lincoln suggests], it would cease to be a Christian Church: the core of Christianity is its provision for salvation from sin. No doubt by the adoption of such a platform many would be recovered to the Church who now stand aloof from it. But this would be not because the world had been brought into the Church, but because the Church had been merged into the world. The offense of Christianity has always been the cross. . . . It would be easy to remove the offense by abolishing the cross. But that would be to abolish Christianity. Christianity is the cross; and he who makes the cross of Christ of none effect eviscerates Christianity. What Christianity brings to the world is not the bare command to love God and our neighbor. The world needs no such command; nature itself teaches the duty. What the world needs is the power to perform this duty, with respect to which it is impotent. And this power Christianity brings it in the redemption of the Son of God and the renewal of the Holy Ghost.[46]

---

[44]SSW, 1:283–84; W, 7:129; SSW, 1:348–55; PS, 66.
[45]Robert Scott and George William Gilmore, *The Church, the People, and the Age* (New York: Funk and Wagnalls, 1914).
[46]SSW, 1:46–47.

The real tragedy of liberal theology, as Warfield saw it, is that it leaves the world without an incarnate and redeeming God, without a substitute to take our sin, without a Spirit to bring us life, and without a reliable, inspired Word to tell us of our saving God. Whether the error be Ritschlian liberalism on the one hand or evangelical perfectionism on the other, Warfield perceived each as eroding not only a system of interrelated doctrine but the gospel itself and a plan of redemption desperately needed by fallen sinners.

Certainly it is beyond coincidence that redemption in Christ was the subject of Warfield's final lecture. One of his students reports it for us:

> On a crisp day in February, 1921, B. B. Warfield after a six weeks' illness, returned to his class for his final lecture. Due to his weakness he asked to be excused from his usual custom of standing to lead an opening prayer, but plunged into a glowing exposition of the third chapter of First John. The discourse quickly gathered about the sixteenth verse as a center. All the eloquence of his Christian heart, all the wisdom of his ripened scholarship focused on the interpretation of that text. "The laying down of His life in our stead was a great thing," said the Doctor, "but the wonder of the text is that He being all that He was, the Lord of glory, laid down His life for us, being what we are, mere creatures of His hand, guilty sinners deserving His wrath."[47]

Without doubt, here we have reached the heart of B. B. Warfield: in a Reformed theology taken to heart and giving rise to the best of Reformed piety—a warm and humble dependence upon the saving grace of God in Christ. Warfield is often known and referred to as the pugilist, the polemicist, or the apologist, and these descriptions are of course accurate as far as they go. His literary output was largely polemic. But these descriptions can also be misleading in that they obscure Warfield's motivation in it all. Warfield did not enter the fray merely out of penchant for debate. At his heart of hearts he cherished a redemptive Christianity, and he could not bear to allow *that* Christianity to be set aside in any degree.

WARFIELD THE AFFECTIONATE THEOLOGIAN

Moving one step further, this redemptive center shows itself in the tones of heartfelt Christian devotion that mark Warfield's work. Warfield's brilliant mind and his broad, careful scholarship have sometimes left him with the reputation of the stereotypical ivory tower scholar, overoccupied with and overconfident in purely intellectual pursuits. Sydney Ahlstrom, for example, characterized the

---

[47]William Childs Robinson, *Our Lord: An Affirmation of the Deity of Christ* (Grand Rapids: Eerdmans, 1937), 123.

Old Princeton theology as "lifeless."[48] But this perception of Warfield is lopsided, and it misses entirely the fulness of Warfield's thinking and writing. No one who has read Warfield widely could be left with such an impression. Warfield said of Calvin, "It was not the head but the heart which made him a theologian, and it is not the head but the heart which he primarily addresses in his theology."[49] So also Warfield—he was a theologian of the heart. His heart beat hot for the things of God, and this passion bleeds through everywhere. He may not have been as noted for revivalistic piety as was Alexander, and he certainly was not as closely acquainted with it—although he did experience a revival while an undergraduate student at Princeton, one that left a deep and lasting impression. He was not as taken with ecclesiastical issues as were Alexander and Hodge. And Mark Noll may not have overstated the matter in saying that "Warfield did not have the pastoral or ecclesiastical instincts as Alexander or Hodge."[50] But such characterizations, alone, can be misleading. Sinclair Ferguson captures Warfield better when he writes: "Warfield, however, was not *exclusively* a scholar. Indeed, for all his learning, he was not even *primarily* a scholar. He was first and foremost a Christian and a minister of the gospel."[51] This, as we have seen, is how Warfield perceives the theologian—he is a preacher of the gospel. And throughout Warfield's sermons and even his most learned articles there is reflected a heart inflamed by gospel truth and taken up with passionate communion with God and an exulting in the blessedness of belonging to Christ. We have seen samples of this throughout this work; one more will suffice for our purposes here. Writing of Jesus' parable of the prodigal son (Luke 15:11–32), Warfield comments:

> To lost sinners like you and me, assuredly few messages could appeal with more overwhelming force. Our hearts are wrung within us as we are made to realize that our Father in heaven will receive our wandering souls back with the joy with which this father in the parable received back his errant son.

This tone is everywhere in Warfield's works. He is indeed convinced of the objective and demonstrable truth of the historic Christian faith, but the subjective entailments of these truths are of utmost importance to him also. Very decidedly he will have neither without the other. He deplores the fact that there are men whose study seems to go no deeper than the academic, and he exhorts his students accordingly. The ministry is a learned profession, and the minister must be

---

[48]Sydney Ahlstrom, "The Scottish Philosophy and American Theology," *Church History* 24, no. 3 (1955), 269.
[49]*W*, 5:23.
[50]David Wells, ed., *Reformed Theology in America: A History of Its Modern Development* (1985; repr., Grand Rapids: Baker, 1997), 16–17.
[51]"Introductory Word" to *HS*, 5 (emphasis original).

learned but "apt to *teach*." Still he says, "Before and above being learned, a minister must be godly." Yet neither will he allow a bare piety without sound theological grounding. He sums this up in a famous passage weighing the respective value of prayer and study.[52]

> Sometimes we hear it said that ten minutes on your knees will give you a truer, deeper, more operative knowledge of God than ten hours over your books. "What!" is the appropriate response, "than ten hours over your books, on your knees?" Why should you turn from God when you turn to your books, or feel that you must turn from your books in order to turn to God? If learning and devotion are as antagonistic as that, then the intellectual life is in itself accursed, and there can be no question of a religious life for a student, even of theology. The mere fact that he is a student hinders him. . . . In your case there can be no "either—or" here—either a student or a man of God. You must be both.[53]

For Warfield the intellectual formulations of theology are important in one respect because they give rise to and shape religious experience. He chides the Christian mystics and liberals alike for arguing that historic Christian doctrine should be discarded, yet that Christian experience and piety are the highest of all religions. They overlook that the touchstone of Christianity is that it is revealed religion. As such it has a doctrinal framework, and it is this, its teaching, that gives Christianity its superior piety and experience. Of course he also stresses that academic learning apart from a heart of zeal fueled by love for God is useless. He emphasizes further that it is the supernatural working of the Spirit of God that enables us to love God and to grasp and therefore enjoy the truths of the Christian faith. The Holy Spirit bears witness with our spirits that we are God's children. This is indispensable also, and Warfield revels in the great work of the Holy Spirit in the believer. But he insists that the Spirit does not work in a vacuum: he works by the Word. Truth by itself will not suffice—truth is not finally understood until it is lived and experienced. Warfield insists on this also. He will surrender neither doctrine nor experience. There is no genuinely Christian experience apart from truth, and it is this depth of Christian experience that characterizes Warfield throughout his writings. If he argues for an inerrant Bible, it is to find in it certain truth about the God whom we can trust. If he explores the mysteries of the Trinity, it is to deepen worship. If he argues for the Calvinistic doctrine of predestination, he finds in it cause for praise and comfort and assurance. If he argues for a clear understanding of the two natures of Christ, it is to

---

[52] *SSW*, 1:369–73, 412; *SSW*, 2:468–96; *SW*, 4.
[53] *SSW*, 1:412.

rest in a uniquely qualified Redeemer and to know and glory in the greatness of his condescending love; only an informed reflection on the redeeming grace of the incarnation "more ardently kindles the affection of faith." If he argues against Pelagian and Arminian and for Calvinistic views of humanity and salvation, it is to heighten our sense of dependence upon and appreciation for divine grace and thereby cultivate piety that is distinctly and thoroughly Christian. If he argues for justification by faith, it is because in no other place can the conscience find rest and be at peace with God and enjoy fellowship with him. When he reads the narrative of Jesus' trials, he highlights not simply the evil of humanity as displayed in Pilate, the priests, and the mob; rather, he adores the contrasting perfections of the One they condemn. For Warfield the academic study of Scripture is to be not only a means to minister to others but also "a religious exercise out of which you draw every day enlargement of heart, elevation of spirit, and adoring delight in your Maker and your Savior."[54]

The "Plan" of the seminary drawn up at its inception combined the goals of the best of academic scholarship and the deepest of devotional piety. Warfield modeled this ideal famously. His personal godliness was prominently noted by those who knew him, and it is unmistakable in his writings. And this godliness was specifically a gospel-shaped piety, cultivated by a mind steeped in Reformed orthodox thought, and characterized by a deep sense of dependence and gratitude. He was, in his heart of hearts, a sinner rescued by divine grace, and it is this consideration that seems to have driven both his devotional life and his polemic endeavors.

Warfield's Contribution

WARFIELD THE REVERED GIANT

In a memorial address, Francis Patton, Warfield's long time colleague at Princeton, eulogized, "It is difficult, of course, to estimate the influence he exerted in this way, but geographically speaking it was widely extended, and I may be pardoned perhaps for saying somewhat extravagantly that his line has gone out into all the earth and his words to the end of the world."[55] Patton proceeded to speak of the continuing effort of the church to construct a perfect theology, and said, "I venture the prediction that some of the choicest stones in that new building will be those which have been hewn and shaped in the Warfield quarry." Charles

---

[54]*FL*, 179–92; *SSW*, 1:146–47, 417, 668, 671; *SSW*, 2:219–79, 468–96, 688–92.
[55]Patton, "Memorial Address," 371.

Brokenshire, a student of Warfield's at Princeton and later a theologian himself, wrote with similar optimism: "Warfield's expositions will live essentially as long as the Word of God is studied and believed and its authority candidly and completely accepted."[56]

In his own day Warfield was recognized as a theological giant. A search through the old theological journals of the day demonstrates very quickly that he was the authority to reference on a wide range of issues. Others expressed disagreement with him only carefully and, with the exception of his most bitter opponents, always with great respect. On the cover of *Bibliotheca Sacra* immediately following his death an added headline proudly announced that Warfield's studies in perfectionism would continue throughout the year.[57] As we mentioned in chapter 1, letters and speakers on the occasion of Princeton Seminary's centennial highlighted Warfield as already a household name at home and abroad and as the institution's brightest light.

Of course in his own day, as in ours, some of Warfield's opponents perceived him as an obscurantist fundamentalist. This is to be expected from his opponents. Still today he is a frequently cited authority, as any quick computer search of recent theological journals will reveal, and he remains in the very highest regard. But one familiar with Warfield is often left with the impression that he is more quoted than read. That is, he is consulted and referenced, but his whole thought on a given subject often seems not well in hand. As we have seen at various points in the previous chapters, this has sometimes resulted in misunderstandings of Warfield. He is still recognized as the champion of the doctrine of inspiration, but clearly his extensive studies on the person and work of Christ, for example, have not been given adequate attention. In short, only a handful of writers have reflected a broad acquaintance with Warfield. David Calhoun has further observed:

> The year 2001 marked the one hundred and fiftieth anniversary of the birth of Benjamin Breckinridge Warfield. That this milestone passed largely unnoticed merely underscores the fact that the most serious omission in the study of American Christianity and theology is the neglect of Princeton Theological Seminary's greatest professor.[58]

It would seem that Benjamin Warfield is both remembered and forgotten. How then shall we assess the contribution and influence of this leading Princetonian?

---

[56]Patton, "Memorial Address," 390; Brokenshire letter to Meeter, 16.
[57]*BSac* 78, no. 309 (1921).
[58]David B. Calhoun, "Foreword," in *BBW*, xi-xii.

WARFIELD'S LIMITATIONS

It is perhaps best to begin with a frank acknowledgment of at least some of Warfield's limitations. Warfield was a powerful theologian and a powerful exegete, but
he was not infallible. Disagreements over denominational differences and such
are to be expected, but on a few occasions Warfield appears uncharacteristically
wide of the mark. For example, few scholars of any eschatological persuasion
would find his treatment of Revelation 20 convincing, and most would judge it
strained. In the words of David McLeod, "Warfield's great exegetical skills left him
when he wrote on Revelation 20:4–6."[59] Similarly, few—whether paedobaptist
or Baptist—would go so far as to say that neither the word *baptizō* nor any other
consideration in the New Testament provides any clue concerning a proper mode
of baptism. Charles Manford Sharpe (1869–1953) criticizes Warfield at length on
this score and finds it ironic that the man who made so much of the importance of
Scripture as normative in shaping our theology could find so little use for Scripture
at this point.[60] Opinions will vary, of course, but it is likely that most would see
Warfield's theological commitments in these cases as controlling his handling
of the biblical text. Warfield's treatment of Calvin's doctrine of creation is highly
questionable also. It is doubtful that he has convinced very many that Calvin's
doctrine of creation was an evolutionary one. Whatever motivations led Warfield
to this conclusion, few would expect Calvin to agree with Warfield's assessment
of him at this point. Impossible as it would be to argue that Warfield was anything
less than a giant among exegetes and theologians, there are a few times when, for
whatever reasons, he seems not to reach his usual level of excellence.

In "Two Theologies Or One? Warfield and Vos on the Nature of Theology,"
Richard Lints draws out the obvious methodological differences between Warfield and his younger colleague Geerhardus Vos. Warfield was very supportive
of the new department of biblical theology at Princeton, and he and Vos were
close friends, taking daily walks together on the streets of Princeton. Warfield
championed the need for the discipline generally and clearly thought highly of
Vos specifically. He was clearly not the student of biblical theology that Vos was.
But Lints overstates the matter just a bit when he says that "the *historicity* of the
Scriptures was so significant for Warfield that he may well have been unable to
see the *historical flow* of the text."[61] Given Warfield's closeness with Vos and his
enthusiasm for his work, it is striking that Warfield's own work did not reflect a

---

[59]"The Fourth 'Last Thing': The Millennial Kingdom of Christ (Rev. 20:4–6)," *BSac* 157, no. 625 (2000):
56n44.
[60]*The Normative Use of Scripture by Typical Theologians of Protestant Orthodoxy in Great Britain and America*
(Menasha, WI: The Collegiate Press; George Banta, 1912), 43–47.
[61]*WTJ* 54, no. 2 (1992): 250 (his emphasis).

more extensive engagement with biblical theology. And it is further strange, as Lints also points out, that while Warfield understood biblical theology as necessarily prior to and foundational to systematic theology, this was simply not the case either in the historical development of theology or in Warfield's own theological endeavor. The strides Vos made showed no great influence on Warfield, but Warfield most certainly *was* able "to see the historical flow" of the biblical text, even if on a more limited scale. Warfield worked at several points to show the biblical-historical development of certain doctrines. Perhaps no area of his work displays this more clearly than in his doctrine of God and of the Trinity in particular, as we have seen. But it is true that his work in biblical theology was nothing like that of Vos, and there is no evidence that Warfield truly grasped or even was extensively acquainted with Vos's contribution. The discipline was young when Vos came to Princeton, his work was in measure that of a pioneer, and it is not reflected to a great extent in Warfield.

It may be worthwhile also to seek to measure Warfield's success in his larger polemic. He took on all comers and diligently fought back the advance of unbelief on all fronts. It might seem in some respects that he was the giant holding back an avalanche. Only three years after Warfield's death, over 1200 ministers and elders, in the "Auburn Affirmation," formally opposed the right of the General Assembly to require its ministers to affirm such fundamentals as the inerrancy of Scripture, the virgin birth of Christ, his substitutionary atonement and bodily resurrection, and his miracles. Just eight years after his death Princeton Seminary was reorganized under the control of theological forces Warfield opposed all his life. And in just another eight years the denomination itself was firmly entrenched in liberalism. The PCUSA today certainly does not share his view of objective revelation, the infallibility of Scripture, and other major points of his theology. Indeed, later professors at Princeton have scoffed at his views.[62] Not surprisingly, his massive emphasis on confessional Calvinism enjoys relatively little hearing in his Presbyterian denomination. From this perspective his defense of the faith certainly failed to secure the objective he desired.

Even if we turn to the more Warfield-friendly evangelical world, we might find a similar failure regarding his studies in perfectionism and higher life teachings. These constitute a major segment of Warfield's literary output. He vigorously opposed all varieties of the higher life teachings, and in his very last published works he sought at length to discredit them. But judging from the continued influence of higher life and Keswick-type teachings within evangelicalism—in the popular teaching of the believer's "two natures," the separation of justifica-

---

[62]Warfield himself saw this coming; see *JGM*, 310.

tion and sanctification, and the "second work" notion of "just surrender and let God" sanctification—it would seem that Warfield has not been heard. Similarly his view of apologetics, in the Reformed world at least, was eclipsed by Cornelius Van Til's presuppositionalism, though Warfield has not been adequately understood on this score. And his very method of polemic is increasingly characterized as rationalistic.

WARFIELD'S INFLUENCE

But other ways of measuring his contribution and influence must not be overlooked. One year after Warfield's death John Mackay reviewed Warfield's extensive work on the doctrine of inspiration and predicted that it had marked an epoch.[63] Certainly no one could argue that Mackay was mistaken in this estimate. Whether in agreement or disagreement, all attention to this doctrine since Warfield must take him into account. For more than a hundred years now it is Warfield's articulation of the doctrine of inspiration that has shaped evangelical thought, as epitomized in the International Council on Biblical Inerrancy. Warfield was indeed a landmark in this regard. We saw that Warfield described Augustine as the church's theologian of grace, Anselm as the theologian of the atonement, Luther as the theologian of justification, and Calvin as the theologian of the Holy Spirit.[64] He meant, of course, not that they invented these respective doctrines but that they were watershed interpreters of them. It was Augustine who first brought out in fulness the biblical teaching of grace. It was Anselm who first articulated the biblical teaching of penal substitution in contrast to ransom-to-Satan theories. And so on. In this respect it could scarcely be doubted that Warfield was and is the theologian of inspiration. It would not be accurate to say that this was Warfield's center or his own major point of theological interest. But this was the defining issue of his day, and Warfield rose to the challenge and, for evangelicals, carried the day. It could scarcely be questioned that it was Warfield who most fully developed the evangelical doctrine of inspiration. Virtually all traditional treatments of the subject since are essentially a restatement of Warfield. Even second- and third-generation works on the subject that reflect little first-hand familiarity with Warfield restate his arguments, having caught them second-hand. And it is widely acknowledged that no opposing doctrine can be taken seriously that does not seek to interact with him in its argument. Whether one agrees with Warfield's position or not, his doctrine of inspiration remains the standard of evangelical thought. If, as is said, all of Western philosophy is just a footnote to

---

[63]Mackay, "Benjamin B. Warfield: A Bibliography," 37.
[64]W, 5:21.

Plato, so also all of the past century's discussion of inspiration and inerrancy is a footnote to Warfield.

In more limited respects the same could be said of Warfield's doctrine of the cessation of the miraculous gifts. Rightly or wrongly, as L. Philip Barnes remarks:

> He more than any other single writer has shaped evangelicals' negative attitude to Pentecostalism and charismatic renewal: this is due in no small part to the fact that he is widely regarded as having given systematic expression to the views of the Reformers, particularly Calvin, on these matters. George Mallone has recently remarked, with understandable exaggeration, that "B. B. Warfield's teaching on the cessation of the gifts has now influenced almost an entire century of the church's life." Warfield's name (in this context) is synonymous with the cessationist view that the gifts were confined to the early church, and consequently are not present or manifest in the church today.[65]

Again, for those who agree as well as for those who do not, it is Warfield's articulation of cessationism that commands attention still today.

Warfield's treatment of the incarnation and two natures of Christ constituted nothing new, substantively, to Christian doctrine. But Warfield unquestionably deepened its exegetical ground for the church to enjoy. It is arguable, further, that Warfield advanced the church's understanding of the doctrine of the Trinity, although the truth of this would be more theoretical than actual, for although he made significant contribution to the study, his contribution does not seem to have been taken up or even recognized by later interpreters of the doctrine.

All sides agree that in the scholarly work of B. B. Warfield, Princeton reached its high-water mark, and it is entirely arguable that what is said of the seminary can be said more broadly in reference to American theology. Of course it is difficult to measure his influence via the 2,700 students who passed through the seminary under his tutelage into denominations and churches, just as it is impossible to measure his influence through the years since via his writings. His example of "earnestly contending for the faith" has inspired countless others to do the same. And if his theological emphases are not heard in his own denomination today, other Presbyterian bodies look to him still as their theological benefactor. Through the history of the *Westminster Theological Journal* scarcely an issue has been published without some reference to him in at least one of its articles. Throughout the resurgence of Calvinistic theology in the larger evangelical scene, Warfield still speaks with commanding influence. In one sense it is arguable that Warfield has not been given his due in that he has not been as widely read as he deserves,

---

[65]"Miracles, Charismata and Benjamin B. Warfield," *EQ* 67, no. 3 (1995): 220.

something this work attempts to remedy. On another level it cannot be denied that to this day his name carries great weight in theological argument—the sheer number of times he is cited in the theological journals is proof enough.[66] Indeed, interest in Warfield seems clearly to be on the rise, as reflected in the increasing availability of his works both in print and in electronic media. In his own day he seldom spoke publicly. Outside the classroom his audience was reached with his pen. As Patton said in his memorial address,

> Through the pages of the *Presbyterian and Reformed Review* and later of the *Princeton Theological Review*, he was speaking regularly to men who waited eagerly to see what he had to say concerning the latest book on New Testament Criticism or the most recent phase of theological opinion.[67]

So also still today, the influence of his writings is clearly being felt. The publication of his works continues, and recent years have also witnessed the republication of some of his material long out of print. PhD dissertations and journal articles on aspects of Warfield show no sign of slowing. David Livingstone and Mark Noll's edited work, *Evolution, Science and Scripture: Selected Writings* (2000), and Gary Johnson's edited work, *B. B. Warfield: Essays on His Life and Thought* (2007), have marked a recognizable step forward for Warfield studies. Biographical works are in the pipelines also. Given all this and the fact that Warfield's works were originally published primarily in periodicals instead of books, it is quite likely that Warfield is being heard more today than ever before.

Indeed, there may be indications that Warfield himself anticipated this and sensed something of his significance in the history of doctrine. He directed in his will that his brother, Ethelbert, see to the republication of his works, an endeavor that took some ten years to accomplish and resulted in the ten volumes readily available today. Warfield himself assisted with the project by keeping a careful record of all his literary output. The Princeton Seminary library houses the Warfield Archives, perhaps the most significant of which are the fifteen volumes of his own collection of "*Opuscula Warfieldii:* Being fugitive pieces published by Benjamin B. Warfield." Most of these bound, hardback scrapbooks, which Warfield kept evidently throughout his career, contain the final (printed) version of almost everything he published throughout his lifetime. In the front of each volume is his handwritten table of contents with a brief description of many of the entries, and each entry is carefully dated and given the appropriate reference data. For

---

[66]A quick search of the current edition of the *Theological Journal Library CD* turns up only thirteen articles focusing specifically on some aspect of Warfield's thought. But a search for references to and citations of Warfield turns up nearly 3,500 hits.

[67]Patton, "Memorial Address," 371.

the most part this is all the information he provided. But sometimes he offered more, and it often seems clear that he was consciously writing notes for those who would come after him to study his works. For example, some of the articles were published anonymously—or with the initials "N.E.D.," the final letters of his first, middle, and last names respectively—and in these opuscula, Warfield named himself as the author, information we would not have otherwise. At certain other points Warfield corrected typographical errors, inserted paragraph breaks, and scribbled other notes of relevance, again intending this information for others who would come after him. He seemed clearly to have at least some sense of his continuing influence, and he anticipated further attention to and republication of his works. He could not have known the degree of continuing interest, of course. But today's rising interest in Warfieldiana certainly vindicates his anticipation. And this is fitting for someone who would be described, with only slight exaggeration, as the one who propelled orthodoxy into the twentieth century.[68]

---

[68]Andrew Hoffecker, "Guardian of the Word," *Tabletalk*, April 2005, 12.

Appendix

A BRIEF AND UNTECHNICAL STATEMENT OF THE REFORMED FAITH

B. B. Warfield

1. I believe that my one aim in life and death should be to glorify God and enjoy him forever; and that God teaches me how to glorify and enjoy him in his holy Word, that is, the Bible, which he has given by the infallible inspiration of his Holy Spirit in order that I may certainly know what I am to believe concerning him and what duty he requires of me.

2. I believe that God is a Spirit, infinite, eternal and incomparable in all that he is; one God but three persons, the Father, the Son, and the Holy Ghost, my Creator, my Redeemer, and my Sanctifier; in whose power and wisdom, righteousness, goodness and truth I may safely put my trust.

3. I believe that the heavens and the earth, and all that in them is, are the work of God's hands; and that all that he has made he directs and governs in all their actions; so that they fulfil the end for which they were created, and I who trust in him shall not be put to shame but may rest securely in the protection of his almighty love.

4. I believe that God created man after his own image, in knowledge, righteousness and holiness, and entered into a covenant of life with him upon the sole condition of the obedience that was his due: so that it was by wilfully sinning against God that man fell into the sin and misery in which I have been born.

5. I believe, that, being fallen in Adam, my first father, I am by nature a child of wrath, under the condemnation of God and corrupted in body and soul, prone to

evil and liable to eternal death; from which dreadful state I cannot be delivered save through the unmerited grace of God my Savior.

6. I believe that God has not left the world to perish in its sin, but out of the great love wherewith he has loved it, has from all eternity graciously chosen unto himself a multitude which no man can number, to deliver them out of their sin and misery, and of them to build up again in the world his kingdom of righteousness: in which kingdom I may be assured I have my part, if I hold fast to Christ the Lord.

7. I believe that God has redeemed his people unto himself through Jesus Christ our Lord; who, though he was and ever continues to be the eternal Son of God, yet was born of a woman, born under the law, that he might redeem them that are under the law: I believe that he bore the penalty due to my sins in his own body on the tree, and fulfilled in his own person the obedience I owe to the righteousness of God, and now presents me to his father as his purchased possession, to the praise of the glory of his grace forever: wherefore renouncing all merit of my own, I put all my trust only in the blood and righteousness of Jesus Christ my redeemer.

8. I believe that Jesus Christ my redeemer, who died for my offences was raised again for my justification, and ascended into the heavens, where he sits at the right hand of the Father Almighty, continually making intercession for his people, and governing the whole world as head over all things for his Church: so that I need fear no evil and may surely know that nothing can snatch me out of his hands and nothing can separate me from his love.

9. I believe that the redemption wrought by the Lord Jesus Christ is effectually applied to all his people by the Holy Spirit, who works faith in me and thereby unites me to Christ, renews me in the whole man after the image of God, and enables me more and more to die unto sin and to live unto righteousness; until, this gracious work having been completed in me, I shall be received into glory: in which great hope abiding, I must ever strive to perfect holiness in the fear of God.

10. I believe that God requires of me, under the gospel, first of all, that, out of a true sense of my sin and misery and apprehension of his mercy in Christ, I should turn with grief and hatred away from sin and receive and rest upon Jesus Christ alone for salvation; that, so being united to him, I may receive pardon for my sins and be accepted as righteous in God's sight, only for the righteousness of Christ imputed to me and received by faith alone: and thus and thus only do I believe I may be received into the number and have a right to all the privileges of the sons of God.

11. I believe that, having been pardoned and accepted for Christ's sake, it is further required of me that I walk in the Spirit whom he has purchased for me, and by whom love is shed abroad in my heart; fulfilling the obedience I owe to Christ my King; faithfully performing all the duties laid upon me by the holy law of God my heavenly Father; and ever reflecting in my life and conduct, the perfect example that has been set me by Christ Jesus my Leader, who has died for me and granted to me his Holy Spirit just that I may do the good works which God has afore prepared that I should walk in them.

12. I believe that God has established his Church in the world and endowed it with the ministry of the Word and the holy ordinances of Baptism, the Lord's Supper and Prayer; in order that through these as means, the riches of his grace in the gospel may be made known to the world, and, by the blessing of Christ and the working of his Spirit in them that by faith receive them, the benefits of redemption may be communicated to his people: wherefore also it is required of me that I attend on these means of grace with diligence, preparation, and prayer, so that through them I may be instructed and strengthened in faith, and in holiness of life and in love; and that I use my best endeavors to carry this gospel and convey these means of grace to the whole world.

13. I believe that as Jesus Christ has once come in grace, so also is he to come a second time in glory, to judge the world in righteousness and assign to each his eternal award: and I believe that if I die in Christ, my soul shall be at death made perfect in holiness and go home to the Lord; and when he shall return in his majesty I shall be raised in glory and made perfectly blessed in the full enjoyment of God to all eternity: encouraged by which blessed hope it is required of me willingly to take my part in suffering hardship here as a good soldier of Christ Jesus, being assured that if I die with him I shall also live with him, if I endure, I shall also reign with him.

And to Him, my Redeemer,
with the Father,
and the Holy Spirit,
Three Persons, one God,
be glory forever, world without end,
Amen, and Amen.

BIBLIOGRAPHY OF WORKS CITED

Ahlstrom, Sydney. "The Scottish Philosophy and American Theology." *Church History* 24, no. 3 (1955): 257–72.

Alexander, Archibald. *The Canon of the Old and New Testaments Ascertained.* Philadelphia: Presbyterian Board of Publication, 1851.

———. *Thoughts on Religious Experience.* 1844. Reprint, Carlisle, PA: Banner of Truth, 1998.

Allis, Oswald T. "Personal Impressions of Dr Warfield." *BT* 89 (Fall 1971): 10–14.

Anderson, Owen. *Benjamin B. Warfield and Right Reason: The Clarity of General Revelation and Function of Apologetics.* Lanham, MD: University Press of America, 2005.

———. *Reason and Worldviews: Warfield, Kuyper, Van Til and Plantinga on the Clarity of General Revelation and Function of Apologetics.* Lanham, MD: University Press of America, 2008.

Aucker, Brian. "Hodge and Warfield on Evolution." *Presbyterion* 20 (1994): 131–42.

Balmer, Randall H. "The Old Princeton Doctrine of Inspiration in the Context of Nineteenth-Century Theology: A Reappraisal." MA thesis, Deerfield, IL: Trinity Evangelical Divinity School, 1981.

———. "The Princetonians and Scripture: A Reconsideration." *WTJ* 44, no. 2 (1982): 352–65.

Balmer, Randall H., and John Woodbridge. "The Princetonians and Biblical Authority: An Assessment of the Ernest Sandeen Proposal." In *Scripture and Truth,* edited by D. A. Carson and John D. Woodbridge, 251–79. 1983. Reprint, Grand Rapids: Baker, 1998.

Bamberg, Stanley. "Our Image of Warfield Must Go." *JETS* 34, no. 2 (1991): 230–42.

Barnes, L. Philip. "Miracles, Charismata and Benjamin B. Warfield." *EQ* 67, no. 3 (1995): 219–43.

Behannon, Woodrow. "Benjamin B. Warfield's Concept of Religious Authority." ThD diss., Southwestern Baptist Theological Seminary, 1963.

"Benjamin Breckinridge Warfield." *PTR* 19, no. 2 (1921): 329–30.

Berkhof, Louis. *Recent Trends in Theology*. Grand Rapids: Eerdmans, 1944.

Breckinridge, Robert J. *The Knowledge of God, Objectively Considered*. New York: Robert Carter & Brothers, 1858, 1860.

Briggs, Charles. *The Bible, The Church, and the Reason*. New York: Charles Scribner's Sons, 1892.

———. *Biblical Study: Its Principles, Methods, and History*. New York: Charles Scribner's Sons, 1883.

———. *Church Unity: Studies of Its Most Important Problems*. New York: Charles Scribner's Sons, 1909.

———. "Critical Theories of the Sacred Scriptures in Relation to Their Inspiration." *PR* 2, no. 7 (1881).

———. *General Introduction to the Study of Holy Scripture: The Principles, Methods, History, and Results of Its Several Departments and of the Whole*. 1900. Reprint, Grand Rapids: Baker, 1970.

———. *Whither? A Theological Question for the Times*. New York: Charles Scribner's Sons, 1889.

Brokenshire, Charles. Letter to John Meeter. June 25, 1942.

Brown, Colin. *Miracles and the Critical Mind*. Grand Rapids: Eerdmans, 1984.

———. *Philosophy and the Christian Faith: A Historical Sketch from the Middle Ages to the Present Day*. London: Inter-Varsity, 1969.

Cairns, Earle E. *Christianity in America*. Chicago: Moody, 1964.

Calhoun, David B. *Princeton Seminary, Volume 1: Faith and Learning, 1812–1868*. Edinburgh: Banner of Truth, 1994; *Volume 2: The Majestic Testimony, 1869–1929* (1996).

Cannata, Raymond. "History of Apologetics at Princeton Seminary." In *Unapologetic Apologetics*, edited by William A. Dembski and Jay Wesley Richards, 57–76. Downers Grove, IL: InterVarsity, 2001.

———. "Old Princeton Doctrine of Scripture." In *Unapologetic Apologetics*, edited by William A. Dembski and Jay Wesley Richards, 120–27. Downers Grove, IL: InterVarsity, 2001. Republished as "Warfield and the Doctrine of Scripture." In *B. B. Warfield: Essays on His Life and Thought*, edited by Gary W. Johnson, 92–107. Phillipsburg, NJ: P&R, 2007.

Carl, Harold F. "Found in Human Form: The Maintenance and Defense of Orthodox Christology by Nineteenth Century American Reformed Theologians." PhD diss., Westminster Theological Seminary, 1992.

Carson, D. A., and John Woodbridge, eds. *Scripture and Truth*. 1983. Reprint, Grand Rapids: Baker, 1998.

Chafer, Rollin Thomas. "A Syllabus of Studies in Hermeneutics Part 1." *BSac* 91, no. 364 (1934): 456–62.

Cho, David. "The Old Princeton Presbyterian Response to the Holiness Movement in the Late Nineteenth and Twentieth Centuries in America." PhD diss., Westminster Theological Seminary, 1994.

Counts, William Martin. "A Study of Benjamin B. Warfield's View of the Doctrine of Inspiration." ThM thesis, Dallas Theological Seminary, 1959.

Cousar, Robert W. "Benjamin Warfield: His Christology and Soteriology." PhD diss., University of Edinburgh, 1954.

Craig, S. G. "Benjamin B. Warfield." In *Biblical and Theological Studies*, xi-xlviii. Grand Rapids: Baker, 1968.

The Daily Dayton Democrat, Dayton, Ohio, July 25, 1876.

Davis, Dennis Royal. "Presbyterian Attitudes toward Science and the Coming of Darwinism in America, 1859–1929." PhD diss., University of Illinois at Urbana-Champaign, 1980.

Dorrien, Gary. *The Making of American Liberal Theology: Imagining Progressive Revelation 1805–1900*. Louisville: Westminster John Knox, 2001.

———. *The Word as True Myth: Interpreting Modern Theology*. Louisville: Westminster John Knox, 1997.

Dulles, Joseph H. *Princeton Theological Seminary: Biographical Catalogue*. Trenton, NJ: MacCrellish & Quigley, 1909.

Duncan, J. Ligon. "Common Sense and American Presbyterianism: An Evaluation of the Impact of Scottish Realism on Princeton and the South." MA thesis, Covenant Theological Seminary, 1987.

Elwell, Walter A., and J. D. Weaver, eds. *Bible Interpreters of the Twentieth Century: A Selection of Evangelical Voices*. Grand Rapids: Baker, 1999.

Erickson, Millard. *Christian Theology*. Grand Rapids: Baker, 1984.

Finlayson, R. A. *The Story of Theology*. London: Tyndale, 1969.

Fuller, Daniel. "Benjamin B. Warfield's View of Faith and History: A Critique in the Light of the New Testament." *JETS* 11, no. 1 (1968): 75–83.

Fuller, Donald, and Richard Gardiner. "Reformed Theology at Princeton and Amsterdam in the Late Nineteenth Century: A Reappraisal." *Presbyterion* 21, no. 2 (1995): 89–117.

Gaffin, Richard, ed. *Redemptive History and Biblical Interpretation*. Phillipsburg, NJ: Presbyterian and Reformed, 1980.

Geehan, E. R., ed. *Jerusalem and Athens: Critical Discussions on the Philosophy and Apologetics of Cornelius Van Til*. Nutley, NJ: Presbyterian and Reformed, 1971.

Gerstner, John. "Warfield's Case for Biblical Inerrancy." In *God's Inerrant Word*, edited by John Warwick Montgomery, 115–142. Minneapolis, MN: Bethany House, 1974.

Gerstner, Jonathan Neil. "Edwardsean Preparation for Salvation." *WTJ* 42, no. 1 (1979): 5–71.

Gleason, Randall. "B. B. Warfield and Lewis S. Chafer on Sanctification." *JETS* 40, no. 2 (1997): 242–56.

Grier, W. J. "Benjamin Breckenridge Warfield, D.D. LL.D. Litt.D." *EQ* 22, no. 2 (1950): 115–22. Republished in "Warfield Commemorative Issue." *BT* 89 (Fall 1971): 3–9.

Gundlach, Bradley John. "'B' is for Breckinridge: Benjamin B. Warfield, His Maternal Kin, and Princeton Seminary." In *B. B. Warfield: Essays on His Life and Thought*, edited by Gary W. Johnson, 13–53. Phillipsburg, NJ: P&R, 2007.

———. "The Evolution Question at Princeton: 1845–1929." PhD diss., University of Rochester, 1995.

———. "'Wicked Caste': Warfield, Biblical Authority, and Jim Crow." In *B. B. Warfield: Essays on His Life and Thought*, edited by Gary W. Johnson, 136–68. Phillipsburg, NJ: P&R, 2007.

Gundry, Stanley, ed. *Five Views of Sanctification.* Grand Rapids: Zondervan, 1987.

Harkness, N. W. Unpublished class notes from Warfield's lectures on systematic theology, 1899–1901. Princeton Seminary library archives.

Helseth, Paul K. "B. B. Warfield on the Apologetic Nature of Christian Scholarship: An Analysis of His Solution to the Problem of the Relationship between Christianity and Culture." *WTJ* 62, no. 1 (2000): 89–111. Republished as "Warfield on the Life of the Mind and the Apologetic Nature of Christian Scholarship." In *B. B. Warfield: Essays on His Life and Thought*, edited by Gary W. Johnson, 108–35. Phillipsburg, NJ: P&R, 2007.

———. "B. B. Warfield's Apologetical Appeal to Right Reason: Evidence of a Rather Bald Rationalism?" *SBET* 16 (Autumn 1998): 156–77. Republished as "A 'Rather Bald' Rationalist? The Appeal to 'Right Reason.'" In *B. B. Warfield: Essays on His Life and Thought*, edited by Gary W. Johnson, 54–75. Phillipsburg, NJ: P&R, 2007.

———. "J. Gresham Machen and 'True Science': Machen's Apologetical Continuity with Old Princeton's Right Use of Reason." *JPH*, 77, no. 1 (1999): 13–28. Also "The Apologetical Tradition of the OPC: A Reconsideration." *WTJ* 60, no. 1 (1998): 109–29. Republished in *B. B. Warfield: Essays on His Life and Thought*, edited by Gary W. Johnson, 54–75. Phillipsburg, NJ: P&R, 2007.

———. "'Re-Imagining' the Princeton Mind: Postconservative Evangelicalism, Old Princeton, and the Rise of Neo-Fundamentalism." *JETS* 45, no. 3 (2002): 427–50.

———. "'Right Reason' and the Princeton Mind: The Moral Context." *JPH* 77, no. 1 (1999): 13–28.

Henry, Carl F. H. *God, Revelation and Authority*. Vol. 4, *God Who Speaks and Shows*. Waco, TX: Word, 1979.

Heslam, Peter S. "Architects of Evangelical Intellectual Thought: Abraham Kuyper and Benjamin Warfield." *Themelios* 24, no. 2 (1999): 3–20.

———. *Creating a Christian Worldview: Abraham Kuyper's Lectures on Calvinism.* Grand Rapids: Eerdmans, 1998.

Hodge, A. A. "Free Will, or Freedom of the Will." Revised by B. B. Warfield. In *Johnson's Universal Encyclopedia*, new edition, edited by Charles Kendall Adams, vol. 3. New York: D. Appleton and Company, 1899.

———. "God." Revised by B. B. Warfield. In *Johnson's Universal Encyclopedia*, new edition, edited by Charles Kendall Adams, vol. 3. New York: D. Appleton and Company, 1899.

———. *The Life of Charles Hodge, D.D., LL.D.* London: T. Nelson and Sons, 1881.

Hodge, A. A., and B. B. Warfield. *"Inspiration."* Edited by Roger Nicole. Grand Rapids: Baker, 1979.

Hodge, Charles. *1 & 2 Corinthians*. 1859. Reprint, Edinburgh: Banner of Truth, 1978.

———. *Systematic Theology*, 3 vols. 1871. Reprint, Grand Rapids: Eerdmans, 1952.

Hoefel, Robert James. "The Doctrine of Inspiration in the Writings of James Orr and B. B. Warfield: A Study in Contrasting Approaches to Scripture." PhD diss., Fuller Theological Seminary, 1983.

Hoffecker, Andrew. "Benjamin B. Warfield." In *The Princeton Theology*, edited by David F. Wells, 65–91. Grand Rapids: Baker, 1989. Republished also in *Reformed Theology in America: A History of Its Modern Development*, edited by David F. Wells, 65–91. 1985. Reprint, Grand Rapids: Baker, 1997.

———. "The Devotional Life of Archibald Alexander, Charles Hodge and Benjamin B. Warfield." *WTJ* 42, no. 1 (1979): 110–29.

———. "Guardian of the Word." *Tabletalk*, April 2005, 12–13.

———. "The Relation between the Objective and Subjective Aspects in Christian Religious Experience: A Study in the Systematic and Devotional Writings of Archibald Alexander, Charles Hodge, and Benjamin B. Warfield." PhD diss., Brown University, 1970. Later published under the title, *Piety and the Princeton Theologians*. Phillipsburg, NJ: Presbyterian and Reformed, 1981.

House, H. Wayne. *Charts of Christian Theology and Doctrine*. Grand Rapids: Zondervan, 1992.

Johnson, Deryl. "The Attitudes of the Princeton Theologians toward Darwinism and Evolution from 1859–1929." PhD diss., University of Iowa, 1968.

Johnson, Gary W., ed. *B. B. Warfield: Essays on His Life and Thought*. Phillipsburg, NJ: P&R, 2007.

Kantzer, Kenneth. "Liberalism's Rise and Fall." *Christianity Today*. February 18, 1983, 10.

Kerr, Hugh. "Warfield: The Person behind the Theology." *PSB*, new series, 25, no. 1 (2004): 80–93.

Kraus, Clyde Norman. "The Principle of Authority in the Theology of B. B. Warfield, William Adams Brown, and Gerald Birney Smith." PhD diss., Duke University, 1961.

Kwok, Man Chee. "Benjamin B. Warfield's Doctrine of Illumination in Light of Conservative Calvinistic Tradition." PhD diss., Trinity International University, 1995.

Lindsay, Thomas M. "The Doctrine of Scripture: The Reformers and the Princeton School." In *The Expositor*, edited by William Robertson Nicoll, 278–93. 5th Series. Vol. 1, London: Hodder and Stoughton, 1895.

Lints, Richard. "Two Theologies or One? Warfield and Vos on the Nature of Theology." *WTJ* 54, no. 2 (1992): 235–54.

Livingston, James C. "Benjamin Breckinridge Warfield." In *Modern Christian Thought*. Vol. 1, *The Enlightenment and the Nineteenth Century*, 315–23. Minneapolis: Fortress, 2006.

Livingstone, David N. "B. B. Warfield, the Theory of Evolution and Early Fundamentalism." *EQ* 58, no. 1 (1986), 69–83.

———. *Darwin's Forgotten Defenders*. Grand Rapids: Eerdmans, 1984.

Livingstone, David N., and Mark A. Noll. "B. B. Warfield 1851–1921: A Biblical Inerrantist as Evolutionist." *Isis* 91, no. 2 (2000): 283–304. Republished in *JPH* 80, no. 3 (2002): 153–71.

Livingstone, William. "The Princeton Apologetic as Exemplified by the Work of Benjamin B. Warfield and J. Gresham Machen: A Study in American Theology, 1880–1930." PhD diss., Yale University, 1948.

Loetscher, Lefferts A. *The Broadening Church: A Study of Theological Issues in the Presbyterian Church Since 1869*. Philadelphia: University of Pennsylvania Press, 1957.

———. *Facing the Enlightenment and Pietism: Archibald Alexander and the Founding of Princeton Theological Seminary*. Westport, CT: Greenwood, 1983.

Lutz, Roland Bruce. "Keeping Out of the Rut." *PSB* 14, no. 5 (1921): 13.

Macintosh, Douglas Clyde. "What Is the Christian Religion?" *The Harvard Theological Review* 7, no. 1 (1914): 16–46.

Mackay, John R. "B. B. Warfield: A Bibliography." *The Expositor Eighth Series*, 24 (July 1922): 37.

Macleod, Donald. "Bavinck's Prolegomena: Fresh Light on Amsterdam, Old Princeton, and Cornelius Van Til." *WTJ* 68, no. 2 (2006): 261–82.

Markarian, John J. "The Calvinistic Concept of the Biblical Revelation in the Theology of B. B. Warfield." PhD diss., Drew University, 1963.

Marsden, George M. *Fundamentalism and American Culture*. New York: Oxford University Press, 1980.

McClanahan, James. "Benjamin B. Warfield: Historian of Doctrine in Defense of Orthodoxy." PhD diss., Union Theological Seminary, 1988.

McLeod, David. "The Fourth 'Last Thing': The Millennial Kingdom of Christ (Rev. 20:4–6)." *BSac* 157, no. 625 (2000): 44–67.

Meeter, John E., and Roger Nicole. *A Bibliography of Benjamin Breckinridge Warfield 1851–1921*. Nutley, NJ: Presbyterian and Reformed, 1974.

Miller, Samuel. *A Brief Account of the Rise, Progress and Present State of the Theological Seminary of the Presbyterian Church in the United States of America at Princeton*. Philadelphia: A. Finley, 1822.

Montgomery, John Warwick, ed. *God's Inerrant Word*. Minneapolis: Bethany House, 1974.

Morrow, Trevor. "Infallibility as a Theological Concept." PhD diss., University of Edinburgh, 1983.

Murray, Iain, et al., eds. "Warfield Commemorative Issue," 1921–1971. *BT* 89 (Fall 1971).

Murray, John. *Collected Writings of John Murray*, vols. 2–3. Carlisle, PA: Banner of Truth, 1978, 1982.

———. "Calvin's Doctrine of Creation." *WTJ* 17, no. 1 (1954): 28–42.

The New Schaff-Herzog Encyclopedia of Religious Knowledge, 12 vols. Edited by Samuel Macauley Jackson. New York: Funk & Wagnalls, 1908–1914.

Nichols, Stephen J. "'The Vital Processes of Controversy': Warfield, Machen, and Fundamentalism." In *B. B. Warfield: Essays on His Life and Thought*, edited by Gary W. Johnson, 169–94. Phillipsburg, NJ: P&R, 2007.

Niebuhr, H. Richard. *The Kingdom of God in America*. 1937. Reprint, Middletown, CT: Wesleyan University Press, 1988.

Noll, Mark A. "B. B. Warfield." In *Handbook of Evangelical Theologians*, edited by Walter A. Elwell, 26–39. Grand Rapids: Baker, 1993.

———. *Between Faith and Criticism*. San Francisco: Harper and Row, 1986.

———. "Charles Hodge and B. B. Warfield on Science, the Bible, Evolution, and Darwinism." *Modern Reformation* 7, no. 3 (1998): 18–22.

———. "Common Sense Traditions and American Evangelical Thought." *American Quarterly* 37, no. 2 (1985): 216–38.

———. "The Founding of Princeton Seminary." *WTJ* 42, no. 1 (1979): 72–110.

———, ed. *The Princeton Theology, 1812–1921*. Grand Rapids: Baker, 1983.

Parson, Burk, ed. "Benjamin Breckinridge Warfield." *Tabletalk*, April 2005.

Patton, Francis Landey. "Benjamin Breckinridge Warfield: A Memorial Address." *PTR* 19, no. 3 (1921): 369–91.

Pearcey, Nancy. *Total Truth: Liberating Christianity from Its Cultural Captivity*. Wheaton: Crossway Books, 2004.

Reymond, Robert. *Faith's Reasons for Believing*. Fearn, Ross-shire : Mentor, 2008.

Richards, George W. "The Mercersburg Theology: Its Purpose and Principles." *Church History* 20, no. 3 (1951): 42–55.

Riddlebarger, Kim. "The Lion of Princeton: Benjamin Breckinridge Warfield on Apologetics, Theological Method and Polemics." PhD diss., Fuller Theological Seminary, 1997.

Robinson, William Childs. *Our Lord: An Affirmation of the Deity of Christ*. Grand Rapids: Eerdmans, 1937.

Rogers, Jack, ed. *Biblical Authority*. Waco, TX: Word, 1977.

———. "Scripture in the Westminster Confession: A Problem of Historical Interpretation for American Presbyterianism." ThD diss., Free University of Amsterdam, 1966.

———. "Van Til and Warfield on Scripture in the Westminster Confession." In *Jerusalem and Athens: Critical Discussions on the Philosophy and Apologetics of Cornelius Van Til*, edited by E. R. Geehan, 154–65. Nutley, NJ: Presbyterian and Reformed, 1971.

Rogers, Jack, and Donald K. McKim, *The Authority and Interpretation of the Bible: An Historical Approach*. 1979. Reprint, Eugene, OR: Wipf and Stock, 1999.

Ruthven, Mark. *On the Cessation of the Charismata: The Protestant Polemic of Benjamin B. Warfield*. Sheffield: Sheffield Academic, 1993.

Sandeen, Ernest R. "The Princeton Theology: One Source of Biblical Literalism in American Protestantism." *Church History* 31, no. 3 (1962): 307–21.

———. *The Roots of Fundamentalism: British and American Millenarianism, 1800–1930*. Grand Rapids: Baker, 1978.

Schultz, Thomas Allen. "The Noetic Effects of Sin in John Calvin's Doctrine of the Knowledge of God, With its Implications for the Apologetic Methodology of B. B. Warfield and Cornelius Van Til." MA thesis, Covenant Theological Seminary, 1987.

Scott, Robert, and George William Gilmore. *The Church, the People, and the Age*. New York: Funk and Wagnalls, 1914.

Selden, William K. *Princeton Theological Seminary: A Narrative History*. Princeton, NJ: Princeton University Press, 1992.

Sharpe, Charles Manford. *The Normative Use of Scripture by Typical Theologians of Protestant Orthodoxy in Great Britain and America*. Menasha, WI: The Collegiate Press; George Banta Publishing, 1912.

Shogren, Gary. "Christian Prophecy and Canon in the Second Century: A Response to B. B. Warfield." *JETS* 40, no. 4 (1997): 609–26.

Smith, David P. "B. B. Warfield's Scientifically Constructive Theological Scholarship." PhD diss., Trinity Evangelical Divinity School, 2009.

———. "The Scientifically Constructive Scholarship of B. B. Warfield." *Mid-America Journal of Theology* 15 (2004): 87–123.

Spencer, Stephen. "A Comparison and Evaluation of the Old Princeton and Amsterdam Apologetic." ThM thesis, Grand Rapids Baptist Seminary, 1981.

Sproul, R. C. "B. B. Warfield Defender of the Faith." *Tabletalk*, April 2005, 4–7.

Stanton, R. L. "Healing through Faith." *PRR* 5, no. 17 (1884): 49–79.

Stevenson, J. Ross. "Benjamin Breckinridge Warfield." *The Expository Times* 33, no. 4 (1922): 152–53.

Stonehouse, Ned. *J. Gresham Machen: A Biographical Memoir*. Grand Rapids: Eerdmans, 1954.

Thomas, W. H. Griffith. "The Victorious Christian Life." *BSac* 76, no. 302–3 (1919): 267–88, 455–67.

Tillich, Paul. *A History of Christian Thought*. New York: Simon and Schuster, 1967.

Trueman, Carl R. "The Glory of Christ: B. B. Warfield on Jesus of Nazareth." *The Evangelical Library Bulletin* no. 106 (Autumn 2001). Republished in Carl R. Trueman, *The Wages of Spin*. Fearn Ross-shire: Mentor, 2007, 103–28.

van Bemmelen, Peter Maarten. "Issues in Biblical Inspiration: Sanday and Warfield." ThD diss., Andrews University, 1987.

van den Belt, Hendrik. "An Apology for the Lack of Apologetics: The Influence of the Discussion with B. B. Warfield on H. Bavinck's Stone Lectures." A paper delivered at the annual conference of the Abraham Kuyper Center for Public Theology in celebration of Herman Bavinck's Stone Lectures, "The Philosophy of Revelation," April 17, 2009.

———. van den Belt, Henk. *The Authority of Scripture in Reformed Theology: Truth and Trust*. Studies in Reformed Theology 17. Leiden: Brill, 2008.

Vander Stelt, John. *Philosophy and Scripture: A Study in Old Princeton and Westminster Theology*. Marlton, NJ: Mack, 1978. This is Vander Stelt's doctoral dissertation from the Free University of Amsterdam.

Van Til, Cornelius. *A Christian Theory of Knowledge*. Nutley, NJ: Presbyterian and Reformed, 1969.

Vincent, Marvin R. "Dr. Stanton on 'Healing through Faith.'" *PRR* 5, no. 18 (1884): 305–29.

———. "Modern Miracles." *PRR* 4, no. 15 (1883): 473–502.

Wallis, Wilber B. "Benjamin B. Warfield: Didactic and Polemical Theologian," 2 parts. *Covenant Seminary Review* 3 (Spring 1977): 3–20, 73–94.

Walvoord, John F. "Is Satan Bound? Part 1." *BSac* 100, no. 400 (1943): 497–512.

Warfield, Benjamin B. *Acts and Pastoral Epistles and Philemon*. The Temple Bible. 1902. Reprint, London: J. M. Dent & Sons, 1930.

———. "*Andover Review*'s Logic and Hermeneutics." *Herald and Presbyter* 45, no. 2 (1884): 2.

———. "The Angel of Jehovah and Critical Views." *TBS* 8, no. 1 (July 1903): 59–60.

———. "The Apologetical Value of the Testament of the Twelve Patriarchs." *PR* 1, no. 1 (1880): 57–84.

———. "Are the Last Twelve Verses of Mark Part of 'The Word of God'?" *The Presbyterian* 53, no. 3 (1883): 8–9.

———. "The Basis of the Proposed Union—Theoretical and Practical." *The Presbyterian* 75, no. 9 (1905): 8–9.

———. *Biblical and Theological Studies*. Edited by Samuel Craig. Philadelphia: Presbyterian and Reformed, 1968.

———, ed. *Biblical and Theological Studies: A Commemoration of 100 Years of Princeton Seminary*. 1912. Reprint, Vestavia Hills, AL: Solid Ground Christian Books, 2003.

———. *Calvin and Augustine*. Edited by Samuel Craig. Philadelphia: Presbyterian and Reformed, 1956.

———. *The Canon of the New Testament*. Philadelphia: American Sunday School Union, 1902.

———. "Children in the Hands of the Arminians." *The Union Seminary Magazine* 17, no. 3 (1906): 167–76.

———. "The Christian Canon." *The Philadelphian* 1 (1887): 300–304.

———. "The Christian Doctrine of Revelation." *The New York Observer* 73 (July 4, 1895): 4–5.

———. "Christian Unity and Church Union: Some Primary Principles." *The Presbyterian Banner* 91 (1905): 103–4.

———. "Christianity and the Resurrection of Christ." *TBST* 8, no. 4 (April, 1908): 277–83.

———. "The Christian's Attitude toward Death." *PrS*. 1892. Reprinted in *Princeton Sermons*, 316–37. Vestavia Hills, AL: Solid Ground Christian Books, 2009.

———. "Convinced against His Will." *TBS*, new series, 3, no. 5 (May 1901): 241–47.

———. *Counterfeit Miracles*. 1918. Reprint, Carlisle, PA: Banner of Truth, 1976.

———. "The Descriptive Names Applied to the New Testament Books by the Earliest Christian Writers." *BSac* 42 (1885): 545–64.

———. "IV. Discussion of Controverted Points [regarding the mode of baptism]" in the article "Baptism." In *NSHEK* (1908), 1:446–50.

———. "Dr. Briggs' Critical Method." *Interior* 14 (February 4, 1882): 2.

———. "Dr. Edwin Al Abbott on the Genuineness of II Peter." *SPR* 34 (1883): 390–455.

———. "Dr. Schaff and the Calvinistic System." *PJ* 17, no. 19 (1892): 290–91.

———. *Evolution, Science, and Scripture: Selected Writings.* Edited by Mark A. Noll and David N. Livingstone. Baker, 2000.

———. "Fact or Fiction?" *The Presbyterian* 76, no. 37 (1906): 4–5.

———. *Faith and Life.* 1916. Reprint, Carlisle, PA: Banner of Truth, 1974.

———. "The Faith of Jesus and Faith in Jesus." *TBS*, new series, 2, no. 6 (December 1900): 353–54.

———. *Four Hymns and Some Religious Verses.* Philadelphia: Westminster Press, 1910.

———. "The Genuineness of Mark 16:9–20." *Sunday School Times* 24, no. 48 (1882): 755–56.

———. "The Genuineness of 2 Peter." *TBS*, new series, 6, no. 3 (September 1902): 179.

———. "The Hibbert Journal." *TBS*, new series, 7, no. 1 (January 1903): 55–57.

———. *The Holy Spirit.* Edited by Michael Gaydosh. Amityville, NY: Calvary, 1997.

———. "The Holy Spirit Our Pledge." *TBS*, new series, 4, no. 6 (December 1901): 359–60.

———. "How Shall We Escape?" In *Lile's Golden Lamp*, edited by R. M. Offord. New York: *New York Observer*, 1889.

———. "Inaugural Address: The Idea of Systematic Theology." In *Inauguration of the Rev. Benjamin B. Warfield, D.D., as Professor of Didactic and Polemic Theology.* New York: Anson D. F. Randolph, 1888.

———. "The Independence of our Lord." *The Herald and Presbyter* 44, no. 21 (1884): i.

———. "Inspiration and the Spurious Verses at the End of Mark." *Sunday School Times*, 25, no. 3 (1883): 36–37.

———. *An Introduction to the Textual Criticism of the New Testament.* London: Hodder and Stoughton, 1886.

———. "Is It Restatement That We Need?" *The Presbyterian* 70, no. 33 (1900): 8.

———. "Jesus' Foreknowledge of His Death." *TBS*, new series, 3, no. 1 (January 1901): 57–58.

———. "Kikuyu, Clerical Veracity and Miracles." *PTR* 12, no. 4 (1914): 531, 533, 547, 585.

———. *The Lord of Glory.* 1907. Reprint, Grand Rapids: Guardian, n.d.

———. "May We Trust Our Gospels." *TBS*, new series, 4, no. 4 (October 1901): 239–40.

———. "Miracle." In *Davis Bible Dictionary*, 504–5. Philadelphia: Westminster Press, 1917.

———. "The New Theology in the Antipodes." *The Independent* 40 (August 9, 1888): 1006–7.

———. "O the Love of God Almighty." *New York Observer*. December 19, 1901.

———. "Paul's Doctrine of the Old Testament." *PQ* 5, no. 3 (1889): 389–406.

———. *The Person and Work of Christ*. Edited by Samuel Craig. Philadelphia: Presbyterian and Reformed, 1950.

———. "Personal Recollections of Princeton Undergraduate Life IV—The Coming of Dr. McCosh." *Princeton Alumni Weekly* 16, nos. 27, 28 (1916): 623–25, 650–53.

———. *The Plan of Salvation*. 1915. Reprint, Grand Rapids: Eerdmans, 1977.

———. "Πνευμάτικος and Its Opposites." *PR* 1, no. 3 (1880): 561–65.

———. *The Power of God unto Salvation*. 1903. Reprint, Grand Rapids: Eerdmans, 1930.

———. "Presbyter." In *A Dictionary of Religion and Ethics*, edited by Shailer Matthews and Gerald Birney Smith, 348. New York: Macmillan, 1921.

———. "The Presbyterian Churches and the Westminster Confession." *PR* 10, no. 40 (1889): 654.

———. "Presbyterian Deaconesses." *PR* 10, no. 38 (1889): 283–93.

———. "Presbyterianism." In *A Dictionary of Religion and Ethics*, edited by Shailer Matthews and Gerald Birney Smith, 348–49. New York: Macmillan, 1921.

———. "The Present Day Depreciation of Christ's Resurrection." *TBS*, new series, 2, no. 6 (December 1900): 357–59.

———. *Princeton Sermons*. Vestavia Hills, AL: Solid Ground Christian Books, 2009.

———. "The Proposed Union with the Cumberland Presbyterians." *PTR* 2, no. 2 (1904): 295–316.

———. "Redemption." In *Hastings' Dictionary of the Apostolic Church*, 2:302–9. New York: Scribner's, 1918.

———. "The Relation of the Presbyterian Principle to the Historic Episcopate." *Methodist Review* 71 (1889): 845–50.

———. "Revision or Reaffirmation: A Letter from Warfield to the Stated Clerk of the General Assembly," June 25, 1900. Reprinted as "Revision or Reaffirmation?" *Daily True American* (June 29, 1900); *Presbyterian Journal* 25, no. 27 (July 5, 1900); *Southwestern Presbyterian* (July 19, 1900).

———. *The Savior of the World*. 1914. Reprint, Carlisle, PA: Banner of Truth, 1991.

———. *Selected Shorter Writings*. 2 vols. Edited by John Meeter. Nutley, NJ: Presbyterian and Reformed, 1970, 1973.

———. "'Sixty Years with the Bible': A Record of Drifting." *TBST* 12 (February 1910): 128.

———. "Some Exegetical Notes on 1 Timothy." *PR* 8 (1887): 500–508, 702–10.

———. "Some Recent Apocryphal Gospels." *SPQ* 35 (1884): 718–19, 724.

———. "Some Rough Notes on Trichotomy." Handwritten lecture notes. Warfield Archives, Princeton Theological Seminary, n.d.

———. "Syllabus on the Canon of the New Testament in the Second Century." Pittsburgh, 1881.

———. "Syllabus on the Special Introduction to the Catholic Epistles." Pittsburgh: W. W. Waters, 1883.

———. "A Symposium on the Problem of Natural Evils." *Biblical World* 31 (January–June, 1908): 123–25.

———. *The Works of Benjamin Breckinridge Warfield.* 10 vols. 1927–1932. Reprint, Grand Rapids: Baker, 1981.

Vol. 1, *Revelation and Inspiration*, 1927.

Vol. 2, *Biblical Doctrines*, 1929.

Vol. 3, *Christology and Criticism*, 1929.

Vol. 4, *Studies in Tertullian and Augustine*, 1930.

Vol. 5, *Calvin and Calvinism*, 1931.

Vol. 6, *The Westminster Assembly and Its Work*, 1931.

Vol. 7, *Perfectionism, Part One*, 1931.

Vol. 8, *Perfectionism, Part Two*, 1932.

Vol. 9, *Studies in Theology*, 1932.

Vol. 10, *Critical Reviews*, 1932.

Warfield, B. B., William P. Armstrong, and Harold McA. Robinson, eds. *The Centennial Celebration of the Theological Seminary of the Presbyterian Church in the United States of America at Princeton, New Jersey.* 1912. Reprint, Eugene, OR: Wipf and Stock, 2001.

Warfield, Ethelbert. "Biographical Sketch of Benjamin Breckinridge Warfield." In *The Works of Benjamin Breckinridge Warfield.* Vol. 1, *Revelation and Inspiration*, v–ix. Grand Rapids: Baker, 1981.

Woodbridge, John. *Biblical Authority: A Critique of the Rogers/McKim Proposal.* Grand Rapids: Zondervan, 1982.

Woodbridge, John, and Randy Balmer. "The Princetonians' Viewpoint of Biblical Authority: An Evaluation of Ernest Sandeen." In *Scripture and Truth*, edited by Woodbridge and D. A. Carson, 251–79. Grand Rapids: Zondervan, 1983.

Woodbridge, John D., and Thomas E. McComiskey, eds. *Doing Theology in Today's World.* Grand Rapids: Zondervan, 1991.

GENERAL INDEX

Abel, 299–300

Abelard, Peter, 293, 295

abiding in Christ, 353

abolitionists, 392

abomination of desolations, 540

Abraham
    circumcision of, 516–17
    faith of, 446

Acts, on deity of Christ, 237–38

Adam, 391
    sin of, 392, 400, 401–3, 414, 442

Adam, Thomas, 465, 481, 488

Adamson, Thomas, 277

adoption, 439

adultery, 347

affection of faith, 567–70

age of the Spirit, 339

age to come, 267, 321

agnosticism, 99

Ahlstrom, Sydney, 55, 567–68

Aiken, Charles Augustus, 37

Alexander, Archibald, 36, 37, 38, 143, 500–501, 568

Alexander Hall (Princeton Seminary), 394

Alexander, James Waddell, 37, 38

Alexander, Joseph Addison, 37, 217, 555

alien righteousness, 442

Allis, O. T., 328

American Whig Society, 28, 29

amillennialism, 536

Amyraldianism, 420

Andover Seminary, 36

angel of Jehovah, 183

angels, 222, 268, 272

Anglicanism, 356

annihilationism, 544

anointing with oil, 363

Anselm, 83, 291, 295, 329, 331, 574

anthropology, 331

antichrist, 535, 540–41

antinomianism, 488

of perfectionism, 469–71
    of Ritschl, 464

anti-supernaturalism, 56–57, 232–33, 460–62, 509

Apollinarianism, 262, 283

apologetics, 19, 79, 80, 81, 550, 551, 564
    as primary, 64–68

apostasy, 540–41

apostles, 127, 135, 528
    and canon, 146–48
    as eyewitnesses of resurrection, 318–19
    on inspiration, 140
    inspiration of, 142–43
    on Scripture, 161–62

apostolic authority, 142–43

apostolic benediction, 188, 196

apostolic gifts, 356–60

application of redemption, 343

Arianism, 189

Arminianism, 53, 59, 77n32, 294, 295, 297, 406, 407, 422, 570
    allegedly in Warfield, 156–57

Armstrong, William Park, 38

Arrowsmith, John, 425

Asbury, Francis, 473

assensus, 452

assurance, 79, 323, 344–46, 350, 352, 429, 431–32, 440, 487

Athanasian Creed, 195

Athanasius, 331

atheism, 97
    evolution as, 370, 371, 375

atonement, 296, 448
    extent of, 309–14, 419–21
    nature of, 310–11
    theories of, 292–96, 309

Auburn Affirmation, 573

Augustine, 55, 69, 83, 119–20, 189, 329, 331, 406, 414, 447, 555, 574
    on biblical authority, 123
    on the church, 514

SCRIPTURE INDEX